I0889319

The Pursuit of the Ideal

SUNY Series in Jewish Philosophy
Kenneth Seeskin, editor

The Pursuit of the Ideal

Jewish Writings of Steven Schwarzschild

Edited by
Menachem Kellner

State University of New York Press

Published by
State University of New York Press, Albany

Printed in the United States of America

For information, address State University of New York Press, State University Plaza, Albany, N.Y., 12246

Library of Congress Cataloging-in-Publication Data

Schwarzschild, Steven.
The pursuit of the ideal : Jewish writings of Steven Schwarzschild / edited by Menachem Kellner.
p. cm.—(SUNY series in Jewish philosophy)
Bibliography: p.
Includes index.
ISBN 0-7914-0219-3.—ISBN 0-7914-0220-7 (pbk.)
1. Judaism—Doctrines. I. Kellner, Menachem Marc, 1946- II. Title. III. Series.
BM601.S39 1990
181'.06—dc20 89-4441
CIP

10 9 8 7 6 5 4 3 2 1

Steven S. Schwarzschild
Frankfurt, 1924 – St. Louis, 1989
II Kings 2:12

Contents

Foreword

It is a pleasure to see this collection of Steven S. Schwarzschild's essays in print. Even the most casual reader will see in them a rigorous intellect and a passionate commitment to Jewish ideals. Imagine a complacent scholar willing to settle for minor adjustments to the prevailing ways of thought and you will be imagining everything Schwarzschild is not. His writing is forceful and stimulating. He is not given to intellectual compromises. He makes demands on his reader because he has already made considerable demands on himself. Before long the casual reader will recognize that Schwarzschild's essays do not satisfy one's thirst for greater knowledge, they enhance it. Having read them, one feels a strong desire to read or reread Hermann Cohen. From Cohen, one is led to the Torah, Ezekiel, and the Talmudic sages, on the one hand, Plato, Maimonides, Leibniz, and Kant, on the other.

What are the ideals to which Schwarzschild is committed? The most prominent among them is his unswerving rationalism. Throughout his writing, there is not the slightest sympathy for obscurantist readings, leaps of faith, or dogmatic appeals to authority. To understand Schwarzschild's rationalism is to understand that *reason* is just another name for *human dignity*. He will not accept any suggestion that commandments must be appropriated in a heteronomous fashion—that God reveals without at the same time educating. He will not accept any suggestion that God is to be dissociated from the moral law and the obligation to treat all of humanity as an end in itself. For Schwarzschild, God is the eternal possibility of enlightenment. It may be said therefore that God is not the One who *is* perfect but the One who *commands* perfection from every rational agent. Apart from rationality, and the moral obligations it imposes, there is no way of referring to or appealing to God.

Rationality also means a refusal to accept things as they are. Reason puts before us the goal of universal human brotherhood. The world as it is puts before us prejudice, violence, social inequality, capital punishment, and religious intolerance. If heteronomy destroys reason from above, then acceptance of the status quo destroys it from below. The discovery of reason is precisely the recognition that what is and what ought to be are distinct. To be rational is to accept the gulf between what is and what ought to be and work toward closing it. It follows that Schwarzschild is the sworn opponent of all who think the gap is already closed. For if the gap were closed, there would be no room to protest injustice and to dedicate oneself to the establishment of a new order. If the gap were closed, in other words, there would be no room for Judaism.

It also follows that Schwarzschild cannot accept any notion of an immanent or incarnate God. If God commands perfection, and according to Schwarzschild there is nothing else He can be presumed to do, one can make no greater mistake than to think God has entered into the world. Ultimately the mistake shows itself in quietude or political conservatism, both ways of thinking that the world does not have to be changed. So we move from the ideal of rationalism to that of human dignity to that of radicalism. When Schwarzschild looks at the world he sees not evidence of perfection but a thousand and one opportunities for reform. In the last analysis, one cannot be a casual reader of his works. From the first few paragraphs to the last word, one cannot escape the serious burdens, moral and intellectual, he puts before one.

Kenneth R. Seeskin

Acknowledgements

The articles included in this volume have appeared over a period of more than thirty years in many different journals. No attempt has been made to assure uniformity of transliteration. The articles appear substantially as they were originally published, with minor corrections and additions made by Steven Schwarzschild. Formulations which were perfectly acceptable when they were written but which offend contemporary sensibilities concerning gender usage have been altered.—Ed.

* * *

Grateful acknowledgement is hereby made to the copyright holders of the articles reprinted in this volume:

Introduction by Menachem Kellner—Steven T. Katz, ed., *Contemporary Jewish Thinkers* (Washington, D.C.: B'nai B'rith).

The Personal Messiah—Toward the Restoration of a Discarded Doctrine—*Judaism* 5 (1956): 123-35.

Do Noachites Have to Believe in Revelation? (A Passage in Dispute between Maimonides, Spinoza, Mendelssohn, and H. Cohen) A Contribution to a Jewish View of Natural Law—*Jewish Quarterly Review* 52 (1962): 297-308 and 53 (1962): 30-65.

The Lure of Immanence—The Crisis in Contemporary Religious Thought—*Tradition* 1966-67: 70-99

On the Theology of Jewish Survival—*CCAR Journal,* October 1968: 2-21.

A Note On the Nature of Ideal Society—A Rabbinic Study—*Jubilee Volume Dedicated to Curt C. Silberman* (New York: American Federation of Jews from Central Europe, 1969).

The Question of Jewish Ethics Today—*Sh'ma* 7/124 (1976) and 7/134 (1977).

Moral Radicalism and 'Middlingness' in the Ethics of Maimonides—*Studies in Medieval Culture* 11 (1977): 65-94.

Jean-Paul Sartre as Jew—*Modern Judaism* 3 (1983): 39-73.

A Critique of Martin Buber's Political Philosophy—An Affectionate Reappraisal—*Leo Baeck Institute Yearbook* 31 (1986): 355-88.

On Jewish Eschatology—*The Human Condition in the Jewish and Christian Traditions,* edited by F. Greenspahn (New York: Ktav, 1986).

Modern Jewish Philosophy—*Contemporary Jewish Religious Thought,* edited by Arthur Cohen and Paul Mendes-Flohr (New York: Scribners, 1987).

Introduction

Steven Schwarzschild is both the last of the major medieval Jewish philosophers and the most modern. Before explaining and defending these statements a few biographical comments are in order.

Schwarzschild was born in Frankfurt on Main in 1924 but grew up in Berlin, emigrating with his parents and brother in January of 1939. He was educated in the United States at the City College of New York, the Jewish Theological Seminary, the University of Cincinnati, and the Hebrew Union College, where he was ordained and earned a DHL degree. His dissertation was on the philosophy of history in Nachman Krochmal and Hermann Cohen. After ordination Schwarzschild served as rabbi of the reconstituted Jewish community in Berlin, ministering to Jews in all parts of the divided city, from 1948 to 1950. He filled rabbinical posts in Fargo, North Dakota and Lynn, Massachusetts before turning to an academic career spent almost entirely at Washington University in St. Louis.

Schwarzschild has characterized himself as a self-conscious German Jew ("Yekke"), a socialist humanist, an opponent of political Zionism on Jewish, socialist, and ethical grounds and as a "quintessential example of the 'symbiosis' of classical Jewish and classical humanist cultures."[1]

Schwarzschild edited *Judaism—A Quarterly Journal* for eight years (1961-69) turning it into the liveliest and at the same time most serious journal of opinion and scholarship in the Jewish world. He was for many years the only active rabbi to hold joint membership in two rabbinical associations, the Reform Central Conference of American Rabbis and the Conservative Rabbinical Assembly. His influence on his contemporaries among scholars, rabbis, and Jewish activists is vast, despite the fact that he is relatively little known in the broader Jewish community. Aside from the obvious impact of his career as editor of *Judaism*, he had important influence as an HUC-educated rabbi who, as such, took Messianism and Halakhah seriously. His oft-reprinted and widely-cited essay, "The Personal Messiah—Toward the Restoration of a Discarded Doctrine,"[2] may be noted in this regard. In addition, Schwarzschild has always been ahead of his time, on the cutting edge of a variety of central developments and insights in Jewish intellectual life. Thus, for example, his book on Franz Rosenzweig and his pioneering studies on Samson Raphael Hirsch and Hermann Cohen were each the earliest serious attention these thinkers had received in English and helped spark an ever-growing interest in them.[3] Schwarzschild's prescience and sensitivity are marked by his unusually sensitive antennae for anti-semitism and political conservatism[4] and evidenced by his warning—as long ago as 1956—of the dangers inherent in triumphalist, Messianic Zionism.[5] As a profoundly committed and deeply learned Jew who is also a pacifist, a socialist and a trenchant critic of Zionism, he has been important to many Jews seeking a way to unite such commitments with their Judaism. The further fact that he fits easily into none of the accepted rubrics of contemporary Judaism (Orthodox, Conservative, Reconstructionist or Reform) has been a source of encouragement to those in the Jewish community who see as dangerous trends which pull Jews apart as opposed to pulling them together.

Schwarzschild's two hundred and more publications—historical, philosophical, and theological studies, essays, reviews, polemics—have the spark of brilliance and profundity. I should like to cite a few examples, even though they can only be fully appreciated in context. Take, for example, this brief, cutting, and trenchant critique of orthodox Marxism: "Indeed, except by philosophic sleights of hand, Marxist dialectics have never been able to get around this dilemma of historical necessity which they posit versus social betterment to which they aspire."[6] Moving from Marxism to Christianity we find the following:

> In Christianity, it is true, God and the world have been so completely separated that they constitute an exclusive alternative: you either choose the world, or any part of it, or you choose God; you cannot have both. This accounts for the well-known other-worldliness of Christianity, its asceticism, its fundamental indifference to social goals, its rejection of reason in favor of 'faith,' . . . Some modern Christians . . . have of course been committed to the world. It can, however, be shown that these have followed 'Judaizing' tendencies, or that their social concerns have been of a deceptive nature."[7]

Schwarzschild's deep understanding of figures in the history of philosophy is exemplified by the following comment on Hegel: "Generally it can be said that Hegel simply stretched out on a horizontal plane, *i.e.*, through history, the originally metaphysical vertical ladder of emanations of the neo-Platonists."[8] Further insights worthy of note here include the explication of the intimate connection between natural law theory and political conservatism[9] (which might explain the force with which Schwarzschild criticizes scholars who seek to impute natural law positions to thinkers like Maimonides[10]), the definition of the *Halakhic* expression *lifnin meshurat ha-din* as "going beyond—actually into the inner recesses—of the letter of the law,"[11] the explication of Maimonides' strange codification of *imitatio Dei* in terms of imitating the rabbis by pointing out that the masses imitate the sages, "the men of philosophical understanding, who in turn emulate God directly,"[12] and his argument that pantheism must lead to the identity of *is* and *ought*, thus making it impossible for Judaism to be pantheistic.[13]

I said above that Schwarzschild is the latest of the major medieval Jewish philosophers. It is now time to explain that claim. In the first place, by 'medieval' I do not mean outmoded or old fashioned. Rather, I mean to place Schwarzschild in the tradition of Jewish thinking which opened with Sa'adia Gaon and reached its highest expression in Maimonides. The common denominator shared by all the medieval Jewish philosophers was their understanding that we could speak intelligibly of a datum called Judaism which had clearly defined, normative and authoritative features, and that this Judaism had to be confronted by and shown to be consistent with some systematic and over-arching view of the universe. Sa'adia did this with Kalam, ibn Gabirol with neo-Platonism, and Maimonides with what he took to be Aristotelianism. Schwarzschild does it with neo-Kantianism.

Schwarzschild is absolutely convinced that Judaism is a consistent, rational system, possessed of authoritative, normative character, and susceptible to clear-cut exposition. His work is studded with expressions like "the original, traditional position of Judaism," "it is established Jewish doctrine that . . ." "authoritative Jewish doctrine holds . . ." "the authentic substance of Judaism," "normative Jewish views," "issues that are Jewish conceptually," "that quintessential Jew . . ." "the differentiating characteristics of Jewish culture," etc.

What is this essential Judaism? In the first place, it involves "an absolute belief in and dependence on the historic revelation at Sinai."[14] Thus, "the most fundamental virtue of the Jew," is to take the Torah seriously.[15] The single most important teaching of this Torah which must be taken seriously is that "truth is above reality—truth is an Ought, not an Is."[16] In other words, the most important characteristic of truth is not its description of the universe as it is but of how it ought to be. This is a reflection of the (neo-) Kantian view that the world in and of itself, the world of the *ding an sich*, of the noumenon, is beyond our ken; the role of science and philosophy is regulative, not descriptive. The "outstanding philosophic exemplars" of this view are, "of course, Judaism on the one hand, which awaits the Messiah and teaches that 'God is the place of the world; the world is not the place of God'; and Kant-Cohen, on the other, who have demonstrated that even the cognition of reality is an ethical imperative."[17] We will return to the issue of the Kantian nature of Judaism or the Jewish nature of Kant below.

We must not view the relationship of God and the world in spatial terms. Judaism adopts the model "of *the will* in trying to conceptualize the relationship between God and the world . . . the explication of the will of God for man we call 'law' or *Halakhah*."[18] Viewing the relationship of God to the world in spatial terms is a pagan or Christian heresy. The cornerstone of Judaism is "the primacy of practical [ethical] reason."[19] This emphasis on volitionalism and ethics (which for Schwarzschild are really the same thing) is what Schwarzschild has called "the Jewish twist" which "literally every single Jewish thinker has felt constrained to introduce . . . into the non-Jewish philosophic system with which he happened to work."[20] Because of this emphasis on ethics "Judaism always advocated, in the name of God absolutely concerned with the world, the greatest possible human, religious attention to the welfare and progress of the world . . . [and] it teaches convincingly that this can be done only under the aegis of a Law put forward by a transcendent God."[21] Schwarzschild summarizes his view of what in an earlier age would have been called "ethical monotheism" as follows: "Classical Jewish thought is committed to the belief in the absolutely transcendent God, who is related to the human world only through his imperatives, and history is, therefore, the enactment of that body of imperatives, to the end of the Messianic achievement, in the interaction of God and Israel, of the Kingdom of God on earth."[22] Schwarzschild's ethical monotheism is thus hardly that of classical Reform Judaism because of its emphasis on *Halakhah* as the body of divine imperatives.

Since Judaism has a clear-cut philosophical view of the world, it can be contrasted with other views, notably Christianity on the one hand and a Christianizing philosophical tendency which Schwarzschild traces from Spinoza through Hegel to Marx on the other hand. Before turning to these critiques, however, it is important to note that if Judaism is defined in terms of its philosophical perspective on the world, then ideas, movements, individuals, and concerns which grow out of or express that perspective can, in an important sense, be called Jewish, whatever their historical, biological, or confessional status. Schwarzschild does not shrink from this conclusion; on the contrary, he enthusiastically embraces it. Many individuals who "do Judaism" are "themselves Jews not by birth or by conversion but by what might be called 'spiritual assimilation'."[23] These "Jewish non-Jews" (as opposed to Deutcher's "non-Jewish Jews") include Immanuel Kant ("the real Kant hailing not from Koenigsburg but from Marburg [the home of Hermann Cohen's—quintessentially Jewish, according to Schwarzschild—neo-Kantianism][24]), J.-P. Sartre, who "ended as a Jew *honoris causa*,"[25] and such alienated Jews as

Ludwig Wittgenstein.[26] This view also allows Schwarzschild to speak of "doing philosophy Jewishly,"[27] to speak of "issues that are Jewish . . . conceptually,"[28] to look for Marx's Jewish theory of usury,[29] and to adumbrate a Jewish aesthetics ("not the aesthetics of Jewish art, but the Jewish aesthetics of art"[30]).

Judaism, then, has a clear-cut philosophical view of its own. This, for Schwarzschild, means that underlying the "blooming, buzzing, mass of confusion," in James' terms, that we ordinarily take for Jewish theological teaching there must be a continuity, systematicity, and consistency to be found by those willing to take the trouble to look.[31] Thus, in an important study on rabbinic views of the Messiah, Schwarzschild says that the crystallization of a systematic, consistent conception of the ideal, Messianic society out of rabbinic sources "needs to be done not only with this aspect as well as the rest of rabbinic eschatology, but with all of Jewish-Rabbinic theology."[32] He goes on to criticize the generally accepted view of the Talmud "as a welter of unsystematic thought" in the following terms: "How unsystematic thought is supposed to underly, or result from, what is conceded to be an extraordinarily systematic legal system is incomprehensible." This last comment is important not only for exemplifying Schwarzschild's view that Talmudic thought is susceptible of systematization but for what it reveals about Schwarzschild's view of the core of Talmudic thought out of which systematic theology is to be spun: *Halakhah*. Schwarzschild, on the basis of his views on the primacy of practical (ethical) reason as the defining characteristic of Judaism, and of the impossibility of ethics without law,[33] has argued for the primacy of *Halakhah* in the elucidation of Jewish theology[34] and has convincingly demonstrated how to do it in several important studies.[35]

As noted above, one of the consequences of Schwarzschild's view that there is a normative and systematic Jewish philosophical perspective is that Judaism can be clearly distinguished from competing religions and, no less important, competing philosophies. Schwarzschild takes great pains to distinguish Judaism from Christianity:

> The doctrine at issue, be it noted, is not the doctrine of sin, original or otherwise. Man's sinfulness is biblical doctrine . . . The doctrine at issue is a basic Christian dualism (Hellenistic and gnostic in origin), between body and spirit, this world and the other world, the kingdoms of the former and the latter. This doctrine leads to Paul's condemnation of the flesh and all that goes with it—to the transfer of God's kingdom from this world to the other and into the heart of man—and to 'Render unto Caesar what is Caesar's and unto God what is God's' . . . It resulted . . . in the divorce of German Lutherans from all political matters, leaving the road open to the princes' ruthless suppression of the peasants' revolt in Luther's time and to the principled indifference of

> the German church as a whole to the rise of Hitler. In such a world, separated from God's direct sovereignty, it is, indeed, true that God's law is ultimately inapplicable. To try to apply it is really hubris . . . Judaism, on the other hand, has never abandoned this world to the devil. This is God's world, created by Him, and His law is specifically and even exclusively meant for it . . . Sin is not a matter of materiality but of errant spirit . . . Furthermore, whatever the total conception of the eschatological state may be in Judaism, none can doubt that the Messianic kingdom is awaited *on this earth*. And thus it follows that, from the Jewish point of view, such matters as foreign policy, like everything else, are directly—not "proximately"—under divine command. Judaism is not only monotheistic but also, in this sense, monistic.[36]

Christianity is intrinsically conservative, surely an "original sin" in Schwarzschild's eyes. This political conservatism is basic to Christianity, and progressive Christians either are not truly progressive or are unconscious Judaizers:[37]

> The reason for this built-in Christian conservatism is . . . the doctrine of the Incarnation. What this doctrine minimally means is that at least one person, at one time and in one place, has been divine. That is to say, the world as it now is, and indeed as it once was, has been at least partly redeemed—and therefore the whole world as it now is is in principle capable of redemption. Cox's only argument with the reactionaries is that they think the entire world is already completely redeemed. The issue between them is one of degree, not of principle.[38]

Schwarzschild criticizes Spinoza, Hegel, and Marx on similar grounds:

> Hegel's basic error consists of having assumed that theoretical reason, rather than volitional ethics, governs history . . . history thus becomes part of nature . . . this is Hegel's version of *Deus sive natura*. This in turn leads to the logical conclusion, which neither Spinoza nor Hegel shirked, that everything that is is necessary and rational and, therefore, in its time and place, is also good. And that, of course, constitutes intellectual and ethical acquiescence to every historical reality, be it good or bad, just or unjust.[39]

Marx failed to free himself of the necessitarian and materialist underpinnings of Spinoza and Hegel. Moses Hess was therefore forced to break "with Marx on ethical grounds, *i.e.*, by holding that socialism was to be the result of the moral will rather than of the inevitable laws of history. Little wonder that he ended as a committed Jew."[40]

The point of all this is that since Judaism = ethical volitionalism (as we have seen) and since Jewish Messianism = revolution (as we will see below) and since Judaism insists on God's transcendence, thus refusing to make the real or material world divine (and thus already in theory perfected), Judaism, while surely socialist and progressive, must reject the (false) socialism and progressivism of Marx, just as it must reject the politically conservative consequences of Christian immanentism.

I said above that the defining characteristic of medieval Jewish philosophy was a view of Judaism as normative, consistent, and systematic and the felt need to confront that Judaism with a systematic, architectonically overarching philosophic view of the cosmos. So far we have seen that Schwarzschild's view of Judaism fully satisfies the first part of this criterion. For Schwarzschild there is also a systematic philosophy with which Judaism must be confronted and which can be shown to be consistent with Judaism. Indeed, for Schwarzschild, this philosophical system is not only consistent with Judaism but for all intents and purposes identical with it. This philosophical system, of course, is Kantianism as canonically interpreted by Hermann Cohen, the founder of the Marburg School of Neo-Kantianism.

Schwarzschild clearly and explicitly identifies himself over and over again as a disciple of Cohen's. "Speaking as a Marburg neo-Kantian,"[41] he says in one place, but speaks as such in almost every place. Perhaps the clearest summary of Cohen' and Schwarzschild's Kant is found in the following critique of Hegel:

> The principle underlying Cohen's rejection of Hegelianism in its original form as well as in its transformed state of socialist materialism is the refutation of the pantheistic doctrine that 'everything that is is rational, and that everything rational is,' on the grounds that, philosophically speaking, this constitutes a confusion of the ideal with the real, of the hypothetical with the empirical, and that, ethically speaking it amounts to a vicious justification of any given *status quo* in history and society. Hegelianism and socialist materialism, in short, are the denial of voluntarism in favor of quietism. Cohen is amazingly radical and consistent in the application of this criterion to all cultural and historical realities.[42]

Kant teaches that reality is never given but must be constructed. The real must not be accepted as the ideal; rather, the ideal, the regulative, must guide our construction of reality. In Jewish terms, this is called Messianism and in Kantian terms, critical idealism. The Spinoza/Hegel/Marx denial of volitionalism (and thus of ethics) must be rejected: "Ethical idealism, *Judaism as well as Kant*, must and does answer this pernicious doctrine with the counterproposition that the rational is never real and that it is man's task on earth to realize it ever more."[43]

Having described Schwarzschild's basic Jewish/philosophic position, we may now turn to an examination of the way in which that basic philosophic/religious orientation finds expression in some specific issues. Among those matters which have consistently attracted his attention are Messianism, Zionism, pacifism, and socialism. Before analyzing his positions on these questions, however, a number of introductory observations are in order.

First, I have noted that Schwarzschild presents himself as a disciple of Hermann Cohen. This is important since, accepting Cohen's "philosophy of origins," we must look for the "essential Schwarzschild" in the "early Schwarzschild." He is not, however, an uncritical disciple. "The live Jew," he wrote at the beginning of his ground-breaking study of Rosenzweig, "never stands still in his Jewishness. If he ever did stand still he would be Jewishly dead; even if he were an extremely pious and learned Jew, standing still he would be an extremely pious and learned dead Jew."[44] Schwarzschild is an extremely pious (not, however, in the terms by which piety is all too often measured today) and extremely learned Jew; but he is by no means a dead Jew. He is constantly growing in his Judaism, whether in terms of personal lifestyle, in terms of his teachers (he counts himself as a disciple, not only of Hermann Cohen but of Samuel Atlas,[45] R. Joseph Soloveitchik,[46] and R. Isaac Hutner[47]), and, most especially in terms of his theological explorations.

This growth, however, is organic, never haphazard. Speaking of Sartre, he says that "truly perspicuous philosophers . . . tend to begin with a unifying vision, or conceptuality, and this original conception, through sometimes fundamental revisions . . . retains its basic philosophical integrity."[48] Schwarzschild is certainly a perspicuous philosopher and his thought, while having undergone some fundamental revisions (particularly with respect to Messianism), expresses a unifying vision and has throughout his career retained its basic philosophical integrity.

This point leads to a second observation. I have just described Schwarzschild in terms he used to describe two other thinkers, Rosenzweig and Sartre. While meticulously adhering to the strictest canons of scholarship in his historical studies, Schwarzschild is so *engaged* a scholar that he is often as revealing about himself as he is about his subjects. This point can be amplified as follows: Schwarzschild has produced a large number of truly important studies in the history of philosophy and of Jewish thought; but he has done so not as an historian, but as a theologian. In Schwarzschild's able hands, historical works always subserve (but are never corrupted by) theological ends. This may explain, in part, why his historical studies, even clothed as they are in all the trappings of academic scholarship, make such lively reading.

Messianism is absolutely central to Judaism: "... the Messianic kingdom is what all of Judaism is for and about;"[49] "Messianic expectation is thus literally the daily and even hourly posture of the Jew;"[50] "... the Messianic vocation of Israel ..."[51] No person half-way literate in the sources of Judaism could deny the truth of these characterizations. For Schwarzschild, however, Messianism is also absolutely central to Kantianism, to reason, to *Halakhah*, and to political and personal ethics. In fact, without too much overstatement we can say that for Schwarzschild, Messianism *is* Judaism which *is* Kantianism which *is* reason which *is Halakhah* which *is* personal and political ethics.

Here we have Schwarzschild on Kant and Messianism:

> It is noteworthy that the two truths which we have hitherto attempted to crystallize have one feature in common: they define the beginning and the middle by the end; *i.e.*, death defines the possibility of life, ultimate divine peace defines the possibility of peace in our time; or, in other words yet, the future defines the past and the present, not the reverse as is usually thought. We are not saying anything new. Kant highlighted this when he distinguished between the reactionary, stand-pattism of the 'is' and the revolutionary ethical 'ought'. And even Kant did not, of course, invent anything; he merely put in philosophical language what biblical religion had always called 'the kingdom of God' or the 'reign of the Messiah'.[52]

As soon as we make ethics a matter of realizing ideals, of always judging the *is* by the *ought*, of constructing the world in which we live not in terms of its present nature but in terms of its future possibilities, when we make ethics a matter of reading the future back into the present—and Schwarzschild's Kant does all of this—we are in Messianic territory.

Since Kantianism is Messianic, so must reason be:

> Reason is thus, I hope to have shown, the companion of faith in all its ways. Reason, in a sense, prepares the path on which faith can walk; reason clears the path once faith has begun to walk it and writes an intelligible record of the distance covered; and when faith has reached its destination, reason embraces faith, and the two companions unite in the kiss of the Messiah.[53]

Halakhah both subserves and is defined by its Messianic end:

> It would not be difficult to show how literally all of the *Halakhah* is either the law of society as it should be—and thus whoever fulfills it in fact establishes, as it were, a small forward bastion of the ultimate future in the present—or the law by which the present society is moved forward toward the Messianic.

> *I.e.* whenever a Jew acts according to the *Halakhah* he either hastens the coming of the Kingdom or actually institutes it at the moment and in the place where he happens to be.[54]

Schwarzschild's view here is entrenched and established Jewish doctrine; perhaps its best-known expression is in the Lurianic concept of *tikkun*.

If *Halakhah* is Messianic, then it can come as no surprise that ethics is as well, since Schwarzschild consistently identifies the two.[55] In terms of political ethics we find the following claim:

> And since the means must be appropriate to the end, the road to the goal, it follows that peaceful action—not war, just and decent action—not exploitation and depersonalization, *Mitzvot*—and not hobbies, timewasters, and flippancies—are the ways in which man must strive to approach his individual and social destination. The opposite or any other action removes us further from the goal and that, therefore, quite literally, must be regarded as reactionary. Contrary to Goethe's dictum, destiny is destination, not character.[56]

We have here a kind of "Messianic imperative" by which Messianic expectation guides our actions in this world.[57] If we wish to bring about the coming of the Messiah then we must behave in ways consistent with that end. In effect, to make the Messiah's coming possible, we must act now as if the Messiah has already come.[58]

Just as our political and social ethics must be defined by the Messianic end, so must our personal ethics:

> But men do play a significant part in the drama of salvation, and they can affect its *denoument* by their lives. Thereupon various Messianic courses of action are followed: vegetarianism, socialism, pacifism—the characteristics of the Messianic kingdom are regarded as commandments for daily living; they, as it were, anticipate the world to come in this world and try radically and piously to 'transform the world in the image of the kingdom of heaven'."[59]

It is no surprise that Schwarzschild, the Messianic Jew *par excellence*, is a vegetarian, socialist, and pacifist.

One of the issues related to Messianism for which Schwarzschild's contribution is best known is the question of the personal nature of the Messiah. In 1956, using Rosenzweig against Cohen (!) Schwarzschild argued both for the actual coming of the Messiah and for the Messiah's personal character in an essay addressed first and foremost to Reform Jews. He was, of course, arguing against one of the important teachings of classical Reform Judaism, which replaced belief in the coming of the Messiah with belief in the advent of a Messianic age. Schwarzschild posited an "intimate connection between the belief in the personality of the Messiah and belief in the personality of God . . ."[60] Although Schwarzschild makes an important philosophical argument in this essay here I want only to cite the ethical argument which he makes for the personhood of the Messiah:

> We have learned from religious as well as nonreligious existentialism, that all moral reality, as distinguished from nature and mathematics, is the reality of persons. Man, the person, is the *locus* of ethics, not ages, ideas, or forces. The Messianic Age is a Utopia; the Messiah is a concrete, though, future reality.[61]

Since the Messianic idea is first and foremost an *ethical* idea, and since humanity in all its concreteness must be the focus of ethics, to depersonalize the Messiah is, in effect, to argue against the ethical focus of Jewish Messianism. And this would be to empty it of its fundamental content, rendering it vacuous.

Precisely thirty years after the publication of this essay Schwarzschild explicitly reversed part of his position in a study which argues on *ethical* (as well as historical and theological) grounds that in order to preserve the ideal, regulative character of Messianic belief we must side with Cohen against Rosenzweig and see the advent of the Messiah as something for which we must work, and toward which we can move ever closer, but as an event which will never actually occur.[62] Schwarzschild uses all his brilliance and insight to show that this admittedly unusual position is actually the teaching of rabbinic Judaism.

I cannot refrain from suggesting that Schwarzschild's position here might reflect not only a revision of philosophical and theological views (which revision brings him closer to his mentor, Cohen), but also his growing disillusionment with Messianic Zionism. To my mind, this is to throw the baby out with the bath water, but that must be the subject of different study altogether.

This observation does bring us to the next topic which I want to discuss, namely, Steven Schwarzschild's views on Zionism. Schwarzschild is well known, in fact notorious, for being the only Jewish theologian of stature in our day to maintain a consistent, radical, and *Jewish* critique of Zionism. Given some of the unfortunate realities in the Jewish world today, and in light of some of the truly ignoble vilification to which he has been subjected, a number of comments must immediately be made. First, Schwarzschild is a Jewish critic of Zionism; that does not make him by any means an enemy of the State of Israel. Second, because he is not an enemy of the State of Israel Schwarzschild has been extremely careful not to wash Jewish laundry in public, keeping his criticisms muted and in the family. Given the strength of his feelings on the subject and the provocations (in his eyes) of Israel and the Zionist establishment, this has often involved great self-restraint. Third, Schwarzschild's critique of Zionism is based, not upon ignorance, but upon a thorough and deep acquaintance with Zionist theory, literature, and history. Fourth, Schwarzschild's critique of Zionism grows directly out of his *Jewish* concerns. Zionism, he is convinced, is bad for Judaism and thus bad for the Jews. Last, Schwarzschild is not and for all intents and purposes has never been a Zionist. But that does not mean that he has never felt the pull of the amazing events of 1948. He, too, like most other Jews, has occasionally "espied the outlines of the figure of the Messiah in the faintest wisps of smoke over the chimneys of Auschwitz and on the skyline of Jerusalem rebuilding."[63] He, too, like many other religious Jews, has been tempted to see the *athalta d'geulah* [beginning of the redemption], but never the redemption itself, in the establishment of the State of Israel.[64]

Why is Schwarzschild not a Zionist? In this connection it is perhaps apposite to quote the famous remark attributed to Hermann Cohen about the Zionists: "Those fools want to be happy!" By this Cohen seemed to mean that Zionists wanted to feel at home in the world, comfortable, not alienated. But the Jew, and here Schwarzschild paraphrases Franz Rosenzweig, must "always and everywhere [be] a stranger except in Judaism and with God and that, as a matter of fact, our commitment to the eventual Messianic Kingdom must perforce estrange us from the existing conditions of the world at all stages prior to that of the Messiah."[65] Our commitment to ultimate perfection and the regulative character of the Messianic utopia forbids us comfort in this dispensation. To feel at home in the present world is to idealize that world and is to be guilty of confusing the world of *is* with the world of *ought*.

Not only does Zionism lead to the confusion of *is* and *ought* but it is also guilty of the kind of materialist immanentism which, as we saw above in our discussion of Schwarzschild's rejection of the Spinoza-Hegel-Marx "heresy," is antithetical to Judaism:

> I argue that Judaism and Jewish culture have paradigmatically and throughout history operated with a fundamental dichotomy between nature ('what is') and ethics (*i.e.*, God and man—'what ought to be'). Pagan ontologism on the other hand, and the Christian synthesis of biblical transcendentalism and Greek incarnationism result in human and historical submission to what are acclaimed as 'natural forces.' Although in the history of Jewish culture such a heretical, quasi-pantheistic tendency asserted itself, first in medieval

> Kabbalism and then in modern Zionism, from a traditionally Jewish standpoint nature remains subject to humanly enacted ends."[66]

A Jew can never feel fully at home in nature, the ultimate *is*. Zionism ignores this fundamental fact of Judaism.[67]

If Jews are not to return to history, does that mean that we have no task in the world? Hardly! "Our task is to be *menschen* and thus—and thus only—to hasten the Messiah's coming, not by force or by magic or by superarrogation."[68] This is so because "the Torah is our business, Israel's survival is God's."[69] This may seem like a recipe for quietism but such is not the case. Zionism may not be the proper expression of true Jewish Messianism but that certainly does not mean (and cannot mean, given the unbreakable tie between Messianism and ethics) that it has no proper, active, concrete expression in this world. This leads us to the last two points in our exposition of Steven Schwarzschild's thought, pacifism and socialism.

Schwarzschild must be a pacifist because of his Messianism: if the Messianic era will be characterized by peace, then the only way to actualize the era (to the extent that it can be actualized) is to act peacefully now. Schwarzschild is also a pacifist because of his belief in God:

> Therefore, when God, the Radical, demands that we seek peace, He demands radically that we radically seek radical peace . . . Because the God of the religious man is the root of all radicalism, the religious man himself is bound to be radical in every respect, including his insistence on peace."[70]

This interpretation of God also underlies Schwarzschild's socialism:

> God is the root of all things. He is *the* radical. Faith is, therefore, by definition radical. Whatever is not radical is not faith. God hates comfortable superficialities. He loves all radicalisms—even His own radical opponents. I am sure He prefers these to His facile believers."[71]

Socialism, which seeks to change the world in light of the Messianic ideals of Judaism, is one of those radical things loved by God and therefore adopted as program and goal by Schwarzschild.

In the preceding survey I have sought to delineate the broad outlines of the thought—as it has developed and been expressed to date—of one of contemporary Jewry's most important theologians. I have suggested that Schwarzschild may be best understood if we fit him in the framework of the great Jewish philosophers of the past, all of whom had a clear-cut vision of what

Judaism is and sought to show that Judaism could and must be successfully confronted with a comprehensive philosophy held by the Jewish philosopher to be substantially true. Schwarzschild is convinced that normative, authoritative, *Halakhic* Judaism is a consistent, rational system primarily characterized by the primacy it gives to ethical concerns. This system, he maintains, can be shown to have been given its canonical "secular" interpretation in the philosophy of Immanuel Kant as exposited by Hermann Cohen. Among the consequences of this position are that Judaism is systematizable, that non-Jews can, in effect, be "spiritually assimilated" into Judaism, and that there are religious and philosophical positions (Christianity on the one hand and Spinoza/Hegel/Marx on the other) absolutely antithetical to Judaism.

Having set forth Schwarzschild's theology to this point, I then discussed four issues—Messianism, Zionism, pacifism, and socialism—on which Schwarzschild has taken important Jewish positions. I tried to show how his position on each of these issues grows directly out of his basic philosophical orientation to Judaism.

Steven Schwarzschild has successfully transplanted to North America the best of a long tradition of Jewish and philosophical reasoning rooted in Europe, immeasurably enriching North American and World Judaism thereby.

–1–

The Personal Messiah—Toward the Restoration of a Discarded Doctrine

Into the first blessing of the Eighteen-Prayer, liberal Judaism has introduced one change which is linguistically minor but doctrinally major. The traditional formulation—He "brings a Redeemer"—now reads, He "brings redemption." This changed liturgical formula persists in practically all authorized liberal prayer books to this day (including the "Conservative" version of Reconstructionism), although the theological reasons which induced the change were among the very earliest issues raised against Orthodoxy at the beginning of the 19th century.

Much, if not most, of the liberal Jewish platform has been modified in these 150 years, and the trend of such modifications has almost unexceptionally been in the direction of a gradual and limited return to the original, traditional position of Judaism. The doctrine of the peoplehood of Israel and the concommitant significance of the earthly Jerusalem for Jewish hopes have long been restored to non-Orthodox religious thinking; the meaningfulness of ritual and ceremonial has been emphatically reasserted; even the validity of the continuous authoritativeness of Jewish law, if not actually reestablished, is certainly increasingly becoming a matter of major concern to Reform Jews. It is, therefore, a little surprising that almost the only basic claim of pristine Jewish liberalism which has not been subjected to this process of reevaluation in the course of time, should be the doctrine of the Messiah.[1]

The reason for this comparative neglect may well be that the doctrine of the Messiah superficially appears to be merely a matter of theory. The question whether the Messianic fulfillment is to be brought about by the instrumentality of a single individual or through the collective progress of humanity seems of little moment when put side by side with such pressing, concrete problems as Zionism, the homogeneity of the Jewish community, the observance of Jewish practice and obedience to Jewish law. If this assumption were correct, it would be perfectly proper to relegate so theoretical a question to the background. And yet, it is very easy to demonstrate tht the Messianic doctrine is not academic at all but, on the contrary, exceedingly "practical";

perhaps it can even be proved that it, too, requires reinvestigation within the framework of contemporary, non-Orthodox Jewish thinking and life.

There were basically three reasons why liberal Judaism in the first half of the 19th century was moved to transform the doctrine of the personal Messiah into the doctrine of the Messianic age—or, to use the phraseology of the Eighteen-Prayer, the doctrine of the Redeemer into the doctrine of redemption. These three reasons can be described respectively as antinationalistic, antimiraculous and optimistic.

In the minds of the early reformers, lay as well as rabbinical, the foremost consideration in favor of the depersonalization of the Messiah certainly seems to have been the fact that they regarded the personal Messiah as inextricably interwoven with the hope of the eventual restoration of the people of Israel from the lands of the Diaspora to Palestine, the reestablishment of the Temple and the sacrificial cult. For the present, it implied the foreign character of Jews in the countries of their domicile. These premises, or implications, of the belief in the personal Messiah they rejected most strenuously. They had begun to receive civil rights in Germany and throughout Western Europe, where Reform had its origin; together with non-Jewish liberals, they continued to agitate for expansion and completion of their citizenship rights; and they confidently looked forward to an early consummation of these aspirations. To declare, at this juncture of history, that they were still awaiting a person who would lead them from their present homes and reconstitute for them a separate nation in a distant land struck them as aiding and abetting their antagonists who insisted on refusing them their civil rights on the grounds that they neither were nor wished to be members of their host nations. Thus, in his report of the pertinent discussions at the Rabbinical Conferences of 1844-1846, Philipson relates that Dr. Mendel Hess identified the personal with the "political" Messiah.[2] Even earlier, the Frankfort Society of the Friends of Reform, in the single substantive statement of its beliefs, had announced: "A Messiah who is to lead back the Israelites to the land of Palestine is neither expected nor desired by us. [The nonexpectation is understandable and, in this context, logical; the undesirability evokes the ironical picture of the Messiah appearing in Frankfort and being received at the city gates by a delegation of respectable Jewish citizens with the urgent request kindly to remove himself since his presence was likely to obstruct current attempts at the complete emancipation of German Jews.] We know no fatherland except that to which we belong by birth or citizenship." And, in another hemisphere as well, many years later, K. Kohler still says: "A complete change in the religious aspiration of the Jew was brought about by the transformation of his political status and hopes in the nineteenth century. The new era witnessed his admission in many lands to full citizenship on an equality with his fellow citizens of other faiths ... He therefore necessarily identified himself completely with the nation whose language and literature had nurtured his mind, and whose political and social destinies he shared with true patriotic fervor. He stood apart from the rest only by virtue of his religion ... Consequently the hope voiced in the Synagogal liturgy for a return to Palestine, the formation of a Jewish State under a king of the house of David, and the restoration of the sacrificial cult, no longer expressed the views of the Jew in Western civilization. The prayer for the rebuilding of Jerusalem and the restoration of the Temple with its priestly cult could no longer voice his religious hope. Thus the leaders of Reform Judaism in the middle of the nineteenth century declared themselves unanimously opposed to retaining the belief in a personal Messiah ... They accentuated all the more strongly Israel's hope for a Messianic age, a time of universal knowledge of God and love of man, so intimately interwoven with the religious mission of the Jewish people ... "[3]

It may be taken for granted that this particular reason for the abolition of the doctrine of the personal Messiah in liberal Judaism need no longer be taken seriously in the middle of the 20th century. In the further pursuit of the argument quoted above, Kohler explains that Eastern European Jewry, still subject to disenfranchisement and persecution, continues to adhere to the Orthodox longing for a Jewish political restoration—that for this reason Zionism was born there, as an answer to anti-Semitism—and that both of these situations are inapplicable to Western Europe in the first place, and must, in the second place, be made superfluous everywhere else by social progress. The irreconcilability of Zionism with liberal Judaism has long been given the lie in theory as well as in practice and need no longer be argued. But one additional observation must still be made in this connection before we proceed to the next point. It is surely an ironical paradox that Reform Judaism eliminated the personal Messiah because it was held that belief in him was inevitably accompanied by Jewish nationalism, while extreme right-wing orthodoxy of the *Aggudat Yisrael* brand rejected Jewish nationalism because it awaited the advent of this very Messiah! The *Aggudah* argued exactly the other way around: the personal Messiah will redeem the Jewish people; therefore, we must not attempt to anticipate by human action what he will do on divine instruction. Reform remained aloof from Zionism because it did not believe in the personal Messiah, the *Aggudah* remained aloof because it did.

This ironical paradox conclusively illustrates the essential *nonsequitur* of Reform reasoning on this point: whether one believes in the personal Messiah or not has nothing whatever to do with Jewish nationalism. Theoretically, there is no reason why the personal Messiah must mean Jewish nationalism and the Messianic age must mean "universalism." It is just as possible, logically, to believe that the Messianic person will bring universal redemption rather than the in-gathering of the Jewish people, and that the Messianic stage in human history will bring with it the national restoration of Israel rather than its complete absorption among the converted nations of the world.[4] Practically speaking, the outstanding Reform Jews who, during the last half century, were also Zionist leaders do not seem to have been inhibited in their Jewish nationalism by their rejection of the belief in the personal Messiah.

In short, not only has the antinationalistic argument against the doctrine of the personal Messiah been refuted in theory and in fact, but it can be shown never to have been a cogent argument in the first place.

A logically more tenable argument against the personal Messiah was the belief that to await him implied in fact expectation of a miracle. Traditionally, in Bible, Talmud, and post-Talmudic Jewish literature, the functions which the Messiah would fulfill were regarded as being indeed miraculous: nature itself would be transformed to accord with moral requirements, human life would be rid of all natural or moral deficiencies, Israel and Judaism would be established in their proper place of spiritual primacy.[5] But such a doctrine ran counter, of course, to the positivistic, scientific outlook of 19th century liberals. As Kohler put it straightforwardly: "Our entire mode of thinking demands the complete recognition of the empire of law throughout the universe, manifesting the all-pervasive will of God. The whole cosmic order is one miracle. No room is left for single or exceptional miracles. Only a primitive age could think of God as altering the order of nature which He had fixed, so as to let iron float on water like wood to please one person . . ."[6]

On closer analysis, however, even on its own premises, this objection to the doctrine of the personal Messiah on "scientific," antimiraculous grounds cannot long be maintained either. In the first place, it is very difficult to understand why the achievement of the Messianic aims by many ordinary people—which is, after all, what the concept of the Messianic age boils down to—is any less miraculous than their achievement by one extraordinary person. Even if it be granted that the state of the world in Messianic times must be considered a miracle from our perspective, a notion which, as we shall see immediately, is not necessary to the doctrine as such, it presumably will be miraculous regardless of the agency through which it is brought about. In one sense, therefore, the transformation of the doctrine does not accomplish this declared aim of rationalization. In the second place, however, it is not at all certain that miraculousness is necessarily one of the ingredients of the Messianic state. Long before the 19th century reformers came along, the medaeval Jewish scholastic rationalists, Maimonides himself at their head, on occasion objected to a supernatural interpretation of this tenet: "Let it not occur to anyone that in the days of the Messiah a single thing will be changed in the natural course of the world or that there will be any kind of innovation in nature. Rather the world will continue to exist as it always has ... The Messiah will come exclusively in order to bring peace to the world ... How all these things will come about none can know until they have actually come about."[7] And yet they certainly anticipated the arrival of the person of the Messiah "though he may tarry, at any time." Therefore, as in the case of the antinationalistic objection to the doctrine of the personal Messiah, here, too, a complete *non-sequitur* in the liberal argumentation must be noted: in fact, people, and often "better people than we," have believed in him without subscribing to his miraculous advent. In theory, Messianism is bound up with miraculousness either in both of its variants, the personal and the collective, or in neither. Thus miraculousness cannot decide the issue between them.

We have stated that miraculousness is inherent in the Messianic doctrine even when it is reformulated in liberalistic, collective terms. Apart from the common-sensical argument already adduced to that effect, no better evidence can be added than that of Hermann Cohen, the man who was rightly described by Klatzkin as "a spiritual giant who guarded the inheritance of an impoverished generation"[8]—the liberal generation. In him, liberal theology, including the depersonalization of the Messiah, reached its grand consummation—and if it failed here it must be regarded as having failed *in toto*.

History was for Cohen the infinite human process of striving for the ideal, and Messianism is the term designating the completion of this infinite process. But how can infinity be completed? If, to use an analogy of which Cohen was fond, the ideal state of the future lies on an axis which the curve of human history approaches ever more closely but cannot actually touch, like an asymptote, then perfection is not an ideal whose reality is guaranteed at some point however far removed, but a mathematical impossibility—and there is no guarantee of success at all; to the contrary, there is only a guarantee of relative failure.[9] The conception of the Messiah as an age leaves humanity swimming desperately in the ocean of history without a shore where he might eventually reach safety. Guttman had pointed out that Cohen's depersonalization of the concept of God had deprived it of the ability to perform the real, historical and ontological function which Cohen himself had ascribed to it.[10] The same must be said of his view of Messianism.[11] In fact, the rational picture presents itself in this manner: that there may be such a thing as history at all, progress must be possible; for progress to be possible there must be a logical guarantee of the eventual attainability of the goal of progress; by

Cohen's own admission the goal of progress, perfection, is unattainable through human endeavor. If, therefore, the goal is to be reached at all, it can be reached only by a divine intercession at the end-point of history. And once the theological, even the philosophical necessity of divine, *i.e.* miraculous intercession is established, it becomes absurd and arrogant to declare the concept of the miraculous, personal Messiah out of bounds. To say that the Messianic state must be miraculously brought about, if at all, but not through the miraculous agency of a person, is clearly a purely arbitrary assertion.

Another, usually unexpressed, reason may have contributed to the hostility which the reformers of the last century felt toward the concept of the individual Messiah. Maimonides had stipulated the belief in the bodily Messiah as a fundamental doctrine of Judaism and declared the denier therof to be a heretic.[12] Taenzer has convincingly demonstrated that Albo relegated this doctrine to a very much lower level of Jewish obligatoriness. On this level, belief or disbelief in the personal Messiah by the individual Jew would be without effect on his full religious status.[13] In effect, Albo proclaimed not only that a Jew need not necessarily believe in the Messiah but actually, by implication, recommended against such belief. The historical conditions under which he lived explain his attitude. By his time, the doctrine had become a serious obstacle to Jewish theological self-assertion, for it was used to good effect by Christians in formal as well as informal religious disputations. "Also the others [!] make out of it [the Messianic doctrine] a basic principle with which to refute the Torah of Moses."[14] Once the principle of an individual Messiah was accepted, and with the narratives of the New Testament difficult to refute in an age bereft of historical or literary criticism, the crucial issue between Jews and Christians seemed to become one of picking the right person to fit the Messianic prerequisities—an unproductive quarrel at best. By eliminating the Messianic doctrine, Albo hoped to prevent further unconstructive controversies and even to strengthen the Jewish position which could then actually turn the argument around: the Messiah having been declared to be irrelevant to true religion, a religion which made him the central test of faith demonstrated its own unauthenticity.

From the Jewish point of view, the phenomenon of Christological Christianity is, of course, only one of many pseudo-Messianisms. By the 19th century there had been many such movements in Jewish history; some of them extremely unsettling. If enlightened, rationalistic, liberal Christians of that era were embarrassed by the traditional claims of Christianity regarding the historical Jesus, as indeed they were, how much more eager must liberal Jews have been to rid themselves of all the theological preconditions which might again lead, as they had done so often in the past, to the recurrence of enthusiastic Messianic claims. One recalls Graetz's immoderate observations on the subject.[15] How easier to answer the claims of traditional Christianity, than to dissociate oneself from Jewish pseudo-Messianisms and the entire Jewish Messianic doctrine, and thus prove the rationality of Judaism. In short, this was Joseph Albo in 19th century disguise.

Perhaps it is no longer necessary to show both the uselessness and the invalidity of this procedure. It is truly a case of throwing out the true gods together with the false ones. If a doctrine is to be rejected because it can be or even has been abused, the very belief in God must be dispensed with, since men have also often represented themselves as God and created havoc by the falsehoods announced in his name. Furthermore, Buber quotes the pointed Chassidic story which compares the pseudo-Messianic movements to wet compresses that keep the patient awake until the doctor comes: "When God saw that the soul of Israel had fallen sick, he covered it with the painful shawl of the *Galuth*. So that it could bear the pains, however, He bestowed upon it the sleep of numbness. Again, so that it would not be destroyed, He awakens it each hour with a false Messianic hope and then lulls it to sleep again until the night will have passed and the real Messiah will appear. For the sake of this work, the eyes of the wise are occasionally blinded."[16] Franz Rosenzweig made the same point in a less anecdotal, more theological and poetic fashion: "The expectation of the coming of the Messiah, by which and because of which Judaism lives, would be a meaningless theologumenon, a mere 'idea' in the philosophical sense, empty babble, if the appearance again and again of a 'false Messiah' did not render it reality and unreality, illusion and disillusion. The false Messiah is as old as the hope for the true Messiah. He is the changing form of this changeless hope. He separates every Jewish generation into those whose faith is strong enough to give themselves up to an illusion, and those whose hope is so strong that they do not allow themselves to be deluded. The former are the better, the latter the stronger. The former bleed as victims on the altar of the eternity of the people, the latter are the priests who perform the service at this altar. And this goes on until the day when all will be reversed, when the belief of the believers will become truth, and the hope of the hoping a lie. Then—and no one knows whether this "then" will not be this very day—the task of the hoping will come to an end and, when the morning of that day breaks, everyone who still belongs among those who hope and not among those who believe will run the risk of being rejected. This danger hovers over the apparently less endangered life of the hopeful."[17] Herein also lies the answer to those who will always worry: if the belief in the personal Messiah as such is granted, why not Jesus? It is true that if I wish to be married I may choose the wrong wife, but does that prove that I should not look for a wife at all and entirely reject the possibility of marriage?

Underlying all these motivations for the depersonalization of the Messiah-concept lay an optimism about the future of the Jewish people and of humanity as a whole. This optimism resulted in the belief that, as already indicated, the redeemer had become not only impossible and undesirable, but also unnecessary. After all, the Messiah was logically and historically a product of need. In the former sense, the anticipation of his coming implied consciously and unconsciously that humanity alone could not master its destiny or reach its goal. Instead, a divine agent would either have to bring about or at least complete the Messainic, *i.e.* perfect, human society. And historically it is true that, as Israel's historic situation became increasingly hopeless, the concept of the Messiah became increasingly supernatural, for the greater the need the more powerful had to be the person who would triumph over it. "The burden of exile narrowed their horizon. They could see no other way of redemption from their abject position than by supernatural events."[18] Or as Baeck put it impressively: "It was especially true in the centuries of despair: only by seeing before him a mirage was many a man able to procure the strength with which to keep on marching through the desert which life had become for him."[19] Now, in the 19th century, it was believed that such pessimism about the nature of man and the prospects of history had once and for all been refuted.

Certainly, the political development of the times seemed to indicate that the Jewish despair which had so largely formed the concept of the Messiah had become a thing of the past. Everywhere and increasingly Jews were being enfranchised and at least promised, often also given, equal rights with their fellow citizens. Physical persecution, except in some God-forsaken corners of Russia, had almost completely ceased. Liberal democracy was making headway everywhere in the West; material and technological developments were fast progressing. And even culturally, the mellowing of Christianity as evidenced by the new liberal theology, Unitarianism, ethical humanism and similar phenomena, persuaded the usually sober I. M. Wise that America would be Jewish within the foreseeable future. Thus Samuel Hirsch declared: "Everywhere the emancipation of mankind is being striven for so that a morally pure and holy life may be possible of being lived by man on this earth.[2-] Auerback agreed with him: "In our days the ideals of justice and the brotherhood of men have been so strengthened through the laws and institutions of modern states that they can never again be shattered; we are witnessing an ever nearer approach of the establishment of the Kingdom of God on earth through the strivings of mankind."[21] Herzfeld chimed in: "The conference must declare what it means by redemption; yes, it should state that we are now entering upon the period of redemption. Freedom and virtue are spreading, the world is growing better."[22] And, of course, the famous Pittsburgh Platform announced: "We recognize, in the modern era of universal culture of heart and intellect, the approaching of the realization of Israel's greatest Messianic hope for the establishment of the kingdom of truth, justice, and peace among all men."[23] In this respect, Wiener summarizes the spirit of the time trenchantly and convincingly: "The new generation was dominated by an almost too gay optimism . . . Transcendent, eschatological ideas receded in the face of the confidence that this world would soon be the scene of divine justice within the moral life of humanity. By the latter was meant above all the completion of equality of civil rights in all countries—which was an understandable preoccupation, though it became embarrassing by being constantly overemphasized." He recalls that for Moritz Lazarus the outcome of the Dreyfus Affair was positively "a Messianic event." Wiener indicts this entire generation of shallowly optimistic, self-centered and self-deceiving leaders when he states: "If it is ever true that religious beliefs are the ideological superstructure of the economic-political conditions of society, then it was certainly true of this class. It interpreted and accommodated religious doctrines in conformity with its enthusiastic attitude toward civil society which it regarded as final, eternal, and divine."[24]

This outlook no longer deserves a reply. The neo-existentialists—Jewish, Christian, and nonreligious—have effectively knocked down this straw man to build up a case for themselves. Rosenzweig, for example, reports the famous incident in which Hermann Cohen is supposed to have pleaded with him that he must expect the Messiah within no more than fifty years.[25] Thus, he wanted to reveal this vapid optimism for the self-deceiving hallucination that it was—and as a symbol his story serves well enough; although we must add that as a truthful report of Cohen's mind it is a thoroughly incredible tale. It belies everything that Cohen stood for in his affirmation of the infinite Messianic process, his violent rejection of all forms of eudaemonism, and even his definition of the Messiah itself. Nonetheless, that the contemporary pessimists have completely and justifiably defaulted this hallucination cannot be disputed. We have learned for a fact that the 19th century was profoundly wrong in its vast overestimation of the social abilities of humanity. If persecution, pogroms and oppression are indeed the rationale for Messianism, then our age is, and by rights ought to be, the most Messianic age of all in the history of Israel.

If, then, we must discard the third main reason which the liberals of the 19th century proffered for the abolition of the concept of the personal Messiah, literally not one of their arguments has been found to withstand critical examination. Their antinationalism has been repudiated by Jewish history; their antimiraculousness has been refuted by the necessities of their own position, not to speak of the views of others; their optimism has been repudiated by general history. Furthermore, it turns out that at least two of their reasons were not logically constructed in the first place. In short but brutal fact, their case against the personal Messiah crumbles at first touch.

We could end the argument at this point. Reigious tradition must always be regarded as valid until, and unless, invincible reasons are brought forth against it. The reasons militating against the traditional doctrine under consideration have been shown to be anything but invincible, and we may, therefore, with good and calm consciences return to the original position. Ours is not necessarily the task to prove the doctrine positively; to refute its refutation ought to suffice. Nevertheless, without venturing to prove its tenability, there are a few hints which may be given toward the construction of the positive case.

The first is a mere technicality. The liberal prayerbooks of the last century have abounded, and still abound, with phrases which must, if they are to be intellectually acceptable, be interpreted very broadly by the Jews who use them. "The Torah of Moses" is a clear cut an example as any, although there are many others. Do liberal Jews believe that "the" Torah was given to, by, or from Moses? As a matter of fact, the very ritual reading from the Torah has become a metaphoric act for most of them. A very high percentage, certainly well over half, of everything read from it, if it is to be acceptable at all, must be homiletically decontaminated of its original historical, theological, moral, or social intent. And nonetheless these things are retained—reinterpreted but retained. Yet the phrase "Who brings a redeemer" cannot be so treated; it must be changed!? All that was required to bring the traditional text into conformity with liberal belief was the interchange of a single letter of the Hebrew alphabet, a *Heh* at the end for a *Vav* in the middle of the word. But this had to be done through a surgical operation on the prayerbook, when much more serious problems were solved with exegetical palliatives. We may assuredly draw two conclusions from this observation: 1. There was more to this than meets the eye; more fundamental interests were involved than those that were expressed; 2. A return to the original phrase is justified if only because it will violate no one's conscience; completely free exegesis will still be offered to anyone who wishes to take advantage of it.

In analyzing the views of Hermann Cohen, we pointed out the intimate connection between the belief in the personality of the Messiah and the belief in the personality of God. For him, as for the liberal mentality in general, the entire concept of personality as such was a terrible stumbling block. As

Kierkegaard and existentialism never tire of pointing out, the existence of the individual personality defies all the universal and theoretical laws of science as well as of idealism. They, therefore, try to dissolve it into general propositions. God as an idea, the Messiah as an age—these are entities with which theoretical reason can deal. The persons of God and of the Messiah, on the other hand, are hard, stubborn, even—as it were— empiric realities that defy classification. But then, so does every individual. And thus, the depersonalization process does not stop with God or the Messiah so far as liberalism was concerned.

A change was likewise introduced into the second benediction of the *Amidah*. "Praised be Thou, O Lord, who bringest to life the dead" seemed to be a liturgical formulation of the doctrine of resurrection, and this doctrine was regarded as outmoded as the reference to the personal Messiah. Do we not know that the body decomposes in the grave? Where would physical resurrection take place in the spiritual world of God? Does not the belief in the eternity of the body imply a vast overemphasis on the material aspect of life? And so the modernistic arguments ran. Therefore, again the liturgical formulation was changed, and so remains to this day: "Praised be Thou, who hast implanted within us eternal life." In this manner, belief in the immortality of the soul was substituted for the concept of resurrection of the body.

The rejection of the belief in resurrection is closely connected with the rejection of the personal Messiah—not only because they both found expression at the very beginning of the *Amidah*. Ever since Ezekiel pictured the Messianic rebirth of Israel in terms of the famous revived bones, one of the traditional marks of the advent of the Messiah in Jewish thought has been the resurrection of the dead.[26] "May the All-merciful make us worthy of the days of the Messiah and of the life of the world to come."[27] And at the Conference of American Reform rabbis in Philadelphia in 1869, the rejection of the one doctrine was immediately and logically followed up with the rejection of the other.[28] Thus, the depersonalization process has gone one step further: God is not a person but an idea or a force; the Messiah is not a person but an age; and each man and woman is not a person but a universal reason confined in an individualizing and debasing body—a state of affairs fortunately remedied in the hereafter!

Herein also lies the most important reason for our time for a return to the personalism of the Messiah. Not only have we reacknowledged the unitary character of the human person: if scientific conclusions have any bearing on this discussion, they tend to assert the indivisibility, even the indistinguishability of "body" and "soul". Martin Buber's philosophy of dialogue is premised on the recognition of persons, human and divine, as the carriers of life.

The outlook of the Bible which deals with "the whole man" is reasserting itself in the form of what is called "personalism." Baeck[29] "describes this outlook in these words: "It is particularly true of prophetic thinking that it is far removed from abstract descriptions and instead envisages the figure of a real human being with its views and deeds. The prophets speak less of a future time than of a future person. The ideal of the future becomes for them an ideal personality . . . The son of David is the future man. As a man of flesh and blood he makes real and vivid what the ideal man ought to be and will be." As Tillich puts it: "Ontology generalizes, while Biblical religion individualizes."[30] And specifically with regard to the Messiah, the "liberal" Wiener puts the case clearly: "It is always the great miracle, the emergence into overpowering visibility of the deeds of God Himself, which charcterize the days of the Messiah—the expression of the personal shaping of world history by the personal God. For this reason so much emphasis is put on the personality of the Messiah . . . It is precisely in the belief in the Messiah that one can recognize the full vitality of a religiosity for which God is personality and His revelation and tangible guidance by means of miracle. One is inclined to say that at this point piety is most distantly removed from everything abstract, from conceptual ideology—and that it rather becomes faith in the true sense of the word, believing confidence in the revelation of concrete facts."[31] We have learned from religious as well as nonreligious existentialism, that all moral reality, as distinguished from nature or mathematics, is the reality of persons. The individual, the person, is the *locus* of ethics, not ages, ideas, or forces. The Messianic age is a utopia; the Messiah is a concrete, though future, reality.

Let us consider one last objection which will be raised against this view. It will be said again, as it has often been said in the past, that reliance on the Messianic fulfillment will lead to moral quietism and passivism. If people expect a divine agent to bring about perfection, they will sit back, relax their own efforts toward the good, and leave to the Messiah the work they themselves ought to do. This has, indeed, often happened. Was it not a delegation of Orthodox rabbis of the *Aggudah* type who requested the British mandatory governor not to withdraw his troops since Zionism was human superorogation anyway, and the Messiah was to come in 1999? But the drawing of an improper conclusion does not mean that the doctrine ought be abolished: It ought rather be protected against false interpreters.

"Perish all those who calculate the end,"[32] was the motto of the Talmudic rabbis who opposed the view that the Messianic time was fixed mechanically without regard to the human contribution to its hastening. They taught emphatically that the arrival of the Messiah was dependent upon human actions: if they were good it would be sooner, if evil—later. "God said: everything depends on you. Just as the rose grows with its heart toward heaven, so do you repent before Me and turn your hearts heavenward, and I will thereupon cause your redeemer to appear."[33] There is even the view, which commends itself on ethical grounds, that the Messiah will appear after the Messianic state has been established, leaving its attainment to humanity but guaranteeing its maintenance thereafter. Even Mendelsohn seems to have held this view.[34] The 19th century proto-Zionist, R. Hirsch Kalischer, stipulated the return to Zion as a prerequisite, not consequence, of the Messianic advent.[35] And even the man who was later to become one of the foremost and most radical leaders of American Reform, Samuel Hirsch, in the days before he went to greater extremes, advanced this same thought. "It is up to us to turn to God, for the Messiah cannot come before we have become completely good . . . No, it is not the duty of the Messiah but that of the entire household of the vanguard against evil, the entire house of Jacob, to wage this battle on behalf of all the inhabitants of the world, and the root of Jesse cannot shoot forth out of its midst until it has fulfilled this duty and carried out its task."[36]

Therefore, not only is it untrue that the doctrine of the personal Messiah must necessarily lead to quietism. On the contrary, it can help in suppressing the peculiar modern variation of pseudo-Messianism. One of the most horrible and disastrous illusions to which modern humanity has fallen prey is that it has actually accomplished the Messianic state. It is on the basis of this self-deception that our contemporary dictatorships have ruthlessly eliminated all dissent, for they maintain that dissent from perfection is, by definition, falsehood. Whereas in the Middle Ages pseudo-Messianisms operated around a central, individual pseudo-Messianic person, in our time it is characteristic of our collectivist and societally-minded frame of references that pseudo-Messianisms take the form of national movements. More that ever, therefore, the absence of the person of the redeemer should constitute a constant warning against such blasphemous exaggerations. This warning is, furthermore, not without its applicability to the present Jewish world situation. The Messianic undercurrent in the history of modern Zionism has in turn led to the far-reaching secularization of "the Messianic thought in Israel," as a result of which, as Leon Roth has pointed out, we no longer ask in the words of the Bible: "Who will recount the mighty deeds of God?" but rather in the words of the Israeli song: "Who will recount the mighty deeds of Israel?" What is even much more dangerous is the hazy notion floating through the minds of a not inconsiderable number of super-Zionists that the establishment of the State itself constitutes the Messianic fulfillment. Here lies the road to certain disaster! When Rabbi Kurt Wilhelm, formerly of Jerusalem and now chief rabbi of Sweden, and this writer dared point out in a series of articles that Jewishly there is a vast difference between *yeshuah*, historical salvaging, and *ge'ulah*, redemption, an Israeli newspaper attacked us vehemently as new *Protestrabbiner!*"[37] If this journalist had only been waiting for the Messiah!

– 2 –

Do Noachites Have to Believe in Revelation?

(A Passage in Dispute between Maimonides, Spinoza, Mendelssohn and Hermann Cohen)

A Contribution to a Jewish View of Natural Law

The Textual Question

Authoritative Jewish Doctrine holds, as is well known, that, in the words of the Talmud, "All the righteous of the nations of the world have a share in the world to come."[1] If to "have a share in the world to come" is the Jewish equivalent of the Christian term "to be saved," as indeed it is, then this doctrine simply states that one does not need to be a Jew in order to be saved but that rather also those who are not Jews but who lead righteous, moral lives will obtain salvation from God. On this doctrine the justified Jewish claim has been based that Judaism emphasizes morality more than belief and that it does not condemn others just because they do not adhere to its law and faith. This position has traditionally been contrasted with the classic doctrine of the Christian church that "outside of the Church there is no salvation."

Maimonides, in his legal code *Mishneh Torah*, states this fundamental Jewish principle in three different places. (He quotes it also in *Perush haMishna'yot, Sanh.* 10:12.) The first occurs in the "Laws of Repentance," chapter 3, 5. At this point he merely quotes it in its original formulation without further elaboration. Thus there seems to be no problem in connection with it as yet. The second time Maimonides refers to it is in the "Laws of Testimony," chapter 2, 10. Here he compares "the righteous of the nations of the world" with Jews who have turned "informers, heretics, or apostates." The latter do not have a share in the world to come,—they are not saved—because they have positively rejected the law of God after having formerly possessed it, while the former, though not Jews, can look forward to their "share in the world to come," for they cannot be regarded as guilty of having rejected something they never possessed in the first place. As Maimonides puts it, "idolators may not have to be rescued, but we also do not need to cause their demise... while these (Jewish rebels) must be destroyed and may not be rescued."[2] Again, the basic doctrinal position, that "the righteous of the nations of the world have a share in the world to come," is not in any manner infringed upon by this formulation of it.

It is in the third place in the *Mishneh Torah* in which Maimonides quotes this principle, the "Laws of the Kings," chapter 8, 10, 11, that his formulation of it has aroused a storm of controversy and a bevy of problems which began in his own days and have not yet abated. Before we enter into a discussion of its implications let it, therefore, be quoted in its entirety and in as literal a translation as possible: "Moses our teacher bequeathed the Torah and the commandments only to Israel,—as it is said: 'Moses commanded the Torah to us as an inheritance of the congregation of Jacob' (Deut. 33:4)—as well as to anyone who wants to be converted (to Judaism) from the other nations—as it is said: 'as for the congregation, there shall be one statute both for you and for the stranger (*ger*, a word which in Talmudic usage came to mean "convert") that sojourneth with you... as ye are so shall the stranger ("convert") be before the Lord.' (Num. 15:15). But he who does not want (to be converted) must not be forced to accept the Torah and the commandments, for thus commanded Moses our teacher on the authority of God: compel all human beings to accept the commandments which were commanded to the sons of Noah (*i.e.*, the seven so-called Noachite laws of human ethics which are incumbent upon all human beings), and anyone who does accept them (and who, the commentators add, is within our jurisdiction in which he can be compelled) shall be killed. (Men, so the argument therefore runs, can and must be compelled to be Noachites, but they must not be compelled to become Jews.) On the other hand, he who does accept them (the Noachite laws) is everywhere called 'a resident stranger-convert' (*ger-toshav*), and he must accept (the Noachite commandments) for himself in the presence of three rabbis (*chaverim*). Anyone who has decided to be circumcised (*i.e.*, to be converted), when twelve months have passed and he is not yet circumcised, is to be regarded as one of the nations."

At this point we must interrupt our quotation from the *Mishneh Torah* in order to clarify the last point made by Maimonides: This point is not really fully relevant to the problem with which we are primarily concerned, but unless it is completely understood it may later cause unnecessary complications in a polemic which is complicated enough as it is. Maimonides here stipulates that a non-Jew who has declared that he wishes to be circumcised and thus to be a Jew but who does not fulfill his promise within one year is to be regarded as reverting to his original status as a non-Jew. So at least the current text of his formulation reads. It may very well be necessary, however, to emend the text. The Vilna edition of the *Mishneh Torah* makes mention in a marginal note of the fact that the Venice edition reads: such a person is to be regarded "as a heretic from the nations." (*meen min ha-umot,* instead of *min ha-umot*). This is likely to be the correct version, for in this statement Maimonides is quoting almost verbatim a statement in Tractate "Idolatry," p. 65a of the Babylonian Talmud. There the text confirms the wording of the Venice edition.

Now this corrected reading may be understood in one of three very different ways. If Jastrow[3] is right in what he says the term "heretic of nations" means, namely "a gentile that has rejected the gods of his people," then such a person could be regarded as not being a Jew, to be sure, but on the other hand as being better than an idolator. Such a person would be, in other words, a heretic against idolatry, perhaps a Noachite, for it might be speculated that he or she must have been a Noachite in the first place before deciding to become a full Jew, and it is to this status of Noachite that he or she reverts when not carrying out the resolve to become a Jew. If the original reading of the text in the *Mishneh Torah* is the one written by Maimonides, then he also might have had a thought similar to this in mind, for he would have mollified the ambiguous talmudic term "heretic of the nations" to read "one of the nations" *i.e.* one of the children of Noah who belongs among the righteous of the nations of the world. On the other hand, the term "heretic of the nations" much more likely implies that such a person is not only not a Jew but is actually worse than those gentiles who never made up their minds in the first place that they wished to be circumcised, for, like the Jewish rebels who were referred to earlier, this person rejected something which was (almost) possessed, whereas no such indictment could be leveled against other gentiles. The commentary *Kesef Mishneh*[4] believes that a "heretic of the nations" is neither a Noachite nor worse than an idolatrous gentile but one "like the rest of the gentiles whom one need neither rescue nor destroy." Also *Lechem Mishneh*[5] holds that Maimonides intentionally lessened the severity of the Talmudic term in order to transform one worse than the common gentile into one on a par with him.

Without attempting to solve this problem, let it be clearly understood that either of these three interpretations is perfectly compatible with the theological formulation with which Maimonides continues his statement in "Laws of the Kings", chapter 8, 11: "Everyone who accepts the seven (Noachite) laws and is careful to fulfill them is one of the righteous of the nations of the world and has a share in the world to come. This is so if he accepts and practices them on the ground that God commanded them in the Torah and that He informed us through Moses our teacher that the sons of Noah (the Noahchites) had earlier been given these commandments. But if he practices them on the basis of his own rational considerations, then he is not a resident stranger-convert nor one of the righteous men of the nations of the world nor one of their sages." [On Maimonides' views on the gentile nations cf. J. Katz, "*Shloshah mishpateem apologaytee-eem,*" *Zion* 24–24 (1958/9), pp. 174-193.]

Here we have arrived at the great bone of contention. Suddenly Maimonides declares that it is not enough to fulfill the seven Noachite commandments—namely, the prohibitions of idolatry, of the improper use of the name of God, [Comp. *Tosfot, Sanh.* 63b: Noachites are later often said not to be prohibited to believe in "theological associationism," e.g., trinitarianism (*shittuf*), etc.; but cf., to the contrary, Schwarzschild, "*De Idololatria.*"] murder, sexual immorality, and of theft, the injunction to establish laws and courts, and the prohibition to eat meat from a living animal[6]—in order to be counted among the righteous of the gentile nations and to acquire a share in the world to come but that, in addition to this, one must also believe that these very laws were revealed in the Mosaic Torah and that there their earlier issuance to Noah and his children was reconfirmed. To the contrary, so Maimonides says, if one believes in and conscientiously performs the Noachite laws because one has arrived at the independent rational conclusion that they are good laws, then one is neither a convert to Judaism nor a Noachite nor even a sage. The problems that arise from this statement are many: from where in authoritative Jewish law does Maimonides derive this doctrine? Why does he stipulate it? What are its implications?

Before we attempt to answer these questions we must again stop in order to do some necessary textual repairing. The manuscript of the *Mishneh Torah* in the Bodleian Library, instead of the printed text which states that someone who practices the Noachite laws for reasons other than that they were revealed to Moses is neither a resident convert-stranger nor a Noachite nor one of their sages, reads: he is "neither a resident convert-stranger nor a Noachite but one of their sages." (*ela* instead of *velo*) This makes much better sense. Obviously, someone who believes in the validity of the Noachite laws not for religious reasons connected with the Sinaitic revelation but for philosophical reasons arising out of logical considerations cannot be regarded as a pious person, but he certainly may, he even must, be regarded as a wise one.[7] Furthermore, the text preserved by R. Joseph ben Shem-Tob, though using the word *aval* instead of *ela* carries the same meaning. Further yet, the *She'elot UTeshuvot* (Responsa) of R. Moses ben Isaac Al-Ashkar, published in 1553 by C. Adelkind in Sabionette, T. Foa contain a section on "Notes on the *Book of*

Beliefs (*Sefer Ha'emunot*)" of R. Shem-Tob ben Shem-tob, in which the correct reading, "but one of their sages," is twice used without further ado, obviously taking it for granted, and not even assuming that a justification for it will be required by the readers.[8]

This emendation of the text does not relieve us of the difficulties that arise from Maimonides' statement, however. It still remains true that he excludes what we might call the philosophical rather than the religious Noachites from the class of the righteous of the gentile nations of the world and thus also from the world to come. All the questions which were previously raised with respect to this dictum, therefore, retain their validity.

We are clearly confronted with Maimonides' definition of what the "righteous of the gentile nations" is (cf. Katz, op. cit., p. 174). Indeed, it is surprising how rarely in Jewish history, during which the Talmudic sentence under discussion has been quoted as often as any, such an attempt has been made. Usually it seems to be taken for granted that we know what such a person is, but in fact Maimonides was no doubt perfectly correct in asking himself whether we can simply assume that one who is generally regarded, or even one who is regarded by God, as falling broadly within the group of human beings who try on the whole to abide by the moral law is necessarily identical with the "righteous of the nations of the world" or with a Noachite. Maimonides, now, in this formulation, adds a prerequisite which is normally not encountered in the relevant Jewish discussions of this subject. This fact has aroused the more interest as Maimonides is not only the greatest philosopher in all of Jewish history but also the outstanding representative of Jewish rationalism, the thinker who most explicitly acknowledged his intellectual indebtedness to non-Jewish, pagan, and Mohammedan predecessors, and who is, therefore, rightly expected to be more appreciative of the merits of non-Jews than most others. Aristotle in particular is venerated by him almost on a par with Biblical authority, and thus, whatever we may eventually come to conclude with regard to Spinoza's polemic against Maimonides, one cannot help but have sympathy with Spinoza's expression of surprise that, in accordance with his rigorous criteria, R. Joseph ben Shem-Tob was entirely right in adding in his book *Kevod Elohim* that "although Aristotle (whom he considers to have written the best ethics and to be above everyone else) has not omitted anything that concerns true ethics, and which he has adopted in his own book, carefully following the lines laid down, yet this was not able to suffice for his salvation, inasmuch as he embraced his doctrines in accordance with the dictates of reason and not as Divine documents prophetically revealed."[9]

The first question, then, which we must ask with respect to this passage is whence Maimonides derived the authority to stipulate it. It is well known, of course, even notorious, that Maimonides did not state his sources for anything in the *Mishneh Torah*. Our inability to trace the material which he used in this instance is another reason for regretting this practice.

Generally it is believed that there simply is no source. R. Joseph Karo in the commentary *Kesef Mishneh*,[10] for example, says: "It seems to me that our teacher made this statement as a result of his own independent thinking (*sebara denafsheh*)—and it is a correct thought." Many centuries later Moses Mendelssohn repeats: "But this addition has no authority in the Talmud."[11] In our own century Hermann Cohen quotes the commentary *Lechem Mishneh* to the same effect.[12] Although these three interpreters agree in assigning the responsibilty for the dictum to Maimonides personally, the first approves of the dictum, while the latter two, like many others, disapprove of it. It may be said that, legally speaking, Mendelssohn and Cohen are no doubt more in the right that the *Kesef Mishneh*: if Maimonides had no talmudic authority for the statement, then, whether he is philosophically or theologically right or not, legally, so far as Judaism is concerned, he would seem to be taking an almost untenable position.[13]

D.H. Joel, on the other hand,[14] believes that he has discovered a source.[15] He refers to a book entitled *Toldot Adam*, chapter 6, p. 35a where the following Midrash is reported: "R. Chassidi said: I have heard that the righteous of the nations of the world have a share in the world to come; we have, however, not been taught that the wise men of the nations of the world are in this position. Who is a righteous man among the nations of the world? He who accepts the seven commandments because they are written in the Torah. A wise man from among the nations of the world, on the other hand, is one who fulfills them because his own reason induces him to do so."[16] Now, a number of aspects are to be noted about this hypothetical source for Maimonides. In the first place, it is quoted in a very late book, several centuries after Maimonides. In the second place, Toldat Adam in turn does not inform us where this Midrash is to be found. In the third place, its text is so close to Maimonides' own statement that it might almost have been composed in order to supply Maimonides with the source which he otherwise did not have. *Sefer Toldot Adam*[17] was written by Ezekiel Feivel; it is a biography of R. Zalman of Volozhin; its first edition was printed in Dyrenfurth in 1801, the second in Danzig in 1845.[18] The subject of Maimonides' dictum on Noachites occurs in this book because R. Zalman was greatly interested in Noachite legislation[19] and proposed some emendations to the *Mishneh Torah*. Altogether, we must be extremely wary of the authenticity of the Midrash: no reference is supplied; its text sounds tailorcut for the purpose; Professor Sonne was quite skeptical of its value.

The Mishnah of R. Eliezer (*The Midrash of Thirty-two Hermeneutic Rules*)[20] also contains a passage which might be regarded as Maimonides' source: having discussed the term "the pious of the nations of the world," it finishes: "But if they fulfill the seven commandments saying: 'We have heard them from somebody or other—or as a result of their own intellectual cogitations—. . . then, even if they obey the entire Torah, their reward will be limited to this world.[21]

There is considerable dispute about the age of this book between Enelow, Mirsky, and Zucker.[22] All, however, seem to agree that it is pre-Maimonidean. Theoretically, therefore, he might have used it. My teacher Samuel Atlas, on the other hand, says[23]: "I do not think that Maimonides would take it as a source for a *halachah* if he did not have a weighty reason for it . . . Consequently, the source in *Mishnat R. Eliezer* does not help matters if we cannot explain Maimonides' view logically and rationally. . . . My considered opinion is that this passage has been added by some commentator on the basis of Maimonides' passage in *Hilchot Melachim*." Indeed, Enelow also states that there are many later Arabic insertions in the book.[24] In any case, it is certainly true that the reason that Maimonides endorsed this unusual view is more important than where he found it.

To Moses Mendelssohn, as we have already seen, this passage in the *Mishneh Torah* is a real and most disturbing problem. (The 19th-century German reformers were naturally very much concerned generally with this problem, for political reasons; cf. Holdheim, *Ueber Die Autonomie der Rabbinen und das Prinzip der juedischen Ehe*, 2nd ed., Schwerin 1847, p. 15.) To him all truth was rational. All people had to have impartial access to it, for he cannot believe that God would be so cruel as to deprive some, regardless of the time in which they live, of the people to which they belong, or of the religion in which they believe, of that which is the highest human good and by which the good life can be attained. For this reason he even rejects the belief in progress, because progess would imply that those who have lived at an earlier stage in human history could know less of the truth than those who lived later. Thus he was a typical representative of the pre-19th century, prehistoricist Enlightenment. Judaism, to Mendelssohn, was not revealed truth but revealed law, the law by which one particular people was commanded to practice the truth which was, for the rest, accessible and comprehensible to all. It is clear, then, that the Maimonidean requirement, that Noachites must not only perform the ethical duties which are expected of them but must also hold a belief in the divine revelation experienced by Israel, had to be profoundly repulsive to him. For this reason he rejected the idea of religious conversion in either direction and instead depended on the Noachite laws. (Ib., III, pp. 43f.

[Cf. Katz, op. cit., p. 173]) If only as a document of genuine human pathetic perplexity the letter to Jacob Emden in which Mendelssohn pours out his heart on this dilemma between what he believes and what the greatly admired and respected mediaeval teacher propounded is worth quoting in full:[25]

> "These things are more difficult for me than flinty rock. Should all the dwellers on earth, from the East to the West, other than ourselves descend into the pit of perdition and be an object of condemnation to all human beings if they do not believe in the Torah which was given as an inheritance only to the congregation of Jacob, especially since this is not at all something expressly stated in the Torah but rather is a tradition among the chosen people or is deduced by its sages from the principles of the Torah ... as Maimonides himself has stated in the ninth chapter, that the Noachite laws are all a tradition in our possession from Moses our teacher and that from the principles of the Torah it can be seen that the Noachites were given these commandments.

Furthermore, according to R. Yehudah, Adam was given only the prohibition of idolatry, and the other six Noachite laws were added only in the time of Noah—the exact numerical opposite of Maimonides' historical chronology—and in this case all humanity up to the time of Noah would have been violators of the basic ethical code. "What shall the nations do on whom the light of the Torah has not shone, and tradition has reached them only through untrustworthy authorities on whom one cannot rely? Could God, heaven forfend, condemn His creatures, destroy them, and wipe out their name when they have done no evil? Can this be called a true concept?"[26] Maimonides arrives at this concept (and here Mendelssohn, taking it for granted that there was no Talmudic authority for Maimonides' dictum, proceeds to try to understand why Maimonides wrote it) on the basis of the belief which he mentions in many places in his books that good and evil are positive, statutory enactments (*mefursamot*)—that they are not rooted or founded on reason. If this is so, then I must not rely for righteousness and wickedness, good and evil, the proper and the improper on a decision of the reason or a verdict of logic, but rather they must be conventions (*mekubalot*) handed down by trustworthy authorities from the first recipient of revelation (*rosh hamekubalim*). It would also seem that according to Maimonides even the knowledge which is called statutory is not known among the nations other than by tradition, a tradition first given to Adam and the sons of Noah, whose source and origin are then forgotten, so that it was only remembered by them as a convention among them of which they did not know from which womb it issued forth ... All this is very strange. I have clear and correct evidence that good and evil, righteousness and wickedness, the proper and the improper are in truth rational." And Mendelssohn ends his letter by once more imploring R. Jacob Emden to let him know what the Talmudic authority was for this—to him—exceedingly distressing statement of the Rambam.

We shall return later to the question, which Mendelssohn discusses, of what the philosophical reasons may have been for Maimonides to demand belief in revelation on the part of the Noachites. We quote his touching letter at this point only because it again illustrates the unsuccessful search for his Talmudic authority by later Jewish teachers. Jacob Emden, it is true, in his reply offers to Mendelssohn several answers to this question.[27] Unlike Mendelssohn's letter which is written in the fluent and felicitous Hebrew of a modern Hebraist, Emden's letter is couched in the typical Talmudic style of the traditional legal disquisition. And the style also reflects the content, for Emden does not actually cite sources but rather engages in casuistic deductions which in his opinion justify Maimonides' stipulation. Mendelssohn, like the *Kesef Mishneh*, he declares, is wrong in believing that we are dealing with a novel concept peculiar to the Rambam. In fact he proposes three solutions. I. Psalm 9:18 states: "The wicked shall return to the netherworld, even all the nations that forget God." Thus not only the sinners but even those gentiles who live moral lives but who forget God or do not believe in Him are condemned to perdition.[28] "Even if they fulfill all the commandments in the world it will not avail them at all because they do not know Him who commands the fulfillment of the commandments." This first derivation, whether substantively correct or not, can hardly be regarded as Maimonides' authority. It is, in the first place, a much blunter though perhaps equivalent statement of the case, and, in the second place, had Maimonides condsidered it his Biblical justification there is no reason in the world why he should not have quoted it himself in a passage in which he quotes several other Biblical verses.[29] 2. Even a Jew who performs a *Mitzvah* for an ulterior purpose rather than for its own sake, *lishmah*, is often condemned by the Talmudic rabbis who exclaim that it would have been better had he never been born. They even go so far as to declare that "a sin committed for its own sake is better than a good deed for an ulterior motive." Now, to do a good deed for its own sake means, Emden says, is to do it "because it is God's commandment, because He instituted it and ordained that His will be obeyed in this fashion." If this is true for a Jew, how much more must it be true for a non-Jew; but a non-Jew who fulfills the Noachite laws without knowing that they constitute the revealed will of God is obviously incapable of complying with this requirement. 3. Those Jewish theologians who hold that "the commandments must always be performed with the proper intention" (*kavanah*) would clearly have to take the same position which Maimonides represents, for one cannot have the proper intention unless one knows what the goal of the intention is to be, i.e., God. But even according to the school which believes that "the performance of the commandments does not require the possession of the proper intentions" (*operans operandi*) a Noachite must be expected to believe in the revealed origin of the Noachite laws, for the rabbinic dispensation for those who fulfill the law without the proper intention only applies to Jews. It applies to them because two good results may be expected to be achieved by the Jew who abides by the law without doing it for the right reason: in the first place, "from fulfilling the law for the wrong reason he may learn to fulfill it for the right reason," and by being punished for fulfilling the law inadequately he will learn his lesson and in the future fulfill it adequately. Neither of these good results can be expected from the unbeliever, for "there is no faith in him." Both these results rest on the premise that he who fulfills the law at least believes in God and His law, though he may not fulfill it for this reason, but a person who does not even believe in divine revelation can hardly be brought to fulfill the law with this fact in mind. He will do it " only for his own advantage and pleasure . . . All the justice and kindness which idolators practice are sinful, because they act in this manner only in order to magnify themselves . . . and so that their temporal rule may be lengthened."[30] The only credit which Jacob Emden is willing to concede to them is that they may be able to obtain earthly credit, but they are certainly not entitled, he concludes, to "a share in the world to come."

Now, whatever one may think of the religious or Jewish validity of R. Jacob's argument, one thing seems clear: the latter two reasons are not in their very nature sources or authorities; they are arguments to buttress Maimonides' position, both revolving around the indespensibility of proper intention in the performance of religious laws. For all we know at this point Maimonides might even have agreed with the reasoning which he follows, but such reasoning does not constitute literary or legal authority. Certainly Mendelssohn, for example, must have remained completely unconvinced by R. Jacob Emden's reply. Their extant correspondence ends at this point, but we can easily imagine what Mendelssohn's reaction must have been: in the first place, he will have said to himself that lots of men believe in God and may even act morally for God's sake without necessarily believing in the divine authority of the Torah; in the second place, he will have answered that the very purpose of the Noachite laws as the natural law valid for all human beings is precisely to provide an avenue of salvation for those who do not happen to be heirs to the Jewish tradtion, and, therefore, all the deductions made from this tradition cannot be believed to be valid for them. We must then conclude that also R. Jacob Emden was unable to supply an answer to the question of

Maimonides' source of Talmudic authority for his statement. We must further conclude, in the absence of other proposed solutions, that the *Kesef Mishneh* was right in the first place: Maimonides added the Noachite requirement of belief in the divine authority of the Torah on his own accord. Or, if one is ready to concede that these sources may after all constitute Maimonides' authority, the problem is merely pushed one step backwards: why did Maimonides use these sources to come to his controversial conclusion when so many other Jewish interpreters who were no less acquainted with them did not utilize them for any such purpose?

If our conclusion is correct, the second question which we must ask of Maimonides gains even further in importance: what were his reasons for this dictum?

Two reasons which were suggested by Hermann Cohen in his polemic against Spinoza must be ruled out. He suggested in the first place that we must weigh the two formulations of the principle that "the righteous of the nations of the world have a share in the world to come" in which the additional requirement is not mentioned against the one place in which this controversial sentence does not occur and implies that the latter is, therefore, of little if any consequence.[31] This is false reasoning. The two sentences in "The Laws of Repentance" and "The Laws of Testimony" may not explicitly state the additional requirement, but there is nothing in these two clauses which contradicts the third. In them Maimonides merely repeats that the "righteous of the nations have a share in the world to come," but he does not explain what constitutes such "righteous." It is perfectly consistent for him in "The Laws of the Kings" to define the righteous of the nations, and then to let the student conclude that it is a person so defined who is referred to in the other two contexts. Furthermore, we must hold in mind the principle which Leo Strauss[32] lays down. Strauss assigns his place to Maimonides in the tradition of esoteric writing in which, during much of antiquity, the Middle Ages, and even in modern times, thinkers who believed that their somewhat unconventional beliefs might draw upon them the wrath of priests, rulers, or mob disguised their views in such a manner that, even while they expressed their doctrines sufficiently clearly for the comprehension of the initiates, the general reader would be oblivious to their true opinions. One of the rules of this kind of Aesopian style is, then, formulated by Strauss thus: "We may establish the rule that of two contradictory statements in the *Guide* or in any other work of Maimonides that statement which occurs least frequently or even which occurs only once was considered by him to be true." Cohen's attempt, then, to justify a virtual omission of the debated clause must be rejected for these two reasons.

Cohen's second explanation of Maimonides' disturbing dictum must also be rejected. For he claims that in the two former instances Maimonides speaks generally of Noachites of whom no requirement is made beyond the seven Noachite laws, while in the statement at issue he speaks of a specific kind of Noachite, namely the *ger-toshav, i.e.* the resident stranger-convert who is a citizen of the Jewish state. This type of gentile, now, Cohen goes on to argue, had to give some additional guarantee that he would always remain a loyal and obedient member of the Jewish society. If he agreed to the ethics of the Noachite covenant by virtue of his own reason alone he might at some future time change his mind for to him equally cogent rational reasons and thus become subversive of civil obedience and peace. This contingency could be prevented only by ascertaining that his submission to the Noachite laws was grounded in a more lasting reason than his own calculations, namely a divine command in whose validity he believed.[33] There is only one thing wrong with this argument of Cohen's: even if his distinction between "the righteous of the nations of the world" on the one hand and the "resident stranger-convert" on the other is correct, even if his definition of what Talmudic law had in mind in the concept of the *ger-toshav* is valid,[34] the wording of Maimonides' disputed statement makes it indubitably clear that he regards the person who does not believe in the divine origin of the Noachite laws in the Torah not only as no resident convert-stranger but also as no "righteous of the nations of the world": ". . . then he is not a resident stranger-convert nor one of the righteous of the nations of the world but one of their sages," and only the righteous of the gentile nations have their share in the world to come. But this is precisely the point which in Cohen's argument is completely missed: even granting Cohen's ascription of political motives to the refusal to let anyone persuaded of the validity of the Noachite laws by reason be considered a stranger-convert, Maimonides also refuses to consider them as morally and religiously righteous members of the gentile nations from the point of view of Jewish law and denies them eternal salvation— and this latter point is what disturbs so many readers of this passage.[35]

Cohen is, of course, an interested party in this dispute. He has three reasons for not wanting to believe that Maimonides could possibly have said what clearly he does say. In the first place, Cohen had unbounded admiration for Maimonides. He regards his as the by far most outstanding Jewish thinker of all time; he discusses his writings and quotes him more often than any other Jewish authority. And Cohen, therefore, is afflicted with the same problem which already Mendelssohn suffered: how could this greatest of all Jewish spokesmen teach a doctrine which neither of them could believe on the basis of their own understanding of Judaism as a rational and thoroughly tolerant faith, on the basis of their own endeavors to bridge the gap between Jews and their non-Jewish fellow Europeans, and on the basis of their own philosophical systems of ethics and truth?

The second reason why Hermann Cohen could not, as it were, believe his eyes when he saw Maimonides' dictum in "The Laws of the Kings," chapter 8, II, is that in his own system of philosophical religious ethics the Jewish concept of the Noachite as the ethical person pleasing to God purely on the basis of natural, rational moral law without religious commitment holds foremost place of pride and glory. The concept of humanity as possessing inherent dignity and value, regardless of race, nation, creed, or social status—the universal dignity of human beings as the cornerstone of moral philosophy and social progress—this concept Cohen rightly believed to have been achieved by Biblical Judaism. Neither the loftiest height of Greek philosophy with its distinction between natural-born slaves and barbarians nor the wide sway of Roman imperial sovereignity over many different nations and religions produced this concept so fundamental to the increasing freedom and welfare of the human race. Only the Bible recognized the dignity of all human beings. "Messianic humanity," Cohen proclaims, "was foreshadowed in the stranger who has equal rights."[36] "This is the great step with which humanity begins, and it begins in the form of law and state, although this state is based on the One God, and although this alien does not profess Him."[37] That Maimonides should infringe upon this universal concept is incredible to Cohen.

Finally, Cohen knew very well that Spinoza used this passage in the *Mishneh Torah*, as we shall see shortly, in one of his most virulent attacks on Judaism. And Spinoza was the archenemy to Hermann Cohen. Spinoza taught not only that nature is God rather than that God is the author of morality, he not only libeled Judaism, he identified right with might, denied freedom—he also advocated submission to, rather than conquest of, reality.[38] Spinoza's attack on Maimonides and through Maimonides on Judaism as a whole had to be annihilated at all costs. We shall also have to refute Spinoza, but Cohen's refutation by vindicating Maimonides on this score does not succeed.

Another reason that has occasionally been adduced for Maimonides' position is that he held not only morality but piety *i.e.*, religious devotion based on religious belief, to be prerequisite to salvation, for Jews as well as for non-Jews. Though this terminological evidence does not seem to be mentioned in this connection, it is, of course, striking that the word usually translated as "righteous person" (*chassid*) means more than merely the good person; it is often in other connections translated as saint or pietist and is derived from the divine quality of *chesed* or grace. Thus, for example, the mediaeval Al-Ashkar[39] interprets the Maimonidean passage to imply that not primarily philosoplical wisdom but religious piety is the criterion for divine acceptability. Dr. Sonne similarly expressed himself: Maimonides, he says, held that belief in *torat moshe misinai*, the divine Mosaic revelation, was indispensable to salvation. This is the religious equivalent of his philosophical tenet that right beliefs are prerequisite to immortality. Now, this is obviously true; it merely restates what Maimonides says in other words in the passage under consideration. On the other hand, it does not help us much in understanding why Maimonides held this view.

A letter is extant from Maimonides to R. Hasdai HaLevy, the Spaniard (of Egypt) residing in Alexandria in which the writer also refers to this problem:[40] "As for what you ask about the gentile nations, you must know that God asks for the heart, and things go according to the heart's intention.[41] Therefore, the sages of truth, our rabbis, may they rest in peace, said: 'the righteous of the gentile nations of the world have a share in the world to come'—if they have attained to that which it is proper to attain of the knowlege of the Creator, blessed be He ... There is no doubt that everyone who has improved his soul with the propriety of the virtues and with the propriety of wisdom in the faith in the Creator, blessed be He, is certainly among the children of the world to come, and therefore the sages of truth, our rabbis, may they rest in peace, said: 'even a gentile, when he busies himself with the Torah of Moses our teacher, may he rest in peace, is like unto the highpriest.' ... There can also be no doubt that the patriarchs, and Noah and Adam, who did not keep any of the words of the Torah, were not children of hell; rather, when they reached and attained to that to which it is proper to progress, they certainly were in the high sphere."[42]

It will be noted that, despite the conciliatory sound of his words, here also Maimonides' insists repeatedly on the prerequisite of faith in God for the attainment of salvation. He does not say so in so many words, but he clearly leaves room for his doctrine that "the virtues" can be acquired only through revelation.

The Historic Question

We turn then to the most important question that arises out of Maimonides' famous statement. Why did he have to make it in the context of his philosophical theology? What is its place in the system?

In the attempt to answer this question we may begin with the observation earlier quoted from Mendelssohn's letter to R. Jacob Emden, that for Maimonides the recognition of good and evil was not a matter of the rational intelligence but rather of convention or statutory enactment. If this is so, Mendelssohn rightly argues, then anyone who claims to believe in the morality of the Noachite laws is not to be taken seriously, is certainly not to be relied on in the long run, for that person believes in a morality which was attained by false and illogical reasoning. And this, of course, correctly represents Maimonides' view of the matter. In his *Treatise on Logic*[43] he proposes that among the judgments which are known to be true without further evidence are, in the first place, "conventions" (*concensus gentilium, mefursamot*) such as "our knowledge of the fact that sexual unchastity is repulsive and that repaying someone who has benefacted us as much as we can is appropriate and right," and, in the second place, "traditions, that is anything accepted from a chosen person or from many chosen persons." It is to be noted that moral cognition as exemplified in chastity and gratitutde is couched in esthetic terminology, as to this day it is commonly held that what is beautiful and ugly is a matter of personal, subjective taste. If there are to be then generally accepted standards of this kind of knowledge, they cannot be arrived at by logical excogitations but rather must be attained by conventions agreed upon by any given society, bequeathed to it by past practices, or imposed by divine or human statutes. And this is exactly what the Rambam in his philosophical ethic teaches. In the *Guide to the Perplexed*, Part I, the entire second chapter is in effect devoted to this question. Maimonides begins by interpreting the Biblical verse "And you will become like God in that you will know good and evil" (Gen. 3:5) very discreetly and ingeniously to mean that only God, and anyone who is like God, can discern good and evil. This knowledge, in other words, is a divine prerogative not properly bestowed upon the human intelligence. "With the reason man distinguishes between truth and falsehood, (this is an intellectual operation) ... but the repulsive and the lovely (and we have already seen that Maimonides identifies moral categories with esthetic ones) are conventions, not rational concepts ... Thus in our language we speak of that which is right and that which is not right as truth and falsehood, but of that which is ugly or lovely we speak as good or bad." Again later in the same chapter he declares: "For the necessary, intellectual existent there is no goodness or evil, only truth and falsehood." In other words, for God the moral and the immoral are not questions of goodness or evil but of rightness and wrongness; it is only for man, with his limited intelligence, that such problems cannot be resolved with intellectual, scientific finality but rather are dependent on less definite judgments which, just because of their indefiniteness, require positive enjoinments for their completion. (B. Netanyahu *Don Isaac Abravanel* [Philadelphia, 1953], Maimonides' view is that natural law cannot satisfy all men's needs; therefore, revelation is required. [Pp. 155f.: *Guide* II/40] "God, through Revelation, grants man an 'addition' to his nature which, in fact, raises man above nature itself." [P. 156])

This view of Maimonides is, of course, an integral part of his Aristotelian inheritance. Aristotle taught.[44] "Now fine and just actions, which political science investigates, admit of much variety and fluctuation of opinion, so that they may be thought to exist only by convention and not by nature. And goods also give rise to a similar fluctuation because they bring harm to many people; for before now men have been undone by reason of their wealth and others by reason of their courage. We must be content, then, of speaking of such subjects and with such premises to indicate the truth roughly and in outline, and in speaking about things which are only for the most part true and with premises of the same kind to reach conclusions that are no better." This view is shared by Maimonides. He teaches in many places that when it comes to ethics and proper human actions the intelligence can only indicate the general direction, set the broad outline, but the details and specifics which are so important if the general principles are to have any meaning whatsoever must be provided by authorities other than reason. This position is concisely summarized in the very clause which follows immediately upon the controverted clause in the eighth chapter of the "Laws of the Kings" and which strikingly is meant to explain it, though it never seems to have been put together with it by the commentators:[45] so far as the six of the seven Noachite laws are concerned that were given already to Adam, "although the reason inclines toward them, it is from the words of the Torah that we learn that they were commanded to him."[46]

An analogy can be drawn between Maimonides' position on this score and his view on the first of the 613 commandments. It is well-known that in his *Book of the Commandments* he lists as the first of the positive commandments the one which enjoins belief in God. This enumeration has often been disputed. For example the *Great Book of the Laws* (*Sefer Halachot Gedolot*), *Zohar HaRakia* (cf. *Megillat Esther ad loc.*) and Nachmanides take the position that this is not to be counted among the 613 commandments; rather that it is the foundation of all the other commandments and cannot, therefore, be regarded as itself one of them. But this is precisely why Maimonides does include it. All the other commandments are dependent for their validity upon this one, and it must, therefore, be put at the very head of the list. Similarly, the fulfillment of the seven Noachite laws is in his judgment dependent on belief in the authority and communication of their Author, and Hermann Cohen's objection, that adding this requirement to the Noachite laws is tantamount to adding an eighth,[47] is no more cogent from Maimonides' point of view than the objection of those who do not wish to see the belief in God included among the total list of 613 commandments.

Finally this circumstance must be recognized in this connection: in chapter 10, 9 of the "Laws of the Kings" Maimonides states: "The basic principle of this entire matter is that it is not permitted to create a new religion and to make laws by oneself out of one's own thinking, but rather a gentile must either become a convert (*ger tzedek*) and take upon himself all the commandments or he may retain his original faith, and then he must neither add to nor detract from it." On the basis of the principle implied in this clause the most interesting modern book on Noachitism was written, Elie Benamozegh's *Israel et L'Humanité*, Paris 1914, a book, it might be added, which was more than a book in that at least in France it brought about a small but important movement of Christian conversions to Noachism.[48] Fundamental to this study is the theory that Noachism is the religion of the gentiles taught by Judaism, itself the religion and the laws of the Jews. In the time especially of the birth of Christianity there existed two tendencies each of which contradicted this theory by attempting to overcome the ethnic particularism of Judaism in an opposite manner: there was the Paulinian attitude which wanted to broaden the validity of Judaism by abolishing its legal requirements not only for gentiles but also for Jews; and then there was the proselytizing attitude among Jews which intended to apply the law not only to Jews but to all people.[49] But the two, Judaism and Noachism, must be kept apart and integral. Only in this way will the truth of Judaism eventually come to benefit all mankind without on the other hand impinging on the sanctity of Judaism or of the Jewish people. Noachism, then, from this perspective is what might be called "the out-patient department" of Judaism, rather than the natural law which exists outside and independent of Judaism.[50] For that reason also, belief in God and in the revelation of the Torah to Israel is indispensable to the legitimate Noachite.

It has been previously mentioned that Spinoza lets loose a vitriolic attack on Maimonides for several reasons, our passage being one of the most prominent in the *Theologico-Political Tractate*. An analysis of Spinoza's polemic against Maimonides' view on this question shall, therefore, represent the last episode in our review of the checkered and agitated history of this controversial clause.

That Spinoza should heartily disagree with everything about this dictum in the *Mishneh Torah* and with all its implications cannot come as a surprise. We have seen, in the first place, that the basic philosophical reason which compelled Maimonides to take this restrictive position toward the Noachites he had learned from his teacher Aristotle; he was ready also for religious reasons to believe that ethics are not a purely rational, philosophic or scientific discipline. Only the barest outline of general ethical principles can be defined by logical methods. The substance of the matter which resides in its details can be obtained only through positive statutes, traditions, or divine commands, none of which are produced by conscious, rational processes. This was the reason, as we have seen, that Noachites could not be trusted to adhere to a system of morality at which they had arrived by philosophic considerations. Now, to the contrary, if Spinoza's system stands for anything it stands for the exactly opposite position, namely that ethics are a purely logical and scientific set of principles which can be elaborated in the smallest details. Indeed, the very title of his major work states as much: "Ethics, demonstrated in a geometric manner;" that is to say, from a small group of fundamental premises, similar to mathematical axioms, by means of logical deductions an entire consistent and adequate system of morality can be developed, even as every mathematical result can be obtained on the basis of the original theses and by means of strictly logical analyses. Thus on the fundamental premise of the very nature of what ethics are Maimonides and Spinoza are worlds apart, and it cannot , therefore, take anyone by surprise that they would violently disagree.

This wide divergency also expresses itself, of course, on the level of the more specific aspects of the actual content of ethics. Thus where Maimonides teaches, as we have seen earlier, that ethics, in order to take on human and livable form, requires a divine addendum in the shape of actual imperatives—that ethics must necessarily be religious ethics and involve a definite religious commitment (for all this is clearly involved in the prerequisite of belief in the divine revelation of the Torah)—Spinoza to the contrary teaches that any rational human being can evolve his own valid moral outlook. Furthermore, according to Spinoza, who himself, of course, adhered to neither Judaism nor Christianity, submitting to the doctrinal or ethical yoke of a religious communion is by no means indispensable to the moral man. Anyone who practices "the virtues of charity, joy, peace, etc., whether he do so by reason of Scripture or on the basis of his own reason, is in effect taught of God."[51]

Thus Spinoza strongly disagrees with Maimonides on the nature of ethics generally and on the indispensability of belief in divine revelation for the validity of ethics in particular. He must, therefore, firmly reject the clause in the "Laws of the Kings" which we have been discussing. And this he does. He goes one step further, however. He writes[52] that "according to Judaism," not just according to Maimonides, a Noachite must accept the authenticity of the Torah, and he then goes on to quote the disputed passage in its entirety and in its unemended formulation.

There are two questions which must be considered in this connection: 1) Why does Spinonza attribute Maimonides' view on this question to all of Judaism, whereas, as we have seen, many of the most outstanding spokesmen of Judaism themselves dissented sharply from it? 2) Was he justified and sincere in quoting the text from the *Mishneh Torah* in its strongest and almost certainly false form?

So far as the second question is concerned, Joel[53] points out that Spinoza does not limit himself to quoting Maimonides but also refers to the little booklet *Kevod Elohim* in which this Maimonidean doctrine is alluded to and supported. Now it happens that this passage as quoted in this book occurs there not in the corrupt form in which we have it in our extant editions but rather in the correct form, reading "but of their sages" rather than "and not of their sages." It follows then that Spinoza who used this book must have known of the correct text and willfully used the incorrect one in order to incriminate Judaism more gravely. (Hermann Cohen quotes this argument of Joel's who, incidentally, had been a teacher of his during his student days and adds that the correct text is also used in the commentary—he must mean either the *Kesef Mishneh* or the *Lechem Mishneh*—and that, therefore, Spinoza maliciously disregarded two pieces of evidence rather than one, but this is not true; these commentaries do not contain the original and correct wording.[54] This circumstance alone, then, ought to make us suspicious of the cleanliness of Spinoza's motivation and of his methods of argumentation in this controversy.

As to the former question, why Spinoza went out of his way in order to give the general non-Jewish public to which his *Tractate* was addressed the impression that Maimonides' individual and certainly somewhat eccentric view authoritatively represented the concensus of Jewish opinion on this subject, Leo Strauss believes that this is a piece of what he indulgently calls "amazing rashness." Strauss proceeds to criticize Spinoza for it and ascribes it to the "irrelevant reason that he (Spinoza) had happened to study it closely in his youth."[55] On the other hand, we must hold more with Joel who believed that Spinoza acted in this fashion not just out of sincere though perhaps erroneous rashness and in honest ignorance of his mistake but out of a conscious and intentional desire to identify Judaism publicly with the one man who on this point happened to be the most "dogmatic" thinker.[56] In other words, we are making the claim that Spinoza knowingly and libelously distorted Jewish doctrine. And our reasons for believing this are three:

In the first place, we have already seen that Spinoza must be held guilty of consciously having chosen a quotation in a text which he was aware to be corrupt just because it displayed the Jewish view on this question in an even crasser light than would have been the case otherwise. In the second place, throughout the *Theologico-Political Tractate* he pursues a policy of what may be called malicious reductionism; that is to say, he defines religion in such a way that having accepted his definition the intelligent reader must reject it. Thus, for example, he denies to the more highly developed religions the right to engage in Biblical exegesis and insists that the Bible must be either taken literally or not at all. The anthropomorphisms which occur in the Bible, therefore, may not be understood in any metaphoric or theological sense but must either be believed or they must lead to a rejection of the concept of God as it is embodied in the Bible. And it is on the ground that Maimonides is, of course, the most outstanding Jewish interpreter who dissolved all forms of anthropomorphisms in as well as outside of the Bible by his theological exegesis that Spinoza polemicizes against him even more vitriolically and frequently than on the ground of his statement in the eighth chapter of the "Laws of the Kings."[57] The point of this entire harangue is not, obviously, that Spinoza wants people to believe that God has anthropomorphic attributes but rather that he wishes them to reject the Bible, and he can accomplish this purpose in no better manner than by insisting on the literal significance of Biblical texts. Thus he reduces the Bible to its most primitive level in order to reject it more easily. This is what we have called *reductio ad barbarum*, and this is also the willful method which he utilizes in his argument against Maimonides' Noachite legislation: by identifying all of Judaism with its most radical expression he expects people to discard it the more eagerly.

The third, last, and most cogent reason for believing that Spinoza intentionally misrepresented Judaism by ascribing Maimonides' view on this question to all of Jewish law is the fact that a doctrine which would exclude non-Jews from all forms of moral or social approbation fits in perfectly with the thoroughly untrue picture of Judaism which Spinoza is at pains throughout the *Tractate* to paint. It is a picture so flagrantly in contrast to the truth that there is even no need to refute it; merely to reproduce it is sufficient for any impartial reader to be convinced of its falsehood. For Spinoza claims that Judaism is profoundly xenophobic. Its religious rites and rituals have been devised primarily in order to distinguish Jews from non-Jews, in order, in this manner, to keep them apart and preserve them as a separate entity, and it is this fact which accounts for the history of antisemitism, for naturally gentiles have reacted to this Jewish xenophobia by reciprocating Jewish hatred.[58] Although Jewish religious ritual was established exclusively in order to mold Jews more tightly together and to strengthen their loyalty to the Jewish state, the Pharisees perpetuated it even after the destruction of the state in order to differentiate Jews from Christians.[59] "Nurtured by daily rites . . . the hatred of other nations . . . must have passed into their nature. Such daily reprobation naturally gave rise to a lasting hatred, deeply implanted in the heart: for of all hatreds none are more deep and tenacious than that which springs from extreme devoutness or piety and it is cherished as pious."[60] Again and again he comes back to this theme: Jewish patriotism is strengthened by a religiously indoctrinated hatred of others, contempt for all gentile fellowmen and by the singularity of one's own religion.[61] In his more oratorical moments Spinoza goes one step further. He exclaims that the very God in whose existence he does not believe, a God who can give laws and revelations, imposed religious and ritual laws upon the Jews "in his anger" in order to make sure that Jews would be held in contempt and hatred by their neighbors and thus would not be able to preserve their own existence and the existence of their state in the face of the enmity to which they would necessarily be exposed.[62] Here he thus discreetly alludes to the Hoseanic passage which states that God gave kings to Israel "in His anger." Indeed, Spinoza continues and now echoes Paul—their laws are a constant reminder to the Jews of their defilement and their divine rejection.[63]

How ideally Spinoza's version and interpretation of Maimonides' restrictive legislation concerning Noachites fits into this mythical picture of Judaism. It too seems to declare that Judaism teaches that non-Jews, people who do not believe in the divinity of the Torah, are incapable of salvation—that indeed, they cannot even be moral. No wonder, then, that Spinoza wants to believe that Maimonides made this point as stringently as possible and that he legitimately represented all of the Judaism which Spinoza wanted so pathetically to reject and to defame.

The Systematic Question

One important aspect of the problem remains to be studied, and perhaps it is the most important. Having established as far as we could what Maimonides said and why he said it, we must ask ourselves what philosophic and religious truth is, also from our point of view today, embodied in his doctrine on this question.

It can fairly be claimed that the fundamental problem clearly involved in the dispute between Maimonides and Spinoza is the problem of the possibility and validity of the concept of natural law. Both philosophers ask themselves within the context of their respective systems whether there is such a thing as a moral law which is known to and applied by all, regardless of whether they are Jews or gentiles, whether they have been given the special boon of divine guidance or not, and regardless of the time and the place in which they live, merely in their capacity of human beings. The traditional term for such a law is "natural law." (F.Y. Baer, *Galut,* Berlin 1936, p. 52 claims that I. Abravanel first identified Noachite and natural law, but Netanyahu, op. cit., pp. 154-157 refutes this claim, Katz, op. cit., p. 174, agreeing with the latter.)

That for Maimonides the question of the Noachite laws was synonymous with the question of natural law can be seen, apart from the general considerations which we have just entertained, in several ways. The Noachite laws in Judaism are known by this name precisely because, all people having perished in Noah's flood, all humanity after Noah must have descended from the only survivor of the flood. Thus Noah is, as it were, a second Adam, the forefather of all human beings, and the laws which devolve upon him and his descendants, therefore, apply to all nations, races, and religions. Maimonides emphasizes this fact by stressing that actually of the seven so-called Noachite laws six were given to Adam and only the seventh was added in the time of Noah, thus underlining the universal, "Adamic" human nature of these laws,[64] although the Talmud records some rabbis who attributed as little as one Noachitic law to Adam.[65] And he inserts the statement that "the reason inclines toward these laws" after enumerating the Adamic laws, before proceeding to the Noachite one. The latter and thus all of the fundamental ethical imperatives, he ends with the phrase: "Thus was it in all the world until Abraham came, "—and then, of course, various additional Jewish commandments were issued.

The identification of Noachite law with natural law for Maimonides can further be realized when two corrolary sources are compared with him. Also for Averroes, whom, of course, Maimonides knew very well, natural law "corresponded roughly to the Second Tablet of the Decalogue but included the command of divine worship,"[66] and such a list coincides almost completely with the Noachite list. Also for Thomas Aquinas, who frequently demonstrates his familiarity with Maimonides by quoting him, the state of nature is that state which referred to all nations prior to the Sinaitic revelation, and this, in turn, is a precise definition of the scope of Noachitic legislation.[67]

At least in the definition of the problem Spinoza agrees with Maimonides. For him, too, this is the problem of natural law. All law, indeed all ethics were, of course, nature for him on the grounds of the famous doctrine of *deus sive natura*. It, therefore, really goes without saying that for him also the issue to be debated was whether there is or there is not such a law which all humanity, *qua* humanity, can know and by which they can attain to the highest good. That Spinoza was concerned with the question of natural law even in the narrower sense of the word can, however, also be demonstrated with historical evidence. We know that he had the work of Hugo Grotius, the acknowledged founder of the modern theory of natural law and an older contemporary and compatriot of his, in his library.[68] Also for Grotius the same distinction between revealed and natural law existed which we have stipulated as differentiating Mosaic from Noachitic law: positive divine (universal) law was embodied in the Decalogue, whereas the gospels, the Christian equivalent of the Torah, were only applicable to their recipients, Christians.[69]

If the issue, then, is the issue of natural law, what is it that is described by this term?

The simplest and certainly also the worst concept of natural law holds that moral behavior should be or is conducted by following the behavior of animate or inanimate nature other than human beings. This idea has been enunciated at various times in the history of philosophy. To the Greco-Roman cynics this was the fundamental criterion of ethics, and since they conceded that by social standards the actions of nature would have to be judged as at best amoral they concluded that the moral person and moral society should also act in this fashion. Under the influence of the biological doctrine of evolution such a philosophy of ethics became popular again toward the end of the 19th century. The advocates of evolutionist ethics proclaimed that even as nature progresses through the processes of the struggle for survival and the survival of the fittest, so also society in its individual as well as its collective aspects would progress toward increased goodness by adhering to these principles. (Isaac Abravanel: "natural law is the law of the jungle" [B. Netanyahu, *Don Isaac Abravanel–Statesman and Philosopher,* Philadelphia 1953, pp. 157, 305, n. 33].) There is more than a little of this belief also to be found in Spinoza. The most characteristic passage in his writings which expresses this point of view is to be found in the *Theologico-Political Tractate*: 'By the right and ordinance of nature I merely mean those natural laws wherewith we conceive every individual to be conditioned by nature, so as to live and act in a given manner. For instance, fishes are naturally conditioned for swimming and the greater for devouring the less; therefore, fish enjoy the water and the greater devour the less by natural right. For it is certain that nature, taken in the abstract, has sovereign right to do anything that she can; *i.e.* her right is coextensive with her power. The power of nature is the power of God, which has sovereign right over all things; and inasmuch as the power of nature is simply the aggregate of the powers of all her individual components, it follows that every individual has sovereign right to do all that he can; *i.e.* the rights of an individual extend to the utmost limits of his power as it has been conditioned. Now it is the sovereign right and law of nature that each individual should endeavour to preserve itself as it is, without regard to anything but itself."[70]

In the second place there is that view of the law of nature which derives moral law not so much from external nature as rather from "human nature," what the Thomists call *natura humana*.[71] In classic philosophy this position was represented by the Stoa. It believed that by analyzing humanity's essential nature of and determining the highest good it would be possible to deduce the principles of individual behavior and of social organization which would best serve this aim. If the cynical-evolutionist interpretation of the doctrine of natural law almost refutes itself by wiping out all differences between brute nature and humanity, by declaring that man ought to do what he is doing, *i.e.*, ethics is not normative but descriptive, then the stoic-Thomist interpretation makes a number of assumptions which in turn cannot be maintained. In the first place, it assumes that human nature is static, determined once and for all everywhere and at all times. "Human nature is the same in all men," postulates Jaques Maritain.[72] But this is not only an unprovable theory; it is the epitome of all moral and social reaction, for it stipulates dogmatically that what humanity is now it must always remain, and thus makes itself the philosophical tool of all those who have resisted human progress by pointing to what they said was the immalleable recalcitrance of human nature. In the second place, this school of thought must always hold that there is such a thing as an essential, permanent, and reliable moral conscience, Thomas calls it the "*synderesis*, a natural *habitus* of the soul" by which good and evil are recognized for what they are, an *irradiato divini intellectus*.[73] Again, this is at best an unprovable claim. Certainly human experience would seem to demonstrate the contrary. What crimes have not been committed in the name of conscience, and sincerely so! (Cf. Schwarzschild, "Conscience," in *Contemporary Jewish Religious Thought . . .*, eds. A.A. Cohen and P. Mendes—Flohr, N.Y.: Scribners, 1987, pp. 87-90.) Furthermore, it dogmatically stipulates the existence of a separate moral human faculty which is rationally undeducible. When Cicero identifies the *vox naturae* with *omnium consensus* he in effect endorses this Stoic position, and here again neither reason nor history justifies such trust in majority agreements. The fact of the matter is that universally people have called that which they believed in and wanted "natural law," whatever the real reasons for their preference. Be it slavery or human freedom, property or selflessness, birth-control or free love, authoritarianism or democracy, they all have at one time or another been identified by their proponents with the very substance of nature and reason. David G. Ritchie amusingly illustrates this truth when he observes that in our language "a 'natural child' means a child born out of wedlock; but an 'unnatural child' is not necessarily legitimate."[74] Justice Holmes said the same thing differently: "The jurists who believe in natural law seem to me to be in that naïve state of mind that accepts what has been familiar and accepted by all men everywhere."[75]

From the point of view of social morality the doctrine of natural law has on balance wrought more harm than good, for it tends to deduce from the fact that something exists that it must also be according to nature—for otherwise it would not be likely to exist in the first place—and that it must, therefore, also be good. Thus the doctrine of natural law usually puts its stamp of approval on every given reality, however repulsive it may be.[76] It is essentially a conservative theory. Spinoza himself illustrates such an attitude based on natural law inertia: whatever form of government a nation happens to have, be it good or bad, free or tyrannical, it is better than what a change of constitution by belligerent or peaceful means could bring about. Keep whatever you have; what you will get through a change can at best be no better and may well be worse. This is so important a principle for him that he would have anyone who violates it punished by death and condemned to eternal infamy.[77] Thus it is that Spinoza, though he opposes monarchy because he believes that it is most likely to lead to tyranny, nonetheless also opposes abolishing monarchy when and where it already exists,[78] and repeatedly he cites Cromwell's Puritan Revolution as his case in point.[79] Leo Strauss correctly characterizes this attitude: "This is a sharpening of an unpolitical realism based on Spinoza's ultimate premises, an affirmation of the real out of nonpolitical motives with later application to politics."[80]

This ramification of the doctrine of natural law is not a peculiarity of Spinoza's; rather it inheres in the very nature of the doctrine. Even one of its ardent latter-day defenders must admit this. He points out that the theory as propounded by Hobbes, from whom Spinoza learned most of his political science, destroys the very possibility of distinguishing between good and bad government, because whatever government is in power—it has been brought about by the operation of nature and is, therefore, unobjectionable. It even destroys the theoretical possibility of resisting any sovereign decree whatsoever, regardless of its possible wickedness, because sovereignty is granted unlimited sway.[81] To give only one more example, Hugo Grotius also teaches such unrestricted acquiescence to established power on the basis of the natural law: "The law of nature further teaches that everyone must be content with what is his, not only because it is otherwise impossible to maintain friendship among men,"[82] again an attitude which even by an admirer of Spinoza's is described as using "the law of nature to provide Grotius with a basis for acquiescence to the social *status quo*."[83]

The objections to the concept of natural law are not limited to moral and political ones, however. Also from the philosophical and epistemological perspective it has been shown to be untenable. For Kant this was an unjustifiable theory. It stipulated a number of things as given, as dogmatically and metaphysically irreducible, which could not defend themselves before the tribunal of human reason. As we have seen previously, natural law assumes human existence as an unchangeable reality, conscience as a divine and infallible faculty, and the moral law as an entity outside of and objectively confronting humanity. But the moral law, so Kant taught, is humanly self-created and self-imposed; it must be autonomous to be moral. Ethics are never given in any existing reality, be this now humanity or nature or revelation; they are ideals, "ought's," tasks to be achieved after they have been rationally defined. Humanity is not a noumenal reality whose permanent character may be assumed to have been formed from its very inception, but perfectible, capable of change and improvement. A competent student of Kant then summarizes his position toward the concept of the natural law in these words: "We have reached the pinnacle of the system with respect to the metaphysical foundation of the philosophy of law. The concept of the natural law is replaced by the *a priori*, or rather by the reason which expands *a priori* into principles."[84] Thus, "however much the concepts of freedom and equality (as taught by Kant) seem to coincide with those of the natural law, however much they are even described as demands of the law of nature, the peculiar achievement of critical philosophy consists of the special manner in which it interprets them. Freedom and equality are ideas which do not designate a "being" but an "ought," not a reality but a task of perfection which is to be attained gradually."[85]

The position of Hermann Cohen with regard to the concept of natural law deserves to be stated fully, firstly because he is the outstanding representative of critical philosophy, secondly because it is not sufficiently known, thirdly because in the dispute between Maimonides and Spinoza with which we are concerned he is not only an interested and significant party but also tended, we may now say wrongly, to fear that in principle Spinoza, whom he opposed, might in this case have made a valid point against Maimonides as whose student he regarded himself. "The danger of scientific dogmatism resides in the philosophical, allegedly metaphysical prejudice that the foundation of morality is to be conceived as a natural law, as a law deposited in our bones. From this common starting-out point onward the paths and the directions diverge. Some say that we do everything out of compassion, others out of revenge. The so-called moral sense is blown in all directions. It is discerned in everything, and it is conceived of as being compulsory since it is revealed in all directions and interpretations. This is alleged to be the only basis for all human concepts and views of ethics, and this basis is found in human psychology, or rather, to be more exact, in physiology, for the senses have always been located within the small confines of these two disciplines . . . When the moral law is conceived as a natural law, as is done by the naturalists of the senses, one is forced to revert to the psyche and to the metaphysics of rational psychology. The proper jurisdiction of ethics, which is derived from the ethos, is lost."[86] "Morality is not supposed to constitute a problem of its own but merely an exudation of nature . . . but we know and understand that this view is a mediaeval error garbed in modern clothes."[87] Thus Cohen's first main objection to the doctrine of natural law is that it identifies ethics with physiology, the "ought" with "being;" it assumes that morality is something that exists rather than something that is to be achieved. A subsidiary weakness of the doctrine which results from this fundamental fault is that it leads to chaos, for all ethical programs have, as we have previously seen, invoked the warrant of nature for their particular theses.

A last and even more crucial objection must be raised against the doctrine of the law of nature, Cohen continues. "Only this is here emphasized, that the ethical personality is not given and may not be presupposed with certain natural tendencies and conditions . . . The ethical subject is not the spirit which so easily becomes a moral ghost. The ethical subject is not simply born and hereditarily determined; rather, however much birth and heredity may have to be taken into account, the person still always remains a new and peculiar problem which cannot be dissolved into its given factors and conditions. The method of purity liberates the concept of the ethical subject from prejudices . . . What meaning could ethics have if the ethical subject could be totally conceived as given, born, and raised in its environment? Ethics would then dissolve in anthropology . . . The method of purity, on the other hand, seeks to determine those conditions and concepts which—we may put it so—bring about the concept of the human being in accordance with the fundamental law of truth. Truth does not consider exclusively or even preferably a theoretical interest in the man of nature; it also demands the ethical interest in the man of culture and of universal history."[88] In other words, contrary to the necessary premise of all theories of natural law, humanity is not a given, permanent reality inaccessible to fundamental change. This is moral counsel of despair and political reaction, quite apart from being rampant empiricism. Though shaped to some extent by the conditions of its physical origin, humanity can be and should be made in the image of rationally self-imposed ethical imperatives. These imperatives are hypotheses in the Kantian sense, ideas produced not by experience but by the reason and thus "purely," though not idealistically in the sense that they either have no relationship to the basic principles or jurisprudence or that they cannot powerfully affect people's real lives. This, contrariwise then, is counsel of hope: humanity is capable of infinite self-perfection; let no one reject demands for reform on the ground that human nature is opposed to it. Subsidiary to this argument runs Cohen's final point, that natural law always defines humanity in terms of its most primitive and original estate; this is a scientific, cognitive, historical endeavor, not an ethical one. The truth of ethics is much more concerned not with what humanity is or was but with what it is and can become under the conditions of culture and history.

Contemporary philosophers of law whose intellectual orientation was signficantly influenced by the fundamental thoughts of Immanuel Kant, of Hermann Cohen and of his Marburg school of critical philosophy have put their teachers' refutation of the doctrine of natural law into practice. Applying it to the concrete reality of jurisprudence they have shown that the idea of natural law is both irrational and injurious and have replaced it with a more persuasive and constructive doctrine. (For the philosophical issues between Cohen, Kelsen, etc., cf. my introduction to Cohen's *Ethik des reinen Willens, Werke,* vol. 7, Hildesheim/ N.Y.: Olms, 1981.) Hans Kelsen is in some ways their most representative spokesman. The law of nature, he declares, is the legal equivalent of the philosophical concept of the noumenon: it is supposed to "lie behind" the phenomenon of the actual, empirical law as its true, substantial, and permanent reality without ever being capable of being reached or even understood in human experience. But, like the idea of the noumenon as such, this is an irrational idea, for, by definition, it cannot be grasped by human comprehension, and it cannot be made or shown to operate in the only universe which humanity inhabits, the universe of phenomena.[89] Furthermore, the philosophers of natural law, whenever they wish to bring their theory down into reality, necessarily and uselessly duplicate the principles of the law, for they must "positivize" the ideal law before it can become effective law.[90] If there were such a thing as a noumenal, "real," natural law it would be uncognizable anyway, and an uncognizable reality is, for human reality which is the only reality that can meaningfully be considered in philosophic discourse, no reality at all.[91] Then again, as we have previously noted, whenever the natural law is brought down from its ethereal speculative heights into the arena of human experience, in other words when an attempt is made to spell out what it presumably commands, it turns out to impose precisely those obligations which the positive law, the law defined and enforced by existing human powers, commands anyway. Thus it justifies and perpetuates positive law and, far from having the revolutionary and rejuvenating effects which are sometimes ascribed to it, it is actually a profoundly conservative force.[92] In this connection Kelsen alludes to Rousseau and claims that his social doctrine of human nature was much less progressive than is generally believed.[93] In the context he cannot take the space to prove his point, but it is a point well worth understanding and affirming, if only because the historical connection between Rousseau and Spinoza has often been made. Whatever use the theoreticians of the French Revolution may have made of his writings, the fact remains that by the time Rousseau finishes defining "the general will" and the citizen's duty of absolute submission to this sovereign, there is not the slightest room left in his state for rebellion against unjust government or resistance to immoral laws. The individual may at most preserve his sense of freedom and righteousness in the privacy of his heart, but any and every public action, even in the sphere of religion, must be unquestioningly subordinated to the dictates of the state. At last Rousseau resorts to the specious freedom which, like Spinoza, defines liberty as resignation into necessity, identifies it with peace of mind, and best summarizes it in the words: "There is no more liberty on earth but in the heart of the righteous man,"[94] and one commentator rightly describes this position, then, in this fashion: "The word *libertas* on the prison gates (and we today would add the inscription on the gate into the Dachau concentration camp) and on the chains of the galley slaves in Genoa seems to Rousseau symbolic of the real meaning of liberty in a civil state."[95] No, Kelsen concludes, the law is human social self-creation according to reason.[96]

Thus the concept of the natural law would seem to be disposed of once and for all. And yet, when all is said and done, there is one last consideration which prevents us from discarding it *in toto*. The philosophical arguments in its favor have not been found to be valid. But the necessities of social morality do impose an ultimate caution upon us. It is not unimportant, for example, that the idea of natural law first seems to have been formulated in the classical age of Greek philosophy as a protest against the positive law of the city with its superstitions and mythologies, its tyranny and unrighteousness. There is a law higher than that of the ruthless rulers, the philosophers declared, and to this law they appealed in the effort to liberate society. Since then it would almost always seem to have been in situations of social stress that the law of nature was brought out again. Grotius expatiates upon it when the Netherlands are locked in combat with England over the freedom of the seas. Erich Cassirer studies it in a book published in Germany in 1919 after the experience of the First World War. Leo Straus advocates its restoration after the experience of the lawlessness of Nazism and the Second World War. He makes no bones that it was this experience which frightened him into feeling the need for some reliable and permanent source of social morality. He refers specifically to Kelsen when he warns that the absence of a belief in natural law is an invitation to tyranny.[97] He persists in believing, or rather in hoping, that natural law is a revolutionary force,[98] for it is presumably something which even the dictator cannot set aside. With some justification he points out that, after all, the historical school of jurisprudential thinking was also meant to have a conservative impact on society since it was developed in the 19th century largely as a reaction to and defense against the forces of the

French Revolution which were, rightly or wrongly, associated with the idea of natural law.[99]

That there remains a last necessity for the idea of natural law from this point of view even the neo-Kantians are prepared to grant to a certain extent. Hermann Cohen does not reject the idea completely but calls it "ambiguous,"—invalid and injurious for the reasons previously stated, but good in the sense that it expresses the impulse to rebellion against legal arbitrariness.[100] In his sense, however, the law of nature must be understood not as a law to be found in nature or even in human nature but rather as a law created by reason in accordance with, if you will, the nature of human ethics. Ernst Cassirer points out that in the thought of Kant and Cohen Rousseau's idea of the state of nature became transformed from the historic, empiric, original human estate (granting that Rousseau himself ever thought of it as such in the first place) into a logical construct, a rational priority, which was philosophically necessary so that all social contracts could be ideally deduced from it and so that it could serve as a norm.[101] And for the same reason even Kelsen, the outspoken advocate of legal positivism, in the end must stipulate a rational, natural *Grundnorm* as a "minimally necessary natural law" to justify the idea of the social contract and to provide a last resort of freedom and morality.[102] "A constitution derives its juridically relevant potency from its presupposed *Ursprungnorm*." (See Erich Kaufmann, about Kelsen, in *Kritik der neukantischen Rechtsphilosophie,* Tuebingen 1921, Aalen 1964, p. 32)

From the systematic-philosophic point of view we thus find ourselves in a real dilemma: we cannot do without the idea of a natural law, and we cannot justify this idea. We ought to have it, and we ought not to have it at the same time. To proclaim it unambiguously, as Spinoza for example did, is to lead us into all sorts of philosophical and moral difficulties, and to reject it completely leads us into grave dangers.

This is precisely the point at which Maimonides' doctrine enters. He has been confronted with this kind of problem before: theology seems to require the belief in creation, and philosophy seems to refute it: in such a situation, he declares the rational position to take is not to rely on the belief more than absolutely necessary—if possible, actually to do without it—but then to try to make it as philosophically acceptable, even as likely as the reason is capable of doing.[103] And this is also the position he takes with regard to the problem of the law of nature: "The reason inclines toward it, and in Revelation it is confirmed;"[104] in other words, it is rationally likely and even necessary but also undemonstrable and dangerous. What in a modern Kantian like Cohen the self-legislating reason had to do to assure the benefits of natural law, in Maimonides naturally Revelation was called upon to perform. This is by no means the same thing, nor is here the place to discuss the merits of the two positions and to weigh them against one another, but Maimonides' view may at least be said to have broken the stranglehold of a doctrine of natural law which regarded itself as being certain, immovable, and irresistable. His view proclaims that for effective law humanity needs more than natural law, and this itself has proved itself to be an important philosophic achievement and a valuable contribution to the history of philosophic progress. In terms of his own philosophy Maimonides held the balance between the doctrine of natural law and the doctrine of positive (be this now divine or human) law, and this, it would seem, is also today as far as the human reason can go.[105] Centuries later Locke expressed the same belief: there is natural law, but it must be assured and affirmed by revelation, and to be able to do this revelation must be preceded by the knowledge of God.[106] And this is exactly what Maimonides said to the Noachite: the fulfillment of the moral law insures you of God's approval: the law of nature provides you with an inkling of the moral law, but by itself it is neither enough nor reliable; to know the moral law you also have to submit to Revelation, and you have to know God. To us he says: the law of nature must be preserved if only so that we will not always be restricted to the fallibilities of the positive law, but this natural law cannot be relied on to reside in the nature around us or in the nature within us; it must come from a higher source. To Maimonides this source was, of course, divine revelation; to Cohen it was reason, or the nature which humanity will in the future make for itself. It is another question—perhaps the most important one—whether on this last score Maimonides or Cohen has more to teach us.

– 3 –

The Lure of Immanence— The Crisis in Contemporary Religious Thought

The Task

The catch-phrases by which the crisis of contemporary religious thought is currently being referred to in Western culture are "the theology of blasphemy" and "the secular gospel." Much that is being written under these and similar titles and about them must be regarded as what the Whiteheadian Protestant theologian Schubert Ogden has called "pop theology." As such it is a fad and not worth taking very seriously (except as a passing sociological phenomenon). Our purpose here will be twofold: a) To extract the authentic religious and philosophical forces that power these manifestations. This is worth doing for at least three reasons: 1) we are likely to learn something about genuine spiritual realities; 2) such realities assert themselves, as we shall see, throughout human history, and we may, therefore, expect to run into them again in the future; and 3) once one is face to face with authentic phenomena, rather than epiphenonema or pseudo-phenomena, one can hope to be able to come to grips with them in a constructive manner. Once they have been discovered, our second purpose (b) will be to try to evaluate these forces from our Jewish vantage point.

I want to state beforehand the conclusion at which I expect us to arrive, so that we know where we are going and are able to organize the evidence in a purposeful fashion. That conclusion can be stated in two sentences: The "theology of blasphemy" and "the secular gospel" are related developments, and they arise out of a peculiarly Christian problematic. The "secular gospel" can, with some serious reservation, be welcomed by Judaism as a partial "Judaization" of Christianity—although even here contemporary Christian theology stands in need of Biblical-Jewish correction[1]—while the "theology of blasphemy" is not only, of course, a most serious theological error but is also likely to vitiate the values of "the secular gospel."

The Basic Theologico-Philosophical Problem

Perhaps the most basic and important problem of all theology is the relationship between the transcendent God and the world. It would seem that there are really only four possible ways of conceiving that relationship: 1) That God is entirely transcendent and, therefore, without relationship to the world. Classically, in the history of philosophy and in Jewish tradition, this has been the conception of Epicureanism—that God may have made the world but since then has withdrawn unto Himself and takes no further interest in His handiwork. Thus, not the denial of the existence of God but the affirmation of His disinterest in the world, his unrelatedness to it, has come to be regarded by Jewish tradition as the hallmark of the unbeliever, the *epikoros*. 2) The denial of God's transcendence altogether and the identification of Him with a part, or the totality, of the universe. This, of course, constitutes absolute immanentism and, in the histories of philosophy and theology, takes various forms of pantheism. The fate of Spinoza—excommunication at the hands of the Jewish community of Amsterdam—tellingly bespeaks the attitude of Judaism to this approach.

At this point the alternatives become more complex. Whereas the first two choose extreme, though opposite, attitudes to our problem—either the exclusive assertion of transcendence or its complete denial—the next two, respectively that of Christianity and Judaism, attempt to define various possibilities of the combination of some sort of transcendence with some sort of divine relatedness to the world.

Christian faith asserts the transcendence of the Biblical God (this is the first person in the trinity) and combines it with His relatedness to humanity's universe primarily through the incarnation, *i.e.*, the second person in the trinity, as well as through other "intermediaries." But it is important to note in what form this relationship occurs. Transcendence as such enters into immanence as such. In the process it does not forfeit its transcendence: the "God-man" remains "all God,"—though He be also "all man." *I.e.*, both transcendence and immanence retain all of their original natures. They merely occur together, in one phenomenon, event, or person. The result of this occurrence is that the world of immanence, in turn, falls apart into two discrete portions—that which becomes identified with transcendence and thereby loses its previous immanentist character *in toto* (remember that the two retained their natures and did not intermix),[2] while the other remains behind, unaffected one way or the other by the event. (This fundamental Christian theological dichotomy may explain the traditional Christian clear-cut demarcation between "the saved" and "the unsaved." There is really no possibility of a middle ground.)

This manner of relating transcendence to immanence possesses one characteristic which needs to be underlined. It operates essentially on what I would call a "spatial model" of the problem—*i.e.*, it conceives of transcendence as being, as it were, physically, spatially above immanence ("the God out there"). If there is to be a connecting link between two "physical" places, this link itself will have to be physical. Furthermore, two physical entities cannot occupy the same place; at best they can be located next and connected to one another. (It should be noted that this understanding of such a relationship between transcendence and immanence does justice not only to a doctrine of incarnation but also to the historically and philosophically related one of intermediaries, *e.g.*, in Philo and in the entire so-called Neoplatonic tradition of the Middle Ages.) The *logoi* or spheres are, as it were, "physically," spatially the connecting links between transcendence and immanence. They themselves are of transcendental nature, despite the connecting function which they perform. Also, it must be remembered that "space" is only a metaphor, or model, for this notion. The relationship between transcendence and immanence is believed to be on the pattern, not in the actual form, of spatial relationships.[2a]

Actually all three alternative ways of conceiving the relationship of God and world that we have so far looked at possess this characteristic of being modeled on spatial relationships. The difference between the first two and the third is only that the first two end by denying all relationship—Epicureanism by, as it were, leaving God "out there" without lines of communication to the world, pantheism by merging the two poles of the relationship into one and thereby destroying the possibility of relationship, whereas Incarnationism retains the reality of a relationship. All three agree that, if there is a relationship, it is constructed on the spatial model; the first two deny that there is one, however, and the third asserts that there is.

The fourth and last way of tackling this problem may be identified with Judaism. It does not employ the spatial model but that of *the will* in trying to conceptualize the relationship between God and the world. The will is not spatial either in human beings or in God. I can will you to do something whether you are near or far, for that matter whether I or you or both of us are physical entities or no. If I have a way of communicating my will to you, by speech or, for all I know, by mental telepathy, then we are in relationship to one another not spatially by volitionally. The explication of the will of God for humanity we call "law" or *Halakhah.*

It is quite easy to prove this proposition from virtually the entire history of Biblical, Talmudic, and mediaeval Jewish philosophical thought. One could, for example, write a history of classical Jewish philosophy in terms of how literally every single Jewish thinker has felt constrained to introduce what I think of as "the Jewish twist," *i.e.*, volitionalism, into the non-Jewish philosophic system within which he happened to work. Let me cite briefly one example from the Kalam, one from Neo-Platonism, and one from Aristotelianism. Saadia Gaon had it easiest in a way, because the Kalam is itself largely a volitionist school of thought. Ibn Gabirol (however Jewish a Jew, so un-Jewish a philosopher that for centuries neither Jews nor Christians realized that the *Fons Vitae* was the work of a Jew), has been accused—with how much justification we need not here investigate—of introducing divine will into his Neoplatonic, necessitarian, emanationist system in a self-contradictory manner. Maimonides, finally, had to cope with the intellectualism of Aristotle, in which not the will but thinking, and logical, *i.e.*, necessitated, thinking, constituted the essence of the Deity. He begins, therefore, by proving that "there is no relationship between God and space" (*Guide* I, 52)—goes on to show that, whereas any one corporeal mode of existence can only produce a single effect of the same nature as its cause, a single will can produce any number of different effects, which he calls "actions" (*ib.*, 53)[3]—and, in the Second Part of the *Guide*, breaks with Aristotle completely on the question of the createdness of the world. Even here, however, Maimonides makes it explicitly and perfectly clear that he is not primarily interested in whether the world was "created" in time or from a primaeval matter or no; the only thing that he is concerned with is whether God is believed to will (*ib.*, II, 25), so that, consequently, "miracles," *i.e.* revelation and its laws, are philosophically made possible.

Judaism's conception of the relationship between God and the world differs from the other three ways which we have considered in that it is constructed on the will-model rather than the space-model. Whereas Christianity requires some sort of quasi-physical, quasi-spatial relationship between transcendence and the world, Judaism conceives of this relationship by keeping God absolutely separate and different from the world but attributing to God ethical concern for it: the God of Israel is absolutely different from the world and absolutely concerned with it.[4]

Maimonides and Thomas on God

We can, at this point of our analysis, begin to make the transition to the modern crisis in Christian theology. Maimonides, as is well known, denies all attributes to God other than negative ones (which, in effect, state that He is like nothing whatsoever that we experience of know of, including space, spatial relationships, etc.) and so-called attributes of action. For the latter we use the phrase "ethical concern for humanity," *i.e.*, laws that, were they the product of human intelligence, express a will for humanity and the world. As part of his "negative theology," he even goes so far as to deny "life" to God. His argument runs something like this: "life," in any but a metaphoric sense, can be attributed only to "sentient" beings, *i.e.* corporeal existences (*Guide*, I, 42); God, however, is not a corporeal and, therefore, "sentient" being (*ib.*, 53, 55)—"life" can, hence, be attributed to God in no real or literal sense (*ib.*, 56ff.) Thus, according to Maimonides, it would be fair to conclude that the God of Israel cannot cease to live because He is not of the genus of entities that have "life," in the literal sense.

Thomas Aquinas, in many ways the Christian counterpart to Maimonides, as is well known, cites and emulates Maimonides more than a few times. Though he goes along with the latter's "negative theology" to a considerable extent, he must, in the end, introduce a "Christian twist" into the system: ultimately he grants the legitimacy of some essential, though only analogical, attributes, of which life is a very important one.[5] And the theological reason that Thomas, the Aristotelian, must part on this score with Maimonides, the Aristotelian, is clearly connected with his Christology: if God really possessed no attributes whatsoever that make humanly experienced and divine essences in any way comparable, then the doctrines of the trinity and, above all, of the incarnation would be completely impossible. In the latter, at least, God is, after all, held to be "in the flesh."[6] It can, therefore, be put this way: the god of Christianity can cease living for the simple reason that he has lived. Indeed, what is surprising about this? It is, after all the most basic of all Christian doctrines that god became man and lived and died as such. (We shall run into this basic doctrine again where we deal with the contemporary theological crisis.)

Spinoza and Hegel

It is at this point that the modern doctrine of "the theology of blasphemy" begins to emerge. Spinoza was rightly excommunicated by the Jewish community because, whether that was the explicit or conscious reason or no, he identified God, "substance," with the world and, therefore, at least in part with matter, physicality, "extension." It followed quite logically that he had to deny will to both God and humanity; they are both part of nature—*deus sive natura*—and they act as their inherent laws require them to.[7] And, while arguing vehemently and even disingenuously in the *Theologico-Political Treatise* against Maimonides, he defines the superiority of Paul of Tarsus over Moses by claiming that the former articulated "truths" while the latter formulated "laws." It was Hegel, the devout admirer of Spinoza (and not that other admirer of his, Nietzsche—as most current writers in "the theology of blasphemy" assert), who then laid the philosophical foundation for the current Christian theological developments.[8]

Hegel propounds the "death of God" in two different ways but for the same end. For him, too, reason and nature are identical. Nature and history are, indeed, "the life of God." He puts it by way of saying that "what is is rational"—*i.e.*, the real, is divine. It is true that the religious and Marxist defenders of Hegel interpret him, in at least some stages of his thinking, to have meant that only what is rational in the real is rational,[9]—but, apart from the obvious tautology in such a proposition, we shall have occasion to note the limited value of such a doctrine that in the actual real, the rational real that is actual in it must be intellected and then brought to complete domination. (I shall call this "the doctrine of *little* revolution.") In "the life of God" ("Mind" or "Spirit"), which we have seen to be nature and history for Hegel, the German philosopher, he now held that in his and our time the "death of God" had been reached. His *Philosophy of History* sees antiquity and specifically Judaism as the stage of the human mind in which God is conceived as an object, outside of and opposed to rationality—the Middle Ages and specifically Christianity as the stage in which God is subjectivized, *i.e.*, he is increasingly located with humanity itself, although still in mythic form and as a *corpus separatum*, as it were—while modernity, finally—*i.e.*, rational philosophy as enunciated by Hegel himself—absorbs the notion of God entirely in mind, spirit, and reason, *i.e.*, in immanence. Philosophy takes the place of religion, and *Geist* takes the place of God. Transcendence has been completely dissolved in immanence. In his relatively early essay "Faith and Knowledge" Hegel thus explicitly speaks of "the feeling on which the religion of modern times (Christianity) rests: God himself is dead"—and goes on to call philosophy "the speculative Good Friday," (*"der Karfreitag der Philosophie"*) *i.e.*, the stage of the development of reason in which the deity is crucified. He ends that essay by speaking also of a resurrection of God—to be sure in the form of philosophical truth. Also in the somewhat later and definitive *Phenomenology* he ends with the philosophic Easter. As Kaufmann[10] rightly puts it: "To put it into our own words: there is no supreme being beyond; the spirit is not to be found in another world; the infinite spirit has to be found in the comprehension of this world . . . 'History comprehended' must replace theology."

The essentially Christian ethos in this conception is philosophically and even biographically perfectly clear. It has been pointed out that Hegel and Nietzsche, in both of whom the proclamation of the "death of God" found its most sonorous heralds, grew up in deeply Protestant environments, in which the opening words of the Luther hymn are most likely to have been very familiar: "God (Himself) is dead"—referring, of course, to Calvary.[11] The trinitarianism of Hegel's periodization of history is a cliché among students: antiquity is God the father, the Middle Ages God the son, and modernity the Holy Spirit. Generally it can be said that Hegel simply stretched out on an horizontal plane, *i.e.*, through history, the originally metaphysical vertical ladder of emanations of the Neoplatonists.

That there was a distinct and conscious anti-Jewish thrust in this entire trend of thought from the outset can be illustrated rather easily. One of the striking features of Hegel's *Philosophy of History* is that, in his schema of history, Christianity is the heir, not of Judaism but, directly as well as indirectly—in the classic Marcionite—Germanic fashion, of Greek culture alone. Unlike the Oriental cultures, says Hegel, Greece recognized man as God (*e.g.*, the ideally human forms of the statues of gods); all that Christianity had to do was to reverse this insight antithetically, to recognize God as man. This god-man could and did die. Thus the foundation was laid, again according to Hegel, for the modern synthesis of the "resurrection" of the rational spirit from the grave of religion. "It may be posited as an advantage of Greek gods that they are represented as men ... But the Greek gods must not be regarded as being more human than the Christian god. Christ is much more a man: he lives, dies ..." (*Cf. The Philosophy of Hegel*, ed. C.J. Friedrich, N.Y. 1953, p. 59.) And Hegel's great contemporary Goethe spelled out the anti-Jewish implications of this view. He, of course, proclaimed himself a pagan. (For a positive Jewish evaluation of Goethean paganism, *cf.* F. Rosenzweig, *Stern der Erloesung*, III, Introd.) To Lavater he writes: Christianity means that "... seeing yourself reflected in it, you worship yourself." In 1774 he publishes an essay "The Eternal Jew" in which he speaks of "the indescribable mischief the 'Jewish nonsense' brought upon us: had we never come to know the melancholy of the Orient, had Homer remained our Bible, how different a form mankind would have achieved." (K. Loewith, *From Hegel to Nietzsche*, p. 21f.) The truth of the matter is that "the theology of blasphemy" is still the age-old resistance of paganism to and the rebellion against the truth of the Hebrew Bible.

Christianity in the 19th and 20th Centuries

The story of how this Christian conception fundamentally affected the further development of the modern spirit is, in turn, well known, at least in outline. Hegel became perhaps the most influential thinker of the 19th century and, if only through Karl Marx, also of the 20th. All that Feuerbach and

Marx had to do was to "set Hegel on his feet," *i.e.*, conceive of the universe to be essentially material rather than "spirit" and combine this doctrine with Hegel's own universal immanentism. The strong tendency of modern Western culture to exclude all transcendent concerns has increasingly manifested itself in all realms.[12] It has finally, in our time, reached Christian theology itself in the form of the "theology of blasphemy." Quite in the spirit of the Hegel of the *Phenomenology*, Thomas Altizer, one of the most prominent spokesmen of that theology, wants to limit Christianity to Good Friday, omitting Easter—so that the deity can not only have died but remain dead: "When god came into the world in the form of Christ, He was no longer transcendent." When Jesus died, with him the deity ceased. He continues: "This was the self-negation of God. The idea of Resurrection is a great mistake of Christian theology. God is immanent in this world now." This has rightly been called a radical *theologia crucis*. Regardless of whether you turn to Paul Van Buren's influential book *The Secular Meaning of the Gospel*, which programmatically wishes to eliminate all transcendence from Christian theology in favor of a completely immanentist interpretation—or Bonhoeffer's and William Hamilton's concern increasingly limited to human and social ethics—or to Cox's *Secular City* in which the deity disappears[13] *de facto* in a flood of technology and historicity—in all of this agitation there is simply the acknowledgement that, so far as at least their Christian faith is concerned, all sense of transcendence has vanished—indeed, it is regarded as injurious to moral and historical goals: immanent reality alone dictates what is to be done.

In conformity with our original definition of the Christian conception of the relationship between transcendence and the world, the specifically Christian character of this problematic can easily be discerned. Christianity had always held that, if God is not "physically" present in the world, the latter is completely bereft of Him, since His will, in the form of His law, was denied from the outset; one, therefore, had to choose between transcendence and immanence; one could not have the former together with the latter. For too long, these contemporary religionists hold, and now no longer tenably either from a philosophical or from an ethical point of view, Christianity had chosen transcendence—"other-worldliness;" now the turn has come at long last to concern oneself with this world, "secularism," and therefore the other, transcendence, has to be let go.

It is not simply a matter of the nonexistence of God. That would be merely old-fashioned atheism. God, they say, must have lived in order to be able to terminate life. Only Christianity, among the Biblical religions, affords the possibility of such a conception. Transcendence enters into immanence while remaining itself. Thus Van Buren can say:[14] "God is only man; therefore Jesus is the deity." And from this beginning Altizer draws the consistent conclusion:[15] "Only the Christian can celebrate an Incarnation in which God has actually become flesh, and radical theology must finally understand the Incarnation itself as affecting the "death of God."[16] And all the really significant spokesmen of this modern temper agree on its essentially Christian character: Nietzsche: "The end of Christianity—at the hands of its own morality (which cannot be replaced) which turns against the Christian God . . ."[17] Heidegger: "It thus becomes clear that Nietzsche's statement about "death of God" speaks of the Christian God."[18] And the Jesuit Jean-Marie Le Blond: "death of God" can only be fully understood in relation to Christianity. It is a question of post-Christian atheism."[19]

G. Vahanian, one of the radical theologians taken most seriously in the current discussion, puts the cards on the table in recognizing, as Paul Ramsey does in the foreword to his book *The Death of God* that immanence is the crux of the problem and that it derives from peculiarly Christian premises: "This, then, is the irony of the cultural tradition of Christianity, it has bequeathed the idea of the death of God. To kill the deity is to become God oneself: this is the meaning of the transition from radical monotheism to radical immanentism which has taken place in Western culture" (p. 230). And he states the typical Christian dilemma in almost paradigmatic form: transcendence must be related to immanence either in substantial form or not at all—an ethical relationship is not even contemplated by him: (p. 210—having discussed Kierkegaard and Nietzsche) "To say that "God is dead" or to assert an infinite qualitative difference between God and man means not only that no ladder leads from man to God; it also means that there is no identity of substance between man and God, and, accordingly, that the problem of human existence is independent of the problem of God."

Jewish Philosophy in the 19th and 20th Centuries

It is most instructive to watch how the Jewish thinkers of the first half of the 19th century, as much under the heavy influence of Hegel as the rest of Europe, nonetheless guarded against this process of immanentization.[20] Formstecher really stipulates only two religious possibilities, paganism and Judaism, between which Christianity and Islam must somehow find their places. The characteristic of paganism is that it worships nature and thereby forfeits freedom, *i.e.*, will, whereas Judaism worships Spirit. Christianity, in its Jewish component, goes out into the world to bring all cultures under the sway of Spirit, but in the process it adjusts itself too much to the paganism with which it must deal. Its doctrine of original sin, says Formstecher, symbolizes its partial abandonment of freedom, *i.e.*, transcendence to nature. Samuel Hirsch, as strict an Hegelian as Judaism has produced, takes a very similar position and expresses it if anything more rigorously: the human Ego and God *are*, in fact, real freedom over against nature and necessity, not the inevitable self-fulfillment of Hegel's spirit which moves in accordance with its own ineluctable laws. Hirsch uses almost the very words of Maimonides when he endorses the Biblical doctrines of miracles and prophecy precisely on the ground that they express the assertion of transcendent freedom, of God's will, rather than logical or rational necessity. Hegel's and Christianity's error, he proclaims, is, again, that they mix pagan submission to nature with the Biblical proclamation of true freedom. One might even say of Moses Hess, who started out as a Hegelian and proclaimed himself "a disciple of Spinoza," that he broke with Karl Marx on ethical grounds; *i.e.*, by holding that socialism was to be the result of the moral will rather than of the inevitable laws of history. Little wonder that he ended as a committed Jew. The only early-19th-century Jewish thinker who really fell prey to Hegelian immanentism and necessitarianism was, paradoxically, the one among them who wrote in Hebrew, Nachman Krochmal. This is also the logic of the otherwise rather random themes with which he deals in the *Guide for the Perplexed of the Times* which has not, it seems, been noted by the historians: Philo, Gnosticism, Ibn Ezra, Kabbalistic emanationism, and Hegel (!)—precisely the lineage of Neoplatonism or quasi-Neoplatonism, against which the mediaevals had to assert the transcendence of God's will.*

If, then, even the Jewish Hegelians of the 19th century preserved Jewish transcendentalism in the face of Hegelian immanentism, it goes without saying that the dissenters from the regnant philosophy of the age recognized the dangers that confronted them with at least equal clarity. Steinheim, in many ways perhaps the most interesting Jewish thinker of that period, argues against the sovereignty of philosophic reason in the name of a higher reason, the reason of Revelation. (He thus assumes the mantle of R. Yehuda Halevy in the depth of the 19th century.) He does not shrink from identifying Christianity with pantheism and pointing not only to the doctrines of predestination and original sin but even the uncreated logos in the trinity as aspects of a misrepresentation of God, Who is in truth free, *i.e.*, transcendent.

And then, of course, occurs the great break in 19th century Jewish philosophy through the person of Hermann Cohen.[20a] He called for the break

---

*It should be analyzed whether in Chapt. 5 of his *Guide* Krochmal also does not try to assert some ultimate transcendence of god over "Spirit," in arguing against Galen and even Maimonieds.

with Hegel (whom, together with Spinoza, he came to regard as the great archenemy not only of Judaism but of ethical reason in general) and the return to the volitionalism of Kant. Cohen resumes the tradition of Maimonides, to whom he devotes much devout attention, and extends the doctrine of negative theology almost to the point where the very personalism of God vanishes. Even during the "systematic" Kantian period of his works, however, God is for Hermann Cohen always the source of ethical freedom—thus ethically distinguished in his protest against Hegel from Kierkegaard's—and certainly during the last period of his life—whatever may be its relationship to the previous period—he even regains the individuality of man in his "correlation" with a personal God. It is at this point in the history of modern Jewish philosophy that Martin Buber starts out with his assertion of the unimpingeable personalism of God Who wills. (Throughout this sketch we have disregarded the, of course, very important problem of the translation of the will of God into Jewish law—it is true that you cannot have Judaism without this, as too many of the men whom we have been discussing forgot, but it is equally true that you cannot have divine law without divine will.) Franz Rosenzweig in turn starts out at this point with his assertion of the individual in the teeth of Hegelian conceptualism. Thus the circle has closed, and the amazingly unilinear thrust of the entire course of Jewish philosophic thought becomes clear: The will of God and of humanity transcends the iron chains of the nature of God, humanity, and the world.

The Social-Secular Gospel

Before we now turn to a Jewish evaluation, critique, and alternative to this historical development of the Christian "theology of blasphemy," we must pay some attention to the so-called "secular gospel" movement. It is intimately related to the former—it represents the philosophical flaw in it—and it will be seen to have to be Jewishly evaluated somewhat differently, all at once.

We have already pointed out that the current desire among these thinkers to extend the process of immanentization also to theology is in large part due to their conviction that the time is long overdue that Christianity concern itself with worldly and human interests rather than with other-worldly, transcendent ones. Here ethico-centrism is at work. Thus Hamilton apostrophizes Bonhoeffer by saying of him that he "has forced us to move from theology to ethics and to see the life of the Christian, in both its private and public-political visibility, as the primary evidence for the truth of the message he bears. Thus, Bonhoeffer's critical influence forces us to take with theological seriousness the problem of speaking up, breaking the silence, leading, serving, getting hurt in the passionate social and political issues of the day."[21] And Van Buren asserts that, in his view, Christianity too long has been preoccupied with the nature of God instead of His effects—acts and attributes of action—and with His law. He prefers to look for God in ethics rather than in nature and, over and over again, demands "ethics and history, not metaphysics and religion."[22]

Jewish Welcome and Critique of Secularity

But it is precisely at the point at which this trend in current Christian thinking comes closest to Judaism, in its ethical emphasis, that the skies tumble down upon it—i.e., the fundamental and original dichotomy between transcendence and immanence, conceived on a spatial model, vitiates it.

Judaism, as we have seen, conceives of the relationship between God and the world subsisting in the Law: God is concerned with the world, while always remaining completely separate from it; He wills the good of humanity and, therefore, expresses His law; this law, which constitutes the link between God and the world—which, one might say, as our classic preachers actually did, "marries" heaven and earth—when realized, transforms the world "in the image of the Kingdom of Heaven." Ethics and God cannot be sundered. Two classical rabbinic dicta, though often misused, illustrate this trenchantly. God is quoted as saying: "Would that they abandon Me but kept My Torah." At first blush the concern with immanent, this-worldly, human matters seem to eject concern with transcendence. However, R. Huna immediately goes on to repair the breach (i.e., ethics require theology): "If they abandoned Me but kept My Torah, by occupying themselves with it, the leaven in it will lead them back to Me." An equally famous and similarly misused dictum by the same teacher immediately follows and displays the same kind of initial dichotomy between theological and moral preoccupation—only to end up by resolving the dichotomy on a higher plane: "Study Torah, even if not for its own (or God's) sake—for by studying it not for its own sake, by occupying yourself with it you will return to do it for its own (or God's) sake.[23]

Christianity omits the connecting link of the law and thereby divorces transcendence from the world. The incarnation restores such a connection, but in a quasi-physical fashion—and this quasi-physical link itself retains, as we have seen, the dichotomy between divinity and humanity. The Christian is, therefore, forced to choose between transcendence *or* the world. And therefore the contemporary Protestant thinkers, with whom we are dealing, again divide themselves into two opposed camps at this point, namely those who affirm only the world and let God go (the secular gospelers) and those who choose only God and let the world go. Altizer, for example, strives for the Nirvana, to leave the world behind, as does his influential teacher, the historian of religion Mircea Eliade, who regards concern with history, politics, ethics, etc., as a perversion of genuined religiosity. Van Buren, Cox, and Hamilton, on the other hand, resolve to be henceforth concerned only with the world. The other-worldliness of the former group is only a reformulation of much traditional Christian consciousness. The exclusive this-worldliness, "secularity," of the latter, in turn, in the absence of a divine Judge, comes to ail of at least three mortal wounds: 1) When there is nothing but the world, the world as it is is divine. We are back with the pantheism of Spinoza and Hegel. The result is a celebration of the real such as has perhaps never before been held in the history of Biblical religion. One must savor the full optimism of Hamilton, based on his estimate of the advance of the social sciences, the arts, and the civil rights movement:[24] "I am persuaded, however, that in addition to cultural factors, the death of God has made this new optimism possible, and it is not an accident, but intended, deliberate, and natural, that the theologies of the death of God should be in themselves optimistic. . . . Not only are there no tragedies around—this could be described as an accident—but there can't be tragedies."

There is no need to be theoretical about this and to compile the Biblical-Jewish record of pessimism about man and his fate, from *Ecclesiastes*—through our sages who "counted and taught that it were better for man never to have been born,"—all the way to Rabbi Soloveitichik who recently wrote: "To the thinkers of the Age of Reason man posed no problem. . . . They saw man in his glory but failed to see him in his tragic plight. They considered the individual ontologically perfect and existentially adequate."[25] We can instead make an historical judgment: Christianity, historically the religion of the West most pessimistic about humanity and the world, in at least one sector turns around to proclaim the unqualified goodness of humanity and the world—indeed, the absence and even impossibility of tragedy—in the very hour in which the Jewish people has sipped of the cup of ineffable, cosmic bitterness to its very last dregs! 2) The absence of transcendence ultimately destroys ethics. As Spinoza and Hegel exemplified, when there is only immanence, whatever is is rational— nature is God—and the real is the good. Ethics means to have an alternative to reality—but this alternative has been eliminated. This validates itself also among these new ethicists. Hamilton, as we have seen, acclaims what is actually happening as what should happen. He approvingly quotes two German Protestant theologians who reject the desire to change the world as the notion that "rape is the only form of engagement."[26] Cox welcomes the new technological age as "the wave of the future."[27] Hans Jonas trenchantly points out that "the being whose fate Heidegger ponders is the quintessence of this world, it is *seculum*. Against this, theology should guard the radical transcendence of its God, whose voice comes not out of being, but breaks into the kingdom of being from without." But the former seminarian thinks of what he still calls transcendence as something that one "sees" rather than "hears," i.e., again as a quasi-physical rather than ethical, entity—welcomed Hitler as divine fate—and took many German Christians and even theologians along with him.[28] How can one ultimately speak of ethics, and even of ethicocentrism, when whatever happens must happen, and when the best that the moral man can be expected to do—as Cox and Van Buren agree with Hegel on his best interpretation—is to discern "where the action is" and to "get with it"? 3) The indigenous Christian antinomianism, or a-nomianism, ultimately eliminates ethics, because, as Kant taught, ethics *is* law. In the absence of law, ethics can at best be laudible sentiment or awaited special divine injuctions. Thus Van Buren distinguishes, in the by now well-known language of the English linguistic analysts, between the verifiable propositions of science and the unverifiable, subjective, however valuable, "blik" of religion. But this is not so much a misunderstanding of religious epistemology as it is a misunderstanding of the philosophical foundations of science. Science works with hypotheses—postulated ideas. These hypotheses "create" the stuff of sensuous experience which constitutes the "problem" for humanity's cognition. "Matter" and "reality," then, are tasks that challenge reason—and infinite tasks at that. Thus it turns out that also scientific cognition is, like faith, an human, ethical, and eschatological enterprise.[29]

The result of this absence of lawfulness which is ascribed to ethics is a) "there is no external criterion by which we might see whether Jesus was in fact obedient," (this is related also to the current wave of the new, "contextualist" morality)[30], and b) that the "kerigmatic message of the hour" may at best be late, as it was even for Bonhoeffer and Karl Barth when the Nazis rose to power, and at worst the confirmation that Hitler embodies the good for Heidegger, and current local political heroes for Cox and Hamilton.

Revolutionary Halakhah

Our Jewish reaction to the current efflorescence of the "theology of blasphemy" and "the secular gospel" can then really be summarized in one sentence: Judaism always advocates, in the name of the God absolutely concerned with the world, the greatest possible human, religious attention to the welfare and progress of this world—and if this be called "secularism," then so be it—but it teaches convincingly that this can be done only under the aegis of a Law put forth by the transcendent God.

By way of analyzing the immanetism of "the secular gospel," we have already had occasion to speak of the indispensability of the Law. Before we finally leave this subject, another point must be made about it, however—this time addressed not to non-Jews but to Jews committed to the *Halakhah*. The *Halakhah* is eternally valid and applicable to the world because it did not originate in Mosaic society, much less in Babylonian or Egyptian society. This is to say, it did not originate from and is not, therefore, exclusively tailor-cut for any past or present society. The *Halakhah* originates with God. God is unchangingly relevant—and therefore so is His Law—to all societies, past, present, and future, until the world will have become what He wills it to be, the Kingdom of the Messiah of our righteousness. The *Halakhah* is the law of the ever-future society and the law that leads every present society in the direction of the ultimate, future society. Surely this is the meaning of the fundamental rabbinic theologumen that in the *Shema* we must first take upon ourselves the yoke of the Kingdom of God so that we may thereafter receive the yoke of its commandments (Ber. 13a).

It would not be difficult to show how literally all of the *Halakhah* is either the law of society as it should be—and this whoever fulfills it in fact establishes, as it were, a small forwardbastion of the ultimate future in the present—or the law by which the present society is moved forward toward the Messianic: i.e., whenever Jews act according to the *Halakhah* they either hasten the coming of the Kingdom or actually institute it at the moment and in the place where they happen to be. Perhaps the Sabbath is the best exemplification of this process. The world was created for the sake of the Sabbath (Gen. 2). The expulsion from the Garden of Eden destroyed the universal Sabbath. The weekly Sabbath is a foretaste of the Garden of Eden restored by the Messiah (Ber. 56)—i.e., on it Jews live as they will live all the time under the Messianic sceptor. But this is not only an individual, rather it is a social, goal. The weekly Sabbath is a small portion of the Sabbatical year, which in turn is a small portion of the Jubilee year, and finally the Jubilee year—with its social egalitarianism—is a small portion, again, of the days of the Messiah. All of the *Halakhic* life of the Jew during the week then leads up to the Sabbath, and all of the *Halakhic* life of the Jew on the Sabbath leads up to the Messianic fulfillment. For that reason our sages can say that if Jews would only observe one or two Sabbaths fully the Messianic Kingdom would have come—for the Sabbath *is* the Messianic Kingdom, and the Messianic Kingdom is what all of Judaism is for and about.[31]

If, then, it be true that Jewish lawfulness is Messianic lawfulness, there is another way of putting this: every given, historical society is by definition infinitely short of what it should be—the infinite being measured by the infinity of the difference between what God wants for humanity and what humanity actually is and does; it follows that the *Halakhah*, in order to be completely realized, requires a total transformation of human society. A commonly used English word for "total transformation" is "revolution." The *Halakhah* is religiously the permanent revolution.

It seems to be important to say this to Jews who are committed to the full sway of the *Halakhah* because some of them these days, confronted with a wide-spread rebellion against law—from civil disobedience in the civil rights movement, through the burning of draftcards, "dirty speech movements" and political revolutions around the world, to an overthrow of previously—at least publicly—accepted sexual *mores*—automatically assume that Judaism stands for law and must, therefore, oppose any infraction of any law. But this is not true. Judaism stands for divine, Messianic, as we have seen—revolutionary law. In each case we ought, therefore, to examine whether a) the rebels against positive law may not in fact, wittingly or unwittingly, be protesting against antiquated law in the name of what we have recognized as "the ever-future law," and b) whether we, for that matter, may not have distorted that ever-future law, through our interpretations and applications, into a replica of present and even past social conventions. (That, in our time, we are often baffled as to what the relevant revolutionary *Halakhah* actually is may be a function of the hiddenness of God, of which we shall speak shortly.)

Jewish Secularity

The immanentization process that we have analyzed we have faulted for failing to understand that immanence without transcendence destroys ethics. But let us emphasize at the same time that concern with this world, rather than pure transcendence, lies at the very heart of Jewish religion. One surely need not adduce all of the *Halakhah*, which is a *Halakhah* for this world, not for another, and for living people, not for the transfigured—one need not adduce all of the prophets of Israel who were passionately immersed in the affairs of their times—to be sure in the name of the transcendent God—in order to prove this proposition.

Indeed, at least two emphases can be derived by Jews from this contemporary concern with secularity which especially "religious Jews" have sometimes of late been tempted to underplay. It has long been a notorious fact that Jews in Central and Western Europe and America since the beginning of the 19th century and in Eastern Europe since the end of that centruy have secularized much more quickly and much more widely than the bulk of Christendom. (This is not the place to trace the whys and hows of this process.) Indeed, even the formulation of a secularistic theology was anticipated by some Jews decades ago, also in this country, under such titles as *The Meaning of God in Modern Jewish Religion* and *Secularism is the Will of God.* What has long been a source of Jewish religious lament now, retrospectively, turns out to have been an ambiguous but sensitive anticipation of the temper of our age which Christians are now trying to catch up with. More importantly, the secular world is—and this is the very heart of Judaism—the concern of God; thus also the secular Jew is a Jew, not made one by separate theological affirmations.

There is, in the second place, a tradition in modern Torah-true Judaism which affirms the value of secularity as a *hakhanah-preparatio* for a new vital faith. It holds that the God of Israel wants humanity to become completely, exclusively human, so that we may thereafter be the worthier of returning to our status as children of God.

Let us mention only three names in this tradition: the Maharal of Prague[32] affirmed humanity's autonomy and held that "there must be a preliminary exploration of the earth, of its physical forces, of its complex interplay of contradictions. In short there must be a pedagogy on the primary level of sensations and perceptions before one can approach the Torah." Rav Kook is, of course, well known to have held that the secularists and materialists are tools in the hand of God, doing His work, who build the physical and material temple of humanity and the world so that He may, thereafter, take up His residence with them the more gloriously. "There is something valuable in present-day materialism. It has a realistic approach to practical problems. For there is danger in abstract ideas, and materialism is a path leading to the later recognition of the Most High, who is above all idealistic theories, the highest and absolute reality, higher than either materialism or idealism."[33]

Finnally, let us adduce a particularly moving expression of this trend, for it comes from a man who, living in the Soviet Union, tried desperately to understand how the universal God of all history could permit—and even bring about—the atheistic Marxism that surrounded him on all sides, R. Yitzchak Krasileshtzikoff. Let me quote a rather lengthy but most provocative passage:[34]

> God wraps Himself in materialism and emanates His light and disperses it from one end of the earth to the other. At this time many see only the sublime material cover, but the time will come when the earth will be filled with the knowledge of God, and the human race will open its eyes to see the spirit and the divine and ethical substance that is hidden in this material. ... R. Yitzchak Abrabanel, in his *Yeshuot Meshicho*, explains R. Nehorary's statement (*perek chelek*) that in the days of the Messiah the kingdom will turn to heresy by saying that when men will no longer adhere to any of their many religions, when they will be rid of all of them, then they will the more easily accept the true faith rather than one that contradicts it. ... The new materialism which denies everything is brought about by Him who calls the generations from the beginning, to make it easier for the perfected and developed mankind to accept the yoke of God's Kingdom. ... To go from monism to monotheism is not so difficult. For to penetrate nature and matter it suffices to find in them the God of all Who is also in him that investigates them.

R. Krasileshtzikoff refers to the Russian Christian philosopher Soloviev and goes on:

> He who calls the generations from the beginning intentionally causes His Godhood to be forgot for a specified period, so that man will acquire an understanding of the knowledge of nature. After this man will realize the glory of the spirit of God that resides in nature and matter.

He even comes to terms ethically with the Marxist doctrine of class struggle by declaring that true human morality can only come about after the class struggle has been overcome.

One might state this profound doctrine that the Maharal and the Russian R. Yitzchak share by saying that God withdraws from humanity the way a father sends his son away to school so that he may grow up and learn to stand on his own two feet. Secularism, they say, is the process of humanity's maturation. And this is virtually the literal kernel of Dietrich Bonhoeffer's doctrine of "the world come of age."

The Hiding God

Therewith we come to the last component of the Biblical, Jewish alternative to the "theology of blasphemy." God hides Himself, we have just been told, in order to let humanity, as it were, get out from under His shadow. But the doctrine of the hiding of God is, of course, much more complex and painful than this. That the time of *The Eclipse of God*, in Buber's phrase, is a time of utter agony by far outweighs its putative pedagogical value. During that time unspeakable horrors transpire—Job-like, humanity feels utterly alone and bereft of meaning—and the world appears if not empty then, worse, filled with filth. This, of course, a pervasive human consciousness in our time, among religionists, writers, artists, and thinkers.

But let us be clear about it: the doctrine of the *e-l mistater* is considerably more searching and more humanistic than that of the "death of God." In the first place, in Jewish tradition it is a hiding, not a hidden God—an *e-l nistar umistater*, not a *deus absconditus*—it is a doctrine of an act, not a state of God, a present process, not a completed one.[35] In the second place, it is a doctrine of an absence, not of an emptiness. The bachelor may regret not having a wife, but surely the widower, bereft of his wife, is suffering infinitely greater pain. In the third place, whereas immanentism declares that there is nothing but that which is and therefore celebrates it, without a need, a possibility, or a desire to change it, those who experience the hiding of God know that there is an alternative and feel called upon humanly to endeavor to overcome their present condition. The hiding manifests transcendence, and out of it the imperative to ethics and revolution sounds forth—the commandment of lightning out of the darkness of the cloud (Ex. 19:16).

We cannot review the history of the Jewish doctrine of the hiding of God—from the cry of the Psalmist (30:7) "Thou didst hide Thy face, and I was confounded"—to the announcement of the prophet (Is. 45:15, which I would translate) "Ahoy Thou hiding God, Thou God of Israel art Savior"*—through the Kabbalistic doctrine that the world and humanity exist only through the process of divine hiding, *tzimtzum*, and are, therefore, perennially in exile (a doctrine which Gershom Scholem has rightly called the extreme opposite of pantheism)—to the mortally wounded outcry of an Elie Wiesel who, in the name of the martyr of the European Holocaust, accuses God of having, as it were, gone AWOL at the height of the battle. We do want to adduce two passages out of our literature because, respectively, they express the historic experience of the Jewish people and the need of our hour.

B. Yoma 69b expresses the experience of the hiding of God in a most radical and daring fashion: "They do not grant halves in heaven." Moses had called God (Deut. 10:17) "great, mighty, and awesome." On the basis alone does the *Halakhah* rule that Jews may so designate God, who otherwise is "beyond all praises." Jeremiah witnessed the withdrawal of God in the destruc-

---

*Note the Radak's extraordinary commentary on this.

tion of the first Temple and dared, therefore, to overrule Moses by refusing to call God awesome. Daniel experienced the further withdrawal of God in the Babylonian oppression and, therefore, refused to call Him mighty. It is true that the Sages decided against Jeremiah and Daniel, but not for any saccharine, homiletical reasons of pseud-optimism about the world—that, after all, there is so much good, too. Rather they propounded an extremely subtle and profound consideration which only underlined further the horror of the world's evils: they held that the fact that the world can at all continue to exist in the presence of such great evil as we witness is ethically and logically incomprehensible except as a result of God's awesome and mighty patience and loving-kindness. At the same time they justified Jeremiah's and Daniel's apparently high-handed actions by saying: "Since these two knew that the Holy One, blessed be He, insists on truth, they would not ascribe false things to Him." Jeremiah and Daniel preferred silence, which is the human response to God's hiding, to speech, which can only be the human response to God's revelation.[36] The rabbis also went so far as to define God's uniqueness precisely by His hidig: they interpreted Ex. 15:11, "Who is like unto Thee among the gods?," as "Who is like unto Thee in keeping silent (after the destruction of the Temple)?"[37]

Martin Buber expressed the need of the hour concisely:

> Fill the horizon that has been declared empty. . . . It would be worthier not to explain it to oneself in sensational and incompetent sayings, the "death of God", but to endure it as it is and at the same time to move existentially toward a new happening, toward that event in which the word between heaven and earth will again be heard.[38]

"And God Heard Their Cry"

Everyone has had God. Some have eliminated Him for themselves through immanentization. Israel still knows Him. Israel still hears Him, commanding the transformation of the world through the Law of the Kingdom of heaven. Our sages, again, characterized the situation aptly: (*Yalkut Shim'oni* to Ex. 2, 169) " 'And God hear their cry' (Ex. 2:24). Collate this with Zech. 10:2: 'For their abomination spoke nullity; therfore, they fled like a flock saying that there is no shepherd.' This can be compared to two boys. The father of one died, and he buried him. The other's father lives. He whose father lives, when he calls out to him 'my father,' the latter answers. 'He whose father has died, when he goes to his father's grave and calls out 'my father, my father' until his strength wanes, receives no answer. So is Israel: their Father lives, and He answers them promptly: 'And God heard their cry:' 'Before they call I will answer' (Is. 65); "Let him call Me, and I shall answer him" (Ps. 91). But as for the nations—"they will cry out to Him, and He will not reply" (Is. 46); and, whereas God answered Elijah, "the disturber of Israel," the false prophets "took the ox that he had given them and slaughtered it and called in the name of Baal from morning until noon, saying: 'Oh, Baal, answer us!,' but there was no voice, and there was no answer" (Kings I, 18:26).

– 4 –

On the Theology of Jewish Survival

Phenomenology of the Jewish Spirit, 1945

When people think in 1968 about Jewish survival it can be assumed that the occasion for their consideration is the Six Day War of 1967 and it continuing consequences. We, too, will want to revert to that episode, but I wish to begin our exploration at another and more decisive point in contemporary Jewish history: the early summer of 1945—i.e., the hour when the Jewish people stood on both sides of the open doors of Bergen-Belsen, of Auschwitz, of Maidanek and Theresienstadt and the other camps of extermination, and when the full weight of what had happened to us there and throughout the Holocaust came bearing down on us.

The reality of the situation at that point was twofold: on the one hand, it was brutally clear that death and destruction, infinite pain and incurable physical and spiritual dislocations had reaped an abundant harvest in our midst. We were on the very verge of expiration; indeed, in some ways we had died, beyond revival. At the same time, we must remember, this condition prevailed, in varying ways and degrees, in all the countries and among all the peoples of the Old World, from the British Isles through the entire heartland of Eurasia to the islands of Japan and beyond. Slaughter and fire, the lie and the eraser had cut a wide swath not only through the peoples but also through the institutions and cultures of these continents. So we looked around us—we saw the scene—and, though with cracked voices and with bitter hearts, we first hummed softly and then sang in a swelling chorus the refrain of the Partisan song: "*Mir zennen do*"—"Never say we have walked our last road;" when all the roads will have been trod, and when all others will have fallen by the wayside, we—or at least a small remnant of Israel, the true "remaining remnant"—will yet present ourselves to proclaim: "We are still here—*mir zennen do*." The greatest, the world-shaking and heaven-rending, the inexpungeably traumatic tragedy of Israel was accompanied, contrapuntally, as it were, by the increasing consciousness of the ineluctable, unextirpatable survival of the Jewish people throughout history—and if through that history then surely throughout eternity.[1]

It is relatively easy to trace the spreading and deepening realization of this truth among Jews over the last twenty-three years. Indisputably the establishment of the State of Israel, in the face of apparently insuperable hostilities and difficulties, was undergirded by the psychology of "the remaining remnant": "We've come through so much—we'll come through this, too' '—together with the historical lesson: "if I am not for myself, who will be for me?" (I remember, for example, the passengers of the Exodus speaking like this, and acting on it, the second time around on their itinerary between West Germany and the shores of Israel.) Again, when one talked with or read the expressions of many of the participants in the Six Day War,[2] almost a quarter of a century later, this immediately post-Holocaust posture was clearly noticeable, usually formulated in just these terms—and this was, in fact, true throughout world Jewry. Even theologically the appropriation of this consciousness, though more slow, can be observed: Eliezer Berkovits ended his notable polemic against "interfaith dialogues" with a rousing peroration to the effect that we, the eternal people, were present and witnesses when the Christian era began—we are still present and witnesses now that it has come to an end.[3] That was several years ago. Last fall this became, as we remember, virtually a stampede among rabbis, community leaders, and among the ranks of Jewry: "The Christian world has again stood passively or even antagonistically. We're on our own. We're going to keep it that way."

The Classic Jewish View

If this is a correct phenomenology of the Jewish spirit after the Second World War, we do not need to stop long to prove that it stands in complete accord and direct line with the classic Biblical, Talmudic, mediaeval Jewish conception of the prospects of Jewish survival and its theology. I take it that the following is a legitimate summary of how our classic teachers envisaged the situation.

The model of the relationship between God and Israel in the Bible is, of course, the Covenant.[4] There are two ways of understanding that Covenant—let them be called the ethical and the metaphysical. The ethical interpretation makes the religious, moral, and historical honor of Israel the prerequisite for God's fulfillment of His part of the Covenant, i.e., the preservation and advance of the Jewish people: if they do not do their share He is relieved of His obligation and will let it lapse.[5] The advantage of this view is obviously the responsibility which it places upon the Jew and the ethical stimulus which it thus constitutes. Its corollary disadvantage is equally obvious: it is entirely too anthropocentric; it claims that history is determined by a large number of individual and collective subjective and irrational factors; it declares in effect that God's providence, or historical forces, can easily be detracked, rerouted, or even stopped cold by essentially trivial human incursions.[6] The metaphysical view, then, represents the other part of the polarity. It speaks of the "eternal covenant"; it assures mankind that as long as the rainbow will be in the sky so long—which is to say eternally—will humanity persist, and it assures Israel that its survival is coeval with God's existence.[7] Here the emphasis is not on humanity but on metaphysical factors—God, the world or humanity as totalities, the overarching purpose of history, etc. Ezekiel and others will thus let ethical considerations ride, at least for the time being, and announce redemption "not for our sakes, but for the sake of His Name". In this interpretation of the Covenant the advantages and disadvantages of the ethical interpretation are precisely reversed: it obviously possesses a view of history which is objective and rational, but correspondingly it tends to lower the status of human ethical responsibility.[8]

These two views are not mutually exclusive, and they are certainly not chronological or Bible-critical *realia*. Their relationship to one another is rather dialectical. The case of Ezekiel just adduced makes this point all by itself and in Biblical terms: ethics are by no means ejected from this historiographical scheme, anymore than historiosophy is absent from, let us say, Amos, for whom, nonetheless, history seems to be a function of ethics rather than vice versa. Certainly for the Bible as such both interpretations of the nature of the Covenant come together in an integral, dialectical unity. God's plan for history is unalterably determined, and man's ethical decisions are indispensable as well as constitutive. If you will, "everything is forseen, but freedom is given". One Biblical formulation of this unity of opposites is the very doctrine of the "returning remnant" of which we spoke at the outset as an historical reality. What the dialectical doctrine states at the very least is that, while Israel's actions are determinative of its survival, it is simultaneously true that this survival is divinely guaranteed in any case.

In classical Rabbinic Judaism this paradoxical view of the matter—empirically verified by Jewish history and doing justice both to the ethics as well as the metaphysics of the problem—becomes considerably more sophisticated and subtle. "*Yisrael Saba*", the eternity of Israel, founded on the eternity of God is taken for granted by all.[9] This in itself is wondrous enough when we remember that Rabbinic Judaism is, after all, largely the product of the destruction of the Second Commonwealth and of the bimillenial fate of Israel in a tragic and always radically tenuous *galut*. The full sophistication of the belief in the divinely guaranteed eternity of Israel becomes clear, however, only when one tries to understand the extremely complex teachings of the Rabbis in which, again, they dialectically synthesize the polar demands of the ethics and the metaphysics of Jewish survival and destiny. In *Perek Chelek, Sanh.* 96b-98a, the *locus classicus* is to be found of Jewish Messianism and thus of the eternity of Jewish life. Especially the debate between Rabbi Eliezer ben Hyrcanus, who advocates the ethical interpretation,[10] and Rabbi Joshua ben Hananya, who advocates what we have called the metaphysical interpretation, is to be noted.[11] By superficial students their debate might be regarded as merely a Billy Graham-like verse-slinging match; the usual but equally superficial view is that the two represent mutually exclusive doctrines, and their debate is then taken as another illustration of the unsystematic nature of Talmudic theology.

The fact of the case is that, by the time the debate is over, in this passage and in a great number of others the final result is precisely the dialectical unity of ethics and metaphysics of which we have spoken. Its lovely poetic metaphor is found in *Midr. Tehillim* 45:3: "Just as this rose grows with its heart toward heaven, so do you repent before Me and turn your hearts heavenward, and, like the dew, I will thereupon cause your redeemer to appear."[12] It takes the form, for example, of saying that Israel must conduct itself morally so that destiny can be fulfilled (ethics) but that God will, if need be, constrain it so to act (metaphysics).

Another frequent way of putting it is to say that God has determined the end but that Israel can, by pious deeds, hasten its advent. (Note the sophisticated nature of this formulation: human evil cannot delay, or frustrate, God's providence, though human good can accelerate it; i.e., God acts, as it were, in a limit-situation fashion.)[13] Perhaps the most highly developed stage of this particular formulation of the combination of the contingency—*cum*-necessity, what Ezekiel Kaufman has called *ratzon vi-hekkre'ach*, of Israel's meaningful existence is to be encountered in the greatest of all Jewish eschatologists, Isaac Abarbanel, who schematizes it by distinguishing between the first period of "the possibility of his coming," when, depending on human actions, the Messiah may come, and the subsequent period of "the necessity of his coming," when he will come regardless of human preparations, by divine fiat.

Of one thing there can, in any case, be no doubt: the Jewish consciousness of our generation that we and our children until the end of days will always proclaim "*mir zennen do*" is a simple perpetuation not only of the experience but also of the classic theology of Jewish history. Whatever the effect on it of the deeds of the Jew and Gentile may or may not be, Jewish survival is guaranteed by God—subject, to be sure, to high costs and to qualifications in detail but not to fundamental anxiety. *Am Yisrael chay vi-kayyam.*

Practical Applications

Let us, at this juncture, try to indicate one sociologico-psychological and one "pastoral" practical application of our theological truism before we return to our main *heilsgeschichtlich* concern in the perspective of the last year.

The sensationalistic notion of "the vanishing Jew" has been widely circulated. With reference to the *galut* Jew in general and the American Jew in particular it serves diverse purposes. Some Israelis and other negators of the Diaspora use it in order to strengthen their exhortations to *aliyah*.[14] I always suspect that certain Christian circles use it because their notion of the religious conquest of Judaism is still very much operative in their minds, if not always on their lips. American mass media use it in order to increase their circulation, which, like most reading matter in this country, depends in large measure on Jewish suburbanite middle-class clientele. Furthermore, it would appear that there is a clinically sick streak in many American Jews who gratify their masochism by reading about their own imminent collective demise. (The fact that they are so interested in reading about it refutes their prediction.) At the same time the diagnosis of Jewry's mortal illness and the prognosis of the death of Judaism come in handy for those who want to justify their own defection from *Clal Yisrael*: they can now point to the public confirmation that their course of action is in line with the *Zeitgeist*, and, indeed, with the inevitable course of history; furthermore, they can legitimately argue against tying up their own and their family's fates in a foredoomed venture.[15]

We will not bother to polemicize against that notion of "the vanishing Jew" at any length. This prediction has been made in literally every single generation of Jewish history.[16] One of the more frequently told such tales is that of Steinschneider who, under historically and culturally similar conditions to our own, is supposed to have asked a rabbinical student why he had come late and, when told that the student had been detained at a Zionist meeting, replied with some anger that, in our time, our only task was to provide a decent funeral for the literary remains of Jewish history. The facts of history—many facts of a very long history—have empirically given the lie to all such predictions, to the point where no reasonable man can, on purely empirical grounds, any longer take them seriously.

No one should mistake this attitude for a vapid or any other kind of optimism: we referred at the outset to the symbiosis of death and resurrection in the barracks of Auschwitz—surely no one who proclaims: "I believe in the coming of the Messiah" while he or his child is walking into the gas chamber can be accused of liberalistic euphoria. Furthermore, we are far from denying the sociological, cultural, and religious evisceration of the Jewish people anywhere, much less in America; on the contrary, we watch its vulgarities and mindlessness with horror. It is perfectly true: according to all the natural laws of history, demography, and sociology the people of Israel cannot much longer endure, and, certainly, it cannot be expected further to be ethically creative. We have no hope in *homo Judaeus*. All that we are saying is that to deduce from this condition the demise of the Jewish people and of Judaism is itself a symptom of the sickness which the thesis claims to be describing: it is to study the Jewish phenomenon according to the "laws of the gentiles"; it is to leave God and His covenantal promise out of account (as Laplace put it to Napoleon). One need not subscribe either to R. Yehuda Halevy's metaphysical biologicism or to Nachman Krochmal's Vicoism to accept the truth with which we, too, have been concerning ourselves—that there is a force at work in our history which overcomes and transcends all these perfectly correct laws of general human history. To put it epigrammatically: it is irrational not to believe in the miraculousness of Jewish history.

The most immediately pragmatic form which the notion of "the vanishing Jew" takes is the widespread worry about intermarriages. Statistics, analyses, papers, books and conferences on this subject proliferate. Parents and rabbis constantly warn young people against its dangers—and the most flagrant of these dangers is supposed to be to the survival of the Jewish people. I always visualize God sitting in heaven, surrounded by myriads of His serving angels, with the instruments of His omnipotent providence at His side, going into a panicky conference with His counselors when news comes through that little Gilbert Shapiro from Scarsdale has, for his own socio-pathological reasons, decided to marry Christine Thomas from Dubuque on the campus of Omaha State Teachers College where they have met: the fate of the world and history, not to speak of the chosen people and its destiny, hangs in the balance! "He who sits in heaven laughs—the Lord mocks them" (Ps. 2:4). There is, obviously, something ridiculous in this picture—even when it is multiplied a thousandfold. The main point, however, is that Gilbert and Christine are obviously not going to make their decision—if decision it be—in terms of Jewish destiny; indeed, if that meant much to them they would not be very likely to have reached their present condition in the first place. What is more, by inveighing against their allegedly great and injurious treason to the ethnic and religious ties of their families and people one is doing exactly what they—like their academic, bohemian, artistic, and intellectual counterparts—are looking for: they are conducting a small-scale raid against their parents, *milieu*, and the God of their backgrounds. They require a father's disapproval so that they can rebel against it and affirm their independence; by imploring their loyalty one confirms to them that, in the first place, the objects of their resentment are very weak and vulnerable and that, in the second place, their attacks are hitting their targets.

I should think that we ought to deal with the problems of intermarriage in the full and confident consciousness of the theologoumen that nothing that anyone, Jew or Gentile, does can ultimately affect the fate of Israel as a whole. When a Jew and a non-Jew come to us with marital intentions—in a period, incidentally, when marriages constitute only a limited portion of connubial relationships—we present to them the full strictness of Jewish law. (I mention only in passing the Reform rabbis who, also in my community, violate conspicuously not only Jewish law but also the explicit consensus of historic and contemporary Reform Judaism and who continue to injure the unity of the people of Israel and the effectiveness of their colleagues by officiating wholesale at mock-Jewish intermarriages.) The inviolability of Jewish law and religious substance affirms their sanctity and viability beyond impertinent individual or collective amputation to the point of death. A Judaism that declares its reliance on God rather than on—never mind kings—effervescent small-fry is considerably more persuasive than a weak beggar going down on his knees to beg for consideration. "The Lord is with me; I shall not fear: what can man do to me? The Lord is for me as my self; thus shall I be witness to my enemies. It is better to rely on God than to rely on man. It is better to rely on God than to rely on princes. All peoples have surrounded me, but I have escaped them. The right hand of the Lord is upright; the right hand of the Lord acts mightily. I shall not die but live and tell of the deeds of God. He has much tried me, but to death He has not given me over" (Ps. 118). Especially in an age in which nothing succeeds as much as success I would hold that Jewish self-abnegation can be cured not with defeatism but only with—if you please—a divine, a Messianic certainty of eventual triumph.

All of this does not, of course, mean that, relying on God's promise, we may lapse into human passivity. Jews have never done this: our metaphysics have always ungirded, not suspended, our ethics. Of course, we want to stop a Jew from defecting, in body or in spirit. But this is so because we hate to see any Jew—or any person deprived of their share in the glory of Israel. We are worried about the incalculable deprivation which such a defection inflicts upon the defecting individual, not upon the people, faith and destiny from which he or she defects; we are anxious for the individual, not for God's providence.[16a] Of course, we want to do everything we can to strengthen, enrich, and disseminate *Yiddishkeit,* but this can be done not by begging unwilling—or, for that matter, even willing—individuals or groups, children, marriageable people, Judaism or God out of their respective troubles. What we must do is to externalize the resplendence of the spirit of God within them—to fan the sparks of the *schechinah* residing in the broken vessels of the Jewish community—to plumb the sophistication of the *sod* within the—usually misunderstood—*peshat* of Jewish reality.

"Not By Power . . ."

We now return to our main theme—the significance of Jewish survival as we experienced it in 1945. The crucial question which—consciously or unconsciously—has arisen for all who have lived since is this: how did this survival, broken yet triumphant, tortured yet exultant, decimated yet fortified, come about? What can we learn about how we are to survive from how we did survive?

At the Eichmann trial the Israeli attorney-general Hausner asked most European-Jewish survivors of the Holocaust who gave testimony: Why did you not resist? Ben-Gurion, among others, said that one of the major purposes of the trial was to purge Jewish consciousness of a haunting guilt-feeling for not having fought back against the Nazis but—as the Biblical phrase, frighteningly transvalued, which is usually cited at this point, goes—having "gone like sheep to the slaughter." Clearly, the premise of the question is, in the first place, that it is better to "fight back" than to die, without physical retaliation or defense, as martyrs, and, in the second place, that the survival of the "remaining remnant" was due to those who, as heroes on the walls of the Warsaw Ghetto, soldiers in the Jewish Brigade, members of the roaming Partisan groups, or after the war as soldiers in the *Haganah* or other military or quasi-military outfits, fought against the Nazis and for the establishment of the State of Israel. There can be little doubt that it is on the basis of essentially such premises that organized Jewry concentrates its memorializations of the victims of the Holocaust on anniversaries of the Warsaw Ghetto Revolt. Hence issues forth also a new worldwide Jewish admiration for heroes of brawn—Israeli, healthy, clear-eyed, wiry boys and girls with machine guns under their arms, Colonels Marcus, tanks and planes on Sunday-school bulletin boards, etc.

This view of how Israel survived its most horrible threat has undergone a rapid escalation. It began, shortly after the war, with the glorification of the Jewish military and paramilitary fighters while the "passive" martyrs were lamented but, for the rest, relatively neglected. From this followed shortly two different but supplementary theses: the Hausner thesis we have mentioned, that there was something, perhaps something crucial, that was demeaning, immoral, possibly even traitorous about not having physically fought back, and the Hannah Arendt thesis that significant elements of the Jewish leadership and communities in Europe had actually collaborated with their people's exterminators. Mind you, even most of those who vehemently argued against the Arendt thesis accepted the premise that to die unresistingly is somehow shameful, and they, therefore, concentrated their attention on revolts in ghettos and concentration camps and on Jewish leaders who were active in the war against the Nazis in order to try to refute Arendt's thesis.[17] The next step in the escalation was, of course, the resolution, in Israel and abroad, not to let ourselves be decoyed into such a situation again but rather, from the outset, to be ready to take arms and other counteraggressive measures against any actual or potential (and thus preemptive) enemy. This was certainly the underlying and usually proclaimed psychological posture immediately before and during the Six Day War; it was part of the *déja-vu*, the *déja-senti* atmosphere of those weeks when the beleaguered spirit of the Second World War was rife in the Jewish community—and it is the source of the predominant "hawkishness" in Jewish circles since then. The last and grotesquely Satanic degree of escalation which this interpretation of the Jewish history of our time has hitherto undergone is the doctrine enunciated in the current wave of Polish, neo-Stalinist Communist anti-semitism—that, by and large, it was the Poles—*mirabile dictu!*—who fought against the Nazis while the ranks of Jewry were shot through with traitors, collaborators, and cowards.

The subject is too painful, and I, therefore, want to try to summarize what is historically and morally wrong with this attitude as briefly as possible. In Israel and in this country a Jewish triumphalism has spread which is not lovely to behold. In the "Movement for the Greater Land of Israel" phrases are slung around which sound most ominous to anyone who has lived through the 'thirties of our century: "liberated territories," "the Greater Israel," "the call of the historic soil," "the metaphysical unity of the people and the land," "the irresistible destiny of the millenia," etc. Policy discussions are held about how to keep the numbers and the fertility of the Arabs (and sometimes even also of the Sephardim) in manageable proportion to those of the rest of Israel—satellite states are proposed as a more liberal way of dealing with the Near Eastern problem than wholesale removal of populations—the Israeli army is further enhanced as the chief tool of integration, education, and decision-making, where the Kibbutz had, surely, been originally cast in that role—generals become cabinet-members and ambassadors, together with previously proscribed terrorist leaders and right-wing chauvinists—let these examples stand for others as well.[18]

In a more technically theological sense the Israeli victory in the Six Day War has produced an immensely aggravated danger of pseudo-faith and pseudo-Messianism. It is by now a cliché how Israeli as well as *galut* Jews without religious faith suddenly came to believe in miracles (performed by a nonexistent God) and thought they were witnessing the *"Atchalta d'Geulah"* —the beginning of the redemption.[19] To which my teacher Prof. Akiba Ernst Simon replied epigrammatically: "I, too, would believe that it was a miracle—if I didn't believe in God so much."[20]

In March 1968 the "Newsletter on Religious and Cultural Affairs" put out by the Consulate General of Israel in New York[21] carried a rather stunning and worrisome summary of this pseudo-Messianic mood in certain circles. The Israeli chief-rabbinate called for *hallel* on the anniversary of the conquest of Jerusalem—the laws of the restoration of the Temple were to be studied (in fact, of course, a great military parade was held)—the possibility of proclaiming Iyyar 28 a permanent holiday was discussed—"Chief Rabbi Untermann reiterated his considered view that "the cardinal duty of *pirsum ha-nes*—publicizing the miracle, made the recital of Hallel on the anniversary of Israel's victory literally a Biblical ordinance *din d'oraita gamur*, and one was also authorized to say the Beracha accompanying it.' " (The Torah Education Department of the World Zionist Organization promised an early publication of Rabbi Untermann's *Mizvat Pirsuma Nissa u-Gedol ha-Shema'ata.*) Here one may ask: why do non-Orthodox Jews hasten to protest against bureaucratic discriminations against them in Israel but not about substantive matters, *ha-omdim bi-romo shel olam*, such as this? Rabbi M. Fogelman of Kiryat Motzkin is quoted: "Is the miracle of our day less than that of Hanukkah?" Rabbi Techorsh, member of the Chief Rabbinate Council, advocated the recital of *"She-hecheyanu"* and *"Al ha-Nissim"*. Rabbi Y. Abuhatzirah, also a member of the Council and spiritual head of Israel's North African community, maintained (and, perhaps, such views can be indulged depending on the history of those who hold them) that last year's "recovery of the Land of Israel constituted the final step before the advent of the Messiah," warranting special readings from Torah and Prophets.[21a]

This is extremely dangerous talk. Theologically I would adduce at least three arguments against it, the first two cited from— if you please—the Satmerer Rebbe's recent *Kunteros al ha-Geulah viha-Temurah*,: 1) "Miracles" are miracles only when they are in accord with the Torah and the *Halachah*; otherwise, like the miracles of the Egyptian magicians, they are deceptions of Satan;[22] 2) Victories in wars, even those of the few over the many, are always natural events, not miracles. Thus Hanukkah celebrates the miracle of the oil, not the victory of the Hasmoneans.[23] Indeed, military victories are special opportunities for the seductions of Satan.[24] I should like to add a third reason for not regarding a victory in war a divine act, and I regret that this kind of thinking is hard to come by nowadays in Orthodox, Reform, or any other Jewish circles: R. Yochanan, the central teacher in the eschatological discussion of *Perek Chelek*, interpreting Jer. 30:6, asks why, in the Messianic fulfillment, "all faces will turn pale."[25] He answers that the angels and Israel will turn pale because the salvation of Israel carries along with it a comparitive demotion of other peoples: "At that time the Holy One, praised be He, will say: 'Those (Israel) are the works of My hands, and the others (Gentiles) are the works of My hands. How can I cause the ones to perish in favor of the others!' "[26] And Rav Pappa (and Rashi *ad locum*) expatiate further on this consideration. It might be argued that, despite their misgivings, all the parties concerned nonetheless pray for the Messianic fulfillment and therefore the corollary derogation of the Gentiles—but it must be remembered that R. Yochanan makes the statement which we have quoted in order to explain why he, like a number of others, exclaims: "*Yatei vilo Itmeneh*"—i.e., R. Yochanan prefers not to experience the Messianic advent rather than be an accessory to the plight of the non-Jews. Much further genuine Jewish morality—or any other—cannot go! Can we say less in the presence of Moslems and Arabs?

Turning to American Jewry, the triumphalism which we have illustrated manifests itself here perhaps more flagrantly than in Israel, perhaps precisely because it is at one remove. Hundreds of rabbis sign full-page newspaper ads insisting that all of the conquered land must be retained by Israel because—if you please—otherwise the Soviet Union will have succeeded in pushing the United States out of its strategic strongholds in the Near East. Liberal Jewish professors, who had been in the vanguard of the movement against the Vietnam War, demand full American political and military commitment on the side of Israel, and, though their dissenting voices are heard on every other subject, a strange silence prevails toward the Israeli government on the delicate but crucial question of Arab-Jewish relations; the center of Jewish attention in this country has now become "Negro anti-Semitism" and campus anarchism where previously it had been equality and peace, etc.[27] I confess with great sadness, that I see a dominant note of rampant self-assertiveness and self-righteousness in world Jewry, which may be compared with the ideology of those against whom Jeremiah prophesied, who thought that their strength lay in their own arms and in alliances with foreign, pagan powers.

One is sorely tempted, at this point, to want to assert one's Jewish 'patriotism" against the inevitable accusations which will be leveled. But let us, instead, go back to the original thesis about the nature of Jewish survival as we witnessed it in 1945, and let us see what happens to the real interests of the Jewish people when that fragmented survival is looked at in another light.

Certainly the Jews in the Warsaw Ghetto had every human right to defend themselves and to fight back. The same is true of all the other military or paramilitary expressions of resistance and counterattack. Rightly do we honor their memories. But let us remember: in the first place, we lament to say that they, too, died—if survival is to be the yardstick of tactical or ethical worth, then we have to mourn to conclude that neither military resistance nor matyrdom availed. In the second place, it has been and is a terrible defamation of the third of the Jewish people who went to their deaths to claim or to imply that because they did not fight back they either did not resist or—God forbid!—collaborated. To be *menschen* in the midst of inhumanity, to sanctify the name of God while surrounded by a flood of heathenism, to study, teach, and pray in a world in which only murder, rape, and brutality reigned, to squeeze a precious drop of life through the sieve of all-consuming death, and finally to go to one's death in ranks of thousands because the world had turned into hell and no longer had a place for decent human beings—who will rise and have the forwardness to claim that this was not, in its way, the greatest, the most admirable, the most heroic form of resistance[28]—that the more than five million who did not, as it happens, resort to guns, knives, stones, and fire did not plant the banner of Israel, God, and humanity fluttering high on the battlefield of history?[29]

Two thousand years of Jewish exilic history had taught the Jewish people that the tree planted by the waters could bend its branches to the storm and afterwards rise up again and grow its fruit for the coming season. One has to be an assimilated, Westernized secularist to see something dishonorable—as Bialik did in "The City of Death" and as so many Jews do today—in crouching in cellars until, it is hoped, the beasts have passed by, in order to save one's own and one's family's lives. To be sure, the gentlemanly thing to do is to stand up straight, meet the badman in the open street and get the first draw on him, but then, as Maurice Samuel has put it, we choose to be Jews, not gentlemen. And, when all is said and done, in 1945 a small but viable remnant from the Holocaust had in fact survived. They stumbled out of the camps, they raised their heads from the floor, they walked blinkingly into the light, they came out of hiding and disguise, and whispered: "*Mir zennen do.*" And this was not a very small minority of our surviving people—it was the overwhelming majority of those who had, by God's unfathomable and cruel grace, somehow or other come through. They *were*, indeed, the Jewish people. They own our unqualified piety and love—as do all those who, to the end and into horribled deaths, exemplified what it is to be Jews, human beings, citizens of "the lands of the living."

It is almost universally said that the Holocaust is an irrefutable blemish on—if not denial of—God. This is true. It is equally true that the survival of the Jewish people—at all times and especially through the Holocaust—is an inexplicable handiwork of His. (It is, incidentally, little less cruel than the slaughter, as Elie Wiesel and others make clear.) We are entitled to put it blasphemously: God was so vicious as to kill us, and He was so vicious as to preserve us; to Him go all blame and all glory. The Jew came out of this furnace—dead or alive—pure as the driven snow. Under the Law those put to death by an [oppressive] government are, regardless of their personal merits or previous conditions, martyrs "for the sanctification of God's name.[30] Again we conclude: we survive by God's harsh decree, and those who survive testify, willingly or no, knowingly or no, gladly or sadly, to His majesty and sovereignty.[31]

Now we can once more jump foward to the Jewish history of the decades since 1945. We presented ourselves—"a brand plucked from the fire"—to the world in 1945, we pressed against the shores of the Holy Land and the doors of governments, and in 1948 the United Nations established the State of Israel. We ought to recall that at that time and for a while thereafter there were no more eloquent protaganists of the United Nations than we Jews. It is one of the sorrier consequences of the superciliousness and arrogancy of the last few years that now in most Jewish circles "the United Nations" is a term of deprecation. One need not have any exaggerated notions of its present capacities or wisdom to perceive the fundamental dangers and immoralities of this attitude. With respect to all three wars that Israel has had to wage since 1948 it is perfectly obvious that the idea that "with the strength of my hand have I acted and with my wisdom, for I am smart—and I remove the boundaries of nations" (Is. 10:13) is foolish even in purely political terms: but for the support that literally all the great powers of our age, the USSR, the U.S. and their satellites in 1948, Britain and France in 1956, and America in 1967, provided, disaster could easily have overtaken us. How long do we think we can live in the Near East surrounded, indeed interpenetrated, by hundreds of millions of Moslems and Arabs in the middle of millions of square miles of hostile territory and, in each blood-letting round, come out victors? (Unlike the Arab countries, we cannot afford a single defeat!) The Jew who is really committed to the survival of Israel not just for another generation but for ever and ever will contemplate the needs of the hour in such a *specie aeternitatis*, however unpopular he may be among his fellows at the moment. And even if it were conceivable that in the longest run the Jewish people could maintain itself in the midst of such a sea of enmity, what human, spiritual and moral price would we have to pay for it? I always remember that when my son was less than ten years old he came home from a summer in an Israeli children's camp and said that his chief impression was of barbed wire all over the country. The transvaluation of all Jewish values which has already seriously set in in Israeli and world Jewry could soon completely overwhlem us.[32] The problem of our Jewish generation and of our children is whether we can live with the ethics and politics of the persecuted, having, in some ways, ceased to be the persecuted.[33] I implore you and me and all of us not to prove Neitzsche to have been right—that morality is the rationalization of the weak.

At this point, finally, I can articulate my own form of Jewish superchauvinism. What we have been saying is simply that the survival of the Jewish people is guaranteed by God—that we need not really concern ourselves with it—that to preoccupy oneself with it is a form of sickness, as health-faddists are invariably sick people[33a]—that to attribute our survival to human instrumentalities including and primarily our own, inevitably leads to the acts of *hybris, ga'avah,* which victimize other human beings and result in unending conflict and eventual defeat—and that, on the contrary, the God Who has brought us this far will also redeem His other promises to Israel. Like the Movement for the Greater Land of Israel I, too, am unable to surrender—*le-atid la-vo*—one inch of the sacred soil of the Land of Israel. We may implicitly believe that in the Redemption not only will the historic land revert to its divinely designated occupants but that, as Rabbinic literature amply proclaims,[34] it will be vastly expanded—yes, Hebron and Jericho, the cedars of Lebanon and the great river: "And He said to me: 'These waters go out into the eastern Galilee, descend into the Arabah, and end in the sea' " (Ez. 47:8). The late Chayim Weizman was asked about this Messianic claim by a member of the Peel Commission when, back in 1936, he was ready to accept the first partition plan for Palestine, and he answered, not facetiously: God made the promise—God, not we, will redeem it. Our task is to be menschen and thus—and thus only—to hasten the Messiah's coming, not by force or by magic or by superarrogation.

The kind of pseudo-Messianism which we have previously had occasion to consider[35] is not limited to the "old fashioned" circles of the Israeli chief-rabbinate.[36] The pop song that became the hymn of the Six Day War is suffused with Messianic connotations: "The *Shofar* sounds on the Temple Mount, in the Old City/And within the caves in the rock rays of the Light shine. . . . etc. Nothing less than the glossy official magazine of French Jewry, *L'Arche,* for Oct.-Nov. 1967 (No. 128) appeared under the red headline: *Jerusalem* 5728—*Le Méssie, va-t-il Arriver?* Inside there is an article by Alex Derczansky still moderately entitled: *"Le Royaume de Dieu Reste à Construire . . . Mais on Sait Maintenant que Godot Doit Arriver,"* whereas Arnold Mandel, one of the intellectual mentors of contemporary French Jewry and presumably a sensitive and sophisticated man, the title of whose article graces the front cover, is quite sure that, at the least, the Messiah son of Joseph, "the political and national Messiah," has arrived *hic et nunc* "on our territory in the Jewish year 5728."

We cannot here analyze the whole complex and profound subject of Jewish Messianology. The least that must be said, however,[37] is that this kind of thinking is grist for the mills of all the "realists," antiutopians, and neoconservative thinkers of our time—Reinhold Niebuhr, Jakob Talmon, Norman Cohn, Hannah Arendt, etc. Their argument invariably boils down to this—that utopianism and Jewish Messianism are forms of *hybris*, idolatry, which claim to be able to accomplish humanly what in truth only God can accomplish and, what is worse, which will always play havoc with human beings who do not completely fall in line with the Messianic claims, on the grounds that they are not only political dissenters but blasphemers who want to undermine the reign of God Himself. This is, of course, a willful and purposeful distortion of the Messianic belief. This belief in fact dictates that people must exert themselves as much as and more than they are capable of doing toward the Messianic goal, in the hope—*nota bene*: not in the arrogantly sure expectation—that God will—in His own good time and for His own good reasons, not in any proportionality to these human efforts: "Not on our righteous acts do we make our petitions dependent"—bring about Redemption. It thus self-evidently subsumes the human part in bringing about the consummation to the onus of human fallibility, inadequacy, and sinfulness and to the divine prerogative of grace. Nonetheless, the "antiutopians" have enough evidence, of course, with which to support their case, by the simple device of procuring it from the rich arsenal of pseudo-Messianisms, which they proceed to identify with authentic Messianism: their evidence of fanaticism, *hybris*, ruthlessness and inhumanity invariably stems from those who violate the fundamental Jewish Messianic dictates: "Do not press the End!"[38] and "May those be devastated who calculate the End."[39]

An apparent contradiction might be pointed to in our argumentation: on the one hand, we reject the view of the antiutopian neoconservatives who advocate, at best, slow, small steps of melioration within the established structures of society—yet, on the other hand, we now raise the old Jewish motto "Do not press the End!"

Here we turn, for the last time, to the dialectical polarity of the ethics and the metaphysics of the Covenant. The ethics of the Covenant do, indeed, require us to act in such a way as to hasten the coming of the Messiah, i.e., to endeavor to establish the radical reign of peace, justice, and goodness on earth. But ethics are concerned with other people, not ourselves. Therefore, with respect to the peace movement, the Black movement, the social movement in our time (movements, that is to say, which are primarily concerned with people other than ourselves) our motto must be theirs: "All of it—here and now!" and on this motto we must act. This must apply, too, to the genuine problems of Palestinian Arabs: no reasonable Zionist has denied the at least partial justice of their case, and the plight of many of their people has lasted much, much too long. The metaphysics of the Covenant, on the other hand, are concerned, as we have seen, with the persistence of the people of Israel throughout history, i.e., primarily with ourselves. This God has assumed as His responsibility. Elie Wiesel quotes a midrash[40] that explains why the Jews opposed to Haman's attempt to exterminate them physically resorted to the spiritual resistance of repentance, fasting, and prayer: "When our physical existence was threatened we simply reminded God of His duties and the promises deriving from the Covenant." In short, the Torah is our business, Israel's survival is God's.[41]

It all comes down to the simple formula of the Levitical and Deuteronomic blessings and curses: if we fulfill the commandments of His will He will bless and keep us—it is not the other way around, that, if we maintain ourselves, He or we will be able to act as He desires us to: "If you walk in My statutes and keep My commandments and do them ... then will I walk Myself in your midst: I will become your God for you, and you will become a people for Me. I am the Lord your God, Who brought you out of the land of Egypt, so that you would no more be their slaves; I will break the bands of your yoke, and I will lead you integrally" (Lev. 26:1-13).

– 5 –

A Note on the Nature of Ideal Society—A Rabbinic Study*

Baba Batra 122a brings a somewhat unusual statement about what Jewish Society will be like under Messianic conditions:

> "It has also been taught in a *Baraita*: In the (Messianic) future, the Land of Israel will be divided for thirteen tribes, while, at the outset, it was divided only for the twelve tribes . . . For the division of the world to come is not like the division of this world. If, in this world, a man owns a cornfield, he does not also own an orchard, or if he owns an orchard, he does not also own a cornfield; in the world to come, however, there will be none who does not own (some property) in the mountainous area as well as in the lowland and in the valley at the same time, for it is said[1] (Ez. 48:31), 'The gate of Reuben is one, the gate of Judah is one, the gate of Levi is one.' God Himself will assign to each of them his portion, as it is said (*ib.*, 29), 'And these are their divisions, says God.' We have learned that, at the outset, it was divided up only for the twelve tribes. Thus we know that the division was made for the benefit of the tribes. Now we have to ask: When it was stated that, in the future, the Land of Israel will be divided for thirteen tribes, for whom will the thirteenth part be? Rav Chisda said:[2] For the prince, as it is said (*ib.*, 19), 'He who serves the city shall be served by all the tribes of Israel.' "[3]

A few textual explanations are in order, first of all. "In the future" and "the world to come" in this passage refer to the Messianic age; the whole

---

*I dedicate this study to Mr. Curt Silberman, President of the American Federation of Jews from Central Europe, on his sixtieth birthday in May 1968. Mr. Silberman was a friend of my late parents, Fritz and Rahel Schwarzschild, over several decades. Their community of Jewish destiny and dedication also brought them together in the Federation. My parents combined in their ideals and life the two highest values of which this paper treats: the faith of Israel and the righteous society. The name of the unity of these two values is "the Messiah." I pray that we all may be privileged to advance the causes of the three persons here mentioned and thus help bring nearer the Kingdom of God.

context, as well as the traditional interpreters, make this perfectly clear.[4] The initial phrases "for twelve tribes" and "for thirteen tribes" are clearly to be taken to mean "twelve parts" and "thirteen parts," as again the subsequent discussion and Rashbam (R. Samuel ben Meir) *ad* "It has been taught" make clear. The "gates" of the tribes correspond to the tribal portions assigned in Ez. 45-48. Finally it must be noted that, in accordance with general Rabbinic practice, Ezekiel's description of the Temple is applied to the Messianic, or "Third" Temple; this is basically due to the fact that there are differences between his prescriptions and those of the Pentateuch for the Temple.[5]

Next, a few substantive interpretations would seem to be called for. It is obvious that this passage implies, as the rest of Biblical and Talmudic eschatology makes perfectly clear,[6] that the Messianic era will be one of economic abundance. As a result, there will also be economic equality for all.[7] Furthermore, the text emphasizes that the ultimate but directly operative authority in the Messianic state will be God alone, not even the Messiah himself.[8] The Messiah is, at the very end of our passage, described literally as a public servant, not a ruler in the usual sense of the word.[9] The Messianic state may, therefore, legitimately be described as a theocratico-democratic society. Finally, it must of course, be added that "the prince," of whom Rav Chisda speaks, is traditionally identified as the Messiah—so Rashbam *ad locum.*[10]

The problem, now, may be formulated in this simple question: why, and for what purpose, should the Messiah, of all people, need all of one-thirteenth of the—Messianically expanded—Land of Israel?[11] Why should the Messiah need so much, or, for that matter, any property, in view of the fact that he will, obviously, rule Israel and the whole world by means of his spiritual power alone?! Maimonides, for example, differentiates the Messianic king from all other kings on precisely this score[12]: "normal" kings need property in order to "compel the appropriate people to be princes" and generals, and "he gives fields, olive orchards and vineyards to his servants when they go to war, so that they can use these places when they can not get their food from any other place;" under Messianic rule, on the other hand, as we have already seen, there is world-wide miraculous abundance,[13] and, furthermore, the Messiah will rule only "by means of the word, through the holy spirit that will rest on him"[14]—, so that he will obviously need none of the "persuaders" of historical kings. Thus we repeat our question: what does the Messiah need so much property for? Surely not for himself, the humble and obedient servant of God and of the people, and, as we have seen, apparently also not for others, inasmuch as everyone will have more than enough anyway, and all future enmities will have been eliminated for the long run?!

We can, perhaps, approach an answer to this question in a somewhat circuitous way: There is an interesting passage in *Abot de Rabbi Nathan,*[15] Variant A, which reads as follows:

> "One verse (Deut. 12:14—speaking of the location of the Temple) says: 'in one of your tribes.' Another verse (*ib.*, 5) says, "from all your tribes." How can this contradiction be resolved? 'In one of your tribes' refers to the tribe of Judah and Benjamin. 'From all of your tribes' refers to Jerusalem, in which all Israel are partners—What part of the Temple was located in the territory of Judah? The Temple-mount, the offices, and the courts. What was located in the territory of Benjamin? The sanctuary, the hall, the Holy of Holies—a triangular strip extended (from the portion of Judah into the portion of Benjamin), and on this the altar was built. Benjamin thus had the privilege of being host to God's presence, as it is said (*ib.*, 33:12), 'Between his shoulders He dwelled.' At the time Joshua said, 'Now that I know that the Temple will be assigned to the boundary between Judah and Benjamin, I will give them the pasture-ground of Jericho.' Who used the produce of that piece of land in all the intervening years (until the Temple would actually be constructed on it)? The Kenites, descendants of Moses's father-in-law, as it is said (Judges 1:16), 'The children of the Kenite, the father-in-law of Moses, came up from the city of the palms.' It was said: when God will manifest His presence He will, in the future, give goodly reward to Jethro and his descendants; and how will the descendants of Jethro nourish themselves? From pottery, as it is said (I Chron. 2:55), 'The families of the scribes that reside at Jabez,' and it says furthermore (*ib.*, 4:23), 'These were the potters who reside on plantations.' They had been prominent people, who owned houses and fields and vineyards, but they gave all that up and went to serve the King of the kings of kings, the Holy One, praised be He. Where did they go? To Jabez, to study Torah—and there they became local residents. At that time Jabez was a goodly and qualified man, a man of truth and righteousness, who sat and taught Torah, as it is said (*ib.*, 10), 'And Jabez called on the God of Israel, saying: "May You, indeed, bless me and enlarge my border, and may Your hand be with me. May You work deliverance from evil, that it may not pain me." And God granted him what he had requested.' "[16]

One important idea emerges from this passage: Jerusalem, the city of the holy Temple—the Messianic Temple included—is, as it were, property of the whole Jewish people. The property set aside for the eventual Temple, or its equivalent, is to be used meanwhile by a group of people who are converts (Kenites). Two characteristics of converts are relevant to this arrangement: in the first place, they are described in the most laudatory terms,[17] and, in the second, they are not, of course, descendants of the twelve tribes, and in the normal course of events they would, therefore, not be assigned to any of the twelve provinces of the country. Special arrangements must, thus, be made for them under the aegis of the chief spiritual ruler.[18] The quasi-Messianic character attributed to Jabez in our quotation—an obscure verse to begin wtih—can easily be overlooked unless one supplements from the Bible the actual phrases adduced in the *Abot de Rabbi Nathan*: he is goodly and qualified (*tov ve-kasher*), a man of truth and lovingkindess (*hassid*), who teaches Torah, and he obtains from God blessing, an enlarged country, divine assistance, and deliverance from evil and pain—surely as comprehensive a catalogue of Messianic conditions as one can hope for! The passage has the additional advantage of being Tannaitic, like the *Baraita* with which we were concerned in *Baba Batra*—and it can surely, then, be argued that, though it speaks directly only of the First Temple, it, in fact, sets up a typology of the relationship between the spiritual ruler and converts.

The tentative answer, then, to our main question would be: the Messiah will require a portion of the Land, not, of course, for his own aggrandizement or power but for the maintenance of gentiles converted to Judaism before and, possibly, in his time. In addition, therefore, to the economically egalitarian and politically democratic features of the Messianic state we would now be face to face with what might be called its universalistic aspect, *i.e.*, the non-Jewish nations of the world will, in one way and one degree or another, be encompassed in its benefits.[19]

The last paragraph in the chapter of *Abot de Rabbi Nathan* with which we have been dealing brings out this feature very concisely and strikingly:[20]

> "Rabban Shimeon ben Gamliel said: In the (Messianic) future all the nations and all the kingdoms will be gathered in the midst of Jerusalem. For it is said (Jer. 3:17), "All the nations will be collected thither for the name of God;" elsewhere (Gen. 1:9) it is said, "Let the waters under the heavens be collected;" as "collection" in the latter verse means that all the waters of Creation should be collected in one place, so "collection" in the former verse means that all the nations and kingdoms will be gathered in one place, Jerusalem.' "[21]

There is a passage in *Ecclesiastes Rabbah*[22] which, at first, would seem to contradict our thesis; on closer consideration, however, it will prove to support it. It reads as follows:

> "All the rivers flow into the sea' (Eccl. 1:7)—all proselytes are proselytes only to Israel; 'and the sea is never filled' (*ib.*)—but Israel never lacks their number,[23] as it is said (Number 23:10)[24] 'Who has counted the dust of Jacob!' In case

one might think that any who have not converted to Judaism in the present aeon will do so in the future aeon, the Bible also teaches (Is. 54:15), 'Behold they will convert[25]—but from here on in 'but not with Me' (*ib.*), *i.e.* they will be separated from Me. To what does 'who will convert with you' (*ib.*) refer? To the present aeon. And 'they will fall upon you' refers to the Messianic aeon. [26]—Rabbi Johanan said 'Furthermore, (a convert will derive his sustenance) from whatever place in which he (happens to) convert—as it is written (Ez. 47:23),[27] "In the tribe in which the convert will live there shall you give him his inheritance." ' "[28]

At first, the implication of R. Johanan's statement, especially as supported by his crucial proof-text from Ezekiel, would seem to be that, in the Messianic state, converts and their descendants will be integrated haphazardly among the twelve tribes—wherever they happen to be at the time of their conversion. In that case, the Messiah would presumably not need any special province of his own in which they could sustain themselves. This, however, cannot be the correct explanation. The question boils down to this: which, in fact, is "the place" in which the respective conversions have taken place? Lots of families originally converted outside of the Land of Israel, as we know, but "the place" can clearly not be there, for we are talking about their settlement within Israel. Rashi's and the Radak's resolution of this difficulty (*ad Ez.* 47:23), in turn, creates what would appear to be insuperable contradictions. They say that converts will be assigned to the tribe among which they were converted in the Diaspora (Rashi) and that the Messiah will inform all parties concerned of their tribal identities (Radak). But then one must ask: if X converts in place A, but place A comprises—as is bound to be the case—native Jews of tribes 1 and 2, to which tribe does X belong? On the other hand, "the place" can presumably also not be among the twelve tribes returned to Israel and on their respective properties, for this restoration will not take place other than by the Messiah himself,—and we have already seen that conversions may not be able to occur after his advent.[29] Even if the latter is not the case, "the place" in which conversions have in fact taken place in the Diaspora must, therefore, be regarded as—*de jure*—the personal territory of the Messiah, the "thirteenth part" which is in the Land of Israel and yet not assigned to any of the tribes. It might be compared to the Jewish theologumenon which imputes the genealogical descent of all converts directly to "Abraham, our father"[30]; so here, their conversion is, theologically, regarded as occuring under the auspices of the Messiah and his eschatological fulfilment. This conclusion might further be buttressed by the very wording of the verse cited from Ezekiel: their inheritance is to be determined "by lot," not by the place in which they happen to have been; but we know that the land will be divided into only thirteen parts, not fourteen, and their lot, separate from that of the tribes, must hence be identical with that of the Messiah.

We have thus added a new element to our outline of the Messianic society. Like the descendants of Jethro who were so highly lauded in the quotation from *Abot de Rabbi Nathan,* the Jews not originally of Jewish parentage are given the special distinction of having their hereditary residence in the holiest of all places, in the Messianically transfigured Jerusalem. Greater "universalism" than this can scarcely be imagined.

Having established our thesis this far, at least tentatively, we can now begin to reap its harvest; *i.e.* we can now try to understand and explain a few interesting but difficult aspects of Jewish eschatology within the *Halakhah.*

In "The Laws of First-Fruit," chapter 4:3, Maimonides rules bindingly that converts, like native Jews, must bring the first fruit of the harvest as a sacrifice and make the Biblically instituted confession that accompanies this act.[31] There are a number of obvious difficulties in his ruling. For one thing, the confessional prayer refers to "my father Abraham" and to "the land which God gave to us;" but, of course, in strictly historical terms these phrases are inapplicable to converts. In addition, a number of statements in the Talmud rule precisely contrary to Maimonides, for the reasons just mentioned.[32] The commentaries *ad locum,* therefore, have to try to resolve this contradiction between Maimonides and his authoritative sources.

The resolution of the problem is two-fold. Textually it is clear that Maimonides prefers to rely on *Yerushalmi, Bikk.,* chapter 1, end, where the ruling is as he lays it down, contrary to the Bablyonian Talmud. This is one of the many instances in Jewish literature in general, and in Maimonides in particular, where the choice of alternative texts constitutes in and of itself an important philosophical and ethical judgment. Maimonides clearly *wants* to establish the absolute equality of converts to Judaism.[33] Logically the *Mishneh LaMelekh,*[34] quoting, among others, the Maharam Ibn Chabib, explains Maimonides's position as follows: it is true that, in the past, converts, who had entered Palestine under Joshua had been insincere[35]; but "just the same, in the Messianic future the converts will have their inheritance amongst the Children of Israel." He then quotes our texts from Ezekiel and *Ecc. Rabbah,* "for the converts that are converted while Israel is in exile are converts of righteousness and do not resemble those converts that converted at the time that Israel left Egypt." (!)

Another difficulty arises from Maimonides' formulation of his ruling in our paragraph. Having stated that converts are the equals of native Jews because they are children of Abraham, our father, he nonetheless adds the short sentence: "Unto Abraham the promise was first made that his descendants would inherit the land."[36] The *Kessef Meshneh*[37] uses this sentence in order to arrive at a conclusion exactly opposite that of the Maimonidean text on which he comments. He takes it to refer to the fact that in the Bible God promises the Land to Abraham before ("first") He declares him "father of the mass of nations," and, therefore, the converts, who are covered by the latter, were not yet included in the former.[38] But, of course, the *Kessef Mishneh* cannot be right in this, for it directly contradicts the first and main point that Maimonides makes in the text under discussion.[39]

Still, the sentence in Maimonides 4:3 which the *Kessef Mishneh* makes use of needs to be explained. Perhaps we may hold that "first" refers to historic times, as contrasted with Messianic times, i.e., "at first" the Land was promised only to Abraham and his natural posterity, but at the last," "in the end of days," it will also have room for proselytes. Another way of reading the difficult sentence is, perhaps, the easiest solution: it does not, from the start, set up a dichotomy between Maimonides' first and second sentences. In the first sentence he declares that converts are sons of Abraham—in the second sentence he declares that Abraham, "in the first place," and his sons (thus including the converts) inherit the Land—and thus also the third and last sentence of the paragragh fits into the presentation, namely that, "in the same manner," also priests recite the prayer at issue, for they, for their reasons, like the converts for their's, have a share in the Land—not, to be sure, by family descent but by legal-theological stipulation.

We are now also in a position to clear up another problem in the *Mishneh Torah. Minhat Chinukh*, commandment 497, raises the following problem and declares that it has no answer;[40] Maimonides codifies the basic proposition of *Baba Batra* 122 from which we started out, i.e. that the Messiah will have one-thirteenth of the Land of Israel, in "Laws of Kings," 4:8; according to the two subsequent paragraghs (9f.), however, a Jewish king who conquers non-Palestinian land owns and may freely dispose of all that he conquers. *Minchat Chinukh's* point is that historical kings may own all non-Palestinian lands conquered, not only 1/13th, as is the case of the Messiah. If the king owns *all* the conquered land and its property, how can he also be restricted to only one-thirteenth of it? The answer to this question is, of course, three-fold. In the first place, "Laws of Kings," 4:8 explicitly refers to the Messianic king alone, whereas the rest of the chapter speaks of all other, non-Messianic, let us call them "normal" kings: i.e. the Messiah acts *de jure*, normal kings act only *de facto*.[41] In the second place, 4:8 speaks of land "which Israel (i.e., the whole people) conquer," where 4:9f. speak of land "which he (i.e., the government alone, unilaterally) conquers." These are, again, *de facto*, not *de jure*, conquests.[42] *De facto* conquests can be used as arbitarily as they were made in the first place,[43] while *de jure* conquests must, of course, be handled according to the strict law of God; i.e., in accordance with the basic legislation of *Baba Batra* 122. In the last place, as we have pointed out before,[44] a normal king requires more property because he has to "force" people into his service and persuade them with gifts,[45] whereas the Messianic king has no need, of course, of such inducements: he rules by the spirit alone.

I want to finish our consideration of Maimonidean *Halakhic* points regarding Messianic society with an item dealing with proselytism. We have noted previously[46] that, according to him as according to all Jewish tradition, one of the chief features of that society is the universal rule of truth, justice, and freedom that will then prevail. The place of Gentiles in the Messianic kingdom, in its specificity, is, therefore, of considerable importance in this context.[47] The chief sections in which Maimonides deals with proselytism are "Laws of Forbidden Intercourse," chapters 13f.[48] and "Laws of Kings," chapter 8-10[49] In the former, a well-known controversial statement occurs. Chapter 13 had laid down the general Jewish legal conditions for conversion. Chapter 14:1f. reiterates the Talmudic warning to potential converts of the responsibilities they are about to assume,[50]—to go on in 2-5 to stress, more heavily than is usual in the classic sources, the compensating benefits of being a Jew—thus reemphasizing Maimonides' fundamental inclination toward proselytism. In paragraph 6 the actual ritual of conversion is finally outlined. In paragraph 7 Maimonides switches to a new, though closely related subject, namely semi-converts (*gerei toshav*) and defines them as people who accept the binding obligation of universal Noachite law.[51] The controversial ruling follows in paragraph 8, namely that such semi-converts may not be accepted at this time, only "in the time when the Jubilee year is reinstituted," which is to say only in Messianic time.[52]

This is a hard pill to swallow. It would imply that no non-Jews can attain to salvation in pre-Messianic times.[53] His great opponent, the Rabad, therefore, immediately contradicts him in strong language: "The author's view is unfathomable and impenetrable." On the contrary, the Rabad asserts, semiconverts may, at the present time, be accepted; the only difference between present-day semiconverts and Messianic semiconverts is[54] that the former cannot obtain all the economic advantages which the latter, under the prosperous economic conditions of the Messianic society, will enjoy.[55] By a great effort, one may interpret Maimonides' statement as, in effect, arriving at the Rabad's position,[56] but more likely it expresses verbatim what the writer intended. In that case it would, at first, appear that in Maimonides' view non-Jews can become semiconverts only in Messianic times—that at that time all people will be either Jews or Noachites, and all will this share, in one way or another, in their economic affluence—or that they can become full converts only in pre-Messianic times.

The latter is, in any case, the generally accepted view. *Yeb.* 24b is the classic source for the doctrine that neither in the time of David and Solomon nor in the days of the Messiah will converts be accepted into Judaism.[57] The obvious and stated reason for this stipulation is that in those periods Israel is extremely affluent, and it must, therefore, be suspected that candidates for conversion have been attracted not by the only legitimate consideration, namely sincere religious conviction, but by ulterior and crasser purposes.

Now, Maimonides, too, of course, warns against, and prohibits, insincere conversions.[58] But it is noteworthy that, though he declares conversions in the time of David and Solomon as invalid in his code, he does not mention the impossibility of conversions inder the Messiah. Indeed, I have not found any place in which he makes mention of this restriction. He does not explicitly reject it, but in "Laws of Repentance," 9:2, for example, and in "Laws of Kings," 11:4 and 12:5, he quietly and repeatedly emphasizes that Gentiles adheres to the Messiah. Indeed, the sentence in which his entire majestic Code culminates declares: "In that (Messianic) time there will be no drought nor war, no envy nor strife; goodness will be widely disseminated; valuables will be as widespread as dust; and the occupation of the whole world will be nought but to know God alone . . . as it is said (Is. 11:9), 'For the earth shall be full of the knowledge of the Lord as the waters cover the sea.' " Furthermore, in "Laws of Forbidden Intercourse," 13:5, he stipulates that when the Temple will have been restored—i.e., in Messianic times (!)—candidates for conversion will again have to bring sacrifices as part of their conversion ritual.[59] It would clearly seem to follow that he does allow conversions in Messianic society—presumably only such, however, as are by the perfected spiritual authority of the time found to be entirely sincere.

It would appear thus that, in fact, Maimonides' view of the future of the Gentiles is that full conversion to Judaism is possible, and even desirable, at all times, pre-Messianic as well as Messianic. The Messiah himself is, after all, a direct descendant of the convert Ruth. Messianic converts would need a place of settlement; it would have to be "in the place in which they are converted,"[60] *i.e.*, in the Messianic province. And thus we would be back with our original tentative, now strengthened, thesis—that the Messiah will have a thirteenth part of the Land of Israel primarily so that even in respect to land-property, converts will be the equals of all native Jews.[61] Semiconverts, or Noachites, or, in other words, potentially all of the rest of humanity, on the other hand, entitled as they are to full economic support, can only be countenanced under the conditions of the prosperity of Messianic society. Within this frame of reference, it also makes sense that "in the Messianic Jerusalem there will be no (permanent) place for semiconverts.[62]

We have tried to crystallize a systematic, consistent conception of the ideal, Messianic society[63] out of some Rabbinic sources.[64] It would seem to have certain necessary features: economic abundance, economic equality, the abolition of private property in land and of the market economy, the universal rule of Jewish monotheism, theocratic democracy, universal truth, justice, and peace.

All of this is intended only as a footnote to "the democratic socialism of Hermann Cohen."[65] For him Messianism was the relgious term for socialism.[66] "The politics of the prophets are nought but what we today call socialism. Their faith is to have justice done to the poor, and their religion is morality."[67] I would want to hold that Cohen was essentially and importantly right. After he had written his *Religion der Vernunft,* Prof. Leo Rosenzweig was asked to compile a collection of actual "Quellen des Judentums" to be appended to it and with which to undergird it. This "Note" is meant to be an addition to Rosenzweig's labors.

– 6 –

The Legal Foundation of Jewish Aesthetics

Treatments of Jewish art invariably feel constrained to begin by discussing whether there even is such a thing as "Jewish art," and, if there is, how it is to be defined.[1] Whatever the answers to these questions may be, this is not the problem to which I want to address myself here. In raising the question of "Jewish aesthetics," I do not wish to look for the philosophical principles, if any, that undergird the actual activities and products that may be classified as Jewish art. Rather, I want to ask whether the philosophico-theological principles that Judaism employs in looking at and relating to the world as a whole also entail principles that determine its aesthetic outlook, and, if so, what these latter principles are. (In any case, I am limiting myself here to the visual arts.)

The distinction can be brought out by a comparison with, for example, Hegel's philosophy of art. Basing his ideas on the reasonable claim that there is such a thing as Christian art, and having discerned certain values in Christianity in general and in its art in particular, Hegel nonetheless did not begin by asking questions about the aesthetic principles underlying Christian art; rather, he derived certain universal aesthetic rules from his general philosophy, and these rules could then be, and were, appropriately instantiated in Christian as well as non-Christian art. Thus my subject is not the aesthetics of Jewish art but the Jewish aesthetics of art.

There should be nothing surprising about such a Jewishly universal aesthetic agenda. Judaism claims to be chiefly concerned with "the Lord of all worlds"—including presumably the world of art in general, as well as the world of Jewish art. In the second place, the Law (*Halachah*) of normative Judaism comprises plenty of material concerned not only with Jews and Jewish affairs but also with human beings in general and their affairs and, indeed, specifically with non-Jews and theirs. It would, therefore, be surprising if Judaism expressly excluded the area of general aesthetics from its purview.[2] Finally, it is only reasonable to expect a Jewish aesthetic to be ultimately rooted in the prohibition of idolatory and of certain types of pictorial representations connected therewith—and that Jewish prohibition of idolatry is, of course, addressed to Gentiles at least as much as to Jews. Indeed, what are classically known as "the seven Noachite laws"[3] are both the model as well as the source of our concern with general Jewish aesthetics: they, like it, address themselves in the name of Judaism to the world at large, and they compromise, among other things, the Jewish prohibition of non-Jewish idolatry.[4]

In the search for normative Jewish views, four thousand years of Jewish history, the vastness of Jewish literature, and the great diversity of Jewish expressions and forms of life would seem to make it difficult, if not impossible, to avoid an arbitrary selection or the impulse to give up on the task because of the apparent lack of consistency in the material. This is bound to be particularly true of a subject which must be conceded to be far from the center of traditionally intense Jewish concern. (This explains in large measure the randomness of the existing literature on Jewish art.) The only promising way of cutting through this thicket is to look not at the multifarious empirical evidence of past history, but at authoritative, normative Jewish law—to extrapolate in as responsible a fashion as possible the principles and implications of this law— and then to measure the facts of history against the results and vice-versa. An appropriate and convenient *locus classicus* for the initial steps in this process is Rabbi Joseph Karo's sixteenth-century *Shulchan 'Aruch*, the accepted codification of presently valid Jewish law—"*Yoreh De'ah,*" "Laws about Idolatry," chapter 141, "Laws about Images and Forms"—which consists of eight paragraphs.[5] We shall simply present its language and that of some of its major commentaries in a way most suitable to a concern with general aesthetics and then draw some compelling conclusions.

First, images that are clearly used by or made for the purpose of idolatry are prohibited for use or enjoyment.[6] So are symbols of state sovereignty, such as stand in front of government buildings with scepter, globe,eagle, sword, crown, or ring.[7] Other images are not prohibited.

Fragments of such images are prohibited only if they show complete parts (such as an entire hand or foot).

Objects bearing images of sun or moon or mythic animals ("dragons"), if reverenced by non-Jews and, therefore, suspect of idolatrous use, are prohibited. If such objects are not used in a reverential manner, they are not prohibited. Even objects that are usually reverenced are not prohibited if it is factually known that the specific ones at issue are not reverenced in an idolatrous manner. There is, however, a school of thought which prohibits any object or image belonging to a class of idolatrously used objects, regardless of whether the particular object is or is not so used. According to Isserles, in Northern Europe, where Gentiles do not in fact worship such objects, the more lenient view is followed. Such objects are then freed for use, but one may not treat them contemplatively, as if for meditative, religious purposes. However, there is even here a more restrictive school of thought.

Fourth, "It is forbidden to draw pictures of any forms appertaining to the sphere of the *shechinah* [the divine presence], such as the four faces facing one another [cf. *Ez. 1*] or the forms of the Seraphim or angels (*'ophanim*) or serving angels. This also applies to the form of a man by himself. It is forbidden to make these, even for a non-Jew. If a non-Jew has made them a Jew is forbidden to contemplate them [religiously]. (*Siftē Cohen:* It is also forbidden to commission a non-Jew to make them, though the Jew does not intend to worship them. *Isserles:* If a Jew finds such an image made by a non-Jew, he may use but not contemplate it.) This prohibition applies only to images in relief, not to engraved or incised ones, such as are stitched into garments or painted on walls. (This permission does not hold for the forms of sun, moon, or stars.) All these forms, whether in relief or inscribed, are permitted for the purpose of study, "to understand and to teach" [for astronomy, for example, or calendaric purposes]. (*Shach:* "It is then clear that all forbidden forms are forbidden only if they represent complete forms, such as a man with two eyes, a complete nose, a complete body, etc., but not half-images, as some painters draw only one side of a form. The latter is not forbidden" *Rosh:* Some permit also the use of otherwise forbidden forms of images if they are in a public place, where no suspicion of idolatry can arise.)

"A seal ring that bears the form of a man—if the form is in relief it may not be worn, though it may be used for sealing; if the form is engraved it may be worn but may not be used for sealing, because in sealing the resultant form would be in relief." (*Shach*: A Gentile may also not be asked to use such a seal.)

"The images of cattle, beasts, birds, fish, trees, grasses, etc. may be drawn, even in relief." (*Commentary*: "Animal forms may not be affixed in synagogues, so that the appearance of bowing to them may not be created.")

"There are those who hold that images of man or a dragon are not prohibited unless they are complete with all their limbs, but the shape of a head by itself or a body without a head is in no wise forbidden. Such may be used if found and even made." (*Isserles:* "This is our actual practice." [Cf. Schach in fourth item, above.])

Finally, "A model of the Temple may not be made of the same size in height, length, and width—a protico like the hall, a court like the courtyard, an altar like the altar, a candelabrum like the candelabrum. Rather, let the candelabrum be made with five or six or eight but not of seven arms, even if the metals are different, even if it does not have the proper cups, ornaments, and blossoms, and even if it is not of the height of eighteen handbreadths."

(*Commentary:* "For all these latter deficiencies would not, *ex post facto*, invalidate such a candelabrum.")

The text we have summarized explicates one principle—that representations of God, divine and mythic beings, humans, and the celestial bodies may not be manufactured, while other natural entities such as flora and fauna do not fall under this prohibition. The principle is qualified by the stipulation that the prohibition applies only to complete images (except for divine beings, of what paritial representations are presumably inconceivable). Incomplete images, on the other hand, such as those which are less than three-dimensional (as in relief), men with only one eye or a broken nose (which, in fact became the chief way of avoiding completely naturalistic artistic representation in Jewish history), or models of the Temple and its main implements (*i.e.*, other sacred objects) that are not exact and complete duplicates of the original—these are not objectionable (of course, only on the premise that they are not used for idolatrous purposes).

It has never been doubted in Jewish history that abstract, nonrepresentation art (in the past, decorative forms, in modern times, abstraction in general) is no way restricted by Jewish religion.[8] This is so obvious that it is not even mentioned in the classical sources. It cannot violate the Second Commandment (*Ex.* 20:4; *Deut.* 4:16-18, 5:8), for it clearly does not "make an image or form of anything that is in heaven above or on the earth below or in the water underneath the earth."

We have thus deduced two of the chief principles of twentieth-century modern art—abstraction and distortion. Now to try to analyze the philosophic-theological principles underlying them.

It must be noted in the first place that all animate and inanimate entities are available to uninhibited Jewish artistic utilization, except for God and humans. Sun, moon, and stars, together with some other items such as mythic animals, are exempt from this proposition, clearly because they are widely used in idolatry. In our aesthetic context this religious consideration may be left aside. Isserles even permits them precisely because in his time and place they are no longer put to idolatrous use.[9] What God, humans, and angelic beings have in common that excludes them from all possible artistic representation is the possession of spirit, or soul; clearly, the thesis of the Law is that spirit as such is unsusceptible to depiction. God, who is all spirit, can, therfore, not be pictured. (Cf. *Deut.* 4:12: "You heard a voice of words, but a form you did not see." *Tanchuma*, "Jethro" 11 and parallels puts this most picturesquely by saying that God is all faces, *i.e.*, He speaks, and does nothing but speak, to everyone.)

Why, then, forbid something that is inherently impossible?: The answer is implied in the question: whenever an artist has created anything at all, and this is then designated as "God" or any kind of representation of God, it is not only a sin in that spirit has been materialized and thus made susceptible to fetishization, but, more important, a philosophical mistake has been made. Something not God has been taken as such; something not all spirit is taken to be God. This is the very definition of idolatry.

The full impact of this Jewish aesthetic principle can, perhaps, be better brought out by a comparison with the basic Christian view of God and the resultant attitude toward representational art. Christian aestheticians often speak of "the art of the incarnation." They reason that, on Christian doctrine, God was adequately embodied in one man (the second person of the Trinity) and is adequately embodied in various components of the actual world that emanate from him (the third person), such as, for example, the church, the *corpus mysticum*. To depict such immanent realities is, therefore, in fact to depict spirit adequately. No artistic transcendence beyond the natural givens is needed in these instances, and the wider a Christian theologian holds that the circle of "fulfilled eschatology" (*i.e.*, realized redemption, the consummated identity of the material with the spiritual) extends in the natural universe and in history, the more numerous are the objects which are worthy and capable of perfect artistic representation through naturalistic means.[10] One may presume that if three-dimensional photography had existed in the time of Jesus, a shapshot of him would adequately show what the perfect spiritual man looks like.

Spirit is to be found, apart from God, also in angelic beings and in humans. They differ from God in that, though also spirit like Him, they have in addition some kind of physical or quasi-physical form.[11] The *shechinah* and various types of angels are really specialized aspects of God. They are, as the Talmudic phrase puts it, "His servants, that serve before Him in the heights." The only part of them that could conceivably be artistically represented is their physical or quasi-physical dimension, and this dimension is precisely what is not divine or spiritual about them. That is, if thus represented, they would not be represented as divine aspects at all.[12] Again, therefore, as in the case of God, the representation of divine aspects would be not only morally sinful but also conceptually nonsensical, and it would once more be a case of falsely taking *pars pro toto*.

Finally there is the human being, par excellence, who "is made in the image of God" (*Gen.* 1:26ff., 5:1), and is frequently spoken of in the Talmud as literally "the ikon of God."[13] The special distinction is that humans are conscious of the fact that they are the *imago* of God.[14] The prohibition of human images is, therefore, so essential that Maimonides and *Sefer Chinuch*, for example, count it as a commandment distinct from the general prohibition of idols.[15]

An undistorted and complete artistic representation of a person thus comprises two theological dangers. First humans are not only spirit but also body. This fact makes an imaging possible. But it is the *anima* in the body, rather than the body as such that makes them the divine *imago*. (For Jewish religious purposes it is important to underline that the issue here is not one of "soul *versus* body" but "soul *in* the body" or, better yet, "ensouled body.") To represent physical appearance as the whole person is, therefore, a misrepresentation. The converse is also true: a "misrepresentation" will in fact be a true depiction. Second, when one sees humanity, one sees God. To "see" God, one must see humanity—though, to be sure, not empirical but "spiritual humanity." To represent the empirical as *tout court* is, therefore, also to misrepresent God. As A.J. Heschel rightly put it: "The idea of man's divine likeness is, according to one opinion in the Talmud, the reason for the prohibition to represent the human figure."[16] And humanity's spiritual nature is held to express itself in moral activities rather than in any aspect of appearance.[17] (This is the sum and substance of Maimonides' philosophical theology, and Hermann Cohen accordingly rephrased the Second Commandment: "Thou shalt not make an image of the moral subject."[18])

There remains only one legitimate way of depicting the human: to indicate in some physical way that the *physis* is only an inadequate manifestation of real nature; and since spirit cannot be pictorially added to the body image, something must be taken away from that appearance. Wishnitzer calls this "the principle of incompleteness."[19]

It has thus become clear that we are talking not only about modern non-representational painting but, in the strict sense, about all non-naturalistic depiction, at least in principle. Religious symbolism before the Renaissance, the play of light over Rembrandt's human figures, El Greco's or Modigliani's elongations, etc., are thus, in varying degrees, legitimized. On the other hand, artistic efforts at "pure empiricism," whether in the Greek clasical form, in its Renaissance revival, or up to French pointillism, must be regarded as, in varying degrees, approximating illegitimacy. Such judgments of degree of success or failure are then the business of the art critic.

The fragmentariness or distortion of the human image in Jewish art is in effect not a reduction but an expansion of the human form. The negative commandment prohibiting the depiction of the complete person is in substance a positive commandment to introduce the human spirit into the human form.[20] In short, the slashed nose is the symbol of the soul.

We want to adduce two episodes to illustrate the fundamental aesthetic principles which we have so far derived. The first is a Talmudic parable[21] that illustrates the prohibition of an exact duplication of the Temple (see p. 111).

The *Mishnah* tells of a king who invited his friends to a banquet. Before they began to eat, they found themselves sitting at a table covered with a magnificient cloth on which abundant fruit and viands were depicted. They feasted their eyes so long on these artificial foods that when the real food was put before them, they had lost all their appetite and fell asleep. The point made by the law and this legendary exemplification is something that might be called the aesthetic law of the identity of indifferents: if two objects, the original and its artistic reproduction, are exactly the same, then art ceases to exist, for in such a case art neither adds to nor detracts from reality but merely reproduces it. It has thus lost all conceivable function. Kant applied Occam's razor to this aesthetic question by enunciating "the rational maxim that unnecessary multiplication of principles is always to be avoided as much as possible."[22] (Cf. the parable, which Lessing used in *Nathan the Wise,* of the genuine ring and its two imitations.)

In Edward Albee's play *Tiny Alice* the model palace bursts into flames at the same time and in the corresponding place as the large-scale palace in which it is kept. The Jew accustomed to kissing the Torah that is clothed in a mantle decorated with a picture of such a Torah might well hesitate to kiss it for fear that what he takes to be the real Torah underneath might also only be another and ritually unacceptable facsimile thereof. What, in truth, is the difference between a pop art duplicate of the front of a soup can and its original on a display shelf? Hegel was surely right when he held that whenever and wherever the ideal is believed to have become identical with the real, "the death of art" has occurred.[23]

The second episode is historical. In 1909 the widow of the well-known Jewish philosopher and ethno-psychologist Moritz Lazarus published a mongraph that her husband had written some time before he died in 1903, *Die Erneuerung des Judentums–Ein Aufruf,* which he had intended as his last will and spiritual testament to Israel.[24] In it (pp. 40-51) the following incident is reported and analyzed.[25] In 1860 the Jews of New Orleans wanted to erect a memorial statue to the famous Jewish-American philanthropist of their city, Juda Touro. They inquired with, among others, Professor Zacharias Fraenkel, the famous Jewish theologian and historian—author of the classic *Darchē HaMishnah,* one of the founders of "Historical (Conservative) Judaism," and at that time director of the pace-setting Jewish Theological Seminary in Breslau—whether their plan was in accordance with Jewish law. Fraenkel answered emphatically in the negative. He cited all the legal evidence which we have surveyed: statues, because they are three-dimensional, are treated more sternly by Jewish law than any other form of the visual arts; human form in statues is most especially forbidden, whether the person concerned be a Jew or not (though sculptured nonhuman forms are permitted); and human sculpture is permitted even in a private place only if the body is somehow malformed or distorted. Interested as he was primarily in what he thought of as the liberalization and modernization of Judaism, Lazarus was utterly outraged by Fraenkel's response. He regarded it as a striking illustration of how Jewish Orthodoxy has become petrified in literalism and has thus alienated itself from what he regarded as modern culture. He excoriated the demand for the deformation of a human sculpture as "horrible:" "Because this thinking is only concerned with verbal formulae, without truth and without life, the most shameless picture of a painting of a chaste Athena whose nose is not torn is forbidden." True, he says, Judaism can never permit a picutorial representation of the divine. "Even the noblest poet of color, Raphael, and even the most powerful speaker who ever struggled for the best expression in stone and color, Michelangelo, succeeded only in depicting Zeus when they intended to represent Jehovah." Even the human may not be reproduced in the synagogue, because that is a place reserved exclusively for the divine and the spiritual. But, for the rest, in the private and non-synagogal life of the Jew, he could see no reason why these ancient prohibitions should be perpetuated.[26] We no longer live among idolators, and as for the Jews themselves "the purely spiritual concept of God and the life in it is not," as he put it, "endangered by 'the calf' but by the gold."

Less than seventy years later it is almost superfluous to point up who was more "modern" and had a better understanding of basic aesthetic principles, Moritz Lazarus with his Victorian-Wilhelminian notion of art and "spirituality" or Zacharias Fraenkel and the Talmudic law prescribing deviations from naturalistic representation. The "chaste Athena" which Lazarus admired would be regarded as embarrassingly maudlin today, while the one-eyed, three-eyed, or otherwise distorted human faces of Picasso express considerably more "the truth and the life" of human beings to us[27] than Lazarus's frozen photographic reproductions.[28]

– 7 –

The Question of Jewish Ethics Today

Every body of law is posited for some specific social organism. The *Code Napoléon* addressed itself primarily to France and its citizens. American law is concerned with the United States and its people. To be sure, every social organism and some of its members enter at some time or other into various relations with other such organisms and some of their members, and, therefore, its body of law must also provide for the manner in which these relations ought to be conducted; but the laws concerning foreign relationships, abroad or at home, will necessarily and properly be a practically subsidiary—however morally significant—part of every body of law.

Mutatis mutandis, Halakhah is the body of law for the Jewish polity. In bulk it is, in its social dimension, concerned with the relations of Jews among one another—whether they live in one state, in more than one state, or in none, in voluntary communities or simply as disparate individuals. *Pari passu* this body of law also has its provisions for non-Jews by themselves and especially in their relations with Jews and *vice-versa*. Thus there are "the Noachite laws," provisions for aliens, settlers, converts, etc., rules "for the sake of the paths of peace" (*mipnay darkhay shalom*—which is to be taken literally, as aiming at the highest social good, peace, and not, as it is usually vulgarized, "as a prudential tactic"), "going into the depths of (within) the line of the law," etc. These "international" stipulations, like their analogues in other legal systems, necessarily constitute a quantitatively minor portion of the entirety of *Halakhah*. Depending on the conditions of Jewry in any particular period they are paid greater or lesser attention and this expanded or left in *status quo ante*; this is jurisprudentially and ethically relatively unimportant. What does matter ultimately, qualitatively, is whether the international legislation (and its appurtenances) are rationaly consistent with the domestic legislation and whether both together make for a moral, humane social and individual life.

Are modern Jewish legal ethics moral or not?

Now, that there would be occasional, and sometimes even serious, inconsistencies between domestic and international legislation in the *Halakhah* (or any other body of law), or at least in its interpretation and application, cannot be surprising in the least. Individual statutes and even basic constitutional provisions come into conflict with one another constantly. That is one, perhaps the most important, reason that we have courts, all the way up to a court of final appeal and interpretation, whose task it is to adjudicate between the conflicting demands not so much of different subjects of the law as of the laws themselves and to arrive at a unified, consistent, and sociomorally desirable legal system. The question is only how good, in terms of both consistency and morality, the developing system of law turns out to be.

It is certainly the case that the vast accumulated literature of Jewish ethics and law can be and often has been interpreted in a selectively restrictive and—ethically—ultimately self-contradictory fashion. But the opposite, expansive, philosophically and ethically ultimately convincing option is always open—and in the end it commends itself more.

Some very few, learned, profound, and sensitive observer-analysts of Jewish law and ethics have tried for some time to raise warnings about what is happening on this score in our era. Thus the late Prof. Leon Roth wrote about "Moralization and Demoralization in Jewish Ethics" (*Judaism*, XI/4, Fall 1962) and the recently deceased Prof. Samuel Hugo Bergman about "Expansion and Contraction in Jewish Ethics" (in *The Quality of Faith*, Jerusalem, World Zionist Organization, 1970). Of the issue that they raised and which their titles outline clearly Bergman rightly said that it is "one of the most burning issues of our life." It is the issue of how, in the present era, the question of the consistency and morality of the *Halakhah* and its implied ethic with respect to both Jews and non-Jews is being handled—and both Roth and Bergman warn that in fact the ethic of the *Halakhah* is increasingly being "demoralized" or "contracted."

In this context *Modern Jewish Ethics—Theory and Practice*, ed. Marvin Fox, Ohio State University Press, 1975 (but for the editor's introduction, papers and discussions at the July 1972 meeting of the Institute for Judaism and Contemporary Thought in Israel) becomes interesting. Precisely the question of contemporary Jewish moralization or demoralization of Jewish (legal) ethics is raised very sharply.

One view: law demands more than the letter of the law

In a contribution that is already gaining fame[1] "Does Jewish Tradition Recognize an Ethic Independent of Halakhah?" Rabbi Aharon Lichtenstein, *rosh yeshivah* of Yeshivat Har Zion in Israel, with his acknowledged credentials of traditional as well as modern Jewish learning, makes essentially one point—that, according to Jewish law, to do no more than what the letter of the law requires is itself a violation of this law (i.e., "the quality of Sodom")[2] and that, to the contrary, to go "within the line of the law" (*middat chassidut—* the quality of [selfless] righteousness") "is part of the fabric of *Halakha*." The interested reader should consider the full evidence and analysis as presented in this study. R. Lichtenstein's conclusion is this: "What I reject emphatically is the position that, on the one hand, defines the function and scope of *Halakha* in terms of the latitude implicit in current usage and yet identifies its content with the more restricted sense of the term (*Halakhah*). The resulting equation of duty and *din* (statute) and the designation of supralegal conduct as purely optional or pietistic is a disservice to *Halakha* and ethics alike."

Despite the cogent case that he makes, R. Lichtenstein will doubtless continue to be contradicted on the usual allegedly logical ground that a supra-legal principle, such as equity, cannot, by definition, be part and parcel of the law.[3] But this is, despite its surface plausibility, a fallacious argument. In the first place, *lifnim mishurat hadin* is "within," not, as the usual rendering has it, "beyond" "the line of the law;" i.e., the very term indicates that we are here dealing with a dynamic function that operates within the system. In the second place, Hermann Cohen proved long ago and in a significantly different connection (*Ethik des reinen Willens*, Berlin 1904, pp. 585-589) that equity is not a factor additional to the *jus strictum* but a judgment procedure which makes sure that the application of the law, statutes as well as procedures, operationalizes ethical values (*'aggadah*).

Another: law is limited; a higher ethic may exist

A contribution by Prof. Ernst Akiba Simon raises serious doubts that R. Lichtenstein's meta-*Halachic* ethics conforms to the sources of Tradition. In fact, the article "The Neighbor (Re'a) Whom We Shall Love" comes to the conclusion that the neighbor whom we ought to love must, according to the *Halakhah*, be a Jew. Simon is, of course, deeply pained by and morally unwilling to accept this. Therefore, he appeals to "a Jewish ethic that is external to the *Halakhah*" and tells the story of Bertha Pappenheim (incidentally, Freud's famous patient "Miss O.[3a] who, when the rabbis of Frankfurt couldn't overcome the problem of *agunot* (deserted wives) cried out to them: "Gentlemen, when the capitalist economy developed to the point where it was no longer possible to observe the Torah's explicit prohibition against lending money for interest your predecessors managed to find within the *Halakha* an acceptable way to circumvent the law. From your failure to act now, I can only conclude that *Halakha*, as you interpret it, places higher value on economic concerns than on the human needs and rights of these pathetic and unfortunate women."

If Prof. Simon's reading of the classic sources of Judaism is correct, then, of course, his appeal to a higher Jewish ethic than the *Halakhah* is imperative. If, in addition, it can be shown, as would appear to be the case, that the nature of classic Judaism rules out the possibility of "a higher Jewish ethic," then anyone committed to a truly human, nonchauvinistic morality will feel compelled to turn his back—however painful this may be—on that classical Judaism. And if, furthermore, the nonclassical, nonstandard, "modernized" forms of Judaism present themselves, as they certainly on the whole do in our epoch, as at least as chauvinistic as Simon understands the classical form to be, then there is only one and even more drastic—and correspondingly more painful—course left open to such a person. Leo Strauss formulated this quandary with great sensitivity in a lecture which he originally gave in Jerusalem[4]: "A mother loves her child because he is her own ... But she also loves the good. All human love is subject to the law that it be both love of one's own and love of the good, a tension which may well lead to a break, be it only the breaking of a heart ... The practical meaning of this idealism is that the good is of higher dignity than one's own ... The Jewish equivalent of this relation might be said to be the relation between the Torah and Israel."

Evidence for Judaism's universalist ethical stance

The present writer, to whom Ernst Simon is a life-long teacher (while most of the other writers in *Modern Jewish Ethics* are his contemporaries and friends), must then want to hold that his teacher is mistaken.

One can, to begin with, wonder what would result if R. Lichtenstein's present thesis were confronted with Prof. Simon's. Unfortunately this confrontation does not take place within the pages of this book.

The evidence from beyond the confines of the book would be too massive and complex to be manageable here. I can cite and consider only two or three *loci classici*. One is the Rabbinic principle[5] that, "the honor/dignity of all human beings (*habriyot*—not only Jews) overrides every prohibition (the weightier of the two basic types of injunctions) in the Torah." What makes this principle the graver and the more relevant to our present concern is that it is derived (Rashi etc.) from *Deut.* 22:4 (and 23:8): "If you see the ox of your brother (!) fall by the way you shall not hide yourself"—i.e., one must not be indifferent to other people's misfortunes. The *Gemara* itself in *Meg.* 3b applies the term "brother" to all human beings. And *Tosfot ad locum* in turn goes out of its way to generalize from the specific issue being treated, the burial of unattended corpses of special Jewish concern, to "all the dead in the world."[6]

Maimonides, in his legal *Code*, "Laws of Sabbatical and Jubilee Years," 13:12f., in a striking and authoritative place, formulates the Jewish doctrine of the universality of human brotherhood on the highest spiritual level in unsurpassable terms: "Every single man among all creatures in the world" (*kol ish ve'ish mikol ba'ay 'olam*—an extraordinary and memorable phrase) is the equal of the Levite tribe, set apart (distinguished) for the whole-hearted service of God, if he, too, "is inspired by the spirit and convinced by knowledge ... to walk straight as God has made him and if he has broken off his neck the yoke of human calculativeness (cp. Ecclesiastes 7:29) ..." Every such human being—also Gentiles—"is sanctified as the Holy of Holies, and God will be his portion and his inheritance forever and ever ..."

A case where morality depends on interpretation

Simon and Lichtenstein both treat one important and specific issue which casts a full light on the nature of the texts with which we are concerned and on the options for their utilization. Both adduce *Mechilta, "mishpatim,"*[6] Prof. Simon regretfully infers from it (pp. 41ff.) that the Jewish murder of a Gentile is treated under Jewish law in a fashion that "may be less severe (than) and certainly not (so) immediate" as that of a Jew, while R. Lichtenstein clearly holds (p. 65)—I should have thought correctly—that "punishment by God" (the penalty stipulated for the former case) is, for religious people, emphatically a more severe condemnation than punishment by a merely human court (the penalty stipulated for the latter case). The Me'iri, for example, resolves the problem of "the perjured witnesses" in capital cases by precisely this consideration.[7] Which of the two juridical authorities comes into force, the human court or God, is then only a *de facto* question of the sovereignity that happens to be involved.

These two ways of reading the same text are by no means necessarily in conflict with one another. The question is only on which the element one wants to put the greater emphasis and therefore, is preferable for use for the purposes of ethics and legal morality.

How the "universalistic" thrust can be advanced is also cogently illustrated by a profound strain in the classical literature which condemns even

Moses in the strongest possible terms for his act of killing a non-Jew (Ex. 2:11f.). This episode is paradigmatic not only because the status of Moses in Judaism is beyond cavil but also because his victim was a brutal taskmaster. Even so, Moses is condemned for his defensive deed by God Himself, and the *Halakhically* significant point is made that he instituted his "cities of refuge" so that he himself could save himself there, like other unwitting murderers, from the death penalty which would otherwise have devolved on him.[8]

The most difficult issue: human survival

The most important ethico-legal text that crops up over and over again in *Modern Jewish Ethics* and in all similar discussions is *Baba Metzia'* 62a—whether R. Akiba is right that if two men have only enough water to see one of them out of the desert, then "I am nearest to myself," or whether ben-Petura is right that both should share the same risk of death. Abner Weiss, of the Society for Justice, Ethics, and Morals of South Africa and Israel, lines up with Achad Ha'am and his late English protagonist Sir Leon Simon on the side of R. Akiba. So does Harold Fisch, of BarIlan University and the Whole Land of Israel Movement. Fisch even goes so far in arguing against Ernst Simon's ethics as to impute a meaning to the term "*chessed*" ("grace"), i.e., "reciprocal obligation," entirely contrary to its historic use[9]; he would use "love" as Erich Fromm condemns Freud for thinking of it—as a pie in the capitalist economy of scarcity that can be divided into only a limited number of slices. And this is then commonly declared to be the normative, authoritative Halakhic standard. Somewhere in the middle of the spectrum Jakob Petuchowski, of Hebrew Union College—Jewish Institute of Religion, and Nachum Rabinovitch, of Jews' College in England, open the door increasingly wider to the option of voluntarily accepting the more altruistic ethic of ben-Petura. Lichtenstein and Simon are joined eloquently by Emmanuel Levinas and Rabbi Louis Jacobs (quoted at length by Petuchowski) in tending to identify normative Jewish ethics with ben-Petura's posture.

In fact the question of B.M. 62a needs to be narrowed down. The Maharsha points up that the proprietary status of the water at issue plays a decisive role.[10] If both men own it together then R. Akiba would agree with ben-Petura: one of them usurping it for himself would violate the fundamental rule that no one's blood is redder than another's (*Yoma* 2:2, *Pes.* 25b) and make himself divinely deserving of death.[11] R. Akiba's decision then applies only where one of the two men either owns the water at issue or takes prior physical possession of it, *de facto*.[12] But this does not really make sense:

regardless of the proprietary question, the equality of all human blood still obtains, and as for physical possession—R. Akiba's view boils down to an ultimate appeal to sheer physical superiority, which is scarcely an answer to a juridicio-ethical question. Maharam Schiff, then, though in fact accepting R. Akiba's view, admits that rationally ben-Petura's should prevail.[13] Furthermore, all would presumably have to follow ben-Petura if they cannot refute R. Lichtenstein's thesis that to act beyond the narrowest requirements of the law is itself a normative requirement of the Halakhah.

Modern anti-semitism and modern Jewish ethics

What may we conclude then at this point of our considerations? It turns out to be by no means a settled matter that Jewish ethics are essentially what Max Weber called "*Binnenethik*" (intratribal ethics); the contrary to be convincingly demonstrated. Therefore, a universalist in ethics need not dissociate from Jewish ethics—though, as we are about to see more fully, it is certainly the case that in order to overcome powerful current tendencies in the restrictive direction the most energetic efforts, intellectual and practical, must be made.

The allegation that Jewish law and ethics are *Binnenethik* and that toward non-Jews Judaism prescribes a purely exploitive attitude has always been one of the chief stocks in trade of traditional anti-semitism. The Christian Middle Ages were full of it, and so is modern anti-semitism. How these banked fires would be stoked if one yielded to the temptation to translate and thus make accessible to a public not privy to Halakhic language and dialectics some of the more chauvinistic exercises published in certain rabbinic and Zionist publications! The consequences could be disastrous. Another historical reminder may then not be amiss.

As part of the rise of the new racist-ethnic anti-semitism in Germany and elsewhere in the 1870's and 1880's, Prof. August Rohling published his notorious *Der Talmudjude* in 1871. Its main thesis was the "Jews are permitted by their religion to cause, secretly or overtly, non-Jews to perish physically and morally." This triggered off a wave of arguments, books, political controversies, and court trials for decades thereafter. One of the chief Jewish scholarly and ethical by-products was Joseph S. Bloch's *Israel und die Voelker nach juedischer Lehre*, Berlin/Vienna 1922. (Its publication so much later and its English translation in 1927 by the editor of the *American Jewish Year Book* occurred in the wake of the anti-semitic campaign of Henry Ford Sr., in which Rohling was resuscitated.) All of the issues broached in our present discussion were treated in its heavy bulk: chapt. 8, "Sacredness of Human Life," chapt. 19, "The Commandment to Love our Fellow-Men," etc. The essential affirmation of Bloch's book is, of course, that Judaism's authoritative ethos is universalistic and humanistic. And it is no historical coincidence that during the same years before and after 1900 the great Rabbi Elie Benamozegh published his studies on Jewish cosmopolitan ethics, every sentence of which gives passionate lie to the new chauvinism which is spreading so widely in our days.

We cannot agree to Jewish chauvinism

One of the legal by-products of the Rohling episode was a trial in Marburg, Germany in 1888, in which the question was raised before the court "whether the Law of Moses is applicable only as among Jews, that it is not applicable to Goyim, and that the latter may be robbed and deceived." Prof. de Legarde of Goettingen[14] argued as an expert in the affirmative and Prof. Hermann Cohen of Marburg in the negative. Throughout the rest of his life Cohen had to come back to this question over and over again, not only for philosophical and ethical reasons but also in order to defend Jewry against recurring spiritual and physcial attacks. As late as during World War I and shortly before his death he had to respond to the famous Protestant Bible Scholar Rudolf Kittel on this score. And when Martin Buber reissued Cohen's "Four Treatises about the Relation between Man and Man according to the Teachings of Judaism" in Berlin in 1935 (Schocken Popular Library, number 20) he stated clearly what was at stake: "It seems important to me to have this man give this testimony about this subject in this hour."

Are we to say that these men, and many others like them throughout the millenia of Jewish defenselessness, lied, or that they totally misunderstood the Judaism to which they devoted their lives, their work, and their very deaths? Are we prepared to stick with the presently ascendant Jewish ethic of chauvinistic self-service, even if or when we may someday, if not today, stand in need of moral protection at the hand of others? In 1935, in the heart of Nazi Germany, the editor of Cohen's essays on Jewish morality toward non-Jews wrote that "vulgarian anti-semitism has, then and now, accused Judaism of applying its ethico-humane principles only to Jews and of commending immoral conduct toward non-Jews." Are Jews who today put forward such a thesis any the less vulgarian? (Kant had a telling phrase for this: "*ethnicismus brutus*") And can they expect anything but egoistic reciprocity in the future?

What about immoral acts by the Israeli military?

We have almost imperceptibly moved from theoretical to political questions. This is inevitable. Also the subtitle of the book under discussion is, after all, "Theory and Practice." Its last section deals with "the contemporary situation"—which, not surprisingly, turns out to mean the State of Israel. Zvi Yaron, of the Jewish Agency, puts it quite correctly: "Israel has by now become a crucial factor in the considerations of Diaspora Jews in their thinking on the contemporary Judaism-ethics issue." And the chief question that is here raised is military ethics, under the entrenched phrase "the purity of arms."

There is surely something frighteningly Prussian about the very phrase "the purity of arms." I cannot here unpack its very terminological implications or its historical parallels and consequences. In any case, the "doves," in this case Me'ir Pa'il, favor it. Although Pa'il reports ("Theory and Practice," p. 216) that "all the quotations (cited in his article) indicate that Jewish Israeli soldiers are making their peace with the perpetration of inhumane acts toward the Arab enemy and civilian population, justifying it as an extreme requirement of national defense," also he, as a matter of fact, puts an apolegetically good face on the facts. The "hawks" at best cast doubts on or even oppose the notion of "the purity of arms." Thus Milton Himmelfarb, of *Commentary* magazine, in a comment filled with the "*golus*-mentality" of servility before the State, says: "To sacrifice even survival to exaggerated moralistic sentimentality borders on idiocy." (How the Right-wingers are permitted prejudicial language!)

Some Jews really say, one may kill the goyim

Since the words here cited were used, the 1973 War has occurred, and much further deterioration has set in. One of the consequences of that was was a booklet put out by the Central Command Headquarters/Israeli Army Chaplaincy and authored by Abraham Avidan (Zamel), military rabbi of the Command, under the title *After the War: Chapters of Meditation, Rule, and Research.* One of its highlights is the rabbi's thesis that " . . . insofar as the killing of civilians is performed against the background of war, one should not, according to religious law, trust a Gentile . . . 'The best of the Gentiles you should kill.' . . ." It took an outraged article in the Mapam newpaper to have the booklet withdrawn by the army, but no principled refutation of its barbarism has been put forward, and insofar as any notice was taken of this occurrence in Jewish publications in this country at all, *tu quoque* evasions were used to muddy the waters.[15] Whatever its administrative fate, the booklet reveals the mind set of some of the more sophisticated religious and military personages; one can imagine, if one doesn't know, its counterpart on crude levels of culture. Thus the question is really not one of "purity of arms" (whatever that may mean) but of the socio-political conditions which make for or against purity of minds and morals. Lest it be thought that these basic problems arise only within a Jewish polity, I want to remind ourselves—without being able to enter into this phase of things—that the moral traffic among Jews is, of course, bilateral and multilateral. Bank affairs, businessmen in high commercial, political, and even religious places, not to speak of ideologists and propagandists, indeed even organized crime, exercise their power here and there—in local affairs, in national, foreign, and international channels.

Jewish self-interest must not destroy Jewish ethics

The fact is that people who feel bound by ben-Petura or *middat chassidut* have, or logically should have, the most serious problems with contemporary Jewish institutionalized behavior and with the rationale offered for it. What is cause and what is effect in this syndrome could itself be debated: does one justify this Jewish behavior because one holds to the validity of ultimate self-interest, or does one adhere to the principle of the ultimacy of self-interest because one wants to justify this behavior? (We are not now raising the question whether this behavior does in fact serve real self-interest.)

When one surveys the historical and literary facts one conclusion emerges quite clearly—and not to one's surprise: the tendency to "moralize" Jewish legal ethics predominates in periods when Jews have relatively little wordly self-interest to defend and when a theory of selfless, universal morality is in fact to their interest (*pace* Nietzsche); on the other hand, when and where they do have a worldly stake—position, money, a state, etc.—then they tend to "demoralize" it and to use it to justify their self-interested behavior. This is only human, all too human. One may ask, however, whether Jewish law and ethics are supposed to be so human. Or are they not supposed to be "divine," absolute? Either way, can something be ethical if it is parochial, or moral if it is egotistical?

One may also point to the fact that even in times of relative Jwish well-being there has always been at least a small minority—moralists, *'amcha*, rabbis, not to speak of prophets—who proclaimed and practiced absolute, universal moral standards as over against narrowly conceived Jewish self-interest. Above all, it is simply a fact that these minorities and the ages of worldly Jewish helplessness defined, in the Talmud and its extrapolations, and for modern times the 18th and 19th centuries of Western Jewish apologetics, the nature of classical Judaism. This is why our evidence tends to come from such sources. And if a Leon Roth, say, then has to hear himself excoriated as a "*golus*-Jew" one may have to draw the consequences.

There is yet a final aspect to this problematic, which is very immediate, practical, and—let us be frank about it—extremely frightening. The boastful affirmation of the legitimacy of self-interest can, of course, easily be turned against one by someone else's self-interest. And Jewish self-interest does not, in the long run, stack up very favorably against the many other and more powerful self-interests in the world. As Rabbi J.B. Soloveitchik puts it in distinguishing the legitimacy ("sanctity") of Joshua's conquest of Palestine from that of Ezra's occupation: "that which results from the force of conquest is annulled by the force of another's conquest."[16] The validity of historic Jewish experience (as much as and more than that of others) and of its theoretical, ethical ideologization is surely undiminished—to say the least—by the events of the 20th century. All who tamper with it tamper with the very existence of the Jewish people.

The question of Jewish ethics today is the perennial question: is it to be *imitatio Dei* or individual and collective *sacro egoismo*?

If we wish to try to advance the resolution of live questions that may be regarded as falling within the sphere of Jewish philosophical ethics, then two issues have emerged out of the discussion begun in *Sh'ma* 7/124, to which I hope I can try to make a further contribution at this time. I would describe them as the question of the place of self-interest within a deontological universalist ethic and the question of the place of martyrdom in contemporary Jewish ethics. I will then turn to these briefly.

It seems to be thought widely that if, for example, one may not become an accessory to another's murder, even at the risk of one's life, one's own life has thereby been devalued. By the same token, it seems to be thought that if one favors universal values one thereby reduces, or perhaps even negates, one's own specificity. But both these inferences are, of course, entirely false. Everything that the prohibition of murder implies about the second person—that you are infinitely valuable, may not be reduced in life or dignity, etc.—it also implies about the first person. And the moral values that are universal are not universal-minus-one (to wit, myself or my national culture); they are valid for me just as they are for you. Practically speaking, the value of my life is vastly enhanced by virtue of the fact that your life, and every other human life, share with my life the unique characteristic of not being subject to another person's disposition. And when the universal value is taken to be the autonomy and dignity of every historic social entity, then the Jewish people and its culture, for example, are possessed of an infinitely higher degree of inviolability than if exceptions could be stipulated to this universalization—for under the latter alternative, who is to say that it is not just the Jews that will be made an exception of? In short, universality does not infringe on but rather heightens—indeed, conceptually it creates—individuality.

Humans are images of God, not means to an end

This is one important meaning of Kant's famous "second formulation" of the categorical imperative in the *Groundwork of the Metaphysics of Morals*: "Act in such a way that you use humanity in your own person (!) as in the person of everyone else always simultaneously as an end, never merely as a means." In his *Ethik* (Berlin, 1904), pp. 303f., H. Cohen called this "the most profound and powerful expression of the categorical imperative." Suicide is, furthermore, famously one of Kant's chief examples of what is prohibited under the moral law. In the *Metaphysical Beginnings of Jurisprudence* he formulated the self-relatedness of the categorical imperative even more bluntly[17]: ". . . to assert one's own value as a human being in relation to others, a duty which is expressed in the sentence: 'Do not make yourself into a mere means for others, but be at the same time an end for them.' "[18] Leaving aside Kant's distinction between the dessert of happiness and its possession— which is not relevant to our present point, the consequence of the categorical imperative from this perspective is that, as Ebbinghaus rightly points out, my own happiness is no less legitimate, though less compelling, than yours. It just may not be more so.

The point of ethics so conceived is that not I or you or she but humanity in all persons—in Jewish language, "the image of God" in all the children of humanity—is to be honored, and to be honored equally, neither you more than I but also not I more than you. Only if a given situation is such as to entail more humanity for me than for you must I act in order to restore the balance. And no less ought you to be ready to bring whatever sacrifice it takes to restore my human equality with you. This is the source of "philanthropy" (in the etymological meaning of the word), and it may, in extraordinary circumstances, push to the point of martyrdom. In martyrdom I do not die for you, nor you for me, but each dies for God, or, phrasing it differently, for the absolute/divine value that inheres in humanness.

Modern restatements of the Akiba–ben-Petura dilemma

Kant then rightly arrives at two conclusions:[19] One is that equity is a legal right, though a humanly unenforceable one: "The claim belongs solely to the court of conscience (*forum poli*, 'the court of heaven')." The reverse of this is that saving oneself at the price of another's life is culpable, though this, too, is humanly unenforceable. Here Kant virtually reconstitutes the scenario of *Baba Metzi'a* 62a: "There could be no penal law assigning the death penalty to a man who has been shipwrecked and finds himself struggling with another man—both in equal danger of losing their lives—and who, in order to save his own life, pushes the other man off the plank on which he had saved himself. For the first man, no punishment threatened by the law could be greater than losing his life. A penal law applying to such a situation could never have the effect intended, for the threat of an evil that is still uncertain (being condemned to death by a judge) cannot outweigh the fear of an evil that is certain (being drowned). Hence, we must judge that, although an act of self-preservation through violence ["violence" means doing injustice to another person's right, according to Kant] is not inculpable (*inculpabile*), it is still unpunishable (*impunible*). ... The motto of the right of necessity is: 'Necessity has no law'; but there still cannot be any necessity that will make what is unjust legal." (*Cp.* Haim Cohn, "Law and Reality in Israel Today," in Wise and Baron [eds.], *Violence and Defense in the Jewish Experience* [Philadelphia: Jewish Publication Society, 1977], pp. 326f.).

In historic fact, Jewish courts have acted as Kant here lays down that individuals should. Indeed, they so acted in an historic context—which numbingly anticipates precisely the Jewish experience of the twentieth century—five centuries ago. R. Solomon b. Adret and others ruled that the Iberian *marranos*, confronted by the choice of baptism or death, should, of course, have opted for death, but the courts cannot afterwords condemn them if they preferred to go on living as public Christians. (*Cf.* H.J. Zimmels, *Die Marranen in der Rabbinischen Literatur*, Berlin, 1932, p. 9 and references. There is also a whole class of violations of Jewish law that are unpunishable—e.g., the wearing of phylacteries on the Sabbath.)

As far as I can see, a curious indecisiveness prevails among contemporary American ethicists about the ethical status of supererogatory acts. J.O. Urmson[20] while expressing some sort of respect for "saints," rather denigrates their importance for ethics. (In an age in which Jews talked differently than we do these days, I would have been tempted to speak of Urmson's typically Anglo-Saxon bourgeois moral mediocrity). John Rawls[21] also waffles on what I dare call the obligatoriness of supererogatory acts, but he at least occasionally comes close to realizing that the line between duties and options (*chiyuv* and *mutar*) may not be so neat: "Some of the duties which justice as fairness counts as supererogatory may be required by the utility principle ..." (p. 117; cp. also pp. 438f.); "Yet although it is true enough that for the sake of justice (*pereat mundus*) a man may lose his life where another would live to a later day, the just man does what all things considered he most wants; in this sense he is not defeated by ill fortune the possibility of which he foresaw ..." (p. 573; cp. pp. 192, 478f., 485, 551) (Rawls' partial derivation from Kant may be given credit for his approximation of a better insight.) At the other end of the spectrum is, *e.g.*, Richard A. Watson[22], who holds that, the world being "a desert island" (p. 118), "the overriding moral principle of equity demands the equal sharing of food even if this leads to universal malnourishment or the termination of the species" (p. 115).[23] Clearly our world requires that more rigorous thinking be done on this subject.

Scripture does not give the self moral priority

What the classic Jewish texts laid down as doctrine millenia ago there can be no doubt, I want to hold. When Maimonides, in "Laws of the Foundations of the Torah," 5:5, codifies the law that all of us must be ready to die rather than hand over one of us to murderers, and when then R. Moses HaCohen of Lunel argues against the Rambam that either way the intended victim will die—let at least the rest of the community be saved.[24], Prof. S. Atlas rightly comments[25] that R. Moses misunderstood the issue: not whether your blood is redder than mine, or mine than yours, but the absoluteness of the command "Do not kill!" is at issue, and "human life is the highest, absolute value, which cannot be calculated. It is not a question of human calculation but of divine imperative (*kabbalah beyadaynu*)." And what Kant refers to as *forum poli* is clearly what the *Halakhah* calls *mittah miday shama'yim* ("death at the hands of heaven"), the ultimate penalty, which occurs in many forms.

In general the sacred texts that have been used in order to claim that, according to Judaism, the self has some sort of moral priority over the other have been, I want to hold, badly misinterpreted. Lev. 19:19 is correctly to be translated, as Hermann Cohen never tired of pointing out, not as "you shall love your neighbor as yourself" (which implies self-love as a model) but as "you shall act lovingly toward your neighbor, for he is like you" (in the image of God). I am glad that Dr. Weber reminded us of Dr. Finkelstein's interpretation of the dabate between R. Akiba and ben Azzai (*Y Ned.* 9) the upshot of which would be, if Dr. Finkelstein is right, that R. Akiba and ben Azzai eventually agree on the *imago Dei* as the objective standard of philanthropy rather than self-love.[26] Hermann Cohen did not understand the outcome of the debate quite this way, and therefore, subscribed to ben Azzai's teaching,[27] but I would prefer to think that Dr. Finkelstein is right.[28] By the same token, then, also the debate between R. Akiba and ben Petura ought to be reconsidered. "Your life comes first," like "like you" in Lev. 19:19, designates an experiential priority, not a moral one. That is to say, it ought to be translated as meaning that "your own life is the first that you know about from experience"—from it you learn about the absolute irreplaceabilty of every human life, your own no less and no more than that of all other humans—now go and act accordingly! I.e., I learn universal ethics from my own universal, ethical obligations. And as, of course, we know from Kant, if from no other source, experience—in this case the experience of my self and its duties—is the occasion but not the source of knowledge. In short, the self has chronological, not ethical priority.

Ben Petura, Akiba: fight for martyrdom or survival?

Between the chronological priority of the self and the ethical priority of the love of the other lies the mediating epistemological priority of the dialectical relationship between the self and the other. By virtually the unanimous agreement of modern Jewish and non-Jewish philosophers, I cannot even know myself as a self other than in the act of recognizing the other as a self. This is the case whether one follows the analysis of Hermann Cohen[29], Buber, Rosenzweig,[30] or E. Levinas[31], and it is true on Kant's, Hegel's, Feuerbach's view, and on that of most current thinkers. Unless one makes this epistemological move, one isolates the self in its own self-consciousness and bars the way to a rational solution of "the problem of other minds."

Ben Petura is really being badly misunderstood. He is apparently widely thought to have held that if I find myself on a desert with another person, and the two of us have only enough water between us to see one of us safely back to civilization, then, other things being anywhere near equal, I ought to seek death so that the other person may survive.

In fact, however, ben Petura is not, as this interpretation would have it, discussing ethics at all. He is engaging in what we would nowadays probably call meta-ethics; i.e., he is analyzing the rational principles that must be taken to underlie moral decisions and actions, not the decision or the action itself. In Halakhic language, he is not "*possek*" here (making an authoritative decision for action).

What is the principle that he is affirming? It is not that I ought to sacrifice myself and that the other person preserve himself. Ben Petura's principle is in fact that each one of the two of us ought to be ready to sacrifice himself rather than see to it that the other die. Altruism[32] is being commanded not to one person rather than the other, but to both.

Imagine the situation: A says to B: "You drink." B says to A: "No, you drink." Now, who drinks? We still don't know. No decision has been made. Presumably a moral competition now ensues us as to who of the two will prefarably die a martyr, and who will reluctantly end up as a survivor.[33]

Also R. Akiba in this discussion has not decided that A should die or B. He, too, is engaging in meta-ethics. The difference between ben Petura's scenario and R. Akiba's is that in the former the struggle between A and B will erupt over who of the two will acquire "the merit" of martyrdom, while in the latter the struggle will erupt over who will end up preserving himself at the expense of another human being.

Martyrdom remains a possibility, distasteful or not

Actually the model situation is such that one does not really know who and how many, if anyone, will die. Whether even by R. Akiba's way of handling the problem I will survive, and whether, therefore, the death of the other person has been "worth it," is, of course, really unpredictable—conditional as it is on so many incalculable external factors: how far the way back to civilization, how strong the constitution of the prospective survivor, how rapacious the wild animals in the desert, etc. By the same token, whether both of us, or even only one, will die if we follow ben Petura's view is equally unpredictable: even if we dont's want to put our faith in divine miracles (and the desert seems always to have been a likely place for such occurrences), wandering nomads—or a helicopter—may come by, an oasis may show up behind the next dune, etc. To let one person die now rather than chance the survival, albeit also the death, of two persons not only raises fundamental moral problems but also seems very unpractical in a world full of contingencies.[34]

Both the history of Jewish martyrdom and a cool analysis of the probabilities of our hypothetical problem show that it is likely that both will die—in one way, however, as martyrs, in the other as frustrated survivors. As Lord Keynes said famously, in the long run we all die. The only question is: how do we die? In our scenario the question is: do we engender a struggle for survival, or do we engender a competition for (unavoidable) martyrdom and its sanctity?

It seems strikingly notable to me that in this entire discussion of Jewish ethics, in which there has been much talk about 'who shall live, and who shall die," almost no one seems to have been willing to talk about the possibility of future martyrdom. I suppose this is understandable: in my generation we have been surfeited with martyrdom, especially Jewish martyrdom. There is surely a heavy surfeit of talk about past martyrdom. We don't want any more of it.[35] But, after all, suffering has been "the badge of our tribe." Who knows what the future holds? Yet even about the possibility of suffering we do not seem to want to think or talk. Are human beings, especially Jews, ever in a position of such privilege, however?[36] Surely one of the most morally distressing phenomena in our times is the fact that no one seems to have any idea anymore about having to draw the line somewhere, beyond which, as a limit, one may not go without losing one's humanity, though, perhaps, saving one's life—not to speak of lesser sacrifices. How many Germans resigned their positions in 1933, without having being forced to do so, rather than being sucked into the maelstrom? How many American government officials resigned rather than carry on the Anti-Vietnam War? What Jews in this country and in Israel have as much as apologized for their fervent advocacy of and coresponsibility with Richard Nixon and all his repulsive misdeeds? (Cp. S. Rabinove, "Vietnam, the guilt we need to face," *Sh'ma* 7/131).

We always have a choice: to be killers or not

R. Baruch Stern wants to make the distinction in Jewish law (*Sh'ma* 7/131) between causing the death of another, which calls for martyrdom, and "seeing" his death, which does not. Now, it goes without saying that before the unfathomable human problems which *churban eropa* (the annihilation of European Jewry) presented to its victims, only respectful listening becomes us; and R. Stern's autobiographical report receives this from me.

R. Stern's reaction, and his *p'sak* (for he makes, in effect, a legal decision), are, however, not the only voice that reaches us. To begin with, in R. Akiba's example, one of the two men is expected to drink the water and thus, at least negatively, cause the death of the other; in R. Stern's case no Jew did anything—it is the Nazi who killed.[37] Furthermore, I would hold that *B. Sanh.* 74a and *Erub.* 13b should be taken together: when you have "counted and taught" that life is not so desirable that "it were better for man to have been born, rather than not to have been born in the first place," it makes sense also to have "counted and taught" that, once born, rather than act inhumanely it is better "not to sin grievously but rather be killed." Most importantly, there were others in Nazi Europe, whose lives, deaths, and judgments evoke the same respect, and who held differently.[38]

In view of the number of attacks that have been directed at me, let me say for once that, after all, I, too, am "a brand saved from the fire;" no one needs to tell me about what is now called the Holocaust. (I have come to feel repulsion at the very word, because of its exploitation among other things.)

I take it that R. Stern understandably did not want to talk about what may be called "the pain of survivorship." It is by now a well-known phenomenon. I remember that when I returned to Europe after the war, in order to work among the *she'erith hapletah* (the surviving remnant), the very first night I was invited to a meeting of the "*Verein der Verfolgten des Naziregimes*" (Council of Survivors of the Nazi Regime), and over the roster a large, red banner was spread, which bore the inscription: "*Die Besten unter uns sind gefallen*" (The best among us have fallen). This is the pain of survivorship: having seen, not, of course, having caused, the death of others. None of the people present wanted to be dead, but all were conscience-ridden that others had died who also had not wanted to die.

Some of us have drawn a conclusion from this experience of our—and all Jewish—generations which I tried to express in these words at the end of my introduction to *Roots of Jewish Nonviolence* (Jewish Peace Fellowship): "I close with a personal confession: the men of my generation have gone through a world war, the Holocaust, Stalinism, and Vietnam—not to speak of other mass blood-lettings. I have seen enough unnatural deaths to outlast a lifetime. I know that I, like all other men, have no choice but to die—only once, but some time. I do, however, have a choice as to whether I will die with human blood on my hands. I am deeply tired of and sickened by killing. I pray with Balaam, inspired by God and seeing Israel (Num. 23:9f.): 'Behold, this is a people that is to dwell solitary . . . May my soul die the death of the righteous and my end be like theirs.' "

Universalism benefits everyone, especially Jews

It goes without saying, too, of course, that, fully in accordance with the *Halakhah*, readiness for martyrdom may, and ought to, become operative only after all "permitted" (i.e., decent) recourses for survival have been exhausted; otherwise the equally wicked sin of suicide will be committed. No one knows better about the penultimate value of survival than Jews who have gone through "the flood of fire": I may confess that occasionally, when I feel really good, I raise my glass silently in a private toast: "I 'intend' (*mekavven*) this drink against those who would have killed me several decades ago. I am just fine, thank you."

Perhaps it is clear that there is nothing pessimistic about this posture. I, for one, have no doubt whatever that the Jewish people will survive and, in time, flourish. We are not discussing the death of the Jewish people; we are discussing the possibility of the death of individual Jews precisely for the sake of the God of Israel. Nothing is so deleterious not only to the values but even to the historic survival of a culture, as the unwillingness of its members to bring "the last full measure of devotion" on its altar. It is in fact the psychopathic desire to survive at every cost which leads to one's own and one's people's death. R. Yehudah HaLevy recognized and taught that willingness to suffer for, is not only the secret of Israel's survival but even of the establishment of the Messianic kingdom.[39] The ineluctable fact is that Jews, like everybody else only more so, will be able to ensure their lives and values fully only when the world as a whole is, Messianically, such that "nation shall not lift up sword against nation ... But they shall sit every man under his vine and under his fig tree, and none shall make them afraid." (Micah 4:3f.) Universalism is in the Jewish, as in everyone else's, interest. This I take to be the significance of the rabbinic dictum that Jewish troubles are only half-troubles; human troubles are fully Jewish troubles.

– 8 –

Moral Radicalism and "Middlingness" in the Ethics of Maimonides

"Extremism in the defense of liberty is no vice; moderation in the pursuit of justice is no virtue."

(Wall-plaque in office of the American Civil Liberties Union, New York; Senator Barry Goldwater, 1964)

"The dishwasher has returned his steak, saying it is too medium."

(Stanley Elkin, *The Franchiser* [New York 1976] p. 316)

Medieval scholastic philosophy (Christian, Moslem, and Jewish) was, of course, molded by Aristotelianism—or at least by what medieval authors took to be Aristotelianism, in fact a sort of amalgam of Aristotelianism and neo-Platonism. With this neo-Platonic Aristotelianism a factor of at least equal weight was combined—"revealed truth," the Bible (Old and New Testaments) and the authoritative teachings of the Church for Christians, the Koran and its authoritative explications for Moslems, and the Torah (Hebrew Bible and its Rabbinic extrapolations) for Jews. As is well-known, scholasticism is then the extended effort to bring these two/three factors into one consistent and persuasive whole, or, for that matter, to differentiate them from one another in favor of one or the other of them. As H. A. Wolfson once put it: "Medieval philosophy is one philosophy, written in three languages, Arabic, Hebrew, and Latin, and among these Hebrew holds the central and most important position."[1] This broad description applies to the ethics of medieval thought at least as much as to any other branch of it.

We want to concentrate here on the situation of Jewish ethics under these conditions. As expected, they, too, were heavily Aristotelian,[2] but at the same time they were afflicted, as they were bound to be, with a number of serious methodological problems. These arose chiefly from two quarters—the inherent problematics of Aristotelian ethics themselves, and the difficulties in trying to fuse Aristotelian ethics with religious, Bible-derived ethics.

Aristotelian ethics are famously the ethics of "the golden mean." As such they are themselves beset by a number of fundamental problems. To begin with, it is not at all clear what the virtues are really supposed to be, what they mean. Even if this question can be satisfactorily answered, it is an at least extremely difficult task to show in Aristotle himself or in Aristotelian meta-ethics how they are arrived at. Further, in the *Nicomachaen Ethics* (the *locus classicus* of Aristotelian and scholastic ethics) Book X climaxes in what may be called an ethic of contemplation, *theoria*, that is not at all "moderate" but explicitly in pursuit of an extremist goal (in fact, a contemplative *imitatio Dei*) and, therefore, perhaps at loggerheads with an ethic of the mean.[3] If and when these difficulties have been overcome, Aristotle himself declares that his form of ethical knowledge is only approximate—not precise, cognitive ("scientific") knowledge[4]—and one is, therefore, left with the troublesome task of making a transition from philosophical ethics to practical morals. Finally, any number of modern philosophers and historians of philosophy have directed attention to serious logical and ethical criticisms that must be leveled at Aristotelian ethics of the mean,[5] and medieval authors were by no means unaware of at least some of them.[6]

There are, too, the problems that result from the marriage of Aristotelian and religious ethics. Intuitively, presystematically, one would expect such a marriage to be extremely difficult, if at all manageable. I will mention here only the most obvious difficulties:

Biblical-Jewish religion directs itself primarily toward God. This God is conceived, certainly by medieval authors, as "infinite," "perfect," etc. He is quite literally the radical *par excellence* (Marx: "to be radical is to go to the roots")—*shoresh hashorashim ("the root of all roots") and 'ikkar ha'ikkarim* (the root-principle of all root-principles").

Bible-derived ethics in Judaism are classically conceived as *imitatio Dei:* "Holy shall ye become, as I, the Lord your God, am holy" (*Lev.* 19:1).[7] Within a theory of *imitatio Dei*, to hold to a doctrine of the mean would then seem to entail that God has to be regarded as acting moderately and that, therefore, we are to act moderately. Logically it might even be taken to follow that we ought to enact moderate imperatives moderately. As we shall see, attempts will actually be made to construct an ethic along precisely such lines. If the famous statement that Senator Goldwater made, for whatever reasons, and that we have placed as a motto of this study, is a formulation of the political application of ethical radicalism, then there is also always the logical and historical possibility to formulate a political program which radicalizes, that is, exponentializes to an infinite power, a morality of moderateness by trying to derive it in turn from an infinite God. The title of Donald I. Warren's *The*

Radical Center: Middle Americans and the Politics of Alienation,[8] just because it really means the same thing as Senator Goldwater's extremist formulation, illustrates this possibility aptly. But under such auspices all sorts of fundamental Biblical texts would in effect have to be rewritten, to say something like "You shall love the Lord, your God, with a moderate part of your heart. . ." (*Deut.* 6:5)[9] and "Be ye temperately integral" (*Gen.* 17:1, *Deut.* 18:13, etc.).[10]

Furthermore, all the well-entrenched components in Jewish law and ethics that make for moral perfectionism, like *mishnat chassidut* (the teachings of special righteousness), *lifnin mishurat hadin* (going beyond—actually, into the inner recesses of—the letter of the law[11]) etc. would have to be stricken from the records. What would one do with fundamental and ever recurring dicta like: "Our sages laid down: those who are humiliated and do not humiliate, who hear themselves reviled and do not revile, who act out of love and rejoice in their afflictions—of them Scripture says (*Jud.* 5:31), 'Those who love God are like the sun when it goes forth in its strength' "?[12] And what would one do with an entire pietistic and moralistic tradition informed with this spirit?

In a more general way it seems intuitively incompatible with an ethic of moderation to stake as much as normative Judaism always has staked on the striving for a Messianically perfected ("repaired") world and on the salvific importance of every last casuistic, pedantic detail of the law of God (in contrast with an Aristotelian proximate ethic).

But, of course, these are only presystematic considerations, which of themselves prove nothing. This study looks at Maimonides as the undoubted epitome of scholastic Judaism and, indeed, as the formulator *par excellence*, among at most a small handful of others, of what fairly may be regarded as classical Judaism, in order to crystalize not where he expectedly follows the conventional pattern of scholastic, Aristotelian ethics but where, less obviously, unexpectedly, and, therefore, the more instructively he deviates from this pattern[13]—at what I have called "the Jewish twist."[14] It will turn out to be the case that Maimonides in fact crafted a philosophic ethic of ultimately perfectionist character. I make no secret of wanting to suggest that this could and must serve as an "ideal type" by means of which other classical formulations of Jewish ethics, basically consistent with it, can be hermeneutically educed from the sources.

Maimonides devoted only one continuous text to ethics as such, the *Eight Chapters*. Here a pretty straightforward Aristotelian ethic of the golden mean is expounded.[15] The one exception which he stipulates is itself quite Aristotelian and of a purely therapeutic character: when a man has fallen into the extreme of one vice he can work toward the restoration of his moral equilibrium by going to the opposite extreme, though the latter by itself is also a vice.[16] Since the negative vices, like stinginess, are harder to cure than their positive counterparts, like wastefulness, it is always better to tilt in the direction of the positive extreme. This is why and how the truly pious "go behind the line of the law."[17]

The logic of the argument breaks down at so early a point as this. Maimonides says that everyone requires such therapeutic compensation of tilting toward the extreme. This, he adds, is particularly true of the pious, all the way up to Moses and the Messiah. Why this should be the case, when logically they would presumably need it least, is incomprehensible. In any event, if everyone has to deviate from the mean at all times it cannot really be said anymore that the mean determines human virtues.

It is instructive to note what the translators have done when they reach this point in Maimonides. Ibn-Tibbon, in his contemporary Hebrew translation from the original Arabic, apparently felt religious or Jewish compunctions about the Greek notion of "temperance" and, therefore, adds to the word *z'hirut* ("prudence") the explanatory phrase *k'lomar yaray chayt* ("to avoid sin").[18] The English translator Gorfinkle goes on to claim apologetically and naively that the doctrine of the mean is standard and normative Jewish teaching.[19] So does Stephen S. Wise, in his translation of Ibn-Gabirol's *The Improvement of the Moral Qualities,*[20] in commenting on Gabirol's utilization of the Aristotelian mean. Wise also quotes Schmiedl to the effect that in time this became *"ein wahrhaft jüdischer Lehrsatz."*[21]

Maimonides' *Eight Chapters* are, of course, his introduction, by way of a general philosophic ethic, to his *Commentary on the Chapters of the Fathers.* Here he deals with classic Jewish texts rather than with Aristotelian theory. When in his *Commentary* he gets to chapter 4:4, "Rabbi Levitas of Jabneh says: 'Very, very humble ("of lowly spirit") be,'" the usually extremely concise Maimonides turns extremely prolix[22] in expounding on the virtue of humility. Relying on the unusual syntax of the injunction and on the equally unusual duplication of the adverb "very," he protests over and over again, in different ways, that ethically and Jewishly it is all together right that the righteous (saintly) "moved away from pride to the extreme of deficiency thereof and inclined completely to humility of spirit, in order not to leave any room whatever for pride in their souls."[23]

A number of characteristics of this perfectionist counsel should be noted. Maimonides starts this exegesis with a cross-reference to his explication of the ethical theory of the mean in *Eight Chapters.* He proceeds very quickly, however, to stipulate humility as a total exception to that theory, as we have noted, and to argue this in terms of *imitatio Dei.* He rehearses at some length the Talmudic principle that "wherever you find God's greatness referred to in Scriptures you also find it immediately accompanied by His humility."

As we have said earlier, intuitively it would seem to be very difficult, if at all possible, to square these two theories of the mean and of *imitatio* with one another. A comparatively simplistic way of trying to accomplish it nonetheless is to be found in *Sefer HaChinuch*, Commandment no. 608, "The Commandment to Imitate the Good and Right Ways of God."[24] This ends up defining these "good and right ways" as "the good and median way, never to be deviated from to either extreme."[25] Although the *Chinuch* is in fact an elaboration of Maimonides' own *Sefer HaMitzvot*, in the latter the identical injunction is handled very differently:

> We are commanded to imitate God to the best of our ability, as the Bible says: "Walk you in His ways!" and repeats: "To walk in His ways," and as is expounded in t. *Sotah* 14: "As the Holy One, praised be He, is called compassionate, so be you compassionate; as the Holy One, praised be He, is called merciful so you be merciful; as the Holy One, praised be He, is called gracious so you be gracious." This has also been said in other words, as when it is said: "After God shall ye walk," which is interpreted to mean that men are to imitate His good activities and honorable qualities, with which actions the exalted God then, metaphorically speaking, adorns Himself—although in fact He transcends the greatest possible exaltation.[26]

Thus Maimonides, conspicuously and unlike the *Chinuch*, makes no reference at all to the doctrine of the mean in defining the commandment of *imitatio*. To the contrary, he places heavy emphasis on the infinite, unattainable, radical character of *imitatio Dei*. (This is further strengthened by the clause about graciousness, which does not in fact occur in *Sotah* and seems to have been introduced by the Rambam quite willfully here.)

Perhaps the most important feature of the radicalization of ethics in Maimonides' commentary to *Aboth* 4:4 is simply the fact that it erupts on the issue of humility. (He also abandons the ethic of the mean with respect to the vice of anger.[27]) It can easily be shown that, throughout Jewish ethical literature, humility is considered as the absolute virtue and is defined in the most extremist, perfectionist, radical terms.[28] And, indeed, perhaps no virtue in the tradition of Biblical religion (Christian as well as Jewish) is more incompatible with the aristocratic ideals of honor, pride, great-heartedness—in short, *megalopsychia*[29]—of the Greek, Aristotelian "gentlemen's ethos."[30] One could lay down the general rule: look for the evaluations of honor and humility, and you will find the fundamental rift between Greek and Jewish ethics down through the ages.[31]

Maimonides' ethical analysis up to this point appears to be an uneasy, tenuous, in the longer run untenable combination of the two doctrines of the mean and *imitatio*. At first sight this also seems to hold for the *Code*. "The Laws of Beliefs" here seem to expound essentially the same self-contradictory synthesis: 1:3 defines the virtues by the mean, and 1:7 actually defines the divine attributes of action, which are to be imitated in morality, in the same way. (This is the textual source for the passage in *Sefer HaChinuch* which we considered above.) The Aristotelian theme of therapeutic tilts, which we found earlier in the *Eight Chapters*, is restated in 2:2. Specific instants of the median practice of median virtues can then be found all through the *Code*: clothing ought to be median (5:9); so ought sexual cohabitation (5:4)—neither too early nor too late in the night, and when one is neither too hungry nor too sated (to which R. Joseph Karo's *Kessef Mishneh* adds the median explanation that children produced by such intercourse will be neither too light-headed nor too heavy-headed); so ought charity ("Laws on Gifts to the Poor," 7:5), etc.

On the other hand, in the *Code* there is also the pull in the radical moral direction. In "The Laws of Beliefs" the practitioners of the ethic of the mean are called "sages" (1:4f., 2:6, etc.), while the higher religious level of moral life is called that of "the righteous/gracious/saintly ones" (*chassidim*) (1:5). This is Maimonides's entrenched terminological distinction between the Aristotelian *homo philosophicus* and the Jewish *homo religiosus*.[32] The saintly ones begin, as in *Eight Chapters*, by deviating from the medium "a little" for compensatory purposes, but, in the very next sentence, they go "to the last extreme" in humility, like in the commentary to *Aboth* 4:4 ("To begin with philosophy [although not *eo nomine*] and to turn almost at once to the Torah may be said to be the law governing the *Mishneh Torah* as a whole," as Leo Strauss put it.[33]) And once this breaking-point of moral radicalism has again been reached, the Rambam once more erupts in extended expositions of perfectionism—the saintly go "behind the line of the law" (1:5); they determine morality by the method of *imitatio Dei*, not by the mean (1:6), in order "to become like God as much as possible"—and this last phrase really means "to the limit of human capacity";[34] ritually admissible food is selected by this criterion ("Laws of Impure Foods," 16:12); etc. Against the notion of the mean Maimonides now pits his favorite Talmudic dictum about "being reviled without reviling ..." ("Laws of Beliefs," 2:3).[35] The principle is that one is to be strict with oneself and lenient with others,[36] and (5:13) "Be of the persecuted, not of the persecutors, of the reviled, not of the revilers, for of such Scripture says: 'You are My servant, oh Israel, in whom I am glorified' (*Is.* 49:3)."

In this ethical radicalism the underlying philosophical theory stipulates a striving toward the infinite *coniunctio* with God through knowledge (3:2f.,

6:2), and this knowledge is quintessentially moral knowledge: the God with whom one strives to be united is defined positively only by the attributes of His (moral) actions, and thus the "beliefs" of the title of the Book in the *Code* are, as its contents make crystal-clear, not theoretical truths but practical virtues. (*Hilchot de'ot* should, therefore, be properly translated really as "The Laws of Morals."[37])

As we now turn to Maimonides' *Guide for the Perplexed*, his philosophical *magnum opus*, we want to show that the apparently unintegrated, unsystematized theoretical theses strewn through and only fragmentarily discernible in his earlier writings and particularly in the *Code* are here formulated fully and brought into rational consistency, so that, among other things, the tension between the ethical doctrine of the mean and that of *imitatio Dei* is creatively overarched.

The results of the lengthy and complex arguments of the *Guide* can be fairly stated in the following summary. Each person's purpose in life is to unite to the greatest possible degree with the deity (through the "conjunction" of his "acquired intellect" with the Active Intellect). The deity, now, is exhaustively described by the totality of His "negative" and actional attributes. The negative attributes have the effect of emptying the universe of God—that is, nothing in or about the universe is in any manner comparable and, therefore, even the less identifiable with God; the universe, and humanity as part of it, are completely "secular." Thus an infinite gap is opened between God and the world. This gap is bridged only by His attributes of action—descriptions of what God does in relationship to the world, not of what He is (in Himself). These attributes of action furthermore possess two features which must be particularly noted: 1) no inference may be drawn from what God does to what He is (so that, for example, He loves, but He is not a lover[38]), and connected therewith, 2) the attributes of action are legitimately imputable to the deity only because and to the extent to which they serve as models which are to be imitated by man in his moral life.

Humanity's moral life in turn transpires initially on two levels—the secular, sociopolitical, physical level, and the spiritual-religious level. At this initial stage the religious *mitzvot* and the virtues of philosophical ethics are determined by the rule of the mean.[39] Once this initial stage has been passed, however, another and higher stage is entered—that of the intellectual union with God. There is nothing moderate about the ethics of this *theoria* in Maimonides, anymore than there had been in Aristotle. Here extremism, radicalism rules. As Simon Rawidowicz puts it[40]: "The man who is wholly absorbed in his efforts to see God . . . this man does not know any 'middle way' between the extremes, any 'golden mean.' It is the absolutely extreme man. Only this man is man to Maimonides."[41]

This is as far as Rawidowicz can take the matter. It is very difficult, if not entirely impossible, to understand why he does not take it to its necessary completion. He is quite aware of where this would lead, for he says: "Without examining here Hermann Cohen's conception of Maimonides' philosophy, we have to state that he was more correct than other scholars in emphasizing the philosophical value of the aforementioned 'conclusion.'"[42] The conclusion referred to is *Guide* III/51ff., the final chapters and the summit of Maimonides' system. To this Cohen rightly drew attention,[43] and the move that is there made is, indeed, radical—in the fullest sense of the word—and revolutionary.[44]

Guide III/51 describes the ideal individual, in the person of Moses, who has fulfilled the social virtues of the mean and gone on to overlay them with the solitary virtues of the intellect that are perfectionist.[44a] Through the latter he aspires to *unio* with God. But it has to be remembered that the deity "is" only negations—albeit negations of privations[45]—except for the attributes of action. One cannot unite with *negativa. Unio* with the deity can, therefore, be brought about only through the positive, that is, actional attributes. Thus, Maimonides concludes in III/52, that "this end (*unio*) is achieved through actions." In III/53, he then uses *Jer.* 9:22f. to define both the deity and the corresponding method of imitating the deity: "Thus said God: 'Let the wise man not boast of his wisdom nor the hero of his heroism; let the rich man not boast of his wealth. Only of this shall one boast: understanding and knowing Me, for I, God, practice grace, justice, and righteousness (*chessed mishpat utz'dakah*) in the earth; for these do I desire,' says God."[46] Maimonides' exegesis is clear: humanity's purpose is to "know" God, but the God who is to be known is knowable only insofar as He practices grace, justice, and righteousness in the world, and to know Him is synonymous with imitating these practices of His in the world: "for these do I desire." And III/54, the final chapter of the final part of the *Guide*, then has for its final and climactic text-sentence this unmistakably grand conclusion: "By virtue of what is man man? . . . The perfection of man . . . is . . . to follow this conception, in the paths toward which he always directs himself, to practice grace, justice, and righteousness, in order thus to come to resemble the actional attributes of God" (end of the book). Salo Baron[47] felicitously calls this "ethical gnosis,"[48] and Julius Guttmann, in talking about this sort of thing, long anticipated my expression by speaking of "the ethical twist."[49]

There can then really be no doubt as to what the Rambam's last word on ethics is. At the end of *Guide* III/52 he had made the traditional distinction between obeying God out of fear and out of love. To obey Him out of fear is identified with practicing the virtues "meanly." From that level one goes on to seek spiritual-intellectual union with Him. This turns out to mean that, again, one practices the virtues—but now not out of fear, meanly, anymore but by imitating Him, that is, out of love. And love is, of course, boundless, infinite, radical: "That great good which is infinite."[50] Indeed, what would the median be between the finite and the infinite? As III/53 puts it (starting with a cross-reference to *Commentary to Fathers,* perhaps 4:4 or 5:7), love is "in excess, where excess [from the mean] is called for." (H. Cohen argues persuasively that at this point Maimonides replaces Aristotle's ideal of "the state of eudemony" with the ideal of "the process of self-perfecting."[51])

Maimonides has thus managed to reappropriate by way of philosophy the classic Talmudic discussion on the priority of theory or practice (t. *Kidd.* 40b): the view that practice is superior to theory is opposed by the view that theory is superior to practice, and both are "sublated" to the effect that "theory is superior to [mindless] practice because it leads to [proper] practice." (*Ad locum* Maimonides does not comment on this discussion in his commentary, but he cross-refers to his "Introduction" to *Sanh.* X.) Generalizing, one could say that Jewish thought in this way comes extremely close to the notion of "the unity of theory and *praxis.*" It is the case, after all, that in scholasticism "actual reason" is activated, active, actional reason.

In any case, there is then here no longer any talk of the ethics of the mean. These have turned into a mere philosophical and moral antechamber (III/51): one first learns about morality and first practices it by the method of the mean; this median practice, however, only serves the purpose of carrying one through the antechamber into the throne-room of the truth, where one learns the higher, real morality and where one enacts it by means of the method of philosophical, intellectual, that is, rational and cognitive *imitatio.* There is then no God but the moral imperative (III/13: "God's will is His essence" and "God is His [moral] attributes"[52]), and there is no truly human life but the radical fulfillment of this imperative.[53]

Following Maimonides' works in their biographical sequence as we have done can convey the impression that his ethical views developed throughout his life from a more simplistic Aristotelian to a more sophisticated Platonizing *imitatio* theory.[54] The facts tend to rebut such an impression, however—with the possibly exception of the truly early *Millot HaHigayon.*[55] Just about everything in Maimonides' *Eight Chapters,*[56] *Commentary to the Mishneh,* and *Code* can be shown to be entirely compatible with the mature reasoning of the *Guide* that we have now arrived at, and Maimonides cross-refers to the former works throughout and frequently—though, to be sure, in the earlier writings his full theory crops up only, as it were, interstitially, in the episodic fashion which their popular, exegetical, or legal character calls for.

Thus, for example, Maimonides states explicitly in his Introduction to *Eight Chapters* (much as this is overlooked or disregarded by commentators and historians) that (Aristotelian) morality is only to serve as the foundation for the higher level of *chassidut* (that is, *Eight Chapters* is, of course, the "introduction" to *Chapters of the Fathers*) and that, indeed, even *chassidut* is to be topped off by "prophecy" (in chapter VII). And Ibn-Tibbon, in his preface to the translation, rightly refers to and at considerable length argues the details of *Guide* III/54 as the consummation of *Eight Chapters* (very much in the manner that we have employed here).

As another example, it is not at all difficult to construct the same metaethic that we have now inferred from the *Guide* with equal rigor from "The Laws of Repentance" in the *Code*. The *Code* 10:1, 5 lays down the obligation to ascend from a prudential ethics ("out of fear") to a deontological ethics ("out of love")—the latter being unavailable to the *homo philosophicus* ("sage") because they are obtained as religious facts, "commanded by God."[57] This is, however, a strikingly sophisticated deontology, as is illustrated by the fact that its "duties" are duties of love (to the point of quoting erotic verses from the *Song of Songs*; 10:3). This love seeks "union" (misunderstood by the *Kessef Mishneh*) with its beloved God through *imitatio* (10:3f.). Such *imitatio* results from that "knowledge" ("knowledge" = connubial love in Biblical Hebrew) "by which He can be known . . . as much as possible."[58] (Herewith ends "The Laws of Repentance," 10:6). In short, in this book as in the *Guide*, the ethics of the mean is to be transcended, really sublated, by an ethic of imitation procured by rational procedures.[58a]

Indeed, even well-known Halakhic conundra in Maimonides can be resolved by means of the ethical axiology of his which we have educed. It is notorious that in *Guide* III/41, 50, he interprets the Biblical principle of "an eye for an eye" literally. This blatantly contradicts not only operative Talmudic law but also the emphatic Mishnaic prohibition to suggest that the Bible ever could have meant anything like that in the first place.[59] It also contradicts, as it cannot help but do, his own legal codification in "Laws of Him who Hurts and Damages," 1:2-6 (although even here the literal interpretation is alluded to) and an explicit statement in the Introduction to his *Commentary to the Mishneh*. The legal difficulties in which he became embroiled as a result can be observed in the flurry of debates about this among all his commentators. The question is why he ever took the risk of putting forward his purely theoretical speculation in the first place—knowing, of course, full well that *de facto* he would have to come out as everybody else does. I suggest that the answer is that the Rambam in effect says this: according to the low-level Aristotelian ethics of the mean, commutative justice requires precise retribution, and thus the Bible is philosophically right with its literal *lex talionis*; on the higher rational level with its ethics of divine imitation, however, which is, of course, the ethics of the Torah, the law acts in accordance with God's leniency and reduces "an eye for an eye" to "the value of an eye."[60]

In the course of Maimonides' development of a full-blown rational ethic a second strain of Aristotelian ethics has also been outgrown. For the Athenian Aristotle, ethics are largely "aesthetic rather than legal."[61] One "looks," as it were, at the existing vices and makes an "aesthetic judgment" as to where between the two vices the virtue lies.[62] *Kalos* then means both "beautiful" as well as generally and ethically "value-laden."[63] The moral imperative is not expected to "give orders" but to "put in order," that is, to make a beautiful arrangement of existing social conditions.

Maimonides, too, had set out to construct his ethic in precisely this manner. Beginning in his most youthful work, moral concepts are *mephursamot,* not cognitive concepts but matters of common consent (*consensus gentium*) that can differ from society to society.[64] Throughout he expects simple people to discover and to obey the demands of morality in this manner. But once people have reached a higher level of understanding they also discover a higher ethic by means of the more sophisticated and "scientific" (that is, cognitive) method of *imitatio Dei.*

Here we must carefully read *Guide* I/2 together with II/30. I/2 is almost universally misinterpreted as claiming that before "the Fall" man was in a nonmoral, purely "theoretical" (that is, intellectual, metaphysical) condition.[65] But this is definitely not Maimonides' point. He specifically refers to the divine "command" of *Gen.* 2:16f., issued before the Fall, thus making it clear that also prelapsarian man was a moral being. "Because of this [our intellect, bestowed by God] he was given commandments. . . . For commandments are not given to beasts and beings devoid of intellect." Before the Fall man learned what it is good and what it is bad to do by means of intellect rather than as a matter of social *mores*; morality was a question of precise truth and falsehood rather than of approximate and quasi-aesthetic "good and bad" in the sense of "pleasant and unpleasant." And the human intellect is, of course, the conceptualizing, cognitive ability which, as the very opening and preceding chapter of the work proclaims (*Guide* I/1), constitutes man's *imago Dei.*[66] Only after the Fall, that is, after forces began to determine humanity other than and inferior to reason, morality also became a matter inferior to reason, namely a matter of established social *mores* (*mephursamot*), with their aesthetic, proximate, and mean qualities. "He, therefore, disobeyed the commandment that was imposed on him by virtue of his intellect" (in favor of using his senses).[67] The gap that was opened between God and humanity by the Fall, that is, by the partial loss of their intellectual bond, can now be bridged only through the reacquisition of this intellectual bond, by philosophical endeavors.[67a] Philosophy "reinstaures" "actualized," "acquired" intellect and through this direct access to God. By means of philosophy the human potential ("hylic") intellect is "realized" and thus conjoined to the Active Intellect (in effect, God). In this way, too, God is re-cognized again, recognized, as He was before the Fall and thus as the model for *imitatio.*[68] Thus also the "scientific" and transcendental status of ethics is rehabilitated to the condition which it possessed before the Fall. We have returned from "conventions" to actional divine attributes through what must be called a lapsarian ethic or an eschatological epistemology.[69]

Thus, cognitive ethics are logically prior to conventionalistic ethics, though chronologically people acquire conventional ethics before they can go on to cognitive ones. Another way of saying this is that the ethics of *imitatio* are logically prior to the ethics of the mean, although actual human experience proceeds in the opposite direction.[71]

Guide II/30 has rightly been called "this very obscure chapter"; it may well be the intentionally most opaque chapter in the whole work. (Compare what Maimonides says about "the work of Creation" in his general introduction to the whole *Guide.*) However, when one has succeeded in unraveling it (with the help of the classic commentators), one can see that it explicates further and reconfirms the thesis of I/2 which we have just educed. To begin with, in original Creation (in the universe as God intended it to be, before the Fall) everything was, of course, in perfect condition. Thus also we were creatures whose sensuousness was ruled completely by reason ("androgyny"), and "the good" was intellectually known to be "practicable" and enduring (rather than the changeable and diverse *consensi gentium* that create *mephursamot*). Shemtov, in his commentary epilogue to this chapter, adds the implied Sabbath-commandment of *Gen.* 2:1f. to the prohibition of *Gen.* 2:16f. as proof that prelapsarian man was also an ethical, indeed an intellectually ethical creature; and he adds that what was "very good' about the creation of man was that he was endowed with reason and will, so that by these latter means he would act morally. Then the feminine half of androgynous man, which is to say his sensuousness,[71a] made itself independent of the male half, which is to say his intellect, thus absolutizing itself, by eating, which is to say using only the bodily powers with respect to the forbidden tree of the knowledge of good and bad (= pleasant and unpleasant = *mephursamot*), and thence forward morality could only be attained in the form of empirical conventions by empirical means. From this "Fall" the Jew rises through the Sinaitic Torah, while humanity in general also rises through the universal equivalent of Torah, which is to say intellect (rational philosophy). When this restoration has been accomplished man has left behind again "the tree of [empirical and, therefore, finite] knowledge" and once more nourishes himself on "the tree of [intellectual and, therefore, immortal] life." (Compare *Guide* I/15 for the use of "Jacob's ladder" as the metaphor of man's descent and rise on the rungs of reason.[71b]) Crescas rightly points out that the ethics of the tree of life are *musskalot* (*intellecta*, intelligibles), rather than *mephursamot*, and Ephodi speaks of "doing the deeds of the intellect." Seth reunites the sensuousness of his mother Eve under the governance of his father Adam's intellect, and he can thus resume the practice of *imitatio*: he models himself on the image of Adam (*Gen.* 5:3), who models himself on the image of God. By way of what might then be called an *imitatio imitationis Dei* the ethics of divine perfectionism have been reconstituted. (This is also how in "The Laws of Beliefs," 6:2 *imitatio Dei* for the masses is explained—as imitation of "the sages," the men of philosophical understanding, who in turn emulate God directly.) As Crescas then correctly summarizes it: "Seth is the true human reason that attains to the knowledge of God and strives for the knowledge of the Torah and for observance of the commandments and reaches true knowledge through his actions. . . ."[72]

What might be called "the *Heilsgeschichte* of ethical knowledge" is then described in this diagram:

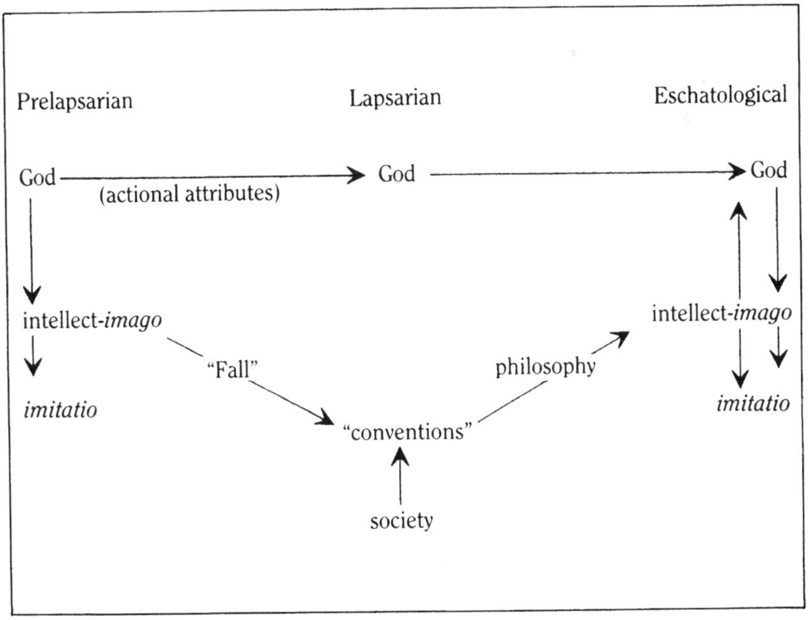

Having thus explicated *Guide* II/30, it must still be admitted that it is chock-full of esotericisms. What "secret" does it disguise? Clearly it is the thesis that Torah = reason = philosophy provides the higher ethic—not any of the ideas which Leo Strauss believes to be Maimonides' "secret doctrine."[73] It must also be admitted that here as well as throughout Maimonides' work, as well as among his best commentators, the doctrine that the higher rational ethics of *imitatio Dei* is the *ultima ratio* of both philosophy and revealed religion is heavily underplayed. But, then, this is the point of esotericism, and, in view of the revolutionary nature of the truth here expounded, we too can easily sympathize with the desire to disguise it.

If we now look back and survey the elaboration of this entire theory of ethics we can observe that Maimonides has in fact worked his way back from Aristotle's doctrine of the mean and of a radical but purely theoretical, contemplative *imitatio Dei* to an essentially Platonic posture.[74] The God of Plato, the highest idea, "the idea of ideas," possesses two features that Aristotle's God lacks; he is, in the first place, identified with "the good" (morality).[75] And, in the second place, this idea, like all of Plato's "ideas," is constructed ultimately on the mathematical pattern, that is, precise rather than, like Aristotle's ethical model, approximate.[76] Thus Maimonides' *imitatio* now possesses these two features: it is certainly practical, rather than theoretical, and it enables him to expound in the *Guide*, however esoterically and problematically, the thesis that the morality embodied in Jewish Law is totally rational rather than either aesthetically proximate or theologically suprarational.[77]

Aristotle had ultimately to find the standards of morality in empirical society, and, therefore, he taught a morality that conforms to a given society. Maimonides, on the contrary, derives his ethics from a God who is not only a God of reason but also *toto coelo* different from any and every given society and whose "will" (the criterion of the moral good) is thus bound to be and in fact is qualitatively different from what in fact is the case. Aristotelian ethics of the mean may then be regarded as an adaptation to the world as it is, while Platonic-Maimonidean ethics of *imitatio* are then world-changing, world-reforming.[78] It turns out that, whether one is Moses ben Maimon or Karl Marx, if one wants "to go to the roots,"[79] philosophy impels one to change rather than merely to understand the world.[80]

In line with the Platonically gained cognitiveness and consequent quasi-mathematical preciseness of ethics, both the philosophical ethics as well as the *Halakhah* of Maimonides acquire an entirely different *timbre* from what could otherwise have been hoped for from an Aristotelian ethic of the mean.

Imitatio Dei more geometrico revolves around the *terminus technicus: middah*. In theology this term is usually rendered as "[divine] attribute." The divine attributes are in all of Jewish literature pre-eminently moral qualities—*a fortiori* Maimonides' "attributes of action." Their purpose is to be emulated by humans, and, thus, when referred to humans, *middah* means "moral quality" or "virtue" (*Guide* I/54). A good classical as well as English term that will then adequately cover both "attribute" and "virtue" and thus fully do justice to *middah* would be "method" (as in "the methods [middot] of Biblical hermeneutics"). *Middah* is thus the method, or rule, of God's behavior and of man's imitation thereof. The Hebrew root means "to measure"; many Biblical, Talmudic, and medieval uses of the word *middah* exemplify this quantitative connotation.[81] Thus it is really "mathematical method." God's ethical quality is the infinite ideal on which men are to pattern their actions; they can do this all the way from zero to "the best of their power"[82] on the ladder of *ma'alot* ("rungs" = virtues).

As for the nature of the *Halakhah*, Maimonides can now claim it to be rational *in toto*—not only the traditionally rational *mishpatim* ("laws") but also the *chukkim* ("statutes")[82a] and even all their finest details (*Guide* III/26, 50, and commentaries).[83] "The Laws of Unlawful Use of Sacred Property," 8:8, puts it very sharply: "*Mishpatim* ('laws') are those injunctions whose reasons are known to us .... *Chukkim* ('statutes') are those injunctions whose reasons are not [yet] known to us."[84]

It would have been easier for Maimonides had he left the technical details of the law as unratiocinated empirical givens. This would have squared not only with Aristotle's proximate ethics but also with the preponderance of Jewish tradition, which frowns on the radical rationalization of *chukkim* and legal specificities. Instead he risked his good standing in philosophical and religious circles in the service of what may be called, with equal justice, ethical rationalism or rational ethics.[85]

In summary we can speak of lower, social, median ethics and of higher, philosophical, rational, radical ethics. On the level of the former Aristotle and the *vulgus* move; on the level of the latter Plato and Torah meet. The higher ethics are occasionally referred to explicitly as "philosophical ethics" or "philosophical moral habits."[86] Also, what appears otherwise as a possible self-contradiction within that same paragraph of chapter II of *Eight Chapters*[87] here finds its explanation: reason is not directly related to good-and-bad in the social sense, unlike the appetitive soul, but reason is so related *via* "beliefs," that is, through knowledge of God, which is in turn ethical. As Altmann suggests, "Maimonides stands solidly in [the] Aristotelian-Plotinian tradition" of, especially, al-Farabi and Avicenna,[87a] in which there is also and especially a will of the intellect.

We have now in effect rehabilitated and further strengthened Hermann Cohen's interpretation of Maimonides' philosophical ethics. Shlomoh Pines attacks Cohen in the following passage:[88] *Guide* III/54 "has sometimes [sic] been interpreted as meaning that—in contradiction to the whole trend of his thought and to many definite assertions occurring in the *Guide* and even in the chapter in question[89]—Maimonides at the end adopted the quasi-Kantian idea that the ordinary [?] moral virtues and moral actions are of greater importance and value than the intellectual virtues and the theoretical way of life. It seems to me . . . that this explanation is completely false." The only evidence which Pines seems to offer for his assertion is the fact that Maimonides has a doctrine of *'ormah 'elokit* ("divine deceit"), which Pines/Strauss take to mean that for Maimonides God equals Nature (Spinoza), behaves "wilily," even ruthlessly—in any case, immorally. But this argument does not succeed.[89a] *The PinesStraussian equation, God equals Nature, is obtained only by means of infinitely malleable methods of esotericist exegesis,*[90] and the notion of "divine deceit" is much better understood in the historical line of moral-practical reason from the legal *'ormah* and *ha'aramah* of the Talmud[91] through Kant's "as if" to the neo-Kantian "legal fiction."

Pines also misinterprets *Guide* I/2. (It is hard to make out whether this is because he does not want to end up having to accept Cohen's general interpretation or vice-versa.) In "Some Traits of Christian Theological Writing in Relation to Moslem *Kalam* and to Jewish Thought,"[92] he claims—wrongly, as do so many others on this point—that for Maimonides there were no ethics before the Fall[93] (actually, there were not, as we have seen, sub-rational, infra-intellectual ethics) and that, generally, "Maimonides had what appears to be a lower opinion of moral judgments" than the Greek commentator on Aristotle, John Philoponus, with whom he there deals.[94] We have seen that this claim is false. It also contradicts what Pines himself had perceptively pointed out in his introduction to the *Guide*,[95] that, if anything, Maimonides affirmed the ultimacy of ethics even more than Plato himself, for Plato's visionary of the sun of ideas returns, after all, to the cave of phenomenal shades. One might add, the man who has come into the throne-room does not leave it again (*Guide* III/51).

It is as difficult to understand Pines as Rawidowicz: why do they strain so hard to argue against Cohen? Pines agrees that Maimonides has "a doctrine concerning the imitation of God that may be all his own,"[96] and he exposits this "saintly, elitist" ethics along the lines blocked out by Cohen: " . . . The theoretical life['s] . . . superiority was proclaimed by Aristotle. However, Maimonides is at pains to show—and this seems to be a Platonic element in his doctrine—that the theoretical life [can be combined with] a life of action. . . . What is more, a life of action [can] constitute an imitation of God."[97] He even realizes that a historical politics of *imitatio* rather than of Aristotelian prudence results from such an ethic of imitation.[98] And the only trouble with this statement of Pines is the supererogatory use of *modus ponens* here and the failure to show how Maimonides' method of *imitatio* is worked out in a rigorous, rational, philosophical manner. One suspects that what lies underneath this unnecessary polemic against Cohen is a Straussian insistence on neo-Conservative politics of "realism" as over against Cohen's politics of ethical socialism.[99]

There is still at least one large gap left between an ethic that is not only radical but also universal and Maimonides' formulation of ethics. Maimonides is conscious of the fact that he has hitherto stipulated a double-tiered meta-ethic—one for the *ignobile vulgus, hoi polloi*, in which a morality of the mean obtains, and the other a morality for the spiritual elite (*chassidim*), where *immitatio Dei* and its radicalism are practiced. Philosophically the latter is the ideal and more desirable, but practically the former is also viable. Now, this is a "highly conservative, if not reactionary" social class-ideology.[100] For Aristotle class-ethics was no problem: it was in fact tailor-made for the class-society of ancient Athens and specifically for the "gentlemen-philosophers," if not philosopher-kings, of this state, who could devote themselves to non-practical *theoria*.[101] For a Biblical religion, however, in which the belief prevailed that "Moses commanded us Torah as the inheritance of the entire congregation of Jacob" (*Deut.* 33:4) and in which "all Israel have a share in the world-to-come" (*Aboth*, motto), even a social and intellectual aristocrat like Maimonides had to build some sort of bridge to his less distinguished compatriots. An elitist theory of ethics is bound to be ultimately untenable in such a context.[102] This will be even more the case in the *Mishneh Torah*, where the Rambam is not expounding personal philosophical views, as in his other writings, but making authoritative *Halakhic* claims. Thus the force of classical Jewish values is bound to mitigate, if not actually to countermand, Greek class-ethics,[103] and Maimonides is confronted with the ideological necessity of, as it were, having to universalize his elitist ethics of saintly *imitatio* so that it will encompass and absorb his populist ethic of the mean.[104]

One method which Maimonides uses to carry out this task is well-established in the secondary literature. This method is contained in his famous "Thirteen Principles of Faith." Salvation is obtained, as we have seen, by dint of philosophical knowledge, but since most cannot be expected to acquire such knowledge, and yet since "all Israel" is divinely destined to attain to salvation, a way must be found of providing this salvific philosophical knowledge to Israel in some popularly digestible form—and this is what the "Thirteen Principles of Faith" offer. They occur then also in precisely the right place—the end of his lengthy philosophical introduction to *perek chelek* and the proper conceptual underpinning to the motto with which the text itself begins: "All Israel has a share in the world-to-come."[105]

A second, perhaps more important but much less noticed, method which the Rambam employs in order to universalize his elitist philosophical ethics for all Israel at least (and for everyone ultimately) is his very unconventional Messianology.[106]

It is a well-known truism that Maimonides' eschatology as presented in the last and climactic chapters of the *Code*, "The Laws of the Kings," chapters 11f., is an unusually sober, realistic, and moderate one.[107] He there depicts the Messianic state without resort to miracles or other apocalyptic features. It is instead a world essentially like the present, though, to be sure, quantitatively much improved (11:3, 12:1f.). The very last sentence of the *Mishneh Torah* then reads as follows:

> In that time there will be no famine or war and no envy or strife—the good will be much poured-out and luxuries as commonplace as dust. The preoccupation of the whole world will be nought but only to know God; therefore, Israel will be great sages, knowledgeable in the things that are at present hidden, who will have attained the knowledge of their Creator to the humanly greatest possible degree—as it is said (*Is.* 11:9): "For the earth will be full of the knowledge of God as the waters cover the sea."

In plain English, philosophy ("knowledge") will no longer be the restricted bailiwick of the philosopher-aristocrats, but, as a consequence of the socio-economic prosperity which will then prevail everywhere, all Israel—and, indeed, ultimately "the whole world"—will "know God"—"know," that is, in the sense of the primacy of moral reason which we have earlier seen to be the only manner in which He is knowable at all. All Israel, without distinction between *hoi polloi* and sages, will adhere to the radical ethics of *imitatio Dei*. (Here then also our original intuition that Jewish Messianism is powered by too radical a thrust to permit a fusion with Aristotelian temperance has been vindicated.)

In the *Guide* there is next to no Messianological discussion. The little that does occur, and this only by allusion, restates the chief point of the end of the *Code*. In III/11, Maimonides also argues, citing *Is.* 11, that the "knowledge" of God which will be universal under the reign of the Messiah will abolish human immorality. But this was alltogether too subtle for Maimonides' opponents. When they accused him of implicit heresy for having neglected eschatology and Messianology in his philosophical *summa*, he wrote his famous *Treatise on Resurrection*. Here he appears to be making up for what is missing in the *Guide*. But in fact he continues to speak an extraordinarily careful language.[108] The eschatology which we have briefly educed from the *Code* is retained in its entirety; it is now only more highly articulated and complex.[109]

Men live and die. At the end of normal history there will be a Messianic reign, during which they will live better and longer because of improved conditions,[110] but otherwise very much as usual. The Messianic generation and the Messiah himself will, in turn, die, as do all men,[111] and then God's "miraculous will" will bring about the resurrection. This aeon of the resurrection, too, is this-worldly and material. In it we will be perfected by means of reward and punishment for our first lives[112] and, in effect, by all becoming philosophers. Philosophy is identical with the "hidden, esoteric" truth of Revelation,[113] and this truth is ultimately ethical: "Examine your deeds ... that their activities always be concerned with the improvement (or deterioration) of their affairs." This-worldliness, ethics and politics, not metaphysics, "is the greatest of all miracles."[114] This applies to Jews and Gentiles alike: "God gave the Torah to man ... in all the earth,"[115] for not only "all Israel" but "all the righteous of the nations of the world have their share in the world-to-come."[116] Through this moralization of their lives in the aeon of the resurrection men conjoin their acquired intellects "as much as possible"[117] with the deity. Contrary to the belief of the fools, "ideas" (*de'ot*, morals) are, of course, much more real than *physis*,[118] and the life of mind, because immaterial, is infinite—ergo immortality. In this manner, by increasing ethical spiritualization the aeon of material resurrection glides imperceptibly into the final aeon of immaterial, spiritual *olam haba*, in which there is external immortality.[119] And this, then, is the ultimate state of affairs: mere human beings have been transformed into eternal thinkers, the people of the mean have turned into emulators of the deity, finite human lives have become infinite moral intellects and thus conjoined to the Active Intellect, bodies have become spiritual, and the world-to-come has absorbed the present world.[120] This ultimate human condition exceeds even the Paradaisical state. It is not a "return" but the ultimate forward-movement. As E. Levinas points out,[120a] "Eden" is beyond where Adam lived. And Moses, as the angelic "pure reason," is, as the proto-type of Messianic man, the eschatological perfection of man which Adam only forecast.

This eschatological scenario of Maimonides displays a large number of extraordinary features. The one that probably strikes the eye most is the thesis that everyone lives in fact not two but three lives: the original terrestrial existence, then resurrected this-worldly existence, and eventually eternal, spiritual, ethico-intellectual life in the world-to-come. But I want to point out two other features.

All Jews, not to speak of non-Jews, will be lifted from the level of *ignobile vulgus* to that of *chassidim* by dint of going through the trials and benefits of the aeon of the resurrection. Thus the Aristotelian picture of the world, in which society remains essentially always the same and internally equibalanced as among its various permanent classes, has now been radically upset.[120b] The historical—and even the extra-historical, eschatological—thrust of Maimonides' Judaism has overcome Aristotelian inertia in the course of transforming ethics from an immanently social concern into a radical, transcendent (or even transcendental) propadeutic to the Kingdom of God. At this juncture, Maimonides' "realism" in Messianism, which at first seems conservative, turns out to have revolutionary implications, for it makes his Messianic doctrine practical in worldly conduct rather than supporting "eschatological delay."[121]

What was said earlier about the philosophic relationship between virtually all of Maimonides' works must here be repeated: the *Epistle on Resurrection* says nothing that is not also said *in nuce* in, for instance, the *Code*. This can be shown not only from the last two chapters of the closing "Laws of the Kings," as we have already done, but also, for example, from the introductory "Laws of Repentance," chapters 8. Here, too, the Messianic reign endows humanity—all nations, not only Israel—with the metaphysical and rational knowledge by virtue of which they enter into the post-Messianic world-to-come (8:7, 9:2). That world-to-come is not "coming" in the sense that it is not yet in existence but rather in that humanity has to come to, grow into it (8:8). Time is, in any case, an accident of motion, and it cannot, therefore, be predicated of the world-to-come, which is purely spiritual and thus eternal (8:1ff.).[122]

Another passage in the *Code* ("The Laws of the Sabbatical and Jubilee Years," 13:12f.[123]) expounds the same doctrine—and perhaps even more majestically.

> 12: [The tribe of Levi] . . . was set apart ['distinguished'] to worship God, to serve Him, and to teach His straight ways and His righteous laws to the multitude, as it is said (*Deut.* 33:10): 'They are to teach Thy laws to Jacob and Thy Torah to Israel.' Therefore, they were set apart from the ways of the world by . . . not benefitting themselves physically . . . 13. But not only the tribe of Levi but rather every single man among all creatures in the world [*kol ish v'ish mikol ba'ay 'olam*] whose spirit has inspired him and whose knowledge has convinced him to set himself apart and to stand before God, to serve Him and to worship Him, to know God, and who walks straightly as the Lord has made him and who has broken off his neck the yoke of the many calculations which human beings pursue [compare *Ecc.* 7:29: "Only see this: I have found that the Lord has made man straight, but they pursue many calculations"], behold he, too, is sanctified as the holy of holies, and God will be his portion and his inheritance forever and for ever and ever, and in this world he will have the benefit of sufficiency for him, as is the case with the priests and the Levites. This is what David, peace upon him, intended when he said [*Ps.*

16:5]: "God is the portion of my inheritance and of my cup. Thou upholdest my lot."

In view of our earlier systematic exposition we need not engage in textual exegesis here but can content ourselves with a catechistic summary of the doctrines clearly enshrined in this passage. Non-material "knowledge of God" comprises on the lower level "straight ways" = "human calculations" = "the ways of the world," that is, the ethics of Aristotle, and on the higher level "the righteous laws" of the Torah. Together these provide a "sufficiency" for this-worldly existence and, above all, immortality. This salvific knowledge of God is emphatically not restricted to any elite—Levitical, Jewish, or otherwise—but is to be provided for what Maimonides not only explicitly refers to as "the multitude" but goes far out of his way to describe in no mistakable or negligible language as "every single person among all worldly creatures." No Jewish authority could conceivably go further than to call all human beings who have reached this stage the "holy of holies."[124]

In our analysis of the relationship between the doctrine of the mean and that of *imitatio Dei* in Maimonides it has been a temptation to identify the former not with Aristotle alone but with Greek philosophy in general and to identify the doctrine of radical *imitatio* with Maimonides' religious, Bible-derived, Jewish posture. It has turned out, however, that this would be too schematic and apologetically facile an analysis. Instead we have to say that Maimonidean Judaism, in its effort to marry Greek philosophy with Biblical religion, was in the end forced to dissociate itself from Aristotelian, median ethics because of the ineluctible requirements of Jewish ethicism and populism and to align itself instead with that part of the Greek inheritance which was permanently molded by the mind of Plato. As David Shapiro puts it: "Without doubt the *imitatio Dei* of Plato is much closer to the outlook of Judaism than that of Aristotle . . ."[125]

By the same token also the meta-political theory of Maimonides is quintessentially a fusion of Plato with Jewish Messianism. The historians declare in concert[126] that it was more than an historical accident that among Jews and Moslems Plato's *Republic* and *Laws* increasingly became the pillar on which they rested their political philosophy, while in the Christian West these works remained unknown—there political theory derived from Aristotle's *Ethics* and *Politics*. In Maimonides, political theory is structured analogously with his theory of ethics: even as the individual moral agent begins with a prudential ethic of the mean and progresses to a transcendental ethic of *imitatio Dei*, so government, too, starts out by merely keeping the antisocial hounds at bay but soon rises to *imitatio Dei* by the ruler and eventually also by the populace (*Guide* I/34 end and 54, end). That is to say, at first what are merely social regulations, *mephursamot* or human *nomoi*, restrain the "war of all against all"; but this war is ultimately extirpated by the law of "Revelation." The latter is concerned not only with the physical but also with the spiritual well-being of mankind, and this total concern is legally enacted by means of God's Torah or philosophically with its equivalent, namely *imitatio Dei* (*Guide* II/40). Government becomes at this point a function of "prophecy," that is, of instituting divine values on earth,[127] for prophets are those men, most preeminently Moses is the man, who convey through the faculty of the imagination the truths of the intellect which transfer divine behavior to the worldly scene (*Guide* II/35).[128] Maimonides uses Platonic ideas, then, precisely as Kant was later to claim[129] they should be rightly understood—not as metaphysical *onta* but as historical regulatives. And Diesendruck's Cohennian claim[130] is borne out: for Maimonides the Torah is ultimately a futuristic, infinite, radical, and regulative ideal. The Platonic "philosopher-king" has been transmuted into the "saint-king." As Leo Strauss rightly puts it,[131] what the *Laws* are in Plato, the Torah is for Maimonides.

Ours is then not only an ethically but also a socio-politically radical understanding of Maimonides' individual and social ethics. It follows that we must agree with one half of Leo Strauss' exegesis and disagree with the other half. We agree that Maimonidean/Jewish classical philosophy is quintessentially an ethico-political enterprise. After all, even the *Chapters of the Fathers* in the *Mishnah* revolve around the ethics of judges, that is, social ethics, and, therefore, so necessarily does Maimonides' *Commentary*.[131a] Every student of the subject must be indebted to Strauss for having crystalized this recognition. It can be summarized no better than by Strauss' reminder that Solomon Maimon spoke of the *Guide for the Perplexed* as a *theologia politica*.[132] What we must emphatically disagree with results from Strauss' stubborn insistence on reading his own theologico-political ideology into the classical texts. His thesis is the "moderation will protect us against the dangers of visionary expectations from politics and unmanly contempt for politics"[133] (a thoroughly Greek sentence!).

Thus, as a matter of widely unnoticed fact, Leo Strauss' entire immensely erudite, complex, and stimulating—though ultimately wrong-headed—work turns significantly on the question treated in the present study. Maimonides and Hermann Cohen are at the heart of it. We can only sketch the broad outline of the debate here.

According to Strauss' own view, the thesis that "moderation" is the supreme philosophical-political virtue is undergirded by the theological truth that, contrary to the spirit of the modern "enlightenment," reason cannot be, and was not believed to be by the classical authors, adequate to Revelation. As a result of this worldly life—the life of reason—may not be expected to become, or to be made, perfect, since perfection is a quality reserved for supernatural subject. Therefore, social life is at best a bad bargain, and conservative "law and order" are the highest political values.

Strauss recognized not only the centrality of political concerns in classical philosophy but also that in Semitic culture Plato was accepted as serving this purpose better than Aristotle.[134] He acknowledged his indebtedness on this score to Cohen. His *Philosophie und Gesetz, Beiträge zum Verständnis Maimunis und seiner Vorläufer*[135] begins with a sentence that quotes Cohen and ends in the same way;[136] indeed, it ends with an extended argument against Cohen's interpretation of the primacy of ethics over metaphysics.[137]

Strauss is simply wrong, however, in his claim that for Maimonides the "law," which is the substance of the *polis* for Jewish and Moslem thinkers, is suprarational.[138] The refutation of this claim, too, can only be sketched here. That men do not know in what the rationality of the law consists does not, according to Maimonides, mean that there is no such rationality.[139] In any case, though we may be now ignorant of such rationality, this does not mean that we shall be ignorant. Maimonides regularly qualifies such ignorance with the phrase "to this day" (for example, *Guide* III/45f.). And though the *ignobile vulgus* may not know all the reasons for all aspects of the law, the *illuminati* certainly do, or at least they can.[140] The very opposite of what Strauss wants to argue is in fact the case: for the great medieval Jewish rationalists (Saadia, Maimonides, Gersonides, etc.) reason = Revelation; from Revelation one could, therefore, derive everything in reason, and equally from reason one could derive everything in Revelation. This is the "secret" of Maimonides' esotericism, not, as Strauss argues, that the Torah is sublated in theoretical philosophy.[141] (This claim of Strauss would, in any case, seem to contradict his other claim, that Revelation is suprarational.)

Strauss is also wrong in limiting Maimonides' eschatology to the most conservative interpretation of "The Laws of the Kings," chapters 11f. (They are conservative enough on any interpretation.) Instead, he should have gone on, as we have shown, to the *Treatise on Resurrection*.[142] In this area the "secret" cannot be and is not, contrary to Strauss, the guarded treasure of a philosophical or any other elite. Political conservatism, in the sense of the rule of the (few) wise and of the trusting obedience of the multitude, is overcome by the power of Maimonides' Jewish populism and Messianism.

In short, when one retains those important points on which Strauss is right and corrects those on which he is wrong, one sees the Maimonidean philosophy is quintessentially ethical and political, that this ethico-political philosophy is rational through and through and that this rational philosophy of social ethics is radically world-changing.

What have we obtained then as a result of our analysis of Maimonides' philosophical ethics that we are not likely to have been aware of before?

We can now be sure that, for reasons of religious/Jewish moral perfectionism and using an essentially Platonizing approach, Maimonides teaches an ethic of Aristotelian moderateness only as an initial and lower stage of ethics. This is still an ethic derived from and thus bound to existing society. From this he goes on to a higher and ultimate stage of moral radicalism, which is determined by *imitatio Dei*. Here moral reason, not sociology, defines the good. The transition from the lower to the higher stage is in fact a cognitive achievement, that is, by coming "to know God" men come to act as God acts, or, to put it differently, philosophy reverses "the Fall of Adam" and messianically rehabilitates prelapsarian perfect man. This, then, is an eschatological, or regulative, ethical epistemology, which, as such, also extends the values of the full knowledge of "the good" to all men universally. If one were to try to bring all this into one short formula for the Maimonidean categorical imperative it might be this: learn to know (philosophical-rationally or religiously) how God acts so as to emulate Him, and spread this knowledge to all humanity to the same end.

– 9 –

Jean-Paul Sartre as Jew*

Introduction

There has long been a large Jewish apologetic literature about "x (anybody or anything whatsoever) and the Jewish question" (whatever that may be)—much so that there is a very old joke about it: a scientific academy put up a prize for the best study of elephants; the French entry was, of course, entitled "The Love Life of the Elephant," the Russian: "The Soul of the Elephant." the German: "Authority in the Elephant Community," and the Jewish: "Elephants and the Jewish Question."[1] Talking about "Sartre on Jews" will inevitably have some characteristics of that type of literature. I shall reduce them as much as possible. In any case, with respect to Sartre this kind of consideration is more legitimate than in most others, for reasons which will be explored and some of which are, anyway, generally well-known.

The phenomenon of the Jew is located even closer to the center of Sartre's works and life than is popularly realized—far beyond his well-known *Antisemite and Jew* (*Réflexions sur la question juive*).[2] My purpose will be to demonstrate that the way Sartre handles the Jewish phenomenon— mostly "the Jew" but eventually even Judaism—proves two important truths about his work: 1) his work displays much more continuity, and even unity, throughout his perfervid and checkered intellectual career than even he fully realized (not to speak of his critics),[3] and 2) the Jew embodies the most important truths of universal human existence as Sartre perceived them. In the end Sartre regarded himself, with no little justification, if not as a Jew then as a "Judaicist."

A good place to start is at the end—the three interviews with Sartre that his last associate, Benny Lévy, published in *Le Nouvel Observateur*, March 1980, very shortly before Sartre's death.[4] Especially the end of the third interview[5] is an astounding document, for our purposes in particular as well

---

*Parts of this study were read at the Washington University colloquium, "The Legacy of J.-P. Sartre," November 20,1980 and at Notre Dame University April 8, 1981.

as in general. It would be memorable as a statement about the significance of Judaism coming from anybody—*a fortiori* when it comes from Sartre.

It was always obvious that Sartre was a thoroughly moral person, not least with respect to everything Jewish: his fight against Nazism—his fight against all exploitation and oppression; his fight against antisemitism; his personal intimacy, even in the bosom of his most immediate family, with Jews (he met Arlette Elkay in Algeria c. 1957 and adopted her in 1965; his (albeit independent, critical) solidarity with the Jewish people in its contemporary struggles even when this created problems for him with other political allies on the Left and in the Third World, etc.[6] Lévy quotes Sartre's marvelous statement:[7] "I am more Jewish than they (the Jews)," in that Jews live in books, not in landscapes. (Compare Chapters of the Fathers 3:9: "Rabbi Jacob said: 'A man who walks down the road, studying, and who interrupts his study to exclaim: "How beautiful is that tree!" or "How beautiful is that furrow!"—Scriptures imputes it to him as though he had forfeited his soul.' ") But not until this very last significant statement of his to Lévy could one discover how absolutely decisive for Sartre's thinking not only Jews but even Judaism are, nor, for that matter, could one until then properly appreciate his radical eagerness always to learn anew.

Before getting down to brass tacks I want to state my general exegetical principle. There can be no reasonable ground for disputing the observation that Sartre proved to be, throughout a long, agitated and productive life, always a thoroughly honorable and serious man. He, therefore, has to be taken seriously. Anyone who has to be taken seriously deserves to have his work interpreted in the most favorable, consistent, and persuasive manner—*lekhaff z'khut*, as one says in Hebrew,—to have it "rationally reconstructed," in Stegmueller's phrase, even by interpreters, like myself, who may disagree with him on some fundamental principles and methods. It is facile to find fault with lots of things that Sartre said and did over eight decades, always intellectually and socially engaged with what was going on around him and always "up front" in deed and in word, but to react in such a manner is to behave like Hegel's and Goethe's famous butler: he concentrates on his master's foibles not because the master is not a master but because the butler is a butler. We can learn from Sartre if we try to understand him on the best possible reading,[8] if only because he tried honestly, though not always successfully or acceptably, to work his way out of the evils, confusions, and stupidities of our complex times.

The Last Interview

The new and striking thesis on "the Jewish question" in Sartre's last interview is that there is a positive, "metaphysical" and "profound Jewish reality" all its own.[9] This reality of the trans-historical Jewish people refutes all of Hegelian/Marxist philosophy of history. Lévy asks: "The history that Hegel put on our map wanted to get rid of the Jew, and it is the Jew who will allow us to get out of this history that Hegel wanted to impose on us?" and Sartre replies: "Absolutely ..." Compare, to the contrary, what Sartre wrote in his preparatory notes for the *Critique of Dialectical Reason*.[10] "If there is a history it is that of Hegel. There can be no other." Here he even imitates Hegel's historiography by omitting Judaism in the genealogy of Christianity, descended from Greek polytheism and Roman monotheism.[11] He goes on to argue, though, thus laying the foundation in 1947 for what he was to say in 1980, that the grand "totalization" of Hegel is, of course, bound to be disputed by other people's totalizations, thus turning every claim to a true historiography into a caricature,[12] and that progress comes about by "living the law" of "approaching the ideal of the project."[13] Of what does Hegelian historiography consist? Of the history of states. Into this Jewry does not fit.[14] Of what does Jewish history consist? Jewish history is produced, so asserts Sartre now, by commitment to the monotheistic God, whose "word" creates a metaphysical life and destiny.[15] This destiny is defined by its end (goal, purpose, *telos, eschaton*), and that telos is a totally new, different, ethical world—in traditional language, the Messianic kingdom of God on earth. Sartre adds, provocatively, that the Jewish conception of the Messianic kingdom is better than the Christian, because it is this-worldly, and on this ground he even professes his liking of the doctrine of the resurrection of the dead.[16] In *La cérémonie des adieux.* ...[17] Simone de Beauvoir reports that Sartre said:[18] "There is a future beyond death, which makes of death almost an accident in the life of the individual that continues without him. ... The maximum of real relations, which do not end in a future where I won't be anymore ... *Rapport* to the future, to hope, to a real life in a real society ... in my head." (She also reports, though in another connection,[19] that toward the end of his life Sartre regarded B. Lévy as his future and that without such a future he would already be dead.) In the *Nouvel Observateur* interview Sartre also prefers Jewish Messianism to the Marxist conception of ideal society, because, while the latter is held to evolve out of past history and is, therefore, afflicted with the wounds and determined by the evils of the past, in Jewish eschatological historiography it is the *summum bonum* that produces incremental truth and goodness in history—in other words, the "pro-jected" infinite future produces the past, not the other way around. The Messianic goal can be attained only through Messianic action, which in turn is defined by law.[20] In short, Messianism tries to remake the world ethically through permanent revolution.

(I want to state, as a serious student[21] of the history and conceptuality of Jewish Messianism, that I regard all this as an entirely correct and superbly formulated summary of the subject. Emmanuel Levinas—no stranger to this issue—therefore, entitled his eulogy on Sartre "A Language Familiar to Us.")[22]

At the tail end of the interview that we have just summarized there occurs what must appear as a curious literary *lapsus*:[23] having just completed his exposition of what he (rightly) regards as Jewish Messianism, Sartre, together with Lévy, suddenly skips to a brief discussion of his auto-biography—specifically what he calls two periods in his life when he was threatened by despair: the destructiveness of the war, and now (or then).

The reader asks: what is the connection (even merely conversationally) between these two subjects? Two answers suggest themselves. The first is explicated in the interview itself: Lévy reminds Sartre that Jews, out of their historical experience, distrust every mob, including revolutionary ones; terroristic violence can easily turn against the innocent; little wonder, therefore, that the hope at the end of the war turned into something approximating despair.[24] Thus, rather than place one's trust in revolutionary violence, we may have to look toward Kant's nonviolent, ethical search for the universal human community.[25] As Lévy puts it:[26] "Are you starting over again at the age of seventy-five . . . ?"

This sequentiality of the argument carries some conviction. But it is also obviously rather dragged in by the hair: the Jew is scarcely the only one on earth to have experienced the fickleness and brutality of men in revolt (what Sartre and Lévy called in felicitous French "*l'homme revolte*").[27] I suspect that something else, and something deeper, is at issue. Precisely the literary choppiness of Sartre's definition of Messianism turns out to be most authentically Jewish: Jewish Messianism is often misunderstood, even by Jews, as some sort of metaphysical, even fatuous, optimism—that things always get better and are bound in the end to lead to success, whereas what Sartre is here proposing is that one pursue the good the more for the invariable triumph of evil—thus, out of despair, because of one's realistic expectation of failure. (This explains the title of the interview: "Today's Hope." My colleague Herbert Spiegelberg correctly points out that "*L'espoir, maintenant . . .*" were better rendered as something like "Hope for the Nonce—in the teeth of history.")[28]

Relatively early in his work Sartre had once concretized the notion of such hopeless hope in a literary figure (a practice which is, of course, characteristic of all of his fiction)[29]—the figure of "Bariona."[30] In this nativity play, written in Stalag XIID in Treves, the Jew Bariona moves from self-defeating solo revolt to hopeless but joyous rebellion against the Romans. He starts out by denying the belief in hope and the future that his pregnant wife holds, but he ends by accepting that belief as a brave lie. Even here Sartre talks a good deal of Messianism and the Messianic kingdom. And in *Les Mouches* he said: "Human life begins on the other side of despair."

The classic and characteristic Jewish formulation of precisely this posture was arrived at in the famous conclusion of the long dispute between the Talmudic schools of Hillel and Shammai: "It were better that man had never been created, but, once created, let him be concerned with his moral life."[31] Jewish evidence for that stance abounds—from before *Ecclesiastes* through the Rabbinic principle that "the righteous have no reward in this world"[32] beyond the hymn at the doors of the gas ovens: "I believe with full faith in the coming of the Messiah, even though he tarry . . ."It was also reiterated in Th. Adorno's view of the necessary self-defeat of reason and that "the whole is the untruth."[33]

In sum, the connection between Sartre's discussion of Jewish Messianism and his subsequent discussion of his personal despair is his (correct) understanding that Jewish Messianic hope arises not in despite of, but because of historical despair.[34]

There is some controversy about how seriously one is to take Sartre's last statements. It is argued, for example, that Benny Lévy's own, somewhat belated, reidentification with Judaism has distorted his representation of Sartre's late thinking. (Since before his Maoist role in the Parisian rebellion of 1968 he had gone under the name of Pierre Victor, [if only to prevent his deportation as an Egyptian—as Bendit-Cohen was deported to Germany,] and only with the publication of these interviews did he publicly revert to his given name.) It is also argued that at the time of the interviews Sartre was no longer quite lucid—that what he said in them is incompatible with what he had believed, in one way or another, all of his life. Raymond Aron, for example, likes the last interviews and, therefore (!), cannot believe that Sartre could have meant them.[35] Aron was Sartre's model for "the authentic Jew" in *Antisemite and Jew*. The two broke shortly thereafter, however. Long before now Sartre had said about him.[36] "*Il travestit ma pensée pour mieux la contester*." And so he does still posthumously.)[37]

These arguments must be rejected, however. Jean Daniel testifies that Sartre expressed his pleasure at the publication of the interviews.[38] My colleague Michel Rybalka informs me that one of Sartre's last concerns, while already in the hospital, was the reception given to the interviews. Emmanuel Levinas, much of whose thought has always arisen in an aloud or silent dialogue with Sartre, rightly says:[39] "The interviews that Sartre gave several weeks before his death are extremely significant. They bring to us an echo of his last thoughts. We have no reason to doubt the exactness of the text." Lévy himself provides some tidbits of evidence for the philosophical continuity between

Sartre's earlier thought and his final statement.[40] I propose to provide much more, and much more substantial evidence, and I will even provide an explanation of why neither Sartre nor Lévy was conscious of the availability of that large-scale evidence.

In any case, the reliability of the relationship between Sartre and Lévy is quite beyond cavil: see *Situations X*, pp. 210-213, *Obliques*, 1978, p. 15, and, in the long interview with the editor of *Obliques*, M. Sicard, references to "my friend Pierre" and to the last, as yet unpublished book, *Power and Liberty*, his long-promised ethic, which the two produced in extended dialogue.[41]

Lévy left his considerable impact on Sartre all right—no doubt about that: Sartre is the first to declare this. But the result is not a misrepresentation or distortion of Sartre's actual thinking. It is a philosophical effect on Sartre, which resulted from the years of their association and of which Sartre was gratefully conscious. This can best be illustrated in Lévy's biting and, withal, loyal attack on Sartre in an article entitled "Apocalypse" in the previously cited special Sartre issue of Obliques.[42] (At the end of the article,[43] Lévy, then still "Victor", declares, while Sartre was very much around to belie it if it were untrue, that the views he presented even then were developed in years of dialogue with Sartre and that the latter approved of that article.) The curve of Sartre's own last development from existentialist Marxism to what must be called Jewish ethicism is here prefigured in Lévy's antiSartre argument. It is a move from "apocalypse" (i.e. terroristic violence, which may and does end in, among other things, Bolshevism)[44]to "Messianism" (i.e. ethics). (The distinction between apocalypticism and Messianism is entrenched in the critical history of religions.)[45] Lévy even recognizes the quintessentially Christian, albeit secularized, trinitarianism in Sartre's and others' conception of "the third-man argument:" the third man "objectifies" the relations between the two subjects, thus producing objectivity. About this Lévy says:[46] "This dyad capped by the third man—we know it. We have long been bugged by the trinity. We have fallen back into Hell." ("Hell is Other People.") "The third man is really the Holy Ghost."[47] "The third as the vicar of totality."[48] In fact, argues Lévy, an objective metaphysics is thus constructed, with a force and a dialectic of its own, which alienates and destroys man's humanity—subjectivity. This has to be eliminated, and "the primordially moral" (i.e. the Jewish and Kantian "primacy of practical reason") has to be put back in its place.[49]

In the same issue of *Obliques* Sartre[50] in effect pleads guilty to Lévy's indictment. He says: "In the end what counts is always morality. . . . I've never stopped being a moral philosopher." He laments what he calls "sociological ethics" (i.e. "the naturalistic fallacy" into which both Hegel and Marx fell), and he predicts that *Power and Liberty* will "leave nothing standing of *Being and*

Nothing and of the *Critique of Dialectical Reason*." In short, the authenticity of the Lévy interviews with Sartre cannot be reasonably inpugned.

There is also Simone de Beauvoir's *La cérémonie des adieux* ... The book is beautiful (if only for its title), and it is moving (if only for Sartre's death scene).[51] De Beauvoir is beautiful (if only for her lifelong devotion to Sartre), and she is touching (if only for her jealousy of Benny Lévy).

She clearly does not like Lévy; indeed, one gets the unmistakable impression that she resents Sartre's lateblooming friendship with him.[52] Further yet, though Sartre had been surrounded by lots of Jews all his life, when Arlette and Lévy belatedly studied Hebrew together and seemed to de Beauvoir to strengthen one another in influencing Sartre in a Jewish direction, one even gets the impression that de Beauvoir somehow feels left out in the non-Jewish cold.[53] Above all, she rejects the last interviews in *Le nouvel Observateur*.[54] But she does not really deny that Sartre's thinking at that latest period in his life was correctly reflected in them—she just disapproves of it, and she blames it on Lévy, on Lévy's own belated "conversion" to Judaism, and on Sartre's emotional and practical dependence on Lévy.

Lévy's reply to de Beauvoir in "Benny Lévy et Sartre"[55] carries conviction.

The Sartre-Lévy interviews are also attacked, by the way, by the Latin-American *literateur* Octavio Paz on ideological grounds. Paz is an old enemy of Sartre's. On "the Jewish question" he displays, apart from utter ignorance, a fundamentally antisemitic strain: "I was surprised by his saying that Judaism, the least universal of the three monotheisms, is the origin and foundation of this hope: Judaism is a closed fraternity. Why was he once again deaf to the voice of his tradition?"[56] (One hears here, between the lines, the old claim to Roman "catholicism.")

One of the most noticeable features of the final interviews is how much Sartre dissociates himself at the end of his life from virtually all of his earlier crucial works—not only his two chief philosophical books but also *Anti-semite and Jew*. Indeed, I think he dissociates himself from them all together too much. I want now to retrace his intellectual life for him in my way.

"Anti-Semite and Jew"

What the self-conscious Jew has always objected to in Sartre's phenomenology of the Jew in this book is that according to it the Jew is nothing in himself. The Jew is completely the product of a world hostile to him. As Sartre puts it:[57] "The Jew is one whom other men consider a Jew." To be sure, the "authentic Jew" transforms the identity that his enemies have imposed on him into his own value:[58] "Authenticity for him is to live to the full his condition as a Jew." "Jewish authenticity consists in choosing oneself *as a Jew* . . ."[59] But what the authentic Jew, or, for that matter, the authentic human being, "chooses," and, furthermore, even what he extrapolates, "projects," therefrom, is still given to him in the first place from the outside, from others, from a hostile world. As Trigano then puts it correctly:[60] "The Jew is the inauthentic being *par excellence*, essentially defined by the glance of the other."

Now, the Jew himself knows better—the Jew, that is, who, as Lévy puts it, has remained a Jew.[61] Conscious of his own particular history and culture, he is much more likely to regard himself as the only truly authentic man there is in the world.[62] Thus, for example, a perennial strain in Rabbinic Judaism (i.e. classical, authentic, and enduringly authoritative Judaism), tends to define "*adam*" = Adam = man as the Israelite.[63]

I may here give my personal testimony. I grew up as an adolescent in the 1930's in Berlin, in the eye of the storm geographically and culturally—the child of an old, equally German and Jewish family and of parents who spent their lives in the leadership echelon of German Jewry. Neither at that time nor at any time since then has antisemitism ever played the slightest role in my life. Of course, the Nazis could tyrannize me, but they and their likes were always so infinitely beneath me—both because they were boors and because they weren't Jews—that they could never reach me where I was, or am. My Jewish substance, to be sure significantly effected by its prehistory in, among other places, Europe, is an inherently extremely difficult but withal totally significating (significance-bestowing) reality. (B. Lévy is, for my generation, a welcome Johnny-come-lately. And the rule is: the more Jewish a Jew is the less is he concerned with antisemitism; the less Jewish a Jew is the more is he concerned with it. On this criterion the Anti Defamation League, for example, has to be evaluated.)

As far as Sartre is concerned, we have to keep in mind that *Antisemite and Jew* started its career as strictly an occasional essay in *Les Temps Modernes* in 1945 in response to the situation immediately after the end of Nazism in Europe.[64] Its original title was *Reflections on the Jewish Question* (i.e. "the Jewish question" was produced by racist Europe), and even then Sartre realized how invidious, because totally external, the very term, "the Jewish question," was: by way of analogy he quotes Richard Wright to the effect that there is no Black question in America—only a White question concerning Blacks.[65] It is under these conditions that Sartre defines the Jew exclusively from the vantage point of the nonJew, and his book was first called *Portrait of an Anti-semite* also in English before it ended up under its present title.[66]

In his last statement Sartre admits the validity and truth of this basic Jewish objection to his *Anti-semite and Jew*. Lévy says: "At the time of this writing (of *Anti-semite and Jew*) you thought that the Jew was an anti-semitic invention."[67] Sartre admits this.

He himself and those who understand him have two historical explanations for this serious mistake. In the first place, during the Third Republic and then during the war it is sociologically only to be expected that Sartre would have known only assimilated Jews—Jews that were thoroughly Frenchified and de-Judaized (like H. Bergson), whose only sense of their own Jewishness was due to their inevitable resistance to antisemitism (a phenomenon that continues to occur wherever assimilated Jews, especially of the educated upperclass, exist:[68] "I am actually not at all Jewish but thoroughly French/German etc.;" or, as Fritz Stern quotes an old French lady, when asked why she did not convert: "*J'ai trop peu de religion pour en changer*," but while Jews are under attack an honorable man will not desert a fortress under siege, although he really doesn't feel at home in that fortress). Now, however, as a result of having become familiar with other types of Jews since the war, Lévy among them especially, and as a result of having read Salo W. Baron's *Social and Religious History of the Jews*,[69] he himself knows better.[70] Even now, though, the definition of the Jew as the product of a hostile world still holds true for those Jews who live in such an embattled world. The fight against anti-semitism is the fight against forcing human beings into inauthentic roles—i.e. forcing them to play roles in society which they (in this case Jews, in other cases victims of colonial, economic, sexual,[71] or racial domination) do not choose to play for themselves. Sartre's loyal support of the State of Israel, alongside his support for the Palestinian struggle, is one preeminent expression of his commitment to the right of all peoples to define, to "make," themselves. He best stated the posture toward Israel when, in 1976, he accepted an honorary doctorate from the Hebrew University—he, who had refused all other formal honors; he said on that occasion:[72] "My acceptance of this degree will no doubt be regarded as a political gesture, and it is one indeed. It expresses the frienship I feel for Israel since its birth and my wish to see this nation prosper in a climate of serenity and peace. . . . For me, as you know, peace can only exist if the Israelis start talking with the Palestinians. For I am also concerned with the fate of the Palestinian people. In fact, the more I am pro-Israeli, the more pro-Palestinian I feel, and vice versa."[73]

Sartre offers a second explanation of his basic mistake about Jewry at the time of *Anti-semite and Jew* in terms of the philosophic views which he then held. He states this explanation with excessive brevity, however, and none too felicitously: "There was the conception of the self, which I deprived of all the individual characteristics that would have come from the interior and which I found for it subsequently on the exterior."[74] The implications of this sentence call for unpacking, and the unpacking will prove once again that what Sartre has to say about the Jew is what he has to say about human beings in general—i.e. that his entire humanistic philosophy is focused in it, whether at the end of his life, when he transcended Hegelianism/Marxism, as we have begun to see, whether in the spirit of his early *Being and Nothingness*, or whether in the spirit of the *Critique of Dialectical Reason*, as I propose also to show.

"Being and Nothingness"

It is, indeed, the case that in *Anti-semite and Jew* Sartre deprived the Jew of all substance of his own, but the fact is that he did the same thing, philosophically, to all human beings, in the wake of his postHusserlian/postHeideggerian existentialist phenomenologism.[75] Husserl had ended up with a "Cartesian phenomenology"—i.e. the basic view that there has to be some sort of substantival, "transcendental" ego, which is the agent of all the intentional acts that constitute the human world. That ego Sartre eliminated in his first philosophical treatise, *The Transcendence of the Ego.*[76] Man—not only the Jew but every man—is not a substantival ego nor any other kind of substance but "nothing," in a world of substances (things)(ergo *Being and Nothingness*), who literally creates himself *ex nihilo*, out of nothing, by means of the reflection of his intentional acts into himself. Thus, man—again not only the Jew but every man—is his self-image as he receives it from the total environment in which he lives. Man's very glory consists of being the hole in the middle of reality:[77] reality is, of course, subject to all sorts of natural laws; man's nothingness bestows upon him his exemption from those laws—his freedom. He is—to switch now to Heidegger's impact on Sartre—"thrown" into the real universe (*"je suis tombé dans le monde"),*[78] and what he makes of his thrown place—indeed, whether he makes anything at all of it or no—determines his degree of authenticity or inauthenticity.[79] As Sartre puts it: "This nothing is *all*, since it is *consciousness* of all."[80] (The newspaper cartoon at the time of his death showing a hand coming out of the grave to write the name "Sartre" on the empty tombstone, illustrated his conception of man very well.) The fundamental difference between *Being and Nothingness* and *Being and Time* is, one can say, that on Heidegger's view time, i.e. history, exhaustively determines the location of man's thrownness (therefore, the absence of ethics in his philosophy)[81] and his self-realization within that "given," whereas Sartre always struggles, as we shall see more fully further on, to extract human freedom, and therewith ethics, from the tight networks of history, causality, science, Marxist dialectics, etc. (the hole in actuality, which Heidegger had plugged up with time), so that the world, from which man receives his self-image, which he can consciously accept and thus authentificate himself, would be at least in small part a world which he himself had intentionally made. Man chooses the meaning of what he is and the situation into which he is thrown, and Sartre ends a passage, in which this notion is explicated, with the statement: "Thus reflective consciousness can properly be called a moral consciousness."[82] As Spiegelberg puts it, in *Being and Nothingness* the nothingness is the enemy of being, while in *Being and Time* he is its property.[83]

In section III, chapt. 1 of *Being and Nothingness,* entitled "Being-for-Others," Sartre constructs what he believes to be the dialectic of the construction of selves. All selves—not only the Jew—are creatures of what others make them. "As I appear to the Other so I am."[84] Therefore, others are necessary for me.[85] I apparently start out as a subject, but I then discover myself to be the object of others, which proves that they cannot be objects, though I had begun by thinking that, as well.[86] (As in Kant's Third *Critique*, for Sartre the art-object is then the best empirical instantiation of the human project.)[87] It is the third man, who looks at both me and my other, that objectifies us both and thus imposes his heteronomy on the both of us.[88] He and I must, therefore, together oppose him and, in a dialectical interaction between us, authenticate ourselves through our own, subjective, intentions ("projects").[89]

Sartre was always painfully conscious of how difficult the philosophical struggle had to be for him of jumping, as it were, over the shadow of both Heidegger and (later) Marx. He admits in his last interview that he did not really succeed in working his way forward to a philosophical ethic until he arrived at his views on Jewish Messianic ethics at the very end of his life. Lévy: "You thought you were opening a moral perspective at the end of *Being and Nothingness* and then you did not write a book offering a solution, but you engaged in a debate with Marxism. One must believe that both things are closely related." Sartre: "Intimately." Lévy: "You believed that by the meaning of history as defined by Hegel and Marxism one could go beyond the dead end to which *Being and Nothingness* led." Sartre: "Yes, only roughly.[90] And then I thought that it was necessary to seek an answer somewhere else, and that is what I am doing now."[91] In other words, the search for an ethics led from *Being and Nothingness* to the *Critique of Dialectical Reason* and from there to Jewish Messianic ethics.[92]

The cause of that lifelong difficulty that Sartre experienced is the fact that he started out with Hegel. Hermann Cohen always pointed out that of all

Hegel's numerous works and courses none ever bore the title "ethics" and that no philosopher in the tradition which collapses immanence and transcendence into one, whether it be Hegel or Spinoza—and we today can add the name of Heidegger here—could produce such a work.[93] (Spinoza's so-called *Ethics* is, of course, an explication of radical naturalistic determinism—*deus sive natura.*) The Frankfurt School suffered the same original fall, and it, too, therefore, struggled manfully—though often only semiconsciously—to regain a Kantian "primacy of practical reason."[94]

What causes surprise and incredulousness on the part of some people at Sartre's last statement, especially insofar as it deals with ethics and with Jews, is that the straight line, leading from *Being and Nothingness* and *Antisemite and the Jew* to the Lévy interviews, was not too conspicuous in the first place. On top of this, Sartre himself did not see it too clearly and, therefore, occasionally tended to obscure it in his self-descriptions.

"Critique of Dialectical Reason"

The major philosophical work that intervened between *Being and Nothingness* and Sartre's final views was, then, the *Critique of Dialectical Reason*, but toward the end of his life Sartre really abjured the latter work as much as in it he had abjured the former.[95] We have earlier heard him say that the promise, at the end of *Being and Nothingness*, that he would now move forward to an ethic was, as seen retrospectively, not fulfilled in the *Critique . . .*, and neither he nor Benny Lévy seems willing, therefore, to remind himself of the important foundation that was in fact laid there for what he wanted to argue in his last days. Perhaps, Sartre was being too hard, too critical, on himself.

The *Critique of Dialectical Reason* (Paris, 1960) is a drawnout exercise in neo—Marxism. Like other, wellintentioned neo—Marxist works in our time, its basic purpose is really to overcome the simplistic naturalism and determinism that afflict orthodox, vulgar Marxism (and, to a significant degree, Marx himself)—what Sartre would call "lazy Marxism"[96]—in favor of a reasonable reconciliation of historico-economic determinism with human freedom and ethics. Sartre wanted to "reconquer man within Marxism."[97] He tried to accomplish this by means of an essentially simple philosophical move: he here holds that between any socio-historical state of affairs A as a cause and a state of affairs B as its effect the human being—still and ever the hole in the universe of being—can, in principle, freely and consciously intervene, so as to alter B into at least, say B′. In this way he proposes existentialism as a "human foundation of Marxist anthropology."[98] Sartre quickly adds, however, that, though this is in principle possible and imperative, the odds are all against a human being actually taking such free and effective action, because of the overwhelming power of natural and social inertia; instead, usually the person lets himself be drawn, and thereby disauthentificated, into the deterministic processes of being.

When formulated like this, the *Critique of Dialectical Reason* clearly does not differ philosophically very much from *Being and Nothingness*, except for the fact that the hole of human autonomy is no longer to be found primarily in the being of some phenomenological metaphysic but rather within the interstices of Marxist history.

Ze'ev Levy proposes an interesting explanation of the place of *Antisemite and Jew* in the development of Sartre's thought from *Being and Nothingness to the Critique* ...[99] Z. Levy argues that in *Being and Nothingness* every individual always possesses the freedom to make himself—inauthentically if he passively accepts the world's assignment, authentically if he actively accepts that assignment and transforms it in accordance with his own, self-created projection. This is a purely individualistic, asocial and ahistorical anthropology. When Sartre, for the first time, tried to apply that philosophical humanism to a social group—and, of all candidates, just Jews—he discovered, Levy thinks, that Jews are an example of historical entities, or the only entity, that possesses no such freedom: history, antisemitism, force, them to be Jews—whether authentic or no; the third alternative, of freely opting out of Jewishness, is foreclosed to them. Thus, as Levy puts it, "the Jewish question did not find a place in his general philosophical system," because it turns out to be a socio-historical question rather than a human one of individual consciousness.[100] Therefore, Sartre, on Z. Levy's view, now had to revise his philosophical stance in general, and he did this in the *Critique* ....

Levy's explanation is interesting, but, unfortunately, incorrect. That it is incorrect can be seen in several ways. For one thing, even in the *Critique* ... consciousness always continues to possess the freedom, and the absurd responsibility, to choose, and this is, indeed, the chief thrust of Sartre's polemic against vulgar-Marxist determinism. As far as this is concerned, the Jew, therefore, would still seem not to have a place in his (revised) philosophy, for he has a neo-Marxist choice no more than he had had a phenomenological one.

In the second place, it is not true that the Jew did not have a place in *Being and Nothingness*. In a section of this book entitled "The Situation" Sartre defines what "the situation" consists of into which every human being "is thrown" and with which he has to cope existentially one way or the other: "my place," "my past," "my environment," and "my fellowmen." The Jew is explicitly named as an example of the human situation so explicated. Those four situational factors share the characteristic of being externally imposed on all of us, not internally produced by us, and they, therefore, constitute "limits" and "negative states" that seriously constrict us. (According to R. Aronson's summary of the unpublished second volume of the *Critique of Dialectical Reason*, what the "situation" is in *Being and Nothingness* is, on the metaphysical scale, "Being-in-itself—i.e. the outermost limits of all human cognition.)[101] We can only "assume" them—i.e. embrace them, by way of *amor fati*, and, as it were, make a good thing out of them. They are, for purposes of authentification, "unrealizables" for us, because they are started out and always remain outside of us, and yet we must strive to realize them—foredoomed though this endeavor has to be.[102]

Sartre cites various examples of human "thrownness" into place, past, environment, and society. A recurring one is the Jew. "The Zionist Jew resolutely assumes himself within his race."[103] Like in *Antisemite* . . ., he has the choice, even within authenticity, to be either a Zionist or a French Jew. (One has to recall that *Etre et Néant* was published in occupied France in 1943. Knowing where Sartre stood, it is the more deliciously satirical that he gives the example of a poster: "Jewish Restaurant. No Aryans Allowed.")[104] "It is only by recognizing *the freedom* of the anti-semites (whatever use they make of it) and by assuming this *being-a-Jew* that I am a Jew for them; it is only thus that being-a-Jew will appear as the external limit of the situation. If, on the contrary, it pleases me to consider the anti-semite as pure *object*, then my being-a-Jew disappears immediately to give place to the simple consciousness (of) being a free, unqualifiable transcendence. . . ."[105] This is the typically neoMarxist, Sartrean, Hegelian master-slave relationship: like master and slave, antisemite and Jew depend on one another to be "recognized" for what they respectively are, though they also want to kill one another.[106] In France in 1943, like in so many other places at many times, it is *de facto*, however, the slave and the Jew who, though theoretically free to deny lordship and anti-semitism, are the only ones to die if they refuse to accept their status. Thus, *de facto*, the Jew only has the choice of either adopting the identity which his enemy imposes on him or death. (In 1943 in Europe the former reduced to the latter, of course.) "Being-a-Jew is nothing outside the free manner of adopting it"[107]—the view which we meet again in *Antisemite and Jew*.

The question that must then be asked of Sartre at that point of his existentialist analysis is why the Jew cannot "look" upon the anti-semite and thus subsume him in his own, objective, Jewish universe, as, according to Sartre, every consciousness is capable of and freely responsible for doing with all external givens. In principle this should be possible, for one would have thought that "being-a-Jew" is unlike place, past, environment, and fellowmen in that attending a synagogue, speaking Hebrew, believing in Maimonides' "Thirteen Principles," etc. is like going to the theater, reading Flaubert in French, or agreeing with Sartre: they are not ineluctable givens but human choices.

One would have thought so wrongly, according to Sartre and according to the Nazi-European world in which Sartre lived at the time! The very sentences quoted from *Being and Nothingness* makes it clear that the Jew at the time was conceived as a member of a "race." That is to say, he was held to have no more choice about being or not being a Jew than a man has to be a horse or to find himself born, "thrown," into a given situation. That is why Sartre's discussion of the Jew occurs in this section, "The Situation," of *Being and Nothingness*: race is a fifth, though unnumbered, component of "the situation." Jewishness is not, contrary to Z. Levy, a socio-historical determination for Sartre at that time and thus a bridge to *Critique of Dialectical Reason*; it was, Sartre was led to believe by the Nazified counter-culture of Europe in the 1930's and early 1940's, a racial and, therefore, ineluctable fate, a "thrownness," a limit, a negative state. "I would not deny that there is a Jewish race . . . among races."[108] (It goes without saying, of course, that Sartre puts no value judgment on race.)

What happened to Sartre on the way from *Being and Nothingness*, via *Antisemite and Jew* and the *Critique of Dialectical Reason*, to his final interviews with B. Lévy, after racism had been intellectually and politico-culturally banished from the contemporary world, is that he learned that "being-a-Jew" is not, and never has been legitimately, an ineluctable, situational, racial given but, though situationally prepared (like all other human existence), ultimately freely chosen or freely rejected as a historico-cultural identity.[109]

In the *Critique* . . . his thinking on this subject still maintains the *status quo ante*. In two extended passages he deals with the Jew in terms now of his neo-Marxism, but still to the same effect. The first of these passages is pp. 315-329. At bottom he is here engaged in reformulating Toennies' distinction between "*Gesellschaft*" ("society") and "*Gemeinschaft*" ("community") in his own (one might add, less felicitous) vocabulary. "*Gesellschaft*" ("*rassemblement*," grouping) is formed for the attainment of an external, material goal. Sartre's example is that of waiting for a bus in a queue.[110] Being external, the goal is not constructed by that grouping; it comes to it, like the bus to those who wait for it, not as its own projection for the future but as already "given" by the past. Lots of individuals are conscripted, "serialized," into the army of workers who labor to attain the goal, by governments, the communications media, etc., but who and what the individuals are is completely uninteresting: they are, if they have "interiorized alterity," thoroughly inauthentic. The Jew in our society is an obvious case of such dehumanization: he is defined by his enemies; he even interiorizes antisemitism as his self-definition; he is thus object, not subject—passive, impotent, material, inert.[111] The self-conscious, self-assertive, self-creating individual (Jew or otherwise) can always opt out of his serialization, and legitimate groups (as distinguished from "groupings"), i.e. "*Gemeinschaft*," can be formed by numbers of such individuals.[112] However, the powers of society, nature, and history are so mighty that normally they even integrate, reserialize, coopt—as the Germans say, "*gleichschalten*"—their very opposition and thus assimilate it to themselves (cp. Herbert Marcuse's "one-dimensional society").

The second "Jewish" passage in the *Critique* ... is to be found on pp. 620-631. With his usual verbosity Sartre here mostly repeats what he had argued in the earlier passage, including the specific Jewish exemplifications.[113] The activity of serialized groupings he calls "the practico-inert," and he repeatedly uses the term "pogrom" for their mass actions under exterior indoctrination. From this one must progress, obviously, to genuine, human—free and self-conscious—action in opposition to the inert. Mass inertia can be expected to be overcome, if at all, only by mass action—revolution,[114] but here it will be a case of authentic human beings forming authentic groups, because they have projected their own, free, self-created purpose, which they try to realize, and which negates its earlier impotence[115] rather than acting as "massified individuals"[116] in a grouping that is the "mineralization of man."[117] In this connection Sartre even advocated the reintroduction of political pluralism, i.e. freedom, in the Soviet Union—although he continued to justify earlier, Stalinist "centralism" for the sake of the abolition of the bourgeoisie.)[118]

In "Materialism and Revolution"[119] Sartre had made the same points: oppressed minorities (Jews being, as always. his favorite example) are created by their oppressors; only when the oppressed Jews "surpass" their interiorization of their oppressors' image of them and take collective, autonomous action not only to abstain from joining their oppressors through the processes of social cooptation but, more importantly, to produce for themselves "a radically new situation," a new future for themselves, do they become an authentic group.

Clearly, Sartre's thinking has remained on a single—if anything, too much an identical—straight line from before *Being and Nothingness* through and beyond the *Critique of Dialectical Reason*: man is absurdly "thrown" into his real situation—he becomes what he is as a result of the forces of the world that operate on him—he is thus a mere object, or, alternatively, he makes himself into what he wishes to be by consciously accepting his inescapable situation and by taking whatever interstitial action he can in order to change the situation with himself in it, thus becoming a subject; all of this transpires both in the metaphysical, cosmologico-epistemological universe and in the historical, socio-economic universe. As far as the Jew is concerned, this means that he finds himself in an anti-semitic world—anti-semites make him what he is—and Sartre in effect calls upon him to become fully aware of his situation, to create his own Jewish values, to group together around, or rather toward, those values, and to create his own Jewish life by revolutionarily working for the realization of a society determined by these values.

The *Critique of Dialectical Reason* is then a curious philosophy—curious, because in effect it is one extended expression of disgust with history; history—quite apart from its (Hegelian) character as a "slaughter-bench"—is seen, after all, to be "the practico-inert," objectified, desubjectified dehumanized, human activities. What is human in history is precisely what is not historical—i.e. ethics, human autonomy.

Once More the Last Interview

Once we have thus reconstituted where Sartre stood on "the Jewish question" in effect throughout his life and what the upshot was at which that thinking arrived, it turns out, as one can clearly see, that there are really only two, and, at that, partial, innovations that one encounters in what Sartre said on the subject in the Lévy interviews. The first is minor and merely factual: Sartre has meanwhile discovered that Judaism has all along done in history precisely what he thought he was newly challenging it to do; the Jews had created their own autonomous culture—a culture, furthermore, which, in the form of Messianism, always strives to do precisely what Sartre wants all humanity to do, that is to create a society in which everyone is self-determined. The second *novum* in the Lévy interview is much more important but also much more difficult: Sartre now stipulates that that Jewish, autonomous culture, which has existed and been activated all along, breaks up the totalization of Hegelian/Marxist historiography and of his own existentialist-phenomenological metaphysics by possessing, from the outset and continuously, its own inherent ethico-cultural, indeed "metaphysical," substance. In other words, Judaism is the only entity which (if one is to take the last interview at its word) is not originally the creature of its environment. It alone seems not to be "thrown" but to be created *ex nihilo*—to be *ab initio* completely "authentic" (except, of course, where it is distorted or even extirpated by antisemitism).

If this is a correct reading of Sartre's last statement, then his final apostrophe to Judaism is, indeed, extraordinary. But it might also, unless explicated with extreme caution, be taken to undermine at its foundation everything that Sartre ever said before throughout his life. Where would that Jewish substance come from—God? Hardly, as far as Sartre is concerned. The Jew, i.e. Jewish man, monadically self-made outside the networks of worldly, human and social, relations in which every man starts out by finding himself? If so, all of Sartre's earlier epistemology and anthropology would be belied. I can and want to think of only one possible answer: Sartre now holds that the Jew, Jewry, is—as he puts it—the only historic entity that "projected" a Messianic goal of autonomous human beings in a true human community not by sublimating, "surpassing," its externally given conditions but out of autonomous human reason alone.

If this is, indeed, what Sartre was trying to get at at the end, he would, of course, have come so closely back to Kant, and away from Hegel and Marx, that the difference would be scarcely worth mentioning. The *Critique of Dialectical Reason* would be purified, at least on this score, of its dialecticism and brought back not even so much to the *Critique of Pure Reason* as to the *Critique of Practical Reason*, with its absolute "primacy of practical reason."

A metaphysical Kantianism of this sort would have finally brought Sartre's metaphysics in line with his ethics. The latter had been basically Kantian long since.[120] He had reformulated the categorical imperative in *Existentialism* quite correctly: "In choosing myself I choose man;" one must ask: "What if all acted like that?"[121] And the Kantian, indeed, the Marburg neo-Kantian, philosophy of history (i.e. the ethical prerequisites of history) had been enshrined even in the neo-Marxist Critique: the goal of history is a society of men as "ends-in-themselves."[122] "The historical revolution depends on the moral conversion ... We act upon situations in the hope of preparing a moral conversion."[123] Further yet, Sartre picks up Eduard Bernstein's "revisionist," neo-Kantian socialism (without knowing that this is what he is doing) by defining socialism as a "regulative idea," to be made binding in the present, as an effort for freedom, not for "happiness."[124] The proletariat is a "project," not an object of cognition.[125] Indeed, man as such is, of course, anticipated by the proletarian, and, therefore, man himself is a pro-ject—still to be invented. "Man is the future of man ... as praxis of all men joined together. Man is to be made."[126] This is in a rigorous way H. Cohen's definition of "humanity" and of "ethics," though less rigorously formulated.[127]) And thus it can come to pass that Sartre's last interview consummates his life and its work in the title's notion of hope, just as Kant's first Critique climaxes in the question that we must rationally ask (B833): "What may I hope for?"[128]

Sartre's Perennial Program

We have drawn a big curve of Sartre's thinking from *The Transcendence of the Ego* to the Lévy interviews. Sartre's oeuvre can thus be seen to constitute a highly interesting and unified enterprise, with human freedom always at its live center and with the Jew always very near that center. Sartre's life itself can be seen to have been a search for human freedom and should be prized as such.

Even the mistakes that he made, philosophically as well as politically, were mistaken paths in the search for freedom. Politically, as a result of the alliance with the Communists during the war and in view of the socioeconomic miseries at end of the war, he thought, for the brief period between 1952 and the occupation of Budapest in 1956, that the Bolshevik party and the apparatus of the Soviet Union were instrumentalities of human emancipation; unfortunately, he continued to defend that posture much too long as having been proper at the time, though he quickly recognized Bolshevik totalitarianism for what it is.[129] (One loves the title, "The Socialism that Came in from the Cold," in *Trois Générations*[130]—although, of course, 1956 is much too long after 1918.) Philosophically, he wanted to rip holes of freedom into the magical fabric of Heidegger's thought and into the straitjacket of conventional Marxism. It took him a while, too, to discover what most others have even failed to discern as yet—that Marxism and Heidegger share a common origin in Hegel's collapse of transcendence into immanence, i.e. of freedom into necessity, and that, therefore, freedom cannot be extracted from Heidegger's Being or from Marxist/Bolshevik determinism. It is entirely in keeping, then, that Heidegger fell to his knees before Hitler, never to stand up again, while Sartre, having bowed to Stalin, quickly stood up straight once more. Sartre never forgot what he had set out to look for in the first place—not intellectual sensibility or revolutionary power but freedom. The original title of his promised, posthumous ethic, *Power and Liberty*, sounds completely suitable, then, to his perennial purpose.[131]

There is always a lot of talk about Sartre's many and often fundamental changes of position during his life. He himself and de Beauvoir knew and said that this is a totally false reading of him. In the opening "Interview" with him in Schilpp's *Philosophy of J.-P. Sartre*[132] he says: "There is an evolution, but I don't think there is a break ... I think that a study of my philosophical thought should follow its evolution." And he refers back to virtually all of his books with some sort of approval. And de Beauvoir quotes him[133] as having said: "I've certainly made lots of mistakes. But not errors of principle ... In principle I agree with my past—I agree entirely with my past," and he cites the "progress" in his works. Even William Barrett speaks of Sartre as "a singularly unitary and consistent personality . . . He is what he is from the start and throughout."

That he seems to many to have changed positions so often is due to his practice of what Nietzsche called "thinking against oneself"[135] and what Walter Benjamin called "thinking against the grain." Sartre himself called it "*décoller de soi*"—"working loose from oneself,"[136] and "thinking in opposition to oneself."[137] I.e., after he had thought through one line of implications of his basic insight he turned to think through another, and perhaps even contradictory, line of such implications, but this does not, of course, constitute self-contradictions as rather, if you please, dialectical explorations and, in any case, enriching self-evolution. As Jeanson[138] says: "Sartre has criticized but never *renounced* any previous work."

One can even observe with relative ease, as we have done, what the identical spring is out of which the entirety of Sartre's oeuvre bubbled forth: it is a "single systematic attitude which consists in always giving precedence to the 'moral' point of view."[139] Jeanson says: "There can be no Sartrean philosophy outside the moral perspective."[140] "I maintained eighteen years ago, and I continue to maintain today, that Sartre's philosophy is a moral philosophy, and all its virtue for us issues from this."[141] De Beauvoir quotes him:[142] "I am always centrally concerned with morality." Rather than speaking explicitly of morality or even freedom she and he speak of "contingency." "*J'ai écrit un Chant de la contingence.*"[143]

In a sentence, J.-P. Sartre was a lifelong and consistent philosophical seeker of (to use the Kantian term) the primacy of practical reason.

In the light of the preceding analysis, one can draw an even bigger curve—from Hegel to Sartre. Hegel produced a philosophical version of Christian, incarnationist, trinitarianly dialectical theology, in which historiosophical determinism took the place of theological providence. Marx tried, for—I might add— good Jewish reasons,[144] to break out of Hegel's metaphysical, so-called "pan-rationalistic," determinism by means of "praxis," but he did this within the context of Hegel's incarnationism, though "set on its feet." Sartre, by means of always insisting on the "nothingness" which breaks holes into the "being" of incarnate, historical and metaphysical, reality, not only recapitulates Marx's "praxis" but regains in addition an ethic beyond naturalism (i.e. Kant). One might say that Sartre has repurified Jewish Messianism of its vitiation by the Christian Hegel and by Hegel's all-too-deJudaized disciple Marx. (Under French historical conditions at the end of World War II this was bound to have and did have great impact.)

But Sartre does all this, of course, in the absence of God. This divine absence transfixed him all of his life. Atheists like Sartre (and Nietzsche and

Kojève) wallow in *furor theologicum*. "It is very distressing that God does not exist."[145] "Man is fundamentally the desire to be God."[146] "*L'absence de Dieu . . . c'est l'ouverture de l'infini. . . .* je ne suis donc plus Moi, mais *absence de moi!* j'attendais cet escamotage et maintenant, sans mesure, je suis gai.)"[147] His is, therefore, a post-theological theology. All the entrenched theological operators and concepts continue to be employed by Sartre (as they were by Hegel and Marx), except that they now function in the absence of God, within a very loose providence, and in a universe which is constituted more by human nothingness than by incarnationist being. In other words, it is really a specifically Jewish post-theological theology. Little wonder that there is a pervasive Jewish vocabulary in all of Sartre's writings.

Lévy uses for example the term "diasporic,"[148] which, indeed, describes Sartre's conception of the self in its preunified, phenomenologically and empirically given, condition.[149] Edgar Morin summarizes all of Sartre as "The Symbol of Wandering."[150] Man as an absurd "stranger/alien" is, if anything, the central humanistic concept of even popular existentialist anthropology.[151] To add another such vocable, it may be remembered that Sartre speaks of the actual self as the sickle of the moon, which we observe empirically only as a part, as a function, of the full moon which we "project" for the future; so the actual self is the empirical reality derived from the "value," constituted by the idea of the self.[152] Hermann Cohen used the Biblical metaphor of the rainbow for the same purpose for which Sartre used the moon: all present actuality is the product of the (Kantian) idea of the (Messianic) future.[153] No wonder at all that a conceptually Jewish post-theological theology should end, with a thoroughly self-conscious, open-minded, and highly literate man like J.-P. Sartre, as it did—with a quasi-Jewish philosophy—what the French have recently taken to call *judéité*. (I suppose, in English one would have to coin the term "Judaity.") On the rising curve of Sartre's life of "Judaity" he was always a "righteous of the gentile nations," but he ended as a Jew *honoris causa*. As he wanted Jewish children (and adopted one), so he even wanted to die like a Jew in the Holocaust, says de Beauvoir—cremated, or "incinerated."[154]

Even then the question of God is not quite so simply laid *ad acta* in Sartre. All seem to agree: Sartre's rejection of belief in God early in life and his replacement of God by man (Sartre) himself (cf. Sartre's introduction to *Descartes*:[155] by being "nothing" I am not subject to God:[156] "freedom is the basis of Being," as it had been in God)[157] continued as a powerful motive throughout Sartre's career. Barth realized relatively early that, humanly and philosophically, what might be called "the possibility of God" lurked somewhere in the depths of Sartre's fascination with "the Nothing" and of his moral passions.[159] Indeed, it is striking that de Beauvoir ends her *Ceremony of Adieus* to Sartre with a lengthy Sartrean (anti)theology[160]: to be sure, *"je n'ai pas besoin de Dieu pour aimer mon prochain,"* and God alienates man from man,[161] but "I have retained in the moral domain a single point of the existence of God, i.e. Good and Evil as absolutes."[162] " 'God exists', as a proposition, is impossible ... It can have worth as an active *positing* and as a practical valorizing." Therefore, "God" is a wager, involving oneself as a human being.[163] "Man loses himself as man," however, says Sartre, "so that God may be born."[164]

It thus turns out that what Sartre is really saying when he proclaims his atheism is what for two-hundred years Kant and H. Cohen's neoKantianism had said all along—except that they regard this as religious faith: belief in God is not a cognitive or pseudo-cognitive act (indeed, pseudo-cognitive belief in God is idolatry) but an ethical, "practical," regulative one. God "is" not, even as the human self "is" not; he ought to be (pro-jected) as man has to pro-ject himself in order to come to be, and all ought's (ought to) flow from this.

Sartre had at least two reasons for not being able to see this rational extrapolation of his own basic viewpoint (leaving aside the perfectly understandable emotional and aesthetic impulse to break with the pieties of the bourgeoise). He believed and always argued that every man wants to be God and that this built-in desire of men is, in the first place, bound to be frustrated and, in the second place, causes the conflicts between men—a war of the (aspiring) gods. Neither of these two objections can really be defended even in terms of Sartre's own considerations.

Regarding the first, Sartre derives his own ethic (as Thomas C. Anderson shows in his good, though not faultless, book *The Foundation and Structure of Sartrean Ethics*)[165] from the move away from the impossible desire to be God toward the desire to universalize human freedom, but he is, of course, the first to admit that such an ethic itself is engaged on a "progressive and never-ending" pursuit.[166] Sartrean pessimism may, therefore, well be engendered by both for their unattainability—or for the Kantian/Marburgian "asymptotic" hopefulness in the infinite pursuit. Regarding the second, it may well be that every man wanting himself to be God inevitably leads to the war of the gods.[167] But precisely by lifting the God-idea out of the realm of even possible Being to the realm of value (exactly what true Biblical religion does) two purposes are accomplished which Sartre seeks to attain: men will not want to "be" God but to "imitate" him, and, furthermore, not only will their common desire to do so not lead to conflicts between them but actually lead to the increasing universal human fraternity under one father that is implicit in Sartre's own humanism. True belief in God was always meant to turn men's minds away from preoccupation with God in favor of preoccupation with humanity ("Wish they would forsake Me and obey My commandments".)[168] This is precisely Sartre's "ethic of deliverance and salvation."[169] And the Lévy interview comes extremely close to stating this ultimate convergence of Sartre's thinking with classical Judaism. (Anderson still awaited a full sorting out of Sartre's philosophical problems.[170] He could not predict Sartre's last turn.)

What really seems to have hindered Sartre from drawing such philosophical conclusions was his existentialist rebellion against rationalism. Rather than, like Kant, showing that rationally—and therefore, "objectively"—man ought to want (autonomously) to be moral, Sartre wanted to show at existentially man must want to be God but ought to want to be free. Anderson rightly finds this to be an internal self-contradiction.[171] (Despite this, Frankena[172] recognizes his deontology, and Frederick Olafson[173] recognizes the kinship between Kantian autonomy and Sartrean freedom.)

In any case, Hermann Cohen's neo-Kantianism and Sartre's Marxist existentialism both resolve religion into ethics and ethics into humanist socialism. The circle of Kant and Sartre, as drawn above,[172] could and should be so closed.

One departs from Sartre with a somewhat mixed feeling. On the negative side, there is some ultimate lack of systematicity in his philosophical work. Not that one cannot show an underlying continuity, and even unity, in his intellectual efforts throughout life, as we have here tried to demonstrate, but one does have to work rather hard to extract such unity, and even then it remains true, as Sartre himself frequently testified, that at any one stage of his conceptual development the results were somehow not quite satisfactory: one has to await the fundamental metamorphosis of the next stage, so that the problematics of the previous stage can be tackled, and so on; the last stage, then, bracketing the unpublished *Pouvoir et Liberté*, remains itself torsoesque, in the "hope" of the Lévy-interviews. Truly perspicuous philosophers, and not only the greatest among them, seem normally to operate differently: they tend to begin with a unifying vision, or conceptuality, and this original conception, through sometimes fundamental revisions and certainly in the face of new evidence, radical counter-arguments, and problematics encountered in its expatiations, retains its basic philosophical integrity. One does not receive the impact of such a single encompassing insight from Sartre, in his continuous concern with "the Jewish question" anymore than in the rest of his labors. He was always somehow in search—sometimes frenetically so.

This constant frenetic search of his must in part explain his life-long volubility. It certainly explains in large part the accusation that his critics level at him, and often he at himself, that he changed his mind on fundamental issues in a fickle way.

But, of course, such a basic intellectual posture could be described more positively as open-mindedness, self-criticism, eagerness to learn, etc. Surely one of the most potent causes of this attitude of Sartre's was his overwhelming desire to "be contemporary"—i.e., as the current jargon puts it, "be with it," to be "engaged" with the real world as it developed around him, intellectually, politically. artistically, in Western Europe no more than on all the continents.

With this last consideration one has already moved to the positive part of the mixed feeling that one tends to entertain toward Sartre's total persona The many things he did, the different views he held, the diverse styles he practiced, were all informed by an almost unbounded literary, by an extraordinary intelligence, and, most importantly, by an unswerving human decency. His treatment of "the Jewish question"—in literary, sociological, political, and philosophical terms, subject to his evolving knowledge and understanding of it—exemplifies his essential ethos: it was always, and still is, an important subject, and he therefore had to come to grips with it; it had to be dealt with substantively, sophisticatedly, courageously, and felicitously; one had to become familiar with it increasingly by means of direct, personal involvement no less than by intellectual means; and, above all, one could never fail one's own humanity and the humanity of other human beings, especially to "the wretched of the earth," what the Bible calls "the stranger, the poor, the widow, and the orphan." If one wants sympathetically to understand Sartre one must begin with this lode-star in his literary story; without it one loses one's way in his glittering panorama.

– 10 –

A Critique of Martin Buber's Political Philosophy

An Affectionate Reappraisal

Introduction

Much has been written about virtually all the vast and diverse aspects of the life and works of Martin Buber. His political philosophy and activities are a striking exception to this state of affairs, although socio-political matters were clearly of fundamental importance to him and although his formal title at the Hebrew University was "Professor of Social Philosophy". In at least some instances this exception is made tendentiously: Buber's reputation is to be used for institutional and political self-advancement, but the nature of his political thought and programme would resist such purposes.[1]

This is not the approach to Buber's written and historical record in the socio-political realm taken in the present study. For anyone coming from a background of rather close personal relations with Buber and his circle[2] and sharing the substance of many or perhaps most of his moral, human, social, Jewish, and even political values, even when differences on fundamental questions—such as his philosophical metaphysic and his attitude towards Jewish religion—emerge, his work in these areas always remains extremely suggestive and valuable, and agreement with him on moral values remains unimpaired. His stance in Zionism (which, of course, lies at the root of his unpopularity before and after his death in many Jewish political circles) could, as a matter of fact, also be criticised for ultimately succumbing to the very views of his opponents.

If then, nonetheless, a critique of Buber's political philosophy here emerges, it does so for the following simple reason. Even granting the validity of his political programme, Buber himself admitted that it thoroughly failed. This is true of his philosophical anarchism (for the fate of which the death of his close friend Gustav Landauer is, perhaps, the best symbol),[3] of his basic pacifism, which, however, he felt he had to suspend, for example, when the Second World War broke out,[4] or whether one thinks of his Zionist binationalism for Palestine.[5] Buber was not very surprised, although he was naturally saddened, by these and other historic failures. In memorable sentences, contradicting the very foundations of the kind of thinking that went into Hegel's famous aphorism that "world-history is world-judgment",[6] he proposed that the ultimate establishment of the Messianic kingdom on earth will be the sum of all the defeats of social morality in history. "The way, the real way, from the Creation to the Kingdom, is trod not on the surface of success but in the deep of failure."[7] Robert Weltsch quotes him: "The history of the created world, as the religion which has faith in history testifies to it . . . is booked in figures other than those of success."[8] Buber called empirical history "this history of disappointments".[9]

But, as really goes without saying, one does not intend failures (though one may be willing to risk them). And the question which besets us, as it plagued him, and as it continues to plague his friends, disciples, and followers, is what the cause of this failure may be.[10] The answer to this question here proposed is the critique. In other words, unlike the Zionist critique of him through the years and unlike the vulgarian Marxist critique, here Buber's programme is basically affirmed and its success desired, while the critique of his political philosophy, though it cannot hope to change present and imminent history under prevailing circumstances, does step forward with the hope that at least in theory it shows a way of such a programme might, in the future, be more effective in actual history.

Phenomenologism

Buber was in some important ways a philosophical phenomenologist.[11] That is to say, he thought that conceptual and verbal analysis had to begin with and be derived from a proper vision of what the world and human beings are really like. As was said in another context, "before there can be adequate theory there must be adequate description".[12] Thus, his start in Nietzscheanism and in what around the turn of the century was called "life-philosophy" stayed with him, in a way, throughout his intellectual career.[13] This explains his opposition to theoreticism as presented by Kant and Kant's renewer Hermann Cohen. (With the latter he, therefore, came into early, however respectful, conflict not only on the question of Zionism[14] but also on notions like God and love.)[15] It also explains some persistent characteristics of Buber's literary style. As do some other phenomenologists and near-phenomenologists, like Emmanuel Levinas in our time, he always writes, for an academician in general and for a philosopher (if this is what, among other things, he was) in particular, uncommonly well, beautifully, poetically, and descriptively (albeit, of course, as has often been mockingly said, with some bombast and unintelligible obscurity).[16] He observed the world with the eye of an artist and then tried to describe it, like an artist.[17] He was, on the other hand, very much the intellectual, the conceptualiser, and this, perhaps, kept his occasional poetry[18] and his one novel[19] from being great literature.[20]

His basic phenomenological stance may also explain the preremptory tone of his basic axioms.[21] When, for example, he wrote the opening sentences of *I and Thou* he thought no doubt that he was formulating an obvious and self-evident observational truth, namely that "to man the world is two-fold, in accordance with his two-fold attitude. The attitude of man is two-fold, in accordance with the two-fold nature of the primary words which he speaks ... The one primary word is the combination *I-Thou*. The other primary word is the combination *I-It*. . . ."[22] Any kind of rationalist, when he reads this, is impelled to ask all sorts of questions: What does this mean? How do you know? How do you prove it? What if I do not make these observations? Above all, how and whence do you derive these claims conceptually and logically?[23] Buber, on the other hand, just lays them down as indisputable verities: "It is not to be proved; it is only to be experienced."[24] And from this he proceeds to build the edifice of the rest of the book, and indeed, of practically all the rest of his vast *oeuvre*—beautifully, as we have said, often persuasively, and almost always very suggestively. Buber's own proclivity for theory tended to detract from the full-blown life of his art, but, on the other hand, his theoretical and practical commitment to reality (and consider how important the word "reality" and its derivatives were in all the different stages of his thinking!),[25] infused his conceptual structures with the Heraclitean fluxibility, the absence of sharp boundaries and of irreconcilable antitheses, logical and otherwise, which may be taken to be the quality of lived reality itself. Everything differs from everything else only in degree, in shade, in nuance. Colours flow together. Tones overlie one another. All objects are somehow connected with one another. People, their thoughts, wishes, attitudes, and values, are all parts of one, though highly complex, configuration.[26]

This kind of basic posture can then also easily be seen to make, given some other ethical factors, for a moral and social programme of what will here be called "incrementalism."[27] This is to say, in the moral as in the physical world, Buber holds, there are ultimately no permanent entities. Here, too, things exist in an ebb-and-flow, and the question is never "this or that?" but "how much of this, and how much of that?" Neither "this" nor "that" is, therefore, ever really wrong, but there may well be a little too much or a lot too little of it. Buber's posture is not only pragmatically and politically but even in fundamental metaphysical principle profoundly irenic, and this may well be the result of a strong penchant for neo-*Chasidic*, quasi-phenomenological panentheism, though, to use the formulation of the Rabbis, "God's world is not His *locus*; God is the *locus* of the world;"[28] in Buber's own formulation: "God compromises, but is not the universe."[29] All reality is, therefore, in some sense divine and, consequently, good.[30] The converse also is the case, namely that God and moral values may not be thought of as "mere ideas" but possess some ontological status.[31] Maurice Friedman correctly understands the implications of this: for Buber the "is" and the "ought" are united in some "ontological life-reality".[32] "Here is the point where the normative imperceptibly emerges from the descriptive."[33]

The fundamental criticism of the equation "is = ought", whether in its Spinozistic or its Hegelian form, which neo-Kantian Cohennians level at such pantheism, and the analytic objection to "the naturalistic fallacy", do not hit the target in cases like Buber's (or Levinas's), because the latter are very careful to lift the "is" of the "ought" beyond nature, have it come from beyond nature, quite literally "from a better world."[34] Whether also in this more sophisticated form the very ground of ethics is not pulled out from underneath our feet is the basic question with which the present study tries to deal.

Moral Incrementalism

Let us look at some of Buber's "incrementalism".

As every intelligent reader of *I and Thou* knows, I-it and I-thou are not two different worlds but two different ways of relating to the same world.[35] Furthermore, according to Buber we cannot and should not try to live in only one of these relationships, but we can and should live in the right proportion of both—as little of the former as necessary and as much of the latter as possible. This is the central incrementalist operator in Buber's thought. From it result incrementalisms in all areas of life.

The question of the nature of evil is all-pervasive in Buber's works.[36] His most systematic statement of this problem is perhaps to be found in his *Images of Good and Evil.*[37] In sum, goodness is thouness, i.e., direction towards one's own otherness, while evil is directionlessness of the soul: "What we call evil is only the directionless plunging and storming of the sparks in need of redemption."[38] What starts out as directionlessness may turn into a "pseudo-direction,"[39] a "course of indecision,"[40] a "wrong way."[41] This wrong way, in turn, goes through several stages, and the last of these is the worst—when it is no longer realised in fact or can be realised by the individual or the group that any direction other than directionlessness, self-directedness, indeed self-absorption, is possible. One might then expect that Buber would stipulate this last stage as absolute, irredeemable, substantive evil, but he does not. Even at this stage a "reorientation" is in principle possible, and repentance, "return," is even now available to the wicked.[42] Buber can tell a large number of impressive tales from the *aggadic* and *Chasidic* repertory that exemplify the ineradicability of the capacity for redemption of even the most abandoned evil, not necessarily or not even prefarably by instantaneous but by gradual, even infinitesimal, degrees of self-redirection.

Buber himslef took many courageous actions during his lifetime that exemplify this belief of his, and he did so often at the cost of harsh hostility from people whom he prized. It has by now been noticed repeatedly that, for example, he remained extremely taciturn, almost to the point of silence, about what is called "the Holocaust," and, though he certainly was sensible of it as any other men and more sensible than most, it did not basically alter any relevant views which he had previously held. This fact is used by some commentators for tendentious political purposes.[43] Properly understood, Buber kept holy silence before this Jewish and human cataclyism, unlike so many who have made a growth-industry of it, while he "confessed that there was not an hour when he did not think of it."[44] In *Images of Good and Evil* he personified the three stages of evil in Adam, Cain, and Persian dualistic evil; in his 1942 essay 'People and Leader'[45] the third place is occupied by Jacob Frank. Frank is here clearly the pseudonym for Hitler, but with the important difference that the Jew Buber picks the Jew Frank as his Hitler-image. In *Gog and Magog* (= *For the Sake of Heaven*)[46] Buber puts on the stage of the *Chasidic* struggle over Napoleon "the demon", whom, in the 'Epilolgue', he explicitly describes as "a demon with bat wings and the features of a judaised Goebbels."[47] (The wise will understand.) In the collection of philosophical essays under the title *The Eclipse of God*[48] the point is that it is not "the Holocaust" but modern immanentist, technological society that has eliminated thou-values, God, from human life. But even in this condition of God's hiding, it is and "eclipse," not "death," which we face, and even a slight shift of the observer's location can, perhaps, let the sun come out again. "The eclipse of the light of God is no extinction; even tomorrow that which has stepped in between may give way."[49] Thus even here evil is not, because it cannot be, ineradicable.

Buber went even further in the speech he made on accepting the Goethe prize of the German publishing industry, repeating, this time before a German audience on German soil after the war, that no one that can be regarded as human is beyond relational restoration.[50] (N.b. his wily formulation.) And I remember the circular that Buber sent also to me, as an unqualified opponent of the death penalty, requesting my signature to a petition to the President of the State of Israel for the commutation of Adolf Eichmann's sentence (not for his pardon).[51]

The problem with Buber's incrementalist position, both in theory and in practice, is, of course, how to determine the right proportion between itness and thouness. Furthermore, who is to make such a determination? What are the criteria by which the determination is to be made?

Buber's answer to these and similar questions is that no predetermined answers to criteria are either possible or desirable. Predetermined considerations would perforce have to be culled from the world of itness, of abstract, theoretical, mechanical rules. Proper answers can be arrived at only in the reality of a personal confrontation of the parties concerned, in the human interaction between them.

Line of Demarcation

This is the Buberian doctrine of "the line of demarcation,"[52] which Ernst Akiba Simon has rightly stressed.[53] There is, as we have seen, the perennial tension in all human life between the "thou" and the "it"; we can never do without both; and the question is always only one of how much there is to be of the former and how little of the latter. Buber defined this "line of demarcation" most concisely, perhaps, in his famous address to the Twelfth Zionist Congress, in 1921, which is shot through with the idea of "demarcation," in the following formula:[54] Only the secret of hourly acting with a continually repeated sense of responsibility holds the rule for such demarcation." In every actual situation, says Buber, there is always, as a matter of fact, too little "thou" and too much "it"; every actual situation is capable of more "thou" than it comprises and viable with less "it" than it possesses. The line of demarcation has to be determined situationally, out of the I-thou which enters the situation and determines the "*quantum satis*," "the sufficiency," that essentially, morally, defines it.[55] As Buber put it:[56] "'*Quantum satis*' means in the language of lived truth not 'either-or' but 'as much as one can.'" It is "*the truth of the boundary*" ("*die Wahrheit der Grenze*").[57]

Buber's doctrine of the *quantum satis* of itness can usefully be shown to correspond to Marx's doctrine of surplus value. Another Buberian designation for it is actually "the political surplus," i.e., the excess of "society" beyond the necessary delimitations of "community." Buber's "political surplus" and Marx's "surplus value" is each, in its respective systematic context, the fountainhead of all social evil.

It is, on the other hand, striking that there is not a single page of concrete economic analysis anywhere in Buber's *oeuvre*, though he was a leading Socialist theoretician.[58] This, too, can be explained in terms of Marx's and Buber's respective outlooks: for Marx social causation is basically economic, and economic analysis of the infrastructure can and must, therefore, be carried out with respect to past and present, while prediction of future social effects as superstructure is at best speculative; for Buber, on the other hand, social causation as infrastructure is basically spiritual, and, in turn, spiritual analysis can and must therefore, be carried out with respect to past and present, while prediction of future economic effects as superstructure is at best speculative. "And he (Isaiah) knows and says: a kingdom of justice will come . . . But he knows nothing and says nothing about the structure of that kingdom."[59]

The parallax between Marx and Buber also extends, then, to the notion of "the line of demarcation." Marx and Bolsheviks hold that, after the proletarian revolution, a transition regime is necessary, while the vestiges and dangers of capitalism are eliminated; this is the same area in society which is defined as lying in the negative, "political," side of Buber's ever-changing, transitional "line of demarcation." This having been said, it has to be added quickly, however, that the reduciton of the transitional stages of "society" as contrasted with "community," Buber's equivalent of capitalism and Socialism, on the one hand, and Communism, on the other, may not be carried out, according to him, in any dictatorial fashion, unlike "the dictatorship of the proletariat" or of its conscious *avant-garde* in the form of the "party."

Ernst Akiba Simon righlty contrasts this Buberian doctrine of "the line demarcation" and of "sufficiency" with Hermann Cohen's Kantian doctrine of the asymptote.[60] For Cohen the ethical and even the epistemological imperative is infinite, and man's task is in every situation to approach that infinity as much as possible. Buber agrees with Cohen that only the actual attempt to reach the infinite will prove how close to it a given empirical situation is susceptible to being brought.[61] Both, therefore, reject a Niebuharian claim that man can know beforehand what his human and moral limitations are and, on the basis, abstain from even trying to push human capability too far.[62] The difference between Buber and Cohen on this score lies then in the fact that Cohen argues the objective rationality of the infinite goal, which, therefore, can also determine the objective legitimacy of any intermediate stage, whereas Buber insists on the ineluctable subjectivity of both.[63] (Even Simon, the loyal, though independent, friend of Buber, dares question this, when he asks[64] whether partial moral moratoriums can always be allowed.) Cohen could, whereas Buber could not, define what the "there" is of the valid Buberian concern with "getting from here to there".

Collapse of Buber's Reasoning

Buber's own repsonse to the question here raised is vacuous, despite its complexity and sophistication. It amounts to saying that there are no answers, and, indeed, that there should not be any answers. Each instance of each relationship is expected to produce its own determination of the proper proportion of itness and thouness, of goodness and evil.[65] Subjectivity, in perhaps its good but certainly also in its pejorative sense, here celebrates a triumph.[66] One may sympathize with people who say that they speak to God every day; it becomes worrisome when they say that God speaks to them every day.

Buber denies, of course, that he is ethically subjectivistic. That which "comes to" a man in a morally problematic situation is not subjective but, he argues, transcendently compelling. Ze'ev Levy has, therefore, spoken of this as neither objectivistic or subjectivistic but as "transjective." But how do the absolute values, which are asserted to be obtained in this way, in fact function? They do not really function at all, as Levy also went on to point out; they come only in the form of subjective "receptions."[67] We are thus back at square one.

The final result of this view of evil and its mutability is that Buber is really incapable of specifying any evil. Perhaps he is also unwilling to do this. (And this parallels his rejection of *Halakhah*, in Judaism, because in his view *Halakhah*, too, claims to make objective rules out of subjective, inter-personal imperatives that arise out of the encounter between an human and a divine thou.)[68]

A concrete political example can illustrate Buber's incrementalism. His lifelong wavering between pacifism and non pacifism results from his basic posture. On the one hand, it was perfectly clear to him (even before *I and Thou* and before the First World War) that killing and war were incompatible with his metaphysical commitment to the ultimacy of person, human, values. At that time and again in the 1920s, 1930s, and 1950s, Buber was a full-fledged member of intellectual, political, and artistic circles which acted on their pacifism. Gustav Landauer, Stefan Zweig, Frans Masereel, Franz Werfel, Romain Rolland,[69] Christian and Socialist radicals, etc., are prominently associated with the pacifist artistic and religious international at the time of the First World War. Buber's affiliation with and intellectual contributions to socio-political ideologies and movements in those decades were clearly of the pacific, if not of the doctrinally pacifist, sort: philosophical anarchism and communitarianism, Arab-Jewish cooperation, even the Jewish peace movement after the Second World War again.[70] On the other hand, one cannot close one's eyes to the fact that in every war that actually erupted he identified himself—however moderately and tragically—with one of the warring sides:

the Central Powers during the First World War,[71] certainly in the Second World War with the Allies,[72] and when the Arab-Israeli war occurred in 1948 he closed his preface to *Two Types of Faith*[73] with this sentence: "The work involved has helped me to endure in faith this war, for me the most grievous of the three. Martin Buber. Jerusalem-Talbiyeh, January 1950." This sentence strikes one as one of the most melancholy sentences imaginable, for it clearly implies a) that two world wars, in all their magnitudes, devastated Buber less than the small Arab-Israeli war, obviously because his life's work was destroyed in the process (as was Judah Magnes's, Ernst A. Simon's, Hans Kohn's, and that of others), b) that he was fully, painfully, conscious of his own historic ineffectiveness, but c), in the context of the present concern, that he was not really in a position, either practically or even theoretically, to say a decisive word in that hour which could even hope to stem the flood.[74] As he put it himself most apodictically: "(w)hen there is war it must be fought."[75] Frankly and simply, Buber's view seems unintelligible. Either killing is, or it is not, incompatible with the single most obvious imperative entailed in the I-thou aspect of the universe—and Buber must and did hold that it is incompatible. How one can then be "incrementalist" about any specific killing is beyond comprehension.[76] One cannot even see how the murderer can ever again move away from having murdered; one certainly cannot see how the victim can incrementally regain his life.

If this is right, then not only is it important in itself, but it also constitutes a methodological breakthrough on Buber's basic philosophical methodology, within his own categories and terms. In other words, it is a fundamental and internal critique. If his incrementalism is conceptually and morally inconsistent with his declared values (so much so that only inconsistent behaviour will square with his inconsistent views), then surely one ought to reconsider the validity and functionality of that incrementalism and of the presuppositions on which it is based.[77]

The State

As a final practical example of Buber's incrementalism we consider his theory of the State. Philosophical anarchist that he was throughout his life, he held that the State is, of course, the very consummation of itness, especially in our advanced technological, bureaucratic mass age. He, therefore, agreed with Marx that the goal of history was the abolition of the State, but not, contrary to Marx, by going through the historical dialectic of alienation, in the expectation that this would produce its own "sublation": "As I do not believe in Marx's 'hatching' of the new configuration, so do I not believe in Bakunin's virgin birth out of the womb of the revolution. But I do believe in the encounter of image and destiny in the plastic hour."[78] Buber taught that, wherever possible, to the greatest possible degree, "community," i.e., social thouness, should be substituted for "society" and the State, i.e., itness.[79] Thus he arrives, at the end of *Paths in Utopia*, at the well-known conclusion that, from this decisive point of view, the kibbutz ("which, despite everything, I dare call 'Jerusalem'") is the "model non-failure" alternative to Moscow.[80] (One wonders whether Buber would still adhere to this view in the light of the subsequent developments of the kibbutz in its Israeli setting.)[81]

Buber realized, again, that men cannot live in community exclusively all the time any more than they can live exclusively in personal thouness. Means must be used, not only ends enacted. By the same token, laws must be instituted in society (however much he thought that his Judaism could do without *halakhah*); mass action is sometimes unavoidable; the State, while it lasts (which is not foreseeably brief), will have to make use of men for its purposes; etc. He mentions specifically the punitive power of the State, propaganda, and the military, whereas bureaucracy is, of course, the very consummation of itness.[82] So here again Buber arrives at incrementalist conclusions: have as much community as possible and as little society as neccessary[83] ("no more State than is indispensable, no less freedom that is allowable"),[84] even as we must accept as much evil as necessary for life, although also no more than this.[85] Though on these and on historically Jewish grounds Buber rejects the validity of the notion of *raison d'état*[86] he, again, acknowledges the reality of "necessary compromises" in this form.[87] Naturally the question cannot be 'centralization or decentralization?' but only: 'In what areas is a greater measure permissible of the decentralization of disposable capacity than the existing measure?' This demarcation must, of course, always be revised and renewed in accordance with changing conditions."[88] Or, describing Landauer's view, he says: "... the degree of incapacity for a voluntary right order determines the degree of legitimate compulsion."[89] And, as we have seen, anything that exceeds the permissible or legitimate amount of society is then "surplus politics", which, like Marx's surplus-value, can almost be quantified and is to be abolished.[90]

The Need for Formal Criteria

Several criticisms of the basic operators in Buber's political philosophy have begun to emerge in the course of our exposition so far. Now these criticisms must be stated more fully, and, above all, traced systematically to the philosophical, metaphysical underpinnings on which they rest.

Because of what we have seen to be Buber's quasi-phenomonologistic, panentheistic, and certainly vitalistic penchant, he insisted on deriving moral and social value from "reality", in one way and to some degree or another. As the Hegelian Marx spurned Kantian "ideas" and "ideals" in favour of what he thought of as "actuality", so Buber distrusted theories, principles, and other abstractions in favour of what he believed to be human realities. In this way he, and others like him, thought they would be able to close the gap between philosophy and life, make theory "relevant" and "lebensnahe". But, of course, "reality" depends on what it is taken to be. As Günther Grass puts it poetically: "noch oder wieder: Federn blase ich leicht/und behaupte, was schwebt."[91]

Christian pessimists like Reinhold Niebuhr and his Jewish disciple Will Herberg, like Hobbes and other socio-political conservatives, look at the world and at man in it, and they conclude that physical and human nature are profoundly corrupt and, therefore, in need of some external discipline—the State, the fear of God, etc. The anarchist tradition, on the other hand, has always proclaimed its belief in the inherent original goodness of man, and Buber, within this tradition, thus held that the improvement of society only required a truer understanding of the nature of man, as the ever-present potentiality of good,[92] and a corresponding re-arrangement of society, in order to pry off the barnacles that had historically encrusted round them.

If one wanted to argue this question of the rather shallow level of overt political history, one could say that the facts of Buber's own lifetime clearly belied his faith. But, of course, like all thinkers, he would have many ways of explaining the facts without being forced into such a conclusion. For one thing, as we reminded ourselves at the beginning of these considerations, he entertained no optimistic views about past or present history: "This is the function assigned to the religious man within the revolution, to perish, perhaps one may say: to perish exemplarily . . ."[93] For another, he could and did, of course, claim that, even if it is not true that history and not his truth was wrong in general, certainly so relatively short and, on just about any ground, so tragic a period as the twentieth century is scarcely a decisive test of his socio-ethical programme. One might wish to accept the validity of such counter-arguments from Buber—although it certainly is paradoxical for people like him, who put so high a value on "realism", to be as unaffected—and unaffecting—of obvious reality as they are in fact.[94]

The issue basically is not between Christian-conservative pessimism and anarchist-liberal optimism about the moral quality of human nature. This is a bootless debate. It assumes on both sides of the argument some eternal essence of humanness, instead of facing the fact that man, like everything else, is an historical product, whose moral quality, too, is determined by historical changes. Worse, either way it consequently makes ethics conditional on the vagaries of such misconceived historical realities. Whatever happens in fact, even in some I-thou event, does not and cannot determine what ought to happen. The very fact that love, sprung from an I-thou relationship, can and occasionally does produce moral monstrosities, like murder, and that "community", as the social embodiment of human relations, is historically an arch-conservative, mythological, and even racist, folkist experience and ideology[95] should put us sufficiently on guard.

It cannot be answered that, if murder or racism be the outcome, the experience that underlies it cannot have been an I-thou relationship: this would be, as we have stated before, a circular argument, and, furthermore, it displays its dependency on formal criteria, as we are about to see more fully, inasmuch as it obviously requires a prior argument for the wickedness of murder or racism.

Here it is believed that men like Buber, Landauer, Hans Kohn (in his earlier stage), a.o., were saved from the invidiousness of their own romantic ideologies only, on the personal level, by the profound decency of their personal characters (that is, their inconsistently held high moral values), and, on the ideological level, by their theoretical inconsistencies.[96]

Not optimism or pessimism about acuality but deontology—formal ethics—turns out to be the issue. That which Buber most wanted to avoid, theoreticism, is, in the first place, unavoidable, in the second, indispensably desirable, and, in the third place, it in fact sneaked back into his value-system. (This was fortunate for his character and historical role, but it is unfortunate for the tenability of his fundamental doctrines.) Not what people do experience as the moral imperative in any situation, be it I-thou or I-it, but what can and must rationally be expected to be the moral values that underlie and result from their lives constitutes ethics. As Hans Kohn, in a perceptive (although somewhat fuzzy and too conciliatory) passage said as early as 1930:[97] "Here formal ethics come into their own. Ultimate goals are to be attained."[98]

History in Buber

One can get at the theoretical inconsistency that Kohn correctly discerned in Buber's ethics in an interesting, lateral way: Buber's *oeuvre* comprises a lot of historical scholarship, Biblical, *hasidic*, intellectual, social, etc. The historiography that he did was clearly and intentionally "objective history", i.e., events subject to public criteria. (And the purpose of historiography for him was the expectation that the responsible individual fit himself into the continuum of his and her history, so that of the Jews, for example, "the Jewish Bible demands that the individual fit his own life into this true history . . . ")[99] At the same time, many observers of Buber have rightly noted a peculiar ahistoricality about his very historiography. Gershom Scholem claims that "he (Buber) has often said that he is not interested in history",[100] and Friedman admits[101] that "Buber's ethics . . . does not decisively depend on [history and historic revelation]".[102]

On the fact of it this seems a peculiar self-contradiction. What brings it about is Buber's combination of Kierkegaardian existentialism with worldliness[103] (religious secularism), i.e., the insistence that the I-thou meeting take place *in* the world, *ergo* in history, and yet that the encounter itself is non-historical. Thus the I-thou enters, as it were, the world of I-it and immediately denatures, dehistoricises, de-ittifies it. (Buber's attitude is, therefore, nowhere near so incompatible with historic *hasidism* as Scholem represents it to be.)[104] Thus, for example, to Buber's way of thinking the historic event at Mount Sinai addresses a thou only for "that specific hour."[105] In other words, there is a "tradition", i.e., history, but then it is a question of "listening" to this tradition,[106] i.e., to discard it except for what, at any given moment, "grabs" you from within it.

It is hard to fathom why a man like Buber, so sensitive to history, wants to break off the power of history so early in his involvement with it. He knows that the subjects that encounter one another in history are greatly formed by their respective prehistories. Therefore, they meet not as non-historical subjects, and their histories enter into their encounter together with them. Their histories are, therefore, part-and-parcel of what emerges from their relationship. It will simply not do, although Buber does it, to permit objectivity, ittishness, to come only to the threshold of the house of the thou; it inevitably crosses into the interior. And the question that arises in the context of Buber's categories is how this factor of objectivity can be synthesized with the subjectivity that should be the essence of the meeting.

It cannot be the task of a critic to offer better alternatives than the thinker's of whom he speaks—even if he could. It is also not at all clear that this can be done within the frame of reference provided by Buber. Nonetheless, the following consideration may serve as a possible supplementation of Buber's philosophy of politics that just possibly may prop it up where it stands in need of propping-up and, within reasonable reach of its own presuppositions, to correct it where it needs correcting. (This is meant as an experiment; it does not by any means commit us to the frame of reference itself.)

Buber's lifelong and massive concern with messianism[107]—unavoidable for anyone involved in Jewish culture—could surely be regarded as the rather obvious third alternative beyond the ittishness of history and the subjectivity of the I-thou. Buber rightly perceives the adumbrations of messianism, "the footsteps of the Messiah" (*ikvot, 'otiyot mashi'ach*), throughout the course of history. But, of course, the consummation of messianism is, by definition, always future. Buber insists more than most others, to the distress of his Christian admirers,[108] that to pull the messianic arrow out of the quiver of the future is a betrayal of the very essence of messianism. And the future is something that man can never "encounter". Human life, religion, is "*Gegenwart*" —present, "over-againstness". If not messianism itself then certainly the messianic consummation, from which alone messianism can, obviously, derive, has to be a concept, an "ideal," an ethico-theoretical construction (precisely in the Kantian sense which Buber so abhors). He abhors it, but in the logic of his own case he cannot do without it. The "advent", "the end of days", is logically incapable of being enshrined in or even produced by the encounter. To the contrary, it is and has to be an objectively set goal, an "*Aufgabe*", task, as both Kant and Hermann Cohen called it. "The yoke of the kingdom of God" has to be shouldered before, according to the rabbis, "the yoke of the commandments" (i.e., moral responsibilities) can be seen to be incumbent.[109] Without the conceptual goal of "the advent" there would be only atomic messianic events, not messianic history, and, at that, it would be difficult to imagine why even these could be called "messianic".

Buber's Aesthetics

Moshe Schwarcz, in his essay 'Martin Buber's Aesthetic Thought',[110] criticised and tried to supplement Buber's aesthetics in a way which in part parallels our suggestion here and in part is identical with it. Schwarcz pointed out that Buber stipulates an "anthropological" drive for perfection—the perfection of a "possible world" which, by definition, cannot be deduced from the real world but is an human construction. The term used traditionally by philosophical aesthetics with which to designate this perfection, as Schwarcz also correctly reminds us, is "the sublime". He refers to classicism and mentions the names of Mendelssohn, Lessing, and—Hegel. Here the *objet d'art* is the actualisation of the human conception of the sublime, perfect world. In the end, probably out of some residual Jewish horror of the imaging of God, Buber rejects too close a connection between faith and art (*'emunah* and *'amanut*) by insisting that the *objet d'art*, while, on the one hand, the only possible human revelation of perfection, also, on the other hand, conceals the quintessentially non-figurative Thou (= perfection) behind itself. (In his 1922 Lectures[111] he cites Goethe, with some reservation: "Das Höchste, das Vollkommenste im

Menschen ist gestaltlos. Man soll sich hüten, es anders als in edler Tat zu gestalten.") Schwarcz concluded[112] that Buber here goes too far: formalistic, abstract, non-figurative art is "transcendental-monotheistic"; i.e., it is in principle capable of pointing beyond itself to the infinite sublime and thus constitutes Jewish art.

Why does Schwarcz carefully avoid the name of Kant in this connection (and *a fortiori* that of Hermann Cohen)? He does mention Hegel, but only with reference to "the spiritual presuppositions of the Judaeo-Christian faith" (whatever that may be).[113] Hegel distinguishes, as a matter of fact, between the (Jewish) art (and religion) of "Erhabenheit" (= "Unaufgehobenheit") ("loftiness"/"sublimity"/"unsublatedness") and the Christian-Greek art of infinite and yet incarnate beauty, and he naturally gives preference to the latter. In Kantianism, on the other hand, it is, indeed, the case that art, in the spirit and according to the very letter of the Third *Critique* (not to speak of Cohen's *Ästhetik des reinen Gefühls*), is the *a priori* creation of objects of perfection—the physical adumbration of the ideal constructions of the postulates at the end of the First *Critique*. Now, it is true that for Buber, unlike Kant and Hermann Cohen, these, as it were, physical ideas are taken from reality, "anthropology", rather than non-empirical reason, but, this important difference aside, it remains also true for Buber as for Kantians that these artistic realisations of perfection and sublimity constitute the normative goals toward which the real world is to strive. As Schwarcz suggested that, had Buber not shied away from the logic of his own essential messianic historiosophy, he would have been able to do greater justice to the role of formal ethics (not unrelated to formalistic aesthetics) in theoretical morality and social philosophy. In fact, he did neither, because he thought that he had to insist on the basic irrationality of the "spirit" behind art and behind morality. He was simply too sceptical about the creative and propelling power of human reason.

Collapse of Buber's Politics

At one decisive point in Buber's life he came awfully close to the insight here recommended. In 1932 he gave a speech, 'About the Ethics of Political Decisions',[114] which is still completely couched in terms of his situational ethics. In one particular sentence he even formulates the point that we have adduced, that for him history leads man to the threshold of the I-thou, but it may not cross that threshold: "Man must prepare himself (for his responsibility), armed with all the 'ought' forged in his group but exposed to the destiny that in the fathomless moment all the armour drops off him."[115] Only a little (but decisive) time later, on 1st May 1933(!), he gave another speech, 'Politics out of Faith',[116] this time, as Ernst Simon puts it plausibly,[117] "apparently at a public Jewish meeting in Frankfurt"—in which occurs the following sentence[118] (which, however, Simon does not cite in his extensive quotation): "*Redemption* [M.B.'s italics] is the completion of God's creation into the *Kingdom of God* ... This tremendous and necessary thought [!] produces the connection of our faith with our personal lives."

It is true that also in this speech the rest of his considerations revolve completely around the centrality of situations. Just the same, and perhaps precisely because of this, it is the more striking that just in the situation of addressing Jews in Nazi Germany on 1st May 1933, Buber feels constrained to designate messianism as a "thought", "Gedanke", whereas at all other times, as far as one can see, every time he uses such vocabulary he immediately goes on to emphasize that he does not mean intellectualistic, rationalistic constructions. It seems that on this occasion, at least, "the situation" was not sufficient for, or not even susceptible to, discerning the imperative of the hour.[119]

Thus, the very messianism to which Buber paid so much attention[120] but whose logical foundations he was unwilling to analyse is in fact the matrix of objective conceptualisation out of which "laws" (*halakhah*) and legal rulings (*p'sakim*) emerge. This is also the deontological framework which Hans Kohn sensed as underlying Buber's ethics (like, for example, the search for "community", etc.) but which Buber did not want to acknowledge. To be sure, a *p'sak* is then the application of a law to a given situation; otherwise, to use the vocabulary which both Buber and Rosenzweig borrowed from Kant,[121] the *Gesetz(deen)* does not become a *Gebot* (*mitzvah*). Also, it is true, the law must be "encountered" by the individual or community and grasped; otherwise, it is performed mechanically, if at all, without *kavvanah*, and, therefore, ultimately to no good, redeeming effect. But it is, when all is said and done, the law, rules, objective standards, etc., that is so met. In the philosophical vocabulary of Kant, "ideas", as infinite goals, are the foundation of both scientific and moral experience.

Rosenzweig and Simon tried to put this point to Buber any number of times.[122] He repeatedly admitted to them—and otherwise—that the law was, indeed, such that it could become a thou.[123] When Rosenzweig and Simon accuse him of doing less than justice to the "it",[124] Buber admits[125] that "in another era I would presumably have been permitted to proclaim the glory of the 'it,' not today ..."[126] Indeed, at one other time he sounds as if he had accepted the point that Rosenzweig had made to him in *The Builders* in 1923: in his *Moses*, pp. 188ff., Buber asserts that Moses rightly "laid down the law", so that it would be available for thou-ish appropriation by individuals and for the community in history. Indeed, here he holds, as we would, that, Jewishly speaking, history is, in fact, the way of the Law towards the Kingdom. But this seems to be an unique expression of sympathy for the Law in Buber's *oeuvre*. (Has the fact that it was published in 1944 something to do with this?) For the rest he always holds to what he had said in *I and Thou* about Moses's law: it is not an "ought", and it becomes operative only "in the presence of the countenance", as "love", and then it produces "as if non-action".[127] Furthermore, Kant long since had made the fundamental point that the law can and does produce a "feeling" all its own, "logos-produced" and *a priori*, extrapolated by Hermann Cohen into a whole *Äesthetik des reinen Gefühls*.[128] This "pure feeling" is, on analysis, identified with *kavvanah* in the context of Buber's dialogicism; it fills precisely the place and the function which Buber assigns to it, but it is not conditional on Buber's subjetivism. This is, however, a route which Buber refused to take.[129]

Buber could not take this route for an interesting reason that arises out of what may be called his (implicit) philosophy of time (and thus of history). The I-thou is for him always "present" (*Gegenwart*)—present, however, in some non-temporal sense, i.e., "eternity". The past is always "it", unless it is drawn into an I-thou ambience, and then it ceases to be past. Past is thus always as such ittish; present is as such always non-temporal. What is the status of the future in this view? It can presumably be only either thouish, but then it is not future, nor, for that matter, any kind of time, or it can be truly time that has not yet occurred, but then it has to be ittish. This last possibility must, however, be rejected by Buber, because otherwise the goal of history would comprise the destruction of humanness as he understands it. Therefore, thouish future turns out to be non-future, indeed, non-temporal.

This is a benevolent way of looking at it, if one wishes, as Buber does especially in his interpretation of *hasidism*, to lift every possible moment in time out of the stream of chronology, to "eternalise" it,[130] in order to emphasize, as it were, metaphysical and ethically decisive, messianic significance. One does this, however, at the expense of the very possibility of time itself and, therefore, of the rationality of a notion of true future. This, too, Buber is naturally not prepared to surrender. The result is that he tries to hold on to both horns of the dilemma—a real and thouish future together with the atemporality of all thouishness. By his own standards this cannot be done, unless one wants to proclaim "the collapse of logos" itself.[131]

So Buber's metaphysic is what Will Herberg rightly called a 'situational ethic".[132] It is sometimes also called an existentialist ethic, and its historical connection with the discovery of Kierkegaard in Germany in the first two decades of the present century is clear.[133] The literature on situational ethics that cropped up in the West in the late 1960s supplies much argument for its arbitrariness, its high degree of principled subjectivity, and moral unreliability. In the hands of good people—and there are many such in every anti-establishment culture—such situational ethics may be devoted to praiseworthy and even compelling values. Certainly this was the case with Buber himself. He, furthermore, vehemently denied that his ethics possessed such individualistic character: "It is an individual ethic, which, however, is bare of all arbitrariness and subjectivity. For the fulfillment of the individual personality is the fulfilment of the will of God, obedience towards the objective truth of being."[134]

The last sentence articulates all the good will but also all the philosophical untenability of his doctrine. No doubt, to Buber God's will commanded humanity. But a) he cannot and does not want to determine what God's will commands other than in what he hears, and we are, therefore, back in the circular argument to which we previously directed attention—no Bible, *halakhah*, church-authority, or rule-governed ethic for him; b) "the objective truth of being" is, of course, an even vaguer notion than that of God's will; and c) "the fulfillment of the individual personality" sends us back, again, to the anarchist optimism about human nature and dogmatic assertions about its potential, of which, too, we have spoken earlier.[135]

To return specifically to the political question with which we are here primarily concerned—a programme is bound to fail which insists in principle on saying to its potential adherents: we have no specific programme, no specific legislation or course of action to purpose, no specific policies to advocate; instead, each of us individually and all of us collectively will, in each moment and in each situation, face up to whatever are the most humane needs that then and there exist, and we will try to satisfy those needs as best we can. No reasonable person would join such a political movement (if it can even be called this). One reason that Gandhi was politically so much more effective with his people and their rulers than Buber was with his is that Gandhi had some clear, unambiguous, and objective goals—independence, unqualified pacifism, rejection of industrialism, etc.—,whereas Buber's programme was, when all was said and done, not only moral but also moralistic. "Sei a mentsh!", while true and important, is simply too vacuous a norm to be, or to be seen to be, helpful in specific situations—and life consists of specific situations.

If situational ethics are unhelpful even in the hands of good people, what must they turn out to be in the hands of the bad? If Buber thought that the First World War was a tragic necessity, what compelling grounds could he appeal to in arguing that Ben-Gurion and certainly Begin were wrong in holding that the Arab-Israeli wars were tragic necessities (to be embraced with varying degree of *amor fati*)? Buber's insistence on the riskiness of "the narrow ridge"[136] foreswore principled resort to any rules, laws or other universal. It is, therefore, possible in principle to draw the line of demarcation, which defines his incrementalism, at almost any point. Simon quotes Buber regarding Arab-Jewish conciliation: "To the extent to which it depends on us, we have to prepare the ground for the present hour."[137] In Simon's introduction to the volume of Buber's collected Hebrew socio-political writings, writing long after the State of Israel was established and the bi-national ideal, therefore, defeated, Simon, while rightly still insisting that the human and historical values of that ideal could and should be fought for even under these new, uni-national circumstances,[138] nonetheless admits (in a marvelous rabbinic pun): "He renders a verdict, but the law does not follow him."[139] It cannot then come as a surprise that some of Buber's closest and most devoted surviving practical disciples in the left-wing kibbutz-movement have been integrated into the Israeli political and military system with no less enthusiasm than anyone else.

Buber and his associates were theoretically extremely conciliatory, though in practice they displayed great moral steadfastness, uncompromising uprightness, and what the Germans call "civil courage". In this study we are concerned with theory only. In this theoretical context Buber wanted—one may perhaps say—to be too much Plato's philosopher-king, i.e., the thinker who also wanted to determine history (in his case, the history of Zionism),[140] and he, therefore, developed an incrementalist theory to underlie the incrementalist actions in which, undoubtedly, a politician does, indeed, have to engage. If, on the other hand, he had been content to be Kant's intellectual, i.e., the thinker who criticises and may at best expect to be consulted by, but does not aspire to be identical with, the statesman,[141] he might have been able to develop the consistent and radical theory which is here being proposed. The politicians who, at best, will make use of the thinkers' theories, will make the necessary compromises more than empirical conditions require anyway. Thus Buber's confusion of his own roles, whether of artist or theoretician,[142] or whether of politician and philosopher, often had pernicious effects on his thinking.

Even with respect to concrete political issues this weakness of Buber's manifested itself. Buber endeavoured throughout his life to "meet" the Arabs and to arrive at a creative *modus vivendi* (in the most literal sense of the phrase) with them. Perhaps because he thought of himself—rightly—as so quintessential a Jew himself, he did not "meet" his fellow-Zionists quite in the same way: it would have been like meeting himself. As a result, he, the Jew, like some others, was always alone among Jews. Suppose for a moment, though, that he had "met" Ben-Gurion or Menahem Begin in a full dialogical way; what might have been the concrete political compromise between them? A "demarcation line" near Hebron rather than either on the Jordan or on the 1948 United Nations lines? Clearly, this is not what Buber had in mind. Perhaps bi-nationalism, or, for that matter, confederation, was, or should have been, "non-negotiable" for him. It may still be the imperative that confronts the semitic peoples of the Near East—and it is an objective historical and ethical imperative, regardless of the perceived sentiments of the politicians at any given moment.

Or, to adduce another specific historic event, take the Eichmann execution.[143] Buber certainly deserved full credit for courageously and intelligently having opposed it.[144] His fullest theoretical statement of why he opposed the death penalty in general appears to have been formulated in 1928, in reply to a questionnaire. The reply consists of three numbered sentences,[145] of which the first two express total opposition on human and social grounds to capital punishment. The third sentence then reads as follows: "Limits must be drawn around society's self-protection, by the criterion of the purpose of this self-protection, and these limits must always be re-examined."[146] What this sentence says is that the death penalty is alleged to have been instituted for the protection of society—that, as the previous two sentences declared, it does not actually serve that purpose—but that it must always be situationally re-examined whether in any given, perhaps extraordinary, case it might not, after all, serve that purpose, and in that case, presumably, the death sentence might be ethically imposed after all.

That Buber did not change his mind on this score is also indicated by what Audrey Hodes[147] reports him to have said at the time of the Eichmann trial: "He would make no exceptions to his basic opposition to the death penalty on principle." The very well-meaning but not very sophisticated Hodes reports, one could guess, Buber's statement almost in *verba ipissima*. He was so impressed, however, with Buber's practical posture that he failed to understand the qualifying phrases "basic" and "on principle".[148] What, in conformity with his statement of 1928 and with his ethics in general, Buber was actually saying was that he, of course, opposed the death penalty, also in the case of Eichmann, but that this was his "basic", not his universal, thesis, and that he held to this thesis "in principle" but not necessarily in every conceivable practical case and situation. Buber's attitude to this problem then comes down to the proposition that he opposes capital punishment in principle and in every actual instance, but he refuses to commit himself to the same stand for all future, unpredictable instances.[149]

In principle one need not deny the logical, philosophical, and ethical possibility of affirming a theoretical principle while rejecting every concrete instantiation of this principle. Thus, for example, Maimonides denied that any report of a divine miracle, even in the Bible, reported a true miracle. They all could, in fact, be explained by quite rational, natural, canons. Nonetheless, he held open the possibility that God's will might in principle work a miracle.[150] To get closer to the present issue, both Bible and Talmud certainly provide for the death penalty, but talmudic statutes in fact make the imposition of the death penalty under the law practically impossible in all cases.[151]

The problem with Buber's attitude is, therefore, neither his personal morality and uprightness, nor the consistency with which he held to his basic ethical stance, nor yet with the logical compatibility of a principled practical opposition with an amount of theoretical flexibility. The problem does reside—again—in the lack of criterion, other than the subjectivity which results from a privatistic I-thou encounter, for when this flexibility is properly to come into force.[152] If, for example, the attorney general of Israel, Gideon Hausner, had relied on Buber's third sentence quoted above and said to him: in the particular, extraordinary case of Eichmann the limits to which society can and should go in protecting itself are drawn on the other side of his execution, the argument could presumably only have dealt with factual questions—whether Buber or Hausner was right about society's need to execute Eichmann in order to protect itself. And this is, of course, precisely what happened. Buber should have been perfectly content with letting the issue turn on precisely such "situational" considerations. Anyone assigned as judge in the dispute between Buber and Hausner, however, would have to insist on knowing what the criteria are on which he is to settle their dispute, and at that point to rely on one's privatistic "verstehen" of Eichmann, Hausner, Israel, and of the world situation would seem to be entirely unacceptable—not to speak of it being unviable.

Buber relied on the moral calibre not only of man in general but of the Jewish people's extra-historical soul in particular—a reliance which persisted across the break from his earlier ethnic mysticism to his later dialogicist philosophy.[153] To the contrary, whether it be with respect to man's nature or to the nature of man's encounters, the declaration of the Psalmist (146:3ff) seems true: "Rely not on princes, on human nature in which there is no salvation ... Man's subsistence is in the Lord, his God ... who works justice for the oppressed, gives bread to the hungry ... God emancipates the imprisoned" (my literal translation). The history of the Jewish people, whether—to use Buber's early dichotomy—"underground" or official, like the history of all other human entities, is much too ambiguous a phenomenon (to put it mildly), and is again so in our time, to permit of any ethical inferences. The ethical activities, on the other hand, that the Psalmist attributed to God, are observable events. Dependent on one's construal of "God", he acts on objectively determinable rules, and thus his acts are susceptible to *imitatio Dei* and to halakhic formulation.

To put the same thing in philosophic rather than in religious language, if Kant's and Hermann Cohen's constructions are correct, then objectively determinable ethical rules and values are in fact available. To be sure, they have to be subjectively appropriated, and, this done, they have to be made incrementally functional under always changing circumstances. But, to try to be specific and political, the abolition of the death penalty, say, or the institution of a non-nationalistic form of society in the semitic Near East, or, for that matter, the abolition of the state and of capitalism as such, would be absolute goals. Human dignity and autonomy would be non-negotiable ideals, not conditional (albeit prized) products of subjective experiences, however much one might have to negotiate their practical, situation-bound realisations.

An Ambivalent Evaluation

Clearly, the critique that has been offered of Martin Buber's social and political philosophy is in the end a philosophically and even ideologically very negative one. This is very worrisome, because, as we said at the onset, this study arises out of the greatest personal respect not only for Buber as a person but also for his practical efforts in society and for his intellectual achievements. One dreads joining the hunting party on Buber that rides these days in several circles, partly for directly political reasons and partly out of academic condescension. Still, if this were all there were to it this would be simply a personal problem. But there is more to it.

Whatever may be people's reactions these days to Buber's "theology", to his aesthetics, historiography, etc., experiences show that his social and political theses continue to provoke people, especially when they are applied to specific issues. His attitude towards the Eichmann trial, for example, or his views on Arab-Jewish relations, or his critique of Marxism, etc., still arouse people's passions, ranging from positive to negative. This indicates, if nothing else, that his is a "live heritage" in the socio-political area.

Furthermore, what reasonable and promising alternatives could one have hoped to offer at the time? Some of the best minds and hearts among Jewish and other social thinkers in his time committed themselves to his, or a very similar, programme in one way or another (as Franz Rosenzweig, a non-Zionist, said even then—though the fact that Rosenzweig remained a non-Zionist and, indeed, a non-Socialist also illustrates that by no means all the best brains thought along such lines). "*Shivat tziyon*", the return of Zion, captured the imagination and idealism of some of the most sensitive people among Jews and Gentiles in the modern world. What seemed to be the viable alternatives to "the Jewish problem" (both external as well as internal) before the Second World War, not to speak of 1945 and after? And even if there were options, is there any realistic reason for thinking that they would have worked out any better than the course actually taken? Buber, like Maurice Samuel and others, realised that the flood-tide of displaced persons that emigrated to Palestine/Israel before and after 1945 could not help but wash out the idealism and the social creativity that resided in the kibbutz-movement, but, again, though the consequences may have been tragic for Zionism, for Jewish history, and for the progress of libertarian Socialism, can one be sure that the political alternatives (which, contrary to the claims of many ideologists, did exist) would have been any more satisfactory in their long-range effects? Certainly the history of pacifism and of the Jewish Diaspora does not promise any greater success than Buber and his associates achieved.

All that can be claimed for the views here presented is that they are internally more consistent and philosophically more valid that Buber's. A practical, immediate failure they almost certainly would have been no less than Buber's. It must, however, be added that, in the longest run, the neo-Kantian operator of the heuristic and regulative "as if" of the infinite and imperative realisability of the "ought" is correct—in short, that "ought" does, indeed, imply "can".[154] This point of view eagerly endorsed Buber's human, moral, and social values, but the claim has been argued that by his conceptions his values could not be achieved, whereas they could be more effectively advanced on the basis of deontological social ethics.

The delicate balance between grateful admiration and philosophical critique can, then, perhaps be formulated as follows: between a more consistent and valid conception than Buber's, accompanied by an human, moral, and intellectual record not at least equal to his, on the one hand, and Buber's conception, accompanied by his record, one would, whatever the qualms, choose the latter and recommend it to others.[155] Buber—whatever his failures and failings, and however basic these may have been—remains one of the truly great Jews and one of the great personages of the century. Few, if any alternative candidates present themselves with the authority to define our essential Jewish humanness, and this because he struggled heroically with just about all the demons—historical, moral, political, cultural and religious— that swarm through the night of our century. As he once said himself: "There is no way in this desert night."[156] Israel once came out of such a nightly struggle wounded but victorious. In the present struggle Buber was defeated. The demons are too strong. But he gave them a good fight. Who could have done better?

– 11 –

On Jewish Eschatology

Introduction

Jewish eschatological doctrine was classically and canonically formulated in the last two of Maimonides' "Thirteen Principles."[1] I quote them here in their foreshortened creedal and liturgical form.[2]

> 12. I believe with full faith in the coming of the Messiah, and, though he tarry, I anticipate him, nonetheless, on every day, when he may come.
> 13. I believe with full faith that there will be a resurrection of the dead at the time that the Creator, may His name be blessed, wills it . . .

A limited explication of these two principles will launch us on our outline of classical Jewish eschatological teachings as a whole.

Messianism

First of all, it is, of course, clear (however wide the ignorance of this in non-Jewish and often even Jewish circles) that classical Judaism authoritatively teaches both Messianism and resurrection. Secondly, as far as this formulation of Messianism is concerned, four points of detail deserve notice. One is fairly obvious—namely, that on Jewish teaching the Messiah has not yet come. Indeed, since the Jews of all generations recite the Maimonidean credo every day of their lives,[3] as will those of all future generations, the logic of this formulation entails that—if one may put it like this—the Messiah will always not yet have come, into all historical eternity. It is his coming, or rather the expectation of his coming, not his arrival, his "advent," that is obligatory Jewish faith. In Maimonides' own words, "Set no time limit to his coming!"[4] (Isaac Abrabanel even makes an argument against Maimonides out of this: a "principle of the faith" would have to be nontemporally true, once the Messiah has come one would no longer "believe" in and "anticipate" his coming; *ergo* . . .)[5]

This leads straight into the strikingly unusual phrasing of the last part of the twelfth principle, taken from Habakkuk 2:3: "*achakeh lo bechol yom sheyavo*."[6] This is usually translated to the effect that "I will await him on any day on which he may come." But the Hebrew is at best awkward if this is to be the sense of it—namely, that we do not know on which particular day he may come, and we must, therefore, be ready for him, as it were, on any day. The wording does not lend itself to this explication. What the text says is not that the Messiah may come on any day but that he does come, conditionally, on every day, on all days. Into all eternity the Messiah comes, conditionally, on every day.[7] "As sustenance comes every day, so does redemption come every day."[8]

The significance of this conception is well caught in the talmudic *aggadeta*, that Rabbi Joshua ben Levi found the Messiah sitting at the gates of Rome, constantly rebinding his wounds, and asked him when he would "come." The Messiah answered: "Today" (*hayom*, lit. "the day").[9] Joshua was flabbergasted at this apparent and extreme adventism, so the son of David explained: "Today—if ye keep God's commandments" [i.e., if all of you transform into actuality all of God's will for the world— this is, or this causes, the Messianic advent).[10]

We can thus also better understand the verb in the imperfect tense—*achakeh*. It is usually translated as "await," but there are several Hebrew terms for this notion. *Lechakkot* is different from, to use the colloquialism, "sitting on one's backside and awaiting developments." It is a very active verb without any quietistic connotations. When one *mechakkeh*, one is doing something very energetically. Compare it to a runner in the starting position of a sprint: he is not running yet; he looks stationary; in fact, however, all his muscles and nerves are highly tensed, so that he can get the fastest possible start the second the gun sounds. "Anticipate," therefore, perhaps comes closest in English to the meaning of the term—anticipate actively and joyfully, the way one makes practical and emotional preparations for the return of a wife who has been away on a long trip, or, in the words of Maimonides, describing the practice of omer, "as is done by one who waits for the coming of the human being that he loves best and counts the days and the hours."[11]

Finally, still dealing with vocabulary, this is, of course, also the strong implication of the introductory phrase to every one of the Thirteen Principles—*'ani ma'ameen be'emunah shlemah*. In English we cannot readily say, "I believe with full belief," or "I have faith with full faith," but this is exactly what the Hebrew does here. "Full" might, in any case, be better rendered as "integral" or something like that. Above all, as Martin Buber taught our age, *emunah* is different from *pistis*.[12] Buber tends to translate it as "trust," rather than "belief" or "faith"; "active interaction between at least two parties" might be a somewhat fuller rendering of the notion in English.

How could we then best, though also somewhat circumlocutorily, translate the meaning of the twelfth principle? "I am totally and actively committed to the postulate of the coming of the Messiah; and, although he will always delay his coming, I will always bend every effort to prepare his coming, for he is on the way on every day into eternity." The religious power of such a proposition was once again, and unforgettably, demonstrated when the Jews in the ghettos, concentration camps, and extermination camps, in Warsaw and among the partisans and the survivors, made Maimonides' twelfth principle their universal anthem.[13]

We ought to dwell for another moment on my earlier assertion that, Jewishly, the Messiah not only has not come but also will never have come—that he will always be coming. This is, to be sure, a radical assertion. It must scandalize Christians, for it flies in the face of the central Christian theologumenon that the Messiah has, in fact, come—at least the first time.[14] (I am leaving aside the even more fundamental deification of the person of the Messiah.) The eternal futurity of the Messiah, translated into operational language, asserts that no smallest time-unit nor any smallest space-unit in the universe is as yet, or will ever have been, redeemed. Indeed, what is asserted is that the universe is always infinitely different from what God wants it to be and what we must, therefore, make it, insofar as this lies within and perhaps beyond our power.

But my radical assertion also scandalizes most Jews. Popularly it is believed by most Jews that, though the Messiah has not yet come, one day, "at the end of days" (better actually: *be'acharit hayamim*—i.e., "in the after-time"), he will have come. In what I daresay was the classical controversy of our century on this score, Franz Rosenzweig had a bit of an argument with Hermann Cohen. Cohen formulated, philosophically and religiously, the doctrine of the eternal delay of the advent.[15] Rosenzweig asserted, to the contrary, that anything that happens in eternity never happens,[16] and, in a beautiful commentary to a Messianic poem by R. Yehudah HaLevy he said that all humanity (or at least all Jews) can be divided into those who have more faith than they have hope, who always figure that very shortly the Messiah will have come; and those who have more hope than they have faith, who always figure that the end-time is still far away.[17] Up to now, says Rosenzweig, the latter have always been right. But someday, on "the day," they will be wrong. Therefore, be very watchful!

Rosenzweig, despite the persuasiveness of the poetic imagination which he shared with R. Yehudah HaLevy, was, I think, wrong. The eternity of the pre-Messianic "interim" is necessary, as Cohen rightly recognized, for at least two reasons: it prevents the mythologization to which, above all, Christianity has fallen prey, of any man or all men ever deifying themselves, and it makes humanity's ethical (and, indeed, scientific) tasks not an interim obligation but a perpetual (if you please, metaphysical) destiny.

Permit me a piece of metahistorical speculation. An entrenched characteristic of very many Christian millenarian movements has always been celibacy; after all, the end is near, and to have children under such circumstances is at best de trop. I know of not a single Jewish counterpart to this![18] History is simply not expected to terminate.

The eternal moral striving that is produced by the eternal delay of the Messianic advent can be deftly summarized here in two ways. Akiba Ernst Simon has written: "After having always again said our no to every claim of redemption that has been proffered to us, we have gone on our long way, the Law on our shoulders and backs, thus remaining with that beloved and endured burden in an unredeemed world—the unredeemed people of redemption and witness of its coming."[19] Nora Levin's full title tells the same story: *While Messiah Tarried: Jewish Socialist Movements 1871-1917.*[20]

Resurrection

Let us move on to the last of Maimonides' principles.[21] The most notable feature of the creedal formulation of the doctrine of resurrection is that it concentrates exclusively on the divine act of volition that is to bring it about. This is also entirely in keeping with Maimonides' own systematic teaching. We must, then, take a glance at his way of handling the tenet of resurrection.

The Thirteen Principles were, as is well known, formulated by Maimonides at the end of the introduction to his commentary to chapter 10/11 (*perek chelek*) of the Mishnah's tractate *Sanhedrin.* This was early in his career (1168). The purpose of formulating such a credo (revolutionary as such an act was at the time and has remained in Judaism)[22] was to make it possible for *hoi polloi* to hold the beliefs which are actually the conclusions of highly sophisticated and esoteric philosophic studies but which are *heilsnotwendig,* i.e., salvifically prerequisite to the (Neoplatonic/Aristotelian) "conjunction" of the human "acquired intellect" with the divine "active intellect," through which alone immortality is achieved.[23] There is thus so early in the exfoliation of Maimonides' systematic views a strikingly paradoxical relationship between the doctrine of resurrection and the doctrine of immortality: you have to believe in resurrection in order to achieve immortality. Curious as such a philosophical tenet may be, it is in fact an entirely accurate restatement of the Mishnaic text which he is here expositing--that anyone who does not believe in the resurrection of the dead, or who, while believing it, does not believe that it is a bibilical doctrine,[24] fails to achieve immortality (his "share in the world to come").

In his *magnum opus*, the *Guide for the Perplexed*, Maimonides never even broaches the doctrine of resurrection. (Thus, immortality is not mentioned in the Thirteen Principles, his popular exposition, and resurrection is not mentioned in the Guide, his technical exposition.) This is, however, in no way incompatible with the position we have seen him take in his *Commentary to the Mishnah*, for not talking about resurrection does not, of course, necessarily imply not believing in it, and, in any case, we have seen that for him resurrection, or at least belief in resurrection, is a propadeutic to immortality. With immortality, in the sense in which we have earlier seen him define it, he does deal in the *Guide*.[25]

Nevertheless, Maimonides had a lot of troubles with his contemporaries.[26] He was accused of heresy for not teaching resurrection. A formal inquiry sent to him became the occasion for his writing the *Treatise on Resurrection*. Here he made his position quite clear, though he gave away nothing either stylistically or substantively. On the one hand, he publicly affirmed belief in resurrection. On the other hand, he made a theological move which is rarely paid attention to: he stipulated two immortalities—the first, between a person's death and his resurrection, and the second, after the death of the resurrected body, for eternity. In other words, resurrection is still an intermediate stage toward immortality.[27]

It must be kept in mind that the problematic we are looking at is not one concocted by the high scholasticism of Maimonides. Maimonides here, as almost always, correctly formulates authentic, classic, rabbinic doctrine.[28] The paramount liturgy, the Eighteen Benedictions, recited three times a day by the Jew, dates back to the mishnaic era and always includes the second benediction: "Thou art mighty forever, O Lord—resurrecting the dead. Thou art great to save. Thou sustainest life with grace, resurrectest the dead with great mercy . . . and He upholdeth His faithfulness to those who sleep in the dust. Who is like unto Thee, Lord of might. . . . the King who resurrecteth the dead and maketh salvation sprout . . . Thou art trusty to resurrect the dead. Praised be Thou, O Lord, who resurrecteth the dead." The "first comprehensive Talmud commentary," by R. Chananel b. Chusiel (d. after 1053), already stipulated belief in the Messiah and in the world to come as "great foundations" (*pinnot*).[29] Clearly here, too, the theological emphasis is placed on the proposition that resurrection is not the result of some kind of natural or divine or even ethical law but that it is a matter of gratuitous, "gracious," beneficence by God. This is the reason that statements about resurrection are always collocated with references to divine power, mercy, and grace (*chesed verachamim*) in relevant Jewish texts.[30]

What in the religious texts is called divine grace is what Maimonides calls God's "will."[31] Such philosophical rather than theological language permits Maimonides to follow an extremely sophisticated set of moves: in the first place, "divine will" may justly be taken to mean, as the rabbis intended, a stipulation beyond natural, rational law; in the second place, however, the cognoscenti will understand that ultimately "will," too, is rationalized by Maimonides: it implies the scholastic identity of will and intellect in the deity, and thus it comes to mean what Kant later was to call "the primacy of practical reason." (This is why Maimonides systematically rejects all miraculous claims, even those in the Bible and the Sinaitic revelation itself, while maintaining the possibility of miracles—as a formulation of the ultimacy of "will" = ethics in the universe.) In other words, Maimonides wants to hold on to both horns of the dilemma: physical existence in any form is bound to be finite and perishable (thus mortal), but it is also prerequisite to infinite, human, moral striving (thus postulatorily resurrectable); he, therefore, teaches a first temporary resurrection on earth and a second resurrection in the "spiritual body" toward and into eternity (which is really indistinguishable from personal immortality).[32] Also in his legal *Code* (intermediate between his *Commentary to the Mishnah* and his *Guide*) he actually implies precisely this doctrine in the climactic last paragraph: in the Messianic age all humanity (Jews and Gentiles, those then living as well as those then resurrected) will live lengthily and in material comfort—thus enabled to study Torah thoroughly and able to achieve the *conjunctio*: "In those days perfection will be widespread, with the result that men will merit the life of the world to come."[33] And a few paragraphs earlier Maimonides declares: "People should never busy themselves with the legends or expatiate on the *midrashim* that deal with these matters [details of the Messianic age] and similar things, and they should not regard them as fundamental, for they engender neither awe nor love" (the two basic religious categories of Maimonides).[34] The last phrase states categorically that, according to Maimonides, eschatology is to be done exclusively as a function of its human heuristics.

Clearly, we find ourselves, via Maimonides, in the very eye of the storm that continues to rage to this day about the dichotomy between the biblical/Jewish doctrine of resurrection versus the Greek doctrine of immortality.[35]

A careful survey of the history of Jewish eschatology would make it clear, I believe, that such controversies, both before and in Maimonides' time as well as in our own, are due to a perennial failure to do with this subject what Maimonides did do with, for example, the subject of divine attributes (anthropomorphism, etc.)[36]—rigorous linguistic analysis of the terminology of Jewish eschatology (e.g., *olam haba* ["the coming world"], *atid lavo* ["the future to come"], *acharit hayamim* ["the after-time"], *ge'ulah* ["redemption"], *yeshu'ah* ["salvation," "help"], *yemot hamashiach* ["the days of the Messiah"], *malchut shamayim* ["the kingdom of heaven"], etc.), followed by conceptual reconstruction based on such linguistic analysis,[37] but what he did only more spottily in the Code with respect to the eschatological vocabulary.[38] What is needed is, in Karl Rahner's phrase, a thorough "hermeneutics of eschatological assertions."[39] I can here only summarize, even in diagrammatic form, what the result of such an unpacking would be.

Man exists in the material world. By ethicizing his life, he incrementally "spiritualizes" himself and thus approaches the (ethical) spirituality of God's world ("the coming world"), which always exists and "comes" to man.[40] He cannot, however, actually attain that infinite (infinitely moral, spiritual) world in the material world by himself. Therefore, at the end of an individual's lifetime his infinite human potential ("soul") is eternalized—on a number of conditions: God's gracious will, whether he or she is a Jew ("All Israel have a share in the world-to come"),[41] or whether he or she is a "righteous non-Jew" ("All the righteous of the nations of the world have a share in the world to come"),[42] etc. That is what is called "immortality." The striving toward total human morality on earth ("the Messianic kingdom") continues beyond any and all individual human lives: this is what we call "history," and it consists of the infinite and, therefore, never-completed spiritualization of the human universe. The regulatively postulated completion of that infinite historical process of spiritualization is what is called "the coming of the Messiah."[43] At this point a new kind of history ensues—call it posthistorical history or intra-Messianic history or, with Karl Marx, human instead of zoological history: all sorts of things continue to happen (the wars of Gog and Magog, other Messianic events, the reinstitution of the purified Law and what it provides for, etc.).[44] We are then here talking about something far different from an undifferentiated "eternity." By the—*per impossibile* (hypothetical)—time that all of these intra-Messianic events have taken place, the dichotomy between matter and spirit, body and soul will be dissolved (i.e., the soul is body and the body is soul). Men will be "spiritual bodies" or "quasi-physical souls" (*gufot ruchaniyot*—cf. Paul's *soma pneumatikos*)[45]—and this is what is called "resurrection."[46] (Up to this time, i.e., until after both "normal history" and post-Messianic history are consummated, only the immortality of the soul, not [contra fundamental Christian doctrine] a single resurrection, obtains).[47] At

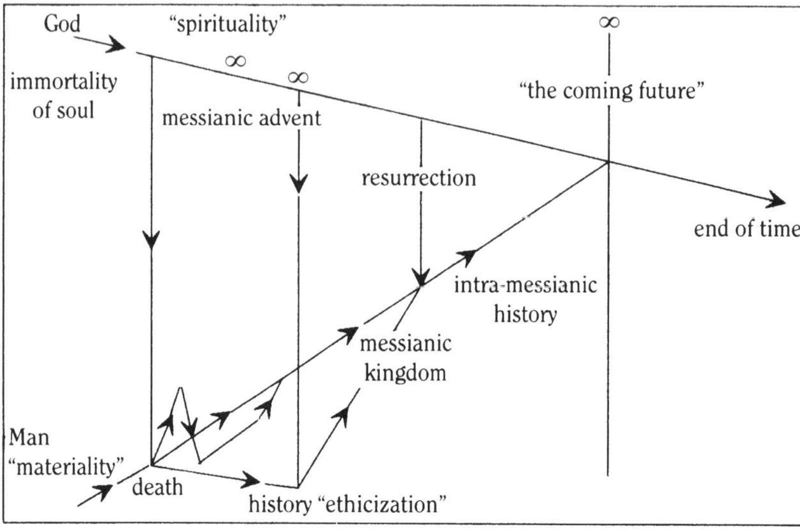

this (regulatively) final point God's world to come will, in "the coming future," indeed, have come, even as the immortal souls and the resurrected bodies will be of the same nature. Saadia Gaon thus held that during the four hundred to five hundred years that the Messianic kingdom would last, men would so spiritualize themselves that, without having to die again, they would slip into the eternal world to come.[48]

Of course, all of this is a radically tenuous synthesis between resurrection and immortality. It could not be maintained indefinitely. Ex-Christian Marranos like Uriel d'Acosta and Spinoza rejected all resurrection together with Christianity and, therefore, subsequently also Judaism. For them religious truth was totally rational and thus excluded all "positivity"—not only history but also temporality as such: the end time is the same as present time. What could be aspired to was, then, what the medievals had called *conjunctio*, the absorption of the rational individual within the infinity of the divine substance. (Though it must be remembered that for Spinoza that substance is both thought and extension = soul and body, and "immortality" is, therefore, for him not totally immaterial.)[49] Under the impact of both Spinoza and Leibniz, Moses Mendelssohn, the first great exponent of Jewish thought under the impact of modernism, then expounded a peculiarly ambivalent conception. His metaphysical rationalism discerned an injustice in the belief that people who happened to live later, say in the Messianic age, should be better off than those who lived earlier, regardless of their moral deserts (as his friend

Lessing's conception of history as the education of the human race implied),[50] and he, therefore, sloughed off the Jewish commitment to Messianic progress, resurrection, etc., adding to his translation of Maimonides' Thirteen Principles, among others, the principle of immortality.[51] On the other hand, his Leibnizian monadology let him claim that the immortal soul would have some "quasi-body."[52] After Kant in particular, such ambiguities were bound to fall apart, and thus Jewish religious "liberalism" in the nineteenth and twentieth centuries discarded resurrection in favor of immortality on allegedly scientific and rationalistic grounds.

My own view, for what it is worth, is that Maimonides was, as usual, wiser than modernity. I would want to argue that we require the doctrine of resurrection, therewith to assert what is nowadays called the psychosomatic unity, or the embodiedsoul/ensouled-body, of the human individual and the infinite ethical tasks incumbent on him or her. (Some current philosophical argument to the effect that spatiotemporal continuity is prerequisite to personal identity reaffirms the traditional affirmation of "quasi-physical" immortality for the purpose of justifying resurrection.)[53] Individual rights as well as duties follow from such "supernatural," i.e., absolute, status: the *Halacha* of respect for human beings is enshrined in the laws of respect for corpses.[54] This is why and how Kant also stipulated what he still (wrongly, by his own standards) called "immortality" in the First and Second *Critiques*. Like Kant, we, too, cannot derive any metaphysical asseverations from such regulative, functional reasons for the belief in resurrection. If we want, religiously, to make such assertions, we have to make them as *theologumenoi* (thus returning to the rabbinic proclamation of God's power and grace as its ground),[55] while philosophically limiting ourselves to regulative, ethical explanations.

Even within the limits of philosophical regulativity we can go a bit further, though. When speaking of the world of resurrection, we are implying some sort of materiality on two scores—that "world" itself and the "spiritual" bodies of the resurrected. Each of these instances of "bodily-ness" is, however, to be taken, even terminologically (in the hermeneutics of eschatology) as strongly homonymic. Whether *olam haba* ("the *world* to come") is to be taken spatially as "world" or temporally as "aeon" needs to be analyzed. By the same token, whether "spiritual body" is to be understood as a body whose substance is spirit (whatever this might mean) or as an entity which acts "spiritually," i.e., morally, also ought to be analyzed. (Consider the transformation of the very notion of "substance" into that of "function" in Ernst Cassirer's book by that title.)[56] In both instances, bodily-ness is translated into terms of "action in time." Thus the regulativity of the entire doctrine is put in the brightest light, and "life eternal" (life always in the "now") is seen to be a quasi-temporal, not a quasi-spatial, conception.

At least two of the most sophisticated philosophical, neoMarxist, and atheist intellectuals of the last generation arrived at precisely our conclusion. J.-P. Sartre ended his life with an interview by Benny Lévy in which he practically declared himself (justly) an honorary Jew and specifically expressed endorsement of the doctrine of resurrection as part of Jewish messianism.[57] And Theodor W. Adorno, in an extraordinarily impressive while typically sophisticated passage in *Negative Dialectic*, sums up our point in the sentence: "Hope clings, as in Mignon's song, to the transfigured body."[58]

Eschatology as Ethics

The two eschatological doctrines, Messianism and resurrection, have all along been seen to interjibe. "Will" has turned out to be the central word and concept that underlies them both. The creedal formulation of the thirteenth principle turned on it explicitly (resurrection as an act of divine will), and the eternal futurity of the Messianic advent (which entails the resurrection) has for its purpose the activation of the human will (as "the image of the similarity of God's structure")[59] in the form of the moralization of the (human) universe. (The fact is that, as we have seen, the [regulative] realization of morality is identical with the resurrection.) "Will" is short for "rational will," and rational will" is, for Maimonides and Jewish philosophy in general as it is for Kant, another way of saying "morality."[60] In brief, Jewish eschatology is the metaphysical as well as ethical absolutization of morality.

Eschatology as a fundamental operator in ethical discourse calls for some, however limited, further unpacking.[61] Messianism as an ethical operator simply declares that, since humanity is to strive to imitate God and thus to endeavor to become like Him, and since they are to undertake these efforts in this world, the ultimate goal of ethics is to establish what is then called "the (Messianic) kingdom of God" on earth. This is, of course, an infinite goal, infinitely (or as Kant and H. Cohen liked to say, asymptotically) to be approached. Far from implying a bracketing of Messianism ("utopianism"), as irrelevant to the daily, historical occurrences of moral problems (i.e., a postponement *ad calendas Graecas*), Messianism in fact operates, therefore, as a direct producer of moral values and as an intermediate criterion of proper action in any and every situation. When men ask themselves how to behave or, indeed, what the standards are to be of their proper behavior, the Messianic end defines the means by which that end can and is to be attained. (This is the point of Kant's *Religion Within the Bounds of Reason Alone*.) As Solomon Schechter put it by way of example: "If the disappearance of poverty and suffering is a condition of the Kingdom of the Messiah, or, in other words, of the Kingdom of God, all wise social legislation in this respect must help toward its speedy advent."[62]

Here once again the *avant-garde* of contempory technical philosophy is trying to catch up as best it can with the entrenched methodologies of Jewish culture (and of Hermann Cohen's Judaistic neo-Kantianism). G.H.v. Wright, in stipulated agreement with Jaakko Hintikka, defines deontic logic as "the study of logical relations in deontically perfect worlds . . . concerned with logical relations between the ideal states the descriptions of which are implicit in norms," and norms " 'bridge the gap' between Is and Ought."[63] *Ethics* in turn is the producer of such norms.[64]

Halacha is then the formalization of the required actions which will take mankind from where we are to where we ought to get—"to 'bridge the gap' between Is and Ought." At this point of the analysis one would have to go into the complexities of Halachic jurisprudence. One of them I will explicate to some extent shortly, namely: does Jewish law enjoin us to act entirely in accord with perfectionist Messianic values or incrementally with the goal of Messianism in view? To mention only two others: what is the notion of a "Messianic Torah," and how does it relate to "the Torah in our hands"?[65] Secondly, what is the status—more importantly, what, if anything, is the function—of *hilcheta dimeshicha*?[66] But these are complicated, technical issues that we cannot go into here. Suffice it to recall the large number of laws that are explicitly defined as possessing Messianic functions: "he who quotes something in the name of its author brings redemption";[67] if Israel observed two Sabbaths, or only one Sabbath, or anyone one of a number of other commandments, just once perfectly—if Israel repented properly only one day[68]—the Messiah would come,[69] etc. The principle of the matter is "to bring near the end" (*lekarev et haketz*). "Great is justice, for it brings redemption near."[70] And the entire complex subject of "*Messianic Halacha*" arrives at the bottom line that it may be dealt with only insofar as currently actionable consequences flow from it.[71] Martin Buber once put it like this: "A drop of Messianic consummation must be mingled with every hour; otherwise the hour is godless, despite all piety and devoutness."[72] All this can be reduced to the formula that Judaism is actionable Messianism.[73]

The theoretical ("aggadic") substructure of the Halachic function of Messianism was paradigmatically formulated in a midrashic passage that is worth quoting at length (and which stands far from alone).

> "There is no God like Jeshurun. who rides the heavens for your help" [Deut. 33:26]: Who, indeed, is like God? Jeshurun— the goodly and praiseworthy

> ones among you. Said Rabbi Berachya in the name of Rabbi Judah b.R. Simon, who said: "You will find that everything that the Holy One, praised be He, will in the future do in the world to come He has anticipated and done through the righteous ones in this world: the Holy One, praised be He, revives the dead—and Elijah revives the dead; the Holy One, praised be He, restrains the rains and Elijah restrains the rains; the Holy One, praised be He, blesses the diminutive—and Elijah blesses the diminutive; the Holy One, praised be He, redeems the barren women—and Elijah redeems the barren women; the Holy One, praised be He, sweetens the bitter—and Elisha sweetens the bitter [2 Kings 4]; the Holy One, praised be He, sweetens the bitter by means of the bitter—and Elisha sweetens the bitter by means of the bitter" [Exodus 15 and 2 Kings 2].[74] R. Berachya in the name of R. Simon said: "'There is none like God.' and 'who is like God? Jeshurun,' the people of Israel, for what the Holy One, praised be He, has written about Himself, 'God is elevated by Himself [Isa. 2:11]. is also applied to Jacob: 'And Jacob remained by himself [Gen. 32:25].[75]

The Talmudic *midrash* reports:

> Rabban Gamliel sat and taught: "Woman is destined [in the Messianic time] to give birth every day, as it is written [Jer. 31:7]: 'She shall conceive and immediately bear child.'" But a certain disciple scoffed at him, quoting Eccles. 1:9: "There is absolutely nothing new under the sun." Rabban Gamliel replied: "Come, and I will show you an example of this in this world." He went out and showed him a hen. Again R. Gamliel sat and taught: "Trees are destined [in the Messianic age] to yield fruit every day, as it is written [Ezed. 17:23]: 'And it shall bring forth twigs and bear fruit': just as there are twigs every day so shall there be fruit every day." But that pupil scoffed at him, saying: "It is written: 'There is absolutely nothing new under the sun.'" R. Gamliel replied: "Come, and I will show you an example of this in this world." He went out and showed him a caper bush. Again R. Gamliel sat and taught: "The Land of Israel is destined [in the Messianic time] to bring forth Lesbian cakes [a pastry] and robes of Melat [fine garments], as it is written [Ps. 72:18]: 'There shall be an abundance of grain in the land.'" [There is an intricate Hebrew wordplay at work here.] But that pupil scoffed at him, saying again: "There is absolutely nothing new under the sun." R. Gamliel replied: "Come, and I will show you an example of this in this world." He went out and showed him morels and truffles, and for robes of Melat he showed him the bark of a young palm tree.[76]

If we may interpret just briefly, Rabban Gamliel clearly expounds the following: the Messianic society is one of universal economic abundance; this will constitute a real novum, a miracle, a qualitative, revolutionary leap. To those who claim that "there are absolutely no nova in the world," he points out that the whole real, even pre-Messianic, world consists, naturally, of nova: life and nature, as over against the inanimate world, are indeed characterized by constant novelty. The whole passage occurs in the context of a polemic against the somewhat Hellenistic book of Ecclesiastes and is part of an extended affirmation of the special nature of human life.[77]

The Messianic doctrine has produced one of the perennial splits in the ethical (and general) outlook of Judaism. One of the entrenched interpretations of the schism between Hillel and Shammai is that the latter's rigorism legislates that people must completely act today as they will in Messianic times, whereas Hillel's leniency formulates the accommodations which people are forced to make under prevailing circumstances in their incremental approximations of the kingdom of God. (Thus it can be true that "these and those are the words of the living God.")[78] One of the counterintuitive results of that interpretation is that ethical rigorism, *mishnat hassidut*—"supererogatory morality," *lifnin mishurat hadin*—"acting within the line of the law" (i.e., not beyond its widest circumference but in its deepest core), etc.,[79] are manifestations of the stern Shammaite spirit, not first or foremost of the humane Hillelite spirit, although also the danger of premature Messianism is thereby run.

This split with regard to the enactment of Messianism in history can be shown to be operative generally in Jewish history and ideology, not excluding the present: one view is that the only, or the best, way in which the universal rule of the Messiah can be established is in situation A to bring about totally Messianic conditions, then to do the same thing in situation B, etc., until the whole world "is filled with the spirit of God as the waters cover the sea" (i.e., to turn every local moral situation into a forward bastion of Messianic conquest), while the other view is that the only, or the usual, practical way of bringing about "the kingdom" is to make situation A a little more Messianic today, even more Messianic tomorrow, etc., to do the same with situation B, etc., until the same result is achieved.

There are many further intra-Messianic problematics: How is the advent to be calculated (if at all)? Is that advent in time or beyond time/history (i.e., in "eternity")? Is there an intra-Messianic, extrahistorical time? And so on. All these apparently metaphysical, eschatological questions can be shown, by dint of "the Jewish twist," to have ethical and even moral functions.[80]

In the *midrashim* quoted at some length above, the function of Messianism slides almost imperceptibly into the ethical function of the doctrine of the resurrection. In the latter the ethical question is raised: What is immortal life like, and how must I act in this life if I am to approximate immortal life as much as possible? (Compare Kant on immortality in the First and Second *Critiques.*) Now, eternal life is, of course, so totally nonempirical that the rabbis could have dogmatically stipulated anything whatever for it without fear of refutation. That they described it in only certain ways implies that these ways are ethically desirable, imitatable ways. For example, perfect justice obtains in the world of eternity. When our earthbound notions and experiences of justice conflict with that perfect justice, we have strong reasons to puzzle, and puzzling values are very weak models for imitation—or none at all.[81] For another example, resurrection is denied to usurers.[82] Z. Shapiro uses the revelation at Sinai as an historical instantiation of resurrection: in both instances men die, in order literally(?) to be resurrected by and in divine truth.[83] As a result the chief classical texts in Jewish ethical (*musar*) literature are built on *M. Sota* 9:15, that morality leads to goodness, goodness leads to holiness, holiness to the holy spirit, and the holy spirit to resurrection.[84]

The function of the Messianic doctrine in Jewish ethics is to be clearly distinguished, I think, from what has come to be called "eschatological verification" in philosophy of religion in our time.[85] The difference resides, it seems, in the following.

"Eschatological verification"—developed from positivism via "analysis"—stipulates the verification of theological statements by some experiential, i.e., in the Kantian sense "sensuous," or at least by some (whatever that might mean) "quasi-sensuous," criterion in the "afterlife"; therefore, the entities referred to, "God," "the personal individual," etc., would have to be sensuous, i.e., material, or at least quasi-material, entities. If, on the other hand, one holds that "the world to come" and all that this comprises are totally immaterial, then (a) such verification is by definition impossible, and (b) to people who accept the notion of such "eschatological verification" is applicable what Maimonides said about ignorant and foolish Moslems who expect a material afterlife.[86]

The eschatological doctrine, as here used, says something else. To use the Kantian distinction, we are making statements that are synthetic a prioris—i.e., they are judgments which cannot themselves be empirically verified but which are, in the first place, logically, analytically true, and which also, as regulatives, make other statements that are a posteriori, synthetically, empirically true logically possible. In other words, we are dealing with "transcendentals" or with "possible-worlds theorizing." Thus, here, statements about life in the Messianic era or in the world to come are not logically self-contradictory or morally counterproductive and, in addition, produce this-worldly ethical injunctions which can both function empirically and be approved of morally.

In our analysis of Jewish eschatology we have hitherto concentrated on its human, ethical significance. This is proper, but it is, of course, also one-sided. It will be remembered that in our diagram the arrows of action go in two directions—one upward set, representing human, moral striving, and the other set downward (the acts of bestowing immortality, sending the Messiah, bringing about resurrection, etc.—all of which are summarized under the theological conception of "grace"), representing divine activities; and it is the dialectical interaction of these two sets of movements in their totality which, alone, leads to the *eschaton*. Thus, humanity and its morality are a necessary but not a sufficient condition for the attainment of the life of the world to come (what Emil Brunner, in Christian terms, called *Anknuepfungspunkte*—i.e., human occasions which God requires for the bestowal of grace), and, by the same token, God's work is a necessary but, for ethical reasons, not in turn a sufficient condition.

This sounds like the extraethical, theological, dimension of Jewish eschatology. It is that. But even this extraethical dimension can be shown, in the hermeneutics of Jewish eschatological assertions, to be of pervasively ethical significance.

It should be noted, in the first place, that all human striving in our diagram—individual life, history, even the Messianic kingdom—is finally consummated by divine action. This is logically necessary once that striving is seen to be a divine norm—divine norms are, by definition, infinite—and human beings cannot, of course, either individually or collectively, attain infinite goals. Thus, "grace" here means: do more, for you have never done enough![87] In the second place, even finite, inadequate, human morality is held to be impossible without divine grace. We are all inextricably and totally embroiled in the necessities of nature—the struggle for survival, the physical and social forces that make us what we are. How then can even one individual, not to speak of a group of individuals (however small), lift itself by its own bootstraps out of that morass?[88]

The paradigm of the indispensability of divine grace for the enactment of even very limited acts of human morality is taken from the Bible, but typically enshrined in the Jewish liturgy. Thus, before the Jew begins to recite the Eighteen Benedictions every day, he silently prays Psalm 51:17: "O Lord, open Thou my lips, so that my mouth may speak Thy praise."[89] In other words, the one smallest thing that it would appear man can do by himself, namely, utter God's praises and ask for His help (the mere activity of making sounds) —even this he cannot do without prevenient grace. Or the liturgy often uses Lamentations 5:21 (and its repetition after v. 22 as the conclusion of the book): "Return Thou us, O God, so that we may [be able to] return; create our days anew as Thou didst create them newly at the outset." "Return" here is the Hebrew term *teshuvah*, usually translated as "repentance." It does mean "repentance" in the narrower sense, but more widely it means "humanly initiated, autonomous, i.e., moral action, *praxis*," of which "repentance" is then only one, though the most characteristic, instantiation. Here again, then, the one human activity which, by its very definition, must be humanly initiated turns out to require prevenient divine grace. This is the point of the extended classical debate between R. Eliezer and R. Joshua as to whether "repentance" (moral action) or God's grace will bring redemption;[90] as Emmanual Levinas points out, the debate remains dialectically open-ended at its conclusion.[91]

Of course, the dialectic of this type of situation is endlessly complex. If I have to pray to be divinely moved to pray and yet I cannot pray until God has moved me to pray, the He and I are in a classical "Mexican stand-off"; neither of us can move until the other has moved first—and nothing can happen. The very fact that these stand-off situations occur in obligatory liturgical contexts throws the first move to the human side: logically I can't pray;[92] I just do. I drop out of the logical situation by taking (moral) action; in this particular situation, I pray. The unsalvageable theological situation is transcended and salvaged by autonomous, human, moral action.[93] Emil Fackenheim put it like this: "Viewed in the light of faith, history is a dialectic of the doing of man and the doing of God. . . . In moments of grace the tension is overcome."[94] Hermann Cohen liked at this point to quote the end of Goethe's *Faust*: "The indescribable—here it is done."[95]

Human beings cannot, of course, know where the curve of their moral striving will be met by the curve of divine grace. They, therefore, have to push the only line under their (partial) control as far as, and further than, they really can. Yet the *hybris of Werkheiligkeit*, of which historic Christian theology has always accused Jewish ethicism,[96] is never even a temptation for at least two reasons. For one thing, as we have already noted, grace is held to be prerequisite for the beginning and certainly for the completion of the infinite moral enterprise. For another, we were careful in our diagram to draw the line of human history, up to the advent of the Messiah, in a number of different possible directions—upward, downward, and going every which way. Rabbinic Judaism is far from wedded to any notion of automatic or necessary progress in history. History may very well go, and (as Jews know only too well) often has gone, in regressive directions. The point is that, as the rabbis classically put it, "the son of David will come in a generation which is either totally guilty or totally innocent."[97] But, of course, for human purposes only the alternative of the "wholly innocent generation" can serve as a regulative. To strive to become a "wholly guilty generation," for the purpose of thus forcing God's hand to send the Messiah at the ultimate nadir of history, ails of a whole slew of terrible sins:[98] (1) it constitutes Sabbateanism, the worst of all Messianic heresies;[99] (2) it violates the fundamental injunction not to rely on miracles;[100] and (3) it obviously is the antithesis of ethics. Still, God's hand cannot be stopped: if and when that nadir of human, historical existence should ever, in God's judgment, have been reached–i.e., when the world has fallen so low that no self-rehabilitation is possible any longer–then God may have to take salvific action. (The descriptions of the condition of the world that would trigger such redemption from the extreme of evil are truly apocalyptic.)[101] Indeed, God's saving hand may force the end at any time that He determines– for example, as Isaac Abravanel canonically formulated this conception, by forcing Israel into an historical situation where it is constrained, rather than morally motivated, to act out the final *Anknuepfungspunkt* of the Messianic advent.[102]

The final upshot, then, of the dialectic of grace and ethics in Jewish eschatology is this: salvation may come about by works or by grace, but, in the first place, grace is indispensable to works themselves, and, in the second place, salvation by grace alone would be such a horrifying experience–morally atrocious and experientially painful–that humanity will not choose it as the way to the goal: "May he [the Messiah] come, but let me not see it!"[103] Thus, ethics remains as the only actionable course. M. Buber puts this by way of saying that men improve the world, while God transforms it. " 'Turning' and 'redemption' belong together. God knows how. I don't need to know."[104]

The meaning of the entirety of the Jewish eschatological vision is then perhaps best summarized in the liturgical phrase: *letakken olam bemalchut shaddai*–"to repair/perfect the world by means of the kingdom of God." This is an infinite task in individual human life, in history, beyond history into the kingdom of the Messiah, and even into the life of the world to come of the resurrection. "The Torah of life and of the love of grace, of righteousness and blessing and compassion and life and peace," i.e., the moral enterprise, is operative into that eternity of the holy God.[105]

Excursus: Messianism in Contemporary Political Debate

By conceptualizing the function of Jewish eschatology in the manner which we have here employed, two entrenched interpretations of what is usually called "Messianism" in contemporary metahistorical discussions have been defanged. The first turns on the alleged distinction between Messianism and apocalypticism. Broadly speaking, apocalypticism is the name of the view that "the end of (normal) history" comes about by a sudden and catastrophic incursion into history by God, whereas Messianism designates the view that there is some organic relationship between human history and its end.[106] As we have just finished seeing, however, no eschatology is possible without a thoroughgoing mixture of grace and morality—that is to say, of divine, incalculable action and of human, rationally moral, efforts. Apocalypticism and Messianism are two points on the continuum of eschatology: in the former, incrementally more emphasis is put on God's, in Messianism more emphasis is put on man's, role in it.[107]

The real dichotomy should be made between Messianism and pseudo-Messianism. Pseudo-Messianism is not a degraded version of Messianism (as superstition is not a degraded version of religious faith), but its antithesis: it contradicts the central Messianic tenet that the Messiah will always be coming in the future (as superstition contradicts the central religious tenet that God is always beyond human and worldly definition) and that ethics is a necessary condition of his coming.

The second metahistorical interpretation of biblical eschatology which our ethical conceptualization has defanged turns on a different dichotomy—between Messianism and utopianism. (Here apocalypticism is either subsumed under Messianism and thus, as we are about to see, disfunctionalized, or it is identified with utopianism and, therefore, rejected.) Utopianism is then defined as the (false) belief that the world can be made perfect, and Messianism is interpreted as the view that we can change the world as we know it either not at all or at best only minimally, leaving the rest to God. By simply leaving out the last phrase, this view can easily turn into secularism. The result of these two definitions is that the thrust toward infinite moralization has been cut down. In Protestant theology the late Reinhold Niebuhr came to represent this view most typically,[108] but in the last generation a large group of Jewish intellectuals, Sir Karl Popper, Hans Morgenthau, Leo Strauss, Hannah Arendt, Jacob Talmon, Norman Cohn, Will Herberg, and Gershom Scholem (several of them closely affiliated with Niebuhr), and by now lesser figures on the political plane, have created a body of thought and policies known as "neoconservatism."

Popper's essay "Utopia and Violence" illustrates this point as well as any.[109] Not a Jew, but the son of Viennese baptized Jews, he is a member of the generation of highly assimilated, German(-speaking), "Jewish" refugees from Europe. The essay here cited was first delivered on the European continent, shortly after the end of World War II. The book in which it is published is dedicated to F.A. von Hayek.[110] the argument of the essay is simple. Violence is, according to Popper, an inherent feature of utopianism, because utopianism claims to know what the ultimate future is and, indeed, when and how it will come about; therefore, utopianism claims the right to force people, against their will and even at the cost of their very lives, to do what is necessary so that it may be realized. Utopianism is the social dimension of the equally wrong philosophy of science which claims that it is progressing toward "truth" (rather than toward the abolition of falsehood). In fact, Popper argues, it is impossible to define ultimate truth or ultimate goodness rationally. Utopians, bereft of reason, therefore, have to resort to violence. The (Popperian) rational man will, on the other hand, "work for the elimination of concrete evils rather than for the realization of abstract goods."[111] And in this fashion Popper settles for "man as he is."[112]

There are some pretty obvious things wrong with this argument of Popper's. In the first place, one can easily imagine "utopians" even as defined and analyzed by Popper (indeed, there are numberless examples in history of such utopians), who believe they know with aboslute certainty what the *summum bonum* is and even when it will be realized, who draw purely pacifist, even quietistic, inferences therefrom, such as that they ought to persuade others peacefully and rationally of their own beliefs or that God will do so in His own inscrutable ways. In the second place, while indicting utopians of irrationalism, Popper admits that his own commitment to (his own kind of) rationalism is irrational: reason can only determine the means to a set end; it cannot, as Max Weber showed, determine ends themselves.[113] Why may violence then not be expected from his own ultimate irrationalism?[114] Indeed, since Popper will not tolerate intolerance (unlike, for example, the ACLU), he may be said to practice violence himself. Above all, Hilary Putnam is entirely right when he says, "The failure to see the primacy of practice leads Popper to some rather reactionary political conclusions."[115]

It is interesting to observe that the Bolsheviks, whom Popper rightly so despises, and he share a common abhorrence of "utopianism." Of course, they abhor it for opposite reasons: Communists think that utopians believe in dreams, i.e., ultimate "values," whereas they deem themselves "scientists" ("in a world of facts"), who "know" what the long-term future will be, while Popper, on the other hand, claims that there are no such things as fundamental laws of history and that no long-term future can, therefore, be rationally projected—i.e., that Communists themselves are utopians.[116]

In fact, utopian socialists, in the historical sense of the term, are usually themselves religious, "Messianic," socialists or secularized Messianists.[117] In technical, especially Jewish, philosophy Hermann Cohen argued convincingly (and in line with Kantianism) that "ultimate value" can and has to be rationally construed, indeed constructed. This is "the primacy of practical reason," and it is the basis of "ethical socialism" (in line with "utopian socialism" except for its rationalism, and in line with "scientific socialism," except for its positivism).[118] It is "rational, ethical Messianism"—and, in this sense, utopian as well as the very foundation of ethics in history. In other words, it is here argued that Popper is entirely right in arguing, as H. Cohen argued in his way, that "futurism" is not only immoral but even irrational, but that Popper is wrong in identifying "joining 'the wave of the future'" with Messianism. It is in fact pseudo-Messianism in our sense—i.e., scientism, superstition, rather than science or rationalism. Messianism and rationality understand values to be infinite regulatives, and from these they derive moral norms.[119]

Thomas Mann, at the end of World War II, said conclusively (and contradicting his earlier, Schopenhauerian lassitude): "In the new situation, I would say, utopia had become a question of practical life."[120]

Turning from K. Popper to the religious side of this argument, and in view of his continuing massive authority, G. Scholem's treatment of Jewish Messianism deserves a few more words.[121] In the first place, Scholem's usual taciturnity about his own ideological agenda must be dispelled.[122] In the second place, it must be articulated what that ideological agenda is. It is, in a word, Zionism—the State of Israel. To undergird that program, Scholem argues that normal Judaism (*Halacha*) is "conservative" (really dead) or Messianic (alive), both of them dangerous and unsatisfying. It is dangerous because it can lead to the dissolution of Sabbateanism or even Frankism, and it is unsatisfying because perennially unrealized eschatology is "life lived in deferment."[123] "This is too high a price to pay for messianism."[124]

There is only one alternative, according to Scholem, for the Jewish people between the death of official Judaism and the danger and frustration of Messianism, namely, the unpredictable realism of the State of Israel.[125] The centrality of this thesis to his entire historiography is brought into focus when one pays attention to his infrequent but repeated outbursts against Hermann Cohen.[126]

In the third place, the question must be asked to what extent Scholem's historiography is determined by his ideology. He certainly overstates the dichotomy between rabbinism (e.g., Maimonides) and Messianism as well as between ethical Messianism and apocalypticism. We have shown above that in Judaism all four of these factors are inseparably linked with one another. Above all, he strains with all his might to break out of what he feels is the unhistoricality of Judaism (which Rosenzweig praised). Therefore, he even occasionally praises Sabbateanism[127] as he certainly endorses Zionism, even though he is aware of some dangers inherent in the later as well. Scholem wants Jewish "realism," vitality, etc. He must, therefore, put out of operation all those forces in Judaism which preserve the wide gap between what is and what ought to be or will be—*Halacha*, Messianism, philosophical ethics, and W. Benjamin's sense of tragedy. The "realism" of Niebuhrian politics and of present-day Jewish "neoconservatives" jibes with his "realism."[128]

–12 –

Modern Jewish Philosophy*

The very notion of Jewish philosophy (even leaving aside the notion of modernity) has been much debated. Isaac Husik, the standard historian of medieval Jewish philosophy, held that starting with the Renaissance there could no more be Jewish (or any other religionist) philosophy than there could be such a thing as Canadian mathematics. Julius Guttmann, the standard historian of the full sweep of Jewish philosophical history, in a way went Husik one better, although to different effect, by esteeming modern "philosophy of Judaism" quite as highly as its medieval predecessor, on the ground that the latter depended on Plato, Aristotle, the Kalam, and Al-Farabi no less than do the moderns on Hume, Kant, and Hegel. The view held here, on the other hand, is that philosophy is Jewish by virtue of a transhistorical primacy of ethics; non-Jewish thought will, of course, sometimes also arrive at such a ethical primacy by rational means to one degree or another, and Jewish philosophy, like Judaism at large, will then gratefully use or bend to its purpose its non-Jewish infusions.

Philosophy that is both Jewish and modern is by general consent dated as having begun with the eighteenth-century German Jew Moses Mendelssohn. The character of the birth of modern Jewish philosophy presages a number of important features of its life history. In the first place, modern Jewish philosophy remained, as it began, in bulk a German-Jewish enterprise until Nazism put an end to German Jewry as well as to German-Jewish philosophizing. During its career it increasingly branched out beyond German Jewry, and it received significant input from elsewhere. At the present time, it is carried on very much in the places where Jewish life is concentrated and under the impact of those cultures—first and foremost the United States and Israel, and then France, Britain, and elsewhere. Mendelssohn is, in the second place,

---

*Reprinted with permission of Charles Scribner's Sons, an imprint of Macmillan Publishing Company, from *Contemporary Jewish Religious Thought*, edited by A.A. Cohen and Paul Mendes-Flohr. Copyright © 1986 by Charles Scribner's Sons.

rightly regarded as symbolically the first "modern" Jew—that is, thoroughly Jewish while reasonably integrated with modern European society and culture—but this is true in a historical, not in a philosophical, sense. Philosophically, he could really more accurately be described as the last Enlightenment rationalist and *Popularphilosoph* (ideologist). Well before Mendelssohn's death, Immanuel Kant had revolutionized the philosophical world, and, though always respectful of Mendelssohn both personally and intellectually, he thus also and in so many words made Mendelssohn's thought a matter of finished history. While the Jewish community leaders in the subsequent period continued to flock to Mendelssohn's banner, Jewish thinkers such as Marcus Herz, Solomon Maimon, and Lazarus Bendavid clustered around Kant and around his philosophical legacy.

The conventional histories of modern philosophy describe fairly enough how German absolute idealism and especially Hegel and Hegelianism used (or misused) especially Kant's *Critique of Judgment*, mostly in order to close the gap that, as they saw and still see it, Kant had opened up between experienced reality and theoretical—to them "metaphysical," truth—the latter heading encompassing matters that are usually regarded as the substance of religious philosophy, including Judaism. Somewhat simplistically one can say that the nineteenth and twentieth centuries attempted philosophically to close the gap between noumenon and phenomenon, rationality and actuality, God and the world, in one of two fashions (which sometimes come to the same thing): either reality was made to disappear into ideality, as in the thought of Hegel, or ideality was made to collapse into actuality, as in Marxism and positivism.

As soon as one sees things in this light it becomes clear that Jewish philosophers and thinkers were likely to want to stipulate some significant reservations about the thesis that the actual is the rational or that there is naught but the actual, for at least two reasons; one historical, the other conceptual: historically, Jews continued to live in a real world that they could scarcely regard from their perspective, at least, as ideal; and conceptually, the absolute transcendence of God and everything he is taken to stand for is firmly embedded in the very foundations of historic Jewish culture. As a consequence, the Jewish Hegelian or quasi-Hegelian thinkers of the first half of the nineteenth century all held, in one way or another, that Judaism differed from Christianity (and paganism) in that it preserved the discreteness of God from nature and, what amounts to the same thing, of the power of reason and moral freedom in the world. This was the principal effect of Solomon Formstecher's religious philosophy and of that of even the most Hegelian of these thinkers, Samuel Hirsch. Solomon Ludwig Steinheim performed a Jewish operation on Hegel in some ways similar to Kierkegaard's Christian operation by identifying reason with necessity and science while attributing truth to revelation, freedom, and "miracles." The Italian Jewish thinker Samuel D. Luzzatto, like his similarly minded German contemporary Samson Raphael Hirsch (both spokesmen for a sort of modern traditionalism), though rejecting Maimonidean rationalism in favor of Judah Halevi's quasi-neo-Platonism, nonetheless insisted, as Mendelssohn had done at the dawn of the Age of Emancipation, on the "liberal" virtues of moral citizenship as derived from "the reasons for the commandments" (*taamei ha-mizvot*). Nachman Krochmal, writing in Hebrew in Russian Poland, tried to elevate Israel above the contingencies of history by subordinating it to the perpetuity of God alone (more or less what Hegel had significantly called Absolute Spirit and what Rosenzweig was to reformulate in the next century).

Historians have noticed that as the nineteenth century grew older the emancipationist thrust of German philosophy grew weaker and had virtually died by the middle of the century. It was, interestingly, usually Jews who, in philosophy as in politics, in the second half of the century sounded (in Otto Liebmann's famous phrase) the call to return to Kant. By general consent it is the greatest of Jewish philosophers of the closing of the nineteenth and opening of the twentieth centuries, Hermann Cohen, who carried out the program in Jewish terms of philosophically restoring the "infinite" gap between ideality and reality and of explicating in technical detail what the actionable consequences of that gap are for science, ethics, aesthetics, religion, and social policy. His disciples were typically Jews—Germans like Ernst Cassirer, eastern Europeans like Samuel Atlas, and, in a more complicated way, the contemporary Rabbi Joseph B. Soloveitchik—so that other schools of neo-Kantianism, which typically sought some sort of compromise between Kantian and Hegelianism, spoke of "the Marburg School" of Hermann Cohen as a Jewish distortion. For Cohen, Judaism was "religion of reason" par excellence, and the task of the Jewish people was to carry its "ethical monotheism" to the ends of the earth.

By the time of World War I, a number of concrete problems of a general philosophical character and of specifically Jewish importance took hold. They all tend to revolve about the complaint that Cohen's, and rationalist "critical" thought in general, was too abstract—that is, that the gap between reason and reality swallowed up received values of history, peoplehood, and individuality. Here the philosopher other than Mendelssohn who, by means of a different periodization, may be regarded as the beginning of Jewish modernity, the seventeenth-century ex-Jew Spinoza, could be invoked, as he had been invoked in the transition form Kant to Hegel: neither Hegel himself nor the early Jewish Marxists such as Moses Hess made a secret of their admiration for

Spinoza, because the motto *deus sive natura* entailed the thesis that truth is to be discerned in, not beyond, reality. Ex-Jews like Henri Bergson, with his espousal of vitalism, and Edmund Husserl, with his rallying cry of "Back to the things themselves!," exemplify this trend in general philosophy. More specifically Jewish, Martin Buber's early Nietzscheanism asserted the decisive realities of mystical experience and of "folkish" culture, and even in his later, "dialogic" thought, "actual man" and "actual experience of God" are superordinated to what Cohen had called pure cognition. Franz Rosenzweig started out under the impact of his German, Hegelian teachers, became a favorite (though always intellectually differentiated) disciple of Cohen's, and then became Buber's closest associate. His magnum opus, *The Star of Redemption*, a thoroughly neo-Hegelian enterprise, proclaims a "new thinking" of the "realities" of humanity, God, and the world, and in his last essay he awards the prize to Martin Heidegger over a "scholastic" Cohen essentially because Heidegger himself had rebelled against (among other things) theoretical reason.

Cohen has remained a significant, though usually unacknowledged, philosophical influence for the rest of the century. This is clearly illustrated by the role he plays in the work of such different thinkers as Cassirer and Rabbi Soloveitchik; among non-Jews in present-day German "transcendental philosophy" and, in the United States, in the thought of Cassirer's student Suzanne Langer. Usually, however, it is radically reinterpreted Cohen (inspired by Rosenzweig's existential reading of him) who is alleged to have broken out of critical idealism in his posthumously published philosophy of Judaism. Emmanuel Levinas, at present perhaps the most creative specifically Jewish philosopher, affirms that Buber and Rosenzweig helped him extricate himself from the Greek, ontologistic thicket of Husserl and Heidegger (*"à partir de Husserl et Heidegger"*). In pre-state Israel and later, Yehezkel Kaufmann and even Jakob Klatzkin, not to speak of Julius Guttmann and other philosophers like Samuel Hugo Bergmann, tried to combine a notion of Jewish "folkish" genius with ethical monotheism as formulated in the nineteenth century. Rabbi Abraham Isaac Kook's kabbalistic panentheism and A.D. Gordon's secular quasi-pantheism arrive at a similar conclusion, though obviously from different philosophical premises.

In the United States the philosophical foundations of even Mordecai Kaplan's Reconstructionism can be seen in at least two ways to be remote and divergent derivatives of the German-Jewish philosophical tradition: Kaplan devoted an entire book to an interpretation of and an argument against Cohen's *Religion of Reason*, and his philosophical teacher, John Dewey, came into American pragmatism from German idealism (as Charles S. Peirce and William James had done). Kaplan, though, makes the historical and social reality of the Jewish people, rather than "reason," constitutive of Jewish religious civilization.

Among the devout there is the temptation to assert an at least equal, if not superior, realm of the numinous beyond the realm of ethics. Thinkers like Judah Halevi in the past and Rabbi Soloveitchik in our time, with his conception of a "higher will," as well as Leo Baeck, with his duality of "mystery and commandment," illustrate such a natural religious pull. When this pull is too powerfully exerted, thinking tends to abandon what can still be called philosophy and becomes theology or even mysticism. The degrees of identification of "the holy" with "the good," all the way from the biblical prophets down to modernist Judaism and contemporary philosophy (compare, for example, Abraham J. Heschel), may then be seen, in our perspective, as the measure of the power of the ultimate and dominate Jewish claim in its many different expressions.

If this reading of modern Jewish philosophy in terms of the struggle between Kantianism and Hegelianism (widely acknowledged in Continental philosophy as a fundamental structure) is accepted, the question arises whether, as would then seem to be the case, Jewish philosophy is only an accommodation to non-Jewish philosophical truth—a tail, so to speak, on the kite of secular philosophy. As we have seen, in itself this would, even if true, not necessarily be an objection; the entirety of Jewish philosophy has been, in a way, a Jewish variant of philosophy at large. Philosophically, furthermore, if reason be truth, and Judaism true, then all rational beings must be capable of the Jewish truth (cf. the Halakhic concept of the Noachites). Still, historically, it should always be noted that in modern as in classical Jewish philosophy the dualism of God and creation, freedom and nature, always tends to reassert itself in Jewish philosophy, in contrast to the Greek assertion of the primacy of metaphysics over ethics.

At the outset of modernity Mendelssohn discerned Jewish particularity in the law, itself an expression of essentially rational morality. We have seen how even the Jewish Hegelians of the nineteenth century and certainly Cohen and his disciples proclaimed Kant's "primacy of practical reason." The traditionalist Jewish thinkers like Rabbi Kook and Rabbi Soloveitchik must, of course, always uphold the centrality of Halakhah. Buber's and Heschel's thought emphasize the ethical and social demands made by the reality of the human-divine encounter. And at the present time all of Levinas' work centers on the ultimacy of the ethical God "beyond essence." (The Hegelians Krochmal and Rosenzweig, in contrast, address themselves perhaps least to ethics.) The claim may thus be made that Jewish philosophy is not finally the tail on the kite but the string that leads it.

– 13 –

Shekhinah and Eschatology

"The *shekhinah* is commandment."

(*Zohar*)

Introduction

I want to propose a definition of "shekhinah" that differs somewhat from what is nowadays the customary one. The purpose of this redefinition, or perhaps this restoration of the original definition, is to avoid the misunderstanding and dangers to which the prevailing definition is easily susceptible. At the same time my definition is intended to highlight the authentic meaning and purpose of the idea of the *Shekhinah* in the total context of Jewish religion.

I propose that "*shekhinah*" be understood as a somewhat poetic, metaphoric name that classical Judaism has given to the idea of the functioning relationship between the transcendent God, on the one hand, and, on the other hand, humanity in general and the people of Israel in particular (the latter as the normatively fullest realization of humanity).[1]

As soon as such a definition is proffered it becomes clear that Judaism has a whole slew of terms and phrases that significantly overlap or are even synonymous with shekhinah: e.g., *ru'akh hakodesh* ("the spirit of holiness"),[2] *k'vod haShem* ("the glory of God"),[3] angel,[4] *memra/yekara,*[5] *bat-kol* ("the daughter-voice"),[6] etc. It would take a more sophisticatedly detailed investigation than, for example, Abelson's[7] to determine what, if any, the minor differences are between all such terms. It is however, clear, in any case, that some of the synonyms or near-synonyms have remained a bit less susceptible to poetic and mystical hyperbole than *shekhinah*.

The Received Interpretation

Before I go into the reasons for and the details of my corrected definition we should look at what has become the widely accepted interpretation of the term that I wish here to surpass.

I take it that generally nowadays *shekhinah* is translated, in one verbal form or another, as "the immanence/in-dwelling of God"—i.e., God insofar as he, as it were, descends from his transcendence and takes up residence (*Shakhon*—"to dwell")[8] in the world or some part thereof, especially among Israel. In short, it is the immanentist aspect of the deity.[9]

In the broad definition that I have just cited I have used the masculine, third-person pronoun with reference to God and his immanence. It must be noted, however, that *Shekhinah* is in fact a Hebrew feminine noun (perhaps *sophia* and *chokhmah* have played a role here), and much heavy weather is made of this circumstance in classical Jewish mysticism and in contemporary radical feminism. (The *Book Bahir,* early Kabbalah, is said by the specialists in the field to have been the first to make *shekhinah* a separate, female power and person[nification] of God.)[10] From this perspective, therefore, a short translation of *shekhinah* is: the immanentist and female aspect of the deity.

One additional feature must be stipulated about this currently accepted characterization of the *shekhinah*: since Israel moves about a great deal in the world, when God resides among them the *shekhinah*, too, must be mobile—from the *mishkan* (the sanctuary" in the desert and before the Solomonic temple), in the temple(s) in Jerusalem, to the places of exile whither the Jewish people is dispersed. A reasonably adequate explanation, then, of *shekhinah* as it is widely understood would appear to be: the immanentist, female, and mobile aspect of the deity.

Critique of the Received Interpretation

Now, what is potentially and sometimes actually dangerous about this conception of the *shekhinah* is, perhaps, most easily illustrated in the above-mentioned assertion of the female aspect of the deity. If properly conceptualized I suppose one can have no objection to what is really intended by it. However we might feel about it in this age of women's liberation, historically it is certainly the case that such character-traits as solicitude, protectiveness, love, etc., that we want to attribute to the deity's relations to humans have been typically regarded as essentially female, maternal, nurturing traits. But I have always liked the reports that the well known Bible scholar of the earlier part of this century, Prof. Moses Buttenwieser, used to insist that the proper meaning of *kadosh* ("holy") was "unique, totally separate, *sui generis,* and, therefore, sexless," and that he then used to translate *Is.* 6:3 as "sexless, sexless, sexless is the Lord of hosts; the whole earth is full of his (!) glory." For our present purposes the point would be that the infinite God is not, of course, subject to the limitations of worldly existence—historical, biological, or metaphysical—and that, therefore, if we often necessarily, metaphorically, and limitedly speak of God in the masculine gender we must also think of him metaphorically and limitedly as feminine—hence the *shekhinah*. If, on the other hand, we take these metaphors literally, above all if we hypostatize them, we do great damage to our concept of God and to the human, religious behavior that is systematically connected with such a conception. In the present instance, for example, God is turned from a spiritual and ethical being into a sort of hermaphrodite, and his worshippers may then well engage in ritual acts of sexuality, from, e.g., the sacred prostitutes of fertility cults, whom the Bible condemns, to orgasm as divine "transport" and to current revivals of pagan practices in religion and daily life. In the *Zohar* and in later Kabbalah this metaphorical sexualization of God occasionally takes on extremely offensive proportions—"holy (sexual) union" between Moses/humanity in general and God/*shekhinah*.[11] The *shekhinah* is here usually identified with the last of the ten *s'phirot, malkhut*;[12] in *malkhut* the other nine s'phirot are brought together again, as they had been unified in the first *s'phirah* (all of them crystalized within the infinite Godhead). It is also the lowest of the ten, closest to the created world. Being female, and yet somehow the male *membrum*, as it were,[13] on the sephirotic body (*adam kadmon*—"the supernal Adam"),[14] it is very hermaphrodite, indeed. Through *d'vekut* ("adhesion, cleaving"—comp. the scholastic notion of *conjunctio*) to the *s'phirah* humans can, therefore, strive to come as near to unification with the deity as possible.[15] The Ba'al Shem Tov, then, the founder of Eastern-European Hassidism, was much attacked for his doctrine, especially in his "Last Will," commending sexual intercourse with the *shekhinah* in some picturesque detail, in the traditional pursuit of *unio mystica*. (This is far from unique in or to Judaism. Comp., for example, the marriage of nuns to Jesus and, indeed, the role of Mary when it sometimes turns into "Maryolatry" in the Roman Catholic Church.) Even Gershom Scholem feels that he has to take his leave at this point. He says: "Dimly we perceive behind this mystical images (sic) the male and female gods of antiquity," of paganism and gnosticism.[16] And he quotes the Talmudic sages: "To cling to the *shekhinah* is impossible."[17]

The dangers of a female god are no smaller than those of a male one.[18] There are, to be sure, less invidious operationalizations of such theological anthropomorphisms—i.e., the "sanctification" of marriage, of nonsexual love, etc.[19] I would be prepared to argue that the conceptualization of the metaphor, as opposed to its literalization, is a better doctrinal foundation for such purposes.

What we have just said about the femaleness of the *shekhinah* applies *pari passu* to its other attributes and, indeed, to the notion as a whole. If, for example, its mobility is meant to designate what is traditionally more abstractly referred to as God's omnipresence (*Ex.* 20:21: "In the whole place where I shall have My name recalled there I shall come to you and bless you"), then presumably the typical theist would raise no objection.[20] But if its mobility is taken with some literalness then presumably God, having taken up residence in one place, is no longer present in another (at least in the same way)—and this blatantly contradicts his infinity and spirituality. The Talmudic rabbis emphatically contradict such localizations of God: the *shekhinah* is everywhere.[21] "No place is empty of the *shekhinah*."[22]

Therewith we come to the nub of the matter. It is almost universally and rightly acknowledged that if Judaism as a religion stands and always has stood for anything it is the insistence on God's absolute transcendence and the correlative rejection of all forms of immanentism, pantheism, incarnationism, etc. This is to say, the God whom Judaism proclaims is totally different from the entire universe and from any of its components. He is, as Hermann Cohen and others emphasized, unique at least as much as he is one. "*Er ist nicht alles, sondern alles ist nicht Er./Das Absolute ist die vollkommene Exemption.*"[23] On the other hand, we would not be dealing with religion at all if this transcendent God had—*pace* epicureanism—no relation to the world, as, for instance, through creation and, more importantly in Judaism, through *Halakhah* ("law," "commandments"—revelation). Thus we have arrived at the decisive question about the nature of the relationship between God and humanity.

In another place[24] I have drawn the fundamental distinction between modeling the God-humanity relationship on a spatial conception, as in the Christian doctrine of the incarnation, in Spinoza's pantheism, and *in nuce* in Philo of Alexandria's intermediaries,[25] and, on the other hand, modeling it on the idea of the "will," i.e., nonspatial volitionalism and its translation into ethics.[26] The *shekhinah* in its more literal interpretation partakes of the spatial model, as we have begun to see. After all, to "in-dwell," like the Hebrew verb *shakhon*, has some almost inevitable spatial connotations: you dwell somewhere, and the preposition "in" calls for the question: where? There can be no doubt that also throughout Jewish history the temptation to veer toward such a literalist understanding has often exercised its dubious charms, especially among more mystically inclined religionists—e.g., in gnosticism, Philo, Christianity, Kabbalah, Sabbateanism, and other heresies (like Spinoza). Not only do such tendencies take what should be used as poetic metaphors literally; in the process they also hypostatize them. I.e., the *shekhinah* as a term of art for God's love, care, and nearness becomes a metaphysical (meta-*physical*), ontic entity that, if it is not actually a part, or aspect, of God, insinuates itself as an intermediary between God and humanity. The Talmud itself warns of such hypostatization—for example, by adding the cautionary term "*kivyakhol*"—"as it were", etc.[27] It was normatively understood that otherwise both Judaism's theological transcendence as well as its absolute monotheism are at risk.

Hypostatization violates what might be called "pure Judaism." Hypostatized entites are virtually by definition quasi-spatial; i.e., they are ideas or functions imagined as though they were objects, and objects are, of course, always in space. If, then, God is located in some (meta-)space, called infinity,[28] and he relates to people, who are certainly in space, through ideas or commands, called *logoi* or angels or sovereignties or the "paraclete," then these intermediaries, too, must be spatial (rather than merely poetic metaphors for the relations between God and humanity [Humean relations being notoriously unperceivable]). Thus, the natural human propensity to think in spatial images has also produced among Jews, over and over again in history, approximations of ideas of self-subsistent intermediaries between God and man—the *shekhinah* not least among them. Philo of Alexandria is the classic formulator of such realistic Platonism with his ladder of emanations. In the *Targumim* not only the "Word" (memra/*logos*) of God but also the *shekhinah* and other intermediaries are inserted between God and humanity—primarily in order to safeguard God's absolute transcendence and his nonanthropomorphism, but in the pursuit of this some additional anthropomorphization paradoxically occurs.[29] R. Saadia Ga'on, in his *Book of Doctrines and Beliefs*,[30] makes sure that the *shekhinah* and "God's glory," etc., keep anthropomorphic notions away from the concept of God, as Maimonides does with respect to angels, etc.,[31] and he stipulates that these intermediaries are "created beings;" i.e., they are effervescent and, therefore, cannot constitute any ultimate barriers between God and man.[32] In R. Yehudah HaLevy the *shekhinah*, the "divine substance" (*'inyan 'elokee*), etc., have, in keeping with his quasimystical, realistic Platonism, a much more metaphysical status.[33] That most bizarre classic of Jewish mysticism, *Shi'ur Qomah*, has precise, astronomic measurements of the *shekhinah*.[34] Blumenthal rightly calls it rabbinic gnosticism.[35] But even this was immediately translated in a "philosophizing" manner, so as to have it express "metaphors for other things"[36]—cosmology, neoPlatonism, and/or pious emotion.[37] Maimonides came to call the *Shi'ur Qomah* an idolatrous insinuation.[38]

That perpetual temptation within Judasism could be traced more fully and widely. For example, even prayer to the intermediary is not always completely excluded,[39] despite Maimonides' fifth, authoritative, dogmatic formulation that we may direct prayer to none but God himself. Still, what has to be stressed in a synoptic overview like ours is that none of such teachings ever attained to anything approaching doctrinal status. As Maimonides put it: they are not "part of the foundations of belief."[40] The intermediaries are almost always only temporary and representational functionaries between the only two real agents involved, namely God and the individual. The classic Jewish insistence that the individual directly faces God, and God alone (*Lev.* 16:30: "before God you shall be pure"), always triumphs over the temptation to think of him as spatially too remote. Christian and other heresies were almost always immediately recognized for what they were by dint of their proclamations of other divine beings. As Solomon Schechter stated it succinctly: in classical, permanent Judaism "establishing an intermediary is considered as setting up of another God, who is the cause of sin."[41] In other words, pure and austere monotheism always carried the day in the end. That, in the meantime, the natural human tendency among Jews to slide off into the spatial model in the form of intermediaries, however limited and short lived, could in turn easily be radicalized into fundamental religious doctrine is exemplified by the impact of Philo, gnosticism,[42] and Kabbalah on Christianity and in Spinoza's pantheism, not to speak of the Christian and even Christological utilization of Kabbalah.[43] (While ladders of intermediaries are one way by which people try to bridge the vertigo that grasps them when they try to imagine the infinite distance between themselves and God, pantheism is another such way: it simply abolishes that distance. Now God *is* the world. Mysticism and Kabbalah in Judaism often risk also this danger.[44] But, in accordance with its essential religious transcendentalism [which the Rabbis expressed by asserting that after the Babylonian exile the root of idolatry was uprooted in Israel], Judaism has always triumphed over that danger.)

At this point we may make the judgment: perhaps earlier modern rationalism and "science of Judaism" overdid their fervent contempt for Kabbalah, but surely the contemporary backlash of overestimating its importance and authenticity, as entrenched by the late Gershom Scholem and his followers, is no less a distortion. (Scholem himself distances himself when the more extreme forms of anthropomorphism occur—e.g., the female side of God and prayer to an intermediary. This is presumably what he had in mind when, in his introductory lecture, he declared: "I shall certainly be the last to deny that [the Kabbalah's] representatives often lost their way and went over the edge of the precipice."[45]

Let it be clearly understood that a critique of a literalist understanding of the notion of *shekhinah* by no means implies a rejection of the notion itself. There is nothing wrong with poetic metaphors as such. They may even be necessary for the human intellect and for human communication—if, but also only if, their function as metaphor is kept at least in the back of one's mind. If one stays aware of the difference between hypostases and concepts, between Platonic realism and nominalism, generally "one can" (as I said in another but related context)[46] "translate mystical thought quite adequately into rationalistic thought, and vice versa."[47] In this perspective, "classical Jewish thought is committed to the belief in the absolutely transcendent God, who is related to the human world only through his imperatives, and history is, therefore, the enactment of that body of imperatives, to the end of the Messianic achievement of the kingdom of God, in the interaction between God and Israel. In the rationalistic terms of the *Halakhah*, of Maimonides and of Hermann Cohen, for example, that basic structure is erected through a *theologia negativa*, which eliminates any divine essence, through *ta'amay hamiztvot*–philosophical ethics, and through a universalistic humanism. In kabbalistic (Chassidic) thought the same conceptual structure is erected through the (negative) withdrawal of the divine name (in the present context, the lifting of the *shekhinah* from Israel–cf. p. 243 below) from the empirical world, the (ethical) purification of the world in preparation for the return of God (and his name) to the world, and the consummation of the process of the return when the Name takes up residence again, as it were (here: the return of the *shekhinah*–cf. p. 244 below) in the human world totally and universally.[48]

In a very different context the great atheist neo-Marxist Theodor Adorno states our present thesis–that hypostatized metaphors may have to be taken literally, so long as one keeps in mind that they are metaphors–even up to the doctrine of God and the theologoumenon of resurrection, and he formulates it so strikingly that it may be quoted here at some length:

> Whoever reifies the transcendent ... lacks imagination, is an enemy of the spirit and hence a traitor to the transcendent. If, on the other hand, the ever so distant and tenuous possibility of realization in existence were to be cut off completely, and ultimately the finite, conditioned, merely existent subject would be deified as its bearer ... In cosmology, heaven and hell as things in space are sheer archaisms. Such archaisms would turn immortality into immortality of spirits, making something ghostly and unreal out of it, which would mock the very concept. ... That is where we are driven by the idea of truth, the highest among metaphysical ideas. He who believes in God, therefore, cannot believe in him. The possibility represented by the divine name is sustained by him who does not believe. ... This is how low the history of a metaphysical truth, which vainly denies history, has fallen. ... By leaving nothing but mere reality it reverts to myth. For it is nothing but the closed, systematic immanentization of what is.[49]

For the purposes of the present study, which is obviously informed by the spirit of Hermann Cohen's neo-Kantianism, the mutual translatability of rationalism and mysticism (while guarding their significant differences–which, in the Jewish context, are in turn radically reduced by their common Jewish ethicist foundation), can be stated even better in the vocabulary of Ernst Cassirer, Cohen's favorite disciple.

In *Language and Myth*[50] Cassirer summarizes his *Philosophy of Symbolic Forms* insofar as our subject is concerned in the very title. Whereas in "Language and Conception" (i.e., conceptualization) (chapt. 3) "the recognition of function precedes that of Being,"[51] and "in this sense, it is something essentially ideal, a 'sign' or symbol, the object of which is not a substantial entity but lies rather in the relations it establishes,"—in "Word Magic" (i.e., myth and mysticism) (chapt. 4) "hypostatization or transsubstantiation" (!)[52] is performed on words, and thus for "every product of subjectivity (i.e., 'mind') so much substantiality."[53] Nonetheless, "The power of metaphor" (chapt. 6) is such that "the resemblances in their results, in the forms that they produce, point to a final community of function, of the principles whereby they operate. . . . (T)he same form of mental conception is operative in both. It is the form that one may denote *metaphorical thinking* [E.C.'s italics] . . ."[54] In logic and conceptualism the extension of words is pursued—in mysticism their intension, "not quantitatively, but qualitatively."[55] This commonality and this fundamental distinction are traced by Cassirer first through "The Successive Phases of Religious Thought" (chapt. 5): "Critical, or 'discursive,' thinking, it is true, finally progresses to a point at which the expression of 'being' appears as the expression of *relation*, so that, to speak with Kant, Being is no longer a 'possible predicate of a thing' and therefore can no longer be an attribute of God. But for mythic thought, which recognizes no such critical distinction, but remains 'substantive' even in its highest reaches, Being is not only a predicate, but at a certain stage of development actually becomes the Predicate of Predicates. . . ."[56] At the very end Cassirer even traces the mystical/conceptualist commonality to poetry,[57] which we, too, see always to be in closest proximity to mysticism.

Improved Interpretation

In short, for a proper understanding of the concept of the *shekhinah*, an act of deliteralization and dehypostatization must be performed.[58] A restatement of this theologoumenon is called for, and this was the reason for my proposed redefinition. Under that redefinition the *shekhinah* is a poetic, metaphoric name for the functioning relationship between God and humanity, and in particular Israel—a relationship that is in turn defined in terms of will, both divine and human ("will" in the Kantian, rational sense, as the rationale and source of ethics). In slightly less abstract terms, the *shekhinah* is the semi-personalized, divine side of the ethical covenant between God and Israel, wherever Israel is, for the sake of the perfection of humanity.

Hermann Cohen, in his essay "The Holy Spirit," states all of our thesis with his usual canonical correctness. The correct Hebrew and the correct conception is, of course, "the spirit of holiness"—i.e., it is not *anything* in itself; it is the spirit of God as the correlation between God and humanity—the foundation of religious ethics. "The spirit of holiness" = "the glory of God" = the *shekhinah* = God.[59] Therefore, it cannot be and is not any sort of intermediary—much less a sort of person, but is "an *attribute* [Cohen's italics], a power, so to speak an organ in God and man. . . . How could the holy spirit mean anything more than a *function?*"[60] As the metaphor for the religious foundation of ethics, and ethics being the foundation for the universal human fraternity, the spirit of holiness necessarily and organically leads to Messianism.[61]

Up to now all my claims oh behalf of the proper understanding of *shekhinah* have been broad and programmatic. Can they be borne out with historical, textual evidence? They can—although here I can do no more, of course, than give a few probative examples from the major eras and genres of Jewish literature.

In a striking and provocative passage (*B. Sukkah* 5a) the Rabbis militate against a quasi-objective conception of the *shekhinah*: "Rabbi Josi taught: 'The *shekhinah* never descended, and Moses and Elijah never ascended.' "[62] (Several Biblical verses are then interpreted accordingly. "Ten handbreadths" distance is stipulated between God and man wherever they meet—I take it, itself a metaphorical way of affirming God's ultimate and unattainable transcendence. All this is typically expounded in the legal and actionable context of the technical details of a proper Tabernacles booth.) And R. Tankhum adds: "God sends the reflection of the *shekhinah* (*zeev hashkhinah*)"[63] (on which people nourish themselves). Indeed, Moses was even totally deprived of the *shekhinah* while and because Israel was being punished for the sin of the golden calf.[64] Sin struck Israel blind, so that they could not see the *shekhinah*.[65] Satan cannot be where the *shekhinah* is.[66] The *shekhinah* is an ethical concept, so that it "dwells" wherever good things are done,[67] and it withdraws from wherever evil things are done.[68] The *shekhinah* dwells wherever morality prevails.[69] "Repentance (*t'shuvah*—really 'morality') is almost a synonym for *shekhinah*."[70] *Aboth deRabbi Nathan* 36: "All the time that the Israelities are immersed in immorality (*p'rutzot be'arayot*) the *shekhinah* keeps away from them . . ."[71] *Gen. R. 8:6:* "Wherever the pious go there the *shekhinah* accompanies them."[72] "Sin ousts the *shekhinah* from its place,"[73] and if it stays with the sinful at all it does so only in order to try to convert them.[74] The greatest sin is, of course, idolatry (i.e., worship of anyone but God), and classically the Rabbis derive all other sins from it. Specific sins and classes of sins are listed that remove the *shekhinah*: adultery, theft,[75] and all sins committed in secret.[76] The sinfulness of idolatry causes the departure of the *shekhinah* (*silluk hashkhinah*)—the "hiding of God's face" (*hester paneem*).[77] On the other hand, wherever justice is carried on there the *shekhinah* is present—e.g., in the courtroom.[78] In one of the great *loci classici* of Talmudic ethics [79] the detailed *imitatio dei* climaxes in the injunction to imitate the *shekhinah*: like God, clothe the naked, visit the sick, comfort the mourners, and bury the dead! Converts who have chosen Judaism are to this day famously brought "under the wings of the *shekhinah*."[80] On the other hand, whenever bad things happen to and are done by Jews the *shekhinah* either goes into exile with them or withdraws from the world alltogether (i.e., it is de-immanentized).[81]

In the medieval period everything I have argued for here was expounded, classically, authoritatively, radically, and convincingly by Maimonides. "There is no relationship between God and space."[82] God is in fact his "will" and his actions[83] for the sake of human *imitatio dei.*[84] The *shekhinah* is a "figurative" way of speaking of God's (ethical) revelations to the prophets,[85] and this, says the Rambam, is also why and how the *Targumim* employ this and similar metaphors.[86] The powerful bottom line of Maimonides' prophetology is that, once a person has acquired the prerequisites for a direct understanding of God's will (rational, as both parties to the relationship are), the rest, as far as the prophet is concerned—the *shekhinah*—is a matter of "intellectual apprehension."[87] "*Shekhinah*" is the poetic, religious term for what Aristotelian philosophers call "the active intellect" (*sekhel hapo'el*).[88] This philosophical explication even precipitates into the law. Like everything spiritual, divine, so also the *shekhinah* (and the angels) may not, of course (because they cannot) be depicted.[89]

Hermann Cohen, here like everywhere, took up the patrimony of mainline, rabbinic, rational/philosophical Judaism. In his previously cited essay "The Holy Spirit" he quotes the three words of *Sifra* to the one word in *Lev.* 11:14, "and ye shall make yourselves holy" (*vehitkadashtem*): *zoo kedushat mitzvah*—"this means the holiness of the commandment."[90] I.e., "the spirit of holiness," which denotes what God and humanity have in common, the bridge across which the two communicate by means of cognition and action, and what is more concretely referred to as the *shekhinah*, is in fact a designation of the commandments that humanity is to fulfill in the pursuit of our moral tasks.

We have noted here from the outset that mysticism and the poetry commonly associated with it are particularly susceptible to the temptation of literalizing and hypostatizing metaphorical language. Kabbalah has, indeed, often succumbed to this temptation. Often enough, too, however, it demystifies and demysticizes itself. It is thus immensely impressive that in the Zohar the one sentence occurs, which recapitulates the equally lapidary, almost identical sentence from *Sifra* that we have just looked at in the rationalist/legal tradition and which states once more in three short Hebrew words everything that the present study propounds: *shekhinah hee mitzvah*—"the *shekhinah* is commandment."[91] (Kantian translation: God is the categorical imperative.) It must thus be noted and stressed that Talmud, Kabbalah, and Jewish philosophy commit themselves as one to three Hebrew words, which formulate the program of ethical monotheism. Thus, for instance, helping the poor constitutes adoration of the *shekhinah*, since the latter is "the poor cousin" of God.[92] Sin, on the other hand, causes the withdrawal of the *shekhinah* into God's secret recesses.[93] Abraham J. Heschel, in succession to Kabbalah and Chassidism and quoting the Zoharic declaration, puts it in modern and his own typically poetic English: the *shekhinah* is God's "immanence in deeds;"[94] it is God's goodness, acting in the world[95]—the "divinity of deeds,"[96] to be imitated in humanity actions.

Abraham ibn Ezra's extended commentary to *Ex.* 32:21f. presents a typical exposition, in the kabbalistic/neo-Platonic vein, of our theme.[97] God cannot be seen. Indeed, "he is not like the universe, nor in the universe, nor with the universe." Even the angels, "the ineffable [72-lettered] name of God" = "God's glory" = "the created light" = the *shekhinah* are still unattainable by perception or, for that matter, by intellectual knowledge. Only the best—Moses—can know them "with the eyes of the mind." The generality of humanity can only cleave to "the creator-God," who is clearly lower on the ladder than the former. The planets and constellations are the creatures of this creator-God, and their laws in turn determine astrologically whatever happens in the world. (In ibn Ezra, typically, science, hard-headed comparative linguistic analysis, and exegetics mix as inseparably with numerology and astrology as Maimonides and *Shi'ur Qomah* sometimes live compatibly side by side.) This is as true of human individuals as it is of collectivities. But—and here come the points in which we are particularly interested in our context—1) ethics overcomes astrology. "There is no constellation that rules Israel," as the Rabbis declared (*ayn mazal le'yisra'el*), "only as long as they keep the Torah" (i.e., do "My good"). If this seems scientifically inconsistent, then ibn Ezra has a lovely parable to tell: a blind man and a lame man cannot stop the course of wild horses or of a flood, but if they know how and where these events will take place they can get out of their way. And 2) all of the above obviously constitutes a neo-Platonic cosmology, and it, therefore, has to be and is explicitly a universalistic doctrine. Israel, to be sure, is "the highest form of humanity," but this is the case by virtue of the fact that they know and live by the laws of the universal God's cosmos. Thus, it is a truth "for all the nations and for those who continue to teach the nations." I.e., even in this (to us) bizarre world view, Judaism is first and foremost an ethical and universalistic enterprise.[98]

In general the treatment of the *shekhinah* by the Kabbalah concentrates on the doctrine that God and Israel are inseverably covenanted—as we now know, if we have not known it otherwise: in the form of commandments or imperatives. God is the head, Israel is the feet of the *shekhinah*[99] In variants on this metaphor, the *shekhinah* is both heavenly and, in *potentia*, earthly,[100] or it is *"k'nesset yisra'el,"* "the *ecclesia* of Israel" itself.[101]

With respect to this mystical doctrine, that the Jewish people *are*, or are part of, the *shekhinah*, it must be kept in the forefront of one's mind (especially in our time, when the temptation to turn Israel into an *ecclesia triumphans* is riding the crest) that the *shekhinah* is either not at all or only in smallest part in this world; it is really in bulk in "the other world"—i.e., it does not describe how anything, including the Jewish people, *is* but how it ought be—how it is only ideally. Israel, in the Jewish context, is always a normative and, therefore, critical concept—not a descriptive and certainly not a self-justifying or self-validating concept. The actual Jewish people is the accusative object of the ideal, normative, regulative Israel of God—the heavenly/Messianic Israel. To put it more simply, Jews are those people who are commanded by, obligated to, God's law to be perfect human beings and who, of course, never in their worldly lives accomplish that task.[102] The Torah is the *definiens*, and Israel is the *definiendum*. As Emmanuel Lévinas says,[103] "I have it from an eminent [Talmudic] master:[104] every time that the Talmud speaks of Israel one is, of course, free to understand by this a particular ethnic group, which will probably, in fact, have achieved an incomparable destiny; but one will in this way also have constricted the general idea enunciated in that Talmudic passage—one will have forgotten that Israel signifies a people that has received the Law and, consequently, a humanity that has arrived at the plenitude of its responsibilities and of its self-understanding. The descendants of Abraham, of Isaac, and of Jacob—that is a humanity no longer in its infancy. . . . Every man that is truly a man is of Abraham's posterity."[105] And Abelson, despite his lack of philosophical sophistication, hits the right terminology: the Rabbis "express this as a doctrine in the 'imperative mood'."[106] He designates the Messianic condition, i.e., the time when the human ideal and human reality will coincide in actuality, when, in the time to come, people will have hearts of flesh instead of hearts and tablets of stone, "as ideal" (to be taken in the Kantian sense of ideal as infinite goal).[107]

Throughout the present study I have presented my argument for the deliteralization and dehypostatization of the *shekhinah* on its merits—i.e., regardless of whether the original notion was intended to be taken literally or no. On the other hand, I have occasionally alluded to the possibility that my proposed redefinition really amounts to the restoration of the original intention deposited in the notion. Let me give only one example of why I think it is more likely a question of understanding properly the original idea rather than a matter of redefinition. If this be true even among the Talmudic rabbis (not to speak of the classic Jewish philosophers of the Middle Ages and modern rationalists, of whom this is obviously true anyway), then the stigma is on those who insist on their hyperbolic enthusiasm.

In *Lamentations Rabba*, proem XV, God is described as walking around among the exiles of Israel (the well-known metaphor of God's mobility with and loyality to Israel in its tragic fate). Twice within the same short paragraph the *terminus technicus "kiv'yakhol"*—"as it were" is carefully attached to the poetic narrative.[108] In proem XXIV then the (as it were) internal, psychological problems are described that afflict God as a result of having punished Israel, which he loves, by dispersing it. The *shekhinah* returns to its transcendence from its immanent residence with Israel. God weeps copiously over the destruction of the Temple. Metatron (another of the angelic intermediaries between God and the world—in this instance very close to, if not identical with, the *shekhinah*) obviously has a more developed sense of divine etiquette than God himself. Metatron says to him: let me weep for you (which is less unbecoming). But God replies: don't hassle me! I want to weep. If you keep on trying to teach me good, divine manners I'll withdraw to higher levels of transcendence, where you, mere Metatron, cannot follow me, and there I'll keep on weeping to my heart's content.

Now, I suppose, if one absolutely insists, one can go on holding that the rabbis of the *'aggadeta* meant this story to be taken literally. To hold that view, however, is really to display a lack of humor beyond literary acceptability. Furthermore, even theologically, to attribute to the rabbis the belief that God has to threaten to flee from his own emissary in order to do what he wants to do is to denigrate those rabbis beyond any degree permissible to a Jew who wants to proclaim his Talmudic orthodoxy or historical comprehension.

Here again the examples could be multiplied almost without end. In short, I have to insist that my interpretation is not only philosophically and theologically but even historically correct.

Eschatology

Almost imperceptibly we have moved quite naturally from the ethical significance of the idea of the *shekhinah* to eschatology. The ethicism of the *shekhinah*, when rightly understood, merges, as in Judaism everything ultimately tends to do, with the ethicism of Jewish Messianism. "The Messianic days," "the coming future," "the kingdom of God," etc., in the present world grow almost organically into "the coming world," eternal life, the resurrection, etc., of "the world to come." The horizontal dimension of the Messianic future in history and the perpendicular dimension of immortality produce, like divergent forces, a diagonal dimension of ethicism in metahistorical eternity. Both together enjoin human beings—Jews first and humanity in their wake—to act in such a manner (i.e., ethically) that we have good reason to hope that we are moving from where we are, steeped in evil, to where we ought be and, indeed, wish to be—that is, in a world which "is good and does good" (*tov umayteev*).[109]

This theologoumenon carries both a practical (*Halakhic*) and a theological (*aggadic*) face. On the *Halakhic* side, all laws have for their purpose, as a matter of fact, "to bring near the end" (*lekarev 'et hakaytz*).[110] By way of specific examples: "one who attributes a quotation to its author brings redemption near"[111]—if Jews kept merely two Sabbaths, or even only one, the Messiah would arrive (the Sabbath being one-sixtieth of the world to come)[112]—anyone who charges interest on money is deprived of salvation[113]—etc.[114] As Steven S. Smith puts it,[115] "ethics is an eschatological optics." In traditional language, Elijah, the herald of the Messiah, brings the *shekhinah* back with him.[116]

On the aggadic side, all moral actions are literally said to be such as "in the future to receive [make one deserving of receiving] the face of the *shekhinah*," according to the Rabbis.[117] In the poetic language of the midrash, the *shekhinah* progressively removes itself from Israel and from the world as these lapse into sin,[118] and she returns ever closer to them as they live in accordance with God's will, until first one part of humanity and its habitat (Israel in Palestine) and then the whole world have achieved, or have been endowed with, Messianic status.[119] The rabbis declare in metaphysical terms that in the world to come people will feed off the "reflection of the *shekhinah*."[120] In metahistorical terms R. Yehudah HaLevy lays it down that the *shekhinah* returns to the world from its heavenly retreat, or to Palestine with the ingathering of the Jewish people from its exile, together with the Messiah.[121] And in fact every Jew recites three times every day the benediction that is part of the core "Eighteen Prayers:" "Praised be Thou, oh Lord, our God, who [in the course of Messianically restoring the Temple] causes his *shekhinah* to return to Zion." According to the early mysticism of *Hekhalot Rabbiti* the *shekhinah*, which is "the prince of the Torah" (*sar torah*),[122] will in the Messianic fulfillment descend again into "the last temple" and from there pervade the world.[123] According to the Kabbalah, "I (God) am like you. In the same plight that you, Jerusalem, are here I am, as it were, above. Just as the holy people do not pilgrimage to you anymore in sacred array, so, I swear to you, I will not ascend on high until the day when your throngs will again stream to you here below."[124] Israel, by cleaving to the *shekhinah,* attains to redemption.[125] According to R. Chayim Vital's *Sha'ar Gilgulim* ("Tractate on Reincarnation") the *shekhinah* can return to the world only after the pre-created souls have lived their earthly lives.[126] Redemption, in turn, implicates all the nations of the world for at least two reasons:[127] 1) the Messianic kingdom extends, of course, over all nations and lands, and 2) the salvation of Israel cannot transpire in the first place without both its soteriological effects on and the soteriological role of the gentile nations.[128] In *Deut. R.*, for example, a thematic red thread is the praise of Esau (= non-Jews), who was, after all, cheated by Jacob—whose human tragedy is described—to whom Israel is unfavorably compared—and whose forgiveness Israel must eschatologically merit.[129] "I call heaven and earth to witness that anyone, whether heathen or Jew, man or woman, slave or handmaid, is capable of possessing the holy spirit according to the actions which he performs."[130] This (though a very late Rabbinic source) was presumably meant as a Messianic proposition: as every person in Israel was grasped by the prophetic spirit at Sinai, so all humanity will be in the messianic hour—*n.b.*, all dependent on their morality. "The *shekhinah* has vanished because of our sins (*Is.* 59:2), but in the future world a new revelation will be vouchsafed to them."[131] And in our own time R. Hutner, having identified the "glory" of God with his goodness (ethics) and with Israel, said: "The mystery of the attribute of 'glory' forces the restoration of the Edenic existence."[132] As Heschel put it,[133] Israel declares the glory of "divine deeds" to the whole world, so that in the end "the world will be full of the knowledge of the Lord as the waters cover the sea" (*Is.* 11:9). And as I have described it elsewhere, [134] *Halakhah* (Jewish law/morality) is the road that we walk of fulfilling the commandments, which leads from where we are to the Messianic goal of the consummation of the socio-ethical tasks toward which we ought strive.

Summary

I began by proposing as a hypothesis that the traditional Jewish notion of the *shekhinah* is a religious metaphor for the functioning relationship between God and Israel, and therewith also with humanity as a whole—a relationship, which is in turn totally defined by ethics. More literalist, hypostatized interpretations of *shekhinah,* as often propounded particularly in mysticism and as widely advocated in the present climate of conservatism and chauvinism, contain serious dangers to the austere, rigorous monotheism of Judaism as well as to the moral progress of society. Ethics, on the other hand, when enacted and effectual, on my definition, brings about what religion calls the kingdom of God. The historical evidence from the sources of Judaism, when properly read and analyzed, verifies that hypothesis. Much more such evidence is readily available.

Afterword

Reading over the studies brought together in this volume it seems to me clear that, although written over a span of more than a quarter of a century, they share certain important common features. (Indeed, rereading the essays—with some pain—even I was surprised to discover how strongly and widely these features appeared.) Most of this common core has already been crystallized in the editor's very selfless introduction.

One of them is concern with the Messiah and Jewish Messianism. The first chapter here announces the theme in its title, and so does the last. (The chapters follow in chronological order of first appearance.) Several essays in between also have such titular references, and others contain significant passages within their text that revolve about this subject.

It might seem to be out of order to cite as a second common feature my perpetual and always deep commitment to Hermann Cohen and Immanuel Kant. (The first of these names occurs often enough, the second more often by implication. Maimonides' name is joined to theirs, but it is the Cohennian Maimonides that is unashamedly put forward.) I mention this pervasive feature in second place because it goes almost without saying that for any "Marburg neo-Kantian" the idea of the Messiah is the practical, i.e., meaningful, way of thinking and talking about God. It is claimed that the advancement of God's reign is the exhaustive function of belief in God in Judaism. Thus the third common prominent feature that the studies in this volume share, even if it were not often explicitly articulated, would have to be, on merely logical grounds, concern with God. (And the fourth common characteristic, namely the ongoing battle against idolatry, is then merely the consequence of the third, although, having just written for separate publication '*De Idololatria*,' I was surprised to discover how often I had had to address myself to this subject in the past.)

Maimonidean, Cohennian Kantianism holds, as do I, that God and Messianism are specifications of what Plato called "the idea of ideas, "the good," God. The pursuit of that idea(1) is then the infinite task that devolves upon people as their meaning. Thus the title that the editor and I came up with for the present collection.

There is another implication in what has been said even so far. Hermann Cohen taught in word and practice that "the truth" that philosophy seeks is, in the first place, also the truth (*'emeth*) toward which Judaism strives and, in the second place, decisively dependent on Jewish monotheism (*pace Religion of Reason out of the Sources of Judaism*). Thus, whereas previously in history Jewish philosophers worked at trying to harmonize two different things, Judaism and philosophy, Cohen showed in a revolutionary fashion that these two things were properly one in the first place; i.e., philosophy has to be ultimately Jewish in some real sense, and, indeed, Judaism is intellectually philosophical. (In an extremely limited way Philo anticipated this view of matters, and Kant suggested something similar in Protestant terms.) I believe this. (Therefore, for me it is not at all anachronistic to have written an as yet unpublished study, "The Jewish Kant." Plato, too, belongs in this line. After all, Christian cathedrals in the Middle-Ages put Plato and Aristotle among their saints—wrongly, I believe, for the former, anyway.)

One ramification of this Cohennian collapse into one of philosophy and what is often called "Jewish thought" is that one cannot be a good Jewish thinker without continuing to do one's homework, as it were, in philosophy (and philosophy here covers, of course, all the standard subfields, including especially the philosophy of science). Again, Maimonides and Cohen, to cite only the greatest of names for this context, said this explicitly and exemplified it in their work. (The Talmudic sages insisted on this, too, in their ways and for their purposes.) If Jewish belief and posture cannot hold their place and, indeed, show their value in the entirety of the logic, "metaphysics," epistemology, philosophy of mathematics, indeed, in the ethics and aesthetics, etc., of the world in which we live—then for which world is it that Judaism is intended? Maimonides presupposed, by and large—though with exceptions— the philosophy and science of others; he merely demanded that they be studied, however critically. Cohen went further: he opened all questions of logic science, ethics, aesthetics, and culture for fresh consideration—to be sure, on Kantian bases—and it is in the framework of such a comprehensive restructuring of the world that the decisive function of Judaism was determined. To cite only two examples out of my work: If I could not satisfactorily handle modern philosophy of infinity, what would I do with all the Jewish religious talk about infinite and eternity; and if I could not explain what a human self is, what would I do with all the Jewish talk about moral responsibility, the soul, etc.?

My friend Prof. Menachem Kellner, in his introduction, thinks of me as a theologian. I suppose what he has in mind is that Jewish religious concerns are, indeed, never out of my mind and often on my lips. Just the same, I think of myself as a philosopher. (When the next volume collects my philosophical studies, published over the years, this will be a little more visible than it is here.) But the difference between Kellner and I on this score is merely verbal: a good philosopher has to be ideally a Jew (as I have learned from Hermann Cohen and believe to be true), and when he or she is an actual (and thoughtful) Jew you can also call him or her a Jewish theologian. (I suppose it would be an acceptable compromise to speak of philosophical theology. On the other hand, both Cohen and his [erstwhile] student, Rabbi J.B. Soloveitchik, *lehibbadel lechayyim*, rightly boggle at the very notion of theology in the context of Judaism—i.e., at the notion that there is anything to be said about "the nature of God." I should just as soon take my stand with them.)

I mentioned earlier in passing that I found it rather painful to reread my writings of years and even decades past. I can only hope that the readers will not have this experience, too. But, then, presumably they do not know beforehand, as I did, what is coming up, which can produce some boredom. Also they do not need to feel the personal responsibility for what is here written, as I do. Furthermore, whatever my many failings, I have successfully trained myuself not to look backward over my life; therefore, to have been forced into the posture of Lot's wife was a wrench for me. I was, on the other hand, relieved to discover that, in bulk, I am willing to say about myself what at one point I quote Sartre as having said: "In principle, I agree with my past."

There was one partial limited detour in my intellectual life, which also leaves its significant traces in the present collection. I started out with Hermann Cohen while I was still in high school, and I am still (indeed, more) with him now. He has been very good company and a very good guide—Jewishly as well as philosophically. The temporary and limited detour went via Franz Rosenzweig. I am not the only one to have fallen prey to this temptation—indeed, Rosenzweig fell prey to himself in this sense. But I recovered. (My forthcoming book, *Martin Heidegger and Franz Rosenzweig: the German and Jewish Turns to Ethnicism*, gives, I am sorry to have to say, further testimony to this recovery.) At the same time, I make every effort not to lose my personal respect for and gratitude to Rosenzweig (and, for that matter, Martin Buber). Quite apart from his (their) personal and intellectual stature(s), the detour via Rosenzweig brought me toward so-called Jewish orthodoxy, even in some ways so-called ultraorthodoxy, where I am intellectually much more comfortable than in Cohen's own (or at least self-perceived) religious "liberalism." (Politically I have to stand at a point where, incredibly, the Satmer Rebbe and Hermann Cohen's ethical socialism meet. Cf. my friend Prof. Harry van der Linden's current *Kantian Ethics and Socialism*. I leave Kellner's interpretation of my attitude toward Zionism to stand on its merits.)

This detour via Rosenzweig is the reason for the only two substantive corrections of what I once wrote to which I must draw attention in this afterword.

My (limited) change of mind on the question of when the Messiah may be expected to arrive has already been discussed by the editor. I still do think and argue that the Messiah ought be conceived as a person, and, indeed, the *Tendenz* of that article continues to express my reasoned view of the matter. But I now know and argue that Cohen was quite right in the first place ("theologically" as well as philosophically—in other words, as a matter of the Jewish sources rightly understood and conceptually) that the Messiah is "an infinite ideal," not in time. To put this somewhat more provocatively, I now sympathize much more with Rav (tr. *Sanh.* 97a), who taught that all "the messiahs" have by now come and gone, and from here on in everything turns on "repentance and good deeds." Kellner believes that I have undergone this change of mind because of all the horrible mischief that has meanwhile been perpetrated by Zionist and Israeli pseudo-Messianists, and I gladly own up to the horror that that misuse of Jewish Messianism arouses in me. (Well over forty years of close personal and intellectual friendship with Rabbi Arnold Jacob Wolf have gone into, among other things, sorting out our respective postures toward Zionism.) But I honestly believe that the more fundamental cause of my retraction is philosophical—that infinite ideals rather than empirical expectation are, or ought be, the incentive to human life and history.

The other retraction occurs in "Moral Radicalism vs. Middlingness in Maimonides' Ethics," n. 64. There I have come to the recognition that again, Cohen (and Kant) was quite right in holding that reason alone suffices for all people to arrive ideally at the truth, and therewith also at the good, and that, contrary to what I argued in the chapter on Noachitism, no necessary surplus of moral cognition remains that calls for revelation or an ultimate intuition to provide. Let it not be misunderstood: the thought underlying this retraction does not, of course, discard Torah (*chass vechalilah*). As I argue at considerable length in another as yet unpublished study of mine, "On Jewish Meta-Ethics," Torah is, as every learned Jew knows, the understanding of a document, the Bible, which is to be taken with infinite seriousness ("divine"), offered by the Sages; in other words, that understanding ("interpretation"—Talmud), itself revealed (i.e., to be taken with infinite seriousness), is a claim on our rationality/reasonableness (in the perspective of the "primacy of practical reason"). In short, again, Judaism ("Torah") and reason (philosophy) work toward the same goal—our knowledge and practice of the good.

I ought say something, I suppose, about how and why I write and do not write.

I used to complain to Rabbi Soloveitchik, as a lot of other people did, that he would not publish. As the years went by I (*lehavdeel*) have more and more adopted his practice (while he has abandoned it). (Thus, for example, the several references I have already had to make to unpublished writings of mine, and my friends and students know that there are a lot of books and studies of mine, some of them decades old, that have never been put in print.) There are a number of reasons for this. For one thing, as has been brought home to me again in having to reread the essays brought together in this volume, it always turns out later that one has made some mistakes in the past or misunderstood some problems. Why perpetuate errors in print and possibly mislead readers? Furthermore, this is necessarily and always the case with humans. There may be a bit of truth in what we believe we have discovered, but there is also always a lot of falsehood in it. Why not restrict our falsehoods as much as possible to at most oral discourse, which is unlikely to be disseminated quite so widely and long? For another, the history of my time has again proved that theoretical enlightenment does not really improve conditions in the world. Things almost always get worse. My goal has increasingly become to try to understand for myself. (Another way of saying this would be that one aims at becoming a *talmid chakham*—literally "a wise student," and no more.) If, then, someone asks how I understand a given problem, other things being equal, I am perfectly willing to say what I think I know or, indeed, to write it down, but otherwise I am entirely satisfied to keep things to myself. (The only cases where I feel I must initiate speech and action are cases of immediate human, moral and social, need—not, again, really in the expectation that I can improve things but simply because this is what it means to me to be "*a mensch*," or, as S.R. Hirsch put it better, "a *Yisroel-Mensch*." As my brother and I always put it to each other: we know that the world is about to perish, but one must dress for dinner anyway.)

When I do write for publication, increasingly I want to write, even for myself and surely for students, in the form of a sort of encyclopaedia-article. One cannot say everything about even a very limited topic, but one can at least try to make reference to whatever is relevant, thus enabling the reader, if he/she wants, to pursue the topic further. Thus my invariably bottom-heavy footnote apparatus, often mainly for the purpose of providing bibliography. Also, I am not really interested anymore in being readily intelligible. Anything simple is *eo ipso* false; the truth, whatever it is, is bound to be terribly complex (J.M. Bochenski, I discovered the other day, put this in an aphorism: "Why should it be simple when it can be complicated.") Thus my long-winded and heavily encapsulated sentences. (Those who mean well by me say that I write English in German. I am, indeed, a thorough-going 'Yekke," but, again, I do not really believe that this is the issue here. For one thing, 18th-century English itself frowned on simplistic sentences of subject-verb-object.) Let others, then, popularize what has been discovered if they, unlike me, feel motivated to be understood.

In the present case a lot could have been changed about these texts. Some I would prefer to alter a bit; a good deal could have been added; much needs further explanation. (My working copies have accumulated much such material.) Also, the editor could have selected other studies of mine, and he could have bunched them topically, rather than chronologically. But, then, in the first place, I would again wish to improve the improved texts a few years later. Also it would take a lot of time and effort, whereas at this time other tasks seem to commend themselves. Perhaps the individual reader will do these things for him/herself.

In philosophy the distinction has long been made between "history of philosophy" and what used to be called "systematic philosophy," which now comes pretty much to the same thing as "philosophical analysis." In plain English, the former is interested in what people used to think was true, while the latter is interested in what is (now believed to be) true. My Kantianism always makes it impossible for me to uphold this distinction to any great degree. We see history, too, of course, through our (epistemological and practical) eyes (= systematically and analytically), and these eyes of ours, in turn, are formed by history (language, culture, the problems inherited by the discipline, the practical problems we are stuck with in our society, etc.). As Ernst Cassirer, that marvelous disciple of H. Cohen once put it (*Essay on Man*, Yale University Press, 1944, p. 178): 'Historical knowledge is the answer to definite questions, an answer that must be given by history; but the questions themselves are posed and dictated by the present, by our present spiritual interests and from our determining moral and social concerns of the present." In other words, history and analysis determine one another—"dialectically," if you will. (If things were left at this we would find ourselves smack in the middle of the notorious "hermeneutic circle," proudly the prisoners of our "prejudices." [Cf. my "Reason and Authority: Contra Gadamer"] The rational thinker will, therefore, raise the "foundational" question of how to exit from that vicious circle of human solipsism. I hold that the Jewish/Kantian answer is that moraliity/"the primacy of practical reason" is imposed on us not "from the world" but from reason/God for the world. This implies rigorously that whatever I see the world and history to be, they cannot, must not, violate decency between human beings; indeed, the former must be at least potentially conducive to the latter. For the rest, as Hillel said in this sort of a situation, "go and learn!") It is in line with this general conception that I study and write. My studies are inextricable mixes of sources and interpretation. Systematic thought tells me what to look for and how to try to understand it—sometimes differently from how the original authors understood themselves (as Kant thought he understood Plato better than Plato understood himself, as Hermann Cohen thought he understood Kant better than Kant understood himself, as Judaism rightly asserts that it increasingly understands the *textus brutus* of the Bible better than those who commit themselves to *sola scriptura*, and as Maimonides insists that the philosophical Jew understands the Sages better than *hoi polloi* understand them). Thus "Judaism" (ideally, regulatively) = philosophical truth (ideally, regulatively), and this is a symmetrical equation. (History is then in a very real sense a normative discipline. This is reflected in what also the educated layman knows—that the historical facts of the past always change in the light of how they are contemporaneously found, understood, and used.) The texts, or "facts," on the other hand, always direct my understanding and challenge it, because they always diverge from our conceptual expectations into infinity. This is, as in the positive sciences, the safeguard against historicistic willfulness.

Only with respect to one of the studies contained in the volume does it seem to me that an essentially bibliographical note need be added, namely "Do Noachites Have to Believe in Revelation?..." It would seem that the fundamental question here at issue will never lead to complete consensus among Jews. The reason for this is that it is an ultimate question: does reason constitute *ultima ratio*, or does revealed faith go at least beyond, if not also against, reason? (It is clear that some form of universalism is implied if the first is believed and some sort of particularism if the latter is believed.) So, not only will people continue to debate this issue, but also their fundamental postures will be revealed in the process. (One would hope that their postures will be reasoned postures, and this itself manifests the aporia of the second of these views.) David Novak has published a full and thorough volume on precisely this subject: *The Image of the Non-Jew in Judaism ...* (Toronto Studies in Theology, vol. 14), N.Y./Toronto: Edwin Mellen Press, 1983). Except for the correction of my study that I have stipulated above, where Novak and I disagree, slightly, I have to persist in my original view. Novak, I think, takes his texts and the tradition too "nakedly," "brutally," unphilosophically. (Also cf. Nahum Rakover, *Hamishpat ke'erekh universalee—deeneem biv'nay no'ach* ["Law as an Universal Value—Laws for the Noachites"], Series of Studies and Analyses of Jewish Law [Hebr.], no. 58, Jerusalem: Justice Department, 1987, as a source book.)

In this connection I also might draw the readers' attention to H.P. Salomon's querrulous "Baruch Spinoza, Ishak Orobio de Castro and Haham Mosseh

Rephael D'Aguilar on the Noachites: A Chapter in the History of Thought," *Arquivos do Centro Cultural Portugues* XIV, Paris 1979, pp. 253-286. Some of the material in it is not without interest. Leaving aside nitpickings, the paradoxical upshot of Salomon's polemic is that d'Aguilar's contemporaneous document, which he publishes, come very much to the same effect as Hermann Cohen's much later argument against Spinoza, and even as far as the actual text under discussion is concerned—Salomon eventually concedes my main point.

I suspect that Salomon's article was influenced by the basic outlook, fairly so or no, of the important book by my very good friend José Faur's *Studies in the Mishne Torah—Book of Knowledge* (Hebr.), Jerusalem: Mossad HaRav Kook, 1978. He rejects my moderately rationalistic interpretation of both Maimonides and of the institution of Noachite law in the original study; (ib., p. 150) how much more would he disagree with the radicalization of this rationalism in "Moral Radicalism . . ."! My reply to Faur is, however, also to be found precisely in the analyses of this latter study.

There are two particularly interesting dimensions to Faur's general outlook. One is that he uses his "post-structuralist" hermeneutics in order to advance democratic, antiauthoritarian, intellectual freedom in, among others, Jewish culture: since all texts are endlessly open-ended, especially, indeed, peculiarly, in the quintessentially Jewish literature of midrash, all responsible interpretations must be given their head. (This is the clearly sincere ethos underlying contemporary French deconstructionism, *pace* Jean Francois Lyotard, and it comprises a consciously Jewish post-World War II attitude.) (That this position of Faur's leads to anything but Halakhic anarchism is not at all so paradoxical as it might seem on the surface: he continues the historical Jewish insistence on absolute freedom of belief and speech [cf., e.g., his *Golden Doves with Silver Dots—Semiotics and Textuality in Rabbinic Tradition,* pp. 62, 66f.], while obedience in action to instituted law is maintained.) This is, of course, a welcome approach to matters. My own differs from it only—but significantly— in that I, like Kant and Kantians generally, argue that the best, indeed, the only, firm foundation for such total democracy of thought is the commitment to the infinite search for the one truth—always in search and thus open-minded, but also dedicated to the one truth and thus reining in anarchism by the bonds of (equally democratic) reason. The famous Enlightenment maxim of Lessing's, which H. Cohen liked to cite, still possesses ultimate power: if God stretches out his right hand to me, holding the truth, and his left, holding the search for the truth, I'll grasp the left. (But it *is* the truth of God/reason—reason as an infinite, regulative ideal.)

The second interesting dimension of Faur's basic view is that he seems to believe that the Sephardic world-outlook differs essentially from the Ashkenazic in that it is non-rational. Although one hates to disagree with so expert a scholar of Sephardic history as he is, I think on this score Faur is simply mistaken—and the facts of history seem to me to prove this—all the way from before R. Saadia Ga'on to beyond his and my common hero Rabbi Elie Benamozegh. (In the latter case, once again, a different vocabulary for the primacy of practical reason. [Comp. my "An Introduction to the Thought of R. Isaac Hutner."])

I guess I ought to finish with something that can look like a grand conclusion. It won't be very grand.

I end the encyclopaedia article on "Modern Jewish Philosophy" with the open question whether under present-day conditions the Jewish people and Judaism can survive healthily. Frankly, I am very pessimistic on both counts. I do try to keep in mind Simon Rawidowicz's warning of mistaking the fact that we are "the ever-dying people:" "A nation dying for thousands of years means a living nation." (*Studies in Jewish Thought,* "Israel—the Ever-dying People," Philadelphia: Jewish Publication Society, 1974, p. 223). Still, who knows? If my pessimism should turn out to be justified (and I pray I may be wrong), even then I want to believe that what I try to do and to say is "for the sake of heaven." I.e., if things go further seriously wrong for the Jewish people and Judaism there will have to be, there ought be, some basis for the reconstruction, for the retrieval, of the Torah, which is, indeed, the only "tree of life" on which the Jewish people can live and grow. I should like to have made some small contribution to this—desperate—option.

Notes

Introduction

1. "Remembering Erich Fromm," *Jewish Spectator*, Fall 1980, pp. 29-33 (p. 29).

2. First published in *Judaism* 5 (1956), pp. 123-35. See below, pp. 15-28.

3. *Franz Rosenzweig (1886-1929)–Guide to Reversioners* (London, 1960); "Franz Rosenzweig and Existentialism," *CCAR Yearbook* 62 (1952), pp. 410-29; "F. Rosenzweig on Judaism and Christianity," *Conservative Judaism*, Winter 1956, pp. 41-48; "Samson Raphael Hirsch–The Man and his Thought," *Conservative Judaism*, Winter 1959, pp. 26-45; "The Democratic Socialism of Hermann Cohen,": *HUCA* 27 (1956), pp. 417-38; "Hermann Cohen Today," *Sh'ma* II/31 (April 21, 1972), pp. 84-87; "The Tenability of H. Cohen's Construction of the Self," *Journal of the History of Philosophy* 13 (1975), pp. 361-84; and many others.

4. See, for one example, "The *Commentary-Monat* Axis," *Menorah Journal* 41 (1953), pp. 87-105.

5. See the essay cited in note 2 above.

6. See "The Democratic Socialism . . ." (above, note 3), p. 421.

7. "Torah for Our Time," I. Eisenstein (ed.), *Varieties of Jewish Belief* (New York, 1966), pp. 243-57, p. 246.

8. "The Lure of Immanence–The Crisis in Contemporary Religious Thought," below, p. 67.

9. "Do Noachites Have to Believe in Revelation?" below, p. 49ff.

10. See, for example, the notes in "Moral Radicalism and Middlingness in the Ethics of Maimonides," below, pp. 309ff.

11. See p. 139 of the essay cited in the previous note.

12. See p. 149 of the essay cited in note 10.

13. "A Critique of M. Buber's Political Philosophy–An Affectionate Reappraisal," below, p. 188.

14. "Samson Raphael Hirsch . . ." (above, note 3), p. 32.

15. Ibid., p. 44.

16. "To Recast Rationalism," *Judaism* 11 (1962), pp. 205-09, p. 209.

17. Ibid.

18. "The Lure of Immanence . . ." below, p. 63.

19. "An Agenda for Jewish Philosophy in the 1980's," *Studies in Jewish Philosophy* I (1981), pp. 55-71, p. 61.

20. "The Lure of Immanence . . ." below, p. 64.

21. Ibid., p. 75.

22. "An Introduction to the Thought of R. Isaac Hutner," *Modern Judaism*, Fall 1985, pp. 237-77, p. 260.

23. "Marrano Professors of Jewish Studies," *Association for Jewish Studies Newsletter*, II/2 (April 1971), p. 6.

24. "An Agenda for Jewish Philosophy . . ." (above, note 19), p. 62.

25. "J.-P. Sartre as Jew," below, p. 181.

26. "Wittgenstein as Alienated Jew," *Telos*, Summer 1979, pp. 160-65.

27. "An Agenda for Jewish Philosophy . . ." (above, note 19), p. 57.

28. "Authority and Revelation," *Studies in Jewish Philosophy* 2 (1982), pp. 45-63, p. 47.

29. "Karl Marx's Jewish Theory of Usury," *Gesher* 1978, pp. 7-40.

30. "The Legal Foundations of Jewish Aesthetics," below, p. 109.

31. See Schwarzschild's comments on Sartre in the essay cited above in note 25, p. 183.

32. "A Note on the Nature of Ideal Society—A Rabbinic Study," below, p. 293.

33. See, for example, "The Lure of Immanence," below, p. 74.

34. "A Philosophy of Mitzvot," (review), *Journal of Biblical Literature* 95 (1976), pp. 519-20.

35. See the essays on aesthetics and Marx cited above in notes 29 and 30 and "The Question of Jewish Ethics Today," below, pp. 117-135. It is worthy of note that Schwarzschild has done more *Halakhic*-based philosophy than any self-proclaimed spokesman of Jewish Orthodoxy other than Rabbi Joseph Soloveitchik.

36. "A Jewish Perspective on International Relations," A. J. Wolf, *Rediscovering Judaism* (Chicago, 1965), pp. 245-85, pp. 258-9.

37. See note 7 above.

38. "A Little Bit of Revolution?" D. Callahan (ed.), *The Secular City Debate* (New York, 1966), pp. 145-55, p. 146.

39. See "Democratic Socialism . . ." (above, note 3), p. 421.

40. "The Lure of Immanence . . ." below, p. 70. For further criticisms of Marxism, see "A Jewish Perspective on International Relations . . ." (above, note 36); "The Messianic Doctrine in Contemporary Jewish History," *Great Jewish Ideas* (Washington, 1964), pp. 237-59; "The New Left Meets the Real Thing," *Dissent*, January-February 1968; and "On Jewish Eschatology," below, pp. 226-228.

41. "Authority and Revelation," (above, note 28), p. 47.

42. "Democratic Socialism . . ." (above, note 3), p. 424.

43. Ibid., p. 422; emphasis added.

44. *Franz Rosenzweig* (above, note 3), p. 5.

45. See the dedication of "Democratic Socialism . . ." (above, note 3).

46. See Schwarzschild's contribution to "The Sixth Annual American-Israel Dialogue," *Congress Bi-Weekly* (February 24, 1969), p. 83.

47. See Schwarzschild's studies of Rav Hutner in *Tradition* 14 (1974), pp. 90-109 ("Two Lectures of Rabbi Isaac Hutner"), in *Modern Judaism* (cited above in note 22), and in the *Encyclopedia of Religion* (New York, 1986), Vol. 6, p. 544.

48. See the article on Sartre below, p. 183.

49. "Lure of Immanence . . ." below, p. 76.

50. "Messianic Doctrine . . ." (above, note 40), p. 244.

51. Ibid., p. 250.

52. "The Necessity of the Lone Man," *Fellowship*, May 1965, p. 16.

53. "The Role and Limits of Reason in Contemporary Jewish Theology," *Central Conference of American Rabbis Yearbook* 73 (1963), pp. 199-214, p. 214.

54. "Lure of Immanence . . ." below, p. 75.

55. See, for example, "Torah for Our Time" (above, note 7), pp. 250-1 and "Do Noachites Have to Believe in Revelation" below, p. 46.

56. See note 52 above.

57. On this subject generally see the present writer's "Messianic Postures in Israel Today," *Modern Judaism* 6 (1986), pp. 197-209.

58. Note how in the passage just cited Schwarzschild identifies *mitzvot* with just and decent actions. Compare note 53 above.

59. "Messianic Doctrine . . ." (above, note 40), p. 256.

60. "Personal Messiah . . ." below, p. 26.

61. Ibid.

62. "On Jewish Eschatology," below, pp. 209-228.

63. "Messianic Doctrine . . ." (above, note 40), p. 240.

64. Ibid., p. 241.

65. *Franz Rosenzweig* (above, note 3), p. 14.

66. "The Unnatural Jew," *Environmental Ethics* 6 (1984), pp. 347-62, p. 347.

67. See the article cited in the previous note.

68. "On the Theology of Jewish Survival," below, p. 96.

69. Ibid., p. 98.

70. "The Religious Demand for Peace," *Judaism* 15 (1966), pp. 1-6, p. 1.

71. "The Role and Limits of Reason in Contemporary Jewish Theology," (above, note 53), p. 200. Compare "On Power in Judaism," *Worldview*, February 1964, pp. 6-10.

Chapter 1

1. The only theologian who seems to have concerned himself with the problem, and he with his customary perspicacity and ardor, is the much neglected Max Wiener, *Der Messiasgedanke in der Tradition und seine Umbiegung im modernen Liberalismus*, in *Festgabe für Claude G. Montefiore*, pp. 151-156.

2. *The Reform Movement in Judaism*, pp. 5, 122, 173-180.

3. *Jewish Theology*, pp. 388f.

4. The identification of the personal Messiah with nationalism was based on the traditional identity of the Messiah as a descendant of David the King. Thus, the Jewish monarchy was believed to be involved and with it all the features of a reconstituted state.

5. Cf. J. Klausner, *The Messianic Concept in Israel*, Jerusalem, 5710, p. 138f.

6. *op. cit.,* p. 165.

7. *Mishneh Torah,* Laws of Kings, 12.1.

8. *Hermann Cohen,* Berlin, 1921, p. 11.

9. Cf. *Rosenzweig,* Glatzer, p. 358: "According to the words of a philosopher whom I regard as an authority even greater than Hermann Cohen, what is not to come save in eternity will not come in all eternity."

10. *Die Philosophie des Judentums,* p. 351.

11. Cf. Cohen, *Religion der Vernunft,* pp. 276-313. I have discussed this point somewhat more lengthily in "The Democratic Socialism of Hermann Cohen," *Hebrew Union College Annual,* vol. XXVII, "Conclusion."

12. Cf. Thirteen Principles, last no.; *Mishneh Torah,* Laws of Repentance, 3:6.

13. *Die Religionsphilosophie Josef Albo's,* pp. 34-37.

14. *Ikarim,* I, 4.

15. Cf. *History,* vol. 10, pp. 190f., 312f., 387f. The Zohar, the source of much late Jewish Messianism he never refers to other than as "the book of lies."

16. Quoted in *Israel-Volk und Land,* p. 31.

17. Glatzer, *Rosenzweig—His Life and Thought, p. 350f.; cf. Rosenzweig, Jehudah HaLevy,* p. 239.

18. Greenstone, *The Messiah Idea in Jewish History,* p. 264f.

19. *The Essence of Judaism,* 4th ed., p. 273f.

20. *Ib.,* p. 178.

21. *Ib.*

22. *Ib.*

23. *Ib.,* p. 356.

24. *Juedische Religion in Zeitalter der Emancipation,* p. 172f.; *Der Messiasgedanke, op. cit.,* p. 153.

25. Glatzer, *loc. cit.; Jehudah HaLevy, loc. cit.*

26. Cf. Greenstone, *op. cit.,* pp. 57-60. Elbogen, *Judaica, Cohen Festschrift,* p. 671 indicates that resurrection precedes the advent of the Messiah.

27. Grace after the meal.

28. Phillipsohn, *op. cit.,* p. 263.

29. *Op. cit.*, pp. 269f.

30. *Biblical Religion and the Search for Ultimate Reality*, p. 39.

31. *Der Messiasgedanke, op. cit.*, p. 154f.

32. *Sanh.* 97b.

33. *Midr. Tehillim* 45:3; cf. generally, A.H. Silver, *Messianic Speculation in Israel*, "Opposition to Messianic Speculation," pp. 195-206.

34. Cf. Wiener, *op. cit.*, p. 170.

35. Cf. Greenstone, *op. cit.*, p. 267.

36. *Die Messiaslehre der Juden,*, pp. 402, 404.

37. *Yedi'ot Chadashot*, 10/3/50.

Chapter 2

1. *Tosefta Sanh.*, ch. 13:2; *b. Sanh.* 105a.

2. Cf. *Abodah Zarah* 26b. I am indebted to Prof. Samuel Atlas and the late Prof. Isaiah Sonne, Hebrew Union College-Jewish Institute of Religion, and Prof. Nahum Glatzer, Brandeis University, for counsel on various talmudic points, but I am, of course, alone responsible for my usage of the material. Cf. also *R.H.* 17a and *Vikúach R. Yechiel miParis*, Thorn 1873, p. 12 (quoted in Jacob Katz, *Exclusiveness and Tolerance ...*, Scripta Judaica III, Oxford 1961, p. 113): "Gehenna will be consumed, but apostates will not be consumed, for they altered the Covenant, as they were of the Jewish faith first, and bore it many days and then cast away the yoke. But the gentiles, who did not accept the Covenant, do not deserve Gehenna to the same extent, if you keep the seven commandments of the Noachides, which were commanded to you, you will be saved."

3. *Dictionary of the Talmud*, vol. 2, p. 776, *viz. meen.* Prof. A. Altmann, Brandeis University holds that this is a purely apologetic and false interpretation. The Lewy dictionary translates the term literally without clarifying its meaning.

4. *Ad locum.*

5. *Ad locum.*

6. *ib.*, ch. 9:1.

7. Cf. *Meg.* 16a: "Whoever states a wise thing even if he is a gentile, is called a sage." *Dtto. Lekach Tov ad* Ex. 7:11.

8. Pp. 181, 192. *Cf. Ziyonei Moharan ad locum; dtto. Ben Aryeh; dtto.* (I am also indebted to the late Prof. Sonne for these references.) *Dtto.* R. Zevi Hirsch Chayes *ad locum.*

9. *A Theologico-Political Tractate,* trans R.H.M. Elwes, vol. 1, N.Y. 1951, p. 80.

10. *Ad locum.*

11. Letter to Lavater, Moses Mendelssohn, *Gesammelte Schriften, Jubilaeumsausgabe,* vol. VII, p. 11, note c.

12. *"Spinoza ueber Staat und Religion, Judentum und Christentum,"* in *Juedische Schriften,* vol. 3, p. 348.

13. Cf. however Ribash, no. 44, and Rosh, Responsa, no. 31: "He who studies Rambam and does not know from where in the Talmud he derived a statement errs if he permits or forbids something contrary to the Rambam, thinking that he knows better." Ralbach 12, etc.: "We may not reject the Rambam's words in any place, even though his words seem untenable to us in view of the *Gemara* as we know it. Rather must we attribute our incomprehension to the limitations of our own mind and understanding." Etc. (S. Glazer, *Book of Mishnah Torah,* vol. 1, N.Y. 1927: "Principles of Rambam.")

14. *Midrash haSohar, Die Religionsphilosophie des Sohar,* Leipzig 1849,—3rd ed. Berlin 1923, p. 9f.

15. The same reference is to be found in *Ziyonei Moharan, loc. cit.,* and in *Ben Aryeh loc. cit.*

16. It may be mentioned that *Toldot Adam* also has the correct reading "but from their sages" rather than "nor of their sages."

17. For the following I am again largely indebted to the late Prof. Sonne.

18. The first edition leaves out the name of the rabbi who states the Midrash.

19. Cf. pp. 11b, 16a.

20. Ed. H.G. Enelow, N.Y. 1933. Comp. C. M. Horowitz, ed., *Pirkay de R. Eliezer,* Brill, 1972.

21. Katz, op. cit., p. 175, n. 5 accepts this as a geniune source.

22. *Ib.,* p. 60; *Hadoar,* no. 39, Heshvan 3, 5722, pp. 738-740.

23. Personal communication to me.

24. *Op. cit.,* p. 18.

25. *Op. cit.,* vol. 16, Berlin 1929, ed. Haim Borodianski, pp. 178f., no. 154, dated Berlin, Oct. 26, 1773.

26. This is a reference to *Kesef Mishneh.*

27. *Ib.,* no. 155, pp. 179-183, dated Altona, November 1773. On Emden cf. M.J. Cohen, *Jacob Emden—A Man of Controversy,* Philadelphia 1937.

28. Cf. *Sanh.* 105a. Compare also *Sanhed.* 107b-110b; *Aboth deR. Nathan,* ch. 36, first part; *Tosefta Sanh.* ch. 13:1-2. But Emden did acknowledge the legitimacy of Christian revelation: cf. Katz, op. cit., p. 167.

29. It might be added that R. Jacob picks one of two views to be found in *Abodah Zarah* 65a quite arbitrarily.

30. Cf. *Midr. Prov.* XIV, 34f., 38b. Unless carefully read Maimonides' letter to R. Hasdai (cf. p. 42) might seem to support R. Jacob's justification in terms of "the heart's intention."

31. *Loc. cit.,* p. 348.

32. *Persecution and the Art of Writing,* Glencoe, Ill., 1952, p. 73.

33. *Loc. cit.,* p. 349; *Religion der Vernunft,* p.386.

34. Benamozegh, *Israel et L'Humanité* (Paris, 1914) p. 618 would seem to support him on this point; also the discussion on p. 596. Also Michael Guttmann, *Das Judentum und Seine Umwelt,* Berlin 1927, pp. 52, 59, 110.

35. How the term "Noachite" differs from the term "resident-convert" Maimonides himself defines and in such a manner as to invalidate this argument of Cohen's: "Who is a resident-convert? A gentile who has taken upon himself not to engage in idolatry together with the other commandments which are obligatory for Noachites even though he is neither circumcized nor baptized; behold, him we accept, and he is one of the righteous of the nations of the world." ("Laws of Forbidden Marriages," ch. 14:7; Cf. also *Abodah Zara* 64b) In other words, a resident-convert is a Noachite who fulfills the obligations of a Noachite.—This passage in *Hilchot Issure Bi'ah* goes on to make the famous and controversial statement that "resident converts are accepted only in the time when the law of the Jubilee year is practiced," not now—which is to say, only in messianic times. (Cf. *Arakin* 29) The Rabad, of course, disputes this view and would restrict the acceptability of resident-converts at the present only to the extent that certain privileges which would devolve upon them in messianic times they could not now enjoy. (*Ad locum*; cf. my "A Rabbinic Note on Ideal Society," this volume, chapter 5.) If Maimonides' original statement were to be left as it first seems to present itself, the clear implication would be that only in Messianic times can there be practicing Noachites, and that then the belief in Revelation would also be prerequisite would presumably be not so much a demand as a self-evident assumption. On the other hand, it is hard to believe that Maimonides could have held that until Messianic times no gentile could be "righteous." Perhaps the solution of this problem lies in Maimonides' exact wording. Ch. 14:7 declares: "Why is a resident-convert called 'resident'? Because we may settle him among ourselves in the Land of Israel." 14:8 then immediately goes on: "We do not accept a resident-convert other than in Messianic times." It is possible, now, that the acceptance mentioned does not refer to the acceptance of resident-converts as such but rather more limitedly to the acceptance of his full residence-rights in

Palestine which is discussed immediately previous to this sentence. (This is also true because conversion in Messianic times must be suspected of ulterior, materialistic motives and would, therefore, violate 13:14). This would then coincide with what Rabad calls the "strict" of the two—according to him—possible explanations. And this also sounds logical, because the practice of the Jubilee year implies residence in Palestine and economic prosperity, whereas in the conditions of exilic distress and poverty residence in Palestine is impossible by definition, and economic help is difficult. This solution would further seem to be supported by the fact that the legislation concerning Noachites is placed by Maimonides in the "Laws of the Kings" immediately prior to, and, therefore, presumably connected with, the last two chapters (11 and 12) which deal with the definition of the Messianic Kingdom. In the very last law of ch. 10 concerned with Noachites, a few words before the discussion of the Messiah begins, Maimonides reiterates: "for behold, we are commanded to support the resident-converts." This, then—not the acceptance of resident-converts as such—is the Messianic aspect of Noachitism.

36. *Loc cit.*, p. 345.

37. *Religion der Vernunft*, p. 141.

38. Cf. the famous essay *"Ueber Staat und Religion, Judentum und Christentum,"* and many other places throughout Cohen's writings; Ernst Simon, *"Zu H. Cohens Spinoza-Auffassung,"* MGWdJ, vol. 79, 2, Breslau 1935, pp. 181-194; Schwarzschild, "The Democratic Socialism of H. Cohen," HUCA, vol. XXVII, pp. 421 f.

39. *Loc. cit.*

40. *Iggrot haRambam*, Leipzig 1859, vol. II, pp. 23f. Prof. Altmann kindly brought this passage to my attention. Guttmann, *op. cit.*, p. 157 also mentions it, and Mendelssohn refers to it. (cf. note 11) Maimonides, in this letter, refers to the *Guide*; it must, therefore, have been written later.

41. Cf. *Sanhed.* 106b; *Ber.* 15af. Cf. also Bernhard Heller, *"'Gott wuenscht das Herz:' Legenden ueber Einfaeltige Andacht und ueber den Gefaehrten im Paradies,"* HUCA IV, 1927, pp. 365-404.

42. Comp. the Christian doctrine of the descent into hell to save these very personages: *"descendit ad inferos."* *"La déscente de Jésus aux enfers" (Dictionnaire de Théologie Catholique*, vol. 4, p. 600): "telle est donc l'explication exacte de l'oeuvre du Christ aux enfers: c'est la libération des justes ou des saints, des Juifs principalement et même des gentils qui accomplirent durant leur vie les préceptes de la loi de la nature ou de leur loi positive et obtinrent ainsi la grâce."

43. Ed. Israel Efros, N.Y. 1938, ch. 8, pp. 39f—Hebrew part.

44. *Nichomachean Ethics*, I, 1094b, 14-23.

45. Ch. 9:1.

46. It should perhaps be added that Hermann Cohen, who was understandably so put out by the original restriction of the definition of a Noachite, rationalist that he is, does not like this Maimonidean view of the inadequate rationality of ethics any better and exerts himself to comment that this view of Maimonides implies no derogation of the autonomy of morality but a high estimate of the rigorousness of reason. (*"Charakteristik der Ethik Maimunis,"* pp. 81-88, *Moses ben Maimon, Sein Leben, Sein Werk, Und Sein Einfluss,* eds. W. Bacher etc., Leipzig 1908).

47. *Loc cit.,* p. 350.

48. Cf. the introduction by Aimé Pallière.

49. Cf. p. 22f.

50. *Ib.,* p. 483. At first glance it might appear that the established doctrine that "he who is commanded to do and does is better than he who is not commanded to do and does" (*Tosefta, Abodah Zarah* 8:4-8, *H. Talmud Torah* 1:13) might here explain Maimonides' position, but this is not the case, for the Noachites are, after all, commanded the seven Noachite commandments. (Cf. Isaac Heineman, *Ta'ame HaMitzvot BeSafrut Yisrael,* Jerusalem 1949, vol. 1, p. 25 and notes).

51. *Theologico-Political Tractate,* p. 80.

52. *Loc. cit.*

53. *Spinozas Theologisch-Politisches Traktat—auf seine Quellen geprueft,* Breslau 1870, p. 56.

54. Cf. *loc. cit.,* p. 347.

55. *Op. cit.,* p. 198.

56. *Op. cit.,* p. 15.

57. Cf. especially *Tractate,* pp. 115ff.: "The falsity of such a doctrine is shown ... for we have shown both by reason and by example that the meaning of Scripture is only made plain through Scripture itself... Therefore, the method of Maimonides is clearly useless ... In conclusion, then, we dismiss Maimonides' theory as harmful, useless, and absurd."

58. *Op cit.,* p. 55.

59. *Ib.,* p. 72.

60. *Ib.,* p. 229.

61. *Ib.,* pp. 230 f.

62. *Ib.,* p. 232.

63. *Ib.,* p. 233.

64. "Laws of the Kings," ch. 9:1.

65. Cf. *Sanhed.* 59b.

66. Leo Strauss, *Natural Right and History,* Chicago 1953, p. 158.

67. *Summa,* I. qu. 102, a. 3 *ad* 12.

68. Cf. Van Rooijn, Servaas, *Inventaire des Livres formant la Bibliothèque de B. Spinoza,* Hague 1883, pp. 147, 183.

69. Cf. P. Ottenwaelder, *Zur Naturrechtslehre des Hugo Grotius,* Tuebingen 1950, p. 119, cf. also I. Husik, "The Law of Nature, Hugo Grotius, and the Bible," HUCA II, p. 400: Grotius speaks of Noachite law; p. 406f.: Grotius quotes our passage from Maimonides on Naochite law. Paul really taught the opposite, that the positive (divine) law applied to Jews, natural law to the gentiles: *Romans* 2:12-24.

70. P. 200.

71. Cf. M.E. Schmitt, *Recht und Vernunft, Ein Beitrag zur Diskussion ueber die Rationalitaet des Naturrechts,* Heidelberg 1955, p. 8.

72. *The Rights of Man and Natural Law,* N.Y. 1943, p. 60.

73. Cf. Schmitt, *op. cit.,* pp. 105ff.

74. *Natural Rights,* London 1895, p. 20.

75. *The Holmes Reader,*ed. Julius J. Marke, N.Y. 1955, "Natural Law" (32 Harvard Law Review, 40-48, Nov 1918, p. 119).

76. Cf. Schwarzschild, "The Democratic Socialism of H. Cohen," *op. cit.,* pp. 421f. N. Isaacs, "The Influence of Judaism on Western Law," *The Legacy of Israel,* eds. Bevan and Singer, Oxford 1944, p. 386: "But natural law is not made by erudition. Even Selden brought back from the Hebrews a mere confirmation of the law of his own country." (Cf. also ib., pp. 383-387)

77. *Op. cit.,* p. 244; *Political Tractate,* p. 356.

78. *Theologico-Political Tractate,* p. 242; *Political Tractate,* pp. 317f.

79. *E.g., Theologico-Political Tractate,* p. 243.

80. *Die Religionskritik Spinozas,* Berlin 1930, p. 221.

81. Strauss, *Natural Right and History, op. cit.,* pp. 192ff.

82. *The Jurisprudence of Holland,* transl. R.W. Lee, Oxford 1926, I, p. 81.

83. Lewis S. Feuer, *Spinoza and the Rise of Liberalism,* Boston 1958, p. 269, n. 14.

84. Erich Cassirer, *Natur- und Voelkerrecht im Licht der Geshichte und der systematischen Philosophie,* Berlin 1919, p. 275.

85. *Ib.*, p. 287.

86. *Ethik des Reinen Willens,* Berlin 1904, p. 94; cf. also p. 247.

87. *Ib.*, p. 240; cf. also p. 421.

88. *Ib.*, pp. 91f.

89. *Die Philosophischen Grundlagen der Naturrechtslehre und des Rechtspositivismus,* Berlin 1928, p. 62. Cf. also I. Husik, "The legal Philosophy of Hans Kelsen," *Philosophical Essays,* Oxford 1952, esp. pp. 315f., 321.

90. *Ib.*, p. 16.

91. Schmitt, *op. cit.*, pp. 32f.

92. Kelsen, *op. cit.*, pp. 33f, 38, 40.

93. *Ib.*, p. 40.

94. Walter Eckstein, "Rousseau and Spinoza," *Journal of the History of Ideas,* V, 3, pp. 281ff.

95. *Ib.*, p. 288.

96. *Op. cit.*, p. 63.

97. *Op. cit.*, p. 4.

98. *Ib.*, p. 93.

99. *Ib.*, pp. 12f.

100. *Op. cit.*, p. 248.

101. *Rousseau, Kant, Goethe,* Princeton 1945, p. 34: *"Je cherche le droit et la raison et ne dispute pas des faits."*

102. *Op. cit.*, p. 67; cf. also Schmitt, *op. cit.*, pp. 103f.

103. Cf. *Guide for the Perplexed,* II, chapters 15-18, 22-25.

104. "Laws of the Kings," ch. 9:1.

105. Compare *Guide,* II, 40: "Though the Torah is not natural, nonetheless it has a natural access."

106. Strauss, *Natural Right and History, op. cit.*, pp. 203-205.

Chapter 3

1. If this be "theological dialogue," then, at any rate, it transpires on a respectable level and has been advocated by at least some thinkers among Jews and Christians.

Thus Paul Tillich has described Jewish transcendentalism as a necessary critique of Christian sacramentalism (*Cross-Currents*, II, 3, p. 41; see also his *Christianity and the Encounter of the World Religions*, p. 87)—and precisely this will largely be our chief point. William Hamilton, one of the major spokesmen of "The atheist theology," has actually extended a specific invitation for such a discussion between Jews and Christians: (I am here omitting some peculiar Christological accompanying features, to avoid distraction) "I would hope it might be possible to set down some theological rules for a Christian, or at least a Protestant, dialogue with the Jew.... A formal kinship exists that could lead to some levels of theological dialogue not made possible by other forms of Protestant theology." ("Radicalism and the Death of God," *Christianity and Crisis*, Dec. 13, 1965.) From the Jewish side, on the other hand, it was significantly Franz Rosenzweig who called upon Jews to provide Christianity with the theological corrections which, for its own sake, it requires. (No one, not even Maimonides, has denied that, though Christianity may be one of the path-breakers of the Messiah [see *Mishneh Torah*, "The Laws of Kings," 11:4 in the uncensored version]. Jews are religiously obligated to induce all men to abide punctiliously by the Noachide commandments [Cf. ib., 8:10].) That it is just Rosenzweig who has issued this challenge is interesting for at least two reasons: 1) His doctrine of "the two covenants" has often been oversimplified (see my *F. Rosenzweig—Guide to Reversioners*, London 1960, pp. 31-36, and "Rosenzweig on Judaism and Christianity," *Conservative Judaism*, Winter 1956); and 2) he is now also becoming an influential theological force in American Orthodox Judaism—see Charles Liebman, "Orthodoxy in American Jewish Life," *American Jewish Year Book*, 1965, p. 46 and *passim*. The crucial relevant passage in Rosenzweig is *Stern der Erloesung*, Frankfurt a/M 1921, pp. 517-520. Much of that passage is not only generally relevant to this subject but specifically adumbrates points which we shall have to bring up.

2. See the so-called Chalcedonian formulation: "... God truly and man truly ... of one substance with the Father in his deity, and of one substance with us in his humanity ... acknowledged in two natures, without confusion, without change ... the distinction of the natures being by no means taken away because of the union, but rather the property of each nature being preserved, and concurring in one person ..." *A History of Christian Thought*, A. C. McGiffert, N. Y. '46, vol. I, p. 285. See the entire chapter XV. In the further elaboration of this Chalcedonian formula dyothelitism was developed, p. 288. (In a fuzzy way P. Lehmann recognizes the connection between Chalcedon and "the secular gospel": "Chalcedon in Technopolis," *Christianity and Crisis*, XXV/12, July 12, 1965.)

2a. For the use of the notion of "model" in current philosophy, cf. R. S. Runder, *Philosophy of Social Science* (Prentice-Hall *Foundations of Philosophy Series)*, 1966, pp. 23-28; and P. Achinstein, "Models, Analogies, and Theories," *Philosophy of Science*, 31/4, Oct. 1964, pp. 328-350.

3. At this point Friedlander, in his annotated translation, claims that a passage has been inserted into the wrong place of the text. But he misunderstands the course

of the argument. (Pines, therefore, makes no such claim.) What Maimonides is saying is that, though the "attributists" are wrong in ascribing even the will to God, they are right in deriving all His many "actions" from one, will-like, source.

4. In this connection it is most instructive to compare H. A. Wolfson's *The Philosophy of the Church Fathers*, esp. pp. 223-232, " 'Eternal Generation,' 'by Will' and 'by Nature,' " and ch. XVI/III, "Orthodox Use of the Analogies of Physical Union." Philo the Jew still used the model of the will in explaining the emergence of the logos from God (p. 223), but increasingly the orthodox, Athanasian Christian faith was forced to use the model of nature, so that finally Cyril of Alexandria exclaimed: (p. 232) "It is monstrous and stupid to think that the Father is a Begetter involuntarily or voluntarily; nay He is so by nature and substantially."

5. Cf. *Summa Contra Gentiles*, I, 33, 96 ff., and *Summa Theologica*, I, 84, 4 where he argues explicitly against Maimonides; cf. also E. Gilson, *Le Thomisme*, Paris 1945, pp. 159, 171f.

6. Jacob Guttmann recognized this logic, if only very *sotte voce*, "Der Einfluss der maimonidischen Philosophie auf das christlische Abendland," *Moses ben Maimon, Sein Leben, Seine Werke und Sein Einfluss*, Leipzig '08, vol. I, p. 183, No. 1.

7. In a dilletantish study which is, however, full of valuable insights, S. M. Melamed could, therefore, subtitle his book *Spinoza and Buddha* "Visions of a Dead God," University of Chicago Press, 1933.

8. "In the beginning was Hegel"—E. Borne, *Atheism*, last chapter.

9. Kaufmann, *Hegel*, pp. 262, 381; R. Garaudy, *Dieu est mort*, p. 6.

10. *Hegel*, p. 162; Kaufmann, however, misrepresents the *Phenomenology*.

11. See H. de Lubac, S. J., *The Drama of Atheist Humanism*, p. 20.

12. There is literally nothing in the current "theology of blasphemy" which has not been stated, usually with much greater clarity and brilliance, in Feuerbach's *Essence of Christianity*. When Van Buren, for example, says: "Jesus is God; therefore God is man" (see below), Feuerbach said: "Not this humble writer but religion says: God is man, man is God." (*Wesen des Christentums*, 2nd ed., 1848, p. XI). And he goes on: (p. XV) "I elevate anthropology to theology, as Christianity, by lowering God to man, made man God." If this is an example of Feuerbach's declaration of the "Death of God" for the sake of immanentization (see L. J. Halle, "Marx's Religious Drama," *Encounter*, Oct. '65, p. 32, note: F. had to destroy the transcendence of Thou for the sake of the I), then the following is an example of doing the very same thing for the sake of the assertion of the moral autonomy of man: "To know God and not to be He, to know bliss and not oneself to enjoy it, this is alienation and a misfortune." (*ib.*, p. 26) (See Nietzsche's famous statement, "if there were a God, how could I bear not being He," and F. Rosenzweig's striking discussion of it, *Stern der Erloesung*, I, p. 27 f)—Marx takes up where Feuerbach

leaves off. What for the latter was a philosophical matter is for the former a programmatic one. Marx underlines Feuerbach's "this-worldliness" ("*Diesseitigkeit*") (see *Marx and Engels on Religion*, foreword by Reinhold Niebuhr, "Theses on Feuerbach," p. 70), and arrives at the same conclusion at which Spinoza's and Hegel's immanentism had to arrive: "Might and freedom are identical." ("The Holy Family," *op. cit.*, p. 65)—It is, perhaps, worth noting the Jewish origin of the three great "immanentists" in Western culture, Paul of Tarsus, Spinoza, and Marx. Like Christianity itself, immanentism would seem to be a specifically Jewish heresy.

13. See my "A Little Bit of a Revolution," *The Secular City Debate*, ed. D. Callahan, MacMillan, 1966.

14. *Op. cit.*, p. 54, etc.

15. *Radical Theology*, p. XII.

16. Cf. also *ib.*, p. 110F.

17. *The Will to Power*, 1, 1-2.

18. *Holzwege, "Nietzsches Wort . . . ,"* p. 199.

19. "The Contemporary Status of Atheism," *International Philosophical Quarterly* V, 1 p. 39.

20. In late 20th-century historiography of Jewish philosophy a certain amount of injustice tends to be done to these men, because they are accused—and largely, of course, with justification—of a) nourishing their thought more with contemporary German philosophy than with authentic Jewish knowledge and understanding, and b) tending to be Reform Jews. Julius Guttmann, on the other hand, in his *Philosophies of Judaism*, repeatedly makes the interesting point that, at least philosophically, though not *Halakhically*, the actual content of their thinking was at least as true to genuine Judaism as were the universally acknowleged classic philosophers of the Jewish Middle Ages, and furthermore the mediaevals were at least as much influenced by non-Jewish thinkers, Aristotle, Plotinus, Averroes, etc., as were the men of the 19th century by Kant and Hegel. (Leo Strauss argues against this, with only partial validity, that, though both groups may have arrived at similar philosophic conclusions, the mediaevals did so on the basis of accepting the reality of Revelation, whereas the moderns did so on the basis of autonomous reason—and that this makes all the difference in the world. Not completely—if, as, for example, Saadia and Maimonides surely did, the mediaevals in fact set up reason as the ultimate criterion of Revelation.) What we are about to point out about the moderns tends to support Guttmann's thesis. It might furthermore be pointed out about these men that, whatever their divergences from Jewish law, their posture against what they regarded as the distortions of Biblical faith at the hands of Christianity was extremely militant, at least as much as that of the mediaevals, and much more than that of most 20th century Jewish thinkers. The accusation of rampant assimilationism on their part must, therefore, be heavily qualified.

20a. Cf. J. Solowiejczyk, *Das Reine Denken und die Seinskonstituierung bei Hermann Cohen*, Berlin 1932.

21. "Bonhoeffer: Christology and Ethic United," *Christianity and Crisis*, Oct. 19, 1964.

22. Van Buren, *op. cit.*, pp. 40ff., 197.

There are a number of other significant motifs in this current literature equally welcome from a Jewish vantage point. In the first place, the content of F. F. Trotter's summary "Variations of the 'Death of God' Theme in Recent Literature," JBR XXXI, 1, Jan. 1965, pp. 42-48, can, in turn, be summarized as crystallizing the themes of antiidolatry or iconoclasm and ethicism (to be sure, immanentist). To these, three additional motifs can be added: 1. The abstract philosophical God is useless for religious purposes—see Altizer, "Nirvana and the Kingdom of God," *New Theology #1*, 1964—echoing R. Yehuda Ha-Levy's and Pascal's distinction between "the God of Aristotle and the God of Abraham, Isaac, and Jacob;" 2. That the absurdity and malevolence of the natural and historical world which we experience contradict the notion of the coherence and goodness of a world stipulated to have been created by God. As Landon Gilkey puts it: "Of course, existence is meaningless, and we must accept and live with our despair." 3. That the God of our culture has been the God of Western civilization—Western civilization is moribund or dead—therefore, so is its God. See Altizer who begins his previously cited essay with these words: "This paper rests upon two crucial assumptions: 1. The foundations of Western civilization—and of Christianity itself—are collapsing about us, and the root ideas and values of this civilization no longer have any validity or relevance to the authentic contemporary man. 2. Christianity as we know it historically has been integrally related to Western civilization, and therefore insofar as Christian theological categories are a product of Western civilization they have neither validity for nor relevance to the contemporary Christian." And surely the Jew, the paradigmatic victim of the malevolence of Western civilization and of the absurdity of an as yet unredeemed world, has utter sympathy with both considerations.

23. *Pesikta deRav Kahana*, ed. Mandelbaum, p. 254ff.

24. Hamilton, *op. cit.*, pp. 160-167.

25. *Tradition*, "The Lonely Man of Faith," Summer 1965, p. 21.

26. Hamilton, *op. cit.*, p. 45, n. 18.

27. Cox, *op. cit.*, p. 6

28. See Jonas' profound and implicitly very Jewish lead article in *The Journal of Metaphysics*, Dec. 1964; and compare Buber's essay on Heidegger in *The Eclipse of God*.

29. See Hermann Cohen, especially ch. 1 in *Ethics of the Pure Will*. Compare also R. Rudner, "The Scientist *Qua* Scientist Makes Value Judgments," *Philosophy of Science*, 20, 1 Jan. 1953, who holds that the scientific hypothesis involves value judg-

ments, "in the typically ethical sense," not only in its practical application but even in its logical status.

30. Van Buren, *op. cit.*, p. 53—his Christological language for whether an action is moral.

31. *Shabbat* 118; compare Ex. R. 25:12.

32. See André Néher, "The Humanism of the Maharal of Prague," *Judaism*, XIV, 3; *Les Puits de L'Exil—La Theologie Dialectique du Maharal de Prague.*

33. *Mussar HaKodesh*, III, p. 27; compare also *Igrot* I, pp. 143, 170, 348, 369. See S. Schechter, *Aspects of Rabbinic Theology*, p. 111: "To a certain Jewish mystic of the last century, R. Moses Loeb of Sasow, the question was put by one of his disciples to the effect, "Why did God, in whom everything originates, create the quality of scepticism?" The master's answer was, "That thou mayest not let the poor starve, putting them off with the joys of the next world, or simply telling them to trust in God, who will help them, instead of supplying them with food." We venture to maintain with the mystic that a good dose of materialism is necessary for religion that we may not starve the world. It was by this that Judaism was preserved from the mistake of crying inward peace, when actually there was no peace; of speaking of inward liberty, when in truth this spiritual but spurious liberty only served as a means for persuading man to renounce his liberty altogether, confining the kingdom of God to a particular institution and handing over the world to the devil." A little later Schechter then actually states our point of the Messianically preparatory function of ethical *Halakhah*: (p. 114) "If the disappearance of poverty and suffering is a condition of the kingdom of the Messiah, or, in other words, of the kingdom of God, all wise social legislation in this respect must help toward its speedy advent."

34. I am quoting from a recent publication, *Shomrey HaGachelet*, eds. T. Harkavy and A. Shauli, N. Y. and Jerusalem, 1966—an essay by one of its editors, Shauli, entitled "On Judaism and Dialectical Materialism," pp. 8-10. Cf. also, "Survey of Theological Literature," *Judaism*, Summer 1967.

35. See A. J. Heschel, *Man is not Alone*, ch. 16, esp. p. 153.

36. See F. Rosenzweig on the relation between divine and human speech, "F. Rosenzweig on Language," R. Horwitz, *Judaism*, XIII, 4, Fall 1964, pp. 393-406.

37. *Gittin* 55b. Compare my "Speech and Silence before God," *Judaism*, X, 3, Summer, 1961, and "Judaism, Scripture, and Ecumenism," in *Scripture and Ecumenism*, ed. L. Swidler, Pittsburgh 1965, p. 120.

38. Buber, *op. cit.*, p. 91—In this book, as well as in many other places in his writings, Buber convincingly demonstrates that it is precisely over the alternative doctrines of "the hiding of God" or "the theology of blasphemy" that Judaism and Christianity must necessarily part, because the doctrine of the incarnation proclaims precisely that in Jesus God came once and for all and completely out of "hiding."

Chapter 4

1. Cf. Emil Fackenheim on what he calls "the *mitzvah* of surviving," *Judaism*, XVI/3, Summer '67, p. 272—One might make a comparison with the famous wisecrack attributed to the Abbé Sieyès: when asked what he had done during the French Revolution, he is supposed to have said: "*J'ai vécu.*" Jewishly one might say that not to have lived but to have "lived above" and thus to have "sur-vived" is at issue.

2. Cf. *Siach Lochamim* ed. A. Shapira, Tel Aviv 5728; cp: M. Rosenak, "Moments of the Heart," *Judaism*, XVII/2, Spring '68, pp. 211-224.

3. "Judaism in the Post-Christian Era," *Judaism*, XV/1, Winter '66, p. 84: "No one can foretell what this new era holds in store for mankind. But we are here at the threshold of the new age. We who were there when the Christian era began; in whose martyrdom Christianity suffered its worst moral debacle; we in whose blood the Christian era found its end—we are here as this new era opens. And we shall be here when this new era reaches its close—we, the *edim*, God's own witnesses, the *am olam*, the eternal witness of history."

4. Cf. e.g., Deut. 26:17, *et. al.*

5. Lev. 26:23f.: "If you walk with Me cavalierly, then also I will walk with you cavalierly." Cf. Ex. 19:5f., Deut. 11:17, 28:24, Joshua 23:16, I Kings 9:7, Jer. 7, especially vv. 4f., 11, 15, 33f., Amos 9:7 and Rashi *ad locum*, Micah 3:11f., etc.

6. Goethe said that "no one is a hero to his butler." To which Hegel replied, "That is not because he is not a hero but because the butler is a butler." I.e., the personal idiosyncrasies, even the ethical failures of a man, cannot ultimately be believed to be history-shaping forces. Otherwise, instead of studying the laws of economics we would have to investigate how a corporation executive liked his eggs on any given morning. Cf. *Phaenomenologie des Geistes*, ed. Lasson, pp. 81, 93, et. al.

7. E.g. Ps. 105:7-10: "He is the Lord our God. His statutes are valid in all the earth. He remembers His covenant forever, the word of His commandment unto the thousandth generation, which He made with Abraham and His oath unto Isaac. He has established it as a statute for Jacob, an everlasting covenant for Israel." Cf. I Chron. 16:16; also Deut. 4:29ff., Is. 49:14-26, Jer. 31-34f.: "Thus says the Lord, Who sets the sun as light by day and the laws of the moon and stars as light by night, Who stirs up the sea so that its waves billow, Whose name is Lord of hosts: If these statutes vanish from before Me, says the Lord, then only will the seed of Israel cease being a people before Me forever." Cf. Gen. 17:7f., Ex. 13:16, Deut. 7:9, 33:27, Is. 54:9f., 59:21, Jer. 30:11, 33:25f., Hosea 2:21f., etc.

8. Thus one arrives at the immoralism—either the reaction of a Hegel or the mechanism of a Marxism.

9. Cf., e.g., Bialik and Ravnitzky (eds.), *Sefer ha-Aggadah, s.v. "Yisrael kayyamim l'olam,"* Cf. *Men.* 53b:11, 24-26. "R. Joshua b. Levi said: 'Israel will not experience complete extinction either in this world or in the text.'" Cf. also A. Marmorstein, *Studies in Jewish Theology*, Oxf. 1950, *"Ha-Emunah bi-Nezach Yisrael bi-Derashot ha-Tannaim viha-Amoraim,"* pp. 1-16.

10. In this passage as well as throughout Rabbinic literature, *Teshuvah* is usually mistranslated as "repentance," whereas in fact, of course, it means "moral conduct" in such instances.

11. For a good beginning of the kind of ethico-conceptual analysis to which this kind of literature ought to be subjected, see Emmanuel Lévinas, "Temps Messianiques et Temps Historiques dans le Chapitre XI du Traité 'Sanhedrin,'" *La Conscience Juive*, eds. E. A. Lévy-Valensi and J. Halperin, Paris 1963. For the theological dialectics of the Talmud, cf. also e.g. J. Petuchowski, "The Concept of 'Teshuvah' in the Bible and Talmud," *Judaism*, XVII/2, Spring '68, esp. p. 184f.

12. Cf. also *Deut.* R. 5:6.

13. Cf. Saadia Gaon, *Emunot ve'Deot* III/7: "Our nation is a nation only by virtue of its *torot*, and since the Creator has declared that the nation will persist as long as the heavens and the earth do, it follows necessarily that its *torot* will persist as long as the heavens and the earth. See Jer. 31: 34f..." Cf. *Kuzari*, II/34: "Do not believe that I, though agreeing with you, admit that we are dead. We still hold connection with that divine influence through the laws which He has placed as a link between us and Him. There is circumcision, of which it is said: 'My covenant shall be in your flesh for an everlasting covenant.' (Gen. 17:13) There is further the Sabbath: 'It is a sign between Me and you throughout your generations' (Ex. 31:13). Besides this there is the 'covenant of the Fathers,' and the covenant of the Law first granted on Horeb and then in the plains of Moab in connection with the promises and warnings laid down in the section 'When you will beget children and grandchildren' (Deut. 4:25). Compare further the antithesis 'If any of yours be driven out to the utmost parts of heaven' (*ib.*, 30:10)–'You shall return unto the Lord your God' (*ib.*, v. 2); finally the song, 'Give ear...' (*ib.*, 32:1), etc. We are not like dead but rather like a sick and weakened person who has been given up by the physicians and yet awaits a miracle or an extraordinary recovery, as it is said: 'Can these bones live?'" (Ezek. 37:3)–*Ib.*, III/10f.: "I have discovered that God has a secret purpose in keeping you in existence... If an evil thought makes a man despair, saying: 'Can these bones live?' (*ib.*)–our greatness having been negated and our history having been forgotten, as it is said: 'Our bones are dried up and our hope lost; we have been condemned' (*ib.*, v. 11)–let him think of the nature of the exodus from Egypt and all that is said in the section 'For how many beneficences unto us do we owe gratitude unto God!' (Passover *Haggadah*). Then he will have no difficulty in imagining how we will be restored to our estate even if all but one of us will disappear. For it is written: 'Fear not, oh worm Jacob (Is. 41:14), i.e., what remains of a man when he returns to be a worm in his grave!"–Cf. also Maimonides, *Epistle to*

Yemen, ed. A. S. Halkin, N. Y. 1952, p. 25: "God has long ago given us the guarantee through His prophets that we will not perish and that we will not cease to be a significant people. As the existence of God cannot be terminated so our disappearance from the world is impossible. It is said (Mal. 3:6): 'For I, the Lord, do not change, and you, the children of Jacob, will not perish' (Cf. *Sotah* 9a). Furthermore, God has informed and promised us that He cannot possibly reject us completely and, though we may disobey Him and turn back His commandments, it is said (Jer. 31:37): 'For God has said: "As much as the heavens above can be measured and the foundations of the earth beneath can be plumbed, so will I reject all of the seed of Israel because of all that they have done"—says the Lord.' This very point was even earlier made known to us by Moses our teacher, peace be upon him (Lev. 26:44): 'Yet for all that, when they are in the land of their enemies I will not reject them, nor will I abhor them, to destroy them utterly and to break My covenant with them—for I am the Lord their God.'" *Ib.*, p. 35: "It has been explained to us by Isaiah, the messenger of the nation, that the sign between us and God and the proof that teaches us that we will not perish is the persistence of God's Torah and His word among us. He said (Is. 59:21): 'As for Me, this is My covenant with them, says the Lord—My spirit which is upon you.'... And it is written (Is. 44:23): 'For You have we been killed at all times and treated as sheep suitable for slaughter.'" Cf. also *Yalkut Shimeoni*, 27b, beginning, to Ex. 19:2, where God's "eternal salvation of Israel" is counterposed to Israel's previsioned "offensiveness and blasphemy," on the basis of its function of "purloining worlds for Him."

14. Cf. the classic writings of Jacob Klatzkin—Cf. *The Zionist Idea*, A. Hertzberg, N. Y. 1960, pp. 314-328, esp. p. 320ff.

15. Arthur Koestler's *Thieves in the Night* was an anticipation of this attitude in our time, and his "Letter to a Parent of a British Soldier in Palestine" (cf. *Under Fire*, ed. D. Robinson, N. Y. 1968) is a proterrorist corollary.

16. E.g. Arthur Ruppin's classic *Die Juden der Gegenwart*, Berlin 1920.

16a. Cf. H. Slonimsky, *Essays*, N. Y. 1967, p. 62: "The individual Jew may drop away, but Israel as a whole is held inexorably fast. Thus Johanan, the prince of the Agada, has the following to say in explanation of God's ontological definition of himself as *Eheyeh asher Eheyeh* 'I can be whatever I may be to individuals, but as for the mass I rule over them even against their desires and will, even though they break their teeth' (referring to Ez. 20:33), (Ex. R., Romm 11b, col. 2).

17. I wish I had kept count of the young Jews with whom I have spoken who, validly or no, are, as a result, finding themselves in the most serious of ethical perplexities now when they have to try to buttress their universal conscientious objections to waging war with Jewish reasoning.

18. There is by now much literature that can be adduced on this score. Cf., *e.g.*, C. Potok's review of a cluster of recent books on the Six Day War in the *N. Y. Times*, June 9, 1968, which ends: "... a new kind of Jew has been in the making during these past

decades, the concept of the exile, with its picture of the cringing, long-suffering Jew (whose picture?!), is now coming to an end . . . " Cf. D. Lang, "After the Sixth Day," *The New Yorker*, May 18, 1968, p. 104. The most frightening religio-political chauvinism comes from Prof. Harold Fisch of Bar-Ilan University: see "Land of Israel Movement," *Congress Bi-Weekly*, 35/3, Febr. 5, 1968, and *Niv HaMidrashiya*, Winter-Spring 1968, pp. 44-49, where he even rather likes Arab intransigence since it leads to Israeli expansion.

19. Mandel, "Le Méssie, va-t-il Arriver?" *L'Arche*, Oct.-Nov. 1967, no. 128, quotes an Israeli: "I don't believe in God, but of one thing I'm sure: this time He was with us."

20. Cf. Maimonides' striking position on miracles, which we cannot here rehearse but which can fairly be summarized as maintaining the possibility of miracles while denying in virtually every single case that one has occurred.

21. Why does this publication always carry the front-page notation: "This publication is for your information and use, in any way you deem fit—therefore, please do not give any credit to the publisher"?

21a. See further relevant *Halachic* discussions summarized in I. Jakobovits, "Survey of Recent *Halakhic* Periodical Literature—The Occupied Territories," *Tradition*, IX/4, Spring 1968, pp. 101-104. Rabbi J. B. Soloveitchik's position represents a humane and wise bright spot in the spectrum. Cf. also *Or Ha-Mizrach*, XVII/3, July 1968, Y. Gershoni, "Is it Halachically Permitted to Surrender Palestinian Territories?" and I. Y. Untermann, "The Commandment to Publicize the Miracle" (Hebrew).

22. *Op. cit.*, p. 69, *et al.*

23. This argument occurs, of course, throughout Jewish history but especially in 19th-century liberalism. I have been sorely tempted to write a review of the Satmerer Rebbe's book to be entitled, for the reason here mentioned as well as others, "The Reform Judaism of Satmer."

24. *Op. cit.*, pp. 34f., *et al.*

25. *Sanh.* 98b.

26. Cf. the famous midrash about God rebuking the angels while Egypt drowns in the Red Sea.

27. Cf. e.g. R. J. Isaac, "Good Guys (Arabs), Bad Guys (Israel): The View from the Left," *Congress Bi-Weekly, loc. cit.*; A. S. Maller, "The New Politics," *The Jewish Spectator*, June 1968; J. L. Teller, "The New Populism and the Jews," *Conservative Judaism*, XXII/3, Spring 1968; M. Wyshograd, "The Jewish Interest in Vietnam," *Tradition*, IX/4, Winter 1966. Quite an interesting bibliography of this new American-Jewish turn away from "the Left" could be compiled—although, on the whole, it is not so much the writers who would make the point, since they almost always were conservatives all along and are merely making use of the new situation for their purposes (like the latter two

mentioned here), as rather the obviously increased receptivity to and respectability of their views among the Jewish community.

28. See Ernst Simon, the very title of whose book tells part of this story: *Creation in the Midst of Destruction–Jewish Adult Education in Nazi Germany as Spiritual Resistance* (German), Tuebingen 1959.

29. Dr. Nathan Eck, of Yad VaShem in Jerusalem, reports the doctrine of Rabbi Nissenbaum of Warsaw that in the past, in order to save one's soul, one had to sacrifice one's life, i.e., in the face of the Inquisition one had to perform *Kiddush ha-Shem* whereas now the Nazis want to exterminate Jewish life, and, therefore, in order to save the Jewish mind one has to perform, above all, *Kiddush ha-Chayyim* i.e., preserve Jewish life. (These questions were discussed at a Conference on Problems of the Resistance held at Yad VaShem the week before Passover 1968.)

30. *Kuzari*, I/113ff.: "Rabbi: 'I see that you are reproaching us with our degradation and poverty. But the best of other religions boast of both ...' The Kuzari: 'This might be so if your humiliation were voluntary. But it is involuntary, and if you had the power you would kill.' Rabbi: '... Yet the majority may expect reward, because they bear their degradation partly from necessity, partly of their own free will. For whoever wishes to do so can become the friend and equal of his oppressor by uttering one word ("*credo*") and without any difficulty ...' If we bear our exile and degradation for God's sakes, as is proper, we shall be the pride of the generation which will come with the Messiah and accelerate the day of the deliverance for which we hope." Cf. also H. Cohen, *Religion der Vernunft*, Frankfurt am Main 1929, ch. XII, last paragr., Engl. transl., *Judaism*, XVII/3, Summer 1968, "From the Classics." This is, all together, one of the most distressing *heilsgeschichtlich* points brought to the fore by the experience of the Holocaust. (Some of the following points have crystallized in my mind as a result of a long and searching conversation on this subject with Dr. Erich Fromm.) It is often argued that "the six million" are not martyrs because many of them were not, of course, practicing religious Jews or even believers in God. The answer of *pietas*, theology, *Halachah*, and historiosophy must be and is that anyone slain as a Jew—on whom the name of God was thus called, whether he knew or liked it or no—is a martyr. If a "martyr" is, etymologically, a witness, then witnesses witness regardless of their own subjective attitude to the content of their testimony. *I.e.*, we are dealing with an objective, rational postulate (cf. footnote 6): it is not that one deduces a martyr's status from the fact that he was a Jew but rather the reverse, the Jew's status from the fact that he was a martyr. (Cf., *Protest: Pacifism and Politics*, ed. J. Finn, N. Y. 1967, pp. 126ff.) See *Encyclopedia Talmudit*, "Haruge Malchut," vol. X, pp. 622-627: "Those slain by a government attain to atonement even though they had been wicked men—see Ps. 79:1f.: 'Thy servants' refers to such as were deserving of death but who, by virtue of the fact that they were killed, are called 'Thy servants.' ... The atonement of those slain by a government is immediate ... as, for example, those who were killed in the destruction of the Temple, who had done all the evils which God hates, as is expounded by the Prophets, and yet Scripture says about them: 'They gave the bodies of Thy servants as food for the fowl of heaven.' ...

Those slain by a government attain to atonement even though they have not done repentance, i.e., even though they were 'killed in the midst of their wickedness.' (See *Sanh.* 47) . . . Those slain by a government are to be properly mourned, and they are not to be deprived of any form of mourning. . . . Referring to those slain by a government that refuses permission to bury them, since it is thus impossible to count the seven and the thirty days of mourning from the time that the grave is closed, one begins to count the period of mourning at the time that hope is abandoned for asking the return of the bodies. . . ." Cf. also the moving words written in 1912 by Rav Kook regarding the HaShomer socialists who lost their lives in defense of the *Yishuv, Zichron*, ed. R. Y. L. HaCohen Fishman, Jerus. 1945, pp. 5-9: he cites *Yoreh Deah*, 340-*Pess.* 50a: "No one can be compared to Jews killed by alien sovereignties," and says: "We are fortune's children when it comes to tears. . . . It is our happiness-*cum*-catastrophe that we may mourn these beloved victims according to our heart's desires, not only out of the emotions of our heart but also by virtue of the *Halachah*. . . . But woe unto us that we are forced to make use of this good fortune."—Another aspect of the current Polish episode into which we cannot, unfortunately, enter is the astounding reconfirmation, which Nazi Germany first supplied in our century on a grand scale, of the eschatological thesis of Isaac Abarbanel (see B. Netanyahu, *Don Isaac Abarvanel* . . . Phil. 1956, pp. 202f., 315f.) and of others that the God of Israel and of universal history stamps His indelible will for the Jewishness of His chosen even on those who most actively deny it—Marranos, communists, etc. Adam Schaff, perhaps the best known Polish academic philosopher, who, in his debate with Sartre, went so far in his self-de-Judaization that he made vulgar anti-Semitic wisecracks, has now—as one example out of many—been removed from official and public life on the ground that he is a Jewish nationalist and—of all things—a Stalinist! I would go so far as to be prepared to argue that the Six Day War lies significantly at the root of the current Czech and French quasi-revolutions and the Polish quasi-counter-revolution. (Cf. *Jews in Eastern Europe*, III/9, May 1968: "World Communist Disunity over Jews and the Middle East.")

31. Let anyone still wishing to quarrel with this thesis look at the case of Richard Rubenstein. Without going into his psychopathology, the least that can be said about his doctrine is that he thinks he has decided to divorce himself from this cruel God—thus he declares Him to be Nothing and teaches a revived religion of paganism, a return to the mother-goddess earth and her Canaanitish ways.

32. Compare what was said in this country during the weeks after the assassination of Senator Kennedy about the psychological relationship between the Vietnam War and the predilection for violence at home.

33. Cf. B. K. 93a, *Lev. R.* 27:5, *Pesikta deRav Kahana* (ed. Mandelbaum), p. 153; cf. generally and importantly, R. Kimmelman, "Non-Violence in the Talmud," *Judaism*, XVII/3, Summer 1968, esp. sect. III. Cf. the very title *The Religions of the Oppressed (A Study of Modern Messianic Cults)*, V. Lanternari, N. Y. 1963. Cf. S. H. Bergman's lovely statement, quoted in D. Lang, *loc. cit.*, about being a minority as a majority, p. 92.

33a. Freud said to Marie Bonaparte: anyone who asks about the meaning of life is already sick.

34. Cf. *Sabb.* 30b, *Ket.* 111b, etc.; also my "A Note on the Nature of Ideal Society—A Rabbinic Study," this volume, pp. 99-108.

35. See p. 95, supra.

36. *E.g.*, Chayim Shevili, *Cheshbonot Geulah* Jerusalem 1967.

37. See also *supra*, p. 96f.

38. *Sanh.* 97a.

39. *Ib.*, 97b.

40. *Judaism*, XVI/3, Summer 1967, p. 281.

41. In G. B. Shaw's *Joan of Arc*, Joan says: "Minding your own business is like minding your own body; it's the shortest way to make yourself sick. . . . I tell thee it is God's business we are here to do; not our own."

Chapter 5

1. *Cf. Baba Kama* 81b and *Tosfot ad locum*. Here this statement is attributed to R. Shimeon b. Eleazar.

2. *Cf.* relevantly on R. Chisda, W. Bacher, *Die Agada der Babylonischen Amoräer*, Strasbourg 1878, p. 70.

3. Ez. 47f. is clearly the text of the *Baraita*. The last eight chapters of this prophet have rightly long constituted a *locus classicus* of Jewish Messianology. (*Cf.* next note) Chapter 36 blocks out the promise of redemption, chapter 37 the resurrection, chapters 38f. the wars of Gog of Magog, chapters 40-48 the map of the Messianic kingdom; chapter 45:1-4: God's portion of the land, with Temple and priestly terrain within it (cp. 48:8-11) (Cp. also B. Levine and W. Hallo, "Offerings to the Temple Gates at Ur," *HUCA* XXXVIII (1967), pp. 49f.); v. 5: Levite territory (cp. 48:13f.); v. 6: Israel's "commons" (cp. 48:15-20); vv. 7-9: priestly terrain (cp. 48:21f.) (Rashi *ad* 45:7 stipulates the doctrine of the Messianic thirteenth part); chapter 47:1-12 describes the eschatological river and its miraculous prosperity, v. 13 the tribal portions (cp. 48:1-7, 23-29), 14-20 the expanded Messianic geography of Israel, and vv. 22f. the place of converts in that society. Finally chapter 48 ends with vv. 30-35, the gates from the city of Jerusalem, "whose name from then on will be 'the Lord is there.' ".

4. *Cf.* L. Ginzberg, *Legends of the Jews*, Philadelphia 1911-1938. IV, p. 234, end. Cp. *Men.* 45a, *Bet Ha-Bechirah* 1, 4.

5. *Cf.* Maimonides, Introduction to *Zera'im* and "Laws of Sacrifices," 2:14f. J. Klausner, *The Messianic Idea in Israel,* London 1956, p. 409 uses this passage to support his thesis that, in Tannaitic times, eschatological terms were used in imprecise and undifferentiated fashion. But see S. I. Forstein, *The Law in Talmudic Eschatology* (unpublished dissertation, Hebrew Union College-Jewish Institute of Religion), 1965, pp. 31-34, etc. It would be useful to crystallize Klausner's ideological axe in his book.

6. Cp. Klausner, *op. cit.*, throughout, and G. F. Moore, *Judaism in the First Centuries of the Christian Era . . .*, vol. II, Cambridge 1946, part VII, chapter 2.

7. *Loc. cit., Tosfot ad* "in this world"; Rashbam *ad* "gate of Reuben"; A. J. Wolf, "Maimonides on Immortality and the Principles of Judaism" (English version of his Introduction to *Perek Chelek* of the *Commentary to the Mishnah*), *Judaism,* XV, pp. 96, 213. *Cf.* also *Midrash Rabbah, beshalakh* 25:3, 7. In this connection, attention may be drawn to an interesting Messianic statement in *Sanh.* 98a: "The Messianic era will not begin", as Samuel said, "until all prices are equal." Rashi, *ad locum,* points out that this could mean either that all prices are equally high or equally low. That interpretation, properly, makes Samuel's statement part of the basic Talmudic discussion on whether the Messiah will come at the worst of times or at the best of times—an important theme in Talmudic eschatology, which deserves separate treatment. (*Cf. ib.*: "R. Johanan said: 'The Son of David will come only in a generation which is completely innocent or in one which is completely guilty. . . .' ") Actually, of course, "all prices" cannot be equal unless they are zero, for only at that point does neither quantity nor quality make any difference. It is interesting to observe how later authorities no longer can, or wish to, understand Samuel's radical socialist thesis, which amounts to an abolition of market prices. The *Maharsha (ad locum)* picks out only the former of Rashi's cited two interpretations, *i.e.* that Samuel is talking about a time when all men will suffer equally. *Cf.* also H. Freedman, *The Babylonian Talmud, Sanhedrin,* vol. II, London 1935, p. 661, n. 10.

8. *Cf.* Isaac Abarbanel's antimonarchic Messianism: *cf.* B. Netanyahu, *Don Isaac Abravanel,* Philadelphia 1953, esp. pp. 173-194. Also the Satmerer Rebbe's *Kuntras al ha-ge'ulah ve-ha-temurah,* New York, 1967, pp. 113f., paragr. 65.

9. *Cf.* Rashbam *ad locum.* Also Ez. 46:10.

10. *Mishneh Torah,* "Laws of Kings," 4:6, footnote. Also Rashi and *Metzudat David ad* Ez. 45:7.

11. *Cf.* note 21. Historical Israel has had only three of the six Deuteronomically instituted "cities of refuge" and will have to provide the others Messianically; *cf.* also J. Sarachek, *The Doctrine of the Messiah in Mediaeval Jewish Literature,* New York, 1932, on Abarbanel, pp. 233ff., 297. Klausner, *op. cit.*, p. 475 argues against the Amoraic and traditional interpretation of the *Baraita*; he suggests that, originally, the thirteenth portion was, in accordance with Ezekiel's provisions, intended for the tribe of Levi. Under Joshua's dispensation that priestly tribe was not assigned a province of its own.

The prophetic text and Talmudic, normative tradition disagree with this, however. (*Cf.* Rashbam *ad* "it has been taught" and following.) They argue, again based on the appropriate verses in the Pentateuch and in Ezekiel, that originally Menasseh and Ephraim were assigned separate provinces, whereas in the Messianic dispensation the two are united as "Joseph"—so that, even with Levi now added, there will still be only twelve tribes. Our question, in any case, is addressed to this traditional interpretation of the *Baraita*.

12. *Loc. cit.*, 4:5f.

13. Cp. also *ib.*, 12:5

14. *Ib.*, 12:3; cp. *Eduyot*, end of tractate; Abarbanel teaches that "anarchocommunism" will prevail: ef. Netanyahu, *op. cit.*, pp. 239, 241f.; "Maimonides on Immortality . . .," *loc. cit.*, p. 214: "All nations will make peace with him, and all countries will serve him out of respect for his great righteousness . . ." and then goes on to quote the famous pacific prophecy of Is. 2:4 and 11:9.

15. Ed. S. Schechter, New York 1945, chapter 35, paragraph 3, p. 104f.—*Cf.* J. Goldin, *The Fathers according to Rabbi Nathan*, New Haven 1955, pp. 144-147 and notes.

16. In the text the proof verses are quoted only fragmentarily. Their cogency becomes clear when read in their original setting.

17. For a thorough study of proselytism in Talmudic Judaism, see W. G. Braude, *Jewish Proselyting in the First Five Centuries of the Common Era . . .*, Providence 1940, and B. Bamberger, *Proselytism in the Talmudic Period*, Cincinnati 1939.

18. In the Law this is a very complex matter. Jethro's descendants are given a very special place, not the same as that of native Jews and higher in some respects. *Cf.* Ginzberg, *op. cit.*, III, pp. 72ff., VI, p. 134, n. 138, pp. 28f., notes 170-172. Cp. *Tosefta, Bikk.* 1:2 (ed. S. Lieberman, N.Y. 1955, p. 286f., and *Tosefta Kifshuta, ib.*, pp. 823-827 and the references there.) The upshot of the discussion would seem to be that, at least *de facto*, the Kenites have the use of special land set aside for them. Even for the other converts the point is that their sustenance would have to be derived from some place, and the location and aegis of this place are what we are concerned with. Cp. Maimonides' ruling, notes 30f. The typology of David = Messiah is beautifully brought out in what seems to be a later Kabbalistic *notarikon: "adam"* = Adam, David, Messiah, and in at least one, rather off-beat place ("Responsum of R. Joseph ibn Shraga to R. Moses Chafetz about the pseudo-Messiah Asher Lemmlein," *cf.* A. Z. Eshkoli, *The Messianic Movements in Israel* (Hebrew), Jerusalem 1956, p. 310f.), this is taken to be the explanation of our passage in *Niddah* 13b (see note 63)—that the Messiah will not come until the identity of Adam = David = Messiah has been enacted in history. (Further on the identity Jericho = Jerusalem, *cf.* Mishnah *Pesachim* 4:8 and E. Urbach, *Ba'ale Tosfot*, Jerusalem 1955, p. 295 and note 80.)

19. The universalistic aspect of the Messianic fulfillment is, of course, an integral part of this Jewish doctrine—from the Bible (esp. *e.g.* Zech. 9-14), the Talmudic stipulations for the Noachites, etc. onward. *Cf. Mishneh Torah*, "Laws of Repentance," 9:2: "To him (the Messiah) all the nations will come to listen, as it is said (Is. 2:2): 'It shall be in the end of days that . . . all nations shall flow toward him!' Etc." A good later illustration can be found in the, for the rest quite self-assertive, Abarbanel—*cf.* Sarachek, *op. cit.*, pp. 236ff. *et. al.* Our main concern here, however, has to be not so much general Noachite monotheism as rather specific Jewish proselytism. Abarbanel does deal with our particular question, but not quite to our end, in *Mashmia Yeshuah*, ed. 1644, pp. 36b, 51f.—see Sarachek, *ib.*, pp. 195f.

20. *Loc. cit.*, p. 106.

21. Generally the notion is that in Messianic times all Israel will be greatly enlarged: *cf. Sabb.* 30b, *Ket.* 111b, etc., Ez. 47:14-20 (cp. note 3).

22. I, *ad* Eccl. 1:7, paragraph 6—Vilna ed. 1887, II, p. 3c.—This passage was pointed out to me by Rabbi J. B. Soloveitchik in a discussion of the problem treated in this paper.—Cp. *Midrash Rabbah—Ecclesiastes Rabbah*, tr. A. Cohen, London 1961, vol. VIII, p. 22f.

23. *I.e.* Israel is always complete, even without its proselytes.

24. The immediate context of this verse from Balaam's prophecy supports the point of the *midrash*, for v. 9 speaks of Israel's incomparability.

25. Compare, however, the usual rendering of this verse. The *midrash* takes advantage of the homonymity of the Hebrew "*ger*."

26. Again, the whole Biblical context in this chapter must be kept in mind. Is. 54 is, of course, a great Messianic text, speaking of the expansion (spiritual and physical) of Israel. The last exegesis refers to the fact that, according to Rabbinic Judaism, it is usually held that all conversions must have taken place before, none will be allowed in, the Messianic era (*cf.* commentaries and sources *ad locum* and Klausner, *op. cit.*, pp. 475-482), to which we shall have occasion to revert (*infra* note 59). This has, in any case, no bearing on our problem; our question is: from what territory will the converts that already exist be nourished? Nonetheless, even the stipulation that no converts will be accepted under the Messiah is not free from significant, and perhaps decisive, qualifications. An impressive proof of this is the commentary to our passage in *Mishnat de Rabbi Eliezer* (a late Kabbalistic-Chassidic supercommentary). It quotes, among others, R. Isaac Luria, the great Kabbalistic authority, to give expression to its "wonderment" at the claim that Israel does not need converts for its completion, "for converts are (parts) of the soul of Israel that had sinned and were caused, by way of punishment, to transmigrate into heathens, but in the Messianic restoration they will return and be reconverted." Compare the end of Eccl. 1:7: "To the place from which the rivers go out, thither they continue to return." The answer is, according to this view, that the souls of

the converts are never missing from the entirety of Israel because fundamentally (in the *guf*, the heavenly repository of all future souls) they were parts of it in the first place; *i.e.* they are not additions but returns to Israel. (Compare the midrashic notion that all converts are actually lineal descendants of Sarah: Ginzburg, *op. cit.*, I, p. 261ff.) From this argument R. Eliezer goes on to conclude—astoundingly—that "therefore, conversions can also take place in the days of the Messiah," *i.e.* he argues that conversions are not really conversions but re-conversions—on grounds of a doctrine of metempsychosis! The logic of his position is, obviously, that all messianic conversions will be legitimate, because they will not—*eo ipso*—be real conversions! Note also Troki's view in *Chissuk Emunah*, that in the end of days there will be only one faith, the Jewish, and one society only, the Jewish; see H.-J. Schoeps, *Christlich-Jüdisches Gespräch in 19 Jahrhunderten*, p. 78, and Formstecher's identical view of the matter in the 19th century, *ib.*, pp. 112f.

27. This is the last verse in chapter 47 and, thus, leads straight into the last chapter of the book which is the text of our chief passage in *Baba Batra*.

28. The rest of the chapter in *Eccl. Rabbah* of which this passage is a part is in its entirety devoted to eschatological interpretations of the verse from Eccl. under consideration. (One of the many desiderata in Jewish theology is a study of the level of classical exegesis which is Messianic, *i.e.* "*sod.*" In it, the entire Bible is turned into eschatology; *cf. e.g.* Maimonides, *loc. cit.*, 11:1: "We need no proof for this (the Biblical authority of the Messianic doctrine) from the words of the prophets, for all the books (of the Bible) are filled with this subject." *Cf. Sabb.* 63b: "All the prophets in their entirety prophesied about nothing but the days of the Messiah;" *Ber.* 34B; *Sanh.* 99a, "Maimonides on Immortality . . . ," *loc. cit.*, p. 212.) Paragr. 7 discusses the eschatological resurrection, paragr. 8 that all Israel will be assembled in the Messianic Jerusalem (*cf. supra, Abot de Rabbi Nathan*, chapter 35, last paragr.), and paragr. 9 that in the Messianic days Israel will be given a new vitality.

29. *Cf.* note 26.

30. *Cf. e.g. Mishneh Torah*, "Laws of First-Fruit," 4:3 and Maimonides' famous and beautiful answer to Rabbi Obadiah, the convert, *cf. Moses ben Maimon—Responsa*, ed. A. Freimann, Jerusalem 1934, pp. 40-42, S. Freehof, *A Treasury of Responsa*, Philadelphia 1963, pp. 28-34, Eshkoli, *op. cit.*, pp. 159f. N. Golb, "Notes on the Conversion of European Christians to Judaism in the Eleventh Century," *Jewish Social Studies* XVI/1-2 (1965), pp. 69-74 and the literature there adduced.

31. *Cf.* Deut. 26:1-11.

32. *E.g. Makkot* 19a, *Bikk.* 1:4, etc. Cp. commentaries *ad locum*.

33. Indeed, in one place in his letter to R. Obadiah (see note 30) he raises converts above the status of native Jews: basing himself on Is. 44:5, he says that native Jews are related to Abraham while converts are, as it were, related to God. It does not seem to

have been noticed that Maimonides is here rephrasing the beautiful parable about converts in *Gen. R.* 8. Cp. also responsum no. 369, Freimann, *op. cit.*, p. 336f. Cp. *Pes.* 87b, *Lev. R.* 2a (Romm ed.)

34. *Ad locum.*

35. Thus, this commentary also eliminates the problem that in "Laws of the Second Tithe," 11:17 Maimonides had just ruled that converts may not pronounce the prayer that accompanies that particular sacrifice: it refers to past inheritances.

36. Rabbi Soloveitchik put this problem to me again. I propose my answer, therefore, with the greatest tentativeness.

37. *Ad locum.*

38. The *Kessef Mishneh* then also adduces Maimonides' statement in "Laws of the Second Tithe," 11:17 (see note 35), to the same effect.

39. Here is another instance, then, of interpretation by selection, for what may be assumed to be a prior judgment; see p. 103f. See on this the important responsum #49 in *Sha'agat Aryeh.*

40. Chief Rabbi M. H. Eichenstein, St. Louis, was kind enough to discuss this problem with me. The text is to be found on p. 137f., Part III, New York edition 1966. This actually corresponds to Commandment 493 in the Chavel edition of *Sefer Chinuch*, Jerusalem 1966, p. 608.

41. Cp. Ridbaz *ad* 4:9. Actually, the *Minchat Chinuch* is very difficult to understand in this section altogether. He claims, for reasons which I find incomprehensible, that the historical kings of Israel also owned "one-thirteenth of the Land." And he asks why the Messiah should be a lesser king than the historical kings in owning only one-thirteenth of the Land whereas they owned—*de jure*—all of it. The point is that he is, of course, not a lesser king but a different kind of king; *cf. infra.*

42. The central Maimonidean source for this distinction is to be found in "Laws of Priest-Offerings," chapter 1. This is an important passage in general and particularly in view of the events pertaining to the State of Israel in our days. I, therefore, want to summarize and analyze it here briefly. (Cp. my "On the Theology of Jewish Survival," this volume, pp. 83-98). Paragr. 2 states that "the Land of Israel" comprises only such territories as have been taken possession of by the head of the Jewish people "with the consent of most (or "the bulk," or "the body") of Israel" (the last translation is best, because, in line with paragr. 26 (see *infra*), it would seem to mean, in effect, all of the Jewish people), not merely by an individual or individuals. Thus territory occupied by individual action, even though it be part of God's promise to Abraham, is not legitimately, *de jure*, Israel. (*I.e.* divine promises come into force only when the human legalities have been observed.) (Cp. "Laws of Kings," 5:6) Paragr. 3 narrows down legally Jewish territory even further: the conquests which King David made, though complying with

the prerequisite of paragr. 2, are also not juridically part of Israel, because outside possessions are not licit until all of the home territory has been completely purified, relieved of pagan remnants—which was not the case in David's time. (Is it in ours? It means that one may not impose the truth on others unless one is oneself perfectly truthful.) Paragr. 5 narrows down the entirely legitimate sovereignty of Israel yet further by another widereaching restriction. Although Joshua's conquest of Palestine satisfied the conditions of par. 2, it, too, was only another sort of *de facto*, not *de jure*, *pro tempore*, not permanent appropriation ("first sanctification," "sanctification *pro tem.*"). The reason for this restriction is that Joshua's conquest took place by force of arms ("conquest") rather than by legal proceeding ("by word of mouth") (cp. Ridbaz *ad locum*) —unlike the repossession in the days of Ezra, which took place by virtue of a (legal) edict of the Persian king and conqueror Cyrus (*cf.* Ridbaz *ib.*). The latter constituted the only *de jure* permanent occupation of Palestine by Jews. (The extremely significant conclusion must be drawn from this stipulation that, as was the case in connection with par. 2, the divine bestowal of Jewish Palestine is made conditional not only on human legalities in general but on the legality of a non-Jewish, pagan, royal disposition!) Maimonides draws the further conclusion from this consideration that all the Temple sacrifices now offered are valid not by Biblical but by Rabbinic stipulation, and used not for the Temple, of course, which is not in existence, but, instead, for the poor. (Cp. 1:16 and Ridbaz *ad* 5. Indeed, the Ridbaz suggests that Joshua failed to take possession of Palestine "by consent" and, therefore, legitimately and permanently, as he could have done, precisely so that these taxes would be channelled later to the poor.) Finally, in par. 26, the end of the chapter, Maimonides prevents the rise of any pseudo-Messianism in his or any other time, at least as far as any *Halakhic* legitimacy is concerned, by stipulating that, even when all the previously cited conditions have been fulfilled—difficult as that may be in itself—Messianic Israel (land and people) will not have been achieved, with all the rights and duties thereunto appertaining, until literally "all Israel," without exception, have been gathered in the Holy Land. (Cp. *Sefer Chinuch, op. cit.*, Commandment 95, last paragr.) (This, presumably, cannot occur under other than Scripturally Messianic conditions.) This makes it impossible, as some have argued, that either "the first sanctification" of Joshua (*cf.* par. 5) or "the second sanctification" of Ezra (par. 26) or any other humanly and, therefore, imperfectly organized "in-gathering of the exiles" can be blasphemously confused with the Messianic fulfillment. (This is, of course, the main point of the Satmerer Rebbe's position, *cf. op. cit.*) The *Kessef Mishneh ad* 5 supports Maimonides' position, but the more militant interpreters state their disagreement—Rabbi Abraham ben Daud, for example, *ad* 26, and the Ridbaz *ad* 5, who points out, among other things, that the Ten Tribes have been despaired of and, therefore, "all Israel" literally cannot be expected to be gathered in. Compare, however, the discussion about the eschatological fate of the Ten Tribes *Sanh.* 10:3, 110b and Klausner, *op. cit.*, pp. 397f., 472-475. Three observations can be made about the Ridbaz' position: 1) Jewish tradition—and history—disagree with him; 2) it is clear from the Talmudic discussions that those, like Rabbi Akiba, who want to give up on the Tribes do so because they press for an immediate, humanly engineered Messianic fulfillment, whereas those who, like Maimonides here, are content to await the reemergence of the Tribes are the purer eschatologists—*i.e.* that the attitude toward the lost tribes is not primarily a matter of historiography or even Scriptural faith but a function of one or another eschatological-historic posture; and 3), clearly, Rabbi Akiba and now the Rabad and the Ridbaz were wrong, Maimonides is right, if for no other reason than that otherwise our stipulated division of the Land into twelve-plus-one parts would make no sense.

43. *Cf.* all of Maimonides' present chapter 4f. *et. al.* His aristocratic, élitist bias extends both to his philosophy (*cf.* J. Guttmann, *Philosophies of Judaism*, New York 1964, Husik, *A History of Mediaeval Jewish Philosophy*, New York 1916, and esp. Leo Strauss in, *e.g. Philosophie and Gesetz*, Berlin 1935) and to his politics. Concerning his politics, note, for example that, unlike many Jewish interpreters, especially Abarbanel, *cf. Netanyahu, op. cit.*, and Sarachek, *op. cit.*, he uses the "statute of kings," I Sam. 8:11-17, in a permissive rather than a prohibitive sense. The *Lechem Mishneh* restricts the king's right to eminent domain only to time of war and then with compensation. On this particular point, however, Maimonides cannot be faulted. The *Lechem Mishneh* is, in fact, entirely in accord with the codifier, as his own commentary to 5:3 makes perfectly clear. (I learned this important fact many years ago from Prof. S. Atlas.) For, here, Maimonides himself rules that the king's eminent domain, without limitations, exists only in wartime. (Cp. his *Book of the Commandments*, negative commandment 363.) Furthermore, since 5:3 directly continues 5:2, where the Sanhedrin's permission is made prerequisite to the type of war under discussion, the king's prerogative is thus further restricted. As the *Lechem Mishneh* points out, Maimonides' ruling differs in these respects from his authoritative sources, *Sanh.* 19a-20b and its Rashi. (*Cf.* p. 90-91.) The increasing democratization of Jewish law of sovereignty can be observed here.

44. *Cf.* notes 12-14.

45. 4:6, 9.

46. *Cf.* notes 19, 26.

47. *Cf.* on this point Klausner, *op. cit.*, pp. 475-482.

48. See tr. L. I. Rabinowitz and P. Grossman, *The Code of Maimonides—Book V*, New Haven 1965, pp. 86-94 and notes.

49. For some major problems connected with the latter section, *cf.* S. S. Schwarzschild, "Do Noachites have to believe in Revelation? . . . ", this volume, and J. Katz, "The Vicissitudes of Three Apologetic Passages" (Hebrew), *Zion*, XXIII-XXIV/3-4, pp. 174-181.

50. *Cf. Yeb.* 47a, *Gerim* 1:1, etc.

51. *Cf. Abodah Zarah* 64b.

52. *Cf. Arakin* 29.

53. "Do Noachites . . . ." p. 40f.

54. *Cf.* "Laws of Kings," 10:12.

55. The *Maggid Mishneh* (*ad locum*) and the *Migdal Oz* (*ib.*), on the other hand, support Maimonides—the latter calling his view as of Sinaitic authority (cp. *Arachin* 29a) (!).

56. "Do Noachites . . . ."

57. Cp. *Yeb.* 76a, end, *Avodah Zarah* 3b, 24a, *Gerim* 1:17, etc. In *Yeb.* the proof text is the verse from Is. which our previously treated excerpt from *Eccl. Rabbah* also uses; see note 22.

58. "Laws of Forbidden Intercourse," 13:14f.

59. The view that conversions will be permitted under the Messiah is far from unparalleled. In *Ber.* 57b, for example, Rabbi Shimeon b. Eleazar (cp., however, Klausner, *op. cit.*, p. 482) declares that ultimately the nations of the world will become proselytes—and he quotes Zeph. 3:9 with which Maimonides ends the penultimate chapter in his Code (11:4, having first said: "The Messiah will restore the whole world to the service of God together."!) We have earlier noted the same opinion in the *Mishnat de Rabbi Eliezer* (see note 26). It might furthermore be noted that the underlying motif for the requirement of "conversion-sacrifices" is to make converts the complete equals of native Jews (cp. *Yeb.* 47b): even as Israel in the desert became Jews through the three-fold ritual of circumcision, immersion, and sacrifices, so does every convert go through the same ritual. ("Laws of Forbidden Intercourse," 13:4.)

60. *Cf.* p. 99f.

61. If I understood Rabbi Soloveitchik correctly, he, in effect, approved of this conclusion.

62. *Cf. Abot de Rabbi Nathan, loc. cit.*, p. 104 top.

63. At this point it may also be legitimate to offer another interpretation of the passage in *Niddah* 13b which is usually adduced as the *locus classicus* of Rabbinic dislike of proselytes. A *Baraita* is quoted that converts and "such as play with young girls delay the coming of the Messiah." This put down of converts is justified with Rabbi Chelbo's oft-quoted statement that "converts are like boils to Israel." The usual reading (*cf.* Rashi *ad locum*) of R. Chelbo's statement is that converts are undesirable because they cannot be relied upon in their fulfillment of the commandments. (There is, however, also that reading which says that they are like boils to Israel because often they are more pious than native Jews and thus cause the latter an uneasy conscience.) (*Klausner, op. cit.*, p. 478.) Leaving R. Chelbo aside, in any case, another view of the matter might be that "converts delay the coming of the Messiah" because, if many or even all humanity must be converted to the truth of Judaism before the Messiah can come, then obviously it will take a long time before this prerequisite can be fulfilled. This view is enhanced by the fact that this is precisely the explanation which the *Gemara* gives of why "playing with little girls" delays the Messiah: whatever the phrase means, it certainly means some kind of sexual behavior without the possibility of procreation,

but "Rabbi Jose said: 'The Son of David will come only when all the souls of the *promptuarium* ("*guf*," *cf.* Klausner, *op. cit.*, pp. 333, 431, and references, and note 26) have been exhausted;' " *i.e.* all those predestined to be Jews must be born—and must be Jews!—before the Advent can occur.

64. Actually, this needs to be done not only with this aspect as well as the rest of Rabbinic eschatology but with all of Jewish-Rabbinic theology. Despite S. Schechter's *Some Aspects of Rabbinic Theology*, New York, 1909, S. Belkin's *In His Image* (London a. New York, 1960), A. Heschel's *Torah Min HaShamayim* ... (London a. New York, 1962) and a few other works, the general view is still that the Talmud is a welter of unsystematic thought; *cf. G. F. Moore, op. cit.*, Kadushin's notion of vague concept-clusters, G. D. Cohen, "The Talmudic Age," *Great Ages and Ideas of the Jewish People*, ed. L. Schwartz, New York 1956, p. 174f., etc. How unsystematic thought is supposed to underlie, or result from, what is conceded to be an extraordinarily systematic legal system is incomprehensible. Rabbi Soloveitchik's teachings in the philosophy of the *Halakhah* would be reduced to nonsense. I would suggest that this notion of a lack of systematic Talmudic theology is due to one or more of the following motivations: 1) Jews and non-Jews often simply do not know the literature properly; 2) particularly Christians like to think of Christianity as having supplied the theology which Judaism lacks; 3) particularly Jews do not bother or are unable, in part because of a, by now, traditional concentration on *Halakhah*, to analyze Rabbinic sources conceptually.

65. *HUCA* XXVII (1956), pp. 417-438.

66. *Ib.*, p. 428; *Religion der Vernunft—aus den Quellen des Judentums*, Frankfurt 1929, p. 26; *Jüdische Schriften* (ed. Franz Rosenzweig), Berlin 1924, vol. I, pp. 313f.

67. *Ib.*; *Ethik des Reinen Willens*, Berlin 1904, p. 528f.

P.S. I gratefully acknowledge the help and criticisms of the learned Rabbi David S. Shapiro. He cannot, of course, be held responsible for anything in this paper.

Chapter 6

1. Cohn-Wiener, *Die Juedische Kunst* (Berlin 1929), p. 1 "Einleitung.—Die Grundfrage—Gibt es eine juedische Kunst? Man ist gewöhnt, die Frage zu verneinen." F. Landsberger, *A History of Jewish Art* (Cincinnati, 1946), p. 3: "I. The Problem of Jewish Art—Is there such a thing as Jewish art? This question is often asked when the subject is mentioned." "Art," *Encyclopaedia Judaica* (Jerusalem, 1971), I, col. 500: "Whether there exists a form of art that can be described as 'Jewish art' has long been a matter for discussion."

2. Cf. C. Roth, "The Problem of Jewish Art," *Judaism,* VI, 118-125; D. Sperber, "Trends in Modern Jewish Art," *ibid.,* XII, 28-35; S. Spero, "Towards a Torah Esthetics," *Tradition,* VI/2, 53-66.

3. Cf. my article "Noachite Laws," *Encyclopaedia Judaica.*

4. The prohibition of idolatry is the first and foremost of "the seven Noachite laws": B. Meg. 13a, etc. Cf. Maimonides, *Mishneh Torah,* "Laws of Kings," 9:2, last phrase: also Gentiles are forbidden to make "images," even for pleasure. D. Shapiro, *Yesodei haDat Ha'Universalit,* New York: Bloch, 1936, pp. 15f. disputes and reinterprets this ruling. Moslem art, like Islam in general, and unlike Christianity, can be shown to conform entirely to Jewish Noachitism. The present exposition, for example, could be duplicated in Moslem terms. Cf. Oleg Grabar, *The Formation of Islamic Art* (New Haven: Yale University Press, 1973)—although one must add that Grabar's philosophical sophistication is quite inadequate to the task—and T.W. Arnold, *The Old and New Testament in Muslim Religious Art* (Oxford: Oxford University Press, 1932).

5. Y. Kahana, "Synagogal Art in the *Halachah*" (Hebrew), in R. Wahrhaftig, ed., *Bet-HaKnesset* (Jerusalem, 1955), pp. 255-308, brings together a very rich collection of the relevant Halachic literature. This survey makes it perfectly clear that the general thrust of Jewish legal thought on art is strongly restrictive. However, we can omit most of that material from consideration in our context, since it impinges on aesthetic criteria only very distantly. Rabbi Joseph Karo belongs distinctly among the more lenient decisors.

6. We are omitting references to the Talmudic sources. They can easily be checked in *Be'er Ha Golah.*

7. Cf. E. Urbach, "The Laws of Idolatry in the Light of Historical and Archaeological Facts in the Third Century" (Hebrew), *Eretz Israel,* V (1958), 199-205, for the anti-imperialist posture expressed in this law. Also Gerhart B. Ladner, "Der Bildbegriff bei den griechischen Vaetern und der byzantinische Bilderstreit," in L. Scheffczyk, ed., *Der Mensch als Bild Gottes,* (Darmstadt: Wissenschaftliche Buchgesellschaft, 1969), pp. 187ff., and J. Phillips, *The Reformation of Images: Destruction of Art in England, 1535-1660* (Berkeley: University of California Press). Political power and idolatry are, or course, ultimately identical.

8. Cf. R. Wishnitzer-Bernstein, 'The New Art and We" (Hebrew), *Rimon,* I (Berlin, 1922), 1. The predominance of geometric designs in ancient Jewish art is striking in B. Mazar, *Beth She'arim: Report on the Excavations, 1936-1940* (New Brunswick, N.J.: Rutgers University Press, 1973), and their sophistication sometimes anticipates Kandinsky (plate IX/1) and "hard edge" (plate XXIII/3). (See my review in American Anthropologist, LXXVI/1.) Cf. in general H.A. Groenewegen-Franfort, *Arrest and Movement: An Essay on Space and Time in the Representational Art of the Ancient Near East* (Chicago: University of Chicago Press, 1951), esp. ch. 1.

9. Cf. Urbach, "Laws of Idolatry," pp. 190f., 198.

10. *Ibid.,* 205a; R. Blum, "Tu ne feras point d'images," *Les Nouveaux Cahiers,* IV/16 (Winter, 1968-69), 50: "... le thème de l'incarnation, propre aux diverses théologies chrétiennes, a eu pour conséquence logique la possibilité de représenter, par l'image et la forme, le Dieu qui s'est fait homme. C'est cette libération de la loi hébraïque...;" also L. Scheffczyk, *Der Mensch,* and S. Schwarzschild, "Survey of Current Theological Literature," *Judaism,* VIII/4, 366ff. The logic of the historic Christian oscillations between iconoclasm and iconography would have to be unpacked separately; for the Jewish factor in this see Ladner, "Der Bildbegriff," pp. 152ff., 171ff., 179, and the literature there adduced. *Cf.* also Edwin Robert Bevan, *Holy Images ...* (London: Allen and Unwin, 1940), pp. 132ff.: "St. John Damascene argued that, since Jesus was (also) a man, God can be depicted." N.b., though, p. 148, note 1 that in the mediaeval chruch it was held that if a raised image showed a person grasping the nose (!) it was regarded as three-dimensional and, therefore, obnoxious.

11. Maimonides holds that they are entirely nonphysical: see "Laws of Repentance," 8:2, and parallels in his writings (including, for example, "Laws of the Foundations of the Torah," 2: 3).

12. Cf. however the extraordinary description of the cherubs in the Temple, *B. Yoma* 54a, and F. Landsberger, "Origin of the Winged Angel in Jewish Art," *H.U.C.A.* XX (1947), 227-54. Lauterbach, ed., *Mekilta* (Philadelphia, 1943), II, p. 287 stipulates the Temple cherubim as a unique exception; commenting on *Ex.* 20:20 (p. 276), it prohibits the representation of God and angels on the same ground. The noncanonical material, such as is here adduced by Landsberger, R. Meyer's in "Die Figurendarstellung in der Kunst des spaethellenistischen Judentums," *Judaica,* V (1949), 1-40, and most especially the massive accumulation in E. Goodenough's thrteen volumes of *Jewish Symbols in the Greco-Roman Period* (New York, 1953-69), can be shown to be not only in some way or degree heterodox but also used by the respective scholars for a more or less unarticulated agenda of their own. (Cf. M. Smith, "Goodenough's *Jewish Symbols* in Retrospect," *J.B.L.* LXXXVI/1 [March, 1967], 53-68.) The depictions of angels or souls that do occur (Mazar, *Beth She'arim,* pp. 61, 80ff., etc.) must and can be explained as folk culture under foreign influences. (For good examples of how Christians enforced their iconographic views on Jews in the Middle Ages, see Américo Castro, *The Structure of Spanish History* [Princeton: Princeton University Press, 1954], pp. 478, 489.) In the debate between J. Jervall and M. Smith, see "On the Shape of God and the Humanity of Gentiles," in J. Neusner, ed., *Religions in Antiquity* (Leiden, 1968), pp. 315-326. Smith is right in holding that for the Rabbis "man" also covered Gentiles, and Jervell is right in holding that man's likeness with God was not believed to be physical. The substance of the present study makes this philosophically clear. (On the last point cf. Scheffczyk, *Der Mensch,* pp. 23, 48, and the article by P. G. Duncker, "Das Bild Gottes—Eine physische Aehnlichkeit?")

13. *Deut. R.* 4:4, *Midr. Ps.* 17: "Make room for the *eikonion* of God. *Cf.* further such references in M. Jastrow, *Dictionary of Talmud Babli ..., sub diyukan. B. Av.*

Zarah 24b reads Ex. 20:20, "You shall not make by My side (*'itti*) a god of silver," as "you shall not make of My symbol (or: sign) ('otti) a god of silver." For the entire concept of *imago Dei*, cf. Scheffczyk, *Der Mensch* and David S. Shapiro, "The Doctrine of the Image of God and *Imitatio Dei*," *Judaism*, XII/1 (Winter, 1963), 57ff.

14. *Abot* 3:18. The notion of "the image of God" must be understood properly. It is not the notion that man is a mirror image of God: if it were, the warning against mishandling God's image would imply homeopathic magic. "Man is made *in, with*, the image of God" (*Gen.* 1:26ff.), i.e., God is conceived as using His own form in order therewith to make man. As a result man resembles Him; the two share, in some respects,the same quality. When something is done to man, it is done to the quality which, as it were, constitutes God—in short, to "the divine in man." The human *imago* is thus like a child that is flesh and blood of its parents. (See Scheffczyk, *Der Mensch*, pp. 24, 26, 80.)

15. Maimonides, "Law of Idolatry," 3:10ff. and the discussion among the commentators, and *Sefer Chinuch*, Commandment 39, 12.

16. *Man's Quest for God* (New York, 1954), "Symbolism," pp. 124ff. See also *Ps.* 115:8: "Like unto them (the idols) will be their makers, everyone that trusts in them;" as the believing man is the image of God, so the idolator is the *imago* of his idol. The human images that do occur in the history of Jewish art (e.g., Mazar, *Beth She'arim*, pp. 77, 152, 183ff.) are rigorously stylized and, at that, under deviationist influences.

17. This is brought impressively home by Jewish law regarding the treatment of corpses. A dead person may not be left unburied, for it is "a blasphemy of God." (*Deut.* 21:23. *Targum Jonathan* and Rashi, *ad locum*, speak of man as "the ikon of God," and Seforno, *ad locum*, states the theory explicitly, in his scholastic theological terms: "The defamation that is inflicted on a man after his death is a defamation of his rational soul, which is the discrete essence that perdures after the death of the body. Therefore, it is a blasphemy of God to leave the body of the executed without burial, for it is a defamation of that eternal essence, which is called God.") A corpse is like a naturalistic portrait—without life. Both may, therefore, not be looked upon. Much less may a portrait of the corpse, dead to the second power, be used. (See Y.Y. Greenwald, *Kol Bo 'al 'Avelut* [New York: Feldheim, 1956], p. 36.)

18. *Kants Begruendung der Ethik* (Berlin, 1877), p. 283. The convergence of Jewish aesthetics with that of Kant can here only be adumbrated. It is best manifested in Kant's apostrophe to the Second Commandment (Cassirer, ed., *Kritik der Urteilskraft*, [Berlin, 1922], p. 347; cf. Schwarzschild, "F. Rosenzweig's Anecdotes about H. Cohen," in H. Strauss and K. Grossman, eds., *Gegenwart im Rueckblick* [Heidelberg: Lothar Stiehm Verlag, 1970], p. 217), as well as in his aesthetic "formalism" ("only the form"; *Kritik*, p. 399) and opposition to "realism" (*ibid.*, #58). Even the distortion of the living face required by Jewish law is encountered in Kant's advocacy of an artistic "one-eyed animal" and other asymmetries and *"grotesqueries"* (*ibid.*, pp. 312ff.). See also Shapiro, "Doctrine of the Image."

19. *The Bird's Head Haggadah* (Jerusalem, 1967), where, for the reasons here adduced, creatures are used for illustration that are men-birds, or birdmen. Wishnitzer

points out that faces are often left empty. (One might contrast this spiritual modesty with sexual prudery, its Western counterpart.)

20. See Walter Kaufmann, *Critique of Philsophy and Religion* (New York: Harper, 1972), p. 374. An analysis of the sculpture of Lipchitz, Epstein, etc., would have to begin at this point. Distortion does not automatically rule out idolatry, as the pagan deformed gods illustrate—the Greek crippled god Hephaestus, the Teutonic gods Odin and Tyr (Zeus), whose right hand had been bitten off by a wolf. The Jewish licitness of distorted animal forms must, therefore, be due to aesthetico-theological rather than religio-cultic considerations.

21. See B. Cohen, "Art in Jewish Law," *Judaism,* III, 171. There are Greek parallels to this story: see Bodmer and Breitinger, *Die Discourse der Mahler,* III, 21st discourse.

22. *Third Critique,* p. 424.

23. José Ortega y Gasset, *The Dehumanization of Art* (Princeton: Princeton University Press, 1965), p. 48: "Art has no right to exist if, content to reproduce reality, it uselessly duplicates it." It would be tempting to block out Ortega's philosophical aesthetic at this point. Let it suffice to say that both his proximity to and simultaneous distaste for the aesthetic here outlined may be due to his acknowledged indebtedness to and fundamental deviation from his sometime teacher Hermann Cohen. (See note 18 above, and my study "The Tenability of H. Cohen's Construction of the Self," *Journal of the History of Philosophy* 13 (1975), pp. 361-384.

24. My copy bears the holograph: To Jacob Schiff, New Year's Day 5670, Stephen S. Wise." For further Lazarus bibliography, see I. Belke, " 'Der Mensch ist eine Bestie . . .' —Ein unveroeffentlichter Brief Th. Fontanes an den Begruender der Voelkerpsychologie, Moritz Lazarus," *Bulletin of the Leo Baeck Institute,* XIII/50 (1974), 32-50.

25. The incident is more fully reported in I.J. Benjamin, *Three Years in America, 1859-1862,* trans. C. Reznikoff (Philadelphia, 1956), I, 320-33; see also *Occident,* XIX; L. Hubner, *The Life of Juda Touro;* Z. Fraenkel, in *Wiener Oestreichische Wochenschrift* #5 (January 29, 1886). In Benjamin's book Fraenkel's response is printed in full, together with corollary responses by Rabbis Judah Leib Rapoport, Samson Raphael Hirsch, and Nathan Adler, and agreement even by the leaders of contemporary American Reform Judaism. (I owe this reference to B.W. Korn, Philadelphia.)

26. The general Halachic view is that, while other considerations may fall by the wayside when it comes to private homes, the fact remains that (Jewishly) paintings are "disgusting" even there and should, therefore, be avoided. See Kahana, "Synagogal Art," p. 300, n. 104.

27. Jean Onimus, in "Art spirituel, art surréel," *Etudes* (Paris, 1959), as a Roman-Catholic, speaks similarly of Picasso's as "a surrealist art which distorts the human face into a grimace as if to take vengeance on it—outstanding example of the misfortune of the modern consciousness which seems to be able to attain to spirituality only through

violence and rebellion." See also H. Sedlmayr's headlong attack, out of his deep, organistic (not to say fascistic) conservatism in art and historiography, on Picasso and the "pure God" in *Verlust der Mitte—Die bildende Kunst des 19. und 20. Jahrhunderts als Symptom und Symbol der Zeit* (Salzburg, 1953), esp. chs. 7 and 8. One might indeed ask about the relationship between various forms of human mimesis in art and various types of "cults of personality."

28. C. Roth, "Representation in Early Jewish Art," *British Journal of Aesthetics*, I/3 (June 1961), though wanting to show that Jews also subscribed to and practiced representational painting, reluctantly admits that "this abstract art, incidentally, is in some ways far closer to the artistic tendencies of our own day than the representational art of Northern European Jewry" (p. 162).

Chapter 7

1. *Cf.* Sid Z. Leiman, "Jewish Ethics 1970-1975: Retrospect and Prospect," *Religious Studies Review* II/2, Apr. 1976, p. 18. Cp. also Lichtenstein's "Toward an Understanding of 'We Suppress the Quality of Sodom'" in *Hebrew Thought in America* (Hebrew), World Hebrew Association, Tel Aviv: Yavneh 1972, p. 374.

2. *Cf. Ezek.* 16:49: "Behold, this was the sin of Sodom, your sister (!): she and her daughters had the pride of satedness with bread and quiet security, but she did not strengthen the hand of the poor and the miserable." Cp. David S. Shapiro, *Studies in Jewish Thought*, N.Y.: Yeshiva University Press 1975, p. 108.

3. *Cf. e.g.* Eugene B. Korn, "Ethics and Jewish Law," *Judaism* XXIV/2, Spring 1975, p. 206. On equity *cf.* Boaz Cohen, "Letter and Spirit in Jewish and Roman Law," in *Mordecai M. Kaplan Jubilee Volume*, English section, N.Y.: Jewish Theological Seminary 1953, esp. pp. 126f., 130.

3a. *Cf.* Dora Edinger, *Bertha Pappenheim—Freud's Anna O.*, Highland Park, Ill.: Congregation Solel, 1968.

4. *What is Political Philosophy?*, Glencoe, Ill.: Free Press 1959, pp. 35f.

5. *B. Meg.* 3b, *Ber.* 19b, *Eruv.* 51b. (Here, as elsewhere, I have learned from my friend R. Simchah Krauss, St. Louis.)

6. Cp. *Gitt.* 61a and Me'iri *ad locum*, Maimonides' *Code*, "Laws of Kings," 10:12, and Rashi *ad II Sam.* 8:13, *I Kings* 11:15, and *Ezek.* 30:13.

7. *Ad Makk.*, ed Sterlitz, N.Y. 1952, p. 9.

8. *Cf.* J.S. Bloch, *Israel and the Nations*, Berlin/Vienna 1927, pp. 172f., and A.J. Heschel, *Theology of Ancient Judaism* (Hebrew), London/N.Y.: Soncino Press 1965, vol. 2, pp. 167, 173, 395, and the sources there adduced.

9. *Cf.* Maimonides' *Guide*, I/54 and III/53; Shapiro, *loc. cit.*, p. 113 and "The Concept of Chessed in Judaism"; G.A. Larne in "Recent Studies in Hesed" in Nelson Glueck, *Hesed in the Bible*, Cincinnati: Hebrew Union College Press/1967, pp. 11f., 16, 18.

10. Cp. Simon Greenberg, "Ethics, Religion and Judaism," *Conservative Judaism* XXVI/4f., Summer and Fall 1972, p. 109.

11. *Cf. Shittah Mekubbetzet ad locum.* (Note the mortifying irony here.)

12. Cp. *B.M.* 2b and Rashi and the early decisors on this.

13. *Cf.* also R. Yehudah Gershuni, " 'Better that Both Drink and Die' or 'Your Life Takes Precedence'?" (Hebrew), *Or HaMizrach* XXIII/3-4, Nissan-Tammuz 1974, pp. 162-168.

14. *Cf.* Fritz Stern, *The Politics of Cultural Despair: a Study in the Rise of the Germanic Ideology*, Berkeley etc.: University of California Press 1974, "Paul de Lagarde and a Germanic Religion," pp. 3-9.

15. *Cf.* Nathan Suesskind, "Tov Sheba-Goyim . . . ," *CCAR Journal*, Spring, 1976, pp. 28f. and n. 2, Uriel Simon, "Religion, Morality, and Politics," *Forum*, nos. 28/29, Winter, 1978, and S.H. Fineberg, *CCAR Journal*, XXIII/4, Autumn, 1976, pp. 96ff. *Cf.* also *SWASIA–North Africa* II/22, June 6, 1975, p. 1, and N. Chomsky, "The Interim Agreement," *New Politics* XI/3, Winter, 1976, p. 28, n. 81: "appalling."

16. 'Al HaT'shuvah, ed. P. Pelli, Jerusalem 1975, p. 302.

17. Cassirer edition, vol. 7, p. 38.

18. Kant has, as a matter of fact, often been accused, and still is, of egotism, of all things. *Cf.* J. Ebbinghaus, "Interpretation and Misinterpretation of the Categorical Imperative," in *Kant*, ed. R.P. Wolff, Doubleday Anchor AP4, pp. 224f.

19. *Loc. cit.*, pp. 35-37.

20. "Saints and Heroes," in *Essays in Moral Philosophy*, ed. A.I. Melden, University of Washington Press 1958.

21. *A Theory of Justice*, Harvard University Press 1971.

22. "Reason and Morality in a World of Limited Food," in *World Hunger and Moral Obligation*, eds. W. Aiken and H. LaFollette, Englewood Cliffs, N.J.: Prentice-Hall 1977.

23. Against Watson cp. Hardin, *ib.*, "Lifeboat Ethics: The Case against Helping the Poor."

24. *Tosfot ad B.M.* 62a discusses another aspect of the same problem.

25. *The Notes of Ramach on the Rambam's Code* (Hebr.), Jerus. 5729, pp. 2f.

26. The universality of the Jewish ethical principle that if I am even merely an accessory to another's murder it is not only his life but my humanity that is destroyed, is strengthened by the Halakhic view which holds that also the non-Jew is religiously obligated to be ready, if necessary, for martyrdom. Limitations of space prevent me from exploring this very interesting question. Meanwhile, *cf. b. Sanh.* 74bf.; *Encyclopaedia Talmudit*, vol. 3, pp. 350ff. (and the sources there adduced); and the case of the Roman soldier by the side of R. Hananyah's martyrdom, in "The Ten Martyrs," in *The Judaic Tradition*, N. Glatzer, Beacon Press BP 316, pp. 175ff. (and its sources).

27. *Religion of Reason*, tr. S. Kaplan, N.Y.: Ungar 1971, p. 119.

28. Will my controversialists, who stake so much on Dr. Finkelstein, also subscribe to the pacifism and progressivism of *The Pharisees* that he once expounded? Just to balance Jewish institutional interests, *cp.* Kaufmann Kohler, "Die Nächstenliebe im Judentum," in *Judaica-Festschrift z. H. Cohens 70 Geburtstag* (Berlin, Cassirer, 1912), pp. 469ff. About this it might be noted that a) it opens and ends with extended apostrophes to H. Cohen's Jewish ethical theses, b) it holds a view emphatically identical with Rabbi Finkelstein's, and c) it makes one wonder what has happened to at least Reform Jewish views on ethics since that time.

29. *Cf.* Schwarzschild, "The Tenability of Hermann Cohen's Construction of the Self," *Journal of the History of Philosophy* XIII/3, July 1975, pp. 361-384.

30. See Rosenzweig's *Star of Redemption*, N.Y., etc.: Holt, Rinehart and Winston, 1971: he accepts Cohen's translation of Lev. 19:19 (pp. 239, 259, 274), and he adds that for the person under Revelation, self and other come to be simultaneously, whereas for the pagan, self precedes the other and really always remains walled off from it (pp. 239f., 346).

31. In the first part of this article, the exceedingly important contribution of Emmanuel Levinas to the volume *Modern Jewish Ethics* unfortunately had to be neglected. His "post-phenomenological" method is too hard to treat together with other vocabularies.

32. I am quite content with Dr. Weber's terminological point (*Sh'ma* 7/126) about "egotism" and "altruism." In any case, I was not discussing R. Akiba's general posture—this would be the task of a broader analysis; I was only talking about *B.M.* 62a.

33. Maharam Schiff sees that this is the bottom line of ben Petura's view and, therefore, rejects it ("there will be no end to the matter"). It is worth reminding ourselves that this entire discussion is only a parenthesis in the wider discussion of usury. The latter is condemned by all parties in increasingly strict fashion. Taking interest on money is held to be identical with murder, and a Jew who does this sort of thing is declared not to be a fitting member of his people. I am tempted to make an offer: if my critics will join me in prohibiting Jews from taking interest I will join them in subscribing to R. Akiba's view.

34. It is a disputed question in the *Halachah* whether one ought or ought not to risk the possible danger to oneself to prevent certain danger to one's fellow; *cf.* R. Gershuni, *loc. cit.*, p. 163.

35. For an analysis of how the contemporary Jewish mind has come to this pass *cf.* my "On the Theology of Jewish Survival," in this volume, p. 90f. Clearly this development has gone further since then.

36. The literature on "suffering" is, of course, vast. For a start *cf.* Schwarzschild, article "Suffering," *Encyclopaedia Judaica*; Montefiore and Loewe, *A Rabbinic Anthology*, London 1938, chapt. 28, "On Suffering;" H.N. Bialik, *Sefer Aggadah*, III/1, chapt. 4/12: "Acceptance of Afflications;" A. Heschel, *Theology of Ancient Judaism* (Hebr.), London/N.Y. 1962, I, pp. 93-110 about the different but positive evaluations of the role of suffering by R. Akiba and R. Ishmael; esp. *Sabb.* 88a-*Yoma* 23a-*Gitt.* 36b.

37. For the distinction between "seeing death" as a *shayv velo ta'asseh* and "causing death" as a *ma'aseh yada'yim cf.* R. Chayim Soloveitchik, *Novellae* ... (Hebr.), Brisk 1936, p. 1. R. Chayim, as Dr. Weber rightly reminded us, equates this distinction with that between "murder by deed" and "killing the other by saving oneself." But this still leaves open ben Petura's option.

38. The literature on Jewish martyrdom is, of course, endless. For a start let me only refer to Jacob Katz, *Exclusiveness and Tolerance*, Oxford University Press 1961, chapt. 6, "The Martyr," pp. 82-91, where typological descriptions are given of "mass suicide and massacre . . . at each other's hand" (p. 88) and where—let it be said, since M. Wyschogrod took a silly swipe at "German Jews" (*Sh'ma* 7/125)—the tragic ideal of martyrdom is historically found to be a peculiarly "Ashkenazi" development; David Daube, *Collaboration with Tyranny in Rabbinic Law*, Oxford University Press 1965, and my discussion of it, "The Imperative of Religious Law," *Washington University Law Quarterly*, Winter 1970, which I ended with the sentence: "A man, or any number of men, must know when to be ready to die rather than commit murder, regardless of any arithmetic calculations to which human life is not susceptible" (p. 109); Louis Jacobs, "Greater Love Hath No Man—the Jewish Point of View of Self-Sacrifice" (pp. 41-47) and "Disinterestedness" (pp. 202-209), *Judaism* VI, 1957; and since it last came to my attention, the discussion of religious martyrdom under the Nazis in Alexander Guttmann, "Humane Insights of the Rabbis Particularly with Respect to the Holocaust . . . ," *H.U.C.A.* XLVI, 1975—one of whose problems is whether, before being martyred, one should recite the short benediction ("Praised be Thou, oh Lord, our God, ruler of the universe, who has sanctified us by His commandments and commanded us to sanctify His name in public") or the long benediction ("Praised be Thou, oh Lord, our God, ruler of the universe, who has sanctified us by His commandments and commanded us to love the glorious and awesome name, who was, and is, and in the future is to be, with all our heart and all our soul, and to sanctify His name in public. Praised be Thou, oh Lord, who sanctifiest Thy name in public"—cp. N. Glatzer, *Faith and Knowledge*, Boston 1963, pp. 120f.).

39. *Kuzari* I/13ff. and IV/23f.; cp. also "Theology of Survival," *loc cit.*, n. 30. Prof. Marc Saperstein has drawn my attention to an anonymous Spanish sermon of c. 1492, in which the following proposition is put forward: "It has long since been proclaimed that 'In Isaac who was to be sacrificed your seed shall be called,' as if he Abraham were sacrificing all future Israel.... It is proper for every Jew to be the father that has to kill his son and to be the son that is sacrificed...." On the other hand, where the wind blows from these days became clear to me again when I heard Prof. H. Ben-Sasson say, at a conference on R. Yehudah HaLevy on 3. 19. 1975 in Jerusalem, that the author of the *Kuzari*, too (he, of all people!), adopted the ideal of *humilitas* from Christianity.

Chapter 8

Parts of this study were read as a paper in the Department of Religion at Temple University on November 3, 1976. I owe thanks to my friend Professor Norbert Samuelson there for having suggested this paper in the first place.

1. "The Needs of Jewish Scholarship in America," in *Harry Austyn Wolfson Jubilee Volume* (Jerusalem: American Academy for Jewish Research, 1965) p. 7.

2. See the ongoing work of L.V. Berman, Hebrew Ethics Project, Department of Religious Studies, Stanford University. For the general (pseudo-) scientific setting of Aristotle's doctrine of the mean, see T.J. Tracy, *Physiological Theory and the Doctrine of the Mean in Plato and Aristotle* (Chicago: Loyola University Press, 1969). (He misunderstands and, therefore, misinterprets Plato, however: pp. 143-53; compare W. Jaeger, n. 74 below). For the complex paths through history of such science see R. Klibansky *et al.*, *Saturn and Melancholy* (London, 1964). Note also the role of the doctrine of the mean in classical Jewish and general climatological theory: A. Altmann, "Yehudah HaLevy's Climatological Theory" (Hebrew), *Melilah* I (Manchester, 1941) pp. 1-7, and N. Allony, "The Reaction of Moses ibn Ezra to 'Arabiyya," in *Etudes Hébraïques, Actes du XXIXe Congrès international des Orientalistes* (Paris: L'Asiatèque, 1975) p. 1f., and in *Bulletin of the Institute of Jewish Studies* (London, 1975) III, 19-24 (note also p. 27: "concerning excess and deficiency").

3. *The Guide of the Perplexed* (ed. S. Pines; Chicago: University of Chicago Press, 1963) p. lxxxvi f.; J.O. Urmson, "Aristotle's Doctrine of the Mean," *American Philosophical Quarterly* X/3 (July 1973) p. 225; also J.D. Monan, *Moral Knowledge and Its Methodology* (Oxford: Clarendon Press, 1968) p. 151. (Allan calls the traditional continuity of Book X with the rest of the *Nicomachaen Ethics* [*N.E.*] "a rickety compromise," *"un compromis toujours précaire, souvent bâtard."*)

4. *N.E.* I, 1, 1094b 14-23.

5. See for example, R. Pucetti, "Aristotle's Golden Tautology," *Ratio* V/4 (December 1964); Hans Kelsen, "Aristotle's Doctrine of Justice," in *What is Justice?* (1960),

reprinted in *Aristotle's Ethics* (edd. Walsh and Shapiro; Belmont, California, 1967); R.A. Gauthier, "On the Nature of Aristotle's Ethics," *ibid.;* Ollé-Laprune, *Essai sur la morale d'Aristote;* and, for our purposes particularly Hermann Cohen, "Charakteristik der Ethik Maimunis," in *Moses ben Maimon*... (edd. W. Bacher *et al.;* Leipzig, 1908) I.

6. *Lechem Mishneh ad Maimonides' Code,* "Laws of Beliefs," 1:5, and, for example, Albo, *'Ikkarim* I/8.

7. See David Shapiro, "The Doctrine of the Image of God and *Imitatio Dei,*" *Judaism* XII/1, now in *Studies in Jewish Thought* (New York: Yeshiva University, 1975). The *Tomer Deborah,* Moses Cordovero's kabbalistic ethic, is in its entirety an *imitatio Dei,* and yet there is no allusion to Aristotelian ethics in it whatsoever.

8. South Bend: University of Notre Dame Press, 1976. See George Dangerfield, *The Strange Death of Liberal England 1910-1914* (New York: Capricorn Books, 1961) p. 17f.: "If there could be such a thing as a Humor of Moderation, then Mr. Asquith was the perfect example of it. ... He was moderately imperialist, moderately progressive, moderately humorous, and, being the most fastidious of Liberal politicians, only moderately evasive ... having married a lady of some wit and more exalted birth than his own who had taught him to be moderately frivolous." See also *ibid.,* p. 4.

9. See the Talmudic and medieval commentaries *ad locum: Sanh.* 74a, "with all your heart" means "unto death"; *Sifré* and Rashi, "that your heart be not divided [*challuk, calculated*] before God"; Ibn-Ezra, "your might" [*m'odcha*] means that "you ought to love God very, very much [*m'od m'od*] [see the discussion of *Aboth* 4:4 below], as much as you can." The entire medieval doctrine of *yichud* (see especially Bachya ibn Pakuda's *Duties of the Heart*) aims precisely at "singlemindedness" (see H. Cohen's "Die Einheit des Herzens," in *Jüdische Schriften* [Berlin: Schwetschke, 1924] III, 213ff.).

10. Maimondies himself discusses these Biblical passages in a crucial place: *Eight Chapters,* chap. 5, end.

11. H. Cohen, "Charakteristik," *op. cit.,* p. 113: "inside of the line of the law"; S. Greenberg, "And He Writes Her a Bill of Divorcement," *Conservative Judaism* XXIV/3 (Spring 1970) p. 132; *Tomer Deborah,* in *The Way of the Faithful: An Anthology of Jewish Mysticism* (trans. Raphael B. Zion; Los Angeles, 1945) p. 32. See generally A. Lichtenstein, "Does Jewish Tradition Recognize an Ethic Independent of *Halacha?,*" in *Modern Jewish Ethics: Theory and Practice* (ed. M. Fox; Columbus: Ohio State University Press, 1975); and my discussion thereof in "The Question of Jewish Ethics Today," above, p. 119.

12. *B. Sabb.*88a, *Yoma* 32a, *Gitt.* 36b, etc.

13. See Samuel Atlas, "The Philosophy of Maimonides ...," *Philosophy* XI/41 (January 1936) p. 63: "Certainly Maimonides stands on the Aristotelian basis; but the points wherein he deviates from the Aristotelian path are not merely in details, but are so fundamental. ... The hall-mark of a thinker consists not in what he has in common with others but what is unique to himself."

14. See my "The Lure of Immanence: The Crisis in Contemporary Religious Thought," above, p. 64.

15. On Maimonides' direct source see Herbert Davidson, "Maimonides' *Shemonah Peraqim* and Alfarabi's *Fusūl Al-Madanī,*" *PAAJR* XXXI (1963) 41, and S. Baron, *A Social and Religious History of the Jews,* VIII, 337, n. 80. But to the contrary see A. Altmann, "The Religion of the Thinkers: Free Will and Predestination in Saadia, Bahya, and Maimonides," in *Religion in a Religious Age* (ed. S. D. Goitein; Cambridge, Massachusetts: Association for Jewish Studies, 1974) p. 37; and L.V. Berman, *Ibn Bajjah and Maimonides: A Chapter in the History of Political Philosophy* (Hebrew, with English summary) (Diss. Hebrew University, 1959) p. 52f. and references there.

16. See *N.E.* II/2, 9 and Kelsen, *op cit.,* p. 108.

17. See below on *Code,* "Laws of Belief," 1:1-6, 2:2.

18. J.I. Gorfinkle, *The Eight Chapters of Maimonides on Ethics* (New York, 1966) p. 22. See Aquinas' "Commentary on the 'Politics,'" in *Mediaeval Political Philosophy* (edd. R. Lerner and M. Mahdi; Glencoe, Illinois: Free Press, 1963) p. 321f.: "A man is called virtuous by reason of a single perfect virtue, namely, prudence upon which all the moral virtues depend. . . ." On the other hand, the Polish Jewish moralist Mendel Lefin (see M.G. Glenn, *Israel Salanter* . . . [New York: Bloch, 1953] pp. 116, 118) copies Benjamin Franklin's boy-scout code of virtues and yet omits "moderation" all together while transmuting "temperance" into "gentleness."

19. Gorfinkle, *op. cit.,* p. 54, n. 1f.

20. New York, 1902, p. 84.

21. See also Simon Rawidowicz, "'Mishneh Torah' Studies (I-III)" (Hebrew), in *Metsudah, VII* (London, 1954) p. 166, n. 113; and Harry S. Lewis, "The 'Golden Mean' in Judaism," in *Jewish Studies in Memory of Israel Abrahams* (New York: Jewish Institute of Religion, 1927) pp. 282-95 (written appropriately, by and for "gentlemen of leisure . . . noble amatures" [sic] [p. 286f.], although Baron, *op. cit.,* p. 339, n. 84, actually takes this seriously!). See also Israel Efros, *Studies in Mediaeval Jewish Philosophy* (New York, London: Columbia Univesity Press, 1974) p. 125 (the unspecified reference here is to Henry Malter, *Saadia* . . ., p. 257, n. 541a), 127.

22. See Maimonides, *The Commentary to Mishnah Aboth* (trans. and ed. Arthur David; New York: Bloch, 1968) pp. 64-70.

23. *Aboth* 5:10-15 all have the quadrapartite structure which lends itself easily to an Aristotelian "mean" interpretation, but Maimonides' commentary to these *mishnayot* does not change the picture. It is worth pointing out that he closes his interpretation of 5:14 by saying: "The purpose of the Torah . . . is the moral virtues." On the other hand, his commentary to 5:10, in which the classic Jewish rejection of the virtue of middlingness as *aurea mediocritas* or as "the quality of Sodom" occurs, plays it very cool and

merely cross-refers to his Aristotelian *Eight Chapters.* (*Cp.* Moses Hess, *Rome and Jerusalem,* Letter 3, n. 2, and Note V, end.) (That the "middling men" [*baynoni'im*] are Jewishly an inferior level of morality is also clear from *R.H.* 16ff.)

24. Ed. C. Chavel (Jerusalem, 1966) p. 826ff.

25. For other "median" statements in the *Chinuch* see nos. 178, 611; and G. Appel, *A Philsophy of Mitzvot*... (New York: Ktav, 1975) p. 93f.; and my review thereof in *J.B.L.*, 95/3 (1976) 519f.

26. *Sefer HaMitzvot,* no. 8; see below *Code,* "Laws of Beliefs," 1:3f. vs. 1:6f.

27. Rawidowicz, *op. cit.,* p. 173ff. makes a case against H. Cohen of the fact that humility is not alone but accompanied by anger as a vice that together break down Maimonides' Aristotelian ethic of the mean. Rawidowicz is in fact right, but this only strengthens Cohen's anti-Aristotelian interpretation of Maimonides, as Rawidowicz himself points out: *ibid.,* p. 174, n. 135.

28. Examples abound: for instance, Gabirol on humility, Stephen S. Wise, *op. cit.,* p. 60ff.; *Reshit Chochmah* (16th cent.), sect. V, chap. 2; etc. See Baron, *op. cit.,* p. 121.

29. *N.E.* 1123f.

30. *Ibid.,* 1113a25-30: *to spandaios,* "the pillar of society"; see V.J. Bourke, *History of Ethics* (Image Books, 1970) I, 41; and Leo Strauss (with J. Cropsey), *History of Political Philosophy* (Chicago: Rand McNally, 1972) p. 245.

31. See *Ber.* 31bf., *Bekor.* 45b, etc.: God Himself is grateful—therefore, be ye grateful, and *Tomer Deborah, op. cit.,* pp. 16f., 29, 37f. *et passim;* and generally Maurice Samuels, *The Gentleman and the Jew* (New York: Knopf, 1950). See J.H. Hertz, *The Pentateuch and Haftorahs* (London: Soncino, 1971) p. 685, *ad Micah* 6:8 (interestingly Hertz here uses a proof-text from H. Cohen). Contrast with all this *N.E.* IV/3ff.; E.M. Forster, *Maurice,* who, speaking of "the gentry," says: "... gratitude being mysteriously connected in their minds with ill-breeding"; and Nietzsche about "slavish virtues," etc.

32. See *Code,* "The Laws of the Kings," 8:11 (uncensored ed.); Schwarzschild, "Do Noachites Have to Believe in Revelation? ...," above, esp. p. 32f. Rawidowicz, *op. cit.,* pp. 167ff., 178; and in *Hebrew Studies in Jewish Thought* (Hebrew) (Jerusalem: Rubin Mass, 1969) p. 453f. and his conclusion p. 464. Rawidowicz makes the additional interesting point that for the Rambam median ethics are "morality" (*mussar*), while what I am calling "radicalism" is "Torah": *Ibid.,* pp. 453, 464; L. Strauss, "Notes on Maimonides 'Book of Knowledge,'" *Studies in Mysticism and Religion presented to G. Scholem*... (Jerusalem: Magnes Press, 1967) p. 277f.

33. Strauss, *ibid.,* p. 275.

34. Rawidowicz, *Metsudah, loc. cit.,* p. 171.

35. See above p. 139. 2:3 also parallels *Eight Chapters* in combining pride with anger as the vices which must be shunned radically and in underlining that Moses was, in the words of the Bible, "very humble." See further "Laws of Torah Study," 7:13.

36. See *Ber.* 22a. Rabbenu Jonah *ad locum* quotes a responsum of Maimonides to the effect that, though after involuntary ejaculation immersion is no longer required in order to be able to engage in study and prayer, he himself always insists on practicing it. See also Rawidowicz, *Hebrew Studies . . ., op. cit.,* p. 463.

37. Strauss, *op. cit.,* pp. 270, 276; R.L. Weiss, "Language and Ethics: Reflections on Maimonides' 'Ethics,'" *Journal of the History of Philosophy* IX/4 (October 1971) p. 430f. Weiss's and C. Butterworth's *Ethical Writings of Maimonides* (New York University Press, 1975) consistently translates "character traits," but this is due to the fact that they never get beyond the most conventional Aristotelian reading of Maimonides' ethics. See also I. Twersky, "Maimonides' Mishneh Torah" (Hebrew) (Israel National Academy of Sciences, V/1; Jerusalem, 1972) p. 18: "The entire work is filled with the strong intention of 'repairing morals and righting actions' ('Laws of Substituted Offerings,' 4:13)."

38. See Fritz Bamberger, *Das System des Maimonides: Eine Analyse des More Newuchim vom Gottesbegriff aus* (Berlin: Schocken, 1935) p. 54; S. Spero, "Is the God of Maimonides Truly Unknowable?," *Judaism* XXII/1 (Winter 1973) 77f. This theory has often been derided as Cohen's logicistic flight of fancy imposed on the Rambam. But, for example, *Guide* I/54: "He [God] does not possess moral attributes; He performs actions that resemble the actions which in us proceed from moral attributes." How this dichotomy is metaphysically maintained and operationalized would require full systematic explication, but that it is not a hyperbolic exercise in fancy logicism is illustrated by the fact that it actually became a commonplace of Jewish piety. See Seligman Beer, *Avodat Yisrael* (Berlin: Schocken, 1937) p. 412 *ad salchan umachalan,* p. 59 *ad rachaman,* and p. 425 *ad chivaryon.*

39. *Guide* II/39, which points to III/27ff., but which also itself adumbrates the higher level of the "perfect."

40. Rawidowicz, *Studies in Jewish Thought* (Philadelphia: Jewish Publication Society, 1974) p. 286.

41. See Leo Strauss, *What is Political Philosophy?* (Glencoe, Illinois: Free Press, 1959) p. 32: "For moderation is not a virtue of thought: Plato likens philosophy to madness, the very opposite of sobriety or moderation."

42. Rawidowicz, p. 277ff.

43. Jewish scholars, perhaps particularly in earlier generations, tended to carry out their often only very partial disagreements as if they were mortal enemies. Actually Rawidowicz essentially agrees with Cohen. He even ends (*Hebrew Studies . . . .*, p. 457; and *Metsudah,* p. 177f.) with a formulation of Maimonides' union with God through ethics. But the way he first fights against Cohen one would not really credit this. (See

Metsudah, p. 173f.) What he seems to have against him basically, as did and do so many other people, is that Cohen "systematizes" the Rambam too much in line with his own philosophical purposes. Rawidowicz asserts the Rambam's simultaneous affirmations of the ethical doctrines of the mean and of *imitatio* (*Metsudah*, p. 179; and *Hebrew Studies* . . ., p. 458), but, unlike Cohen, he does not show how this can be done, and it, therefore, remains a magical juggling-act.

44. Bamberger, *op. cit.*, p 42, uses the very word "revolution" in this connection.

44a. See S. Atlas, "Moses in the Philosophy of Maimonides, Spinoza, and S. Maimon," *H.U.C.A.* XXV (1954), esp. I, 369-80.

45. See Z. Diesendruck, "Maimonides' Theory of the Negation of Privation," *PAAJR* VI (1934-1935); H.A. Wolfson, "Maimonides on Negative Attributes," in *Jubilee Volume in Honor of Louis Ginzburg (English Part) (New York: American Academy for Jewish Research, 1945) p. 424ff.; Bamberger, op. cit.*, p. 42f.; Spero, *op. cit.*, p. 72f. and *ibid.*, XXII/3 (N. Samuelson) p. 361.

46. The use of *Jer.* 9:23 for an ethical definition of the knowledge of God is apparently first made by Joseph ibn Zaddik. See I. Husik, *A History of Mediaeval Jewish Philosophy* (New York: McMillan, 1930) p. 146ff.; Baron, *op. cit.;* and L.V. Berman, "The Political Interpretation of the Maxim: The Purpose of Philsophy is the Imitation of God," *Studia Islamica* XV (1961) 54, n. 14. Abraham ibn Daud also follows this line: see J. Guttmann, *Philosophies of Judaism* (Philadelphia: Jewish Publication Society, 1964) p. 426, n. 125. For the midrashic use of *Jer.* 9:23, see, for example, *Numb. R.* "mattot," 22:7.

47. Baron, *op. cit.*, p. 118f. Berman, *op. cit.*, p. 59f, is one of the very few historians, apart from H. Cohen, to have rightly so understood the end of the *Guide*.

48. See D. Shapiro, *Studies in Jewish Thought*, p. 262.

49. See above p. 67 and Guttmann, *op. cit.*, p. 118. See also Nahum Glatzer, "Faith and Action," *Judaism* XVII/1 (1968) 56, 60f.

50. *Code*, "Laws of Repentance," 8:6 and "Laws of the Foundations of the Torah," 2:2: "[God's] wisdom . . . which is . . . infinite . . ."

51. Cohen, "Charakteristik," p. 121ff.

52. *Eight Chapters*, chap. 8, end.

53. See Z. Diesendruck, "Die Teleologie bei Maimonides," *H.U.C.A* V (1928), esp. pp. 489-533—a very sophisticated neo-Kantian analysis. A.J. Heschel, "The Last Days of Maimonides," in *The Insecurity of Freedom* (J.P.S., 1966), also sees the real point, though he somewhat sentimentalizes it.

54. For example, Rawidowicz, *Metsudah*, pp. 164, 171, 174; and *Hebrew Studies* . . ., p. 450.

55. See Strauss, *What is Political Philosophy?*, p. 163.

56. See H. Davidson, *op. cit.*, pp. 40, n. 19, 49.

57. See n. 32.

58. See n. 34.

58a. *Cf.* Chaim Wirszubski, *Three Chapters in the History of Christian Kabbalah* (Hebrew), Jerusalem: Mossad Bialik, 1975, pp. 16-19: Maimonides takes the "beloved" in the *Songs of Songs* to be not Israel, but the soul, and (III/51) the kiss of the lover is then the conjunction of the intellect.

59. *B.K.* 83f.

60. Note the phrase that Maimonides adds: (Ibn-Tibbon) "The financial loser is to forgive and be lenient to the culprit"—(Al-Charizi) "The injured party [in general] may [!] forgive the culprit." Rabbi J.B. Soloveitchik has interpreted this difficulty in Maimonides in the same way: see A.J. Greenburg, *'Itturay Torah,* vol. "Leviticus" (Tel Aviv: Jabneh, 1969) p. 137. Another teacher of mine, Samuel Atlas, offers a morally equally-convincing but differing explanation in *The Novellae of Rabad to Babba Kama* (Hebrew) (London, 1940) p. 364, n. 3 and the *Addenda* thereto (Jerusalem, n.d.) p. 408.

61. Gauthier, *op. cit.*, p. 22f. See Ollé-Laprune, *op. cit.*, pp. 86f., 99; H. Grant, *The Ethics of Aristotle* (4th ed., 1885) I, 207f. See also G. Lukacs, *Die Eigenart des Aesthetischen,* I, 307f.: "The methodological center of [Aristotle's] ethics turns out to be a problem of correct proportionality . . . therewith the question . . . touches upon . . . the basic interrelationship of ethics and aesthetics."

62. Gauthier, *op. cit.*, p. 25.

63. *Ibid.*, p. 20.

64. *Millot HaHigayon* (ed. I. Efros; New York 1938) p. 47ff.; Efros, *Studies in Mediaeval Jewish Philosophy*, p. 75f.; my "Do Noachites . . . ," pp. 36f., 42f., 58. In the light of the present study my conclusion in "Noachites" calls for serious modification. In the latter I concluded that on Maimonides' view ethics had to be, however vestigially, ultimately transrationally "theonomic." (This paralleled my understanding of Kelsen's "Grundnorm.") This conclusion can now be seen to have to be dropped. Therefore, Maimonides' statement that those who accept the Noachite laws on their own ratiocination rather than as divinely revealed are "not of the righteous but of the sages of the nations of the world" can be seen to mean that they, like Aristotle, do not know God—cannot, therefore, act in imitation of Him—and also cannot, therefore, arrive at intellectual *conjunctio*, which provides immortality. That is, Aristotelian ethics pure and simple, without God ("revelation"), are not salvific. On the other hand, one can, of course, come to know God, as much as He is knowable, by means of philosophy, as Maimonides goes out of his way in the opening chapters of *Guide* II to prove (at the expense of the Kalamite proofs from *creatio*): a "sage," then, who practices ethics as

a matter of *imitatio*, philosophically arrived at (and who would, therefore, realize that Israel can know about the higher morality as a result of revelation, while "the sons of Noah," like himself, too, learned it from God—though without Torah) does have, in turn, his "share in the world-to-come." This, as a matter of fact, is precisely what the Rambam writes to R. Hasdai HaLevy ("Noachites," p. 42; and I. Twersky, *A Maimonides Reader* [New York: Behrman House, 1972] p. 478): "There is no doubt that every man who ennobles his soul with excellent morals and wisdom based on faith in God certainly belongs to the men of the world-to-come." This also explains Maimonides' codification of *Meg.* 13b in "Laws about Idolatry," 2:4 that "whoever rejects idolatry is [tantamount to] one who believes in the whole Torah"—that is, rejection of idolatry is, of course, a) rational, the philosophic thing to do, b) the first of the Noachitic, universal imperatives, and, therefore, c) in effect identical with "true faith."

65. Marvin Fox, "Maimonides and Aquinas on Natural Law," in *Dinay Israel* (Tel Aviv, 1972) III, v-xxxvi, now in *Studies in Maimonides and St. Thomas Aquinas* (ed. J. Dienstag; New York: Ktav, 1975) thus completely misses the point exposited in the present paragraph. (See Dienstag, *ibid.*, p. 85ff.) But then he always has an axe to grind—to prove his own "Orthodoxy" by turning all the great Jewish rationalists into fideists or rejecting them. See his "On the Rational Commandments in Saadia's Philosophy: A Reexamination," in *Modern Jewish Ethics;* "Law and Ethics in Modern Jewish Philosophy: The Case of Moses Mendelssohn," *PAAJR* (1976) 1-14; and "Philosophy and Religious Values in Modern Jewish Thought," in *The Role of Religion in Modern Jewish History* (ed. J. Katz; Cambridge, Massachusetts: Association for Jewish Studies, 1975) pp. 75f., 90. A good, indubitably "Orthodox" as well as rational and ethical reply to Fox's personal program can be found in David Shapiro, "God, Man and Creation," *Tradition* XV/1-2 (Spring-Summer 1975) 38; and David Hartman, "*Halakhah* as a Ground for Creating a Shared Spiritual Language," *Tradition* XVI/1 (Summer 1976) 18ff. Samuel Atlas wittily characterizes Fox's fideist view as holding that nothing can be "religious" unless it is idiotic and that, therefore, God is an idiot. One wonders whatever became of the fourth benediction in the Sh'moneh 'Esreh. Thus here Fox acknowledges (p. 84) the textual and philosophical importance of my "Noachites" but then proceeds to disregard it for the purposes of his own theologizing. See also his "Prolegomenon" to A. Cohen, *The Teachings of Maimonides* (New York, 1968) pp. xlif. The present study refutes Fox on both counts. Also Efros, *op. cit.*, pp. 75, 166, misses this point entirely. He fails to show for Maimonides (p. 75, n. 22) that moral laws are regarded as nought but conventions, and, like Fox—though somewhat more sophisticatedly—he resorts to a dubious use of Aristotle in order to stipulate an eventually quasi-supernatural discernment of the moral imperative on the part of Maimonides (p. 76). Finally, also Ben Zion Bokser, "Morality and Religion in the Theology of Maimonides," in *Essays on Jewish Life and Thought... in Honor of S. W. Baron* (New York: Columbia University Press, 1959) has most of the relevant texts, but he does not really understand their philosophical impact. He, too, apparently thinks that divine intercession, rather than rational *imitatio*, is held by Maimonides to cause the ascent from ethics of the mean to perfectionist ethics: pp. 147, 150, 152f. See also his "Reason and Revelation in Maimon-

ides" (with its apostrophe to Leo Strauss) in *H.U.C.A.* XX (1947). This is also the erroneous interpretation of B. Netanyahu, *Don Isaac Abravanel–Statesman and Philosopher* (Philadelphia, 1953) pp. 53, 155f. (Netanyahus have a way of being wrong.)

66. See L.V. Berman, "Maimonides on the Fall of Man" (abstract), *Association for Jewish Studies Newsletter* (June 1976) 13f. It comes very close to without actually reaching the conclusions of the present study. With an eye on current Jewish theologico-ethical discussions, this Maimonidean apostrophe to the notion of *imago Dei* (which is entirely typical of all mainstream Judaism: see Chapter 6 of this volume, 113., n. 13ff.) may be contrasted with Isaiah Leibowitz's quasi-Kierkgaardian derogation of this notion. In *Judaism, Jewish People, and State of Israel* (Hebrew) (Jerusalem: Schocken, 1976) p. 317, Leibowitz goes so far as to say that if man is "the picture of God" he is "like a picture that we hang on a wall, that is nothing but a canvas moistened with colors ... Man as such is no value or end."

67. See *The Commentary of R. Bachya ben Asher on the Pentateuch* (Hebrew) (ed. C. Chavel; Jerusalem: Mossad HaRav Kook, 1971) I, 77f. *ad Gen. 3:6*, which embodies precisely this Maimonidean thesis. At this point Maimonides' rationalist meta-historiography and meta-historicist philosophy of law should really be explicated: the rational moral law was operative before Adam's Fall, and it will, therefore, also be operative after the Messianic overcoming of the Fall, that is, the Torah is not changed nor invalidated by the Messianic advent. See Schwarzschild, "A Jewish Eschatological Liturgy," *C.C.A.R. Journal* XXIII/4 (95) (Autumn 1976) 25.

67a. I. Berman, in *Ibn Bajjah ...*, understands this and puts it well, pp. xxx, 186f. See also pp. v, 199, and his proper rejection of Vajda's conventional misunderstanding of this on p. 202, n. 5: "Intellectual perfection is a necessary condition for the imitation of the works of God, for without sound knowledge of that which is to be imitated there cannot be faithful imitation."

68. It is thus more than a triviality that on the question of the "acquired intellect" Maimonides deviates from his *Vorlage* in Alfarabi: see H. Davidson, *op. cit.*, p. 38, n. 16.

69. Few, if any, have recognized the epochal move that is here being made. Frances Yates, in, for example, "Science, Salvation, and Cabala," *N.Y. Review of Books* (May 27, 1976) 27ff., and the wider literature to which she there refers, does not realize that what she rightly recognizes as the eschatological sources of the scientific and social revolutions of the sixteenth and seventeenth centuries, Kabbalistic and Puritan millenarianism, stem directly and indirectly from this eschatological epistemology of scholastic rationalism. The role of Maimonides in the Kabbalah, Christian Renaissance, in Leibniz (see A. Foucher de Careil, *Liebnitz, la philosophie juive et la cabale* [Paris, 1861] and "re" Raphael Levy, secretary to Leibniz and Hebrew writing Jewish scientist, *cf.* Steven Schwarzschild, "Two Lives in the Jewish 'Fruhaufklarung': Raphael Levy Hannover and Moses Abraham Wolf,' *Leo Baeck Institute Yearbook* 39 (1984), pp. 229-276), and Newton (see F.E. Manuel, *The Religion of I. Newton* [Oxford]), for exam-

ple, is in fact not too hard to trace. Thus, the content of *Guide* II/30, which we are about to treat, is noted by Yates in Jean Bodin's *Heptoplomeres*, but, though she thinks of Philo of Alexandria and of the *Zohar*, she does not seem to know Maimonides. See "The Mystery of Jean Bodin," *N.Y. Review of Books* (October 4, 1976) 47, and n. 72, below on Liebeschütz.

70. See *Guide* II/30, beginning and III/27, beginning. See Kant's famous distinction between the logical and chronological priorities of reason and experience at the very beginning of the First *Critique*.

71. See *Moses ben Maimon, Führer der Unschlüssigen* (trans. and annotated by Adolf Weiss; Leipzig: Felix Meiner, 1924) II, 207, n. 45. Neither this Weiss translation (*ibid.*, p. 215, n. 88) nor M. Friedländer's English translation (New York: Hebrew Publishing Co., n.d.) p. 156, n. 5, understands the Maimondidean ethic of prelapsarian man. Compare D. Nelson, "Animal Imagery in Marcabru's Peotry," *Studies in Medieval Culture* XI (1977), p. 51.

71a. See J. Higgens, "The Myth of Eve," *J.A.A.R.* 44/4 (1976) 639ff.

71b. For the universality of the Jewish motif of the eschatological tree of life, *cf.* Zofja Ameisenowa, "The Tree of Life in Jewish Iconography," *Journal of the Warburg Institute* II/4 (April, 1939), pp. 326-345.

72. Despite Maimonides' dislike of Al-Rāzī (*Guide* III/12 and Pines, *ibid,* cxxxi f.), some connection between his theory here explicated and Rhades commends itself: see Lenn E. Goodman, "Rāzī's Myth of the Fall of the Soul: Its Function in his Philosophy," in *Essays on Islamic Philosophy and Science* (ed. G.F. Hourani; Albany: State University of New York Press, 1975) (Comp. also by the same author, "The Epicurean Ethic of Muhammad ibn Zakariya' al-Razi," *Studia Islamica,* XXIV, pp. 5-26.) The doctrine of *Guide* I/2 and II/30 here adduced quickly entered into the Kabbalah: see Seymour Cohen, *The Holy Letter: A Study in Mediaeval Jewish Sexual Morality* (New York: Ktav, 1976), where, too, humans knew ethics through the intellect before the Fall (p. 44), man is form and *sophia* (pp. 48, 145), woman is matter and understanding (pp. 79, 145), their copulation/conjunction produces knowledge (p. 44), and meanwhile "middlingness" is the proper standard (pp. 74f., 81, 83, 97f., 143, etc.). Neither Cohen nor M. Harris, "Marriage as Metaphysics: A Study of *'Iggeret Hakodesh,*" *H.U.C.A.* XXXII (1962), however, recognizes the relationship of all this to Maimonides. In the *Raya Mehemna* component of the *Zohar*, then, the Maimonidean doctrine of the Messianic return to the tree of life from the post-lapsarian tree of the knowledge of good and evil becomes central. And generally in Kabbalah the problem of the Fall turned, consistently enough, into a broader doctrine of *felix culpa.* All this entered into Christian mysticism through Meister Eckhart at the latest, explicitly deriving itself from Maimonides: see Joseph ben Shlomoh, "The Problem of Pantheism in Theistic Mysticism—R. Moses Cordevero and Meister Eckhart," in *Revelation, Faith, and Reason. A Collection of Papers* (Hebrew), edd., M. Hallamish, M. Scharcz, Ramat Gan: Bar Ilan University Press,

1976, 71-81, and Liebeschütz, "Meister Eckhart und M. Maimonides," *Archiv für Kulturgeschichte* 54 (1972) 86-88. Liebeschütz does not seem to be aware, however, of the role of *Guide* II/30 in this. On the other hand, he claims, quite credibly, that he can trace this exegesis of *Gen.* 3 in the neoPlatonic tradition through Augustine and Ambrosius back to Philo of Alexandria—an interesting and ironic underground path of Jewish thought. (See also Harris, p. 210ff.) (In any case, Maimonides had at least one Jewish neoPlatonist intermediary through whom these notions reached him: see Yehudah HaLevy, *Kuzari*,, IV/25, middle.) Eckhart had trouble with the censor of Cologne about this allegorizing exegesis. (Liebeschütz, p. 88, n. 64). The classic commentators here make the distinction between social ethics and individual morality—respectively outside and inside the Garden of Eden: see Ernst Bloch, *Avicenna und die aristotelische Linke* (Berlin: Ruetten & Loening, 1952) pp. 25-30; *Mediaeval Politial Philosophy*, pp. 19, 123ff., 134ff.; Henry Corbin, *Avicenna and the Visionary Recital* (New York: Pantheon, 1960) pp. 123-64. That the Maimonidean doctrine of man's self-redemption through reason is still powerfully operative today can, perhaps, best be illustrated in Karl Marx: *Grundrisse* (trans. M. Nicolaus; New York: Random House, 1973) p. 611f.: Marx condemns Adam Smith for conceiving of work only in (capitalist) terms of *Gen.* 3:19 as a "curse," whereas genuine (socialist, redeemed) labor (*felix culpa*) is self-realization, real freedom, "creative activity," and this is similar to, though different and higher than, "the pastoral etc. state, which it has lost."

73. See p. 159 below. I can find no discussion of this chapter or its content by Strauss.

74. If Werner Jaeger's explication of Aristotle's works and development away from Plato is right (and it continues to make good sense to me) (see Monan, *op. cit.*, pp. 42-44, 47, etc.), then one could say that Maimonides traced Aritotle's way back to Plato, whence he came. See *Paideia* (New York, 1944) II, 395,n. 20 for Jaeger's basic agreement with the Marburg School's interpretation of Plato's "ideas."

75. *Republic*, 509; *Timaeus*, 29f.; *Gorgias*, 503e. In *Meno* 88 Plato's virtues are median, but "knowledge" is not susceptible to the middlingness; the end of the *Meno* derives knowledge from the gods', of course, and, therefore, also morality entailed in this knowledge is divine, not median. See Paul Shorey, "The Idea of Good in Plato's *Republic:* A Study in the Logic of Speculative Ethics," in *Studies in Classical Philology* (University of Chicago Press, 1895), I; C. G. Rutenberg, *The Doctrine of the Imitation of God in Plato* (New York: King's Crown Press, 1946). David Novak, *Suicide and Morality* . . . , New York: Scholars Studies Press, 1975, p. 33 argued against God = good in Plato, but he fails to convince me. *Cf.* H.A. Wolfson, "The Knowability and Describability of God in Plato and Aristotle," *Studies in the History and Philosophy of Religion* I Cambridge: Harvard University Press, 1973, pp. 98-114.

76. See "Charakteristik," p. 65ff.; and Shorey, *op. cit.* (The differences in style, culture, and even philosophy between Cohen and his contemporary Shorey only underline the closeness of the conclusions about Plato at which both arrive.) See Paul Natorp, *Platons Ideenlehre* . . . (Leipzig, 1921) p. vi. This is also the philosophical crux for

Emmanuel Levinas, who is aware of his relationship to Cohen: *Totalité et Infini* (Hague: Nijhoff, 1961) pp. 43 *et passim.*

77. For the rational autonomy of ethics in Judaism in general see Louis Jacobs, "The Relationship between Religion and Ethics in Jewish Thought," in *Religion and Morality* (edd. Outka and Reeder; New York: Anchor Books, 1973) p. 155ff.; and *A Jewish Theology* (New York: Behrman House, 1973) pp. 231-42.

78. Cohen, "Charakteristik," p. 85 daringly and convincingly connects Aristotle's societal definition of the good with Hegel's notorious equation of the rational with the actual. See also Pines, *Guide, op. cit.,* p. lxxxviii; and A. MacIntyre, *A Short History of Ethics* (New York, 1966) p. 67f.

79. See p. 138 above.

80. The last of Marx's 1845 "Theses on Feuerbach."

81. "Charakteristik," p. 99; M. Buber, *Two Types of Faith* (London: Routledge and Kegan Paul, 1951) p. 152.

82. See n. 34 above.

82a. I can find no evidence that the philosophic literature has taken cognizance of *R.H.* 25b, where the *gemara* treats *chok* not as an irrational "statute" but simply as the peremptory legal conclusion of the rational, discursive process that leads up to it (*mishpat*).

83. See also "The Laws of Heave-Offerings," end; Y. Heinemann, *Ta'amay Ha-Mitzvot beSifrut Yisrael* (Jerusalem, 1954) I, 81f.; and Baron *op. cit.,* VI, 375, n. 110.

84. Maimonides goes on to cite the example of the sacrificial laws in the Bible as *chukkim.* In the *Guide* he certainly goes to great length to give historical, "rational" grounds for them!

85. W. Kluxen, "Literargeschichtliches zum lateinischen Maimonides," *RThAM* 21 (1954) 23-35, points out that the thirteenth-century Latin translation of the *Guide,* which was the source of its general philosophic influence in the West, was entitled *Dux Neutronum vel Dubiorum* (Paris, 1520; Frankfurt, 1964), that is, the *Guide* was taken to pursue the purpose of leading men away from "neutrality," middlingness.

86. Weiss, *Ethical Teachings,* pp. 107f., 111.

87. *Ibid.,* p. 64f.; Gorfinkle, *op. cit.,* English p. 48f., Hebrew, p. 15.

87a. See "Religion of the Thinkers," p. 44.

88. *Guide* (Chicago, 1963), p. cxxii.

89. Suddenly the Straussian esotericist interpretation of Maimonides is dropped and alleged *verba ipsissima* are taken at facevalue.

89a. See Altmann, "Religion of the Thinkers," pp. 41ff., 145. (Altmann concedes part of the argument to Pines, which to me seems unnecessary.)

90. See M. Fox, "The Guide . . ." (review) *J.H.P.* III/2 (October 1965) 265-74; and his "Prolegomenon," p. xx (although he then goes on to engage in precisely the same esotericism: pp. xli f.); Baron, *op. cit,* VIII, 314f., n. 28; Erwin Rosenthal, "Political Philosophy in Islam and Judaism," *Judaism* XVII/4 (1968) 432; and Hiram Caton, "The Problem of Descartes' Sincerity," *Philosophical Forum* II/3 (Spring 1971) 360 *et passim.*

91. See Samuel Atlas, "Ha'Ormah hamishpatit beTalmud," in *Jubilee Volume in Honor of Louis Ginzburg,* Hebrew Part (1946) pp. 1-24; and "Kol demekaddesh ada'ata derabbanan mekaddesh,"*Sinai* LXXV (Sivvan-Tammuz, 1974) p. 132ff.

92. *Proceedings of the Israel Academy of Science and Humanities,* V/4 (1973).

93. *Ibid.,* p. 19.

94. *Ibid.,* p. 21. In any case, Pines himself admits that the connection between Philoponus and Maimonides is very farfetched.

95. *Op. cit.,* p. xci.

96. *Ibid.*

97. Encyclopaedia of Philosophy (New York: MacMillan, 1967) V and VI, 133.

98. *Ibid.*

99. See p. XX below. Heinemann, *op. cit.,* p. 86ff., just misses the point. He realizes that the concluding chapters of the *Guide* retroactively transform all that precedes them, but he thinks this is a matter of "feeling" *versus* intellectualism. The point is not that rational knowledge *produces* morality, but it *is* morality. See *ibid.,* p. 156, n. 49; J. Guttmann, "The Religious Motifs in Maimonides' Philosophy," in *Religion and Knowledge: Essays and Lectures* [Hebr.] (Jerusalem: Magnes Press, 1955) p. 91. The apologetic and religious purpose which Heinemann wants to serve is intimated in his references to Hermann Cohen: pp. 93, 156, n. 141. The view that the knowledge of God produces, rather than being identical with, the higher morality is a step in the right direction, but it is not sufficient. The better interpreters, including L. Berman and A. Nuriel, "The Divine Will in the *Guide*" (Hebr.), *Tarbiz* 39 (1970) 39-61, for this reason wrongly think that when Maimonides says (*Guide* I/2, end) that God's "intention and wisdom cannot be fully attained" by human beings he was saying that human reason, because of its imprisonment in matter, cannot reach God. His real point is, however, in the context, that man's submission of his reason to the senses transforms rational ethics into conventional morality; reason not so distorted, not "fallen" but rehabilitated through philosophy, should and can "attain to the Lord of the will" [!]. After the present study was already in galley my friend David Hartman's *Maimonides: Torah and Philosophic Quest* (Philadelphia: J.P.S., 1976) reached me. He, too, comes quite close to the conclusions that I am here producing, including his (muted) disagreeemnt with Pines:

see esp. pp. 26, 188f., 191, 198f., 200, 204, 211, 263, n. 48; p. 205: "Maimonides ends the *Guide* exactly as he began his earliest legal work. By distinguishing between morality before and after knowledge of God, Maimonides is expressing a key theme of his philosophy: theoretical knowledge of God affects practice. . . . Knowledge of God . . . is necessary in order . . . to become a person whose actions reflect the principle of *lifnim mishurat hadin.*" Hartman does not see, however, that the moral "will" *is* God (p. 196), and he still concedes too much to Pines in understanding Maimonides' "world-to-come" as supra-ethical (p. 203f.).

100. See Shapiro, *Studies in Jewish Thought*, p. 261.

101. For the contrast between Aristotle's "natural slavery" and Plato's social view of slavery and for a Jewish context, see David Ben-Gurion, "Slavery in Plato's Writings," in *Askolot—Collection of Investigations into and Interpretation of Classical Culture* (Jerusalem: Magnes Press, 1955) II, 1-15. Tracy, *op. cit.*, p.286ff., speaks of Aristotle's "Principle of Natural [!] Subordination." My colleague and friend Robert Barrett proposes that Aristotle's moral virtues function very much like his "natural kinds" in scientific theory. And it is, of course, notorious that social classes are in Aristotle's view precisely this—natural, ineluctable kinds.

102. I. Twersky, *Rabad of Posquière . . .* (Harvard University Press, 1962) p 48; *Lechem Mishneh ad Code,* "Laws of Beliefs," 5:4, etc. The *Tomer Deborah,* p. 32ff., actually has distinct Kabbalistic names for the Jewish *vulgus* and elite respectively: Jacob and Abraham. Unlike the rationalist Maimonides, it does not seem to make any effort to overcome this elitism.

103. See Rawidowicz, *Metsudah,* p. 177f.; and *Hebrew Studies . . .,* p. 461, n. 185.

104. Twersky, "Maimonides' Mishneh Torah," p. 4, n. 16; Heinemann, *op. cit.,* p. 157, n. 152.

105. See Julis Guttmann, *Philosophie des Judentums* (München, 1933) pp. 200-203; L. Berman, *Ibn bajjah . . .*; and A. Hyman, "Maimonides' '13 Principles,'" in A. Altman (ed.), *Jewish Mediaeval and Renaissance Studies* (Cambridge, Massachusetts, 1967) pp. 138-44.

106. Cohen, "Charakteristik," sect. VII, brings Messianism into the ethical question in a significant way. (He does not use the *Treatise on Resurrection.*) This is also true of Weiss, *Ethical Teachings . . .*; and Eliezer Schweid, *'Iyyunim beshmoneh p'rakim* (Jerusalem: Jewish Agency, 1965) p. 28. As far as I can see, none of Cohen's critics (Rawidowicz, Pines, least of all Strauss) pays any attention to this aspect of the matter. The politically wise will understand.

107. Twersky, p. 11.

108. See J. Finkel, "Maimonides' Treatise on Resurrection," in *Essays on Maimonides* (ed. S. Baron; New York, 1941) p. 144f. The question of Maimonides' own attitude

to adventism, is, of course, very complex: see S. Zeitlin, *Maimonides—A Biography* (New York, 1955); A.J. Heschel, "Did Maimonides Believe that he was Worthy of Prophecy?" (Hebrew), in *Jubilee Volume in Honor of L. Ginzburg*, Hebrew Part, p. 159ff.; Twersky, p. 5, etc.

109. The *Treatise* often cross-refers to *Perek Chelek, Code,* and ends with an emphatic cross-reference to the *Guide.*

110. Maimonides here cross-refers to Aristotle and his own *Guide*; see *'Igrot ha-Rambam* (ed. M.D. Rabinowitz; Tel Aviv, 1951) I, 369, 372ff.

111. *Ibid.,* p. 199.

112. *Ibid.,* pp. 359, 363.

113. *Ibid.,* pp. 347, 356.

114. *Ibid.,* pp. 388f., the very end of the *Treatise.*

115. *Ibid.,* pp. 382, 385, although the editor tries to explain this away.

116. See "Noachites," p. 29ff.; and Jacob Katz, "The Vicissitudes of Three Apologetic Passages" (Hebrew), *Zion* XXIII-XXIV/3-4 (1958-1959) 174-81. For Maimonides' Messianic universalism in general, see my "A Note on the Nature of Ideal Society—a Rabbinic Study," this volume, chapter 5.

117. *Treatise,* p. 380f.

118. *Ibid.,* p. 354.

119. *Ibid.,* pp. 351, 364; Rabinowitz, p. 199; Finkel, *op. cit.,* p. 100.

120. *Ibid.,* p. 349.

120a. In *La Conscience Juive* (edd. Lévy-Valensi and Halperin; Paris, 1963) p. 275.

120b. L. Berman, *Ibn Bajjah . . .,* p. 109, rightly uses the word "revolutionary." See also *ibid.,* p. 106ff., that the purpose of the *Guide* is to lead to the best state. "The Torah of Moses is the superior state of Plato's *Laws . . .*" (*ibid.,* pp. 200, xxxv). On p. 188, n. 3, he has a better text for *Guide* III/29: "The intention of the Torah is that all men in that [eschatological] time shall be perfect."

121. See Schwarzschild, "On Power in Judaism," *Worldview* VII/2 (February 1964) 6ff.

122. Maimonides here argues also against the conventional Moslem view of the material paradise (*ibid.,* 8:5). The Rabad (*ad* 8:4), on the other hand, tries to srike a perhaps more conventional middle position by raising the possibility of "spiritual bodies."

123. This is the last chapter and the last laws of the entire "Order Seeds" (one of the six "orders" of *Mishnah and Mishneh Torah*), chapter 13, paragr. 13. Even if one shrinks from Leo Strauss's neokabbalistic numerology, one cannot quite help noting Maimonides' predilection for 13 and for formulating important, basic principles at the very ends of his works and their subsections. (My attention was again drawn to this passage by my friend Rabbi Simcha Krauss.)

124. The Ridbaz makes a point of emphasizing that this entire proposition is Maimonides' "own [personal] ratiocination." See L. Berman, *Ibn Bajjah . . .*, p. 190.

125. "The Image of God . . . ," p. 68; see also M. Lazarus, *Die Ethik des Judentums* (Frankfurt a/M: Kauffmann, 1898) p. 387f.

126. "Charakteristik," p. 132: "Averroes translated Plato's *Republic.* (*Cf.* Munk, *Mélanges,* p. 314.) Did Maimonides read it? Anyway, we would know that their agreement has its roots in their Messianic congeniality." See also Leo Strauss, "Quelques remarques sur la science politique de Maimonide et de Fârâbî," *R.E.J.* C (1936) 4; Ernst Fortin, *History of Political Philosophy,* p. 224ff.; S. Pines, *Encyclopaeda of Philosophy,* p. 133; *Guide,* p. lxxxvi; A. Hymann and J. Walsh, *Philosophy in the Middle Ages, the Christian, Islamic and Jewish Traditions* (New York: Harper & Row, 1967) p. 5; *Mediaeval Political Philosophy,* pp. 16f.; Ernst Bloch, *op. cit.,* p. 206. See R. Klibansky, *The Continuity of the Platonic Tradition During the Middle Ages* (London, 1939).

127. Maimonides here, as in other respects, follows the Platonizing Al-Farabi: see *Mediaeval Political Philosophy,* p. 77 *et passim*; L. V. Berman, *Ibn Bajjah . . .*; "The Political Interpretation . . ." pp. 56f., 60; and "Maimonides, Disciple of Alfarabi," *Israel Oriental Studies,* 4 (1974) 171; and Rosenthal, *op. cit.,* p. 435.

128. When Weiss, *Ethical Teachings . . .*, p. 14 *et passim,* and other disciples of Leo Strauss then identify "the prophetic life" with Aristotelian contemplation, *theoria,* they contradict their own, or Strauss's, correct insight that prophecy is quintessentially a political, that is, a moral function. See Berman, *Ibn Bajjah . . .*, p. 209, n. 66.

129. "The Trascendental Dialectic," Book I, section 1, "The Ideas in General."

130. *Op. cit.,* p. 529.

131. "On Abravanel's Philosophical Tendency and Political Teaching," in *Isaac Abravanel* (edd. Trend and Loewe; Cambridge, 1937).

131[a]. See Schweid, *op. cit.,* pp. 33f.

132. *Ibid.,* pp. 98ff.; "Der Ort der Vorsehunglehre nach der Ansicht Maimunis," *MGWJ,* LXXXI (1937) 104, n. 34; *What is Political Philosophy?* p. 168f.; Berman, "The Political Interpretation . . . ," p. 59, resumes referring to the *Guide* as "the theologico-political treatise." R. Lerner's study of Maimonides' political philosophy (L. Strauss and J. Cropsey, *History of Political Philosophy* [Chicago, 1972]) is altogether too simplistic, when not wrong (esp. p. 220).

133. *Liberalism Ancient and Modern* (New York: Basic Books, 1968) p. 24. (I am indebted to the unpublished dissertation of Stanley Weber, "Leo Strauss on Jerusalem and Athens," MacMaster University, 1975, for bringing together much of the rlevant Strauss material in handy fashion—though I am bound to regard several of its fundamental theses as false.)

134. "Abravanel," 96f.; *Persecution and the Art of Writing* (Glencoe, Illinois: Free Press, 1952) p. 9, etc.; "Fârâbi's *Plato,*" in *Ginzburg Jubilee Volume,* p. 364; "Jerusalem and Athens," *Commentary* (June 1967) 20; etc.

135. Berlin: Schocken, 1935 [!].

136. *Ibid.,* pp. 9, 122. See also his "Preface to the English Translation" of *Spinoza's Critique of Religion* (New York: Schocken, 1965); *What is Political Philosophy?,* p. 17; and my "Franz Rosenzweig's Anecdotes about Hermann Cohen," in *Gegenwart im Rückblick: Festgabe für die Jüdische Gemeinde zu Berlin ...* (Heidelberg: L. Stiehm, 1970), p. 216, n. 13.

137. *Philosophie und Gesetz,* pp. 119-22.

138. *Ibid.,* pp. 5f., 56, 65, etc.; *Die Relgionskritik Spinozas ...* (Berlin: Akademie-Verlag, 1930) p. 142; etc.

139. See above; and *Treatise on Resurrection,* p. 392.

140. See also "The Laws of Substituted Offerings," 4:13.

141. *Guide,* Chicago, p. xliv. By the same token, Cohen did not dissolve Judaism in philosophy but Judaized philosophy.

142. See "Abravanel," p. 109. Correspondingly Strauss cannot like the millenarianism of Abarbanel, which is, however, much more typical of Jewish eschatology than Maimonides'.

Chapter 9

1. Since writing this, I have found this story again in J. Frank, "His Jewish Problem," *New York Review,* December 4, 1980, pp. 43f.

2. *Réflexions sur la question juive,* 1946—*Anti-semite and Jew,* tr. G.J. Becker, (New York, 1948.)

3. Cp. Schwarzschild, "The Tenability of H. Cohen's Construction of the Self," *Journal of the History of Philosophy,* XIII/3 (July 1975), p. 383, n. 109.

4. "Today's Hope: Conversations with Sartre," *Telos,* no. 44 (Summer 1980), pp. 155-180, and "The Last Words of J.-P. Sartre," *Dissent,* (Fall 1980), pp. 397-422. References to the interview, unless otherwise indicated, are here to the *Telos* version.

5. *Telos*, loc. cit., pp. 176-181.

6. Cf. e.g. the special issue of *Les temps modernes, "Le conflit israélo-arabe,"* XXII (Summer 1967), with Sartre's moving foreword (pp. 5-11): he had hoped to put together a balanced and helpful symposium, in which all the sides to the Near Eastern conflict would be represented, but now, May 1967, the pot is threatening to boil over again, —and when the Jewish people is again at stake he has to commit himself. Cp. also *Situations*, X (1976), pp. 221f.

7. *Telos*, loc. cit., p. 205; also "B. Lévy et Sartre," *Libération*, (January 16, 1982), p. 10.

8. In *Situations X*, op. cit., p. 208, Sartre insists, with his usual emphasis on individual autonomy, that, while he's alive, he may change his mind, and, in any case, he wants to interpret himself. After his death his readers may interpret him. That attitude of his may also, at least in part, explain the immense flood of words and deeds that spouted forth from him during his lifetime. Cp. "La grande Morale" (=notes of 1947 for the *Critique of Dialectical Reason*), in *Obliques*, Sartre-issue, (1978), p. 261, no. 68: death is "the impossibility to *correct* one's work and the impression it makes. Purely one proposition. Thus one *delivers oneself to the others* . . ."

9. *Telos*, loc. cit., pp. 176f.

10. Cf. *Obliques*, loc. cit., p. 251, no. 9.

11. Ibid., p. 258, no. 53.

12. Cf. n. 10.

13. Cf. n. 11.

14. Ze'ev Levy, *Spinoza's Interpretation of Judaism—A Concept and its Influence on Jewish Thought* (Hebrew) (Tel Aviv, 1972), chapt. 5, "Sartre's View of the Jewish Question," p. 131, perceptively recognizes this issue. For Hegel, for whom history is nought but the history of states, classical, i.e. exilic, Jewry cannot be historical. Franz Rosenzweig, the great Jewish philosophical theologian of this century, Hegel-disciple, and Heidegger-admirer in 1929, therefore stipulated the extra-historicality of Jewish existence. (Cf. Schwarzschild, "Rosenzweig on Judaism and Christianity," *Conservative Judaism*, (Winter 1956), p. 54: "The Star . . . ," *Thomist*, XXXV/4 (October 1971), pp. 734f.) If, however, historicality is quintessentially social and non-political, perhaps even anti-political, then not only is Jewish diasporic existence (*pace* N.N. Glatzer, *Untersuchungen zur Geschichtslehre der Tannaiten*, (Berlin, 1933)) the very paradigm of historicality but also, as Sartre here says, all of Hegel's philosophy of history has been annihilated in one fell swoop. In that case, on the other hand, the Jewish authenticity of the new state-fetishism of Israel, practiced by most contemporary Jews (including people like Z. Levy and E. Levinas, who are in dialogue with Sartre) must seriously be doubted. (I might add, as an anti-Zionist Jew, that it would be quite disturbing if the anti-Zionism that I advocate were to be put forward by non-Jews, or nonArabs—a bit,

perhaps, as Sartre might have felt about, say, American anti-French attitudinizing at the height of his own pro-Algerian, anti-French activities. Sartre's carefully balanced support of Zionism was, thus, just the right posture for a sensitive man in his position.) The Czech writer Milan Kundera has formulated this point in the following memorable passage (*New York Review of Books*, January 22, 1981, p. 21):

> In Hasek's famous novel, while the successor to the Hapsburg throne is being murdered in Sarajevo, thus starting the First World War, Svejk is at home with Mrs. Muller and tends to his rheumatic legs. "So, they've killed our Ferdinand," she says. Svejk is surprised. "Ferdinand? Really? But which one? The one who used to pick up dog turds? Or that apprentice hairdresser who once drank the hair lotion by mistake?
>
> This is not ignorance or stupidity speaking, it is the refusal to concede History a value, to grant it seriousness. The depth of blasphemy contained in *The Good Soldier Svejk* has never been fully assessed: what is to my mind the greatest comic novel of our century was written on the most cruel subject one could imagine—war.
>
> It is not war that is grotesque in Hasek's novel, but History, that is to say the concept which pretends to rationalize the irrational stupidity of war, pretending to give it sense. European thought formed by Hegel and by Marx conceives of History as being the embodiment of reason, seriousness par excellence. The unserious, the absurd only have a place on the edge of History, or against the background of its seriousness.
>
> *The Good Soldier Svejk* brutally disrupts this order of things and asks a question: what if that rationalization which means to present the chain of events as reasonable were only a mystification? What if history were simply stupid?
>
> At the time that Svejk was wondering whether the murdered Ferdinand was the same fellow who used to pick up dog turds, Kafka wrote in his diary: "Germany has declared war against Russia. Afternoon, swimming pool." He undoubtedly did not experience war as a German did, conscious of belonging to a great nation engaged in the making of history, but as a Jew from Prague, who knew that neither the Jews nor the Czechs were making history, but were submitting to it.
>
> Just as Beckett strips man to his biological essence, Kafka strips history to the bare will for power, which is ahistorical and has no content outside itself.

The notion of Jewish historical exceptionalism, or even uniqueness, is, of course, well-entrenched in Jewish as well as non-Jewish historiography. The special character of Jewish history is obviously central to the Bible, and it remained so until at least modern times. Cf. J.L. Talmon, *The Unique and the Universal*, (New York, 1965), e.g. p.

65: "In Western Christian civilization's vision of history, the Jew occupied ... at least a unique place.... He embodied a great mystery." In Christian culture this Biblical topos, appropriately emended, is equally widespread. In post-Christian culture the names of Isaac LaPeyrère and Giambattista Vico symbolize one way of secularly handling Jewish historical exceptionalism: cf. Richard Popkin, "The Marrano Theology of Isaac La-Peyrère," *Studii Internationali di Philosophia*, V (1973), pp. 105ff.

15. *Telos*, loc. cit., p. 178.

16. Cf. also "B. Lévy et Sartre," in *Libération* (Jan. 16, 1982), p. 12.

17. (Paris, 1981).

18. Ibid. pp. 536-538.

19. Ibid. p. 152.

20. Loc. cit., p. 179. H. Barnes had talked about Sartre's pervasive messianism as early as 1968: cf. T. Busch, "'La Nausee': A Lover's Quarrel with Husserl," *Research in Phenomenology* XI, 1981, pp. 21ff.

21. Cf. my "On Jewish Eschatology," in this volume.

22. Cf. n. 20.

23. Ibid., pp. 180f.

24. Cf. Sartre's original interview, in French, loc. cit., p. 115.

25. Ibid., p. 104.

26. Ibid., p. 115.

27. *On a raison de se révolter* (Paris, 1974).

28. Cf. also Spiegelberg's "Sartre's Last Words on Ethics ...," *Research in Phenomenology*, XI (1981), pp. 90-107.

29. Cp. Marjorie Greene, *Sartre*, (New York, 1973).

30. M. Contat and M. Rybalka, *Les écrits de Sartre* (Paris, 1970), appendix, "Bariona," and Renate Peters, *Obliques*, op. cit., "Bariona entre Brecht et Sartre," pp. 131-137.

31. B. *'Eruvin*, 13b.

32. Cp. *Tanhuma*, "Genesis," paragr. 1, f. 7a; *b. Kidd.*, 39b; cf. Joseph Dan, "Samuel, Lilith, and the Concept of Evil in Early Kabbalah," *AJS Review*, V (Cambridge, 1980), p. 34: "The creation of our world is therefore described as a compromise, a reluctant one, by God." This view is here elaborated in terms of Kabbalah, but it can be much elaborated from throughout Jewish culture.

33. This, like so much else in Sartre as well as the Frankfurt School, is a profoundly Kantian topos; cf. Schwarzschild, "The Tenability . . . ," loc. cit. But neither of them ever fully recognized this, because they did not know Marburg neo-Kantianism and understood Kant only through the distorting lenses of Hegel, the post-Hegelians, and of the conventional school representations of Kant. This is a problem that cries out for full treatment. Cf. below, n. 120.

34. H. Spiegelberg has suggested the possibility that Sartre's interest in the Messianic Kingdom may be a reflection (however unconscious) of his youthful connections with his "uncle," Albert Schweitzer, and the latter's classic treatments of Biblical eschatology. (Schweitzer's wife Helen was the daughter of Harry Bresslau—a Jew, albeit a very Germanic one: cf. *Der Berliner Antisemitismusstreit*, ed. W.B. Gehlich, (Frankfurt, 1965), pp. 52ff.)

35. *Telos*, loc. cit., p. 206. De Beauvoir agrees with Aron: *La cérémonie des adieux* . . . , loc. cit., p. 151.

36. *Situations X*, op. cit., pp. 188f. For Aron on Sartre cf. *History and the Dialectic of Violence*, (New York, 1975), *Marxism and the Existentialists*, (New York, 1969), *Opium of the Intellectuals*, (London, 1957), and R. Neudeck, "Man muss für sich selbst und für die Anderen leben," *Merkur*, no. 379 (December 1979), pp. 1208f.

37. J.-P. Enthoven argued rightly in *Le Nouvel Observateur*, no. 807, April 28-March 4, 1980, "Sartre et Aron, enfin . . . ," p. 111, that Aron could now have said: "you see, I was right," and Sartre ultimately admitted it, but, instead, he preferred to doubt that Sartre ever said what Lévy reports him to have said—so that he, Aron, could go on attacking him. Cf. also William Gass, "Theatrical Sartre," *New York Review of Books*, October 14, 1976, where, failing to understand Sartre, he accuses Sartre, in his own meretricious and baroquely metaphoricist style, of constantly changing his mind.

38. *Telos*, loc. cit., p. 185.

39. Ibid., p. 201. Levinas introduced Sartre to Heidegger: cf. Herbert Spiegelberg, *The Phenomenological Movement—A Historical Introduction*, (Hague, 1965), vol. 2, p. 752, n. 462 (1). For Lévy on Levinas, cf. "B. Lévy et Sartre," loc. cit., p. 11.

40. *Telos*, loc. cit., p. 206.

41. Cf. Neudeck, loc. cit., p. 1213 that the title *Power and Liberty* had been dropped.

42. *Obliques*, op. cit., pp. 265ff.

43. Ibid., p. 280.

44. Ibid., pp. 272f.

45. I happen to believe that the apocalypticism-Messianism distinction is mistaken and that the real demarcation line has to be drawn between Messianism and pseudo-Messianism—but this is another question: cf. "On Jewish Eschatology," loc. cit.

46. *Obliques*, loc. cit., p. 273.

47. Ibid., p. 275.

48. Ibid., p. 279. A more important instance of (virtually Sartrean) Hegelo-Marxist, technically philosophical, Jewish, dualistic protest against secularized trinitarianism is Alexandre Kojève. Cf. his *Kant*, (Paris, 1973), p. 82: "We shall see that effectively Kant's refusal to introduce into his *system* a *third* part, with respect to the Third *Critique*, determines the difference between his system (dualistic, i.e. theist) and the Hegelian system (trinitarian, i.e. atheist);" ibid., p. 65: "Without any doubt, this Kantian 'problem' is one of the many forms of the famous conflict between 'Athens' and 'Jerusalem.'" (Cp. also pp. 9, 36, 50f., 193f. about the [alleged] "Judeo-Christian anthropology".) What makes this so Sartrean—quite apart from their shared Hegelo-Marxism—is that one can trace in Kojève the Kantian genealogy of Sartre's conception of man as "nothing." It is launched when Kojève says (ibid., p. 195): "As Hegel says, not to be (in the sense of 'free') is what man is (as 'necessary' or 'given') and being ('freely') what he is not 'necessarily'." Once this is stipulated, one goes back to Kant's extraordinary categorial table of nothingness (First *Critique*, B348). I have always tended to think of that table as one of Kant's frequent, but universally, ignored, jokes: a schematized nothing! (Cp. the humorous article by P.L. Heath, "Nothing," *Encyclopedia of Philosophy*, Vol. 5, pp. 524f.) By Kojève (and his likes) this joke is taken with deadly (Hegelian-Marxist) dourness; by means of a "violent distortion of Kant" (ibid., pp. 19, 40, 164) "nothing" is here really, and seriously, extended over the table of transcendental categories and thus made to produce persons: ibid., pp. 131ff., 164, 176f., 188, n. 1, 192ff. The whole purpose of this strained exercise is, of course, to bring human freedom back into the phenomenal world (cf. pp. 82, 95, 103, 129, 172)—the quintessentially Hegelian-Marxist project of collapsing transcendence into immanence, which is then (half-rightly) taken to be the "('moral') Judaic anthropology of *liberty* (of negativity) (implicitly atheist) *versus* discursive theism (of identity) of Greek or 'pagan' origin. . . ." (Ibid., p. 51—cp. pp. 33f., 124) (The fact is that also Hermann Cohen [*Kant's Theorie der Erfahrung*, 2nd ed., p. 435] uses the "*nihil privativum*" of Kant's table of categories of nothingness to produce what he calls "intensive magnitude" = the infinitesimal, which lies at the heart of his entire philosophical system, but here the "nothing" is, of course, not in the world but in reason.) (Cp. also M. Greene, op. cit., pp. 205-212 for the role of the Kantian modalities in Sartre.) From Sartre's man as nothing and need one has to go on to E. Levinas' man as "desire" (the Hebrew "*chafetz*": cf. *Totalité et infini* . . . , (Hague, 1961), pp. 3, 21, 34, 88f., 130-142, 191) "desire" as the enjoyment of the "elements" and "disinterested desire"—goodness, which establishes relations.

49. One could show that Marx's *Critique of Hegel's 'Philosophy of Right'* seeks to eliminate Hegel's trinitarianism of metaphysics and to replace it with the dualism of ethics *versus* nature.

50. Loc. cit., pp. 14f.

51. Op. cit., pp. 152-155.

52. Ibid., pp. 54, 85, 98, 118, 126, 140-148, 357f., 470ff. *et al.*

53. Ibid., p. 151.

54. Ibid., pp. 150ff.

55. *Libération*, Jan. 16, 1982, pp. 10ff.

56. "Sartre in Our Time," *Dissent*, loc. cit., p. 429.

57. *Antisemite . . .* , op. cit., p. 69.

58. Ibid., p. 91.

59. Ibid., p. 136.

60. *Telos*, loc. cit., p. 201; cp. Levinas, ib., p. 200.

61. French interview, loc. cit., p. 115.

62. Cp. E. Fackenheim, *Encounters between Judaism and Modern Philosophy—A Preface to Future Jewish Thought*, (New York, 1973), pp. 207f., N. Goldman, *The Jewish Paradox*, (New York, 1978), p. 13, and Harold Rosenberg's "Does the Jew Exist? Sartre's Morality Play about Anti-Semitism," *Commentary*, Vol. 5 (1949), reprinted in A.A. Cohen, *Arguments and Doctrines . . .* , (New York, 1970), pp. 3-23. (This was a very penetrating article, much of whose criticism of Sartre Sartre was later to accept. At the time it caused a break between Rosenberg and his friends on the *Partisan Review*. It also makes the point that in the Jew, Sartre really describes himself [though "I'm not suggesting that he is secretly a Jew" (p. 22),] a point which the present study emphasizes and which B. Lévy ["B. Lévy et Sartre," loc. cit., p. 11] also makes.)

63. Cf. b. *Yebamot*, 61a, *R. Numbers*, 5:3 and parallels; cp. L. Ginzberg, *The Legends of the Jews*, (Philadelphia, 1945), vol. V, pp. 66ff., nn. 6, 8, and p. 178, n. 28; N.M. Bronsnick, "Ye are called Adam" (Hebr.), *Or HaMizrach*, XXVII/1 (October, 1978), pp. 62-71; A'd'm'=A'braham, D'avid, M'essiah (Scholem, *Encyclopedia Judaica*, vol. 6, col. 881); cp. also the Maharal's "*l'homme-Israël* [A. Neher, *Les Puits de l'Exil*, (Paris, 1966), p. 87] and S.R. Hirsch's "*Yisroelmensch*."

64. *Portrait of an Anti-semite* thus still strictly continues the line which Sartre had taken in "Childhood of a Leader." That essay was written in 1938/39 but published as late as 1947 in *Revue Juive de Genève*: proassimilationist but anti- antisemitic.

65. Cp. J.L. Borges, "Dr. Americo Castro is Alarmed," in *Other Inquisitions . . .* , (Austin, 1964), p. 26: "The word *problem* may be an insidious *petitio principii*. To speak of the *Jewish problem* is to postulate that the Jews are a problem; it is to predict (and recommend) persecution, plunder, shooting, beheading, rape, and the teaching of Dr. Rosenberg's prose. Another disadvantage of fallacious problems is that they bring about solutions that are equally fallacious."

66. The North-African French-Jewish intellectual Albert Memmi did the same thing from the Jewish side: *Portrait of a Jew,* (Paris, 1962), for which another Arab-Jewish intellectual, Elie Kedouri, attacks him vehemently: *Arabic Political Memoirs and other Studies,* (London, 1974). Cp. N. Rejwan, "E. Kedouri and Modern Islam," *Midstream* October, 1982, pp. 51-54.

67. *Telos,* loc. cit., pp. 176f.

68. Ibid., p. 177, Trigano, ibid., p. 201, and F. Stern *Gold and Iron—Bismarck, Bleichröder . . . ,* (New York, 1977), p. 469. Such "defensive Jews" (cf. Gerald N. Izenberg, *The Existentialist Critique of Freud . . . ,* (Princeton, 1976), pp. 312-318), what the Germans called "Trotzjuden," i.e., alienated Jews who refuse baptism out of a sense of "honor" toward their disadvantaged brethren (cf. Peter Loewenberg, "Walther Rathenau and Henry Kissinger . . . ," *Leo Baeck Memorial Lecture,* no. 24 (New York, 1980), pp. 7f.), can be illustrated in France in such persons as H. Bergson, Simone Weil, and even after World War II Jean Améry, "On the Necessity and Impossibility of being a Jew," *New German Critique,* no. 20 (Spring-Summer, 1980), pp. 15-20 (=*At the Mind's Limits—Contemplations by a Survivor of Auschwitz and its Realities,* (Bloomington, 1980) (Améry accepted Sartre's early, negative definition of the Jew: pp. 86, 94, 98, and, unlike Sartre himself, never went beyond it; this was Améry's tragedy), in Germany Günther Anders (!), "Anti-semitism without Jews," in *Mein Judentum,* ed. J.-H. Schultz, (Stuttgart, 1978), pp. 60f.

69. Salo Baron's *Social and Religious History of the Jews,* (New York, 1952ff.) as yet uncompleted, is in its eighteenth volume: *Histoire d'Israel. Vie sociale et religieuse,* vols. 1-5 (Paris, 1956-64). It is, in any case, passing strange that Baron's *History* should have made such an impact on Sartre (and Lévy). To be sure, it is generally regarded as the standard history of our time, a legitimate successor to Heinrich Graetz's standard-work of the last century—whatever criticisms one might wish to level at it (cf. the review by J. Neusner, *Judaism,* XV/1 (Winter, 1966), pp. 120ff.), but for Sartre's present purposes (i.e. to learn that Jews have long had a positive internal culture of their own) surely any of the numerous conventional Jewish histories would have sufficed. Why then just Baron? The answer might well be: why not? I.e. Sartre (and Lévy) ran across it more or less by accident. Either way, an historical analogy can here serve: Moses Hess, Karl Marx's erstwhile companion and teacher, had close relations in later life with Graetz and, indeed, translated Graetz's first volume into French. (*Sinai et Golgotha ou les origines du Judaisme et du Christianisme . . . ,* par H. Graetz, traduit et mis en ordre par Maurice Hess, (Paris, 1867)); E. Silberner, *M. Hess—Geschichte seines Lebens,* (Leiden, 1966), pp. 635, 642; "H. Graetz's Briefe an M. Hess," *Annali dell' Instituto Giangiacomo Felbrinelli,* (1961), pp. 326-400; *Western Socialism and the Jewish Question* [Hebrew], (Jerusalem, 1955), pp. 202-216; "M. Hess als Begründer und Redakteur der Rheinischen Zeitung," *Archiv für Sozialgeschichte,* IV (Hanover, 1964); R. Michael, "Graetz und Hess," *Leo Baeck Institute Year Book,* IX [new York, 1964].) This was organically related to Hess's Zionist program as expounded in his *Rome and Jerusalem,* (Leipzig, 1862), the first great proto-Zionist book. One might then, as a question, for-

mulate this equation: Graetz: Hess (<Marx) = Baron: Sartre (<Marx)? Putting it like this, several features are revealed: 1) the only non-Jew in the equation is Sartre; 2) Marx is what Hess and Sartre have in common in their receptiveness to Jewish history; 3) all five are, of course, different from one another, and their differential relations among one another would deserve analysis; 4) Hess and Sartre had long since encountered Marx when they experienced their respective Jewish historian's influence; 5) the line in modern intellectual history goes from Spinoza to Hegel and from both of these to Marx, Hess, and to Sartre: in this line the non-Jews are Hegel and Sartre. Z. Levy, op. cit., p. 122 rightly draws attention to the parallelism between Marx's famous/notorious "On the Jewish Question" and Sartre's "Reflections . . ."—In view of the nature of the subject under discussion, it is perhaps useful to compile an initial bibliography of Hebrew studies of Sartre: J.-P. Sartre, *Selected Writings*, 2 vols. (Hebrew), ed. M. Brinker, (Tel Aviv, 1972). Y. Yovel, "Lucidity and Synthesis in Sartre's Philosophy," (Hebrew), *Iyyun*, XXIII/2-3 (April-October, 1972). (*Iyyun*, the Israeli philosophical quarterly, has English synopses of its articles.) Levy, op. cit. Michael Sukale, "The Ego and Consciousness in Rival Perspectives. A Study of Husserl and the early Sartre" (Hebrew), *Iyyun*, XXII/4 (October, 1971). Ora Segal, "Freedom and Necessity in Sartre's Philosophy" (Hebrew), *Iyyun*, XVI/1-2 (January-April 1965). Tzvi Magen, "Sartre and the Jewish Question" (Hebrew), *Kivvunim*, 2 (February 1979) (Austrian Chancellor Kreisky as the embodiment of Sartre's inauthentic Jew). J.-P. Sartre, *Reflections on the Jewish Question* (Hebrew), tr. and epilogue by M. Brinker, (Tel Aviv, 1978). Martin Buber, *Eclipse of God*, (New York, 1952), pp. 87-94 (straight Buber), cp. the ecstatic W.B. Goldstein, *J.-P. Sartre und M. Buber* (Jerusalem, 1965).

70. Sartre's interview in French, loc. cit., p. 134.

71. *Being and Nothingness—An Essay on Phenomenological Ontology*, tr. H. Barnes, (New York, 1966), chapter "Bad Faith," the example of the homosexual.

72. *New Outlook*, (December 1976), p. 13. For his refusal of the Nobel Prize cf. *Le Monde*, Oct. 24, 1964; Contat and Rybalka, *The Writings of J.-P. Sartre*, I, pp. 451-454. Cp. also de Beauvoir, op. cit., pp. 318-322.

73. Cf. Neudeck, loc. cit., p. 1219: "I was always a partisan of both positions—of the Jews and of the Palestinians . . ." Before 1948 Sartre came to the support of M. Begin's wing of Zionism—in 1966 he said: "We are living the Arab-Jewish struggle within ourselves"—he travelled to Israel just before the 1967-War—after 1970 he sympathized increasingly with the Arab side—and his last trip outside France took place in 1979, to Israel.

74. *Telos*, loc. cit., p. 177.

75. On Sartre's relationship to Husserl and Heidegger, cf. Spiegelberg, loc. cit., pp. 458-463, Greene, op. cit., chapt. 3, and Neudeck, loc. cit., p. 1212: Sartre read Heidegger for the first time while in a P.O.W. camp but later drastically changed his initially indulgent attitude toward him.

76. *The Transcendence of the Ego—An Existentialist Theory of Consciousness*, tr. F. Williams and R. Kirkpatrick (New York, 1957). The original appeared in 1936/37. Cp. Schwarzschild, "The Tenability . . . ," loc. cit.

77. *Critique de la raison dialectique*, p. 173: *"le tout est la déchirure du tout;" Being and Nothingness*, p. 94: "fissure in being" p. 96: "This hole of being;" cf. Wilfrid Desan, *The Marxism of J.-P. Sartre*, (New York, 1966), p. 84.

78. *Etre . . .* , op. cit., p. 349; *Being and Nothingness*, op. cit., p. 289. (Is "fallen into the world" the secularized form of "the Fall"? Cf. *Being and Nothingness*, op. cit., p. 627.)

79. I take it that Sartre's condemnation of Flaubert in *The Family Idiot* boils down to the argument that Flaubert accepted himself only as what others regarded him as being and that, therefore, he was the totally determined, unfree man, without a future because without autonomous *praxis*. M. Greene, in *Sartre*, last chapt., expresses her expectation that after *The Family Idiot* something really new would come from Sartre; she expected the wrong thing—we know now that the Lévy interviews were in the offing.

80. *Transcendence . . .* , op. cit., p. 93; *Being and Nothingness*, pp. 97, 101.

81. Cf. Gerold Prauss, *Erkennen und Handeln in Heideggers 'Sein und Zeit'*, (Freiburg/Munich, 1977), pp. 46, 95, 101; Hans Ebeling, "Die Bedeutung der praktischen Selbstbeziehung in der neueren Heidegger-Kritik," *Philosophische Rundschau*, XXVI/1-2 (1979), p. 141; Luk Baukaert, "Ontology and Ethics: Reflections on Levinas' Critique of Heidegger," *International Philosophical Quarterly*, X (September, 1970); Steven Gans, "Ethics or Ontology: Levinas and Heidegger," *Philosophy Today*, XVI (Summer 1972).

82. *Being and Nothingness*, op. cit., pp. 101ff., 116.

83. Op. cit., p. 468; cp. Klaus Hartmann, *Grundzuege der Ontologie Sartres in ihrem Verhaeltnis zu Hegels Logik—eine Untersuchung zu 'L'être et le Néant*, (Berlin, 1963), p. 30, n. 91: "It is only reasonable that the ideological paths of Sartre and Heidegger have to be completely different, for Sartre finite-absolute freedom, for Heidegger 'obedience to Being.' " Cf. also Karl Barth, *Kristlische Dogmatik*, III/3, 1950, paragr. 50 (= "Gott und das Nichtige," in *Heidegger und die Theologie—Beginn und Fortgang der Diskussian*, ed. G. Noller [Theologische Bücherei, vol. 38,] (Munich, 1967), pp. 197-225), p. 208: "Sartre ist—etwas summarisch ausgedrückt—im Gegensatz zu dem in Tiefsinn verharrenden Deutschen Martin Heigegger—der Typus des ewigen französischen *débrouillard* . . ."; p. 217: Sartre has the nothing behind him (i.e. he overcomes it), while Heidegger has it in front of him (i.e. this is where he has to end up). Cf. also François Bondy, "The Question of Heidegger in France," *Merkur*, pp. 189-192, and Pierre Bourdin, *L'ontologie politique de M. Heidegger*.

84. *Being and Nothingness*, op. cit., pp. 290, 319.

85. Ibid., p. 291.

86. Ibid., pp. 93, 297, 312, 331, 626. Francis Jeanson, *Sartre and the Problem of Morality*, (Bloomington, 1980), pp. XII f.: "He who looks at me must be free, so that I, looked at, can be free."

87. Cf. C.D. Tenney, "Aesthetics in the Philosophy of J.-P. Sartre," in *The Philosophy of J.-P. Sartre*, ed. P.A. Schilpp, (La Salle, [ILL.], 1981), pp. 112-138, a superb exposition but, unfortunately, a bad critique.

88. *Being and Nothingness*, pp. 322, 354; *Critique* . . . , op. cit., p. 192.

89. Ibid., pp. 105, 111f.

90. Cp. Desant, op. cit., p. 255; *The Problem of Method*, tr. H. Barnes, (London, 1963), intro., p. xxv.

91. *Telos*, loc. cit., p. 158.

92. *Telos*, loc. cit., pp. 162f., 171f.

93. Cf. Schwarzschild, "The Democratic Socialism of H. Cohen," *H.U.C.A.*, XXVII (1956), p. 421.

94. Cf. Schwarzschild, "Adorno and Schoenberg," forthcoming. There are other important connections here, as usual. Moses Hess, too, called himself "a Spinoza disciple" when he published him *The Holy History of Mankind*, (Stuttgart, 1837), but he, too, ended up contradicting Spinoza on the glories of Jewish culture. (Cp. n. 69 above and Silberner, *M. Hess* . . . , op. cit., pp. 332f., Horst Stuck, *Philosophie der Tat*, (Stuttgart, 1963), pp. 202-206; Th. Zlocisti, *M. Hess*, (Berlin, 1921), vol. I, pp. 51, 53f., 57, 137) Adorno, also, declared in *The Authoritarian Personality*, (New York, 1950), last chapter, that "anti-semitism has nothing essential to do with the Jew," although at least his lifelong associate Horkheimer revised his estimate of Judaism in a fundamental, positive direction at the end of his life: cf. *Die Sehnsucht nach dem ganz Anderen*, ed. H. Gumnior, (1975), and *Porträts deutsch-jüdischer Geistesgeschichte*, ed. Thilo Koch, (Cologne, 1962), pp. 255-272.

95. *Telos*, loc. cit., p. 170. In 1976 he still defended the *Critique* . . . *: cf. Situations X*, op. cit., p. 153.

96. *Problem of Method*, op. cit., p. 49.

97. Ibid., p. 83.

98. Ibid., p. 176.

99. Op. cit., pp. 123, 132ff., 140.

100. Ibid., pp. 134f. De Beauvoir (op. cit., p. 495) seems to be saying the same thing.

101. In "Sartre's Turning Point: The Abandoned *Critique de la Raison Dialectique*, Volume Two," in Schilpp, op. cit., pp. 696ff. Here, too, it seems, anti-semitism (this time in its Soviet-Russian form) is a central consideration for Sartre.

102. *L'être et le Néant,* op. cit., p. 647. Ora Segal, loc. cit., therefore, argues that there is, anyway, an irresolvable self-contradiction in the notion of the freedom to perform unfeasible necessities. Basically, Segal does not understand the difference between a self-contradiction and a paradox.

103. *L'être* . . . , op. cit., p. 614; cp. ib., pp. 641f.; *Being and Nothingness,* op. cit., pp. 649f.

104. *L'être* . . . , op cit., p. 642.

105. Ibid., pp. 644f.

106. Ibid., pp. 293ff. Cp. Werner Becker, *Idealistische und materialistische Dialektik—das Verhältnis von 'Herrschaft' und 'Knechtschaft' bei Hegel und Marx,* (Stuttgart, 1970).

107. Ibid., p. 647.

108. *Reflections* . . . , op. cit., p. 78. Cp. Améry, op. cit., p. 88 for another prisoner in Auschwitz who demonstrated the same understanding and O. Mandel, "Being and Judaism," *Georgia Review* XXXVI/3, Fall 1982, pp. 557-585.

109. There have also always been Jewish temptations to racism. The classical case is. R. Yehuda HaLevy: cf. C. Dover, "The Racial Philosophy of Y. HaLevy," *Phylon—The Atlanta University Review of Race and Culture,* XIII/4 (December, 1952), pp. 312-322.

110. L. Abel, in "Sartre and Metaphysical Stalinism," *Dissent,* (Spring 1961), pp. 145f., parallels Joyce's Bloom taking his cuckhold's place in bed next to his wife. Cp. also W. MacBride, "Sartre and Lived Experience," *Research in Phenomenology* VI, *op. cit.,* pp. 84-88.

111. *Critique* . . . , op cit., pp. 317-321. Cp. Anderson, op. cit., chapt. 5.

112. Ibid., p. 329.

113. Ibid., pp. 620-623.

114. Ibid., pp. 625-627.

115. Ibid., p. 325.

116. Ibid., p. 622.

117. Ibid., p. 627.

118. Ibid., pp. 629f. Cp. also the soft revision here of his earlier views on the invasion of Hungary by the U.S.S.R., p. 485, and his *The Ghost of Stalin,* (New York, 1968). The internal discussions among party-loyal Marxists at the time are, as always, intellectually and morally atrocious. Cf., e.g., Adam Schaff, *Marx oder Sartre? Versuch einer Philosophie des Menschen* (Frankfurt o/M, 1966) (the second edition of the Polish

original appeared in 1962) (= "Marxism and Existentialism," *Monthly Review*, XIV (May-June 1962), and "Individual Determinants of Happiness," *Polish Perspectives*, (V/2 [February 1962].) Though Schaff participated in the Gomulka "thaw" at the time, and himself a Jew, he attacks Sartre on simplistic party lines and, in the process, engages in Jewish anti-semitism (cf. pp. 26f., 32f.). Schaff is a perfect example of someone who, as one says in Hebrew, "skips on two threshholds," i.e. tries to play both sides against the middle. One hopes that the current Polish workers' movement, with its admirable courage and intelligence, will have a better fate. Toward that end it may have to keep its distance from so-called "intellectuals," both in the church and in the party.

119. *Situations III*, (Paris, 1946), pp. 133-225, esp. pp. 177-179 (= *Politics*, July-August 1947), pp. 161-172).

120. Cp. n. 33 above. Also Cf. K. Barth, op. cit., p. 211; Jeanson, op. cit., p. XIV: "Morality of revolution, in the sense that there is a revolution in Descartes and Kant, and an evolution in Leibniz" ibid., p. 22, n. 4.

121. *Existentialism*, (New York, 1947), pp. 21f. Cp. Neudeck, loc. cit., p. 1221: "One must realize oneself by giving oneself to others."

122. Cf. Jeanson, op. cit., pp. XVI, 265, 268.

123. "La grande Morale," loc. cit., p. 261, no. 68.

124. Ibid., p. 262 (though there is here still some Bolshevik exceptionalism in favor of revolutionary violence).

125. Jeanson, op. cit., p. XV; ibid., p. XVII: "Definition du proletariat," in *Lignes de depart*, (Paris, 1963), p. 134: "The task of the proletariat is not in history; it is to effect the conversion of history."

126. Cf. Jeanson, op. cit., pp. XXVI, 35, ibid., p. 214: *"To exist is to be a problem for oneself;"* ibid., p. 268: "unconditional morality is the obligation to invent humanity."

127. It may be noted that the "Introduction" to *Being and Nothingness*, "The Pursuit of Being," "I, the Phenomenon," says that it wishes to be an argument against Kant and is in fact precisely H. Cohen's neo-Kantian reading of Kant—e.g. the noumenon as an infinite series, the use of Poincaré etc. (It might be worth investigating how much Kant, and what kind of Kant, Sartre learned as a student from his [Jewish] professor, Brunswick.) Cf. also J. Vuillemin, "La dialectique negative dans la connaissance et l'existence [Note sur l'épistemologie et la métaphysique de Nikolai Hartmann et J.-P. Sartre"], *Dialectica*, 4 (1950), pp. 21-42.

128. Cf. C.H. Peters, "I. Kant on Hope," Washington University Ph.D. dissertation, Dec. 1975; also Jeanson, op. cit., p. 22, n. 4.

129. *Situations X*, op. cit., pp. 182ff.; *The Ghost of Stalin*, (New York, 1968).

130. A Lieben, (Paris, 1970).

131. Cf. n. 41 above.

132. Op. cit., pp. 12-38.

133. Op. cit., pp. 504, 531.

134. *The Truants–Adventures among the Intellectuals*, (New York, 1982), p. 120.

135. *Human–All Too Human*, preface.

136. Jeanson, op. cit., p. 264.

137. Schilpp, op. cit., p. 12.

138. Op. cit., p. 35.

139. Jeanson, op. cit., p. X; cp. also p. XXV.

140. Ibid., pp. 13ff. and T. Busch, loc. cit., p. 21f.

141. Ibid., p. 265; cp. also pp. 261, 269f. Anderson, op. cit., e.g., p. VIII makes the same assertion.

142. Op. cit., pp. 40f.

143. Ibid., pp. 181f.

144. Cf. Schwarzschild, "Karl Marx's Jewish Theory of Usury," *Gesher* (Yeshiva University, New York, 1978), pp. 7-40.

145. *Existentialism*, op. cit., p. 26: *"Il est très gênant que Dieu n'existe pas."*

146. *Etre et Néant*, op. cit., p. 654; *Existentialism is Humanism*, op. cit., pp. 33f.

147. "La grande Morale," loc. cit., p. 255, no. 36. Cp. H. Barnes on Sartre's religious concerns in her introduction to *Being and Nothingness*, op. cit., pp. XXXIV-XLIII.

148. *Telos*, loc. cit., p. 125, and "B. Lévy et Sartre," loc. cit., p. 10.

149. *L'être* ..., op. cit., p. 183.

150. *Telos*, loc. cit., pp. 196f.

151. Ibid., p. 206.

152. *L'être* ..., op. cit., pp. 130, 136. (Cp. his pervasive use of the moon metaphor [de Beauvoir, op. cit., pp. 308-310] and his *femme lunaire" [ib., pp. 334f., 380, et al.]* [*Cp.* Schwarzschild, "Adorno on Schoenberg," forthcoming.] Cp. b. *Hullin* 60b and the Jewish liturgy of the Blessing of the New Moon: "May it be Thy will, o God ... to complete the sickle of the moon, without any subtraction...."

153. *Religion of Reason out of the Sources of Judaism*, tr. Simon Kaplan, (New York, 1972), p. 251; cp. H. Cohen, *Ethik des reinen Willens*, (reprinted: Hildesheim and New York, 1980), intro. Schwarzschild, n. 21.

154. Op. cit., p. 153.

155. (Paris, 1946).

156. Ibid., p. 33.

157. Ibid., p. 50.

158. Cf. Jeanson, op. cit., pp. 257f.

159. Barth, loc. cit., pp. 257f.

160. Op. cit., pp. 551-559.

161. Ibid., p. 558.

162. Ibid., p. 551.

163. Cf. Jeanson, op. cit., pp. 206, 208.

164. Schilpp, op. cit., p. 39.

165. (Lawrence [Kansas], 1979), e.g. p. 29.

166. Ibid., p. 59.

167. Cf. K. Barth, op. cit., p. 213.

168. *Hagigah* 1:7.

169. *Being and Nothingness*, op. cit., end.

170. Op. cit., p. 120 *et al.*

171. Ibid., pp. 29, 37.

172. *Ethics*, 1973, pp. 16, 23.

173. *Principles and Persons*, (Baltimore, 1970), p. 203, as quoted by Anderson, op. cit., p. 157, n. 21.

174. Cf. above, p. 56.

Chapter 10

1. Cf. e.g., the reports on the Buber Conference at Ben Gurion University, Beer-Sheba, Israel, in *Ha'aretz*, 9th January 1978, 'Buber's Living Teachings'; *New Outlook*, February-March 1978, pp. 55-62; *Allgemeine Jüdische Wochenzeitung*, Düsseldorf, XXXIII, No. 5 (20th January 1978), p. 5; XXXIII, No. 9 (3rd March 1978), p. 9; etc. (This policy of using Buber for Israeli political purposes contrary to his own has a long prehistory: cf. A. Ernst Simon, 'Religion und Staat in Israel', in *Religion und Politik in*

der Gesellschaft des 20. Jahrhunderts, eds. Talmon and Siefer, Bonn 1978, p. 151: Ben-Gurion "wanted to make use, as far as possible, of the worldwide fame of his opponent [Buber] for the prestige of the state".) The work of this conference has now been published: Haim Gordon and Jochanan Bloch (eds.), *Martin Buber–A Centenary Volume*, New York 1984. The central figure in the controversy about the omission of socio-political subjects at the Beer-Sheba Conference was Professor Bloch of Ben Gurion University. To see part of the involved personal relations that entered into that controversy, cf. his *Die Aporie des Du. Probleme der Dialogik Martin Bubers*, Heidelberg 1977, p. 317.

2. Cf. Schwarzschild, 'Martin Buber. Jewish Education as Spiritual Resistance,' *St. Louis Jewish Light*, 2nd August 1978, p. 16A.

3. Cf. *Paths in Utopia*, Boston 1958, chapter 6. For an example of Buber's influence on the formation of Jewish anarchistic Socialism cf. Arie Wolf, 'Arnold Zweigs Ostjudenbild', in *Bulletin des Leo Baeck Instituts*, 67 (1984), p. 25, and comp. Maurice Friedman, *Martin Buber's Life and Work*, vol. III, New York 1983, p. 24.

4. Martin Buber and Judah L. Magnes, *Two Letters to Gandhi*, Jerusalem 1939. Buber had long seriously wrestled with Gandhi's role and views: cf. e.g., 'Gandhi, die Politik und Wir', in *Die Kreatur*, III, No. 4 (1930).

5. Cf. e.g., *Towards Union in Palestine. Essays on Zionism and Jewish-Arab Cooperation*, eds. M. Buber, E. Simon, Jerusalem 1947.

6. Jakob Taubes's article, 'Martin Buber und die Geschichtsphilosophie', in Paul A. Schilpp and Maurice Friedman, *Martin Buber*, Stuttgart 1963, pp. 398ff., revolves around a confrontation of Buber and this Hegelian dictum. Taubes curiously identifies St. Paul with Hegel on this score. (Cf. Kierkegaard's reply to Hegel that only before God, not for men, is world-history world-judgment: S. Crites, *In the Twilight of Christendom. Hegel versus Kierkegaard on Faith and History*, American Academy of Religion, 1972, p. 61)

7. *Israel and the World*, New York 1948, 'Biblical Leadership', p. 133. Comp. also Hannah Ahrendt, *Lectures on Kant's Political Philosophy*, Chicago 1982, appendix by Ronald Beiner, p. 127.

8. Schilpp, *op. cit.*, 'Bubers politische Philosophie', pp. 389f.; 'Gandhi, die Politik und Wir', *loc. cit.*, p. 333; cf. also *ibid.*, pp. 334, 341 *et passim*.

9. *The Prophetic Faith*, New York 1949, p. 224; cf. the whole passage pp. 222-230. Cf. also 'Die Forderung des Geistes und die geschichtliche Wirklichkeit' (his inaugural lecture at the Hebrew University, 1938), where, speaking of *Isaiah* 6, he says (*Werke*, vol. I, Heidelberg 1962, p. 1065): "Der Träger des Geistes erfährt hier am Anfang seines Weges, dass er scheitern muss . . . Das Scheitern gehört zu dem Weg, den er zu gehen hat."

10. This is thus—all proportions and differences guarded—the question that Gershom Scholem raised on Buber's 75th birthday (cf. A. Ernst Simon, *The Line of*

Demarcation. Nationalism, Zionism, and the Jewish-Arab Conflict in Martin Buber's Thought and Work, (in Hebrew) Giv'at Havivah/Israel, Center for Arab Studies, 1973, pp. 40f.), why "ultimately it may be thought that perhaps also Buber is to be counted among those toward whom the poet's blessing turns: 'Blessed are those who sow and reap not'". As Simon adds (cf. also his 'Scholem und Buber', *Neue Zürcher Zeitung*, 11th June 1967, sect. iv), the poet referred to is Abraham ben Isaac Sonne. Buber, in his reply to Scholem, finished the line: "Blessed are those who sow and reap not, for they have a long way to go."

11. Husserl is reported to have exclaimed in 1920: "Buber, das ist doch eine Legende!" See Hans Lamm, 'Bubers Standort im Geistesleben des 20. Jahrhunderts', *Allgemeine Jüdische Wochenzeitung*, XXXIII, No. 5 (3rd February 1978), p. 5. For Buber's view of Husserl cf. *Das Problem des Menschen*, Heidelberg 1948, pp. 85-88. He calls Husserl "a Jew of German culture". (*Ibid.*, p. 85) Here the entire complicated, triadic relationships between Husserl, Buber, and Emmanuel Levinas would have to be disentangled. Cf. A. Tallon, 'Intentionality, Intersubjectivity, and the Between. Buber and Levinas on Affectivity and the Dialogical Principle', *Thought*, [Fordham University Quarterly], September 1978, Martin Buber Commemorative Issue, pp. 293ff.

12. Tallon, *Loc. cit.*, p. 296.

13. Buber's first literary project was to translate Nietzsche's *Thus Spake Zarathustra* into Polish, in 1895. The project was not carried out. (David Biale, *Gershom Scholem. Kabbalah and Counter-History*, Cambridge, Mass. 1979, p. 43 and Friedman, *Martin Buber's Life and Work*, vol. I, *op. cit.*, pp. 29ff., 40, 137f., 325, etc.) Cf. also Baruch Kurzweil, 'The Influence of "Lebensphilosophie" on Hebrew Literature at the Beginning of the 20th Century', in *Our New Literature. Continuity or Revolution?*, Jerusalem 1971 (in Hebrew), pp. 225-270, and *Facing the Spiritual Perplexity of Our Time* (in Hebrew), ed. Moshe Schwarcz, Ramat Gan, Bar Ilan University, 1976, p. 108: "Without taking into account the factor of German culture from the beginning of twentieth-century philosophy: *Lebensphilosophie*, Dilthey, the Stefan George circle, Heidegger, the investigatiors of mythology and myth—not to speak of German poetry—, one cannot understand Buber's place at all ..." Buber discusses his beginnings in "Lebensphilosophie" in Schilpp *op. cit.*, 'Antwort', p. 601. Cf. also Nathan Rotenstreich, in *Martin Buber. A Centenary Volume, op. cit.*, p. 474. As late as in *Prophetic Faith* he still speaks of Israel's "pre-Sinaitic soul". (Cf. Will Herberg, *The Writings of Martin Buber*, Meridian Books, 1965, p. 254.) When Scholem argues that Buber's famous break between his earlier mysticism and his later dialogicism really only amounts to verbal flimflam, even Ernst Simon largely concedes the point: *The Line of Demarcation, op. cit.*, p. 49, and 'Scholem and Buber', *loc. cit.*, sect. 1; indeed, he puns eruditely: "It follows that if this be Torah, then, as is the exegetical rule for the Torah, there is no temporal sequence here." (*Ibid.*, p. 48; cf. also Friedman, *Martin Buber's Life and Work*. vol. I, *op. cit.*, pp. 93, 301, *et. al.*) The overwhelming impression one derives from Paul R. Flohr's, 'The Road to *I and Thou*. An Inquiry into Buber's Transition from Mysticism to Dialogue', in *Texts and Responses ... to Nahum N. Glatzer*, eds. M. Fishbane and P.R. Flohr, Leiden

1975, pp. 201-225, is that, directly contrary to the author's own thesis, all the armamentarium of Buber's "dialogicism" is completely taken over from his mysticism. In any case, the distinction between the two, which is standard practice among Buberians, depends on definitions that are not beyond dispute.

14. *Volker/Staaten und Zion. Ein Brief an Hermann Cohen und Bemerkungen zu seiner Antwort*, Berlin-Vienna 1917.

15. 'The Love of God and the Idea of Deity', in *Israel and the World*, New York 1948 and in *The Eclipse of God*, New York 1952. For the relationship between Hermann Cohen and Buber cf. Further Rivka Horwitz, *Buber's Way to 'I and Thou,'* . . . , Heidelberg 1978, pp. 166-170, 254ff.; Biale, *op. cit.*, pp. 80f., 109ff., 151, 186, 203; and Friedman (who totally misses it), *Martin Buber's Life and Work, op. cit.*, vol. I, pp. 205, 215-219, 399, vol. II, p. 149, his indexed references to Paul Natorp, *et al.* T. Weiss-Rosmarin, *Sh'ma* 4, No. 68 (22nd February 1974), pp. 61f. rightly says: "Buber repressed what Cohen had taught." This is even true of the very "I-thou" nomenclature that made Buber famous: cf. Hermann Cohen, among other places, 'Charakteristik der Ethik Maimunis', in *Moses ben Maimon. Sein Leben, sein Werk und sein Einfluss*, eds. W. Bacher, *et. al.*, Leipzig 1908, vol. I, p. 120: "For this self there is no I without thou. *Re'a* is what the other is called; he is like thou; *he is the thou to the I.* (Cohen's itals.) The self is the result of the eternal relationship between I and thou—the infinite ideal of this relationship . . ."

16. Cf. Eliezer Berkovits, *Major Themes in Modern Philosophies of Judaism*, New York 1974, pp. 84ff. says that Buber "testifies" rather than argues; cf. also Schwarzschild, *Judaism*, VII, No. 3 (Summer 1958), p. 282 (review of Arthur A. Cohen, *Martin Buber*, London 1957), and Friedman, *Martin Buber's Life and Work*, vol. I, *op. cit.*, p. 226. Comp. also notes 21 and 24 below.

17. His first book was *Jüdische Künstler*, Berlin 1903—part of his earlier philosophico-ethnic view that a "people's soul" ("Volksseele") expresses itself in all areas of culture, especially the less intellectualised, "populist" ones. Cf. also, e.g., his contributions to Gustav Landauer's *Masken*, the publication of his *avant-garde* theatre in Düsseldorf. For Scholem on Buber as primarily an artist, cf. *The Messianic Idea in Judaism* . . . , New York 1971, 'Martin Buber's Interpretation of Hasidism', p. 23. Cf. *Werke, op. cit.*, vol. III, p. 968: "I had to tell the stories, which I had assimilated within myself, out of myself, just as a true painter assimilates the lines of the model within himself and accomplishes the true picture from his creative memory." Cf. also Steven Katz, 'Martin Buber's Misuse of Chassidic Sources', chapter 2 of *Post-Holocaust Dialogues. Critical Studies in Modern Jewish Thought*, New York 1983; and Horwitz, *op. cit.*, pp. 58ff. Cf. section IX, pp. 377f. below.

18. E.g., 'Elijah', *Ost und West. Illustrierte Monatsschrift für modernes Judentum*, ed. Leo Winz, vol. IV, Berlin 1904, col. 817, and the string of poems from then on through the end of his life: *Nachlese*, Heidelberg 1965, pp. 11, 18-22, 25f., 264ff., 257f.

19. *For the Sake of Heaven*, tr. L. Lewisohn, Philadelphia 1946. (For Friedman's vast over-estimation of the novel cf. his *Martin Buber's Life and Work*, vol. II, chapter 16, pp. 309-325, and p. 35)

20. This may explain, at least in part, why Buber had so much trouble getting *For the Sake of Heaven* published as a book in German. It started out as Hebrew newspaper instalments.

21. *New York Times*, 9th February 1978, quotes Walter Kaufmann as saying that Buber "approximates the oracular tone of false prophets" (cf. also his translation of *I and Thou*, London 1970, pp. 19, 23f. and *passim*; 'Buber's Failures and Triumphs', in *Martin Buber. A Centenary Volume, op. cit.*, pp. 8, 19; also his 'Martin Buber. The Quest for You,' *The Jewish Spectator*, Spring 1980, p. 23: "... the style which is affected rather than ruthlessly honest ... influenced by the prose of Nietzsche's *Zarathustra* without remotely approaching its riches or its irony", and his—as usual—fuzzy, anecdotal, but correct Buber-chapter in *Discovering the Mind*, vol. 2, New York etc. 1980), while Robert Smith describes it as "religious poetry".

22. *I and Thou*, tr. by R.G. Smith, Edinburgh 1937, p. 3. One of the more striking features of Buber's vast and variegated output is the fact that, while the notion of "relation" is clearly the cornerstone of his intellectual edifice, neither he nor any of his followers has, as far as one can see, dealt with the important technical studies of the logic and of the history of the logic of relations since before Leibniz until after Bertrand Russell. (The current consensus in this field world probably be helpful to Buber's purpose.)

23. Cf. Schwarzschild, 'To Re-cast Rationalism', *Judaism*, XI, No. 3 (Summer 1962), pp. 205-209.

24. *Eclipse of God, op. cit.*, p. 164. Cf. also Steven T. Katz, 'Martin Buber's Epistemology. A Critical Appraisal', in *Post-Holocaust Dialogues ..., op. cit.*, pp. 13f. Bloch calls it "postulating" (*op. cit.*, p. 296) and rightly elaborates on the importance in Buber of "showing". (*Ibid.*, pp. 17ff.) Cf. notes 16, 21 above. Buber himself tries to handle the problem of language, to which Bloch legitimately draws attention, in another way. (Cf. note 1 above.) He insists on the centrality of language, but language cannot, indeed, "denote" thous. It can, on the other hand, be expected to circumlocute thous—i.e., circle ittishly around them, use poetic locutions and neologisms in order to "awaken us from our dogmatic (ittish) slumber," open the window (to use Buber's metaphor) and point to the thou ostensively, without denoting it. (Comp. Kierkegaard having to write in all sorts of indirect, pseudonymous, ironic and other ways, in order to avoid objectifying what he is talking about, namely subjectivity, by virtue of the very fact of talking about it: Crites, *op. cit.*, p. 28. Also the connection between Buber's "showing" and Wittgenstein's "unspeakable" "showing" should be taken into account here: cf. Schwarzschild, 'Wittgenstein as an Alienated Jew', *Telos*, No. 39, Spring 1979.) The difficulty of Buber's style may thus be seen to stem from his desire to bespeak the unspeakable. In short, where Bloch celebrates a triumph of irrationality, Buber himself

prefers at least to hold on to the paradox. Bloch's book (cf. note 1 above) as a whole makes a couple of points quite clear. One is that, when Buber's basic notions and his intellectual procedures are followed to their bitter end, as Bloch does not unsuccessfully, utter mystification results. Even language itself, so fundamental to Buber's dialogicism, vanishes, because whords are, of course, rules—to be invoked whenever "the same" objects are to be referred to, but, according to Buber, no two objects or object-situations are ever the same, and words cannot, therefore, get a grip on them. (*op. cit.*, pp. 29ff.; also *I and Thou*, tr. Kaufmann, *op. cit.*, p. 83 for what might be called Buber's epistemological anarchism.) The question of language in Buber is handled much better and more constructively by Moshe Schwarcz in 'Martin Buber's Conception of Myth and the Problem of Demythologization in Our Time', sect. 5, 'Language and Myth', in *Language, Myth, Art* (in Hebrew), Tel-Aviv 1966, pp. 247ff. Cf. also Roger Moser, *Gotteserfahrung bei M. Buber. Eine theologische Untersuchung*, Heidelberg 1979: since every relationship is unique, so is every word (p. 253), arising out of always unique "situations" (p. 249); there are, therefore, "authentic" and "inauthentic" ("eigentlich", "uneigentlich") words, both arising out of "das schweigende Grundwort" ("the silent foundational word"), of which the former is "preaccoustical, silent forthrightness between I and you" (pp. 247f.). At every important point in Bloch's close analysis, on the other hand, he triumphantly declares that he has arrived at rationally entirely self-contradictory and even unspeakable, incomprehensible, but true conclusions—what he calls (*op. cit.*, p. 315) "the collapse of the logos". (A comparable extrapolation of Buber to his extremes was A. Maisel's *Thought and Truth: A Critique of Philosophy. Its Source and Meaning*, New York 1956, and my review, 'The Realities of the Human Spirit', *Circle-Jewish Bookland*, September 1957.) The second point is that what results from such philosophical self-destruction is, of course, a lapse back into mindlessness, "natural" living (*ibid.*, pp. 287-315), what Bloch repeatedly calls "thinking with the stomach" (*ibid.*, pp. 292f.). Robert Wood, 'Buber's Conception of Philosophy', *Thought*, *op. cit.*, p. 314, quotes Buber as thinking with the fingertips, not "with the brain alone". Here everybody does what he has to do. "Lebensphilosophie" has come back with a vengeance. (Cf. note 13 above). And this is, of course, Bloch's political point. (*Ibid.*, pp. 171, notes 150 and 295.) He is both intellectually and politically the (reverse) mirror-image of Buber. (After this study was first written Professor Y. Bloch died, on 26th February 1979.) Cf. Horwitz, *op. cit.*, p. 123: "Ich appelliere an nichts anderes als an das, was jeder Einzelne von Ihnen unmittelbar von sich weiss, wenn er es nur wissen will ... Das ist die Grenze, diese Grenze kann ich nicht durchbrechen." For the decisive role of their respective views of language in the differences between Buber and Scholem cf. Biale, *op. cit.*, pp. 89f.

25. Cf., e.g., Friedman, *Martin Buber's Life and Work*, vol. I, *op. cit.*, chapter 8 on "Realization".

26. Cf. Bloch, *op. cit.*, p. 24: "[d]ie Wirklichkeit ... eingebunden ist ... in das gestaltige, färbige, tönende, einzigartig lebende und anwesende Sosein der Konkretheit."

27. J. Woocher, 'Martin Buber's Politics of Dialogue', *Thought*, *op. cit.*, p. 250 *et passim*, uses the term "liberal incrementalism".

28. *Genesis Rabba* 68:9. Buber cites this talmudic adage in the course of his 'Spinoza, Sabbatai Zvi, and the Baal-Shem', *The Origin and Meaning of Hasidism*, ed. and tr. by M. Friedman, Harper Torchbooks, 1966, p. 96.

29. *Ich und Du*, Berlin n.d., p. 111. "Gott umfasst das All, und ist es nicht." This is quoted by Berkovits, *op. cit.*, pp. 126ff., Herberg, *op. cit.*, p 57, Steven T. Katz, 'E. Berkovits and Modern Jewish Philosophy', *Tradition*, XVI, No. 5 (Fall 1977), p. 119, and cf. James Brown, *Subject and Object in Modern Theology*, New York 1955, pp. 137ff.

30. This explains his strikingly ambivalent discussion of Spinoza in 'Spinoza, Sabbatai Zvi... *loc. cit.*, "Panentheism" is surely the correct term for the view that "God transcends the universe but dwells in it", (*Ibid.*, p. 96.) Buber's dislike of religion is justified precisely by his argument that God dwells in the whole world, not just in some part of it called "religion". For Buber on Spinoza, Kant, and Hegel cf. also his *Eclipse of God, op. cit.*, pp. 22-30. Cf. Horwitz, *op. cit.*, pp. 236f.

31. Cf. *Origin and Meaning* ... , *op. cit.*, pp. 100f. The view that evil is nothing has, of course, a long pre-history in Jewish as well as non-Jewish philosophy. In Jewish culture Maimonides is its most important spokesman. It is, perhaps, not so much the doctrine of the nothingness of evil as the panentheism combined with it in Buber that presents us with our present problem: for Maimonides evil was nothing, but then, in some real and neo-Platonic sense, the entire actual, material universe was itself metaphysically nothing to him and this somehow evil, whereas for the quasi-Spinozist Buber the latter is, of course, not true.

32. 'Die Grundlagen von Martin Bubers Ethik', in Schilpp, *op. cit.*, pp. 158f.

33. *Ibid.*, p. 155. And, as Buber and Friedman go on to emphasise, the "norms" here spoken of may never by turned into "maxims", i.e., rules—as usual, an explicit dissociation from Kant. (*Ibid.*, pp. 158f.)

34. Therefore, in ethics as in art and everywhere else, Buber always goes out of his way explicitly to reject Kantian conceptualism. Under the influence of Nietzsche, Dilthey, Bergson (cf. 'Bergson's Concept of Intuition', in *Pointing the Way*), etc., at the turn of the century (cf. Hans Kohn, *Martin Buber. Sein Werk und seine Zeit. Ein Versuch über Religion und Politik*, Hellerau 1930, pp. 227f.), wanting to talk the language of "Lebensphilosophie", he takes occasion to administer side-swipes at theoreticism in general and at Kant in particular: e.g., "the command inherent in a gunuine norm never becomes a maxim ..." (Herberg, *op. cit.*, p. 20, citing from *Between Man and Man*, tr. by R. G. Smith, London 1947); "Representation of an idea, I say, not of a rigid principle, but of a living form that wants to be shaped in the daily stuff of the earth ..." (*Paths in Utopia*, Beacon Press, 1958, p. 47). Cf. also Katz, 'Martin Buber's Epistemology', *loc. cit.*, pp. 27ff.

35. Cf. Katz, *loc. cit.*, pp. 29ff.

36. Maurice Friedman's *Martin Buber. The Life of Dialogue*, Harper Torchbook, 1960—his earlier standard and exhaustive, albeit also entirely uncritical, survey of Buber's life and works—could easily be restructured around the question of evil in Buber.

37. *Good and Evil*, New York 1953 = *Bilder von Gut und Böse*, Cologne 1952, (in Hebrew) Jerusalem, 1962. Cf. also Horwitz, *op. cit.*, pp. 63f.

38. *Origin and Meaning . . .* , *op. cit.*, p. 98. Cf. also *ibid.*, pp. 102ff. On p. 101 Buber makes clear the *kabbalistic* basis of his phrase "the sparks in need of redemption". Cf. also *Good and Evil, op. cit.*, pp. 125ff.; *Two Types of Faith*, tr. by Norman P. Goldhawk, London 1951, pp. 63f. Cf. also the *Kabbalistic* terminology in his letter to Hugo Bergmann of 4th December 1917, quoted by Kohn, *op. cit.*, pp. 333f. and by Flohr, 'The Road to *I and Thou . . .* ', *loc. cit.*, pp. 224f. Buber puns in German, that "the just" ("das Gerechte") is "the directed" ("das Gerichtete") and "the judged". (Horwitz, *op. cit.*, pp. 64, 263.)

39. *Good and Evil, op. cit.*, pp. 130, 140.

40. *Ibid.* p. 134.

41. *Ibid.*, p. 59

42. Cf. Friedman, *Life of Dialogue, op. cit.*, pp. 104ff and 112f.

43. Cf. Harold Fisch, 'Buber's Interpretation of Zionism', *Forum* (Jerusalem) I, No. 26, (1977), pp. 24f.; David Glanz, 'Buber's Concept of the Holocaust and History', *ibid.*, Nos. 30-31 (Spring-Summer 1978).

44. M. Friedman, 'The Intellectual Challenge Buber has Left Us', *Thought, op. cit.*, pp. 341f.

45. *Pointing the Way, op. cit.*, pp. 158ff.

46. Heidelberg 1949, p. 405.

47. Cf. Herberg, *op. cit.*, p. 238, *Good and Evil, op. cit.*, pp. 58f., 133ff.

48. Contrary to Katz (*loc. cit.*, p. 121), *The Eclipse of God* contains essays from well before until well after the Second World War, and the reality of "the Holocaust" has, therefore, been well integrated into Buber's worldview here. No later than 1922 Buber spoke of the then present time as "the moment of the deepest historical valley". (Horwitz, *op. cit.*, pp. 50, 126, 131, note 12).

49. Herberg, *op. cit.*, p. 113.

50. *Das echte Gespräch und die Möglichkeit des Friedens*, Heidelberg 1953 = *Men of Dialogue. Martin Buber and Albrecht Goes*, eds. E. Rollins and H. Zohn, New York, 1969, pp. 20ff.

51. Cf. Simon, *The Line of Demarcation . . .* , *op. cit.*, p. 46. Buber was not concerned really with Eichmann's fate but with the spirit of Israel as it would realise itself in that first and hitherto only execution.

52. *Ibid.* Cf. the review by Abraham Shapiro, 'The Line of Demarcation', *Forum* (Jerusalem), Nos. 32-33 (Fall 1978), pp. 171-176.

53. Cf. his 'Martin Buber. His Way Between Thought and Deed', *Jewish Frontier*, February 1948 (= *Aufbau*, New York, 20th February 1948, pp. 7f., in German); 'Martin Buber, der Erzieher,' Schilpp, *op. cit.*, pp. 500-503; 'On Martin Buber's Political Path and National View,' *loc. cit.*, pp. 37f.; also Friedman, 'Martin Buber and the Social Problems of Our Time,' pp. 238ff.; and *idem, Martin Buber's Life and Work, op. cit.*, vol. I, pp. 256, 268, 341, vol II, pp. 18, 117, 135, 150, 249, vol. III, p. 207.

54. *Israel and the World*, p. 216; cf. also *I and Thou*, pp. 110f.

55. *Ibid.*, and *Martin Buber's Life and Work*, vol. 3, *op. cit.*, p. 6.

56. Quoted from 'Geltung und Grenze des politischen Prinzips,' in *Hinweise* by Robert Weltsch; 'Bubers politische Philosophie,' Schilpp, *op. cit.*, pp. 391f. Cf. also *Good and Evil, op. cit.*, last sentence, p. 143.

57. *Nachlese, op. cit.*, p. 75: Buber's italics. Here Buber's heavy dependence on Franz Rosenzweig also strikes the eye. Buber was quite conscious of this, but especially the non-Jewish secondary literature that deals with Buber, if it is aware of this at all heavily mutes it—presumably because it is largely ignorant of and uninterested in Rosenzweig (a typical "de-Judaisation" of Jewish literature at the hands of "general culture"). Friedman plays down the decisive role of Rosenzweig in Buber's thought for his hagiographic reasons: cf. *Martin Buber's Life and Works*, vol. I, *op. cit.*, chapter 14 and 'note,' pp. 322, 408-411, 418, 422.) The very notion of "relation" in Buber's sense is, of course, the essence of Part II of Rosenzweig's *Star of Redemption*. (Cf. Schwarzschild, 'The Star of Redemption' [review], *The Thomist*, XXXV, No. 4 (October 1971), pp. 728-737) (Rosenzweig in turn obtained and transmuted this notion from Hermann Cohen: cf. Schwarzschild, 'The Tenability of Hermann Cohen's Construction of the Self', *Journal of the History of Philosophy*, XIII, No. 3 (July 1975), p. 363, note 7). That divine revelation is exclusively sheer relation, without any legitimately objectifiable consequences, is also part of Rosenzweig's notion of relation. (Cf. *The Thomist, loc. cit.* Cf. Herberg, *op. cit.*, p. 61 to the effect that, according to Buber, no "ought's" are produced by the man-God encounter.) And finally with respect to the present point, that human actions have to be ethically "incrementalist" is derived from Rosenzweig's doctrine of "I can . . . as much as possible." (Cf. Schwarzschild, *F. Rosenzweig. Guide to Reversioners*, London 1960, pp. 41f.) About all this it is to be noted that in each instance Buber is more subjectivistic than Rosenzweig—which also accounts for their partial disagreements.

58. Friedman, *Martin Buber's Life and Work, op. cit.*, vol. I, p. 341 and vol. III, p. 73ff. has some unhelpful references to the economic dimension of Buber's thought. In

Martin Buber. A Centenary Volume, op. cit., J. Bloch, p. XVII and especially Haim Gordon, in his 'Existential Guilt and Buber's Social and Political Thought,' p. 226 and note 25 criticise the absence of concern with economics on the part of Buber, unlike, say, Thoreau.

59. Die Forderung des Geistes', *loc. cit.*, p. 1066; cf. also *ibid.*, p. 1068.

60. Martin Buber, der Erzieher', *loc. cit., ibid.* Cf. also Buber's sentence: "Die Geschichte ist eine geheimnisvolle Annäherung." (Horwitz, *op. cit.*, p. 152, the very end of the lectures, and its use in *I and Thou*).

61. Friedman, 'Die Grundlagen . . . ', *loc. cit.*, pp. 169f.

62. Cf. Schwarzschild, 'The Religious Demand for Peace', *Judaism*, XV, No. 4 (Fall 1966), pp. 413f.; and R.D. Hyslop's Niebuhrian answer, which follows that article.

63. Kant himself sometimes spoke of God as "the God of the (infinite) limit"—"der Grenzengott."

64. *Loc. cit.*, p. 505, note 159. Simon, however, subscribes to such "occasionalist" pacificism himself: cf. his 'Erziehung zum Frieden in Kriegszeiten—dargelegt am Beispiel Israels' (1970), in *Entscheidung zum Judentum* . . . , Frankfurt a. Main 1980, pp. 363, 366.

65. Cf. Herberg, *op. cit.*, p. 30.

66. Cf. Katz, *loc. cit.*, pp. 38-41.

67. Cf. his 'Man and Society in Martin Buber's Thought,' *Shdemot*, 1978, No. 9, pp. 84f.; and *Martin Buber's Life and Work*, vol. 2, *op. cit.*, p. 108.

68. Cf. F. Rosenzweig, *On Jewish Learning*, ed. N. Glatzer, New York 1955, esp. pp. 111, 115, etc. and Friedman, *Martin Buber's Life and Work*, vol. 2, *op. cit.*, chapter 3, 4. There is, of course, a *Chasidic* backdrop to Buber's distaste for the law. That also in authentic *Chasidism*, not only in the acculturated, Buberian form of it, some rather extreme forms of antinomianism can crop up: cf. J. G. Weiss, 'Eine spätjüdische Utopie religiöser Freiheit', *Eranos Jahrbuch* XXXII (1963), Zürich 1964, esp. pp. 242, 245, *et passim*; and Schwarzschild, 'An Introduction to R. Isaac Hutner's Jewish Thought', *Modern Judaism*, Fall 1985. More generally, the school of Ishbitz went about as far in antinomianism and in denying the ultimate reality of sin as one can go: cf. A.J. Heschel, *Kotzk. The Struggle for Integrity* (in Yiddish), Tel-Aviv 1973, vol. I, pp. 635f.; and J.G. Weiss, *loc, cit.*, pp. 234ff.

69. A comparison of Rolland's attitude with Buber's at that time is revealing. While the former was an opponent of the war and Buber was a proponent, their basic attitude was the same: everybody has to be "true to himself" (whether this leads him into the army or into conscientious objection); cf. Stefan Zweig, another member of the same artistic group, *Romain Rolland. Der Mann und das Werk*. Frankfurt a. Main 1921, pp. 235ff. This is, of course, a description of the problem, not an answer.

70. Cf. M. Friedman, 'Martin Buber on Peace', *Tidings* (Jewish Peace Fellowship), (Winter 1955); *idem*, 'Martin Buber and the Covenant of Peace', *Fellowship*, 1st January 1960; and *idem*, 'Martin Buber and Pacificism', *Shalom*, Winter 1968.

71. *Martin Buber. Briefwechsel aus sieben Jahrzehnten, I: 1897-1918*, Heidelberg 1972, pp. 63-67 (introduction by Grete Schaeder), and No. 306, pp. 433-438. Cf. Schwarzschild, '"Germanism and Judaism". Hermann Cohen's Normative Paradigm of the German-Jewish Symbiosis', in *Jews and Germans from 1860 to 1933. The Problematic Symbiosis*, ed. D. Bronsen, Heidelberg 1979, p. 207, note 32, and Kohn, *Buber . . ., op. cit.*, pp. 163ff. Cf. also the in effect generally very critical A. A. Cohen, 'Martin Buber and Judaism', in *LBI Year Book XXV* (1980), pp. 292f.; also *Briefwechsel, ibid.*, for the "patriotism" of Rabbi N. Noble, Hugo Bergmann and other Zionists during the First World War. Flohr's 'The Road to *I and Thou: . . .*,' *loc. cit.*, is in its entirety concerned with Buber's endorsement of German arms during the First World War (= Flohr, *Von der Mystik zum Dialog. M. Bubers geistige Entwicklung hin bis zu 'Ich und Du'*, Königstein/Ts. 1979, pp. 14, 131-140, *et. al.*). Flohr's study makes a number of things clear, even against the author's intention: 1) The bombast and aggressiveness of Buber's enthusiastic support of the German cause exceeds all tolerable proportions. 2) Contrary to Flohr's thesis, Buber never really rescinded his effusions on this subject, although he later tried to cover his tracks (cf. his omissions in later editions: *ibid.*, notes 53, 87, 89), and his followers continue to this day to act similarly (cf. Kohn, *op. cit.*, pp. 164ff. and notes, with what is, under the circumstances, a particularly outrageous attack on Hermann Cohen for his "state fetishism" [Cohen's support of the German arms at the time was much more modulated than Buber's] and pp. 217f., and Flohr's article itself, which has something of an air of mystification about it). 3) Flohr's thesis, that Gustav Landauer's argument against Buber's support of the war (which Landauer described as "aestheticism") was what moved Buber out of "mysticism" into "dialogicism" fails of proof and is not logically persuasive: there is no correlation between *Erlebnis* ("experience") and war or between *Begegnung* ("meeting") and anti-militarism. (A. A. Cohen, 'Martin Buber and *Der Jude*', *Midstream*, June/July 1980 [= *The Jew. Essays from Martin Buber's Journal 'Der Jude' 1916-1928*, University of Alabama Press, 1980], pp. 31f. accepts Flohr's untenable thesis.) Let it be said to Gershom Scholem's credit that he, like Gustav Landauer and Walter Benjamin, took the position of conscientious objectors in the First World War: therefore refused to cooperate on Buber's *Der Jude*, and, again like Landauer, blamed Buber's linguistic pomposities at least in part for his militaristic metaphysics. (Biale, *op. cit.*, pp. 58-65, 103f.) (Levinas also regards the early Buber as too "aestheticistic".) Cf. also the Israeli pacifist Nathan Chophshi, *With Heart and Soul. In the Crisis of Nation and Man* (in Hebrew), privately published, 1965, pp. 177f. and 216f. against Buber's "realism" on the 1956 War, and p. 227 even against Magnes during the Second World War: "What is the power and what is the value of pacifism if it is limited to peacetimes!" Cf. my review of Friedman's *Martin Buber's Life and Work*, in *Judaism*, XXXIV, No. 4 (Fall 1985).

72. Cf. note 4 above. Judah L. Magnes joined him in this posture, although in the First World War he had been a conscientious objector and activist. Leo Baeck shared Buber's equivocating on all these occasions. (Ernst Simon, 'Baeck's and Buber's Social and Political Thought. Paradigms for Today?', *Leo Baeck Memorial Conference on Jewish Social Thought,* American Federation of Jews from Central Europe, ed. H. A. Strauss, New York 1974, p. 13. Simon answers the question of his title thus [*ibid.*, p. 10]: "As to the values held by either man in relation to society I do not believe that they will serve as paradigms for today.")

73. Tr. N. P. Goldhawk, p. 15.

74. For Buber's vacillating on pacifism, cf. Herberg, *op. cit.*, p. 22. Also Aubrey Hodes, *Martin Buber. An Intimate Portrait,* New York 1971, p. 99, quoting Buber: "When there is war, it must be fought." Cf. note 75 below. Herberg, under Niebuhr's influence, exaggerates his equivocation into positive hostility, speaking of "the cult of pacifism." (*op. cit.*, p. 22.).

75. Friedman, *Martin Buber's Life and Work,* vol. III, *op. cit., p. 25; cf. also ibid.*, pp. 8, 159, vol. II, p. 292.

76. There is an anlogous paradox in Emmanuel Levinas. He, even more emphatically than Buber, is philosophically committed to the proposition that "Do not murder me!" is the first, major, and fundamental incursion of "the infinite" into "totality." Furthermore, from his (disputed) asymmetry of "the other" and "the I" he derives an elaborate view of moral existence as "persecution," "hauntedness," etc.—yet this is accompanied in Levinas by an unambiguous identification with official Zionism and the State of Israel (cf. *Difficile Liberté,* Paris 1963: 'Etat d'Israel et Religion d'Israël,' 'La Pensée juive d'aujourd'hui')—whether this be right or wrong in itself. As also D. Awerkamp, *E. Levinas. Ethics and Politics,* New York 1977, points out, Levinas has, of course, a place for the State and, indeed, totality in his ethics (cf. *Difficile Liberté, op. cit.*, pp. 193ff., 242, 244), but how the violence of war can be reconciled with Levinas's most fundamental insight seems philosophically entirely incomprehensible. Awerkamp quotes (*ibid.*, p. 37) "Les Vertus de Patience": "The hand which grasps the weapon must always suffer by the very violence of the gesture. The anesthesia of this suffering leads the revolutionary to the frontiers of fascism," and (*ibid.*, p. 38) 'Transcendence et Hauteur': "The fundamental contradiction of our situation (and perhaps of our condition) ... is the simultaneous necessity both of the hierarchical structure taught by Athens and of the *abstract* and somewhat *anarchic* ethical individualism taught by Jerusalem (the author's italics), in order to suppress the violence. Each of these principles, left to itself, only hastens the contrary of that which it wishes to insure." One may suppose that here, too, as in Buber, there is the incrementalism of the proper balance between what he, as well, calls "Athens" and "Jerusalem" that is at the bottom of it.

77. Paul Tillich, *Politische Bedeutung der Utopie im Leben der Völker,* Berlin 1951 (Schriftenreihe der Deutschen Hochschule für Politik Berlin), p. 19, made an

entirely analogous point about John Dewey: "I said, 'How can you avoid the criticism that you have no norms, e.g., against Nazism (and Dewey is a prominent fighter for humanism against everything totalitarian, etc.)?' ... He could not answer and basically more or less agreed when I said: 'These norms come from the still unbroken tradition of Anglo-Saxon humanism. That is to say, the fortunate inconsistency of the Anglo-Saxons has preserved them from the European fate ... "

78. *Der utopische Sozialismus* (= *Paths in Utopia*), Cologne 1967, p. 248. I do not believe I understand a single word in the last sentence: "Wie ich nicht an Marxens 'Ausbrütung' der neuen Gestalt glaube, so glaube ich nicht an Bakunins Jungfernzeugung aus dem Schoss der Revolution. Aber ich glaube an die Begegnung von Bild und Geschick in der plastischen Stunde." (It is the last sentence in the book. Cf. also *Nachlese, op. cit.*, Bemerkungen zur Gemeinschaftisidee" [1931, p. 81].) In an article appended then to *Der utopische Sozialismus, ibid.*, p. 265, Buber says: "Daher beginnt mit Marx die Bewegung eines Sozialismus, in dem das soziale Prinzip nur noch als letzte Zielsetzung, nicht im realpraktischen Entwurf existiert."

79. *Ibid.*, p. 233. A number of ramifications of this political philosophy may be noted. 1) The "community/society" distinction is, of course, the classic contribution of Ferdinand Tönnies. Cf. Buber's reference to Tönnies, *ibid.*, p. 259; Kohn, *op. cit.*, pp. 188-210 on Buber, Tönnies, and Landauer; Weltsch, *loc. cit.*, pp. 386ff.; Friedman, 'M. Buber and the Social Problem of Our Time', *YIVO Annual*, XIII (1958-1959), p. 237, and *Martin Buber's Life and Work*, vol. I, *op. cit.*, pp. 232, 238; Paul R. Flohr and Bernard Susser, 'Alte und Neue Gesellschaft. An Unpublished Buber Manuscript', *AJS Review*, I, Cambridge, Mass. 1971, and Paul R. Mendes-Flohr, 'Martin Buber's Concept of the Centre and Social Renewal', *Jewish Journal of Sociology*, XVIII, No. I (June 1976), pp. 17f. (The latter authors usefully point up the religio-historical dimension which Buber adds to the "Gemeinschaft/Gesellschaft" dichotomy by extrapolating "Gemeinschaft" to "Gemeinde": *loc. cit.*, pp. 18ff.) For the personal relations between Buber and Tönnies, cf. E.G. Jacoby, *Die moderne Gesellschaft im sozialwissenschaftlichen Denken von Ferdinand Tönnies*, Stuttgart 1971, p. 302, note 12. Buber's qualified Spinozism may then also be seen as parallel to Tönnies's: cf. Alfred Bellebaum, *Das soziologische System von F. Tönnies unter besonderer Berücksichtigung seiner soziographischen Untersuchungen*, Meisenheim am Glau 1966, pp. 108ff. and 166-182. For Tönnies on Hermann Cohen, on the other hand, cf. his 'Ethik und Sozialismus', *Archiv für Sozialwissenschaft und Sozialpolitik*, XXVI (1910), pp. 895ff. And for a very Cohennian treatment of "Gemeinschaft," "Gemeinde," etc., which also exemplifies how widespread this discussion was at that time, cf. Albert Görland, *Ethik als Kritik Der Weltgeschichte*, Leipzig-Berlin 1914, pp. vi, 159, 194, 315, *et passim*. (Cf. Flohr, *Von der Mystik ..., op. cit.*, p. 82, p. 106, note 265, and p. 188, note 5, for how Buber goes beyond Tönnies and another Cohen-disciple, R. Stammler, in apostrophising "community".) 2) I would want strongly to argue (cf. Schwarzschild, 'Germanism and Judaism', *loc, cit.*, p. 191 and T. Keck, *Kant and Socialism. The Marburg School in Wilhelmian Germany*, dissertation, University of Wisconsin, Madison 1975, pp. 184, 187, 306ff.; cf.

A. E. Simon, 'Glaube, Religion und Gesellschaft', in *Religion und Politik, op. cit.*, pp. 22f.), though I can here only state, that the ideal of "community" is inextricably connected with the model of "the organic state", and thus, in cases like Buber, Tönnies, and Landauer, it is an unwitting, romantically anarchist, contribution to the rise of fascism. Even Simon once admitted this: 'Martin Buber, his Way between Thought and Deed', *Jewish Frontier*, February 1948, p. 27, speaking of Nazis: "Buber, of course, does not speak their language—how could he, and how could they—but he uses partly the same vocabulary , and Alfred Rosenberg dared to quote him in Nuremberg." Cf. Schwarzschild, *Judaism*, VII, No. 3 (Summer 1958), p. 282, and notes 96, 143 below. Thus, for example, also Heinrich Schmidt's *Philosophisches Wörterbuch* in the 1943 edition (!) co-opts Tönnies, despite his personal insulation against the Nazis, for Nazi "Volksgemeinschaft", because "community" of "birth and blood" resists the "degeneracy" of the "city" in "society". The same thing had been done to him immediately in 1933 by some of his own associates: cf. Jacoby, *op. cit.*, pp. 250f. For Tönnies's argument against Kantian societalism cf. *Archiv für Sozialwissenschaft . . .* , *loc. cit.*, pp. 905ff., 910ff., and 928f.; for Kant on society vs. community cf., among others, *Metaphysical Foundations of Law, Werke*, Cassirer edn., vol. 7, p. 113. On the romantic, anarchist side of the communitarians. It stands to reason that Landauer was a friend of Peter Kropotkin's and Buber a (qualified) admirer of Gandhi. 3) E. Berkovits's and some others' criticism of Buber to the effect that his individualistic "I" is alien to Judaism's "we" (*op. cit., pp. 97-100, 102-104*) is simply false on all counts. (Cf. Herberg, *op. cit.*, pp. 20ff.; Friedman, *Life of Dialogue . . .* , *op. cit.*, pp. 208f.; *Problem des Menschen, op. cit.*, pp. 115f.) "Wes", too, according to Buber, experience thouness—so preeminently so, in fact, that he stipulates an "essential we". (Mendes-Flohr. *loc. cit.*, p. 20). 4) The "Gesellschaft/Gemeinschaft" dichotomy corresponds to and is causally connected with the equally Germanic dichotomy of "Zivilisation/Kultur" ("civilisation/culture"), and Buber accepts the latter, therefore, as well. (Cf. M. Schwarcz, *op. cit.*, 'Martin Buber's Aesthetic Thought', pp. 316ff.). Buber's necessary lapse from thouishness to ittishness, and the ever-recurring necessity to lift oneself out of it, is his equivalent of Max Weber's dialectic in political sociology between charisma and bureaucratic routinisation.

80. *Paths in Utopia,* p. 142: "[I]n a world of partial failures, we can recognize a non-failure—and as such it is a signal non-failure."

81. In a letter to me Professor Ernst Simon answered this question as follows: "Today he would perhaps omit the adjective 'signal' ('model'), but the rest he would maintain—and in my opinion largely with justification." Buber's profound ambivalence is, perhaps, best expressed in the striking sentence which H.T. (Hans Tramer) quotes from a letter that Buber wrote to Eduard Strauss at the beginning of 1948 (!): "Ich verlasse dieses unselige Land nicht." ('Eduard Strauss und seine Freundschaft mit Franz Rosenweig und Martin Buber', in *Bulletin des Leo Baeck Instituts, XVI– XVII, Nos. 53-54 (1977/1978), p. 158.* [Tramer, long-time editor of the *Bulletin,* died shortly after writing this article. I may add that my late father was Eduard Strauss's closest friend.]).

82. *Der utopische Sozialismus . . ., op. cit.*, pp. 267f.

83. *Paths in utopia, op. cit.*, p. 134: "The fatal question does not take the form of a fundamental either-or [*pace* Kierkegaard!]; it is only a question of the right line of demarcation that has to be drawn ever anew . . . Representation of an idea, I say, not rigid principle, but of a living form that wants to be shaped in the daily stuff of this earth . . ." (Also Herberg, *op. cit.*, pp. 126, 128: Friedman, *Life of Dialogue, op. cit.*, pp. 208-222). And Herberg, in his right-wing old-age, although otherwise an almost unbounded admirer of Buber's, thought that the degree of communitarianism that Buber insisted on at that time was already far too much: *op. cit.*, pp. 23ff.; and his review of Friedman's book in *The New Republic*, 16th January 1956, p. 28.

84. *Paths in Utopia, op. cit.*, p. 104.

85. Friedman, *Life of Dialogue, op. cit.*, p. 145; Herberg, *op. cit.*, pp. 22f.

86. *Israel and the World, op. cit.*, p. 236: "What is wrong for the individual cannot be right for the community; for if it were then God . . . would no longer be the Lord of peoples, but only of individuals."

87. Here the influences of Buber and of Reinhold Niebuhr conjoined in Herberg. (cf. note 62 above.) "Original sin" in the form of human finitude and the practical necessities of life, each in itness, compels compromises, the lesser of evils, in human life. (cf. the Niebuhrian critique of Buber by Ray Branson, 'The Individual and the Commune. A Critique of M. Buber's Social Philosophy', *Judaism*, XXIV, No. 1 [Winter 1975].) The result would seem to have been a commitment to democracy on the part of each of the three religious thinkers here considered—Buber, Niebuhr, and Herberg—but with political conservativism increasing in the order named. (cf. note 62 above and Kenneth W. Thompson, 'Niebuhr's Conception of Politics', *Interpretation*, 6, No. 2, [May 1977].) *Re* Herberg's critique of Buber, cf. Schwarzschild, *Judaism*, IX, no. 3, (Summer 1960), p. 274. Buber's anarchist optimism about human nature differentiates him from the theological pessimism of the other two. Cf. Buber's reply to Niebuhr's critique of him in a letter to M. Friedman, *Life of Dialogue, op. cit.*, p. 222: "There is indeed a norm of justice . . . But man tends to accept and to realise this norm only in general and abstract laws . . . I cannot see the God-willed reality of justice anywhere other than in 'being just,' and this means of course: being just as far as it is possible here and now . . ." (*N.B.* here again the "incrementalism" and the "situation-ethics" in terms of which Buber couches his reply to Niebuhr.) Cf. also Friedman, in *YIVO Annual, loc. cit.*, p. 241, and *Martin Buber's Life and Works*, vol. III, op. cit., pp. 188f., 200-202.

88. *Der utopische Sozialismus, op. cit.*, p. 269.

89. *Paths in Utopia, op. cit.*, p. 47. The language of "degrees" always pervades his discussions of this subject: *ibid.*; and Friedman, *Life of Dialogue, op. cit.*, pp. 213f.; and *Prophetic Faith, op. cit.*, p. 295.

90. *Der utopische Sozialismus, op. cit.*, pp. 268f.; *Paths in Utopia, op. cit.*, p. 47. There is then so close an analogy between Buber's doctrine of evil (cf. pp. 361-364 above) and his doctrine of the State that they end up being one-and-the-same. Evil and the State are both nothings, privations, the absence of thouness and of community respectively. The State is really "absolute evil", insofar as Buber can have such a thing. But evil = the State must be lived with minimally, and it must be maximally redirected. (Cf. Kohn, *op. cit.*, pp. 205f.).

91. *Der Butt* ("The Founder"), Luchterhand 1977, p. 116. "Still or again: I lightly blow feathers/and assert what floats." On Buber's optimism cf. N.N. Glatzer, 'Buber as Interpreter of the Bible', in *Essays in Jewish Thought*, University of Alabama Press 1978, p. 203.

92. Cf. Martin Buber, *The Knowledge of Man ...*, ed. M. Friedman, transl. R.G. Smith, New York 1965, pp. 83f., about the "unfolding" of human potentialities. (Buber there also cross-refers to his *Between Man and Man*, "dialogue", esp. pp. 4-6 and on p. 87 to the meeting of intellectuals just before the First World War: cf. above.)

93. Kohn, *op. cit.*, pp. 236ff., talking about Landauer.

94. Woocher, *loc. cit*, p. 256: "Buber believed he was offering a superior *Realpolitik*, superior because it was rooted in full reality of interhuman relationships ... We may readily acknowledge that by conventional criteria Martin Buber was not a 'successful' political actor"; comp. also Menahem Doron, "Martin Buber's Address "Herut" and Its Influence on the Jewish Youth Movement in Germany', *Martin Buber, A Centenary Volume, op. cit.*, pp. 244, 247.

95. Kohn, *op. cit.*, pp. 192-196: while broaching this problem and rightly even drawing attention to the connections of communitarianism with vitalism and romanticism, Kohn tries half-heartedly to extricate Buber and Landauer from this morass.

96. Cf. Kurzweil, *Spiritual Perplexity, op. cit.*, p. 111: "His faith in man, in his honor, that he is created in the image of God, this served him as a regulative against the danger of German irrationalism and of myths." But compare Joachim Doron, "Rassenbewusstsein und naturwissenschaftliches Denken im deutschen Zionismus während der wilhelminischen Ära', in *Jahrbuch des Instituts für deutsche Geshichte*, IX (1980), Tel-Aviv University, p. 421, where Max Brod is quoted as having said: "Wir streichelten die Höllenhunde, die an ihren Ketten zerten!"

97. *Op. cit.*, pp. 231-235.

98. *Ibid.*, p. 233.

99. *Prophetic Faith, op. cit.*, p. 243.

100. *The Messianic Idea in Judaism ...*, New York 1971, p. 230. Scholem repeatedly called Buber "a religious anarchist". Simon accepts this description. (Cf. note 135 below.) Actually Buber's religious as well as his political anarchisms derive from a metaphysical

anarchism, which can, perhaps, best be seen in its extrapolation in Levinas, who often stresses that the experience of the other is an-archic, i.e., prior to the beginning of logos, etc.

101. Die Grundlagen. . .',*loc. cit.*, p. 164.

102. Cf. also A.A. Cohen, *The Natural and the Supernatural Jew*, New York 1962, pp. 170-172; Jacob Agus, *Modern Philosophies of Judaism*, New York 1941, pp. 241ff.; Franz Freiherr von Hammerstein, *Das Messiasproblem bei Martin Buber*, Stuttgart 1958, p. 85 and note 93; Simon, 'Glaube, Religion und Gesellschaft', *loc. cit.*, p. 16: "a certain tendency not to take concrete historical process too carefully". Cf. Also S. Poppel, 'Martin Buber, The Art of the Unpolitical', *Midstream*, XX, No. 5 (May 1974): "History either in the past or the future was not the realm of providential intervention." (P. 15) "This negative attitude towards history is preserved in the work of Emmanuel Levinas . . . There are also significant parallels with Paul Tillich's well-known notion of *kairos*." (P. 16) Also Martin Jay, 'Politics of Translation. Seigfried Kracauer and Walter Benjamin on the Buber-Rosenzweig Bible', in *LBI Year Book XXI* (1976), pp. 21f., about the attack on the ahistoricality of Buber's language by the Frankfurt School. Biale, *op. cit.*, pp. 81-86; p.85: "Buber's linguistic skepticism resulted in his disparaging of history and tradition. If language is incapable of communicating the essence of the revelatory expereince, then how can a tradition based on revelation have any authority? Tradition is merely conventional and artificial; it is part of the linguistic realm of Erfahrung, since it cannot effectively communicate Erlebnis." P. 166: "Even though he urged a return to the plane of historical action, the category of history served for Buber more as a metaphor for the existential present than for an historical continuum." P. 168: "The historical phenomenon consequently loses its historical context and background." P. 202: ". . . Buber's unhistorical rendering of historical moments". Also cf. Kurzweil, in *Spiritual Perplexity*, *op. cit.*, pp. 76ff., 80f., 84f. O. Pöggeler, 'Hegel's Interpretation of Judaism', *The Human Context*, VI, No. 3 (1974), p. 556: "It was precisely in the name of a God who 'made demands in history'that the prophets of Israel shattered every kind of demand for security. Admittedly Buber shifted the grounds on which the question was posed in a way which no longer admitted of any real discussion." Friedman, *Martin Buber's Life and Work*, vol. I, *op. cit.*, pp. 424f. and references: "Casper holds that Buber lacks both a past and a future that can be taken seriously as a reality of creation . . ." Cf. also S. Katz, 'M. Buber's Epistemology . . .', *loc. cit.*, pp. 44ff.

103. Cf. 'The Question of the Single One', in *Eclipse of God*, *op. cit.*

104. Cf. 'Martin buber's Interpretation of Hasidism', in *The Messianic Idea . . .*, *op. cit.*, *ibid.*; also Biale *op. cit.*, p. 167: "Scholem's position appears to be much closer to Buber's than he may be willing to admit." Generally for the relations between Buber and Scholem cf. *ibid.*, pp. 12, 43-47, 56-60, 81-86 *et passim*; and Friedman, *Martin Buber's Life and Work*, vol. III, *op. cit.*, chapter 12, *et al.*

105. *Prophetic Faith*, *op. cit.*, pp. 192, 194; 'Biblical Leadership', *loc. cit.*, p. 133. Cf. Glatzer, *loc. cit.*, pp. 204f. Glatzer cites Rylaarsdan (*ibid.*, p. 203): "Basically his interpretation of the Old Testament is a documentation of his own views."

106. Cf. Friedman, 'Die Grundlagen . . .', *loc. cit.*, p. 162.

107. Cf. e.g., *Kingship of God*, New York 1967, and Hammerstein, *op. cit.*

108. *Ibid.* Cf. also Friedman, *Martin Buber's Life and Work*, vol. III, *op. cit.*, chapter 4 and "Note" and pp. 46ff.

109. *Berachot*, 13a.

110. In *Spiritual Perplexity*, *op. cit.*, pp. 326ff. Comp. S. Schwarzschild, 'The Legal Foundations of Jewish Aesthetics', in this volume.

111. Horwitz, *op. cit.*, pp. 61.

112. In *Spiritual Perplexity*, *op. cit.*, pp. 331f.

113. *Ibid.*, p. 327.

114. *Nachlese*, *op. cit.*, pp. 235ff.

115. *Ibid.*, p. 237: "Zu [seiner Verantwortung] muss er sich selber aufmachen, ausgerüstet mit allem in der Gruppe geschmiedeten Sollen, aber ausgesetzt dem Schicksal, dass im abgründigen Augenblick alle Rüstung von ihm abfällt."

116. *Ibid.*, pp. 192ff.

117. 'The Living Legacy of Martin Buber', (In Hebrew) *T'futzot haGolah*, Nos. 83-84, Jerusalem 1978, p. 75.

118. *Nachlese*, *op. cit.*, p. 192.

119. Cf, Jacob Fleischmann, 'Le problème de M. Buber', *Revue philosphique de France et de l'étranger*, Paris 1959, no. 3: 'What is the relevance of a theory which falls silent when the decisive word needs to be said? What becomes of man when he is orientated by uncertainty?"

120. E.g., *The Prophetic Faith*, *op. cit.*, chapter 5.

121. 1st *Critique*, Cassirer edn., p. 545.

122. *Judaism*, VII, no. 3. *loc. cit.*; and Schwarzschild, *Judaism*, VIII, No. 2 (Spring 1959), pp. 168-170. Cf. Horwitz, *op. cit.*, pp. 227f., 254. (On p. 227 there is a bad printing error, which can be corrected with the text of p. 154. Notice in the latter also the extremely clever and literate discussion of Hermann Cohen.)

123. E.g., *The Prophetic Faith*, *op. cit.*, p. 215, against Korach's biblical denial of this claim (but see *I and Thou* [Kaufmann edn.], chapter 'The Contradiction', pp. 180ff. on Moses and Korach).

124. Simon, 'Martin Buber, der Erzieher', *loc cit.*, p. 503, and 'Scholem und Buber', *loc cit.*, sect. iv.

125. Schilpp, *op. cit.*, 'Antwort', p. 602.

126. Cf. also Bloch, *op. cit.*, chapter 6, 'The Relation of the Thou to the It', and pp. 289f., note 19 and p. 306.

127. *I and Thou*, Kaufmann edn., *op. cit.*, p. 153.

128. 2 vols., Berlin 1912.

129. Cf. also his rejection of "inorganic", "abstract moral or social postulates" at the end of his 1921 Zionist address: *Israel and the World, op. cit.*, p. 225.

130. Schwarzschild, 'The Star of Redemption' (review), *The Thomist*, XXXV, no. 4, (October 1971), p. 732. For the desire to escape from temporality, which, in the wake of Kierkegaard (cf. Crites, *op. cit.*, pp. 74, 81) and Nietzsche, informed German culture generally at the turn of the century and thus also heavily influenced Buber and Rosenzweig; cf. Jakob Taubes's introduction to Franz Overbeck, *Selbstbekenntnisse*, Franfurt a. Main 1966. Buber's 1922-lectures, published by Horwitz (*op. cit.*), also makes this philosophy of time/timelessness quite clear. "Religion is a present, which cannot become past ... absolute present." (*Ibid.*, p. 48.) "Religions come into existence when duration replaces eternity". (*Ibid.*, pp. 166f.) "Present" is always momentary but also always eternal. (*Ibid.*, pp. 104, 234f.) Here Horwitz herself makes the connection with Rosenzweig, a connection which her book in general rightly stresses. (Cf. *ibid.*, 183ff., 214ff., *et passim.*) This connection between the two can also be shown to extend to Buber's contrast between "Gegenwart" and "Gegenstand". It should especially be noted that in all of these fundamental passages Buber talks a great deal about past and present but not at all about future. (Friedman argues vehemently [too vehemently] against Horwitz's derivation of *I and Thou* from Rosenzweig. *Martin Buber's Life and Works*, vol. I, *op. cit.*, pp. 298-301, 408-411.) This is unfortunately part of Friedman's hyperbolical insistence that everybody is derivative to Buber—Buber derivative to no-one. (I may add some private evidence here. I have in my possession the hand written notes that my late mother took during Buber's course in the Frankfurt *Lehrhaus* on "Arch-Forms". [Cf. Rosenzweig's letter to my parents,then just about to marry, in *Living legacy. Essays in Honor of Hugo Hahn*, ed. B.N. Cohn, New York, Congregation Habonim, pp. 52ff.] These notes tend to support Horwitz's argument strongly.) A very similar philosophy of time/timelessness has been shown to underlie Rudolf Bultmann's philosophical theology: Roger A. Johnson, *The Origins of Demythologizing. Philosophy and Historiography in the Theology of Rudolf Bultmann*, Leiden 1974, pp. 21, 24, 68 *et passim.* Its perverse derivation from Hermann Cohen is also something that Bultmann has in common with Buber: cf. *ibid.*, chapter 2: 'The Philosophical Origins of Demythologizing. Marburg Neo-Kantianism'. And of course, the entire ambience of the German turn from rationalism in the First World War, as brought to a head in Heidegger, characterises this whole intellectual trend. (Cf. also Bultmann's and Buber's replacement of "Erfahrung" with "Erlebnis": *ibid.*, p. 58 etc.)

131. Cf. notes 1, 24 above, *re* J. Bloch. A close reading of Buber's letter to Bergmann (cf. note 38 above) brings out his philosophy of time (or rather of timelessness) very clearly. What Buber calls "messianism" is never future but always functions in the present. He calls this "absolute future", and it turns out to mean "eternalisation" in my sense. He calls this "allzeitliche Messianität", "omnipresent messianity". "All times are redemption-immediate." (Kohn, *op. cit.,* pp. 84f. Cf. for this Ranke's famous doctrine that every historical hour is, as it were, "immediate to God'.) Only "in this sense", i.e., in the sense that eternity, timelessness, inheres every time period, "is time greater than eternity". (He here uses the term "Menschendauer", which is presumably an allusion to Bergsonian *durée.) Cf. Poppel, loc. cit.,* p. 15: "Hostile to historicism, [Franz Rosenzweig] and Buber also had little patience with any really future-orientated religiosity, despite their stress on the messianic side of Judaism."

132. *Op. cit.,* p. 20.

133. *Eclipse of God, op. cit.,* chapter 7; Freidman, *Life of Dialogue, op. cit., passim.* Like so much else, these things tend to precede their American avatars by about half-a-century.

134. Quoted in Kohn, *op. cit.,* p. 232.

135. Buber formulates his actual subjectivism often and in different ways: "Oh you secure and safe ones, who hide yourselves behind the ramparts of the law [or theology or of ethics], so that you will not to have to look into God's abyss . . . Of God's will we know only the eternal; the temporal we must command for ourselves." (Herberg, *op. cit.,* p. 19, quoting *Der heilige Weg,* 1920.) "God has truth but no system." (Simon, 'Introduction to Martin Buber's Political Way . . .', *loc. cit.,* p. 10). "Therefore, I still oppose 'situations' to 'principles', the 'unclean' reality to 'pure' abstraction. . . . that one wins from [situations] from time to time as much truth and justice as one can." (D. Saperstein, 'Martin Buber's Theory of Poltiics', MA-thesis, Hebrew Union College-Jewish Institute of Religion, New York 1973, quoting from 'Reply to my Critics', Schilpp, *op. cit.,* English edn., p. 722); etc. The criticisms of his subjectivism are no less manifold: Schwarzschild, *Judaism,* VIII, No. 2 (Spring 1959), pp. 168, 170; N. Rotenstreich, in Schilpp. *op. cit.,* pp. 122, 131, and Buber's reply, *ibid.,* p. 722; M. Fox, 'Einige Probleme in Bubers Moralphilosophie', Schilpp, *op. cit.,*; Berkovits, *op. cit.,* pp. 87f.; for Scholem on this point: Simon, *The Line of Demarcation, op. cit.,* pp. 44, 49, 'Martin Buber's Interpretation of Hasdism', *loc, cit.,* p. 245. It is then only fair play that Simon rightly attributes "religious anarchism" to both Buber and Scholem: 'Religion und Staat in Israel', *loc. cit.,* p. 179; also, T. Friedman, 'Gershom Scholem . . .', *Conservative Judaism,* XXXII, No. 2 (Winter 1979), pp. 78f. Cf. also Biale, *op. cit.,* pp. 3, 94-100, *et passim.* Baruch Kurzweil's vehement attacks on Scholem are based in part precisely on the claim that Scholem, unlike Buber, hides his anarchism under a mantle of historical objectivity. (*Ibid.,* pp. 172, 192.) Simon himself always tries to find some middle-way between Buber and Scholem: on the one hand, he calls Buber's position "A believing occasionalism" ('Martin Buber, der Erzieher', *loc. cit.,* p. 499) and says: "Education for 'compromise,'

which Matthew Arnold expected of the adult citizen of a mature democracy, is for Buber not only the goal but the basis of character-education" (*ibid.*, p. 502); on the other hand, Simon sometimes goes so far as to speak, for example, of Buber's "radical subjectivism ... which occasionally borders on arbitrariness (nihilism) (*shririyut!*)". (*Lines of Demarcation, op. cit.*, p. 54. Cf. note 72 above).

136. The metaphor of "the narrow ridge", whatever else might be said about it, is presumably derived from the rabbinic simile that the Torah is like a ridge between fire on one side and ice on the other, to which man had better keep if he wishes to avoid dying from heat or cold. (Cf. *Aboth de Rabbi Nathan,* ed. S. Schechter, New York 1945, p. 86, and the cross references there enumerated.) It is typical of Buber's exegesis, i.e., removing the legal sting and spiritualising such texts, as Scholem also pointed out with respect to his exegesis of *hasidic* texts. In the present instance Buber really turns the simile upside-down: in all its variants (cf. Levy, *Wörterbuch über die Talmudim und Midraschim, sub* "sh'veel" and "astrateya"), it is precisely the Torah, i.e., the law with its objectivity and specificity, that saves man from the dangers of subjectivity.

137. *The Line of Demarcation, op. cit.*, p. 43.

138. About Martin Buber's Political Path ...', *loc. cit.*, p. 31.

139. *Ibid.*, p. 43.

140. This explains, at least in part, his attraction to people like Dag Hammarskjoeld: *Nachlese, op. cit.*, pp. 33-36, and Friedman, *Martin Buber's Life and Works,* vol. III, op. cit., chapt. 13, and to Ben Gurion himself (cf. Friedman, *ibid.*, chapter 14).

141. 'Toward Perpetual Peace', Cassirer edn., p. 456. In 'Die forderung des Geistes ...' Buber himself operates with this contrast between Plato and Kant. (*Op. cit.*, pp. 1061-1069.) He tries to make a case that Isaiah is a third model figure, which in a sort of Hegelian manner, "sublates" that contrast—a figure, furthermore, which he obviously adopts as his own ideal.

142. Cf. notes 17-20 above.

143. Cf. note 51 above.

144. Cf. Max Horkheimer's equivalent position on "this question of the day": *Die Sehnsucht nach dem ganz Anderen,* Hamburg 1970/1975, pp. 47f., and Julius Carlebach, *Karl Marx and the Radical Critique of Judaism,* London, etc. 1978, p. 418, note 93. (Comp. S. Schwarzschild, 'Karl Marx's Jewish Theory of Usury', *Gesher,* Yeshiva University, 1978, pp. 7-40). Scholem, too, opposed the execution: cf. Hannah Arendt, *The Jew as Pariah,* ed. R.H. Feldman, New York 1978, pp. 244f.

145. *Nachlese, op. cit.*, p. 218. For Buber on the death-penalty in the U.S.S.R. cf. Friedman, *Martin Buber's Life and Work,* vol. 3, *op. cit.*, pp. 323f., 403: "in each particular case".

146. "3. Dem Selbstschutz der Gesellschaft müssen durch seinen Zweck die Grenzen gezogen sein, und sie müssen immer neu nachgeprüft werden."

147. *Op. cit.,* p. 113. For Hodes (and Kohn), cf. Sander Gilman, 'Rediscovery of the Eastern Jews. German Jews in the East, 1890-1918', in *Jews and Germans . . ., op. cit.,* p. 363, note 9.

148. On Hodes cf. also *Martin Buber's Life and Work,* vol. 1, *op. cit.,* p. 396.

149. In his two short essays on Henry Thoreau (*Nachlese, op. cit.,* pp. 215ff.) one can follow Buber's *modus operandi* along precisely the same lines with respect to civil disobedience.

150. *Guide for the Perplexed,* Pines edn., p. 499: "For everyone who seeks the truth . . . will seek out the beliefs that are so firm that when one has them one pays no attention to the man who tries to compete through working a miracle." Even the revelation at Sinai turns out ot be a *façon de parler,* since God has, of course, no organs of speech (*ibid.,* I/46), and it is "a parable for some (rational) notion" (*ibid.,* p. 437). *A fortiori* is it the case that Maimonides gives natural, scientific explanations for every, even biblically, alleged miracle. Yet that "only will alone" (*ibid.,* p. 452), "volition " both human and divine, is operative in the universe (for purposes of ethics) has to be affirmed and, in this sense, the possibility of miracles. Cf. Schwarzschild, 'Moral Radicalism and "Middlingness" in the Ethics of Maimonides', this volume, p. 155; and A. Altmann, 'Maimonides and Thomas Aquinas. Natural or Divine Prophecy?', *AJS Review,* III (1978), Cambridge, Mass., Association for Jewish Studies, p. 8 and p. 17: "In Maimonides's view even Moses's prophecy was the natural result of a specific disposition which, though unique, was still natural." Cf. also Lawrence Kaplan, 'Maimonides on the Miraculous Element in Prophecy', *Harvard Theological Review,* 70, Nos. 3-4 (June-October 1977), p. 255.

151. Cf. M.M. Kellner, *Contemporary Jewish Ethics,* New York 1978, on the classical sources regarding capital punishment: pp. 309-333, and S. Schwarzschild, 'Kantianism on the Death Penalty (and Related Social Problems)', *Archiv für Rechts- und Sozialphilosophie,* LXXI, 3 (1985), pp. 343-372.

152. Cf. Kurzweil, in *Spiritual Perplexity, op. cit.,* p. 94: "In the absence of a normative criterion—and Buber has none such—inevitably the way is open to 'autarchy of the soul' ". Kurzweil rightly explains Buber's unpopularity with most religious Jews and his popularity with many Christians on the basis of this antinomianism of his. (*Ibid.,* pp. 94, 100, 109.)

153. Cf. S. Schwarzschild, 'Martin Buber's Zionism. Its Bearing on Pacifism', *Jewish Peace Fellowship Tidings* (mimeographed), September 1947, p. 6.

154. Cf. in current terms of technical, "deontic logic", Aziza Al-Hibri, *Deontic Logic,* Washington D.C. 1978, pp. 18ff., 50ff., 103.

155. Other serious and devoted students of Buber's have arrived at the same respectfully ambivalent conclusion. Walter Kaufmann, 'Martin Buber. The Quest for You', *loc. cit.*, pp. 26,28: "At every turn my admiration and love for Buber are fused with critical reflection . . . I love Buber but feel that love does not entail agreement anymore than agreement entails love." Kurzweil, in *Spiritual Perplexity, op. cit.*, p. 89: "He determined our way also when we struggled against him and when our ways parted"; also *ibid.*, pp. 64, 91, 110. Francis Jeanson, *Sartre and the Problem of Morality*, Bloomington 1980, articulated the same attitude of discipleship and deep dissent towards his teacher.

156. In the last sentence of the 'Nachwort' to *Gog und Magog*, Heidelberg 1949, p. 408; the German edition of *For the Sake of Heaven*, Philadelphia 1945.

Chapter 11

1. For the sake of compactness I shall here omit consideration of principles 10 and 11 (individual providence and reward/punishment), though they obviously are of one piece with their successors. (Maimonides handles them with the same sophistication as the others, see n. 105 below.) The full English text of the Thirteen Principles is found in A.J. Wolf, trans., "Maimonides on Immortality and the Principles of Judaism." *Judaism* 15 (1966): pp. 96 ff., 213 ff. (= I. Twersky, *A Maimonides Reader* [New York: Behrman House, 1972] pp. 422 f.). Maimonides' "catechism" possesses universal Jewish authority (the Yemenites inserted Maimonides' name into the *Kaddish* prayer for early redemption: "In your life and in the life of our teacher Moses ben Maimon" [*Kovetz Teshuvot haRambam* (Leipzig, 1859), pp. 8 f.])—which is not to say that it cannot be or has not been disputed (cf. M. M. Kellner, "R Isaac Abravanel on the Principles of Judaism," *JAAR 45*; n. 4, Supplement [December 1977]: n. 1); it does say that no one can fail to consider it with the highest degree of seriousness. For the place of the Thirteen Principles within Maimonides' total philosophical system, see S. Schwarzschild, "Moral Radicalism and 'Middlingness' in Maimonides' Ethics," in this volume p. 153 and note 105. A brief history and a very good historical theology of all of Maimonides' Thirteen Principles is Louis Jacobs, Principles of the Jewish Faith: An Analytic Study (New York: Basic Books, 1964); for our principles, see chaps. 12-14 (cf. also Jacobs, *A Jewish Theology* [New York: Behrman House, 1973], chaps. 22-23]. See also M. M. Kellner, *Dogma in Medieval Jewish Thought* Oxford: Oxford University Press, 1986, in Hebrew as *Torat ha-Ikkarim* . . . (Kibbutz-Me'uhad, forthcoming), chap. 1 on Maimonides.

2. I translate these two sentences as literally as possible and with an eye toward their most sophisticated explication. Seligmann Baer (*Siddur Avodat Yisrael* [Berlin, 1937], p. 154) adduces Samuel David Luzzatto (introduction to Mahzor Roma, p. 18) to attribute the *Yigdal*, a hymnal formulation of Maimonides' Principles, to Daniel b. Judah Dayyan early in the sixteenth century; the credal formulation here used appears first in the 1566 Venice Haggadah (cf. A. Altmann, "Articles of Faith," *Encyclopaedia Judaica*, 3:656). Zalman S. Shapiro (*Treatise on the Thirteen Principles* [Hebrew;

Denver, CO, 1959], pp. 24, 27) interestingly assigns the credal form to use by the masses, the philosophically more technical hymnal form to potential students, and *Adon Olam* (another hymnal version of considerable technical sophistication) to the scholars, thus "rationalizing" the liturgical repetitiousness of all three versions in the prayer book.

3. Cf. Baer, loc. cit.; "They are accepted in all the dispersions of Israel." See also the legal code of my family's hometown, Frankfurt o/M, *Joseph Ometz*, §60: "In Germany the custom is to recite *Yigdal* after every prayer, for it is a beautiful hymn, structured according to the thirteen principles of our faith. Therefore, it is good to learn its grammatical explanation and to recite it with devotion."

4. Wolf, op. cit., p. 341. Maimonides here recapitulates the classic Talmudic prohibition of predicting the time of the Messiah's advent: B. Sanh. 97b: "Perish all those who calculate the 'end'!" (Cf. also ibid., 99a-b.) This is a prohibition which has, however, been violated more frequently than one can count—with all sort of excuses—even by Maimonides himself. S. Zeitlin ("Maimonides," *American Jewish Yearbook*, vol. 37 [1935], pp. 78 ff.) even suggested that Maimonides codified the laws that would be operative again only in Messianic times because he expected those times imminently. Cf. also A.J. Heschel, "Did Maimonides Beleive That He Was Worthy of Prophecy?" *Louis Ginzburg Jubilee Volume* (New York: American Academy of Jewish Research, 1954), Hebrew sec., pp. 159-188.

5. *Rosh Amanah*, chap. 5, objection 8.

6. Cf. Rashi's extended treatment of Hab. 2:3, in which he summarizes the bulk of classical Jewish speculation regarding the Messianic advent, and also E. Urbach, *The Sages* (Hebrew) (Jerusalem: Magnes Press, 1969), p. 607.

7. Cf. the fifteenth benediction in every Amidah recited by the Jew; " . . . for upon Thy salvation we do hope all the day/on every day," and also S. Schwarzschild, "The Messianic Doctrine in Contemporary Jewish History," in *Great Jewish Ideas* (Washington, D.C.: B'nai B'rith, 1964), p. 246.

8. *Gen. Rab.* 97, 94a.

9. *B. Sanh.* 98a, *Targum Jonathan* to Gen. 35:21 and Exod. 13:43. Cf. also A. Berger, "Captive at the Gate of Rome: A Messianic Motif," *Proceedings of the American Academy for Jewish Research* 44 (1977), and the intellectualized interpretation of this *'aggadeta* by R. Isaac b. Yedaiah (13th cent., Provencal) in Marc Saperstein, *Decoding the Rabbis: A 13th Century Commentary on the Aggadah* (Cambridge, Mass.: Harvard University Press, 1980). pp. 102-117.

10. Compare Maimonides, Code, Laws of Repentance 7:2. In the *Star of Redemption*, Franz Rosenzweig uses this text for his particular theological purposes—namely, that Israel, in its religious life, lives outside of time/history, i.e., in eternity at all times [New York: Holt, Rinehart & Winston, 1971], pp. 289-293.

11. *Guide of the Perplexed* 3:43, ed. S. Pines (Chicago: University of Chicago Press, 1963), p. 571.

12. *Two Types of Faith* (London: Routledge & Kegan Paul, 1957). Wilfred Cantwell Smith picks up this Buber-caterogization, although he gives only passing credit (*Faith and Belief* [Princeton, N.J.: Princeton University Press, 1979], p. 325, n. 65), and he universalizes and quite unduly exaggerates it.

13. Cf. Schwarzschild, "Messianic Doctrine," pp. 237 ff.

14. Hegel's perpetual haranguing of "bad infinity" in favor of "good (i.e., completed, or completable, 'actual') infinity" and all its subsequent philosophical as well as even mathematical (e.g., Georg Cantor) ramifications are modernist reformulations of this Christian doctrine. Cf. my "The Religious Stake of Modern Philosophy of Infinity," *Annual of Bar Ilan University* 22-23 (1987), pp. 63-84.

15. Cf. S. Schwarzschild, "The Personal Messiah—Toward the Restoration of a Discarded Doctrine," this volume, p. 19. "The Democratic Socialism of Hermann Cohen," *Hebrew Union College Annual 27* (1956): 436f.; and my introduction to Cohen's *Ethik des reinen Willens* (Hildesheim and New York: G. Olms, 1981), pp. xxiff. (M. Buber, too, says: "In our [Jewish] view redemption occurs always, and none has yet occurred"—cf. Maurice Friedman, *M. Buber's Life and Work: The Late Years, 1945-1965* [New York: Dutton, 1983], 3:50.) It should be noted that the assertion of the personhood of the Messiah, as over against the notion of "the Messianic age," is logically and theologically independent of the affirmation that one day he will have, in fact, come; cf. S. Schwarzschild, "Personal Messiah," p. 17. What I wish to confess in repeating this point is that, with respect to the article just cited, which has often been reprinted, translated, and used (recently, for example, in Ze'ev Lévy, *On the Relationship Between Jewish and General Philosophy* [Hebrew] [Tel Aviv: Hakibbutz Hame'uchad, 1982], pp. 247 f.), I have been forced to change my mind. I continue to argue for the personhood of the Messiah, as I did there, but I have come to see that the other argument there (actually Rosenzweig's argument—cf. nn. 13 f.), that the Messianic advent has to be in time rather than "in infinity," is erroneous for at least two reasons: (1) it is philosophically mistaken (H. Cohen was, after all, right [cf. *Ethik*, pp. xxiv f.]), and (2) it is historically invidious (for example, the pseudoMessianism of Zionism and the State of Israel is precluded by the doctrine of the Messiah's eternal coming). I am, indeed, now prepared to argue that even the denial of the expectation of the personal Messiah in the classical Jewish sources (for example, the silence about this in several biblical books and the statement of the amoraic Rabbi Hillel that "he had already been consumed" [*B. Sanh.* 99a, Rashi ad locum = *Midr. Ps.* 107, and I. Abrabanel, *Yeshu'ot Meshiho* (Königsberg: 1861), pp. 26a ff.; cf. A.H. Silver, *A History of Messianic Speculations in Israel* (New York: Macmillan, 1927), p. 197, Rav's statement that "all the 'ends' have been exhausted, and the matter now depends solely on repentance and good deeds." B. Sanh., 97b, etc.]) and the derogation of the whole doctrine, one way or the other (for example, by Albo, *Ikkarim* I/4, IV/35:1; cf. Urbach, op. cit., p. 612, n. 10; Schwarzschild,

"Personal Messiah," p. 20; and Kellner, *Dogma*, chap. 1, n. 244, who here comes to the conclusion that "Maimonides' emphasis on the dogmatic importance of belief in the Messiah is unique in the literature of medieval Jewish dogmatics") ought to be understood in the same way: these teachers, too, really want to say that such an advent is not to be counted on as an operational factor in Jewish ethics of history. I am always puzzled why it is that Julian the Apostate's concrete attempt to restore the Jerusalem Temple left no traces in rabbinic literature. (Cf. Y. Levi, "Caesar Julianus and the Building of the Temple" [Hebr.], Zion 6 (1940-1941): 1-32 and F. Blanchetière, "Julien Philhéllène, Philosémite, Antichrétien: L'affaire du Temple de Jerusalem [363]," *Journal of Jewish Studies*], 31, no. 1 [Spring 1980]: 60-81.) None of the historical experts comes up with any solutions. It may be a weak, *e silentio*, argument, but I like to think that the rabbis did not take Julian seriously because, since he had come, he could not be the Messiah.

16. Cf. Schwarzschild, "Personal Messiah," p. 21 and "F. Rosenzweig's Anecdotes about H. Cohen," in *Gegenwart im Rueckblick—Festgabe f.d. jüdische Gemeinde zu Berlin 25 Jahre nach dem Neubeginn*, ed. H. Strauss and K. Grossman (Heidelberg, 1970), pp. 210 f.

17. *Jehuda Halevy—92 Hymnen und Gedichte deutsch* (Berlin: L. Schneider, n.d.), p. 239.

18. Cf. S. Schwarzschild, "Jenseits von Sein und Zeit" (review), *International Studies in Philosophy* 14, no. 1 (1981): 102 ff.

19. *Entsheidung zum Judentum—Essays und Vorträge* (Suhrkamp, 1980).

20. (New York: Schocken, 1977). Her English title reproduces the Yiddish locution of not using an article with the name "Messiah": after all, the name of any other individual also does not take an article.

21. Maimonides himself refers back to his entire introduction to the Principles for the doctrine of resurrection. He is right: his entire exposition there deals with eschatology.

22. Cf. Kellner, *Dogma*, loc. cit.

23. Cf. Maimonides' *Code*, Laws of Repentance 8:3, and Schwarzschild, "Moral Radicalism," pp. 143 f.

24. *M. Sanh.* 10:1 (It seems actually, on the latest evidence, that the phrase about having to believe resurrection to be "taught in the Bible" is not part of Maimonides' own text in his *Commentary to the Mishnah*; cf. ibid., ed. R. Joseph Kafich [Jerusalem: Mossad HaRav Kook, 1963], vol. 4 ["Nezikin"], p. 165). Or in the vernacular: if you don't believe in it, you won't get it. Presumably this Talmudic dogma contradicts both Sadduceeanism and Greek spiritualism. Note carefully Maimonides' wording (Wolf, op. cit., p. 31): "We are to believe as a fact that . . . " Such a formulation is significantly different from saying "it is a fact that . . . " Also, it leads straight into Maimonides' logic of what he calls "necessary truths," themselves a component of the complex history of

pias fraus and "fiction." (Cf. S. Schwarzschild, "Introduction," p. x in Cohen, *Ethik*; Moshe Silberg, *Talmudic Law and the Modern State* [New York: Burning Bush, 1975], chap. III, "Evasion of the Law"; and my late teacher, Samuel Atlas, *Pathways in Hebrew Law* [Hebrew] [New York: American Academy of Jewish Research, 1978], "Evasion and Fiction," pp. 265 ff., esp. pp. 267 f., for the philosophy of fiction, and "Whatever the Rabbis Sanctify is Sanctified" [Hebrew], *Sinai* 75 [Sivan–Tammuz 1974]: 135 f., 141; Y.S. Zuri, "Legal Conceptualization in Jewish Law," [Hebrew], *Festschrift for B.M. Levin* [1940], pp. 174-195; M.A. Amiel, "The Concept of Potentiality in the Halakhah" [Hebrew], *Sinai 7* [1943]: 20-33; A. Karlin, "Ex Post Facto Law" [Hebrew], *Sinai 14* [1951]: 129-142 and "De Jure Personality," *Sinai 2* [1939]: 445-452; Solomon Goldman, "The Legal Fiction in Jewish Law," in *Presentation Volume to William Barron Stevenson*, ed. C.J. Mullo Weir, (Studia Semitica et Orientalia 2 [Glasgow, 1945]).

25. Arthur Hyman ("Maimonides' Thirteen Principles," in *Jewish Medieval and Renaissance Studies*, ed. A. Altmann [Cambridge: Harvard University Press, 1967], pp. 134 ff.) argues that Maimonides does not deal with the subjects of principles 12 and 13 because he does not regard them as philosophical, i.e., rational. Kellner (*Dogma*, chap. 1, nn. 239-241) convincingly argues that Hyman is mistaken about this by pointing out that principle 13 is the only one of all of them that employs all three of the epistemic terms in Maimonides' vocabulary—"knowledge," "faith," and "sincere affirmation."

26. Cf. esp. Rabad *ad* "Laws of Repentance" 8:1 ff.; D. Silver, *Maimonidean Criticism and Maimonidean Controversy* 1180-1240 (Leiden: E.J. Brill, 1965), pp. 109-135; Jacobs, *Principles*, pp. 407 f.; and Z.S. Shapiro, *op. cit.*, p. 13: "The heavens and the earth have long quaked with the arguments against the Thirteen Principles."

27. Cf. "Moral Radicalism," pp. 154f. Saadiah Gaon and Ibn Ezra (ad Dan. 12:2) make similar stipulations. The purpose is in each case the distinction between normally physical existence in the Messianic realm, on the one hand, and existence in a "spiritual body" in the world-to-come, on the other hand (cf. below). Gersonides, as usual, exponentializes Maimonides' rationalism. He does not mention the Messiah at all in his magnum opus, *The Wars of the Lord*. He, too, makes the will central to the Jewish enterprise (M. Kellner, "Gersonides on Miracles, the Messiah and Resurrection," *Da'at* 5 [Winter 1980]: 33, n. 114), and, therefore, Jewish morality brings the Messiah (ibid., pp. and 30, nn. 106 and 109). One might note with curiosity that Euridice is resurrected twice in Gluck's *Orfeo and Euridice*.

28. On rabbinic doctrine cf. Arthur Marmorstein, "The Redemption-Idea in The Teachings of the Tannaites and Amoraites" in his *Studies in Jewish Theology: The A. Marmorstein Memorial Volume*, ed. J. York (Oxford University Press, 1950), pp. 17-76; see also pp. 145-161 ("The Doctrine of the Resurrection of the Dead in Rabbinic Theology") and pp. 162-178 ("Participation in Eternal Life in Rabbinical Theology and Legend"); S. Lieberman, "Some Aspects of After Life in Rabbinic Literature," in *Texts and Studies* [New York, 1974], pp. 235-272, and H.J. Matt, "An Outline of Jewish Eschatology," *Judaism* 17 (Summer 1968): 186-196. (The article on "Eschatology" in vol. 6 of

the *Encyclopedia Judaica* has a good summary of the subject in biblical literature—and next to nothing else!)

29. Cf. Altmann, op. cit., col. 655.

30. Cf. Schwarzschild, "Messianic Doctrine," pp. 254f.

31. Cf. S. Schwarzschild, "The Lure of Immanence—The Crisis in Contemporary Jewish Thought," this volume, p. 65.

32. Cf. S. Schwazschild, "Moral Radicalism," n. 122, and Maimonides, Laws of Repentance 8:7 and 9:1.

33. *Code*, Law of Kings 12:5; cf. Twersky, op. cit., pp. 414 f. The continuity of Maimonides' thought throughout his life is thus reconfirmed. (Cf. Twersky, op. cit., p. 387.)

34. Ibid., 10:5.

35. Cf. Oscar Cullmann, "Immortality of the Soul and Resurrection of the Dead," in *Immortality and Resurrection: Death in the Western World: Two Conflicting Currents of Thought*, ed. K. Stendahl (New York: Macmillan, 1965), pp. 9-53. I think Cullmann's dichotomy is valid. I also think, however, that his claim to the doctrine of resurrection in the New Testament and early Christianity misfires (cf. J.D. Tabor, "Resurrection and Immortality," in *Christian Teaching: Studies in Honor of LeMoine G. Lewis* [Abilene: Abilene University Press, 1981]).

36. *Guide*, I.

37. There is a beginning of this in Joseph Klausner, *The Messianic Idea in Israel* [London, Allen & Unwin, 1956], especially pt. III, and in S. Forstein, "The Law in Talmudic Eschatology" (diss., Hebrew Union College—Jewish Institute of Religion, 1965).

38. Laws of Repentance 8:4 re "soul," 8:5 re "perishing," and 8:8 re "coming."

39. *Theological Investigations* (Baltimore: Helicon, 1966), 4:323-346.

40. Cf. *Code*, Laws of Repentance 8:1 ff. and 8:8.

41. *M. Sanh.* 10:1.

42. T. *Sanh.* 13:2 Cf. S. Schwarzschild, "Do Noachites have to Believe in Revelation?" this volume pp. 37f. "An Eschatological Liturgy," *CCAR Journal 23*, no. 4 (Autumn 1976): 22-26; Jacob Katz, "The Vicissitudes of Three Apologetic Passages" (Hebrew), *Zion* 23-24, nos. 3-4 (1958-59): 174-181.

43. The Hebrew word for "coming" (as in *olam haba, bechol yom sheyavo*, etc.), here needs to be unpacked in its eschatological usage. (Cf. nn. 37 ff. above.)

44. Aggadic literature is full of the things that God does in His eternity and, indeed, of the things that people do in their eternal lives. Above all, the latter continue to

"strive"—i.e., they "grow"—intellectually and morally; cf. Maimonides' interpretation of the rabbinic dictum (*B. Ber. 17a*) that, though "there is no eating or drinking or sexual intercourse in the world to come, the righteous will sit, wearing crowns on their heads"—i.e., there will still be something beyond themselves, namely, the "Idea" of God and imortality—and, therefore, "they will drink in the effulgence of the presence of God"—i.e., they will enjoy greater, namely spiritual, pleasures: study of Torah. (Twersky, op. cit., pp. 411 f. and Laws of Repentance 8:2, "the crowns" are "knowledge.") Cf. also Emanuel Levinas, "Temps messianiques et temps historiques dans le chapitre xi du Traité 'Sanhedrin,'" in *La Conscience Juive*, ed. E.A. Lévy-Valensi and J. Halpérin (Paris, 1963). (For an adumbration of Levina's eschatology cf. S. Schwarzschild, "S. Strasser, 'Jenseits von Sein und Zeit,'" *loc. cit.*, last paragragh.) Cf. Kant's *Religion Within the Bounds of Reason Alone* in *Immanuel Kants Werke* ed. H. Cohen et al. (Berlin: B. Cassirer, 1923), vol. 6, ed. E. Casirer, p. 283: "This notion of a history of afterlife, which is itself historical, is a beautiful ideal of the ... future epochs of the world, ... toward which we look forward in continuous progress and approximation."

45. 1 Cor 15:44 (cf. J.T.A. Robinson, *The Body: A Study in Pauline Theology* [London, 1952], p. 28, on *sarx* ["flesh"] vs. *soma* ["body" = person].) Cf. also Klausner, op. cit., p. 270 on the Wisdom of Solomon; ibid., p. 300 for the Book of Enoch: the "spiritual bodies" are bestowed like "the garments in the wilderness"; Albo, *Ikkarim* II/1 on Saadiah; Maimonides' *Guide* 2.30, and the end of the Rabad's (typically vehement but suddenly conditional) polemic against Maimonides' Code, Laws of Repentance 8:2; B. Safran, "Rabbi Azriel ..." in I. Twersky, ed., *Rabbi Moses/Nahmanides (Ramban): Explorations in His Religiou and Literary Virtuosity* (Cambridge: Harvard University Press, 1983) p. 86; Manasseh b. Israel, Nishmat Hayyim, chap. 1; G. Scholem, *Shabbetai Zvi* (Tel Aviv: Am Oved, 1956/57), p. 57, on "spiritual body" (English trans., p. 73).

46. Cf. Nachmanides, *Gate of Reward* in the *Zohar*, on "spiritual bodies." Also cf. E. Urbach, *The Sages*, p. 591, about the "intermixed," rather than metaphysical, character of *olam haba* and about the distinction between individual salvation and historical or posthistorical redemption.

47. *B. Shab.* 152b f. and Rashi *ad locum*; also on Maimonides' Code, Laws of Repentance 8:7.

48. *Book of Beliefs and Opinions*, trans. S. Rosenblatt (New Haven: Yale University Press, 1948), pp. 218, 431, 433. f. Cf. *B. Niddah* 61b, *Tosfot*, where the Messianic age and eternal life are collapsed into one. The rabbinic split of the Messiah into two Messiahs, the Son of Joseph and the Son of David, also basically expresses the two dimensions of this single eschatological entity—the physical and the spiritual. Max Brod, a goodly man who is too little known in this country for all but his relationship to Kafka, devoted, in our time, the whole second volume of his *Diesseits und Jenseits* (Winterhur: Mondial-Verlag, 1947), which was written in a very personal vein in Palestine during World War II, to "The Immortality of the Soul, the Justice of God, and a New Politics." (Brod's philosophizing is, unfortunately, always rather amateurish and quasi-

pantheistic.) His doctrine of immortality, attached to the rabbinic doctrine of "death by God's kiss" and to Maimonides' "conjunction" (chap. 6, M), is heavily ethical, even politically socialist (ibid., p. 334). Yet even he raises the possibiity of a quasi-material immortality (i.e., resurrection), which eventually would gravitate toward God (ibid., pp. 294 ff.).

49. Cf. *Ethics,* 3.11f. and 5.20 to the very end and climax of the work; compare H.A. Wolfson, *The Philosophy of Spinoza* (New York: Meridian books, 1965), 2:284-325, 349F. (on d'Acosta, pp. 323f.).

50. For Kant's argument against Mendelssohn on this score cf. his "On the Old Saw: This May Be Right In Theory But Won't Work in Practice," in *Kant's Gesammelte Schriften* (Berlin: Reimer, 1907), 6:392 f., and "Ideas for a Cospmopolitan History in Pragmatic Perspective," "Third Thesis," as well as H. Arendt, *Lectures on Kant's Political Philosophy* (Chicago: University of Chicago Press, 1982), p. 77. There is an extraordinary current debate among neo-Marxists, which duplicates this discussion and which owns up to its deeply Jewish charater: cf. Helmut Peukert, *Wissenschaftstheorie-Handlungstheoie-Fundamentale Theologie* (Duseldorf: Patmos, 1976), pp. 280 f., and *Habermas: Critical Debate,* ed. J.B. Thompson and D. Held (London: Macmillan, 1982), pp. 246 f., as to whether an ideal society can be happy remembering or forgetting the suffering of the past.

51. Cf. Isaac Heinemann *Ta'amay haMitzvot beSifrut Yisráel* (Jerusalem, 1961), 2:15 and A. Altmann, *Moses Mendelssohn: A Biographical Study* (Philadelphia: Jewish Publication Society, 1973), pp. 171-186. Cf. E. Schweid, "The Educational and Political Justification of Commandments of Belief According to Maimonides" (Hebrew), *Táam veHakashah* (Ramat Gan: Massada, 1970), pp. 80-104.

52. Altmann, *Moses Mendelssohn,* p. 183.

53. Cf. T. Penelhum, *Survival and Disembodied Existence* (London: Routledge & Kegan Paul, 1970) and A.G.N. Flew, "Is There a Case for Disembodied Survival?" *Journal of the American Society for Psychical Research* 66 (1972): 129-144.

54. Cf. C.Z. Reines, "*Kvod haMet*" (Hebrew), *Sinai* 53 (Tammuz-Av, 1936): 193 ff., esp. p. 193, n. 6: "This myth (of resurrection) entered, as is known, into Christianity, which assigned a mythological-mystical meaning to 'resurrection,' whereas Judaism assigned to it moral and symbolic meaning, connected with the Messianic conception." Reines concentrates so much on the moral significance that he, Orthodox Jew that he was, nonetheless somewhat neglects the sheer physical integrity of corpses; for this cf. Y.Y. Greenwald, *Kol Bo'al Avelut* (Hebrew) (New York: Feldheim, 1956).

55. S.L. Steinheim distinguished between naturalistic doctrine of immortality, offered by reason, and the doctrine of immortality by grace, offered by revelation: cf. N. Rotenstreich, "S.L. Steinheim—Philosopher of Revelation," *Judaism* 2, no. 4 (1953): 332f.

56. Chicago: Dover, 1953 (really *Substantial Concept and Functional Concept* [Berlin: Cassirer, 1910]). "Dimensionless bodies" is a notion used by the Kalam, which

is rehabilitated in Leibnitz's monads—mathematized at that time in the infinitesimal calculus (cf. S. Schwarzschild "Two Lives in the Jewish 'Frühaufklärung'," *Leo Baeck Institute Year Book 29* [1984], pp. 102 and 104)—taken further in Marburg neo-Kantianism in the form of "intensive magnitudes," and surely a legitimate scientific problematic at this time both epistemologically as well as in the burgeoning field of subatomic physics. The realms of ethics and of science must, to be sure, be carefully distinguished, but not sealed off, from one another.

57. Cf. *Telos* 44 (Summer 1980): 179 (compare S. Schwarzschild, "J.-P. Sartre as Jew," this volume, p. 163.

58. Frankfurt, 1966, pp. 389-392. Generally, the role of the "Frankfurt School" in contemporary, avant-garde Messianism is a subject that cries out for full explanation. E.g., T.W. Adorno even gets to resurrection: "Thus the center of Benjamin's philosophy is the idea of the salvation of the dead as the restitution of deformed life through the perfection of its objectification." (*Über W. Benjamin* [Suhrkamp, 1970], p. 29.) Jewish Messianism is this-worldly, social. "Utopia is the center of his theory" (p. 79). As for Adorno himself, cf. his *Minima Moralia* (Suhrkamp, 1951): "Philosophy as it can only be seen responsibly done in the face of depair would be the attempt to regard all things from the perspective of redemption" (p. 113). Walter Benjamin's part in the school and the importance of his friendship with Gershom Scholem are well known: Benjamin's "Theological-Political Fragment" (*Schriften*, ed. T.W. Adorno [Frankfurt, 1955], 1:511 f.)—Adorno dates this fragment ca. 1920 (*Über W. Benjamin*, p. 168, n. 19). G. Scholem, on the other hand, dates it as the very end of Benjamin's life (Scholem, *On Jews and Judaism in Crisis* [New York: Schocken, 1976], pp. 180, 199, 231), See n. 108 below. I cannot decide this issue between Adorno and Scholem. Each of them, no doubt, thinks that it has something to do with his respectively more Marxist or more Kabbalistic reading of Benjamin. (Cf. Über W. Benjamin, pp. 91 ff.) I think they both overdo their respective theses. (Cf. also Benjamin's famous "Angelus Novus," *Illuminations*, ed. H. Arendt (New York: Harcourt, Brace, & World, 1968], pp. 12f., 257 f., and Scholem, *op. cit.*, "Walter Benjamin and His Angel.") is perhaps the most profound and relevant formulation of Jewishly, radically pessimistic Messianism in our tragic century. Ernst Bloch's *The Principle Hope* (Suhrkamp, 1959), occupies an even more curious position in contemporary thought: Bloch himself and Jews and Judaism have been only dimly aware of one another and their inner connections, while Christian "theology of hope" (Möltmann, etc.), "theology of liberation," etc., are, in turn, only dimly aware of the (partial) Judaization which they underwent in the process of learning from Bloch. (Cf. Michael Landmann, "Das Judentum bei E. Bloch und seine messianische Metaphysik" in *Jüdische Miniaturen* [Bonn: Bouvier Verlag Grundmann, 1982], 1:161-182.)

59. B. *Ket* 8a. Compare the third benediction of the wedding ceremony (and its many commentaries). The whole benediction fits our present concern: "Praised be Thou, O Lord, our God, King of the world, who created man in His image, in the image of the similarity to His structure, and perfected for him therefrom a timeless edifice." Cf. S. Atlas, "*Dina D'Malchuta* Delimited," *Hebrew Union College Annual* 46 (1975):

280, n. 9, and Boaz Cohen, "Law and Ethics in the Jewish Tradition," in *Law and Tradition* (New York: Jewish Theological Seminary, 1959,), p. 187, n. 28, middle.

60. Cf. Kant's distinction between *Wille* and *Willkühr*: L.W. Beck, *A Commentary on Kant's Critique of Practical Reason* (Chicago: University of Chicago Press, 1960), pp. 176-208.

61. For a discussion of the contemporary Jewish philosopher E, Levinas's ethics as an eschatological "optics," cf. Steven G. Smith, *The Argument to the Other: Reason Beyond Reason in the Thought of K. Barth and E. Levinas* (Chico, Calif.: Scholars Press, 1983), pp. 85, 168.

62. *Some Aspects of Rabbinic Theology* (New York: Behrman, 1936), p. 114.

63. "Is and Ought," in *11th World Congress of Philosophy of Law and Social Philosophy* (Helsinki, 1983), "Plenary Main Papers and Commentaries," pp. 16-17.

64. Ibid., p. 25. (Fundamental disagreement still separates me from Hintikka.)

65. Cf. Schwarzschild, "Jewish Eschatological Liturgy," pp. 25 f.

66. Cf. the article "*Hilkheta dimeshicha,*" *Encyclopedia Talmudit* (Hebrew), 9:388 f. The material here would have to be carefully conceptualized.

67. *B. Meg.* 15a.

68. *Exod. Rab.* 25:16.

69. *B. Sabbath* 118b, *B. Sanh.* 97b f., *B. Abod. Zara* 3a, *B. Ber.* 57b; *Midr. Psalms*, ed. Braude, 2.137; Klausner, op. cit., pp. 427 f.; A.J. Heschel, *The Sabbath* (Philadelphia: Jewish Publication Society, 1952).

70. *B.B. Bat* 10b.

71. Cf. article "*Hilkheta dimeshicha,*" *Encyclopedia Talmudit* (Hebrew), loc. cit.

72. Will Herberg, ed., *The Writings of Martin Buber* (New York: Meridian Books, 1956), p. 311; cf. also R. Isaac Hutner, *Pachad Yitzchak*, vol. "Day of Atonement" (Hebrew) (Brooklyn, N.Y.: Gur Aryeh, 1978), lecture 5, pt. I, par. 2: "The belief in the end-time perceives anticipations of the future in the present" (see also my "Two Lectures of R.I. Hunter," *Tradition* 14, no. 4 [Fall 1974]: 93, and "Introduction to the Thought of R. I. Hunter," *Modern Judaism*, [Fall 1985], pp. 225-227), Ernst Bloch, "Resistance and Peace" in Z. Batscha, ed., *Materialien zu Kantz Rechtsphilosophie* [Suhrkamp, 1968], p. 374: "Therefore, distant goals must be present in every nearby goal more than implicitly—namely, they must emerge as more than *sine qua non* and as participatory"; Benjamin. "Theses about the Philosophy of History," op. cit., AB appendix to thesis 18: "Every second is the narrow portal through which the Messiah may enter."

73. For a detailed example of Messianic expatiation of *Halachah* cf. S. Schwarzschild, "A Note on the Nature of Ideal Society—A Rabbinic Study," this volume.

74. Cf. *B. Ta'anit* 2a f.: "God has kept three or four keys to himself—the keys to rain, birth, resurrection . . . and has not handed them over to a messenger" (*shaliach*; Rashi as locum repeats the phrase three times: *velo shaliach*! [Compare the repeated refrain, "God Himself—not a messenger,' " etc., in the *midrash* to Deut. 26:5-8 in the Passover Haggadah.]) *Tosfot* ad locum reconciles this statement with ours by saying that Elijah did, as a matter of fact, have the keys to rain and resurrection—he did not hold on to them permanently. Rashi reconciles the two passages by saying that no one human being ever shall have all three keys.

75. *Gen. Rab.* 76:1 and the parallels there cited.

76. *B. Shab.* 30b, cf.*B. Ket* 111b.

77. If J. Klausner is right, this *midrash* is especially titillating, for he claims that "the certain disciple" of R. Gamliel was Paul of Tarsus (*Messianic Idea in Israel*, p. 107). See also *Pirke deRabbi Eliezer*, ed. Friedlander, pp. 415 f., for a similar argument: again it is a matter of the novum of the resurrection against the "Greek" doctrine that "there is nothing new under the sun"; again the identity of one of the polemicists is left in doubt, but this time the later, medieval, Aristotelian concept of the sublunar world is invoked, so that the righteous will be resurrected "above the sun," while the wicked will cease to exist "under the sun," where there is really nothing new.

78. Cf. *M. Eduyot* 1:13, where Shammai insists Messianically that there can be no half-slaves, whereas Hillel, "for the sake of the (gradual) improvement of the world," permits them meanwhile; Shammai famously would light all eight Chanukkah candles immediately on the first night, whereas Hillel (and we) "build up" to them; Shammai insists on a total, rigorous, Messianic Sabbath (cf. M. Buber, *To Hallow This Life*, ed. J. Trapp [New York: Harper & Brothers, 1958], p. 97) rather than treating the Sabbath as "a foretaste" of the world to come (*B. Abod. Zara* 3a, *B. Ber.* 57b), and stolen property has to be returned to its rightful owner, regardless of invidious consequences (*B. Gitt.* 55a).

79. Cf. S. Greenberg, "And He Writes Her a Bill of Divorcement," *Conservative Judaism* 24, no. 3 (Spring 1970): 132.

80. Cf. S. Schwarzschild, *On Jewish Meta-Ethics*, chapter "Messianism," forthcoming.

81. Cf. S. Schwarzschild, "Justice," in *Encyclopaedia Judaica* (Jerusalem: Keter, 1971). For the ethicization of the Jewish vision of the world to come, see idem, "Eschatological Liturgy," p. 26.

82. Cf. S. Schwarzschild, "K. Marx's Jewish Theory of Interest," *Gesher* (New York: Yeshiva University, 1978), n. 53. Also the doctrine of reincarnation, which pops up in Jewish mysticism, is in fact a doctrine of renewed opportunities for self-remortalization (cf. "Eschatology: Kabbalah," *Encyclopaedia Judaica*, loc. cit.).

83. Shapiro, "Treatise," p. 16.

84. Maimonides' *Eight Chapters*, beginning; *Sefer Chassidim* (S.A. Singer, *Medieval Jewish Mysticism: The Book of the Pious* [Northbrook, Ill., 1971], p. 15); M. H. Luzzatto, *Mesillat Yesharim*, etc.

85. Cf. John Hick, *Philosophy of Religion*, 2d ed. (Englewood Cliffs, N.J.: Prentice-Hall, 1973), pp. 90-95, and idem, "Eschatological Verification," in *The Logic of God/Theology and Verification*, ed. M.L. Diamond and Litzenberg Jr. (Indianapolis: Bobbs-Merril, 1975), sec. 6.

86. *Code*, Laws of Repentence 8:6.

87. This need for grace in the performance of even a single, limited moral action is expressed, for example, in the rabbinic principle, variably instatiated, that the fulfillment of one important commandment is accounted as though it were the fulfillment "of the whole Torah" (*B. Kidd* 40a. for the denial of idolatry; *B. Chullin* 4a for Sabbath observance). See nn. 68-70 above.

88. Cf. S. Schwarzschild, "On the Theology of Jewish Survival," this volume, p. 97 and S.H. Bergman, *Faith and Reason* (Washington, D.C.: B'nai B'rith Hillel, 1961), p. 50, on Hermann Cohen's "correlation": correlation is . . . the narrow ridge between two dangerous abysses: man's activism, his trust in his own power, his confidence that heaven is not needed . . . and an attitude exemplified, for instance by Luther who makes man the passive recipient (or non-recipient) of divine grace . . . . Cohen, in rejecting both extremes, follows the tradition of classical Jewish thought." Compare also R. Yehuda HaLevy's dialectic of grace and works: the influx of grace must be prepared, even on the part of Jews who are metaphysically equipped for this, by the fulfillment of the commandments.

89. Cf. *B. Ber.* 4b.

90. *B. Sanh.* 97bf. = *Y. Ta'anit* 1:1, 63d.

91. "Temps messianiques," loc. cit.

92. Sometimes Ps. 65:2 and Deut. 32:3 are added to Ps. 51:17. I suspect that Ps. 65:2 is expected to be the overtone to Ps. 65:3: "Unto Thee [O God] silence is praise." (N.B. the recurrence of the word "praise" in Ps. 65:2 and Ps. 51:17.) Thus prayer somehow emerges out of the necessary silence between man and God that precedes and underlies prayer. (Cf. S. Schwarzschild, "Speech and Silence before God," in *Understanding Jewish Prayer*, ed. J. Petuchowski [New York, 1972], pp. 84-99 and 167-170). Indeed, at their end the Eighteen Benedictions fade back into the silence out of which they emerged, in the words of the coda, also silently recited by the individual: "Let my soul be silent and like dust unto all" (*B. Shabb.* 88b, *Tosfot* to *B. Ber.* 17a). N.B. the use of the word "my lips" at the end, as at the beginning. Cf. also I. Frimer, "The Recital of 'O Lord, open my lips . . .'" *Or Hamizrach* 34/1-2 (120-21; September 1985), pp. 87-93.

93. The dialectics does not, of course, dissolve so simply. Man takes autonomous action (by praying), but he gets this prayer from the Bible, which is "graciously" revealed.

Many similar liturgical situations occur. For example, "Our Father, merciful Father, merciful One, be merciful by putting it into our hearts . . . to keep, to do, and to fulfill in love all the words of learning of Thy Torah."

94. *Quest for Past and Future* (Bloomington, 1968), pp. 90, 202; cf. also ibid., "Judaism and the Idea of Progress," pp. 83-95, and "Human Freedom and Divine Power."

95. *Ethics of the Pure Will* (Berlin: Cassirer, 1904), p. 407.

96. There is, in any case, a pervasive hybris ("counter-snobbery") in "salvation by grace": the *ecclesia triumphans* boasts of being saved because it is poor in works!

97. *B. Sanh.* 97a and *Midr. Pss.* 45:3. The "or" in the Hebrew sentence should probably be taken as an inclusive, not as an exclusive, i.e., "and/or." Cf. S. Schwarzschild, "From Critical to Speculative Idealism" (review), *Journal of Bible and Religion* 34 (January 1966): 65 f.

98. Cf. S.D. Goitein, "'Meeting in Jerusalem': Messianic Expectations in the Letters of the Cairo Geniza," *AJS Review* 4 (1979): 52 ff.

99. Scholem, op. cit., pp. 76 f. (Nathan Shapiro, in Spinoza's and Shabbetai's time).

100. *B. Pesah,* 64b.

101. Cf. *B. Sota,* end, the biblical notion of "the terrible day of God," and the rabbinic notion of "the birth pangs of the Messiah." Cf. also R. Aron Rote, as exposited in S. Schwarzschild, "Speech and Silence before God," *Judaism* 10, no. 3 (Summer 1961): 199.

102. Cf. Schwarzschild, "Survival," p. 97.

103. *B. Sanh.* 98b.

104. Maurice Friedman, *Martin Buber's Life and Work: The Late Years 1945-1965* (New York: E.P. Dutton, 1984), p. 103.

105. We can finally integrate principles 10 and 11 into Maimonides' eschatology. Principle 10 asserts, against then current Aristotelianism, divine *providentia individualis* for human beings alone, through the reason that God and humanity share (cf. *Guide* 3.17 f.). Principle 11, "reward and punishment," can then draw the conclusion that reward consists of immortality (by virtue of the *conjunctio* of the human spirit with the divine), while punishment consists of the absence or reward (*theologia negativa*) (cf. Twersky, op. cit., p. 412—Laws of Repentance 8:5). Albo makes the doctrine of reward and punishment (i.e., the ultimacy of moral responsibilty) fundamental to Judaism (unlike the Messianic doctrine, cf. n. 15, end, above) and inserts the Messianic kingdom on earth and physical resurrection as intermediate stages between normal life and immortality (just like Maimonides) only so that immortality can follow the elimination of the guilt/punishment phenomenon. (*Ikkarim* 1:23, 4:30, and 31:9).

106. Cf. M. Friedman, *Martin Buber's Life and Work: The Middle Years 1923-1945* (New York: E.P. Dutton, 1983), p. 313 and *The Late Years, 1945-1965,* p. 211.

107. Lou H. Silberman argues very well against the simplistic Messianism-apocalypticsm dichotomy in "The Human Deed in a Time of Depair: The Ethics of Apocalyptic," in Essays in *Old Testament Ethics,* ed. J.L. Crenshaw and J.T. Willis (New York: Ktav, 1974), pp. 193-200, and "Apocalyptic Revisited: Reflections on the Thought of Albert Schweitzer," *JAAR* 44, no. 3 (176): 489-501.

108. Cf. *The Nature and Destiny of Man* (New York: Scribner's, 1946), 2:270: "eschatological irresponsibiltiy," and S. Schwarzschild, "Survey of Current Theological Literature," *Judaism* 7, no. 4 (Fall 1958): 363-367.

109. *Conjectures and Refutations: The Growth of Scientific Knowledge* (New York: Harper Torchbooks, 1963), chap. 18, pp. 355-363.

110. There are all sorts of personal, philosophical, political, and/or even family connections among the members of the inner circle of assimilated Viennese Jews—including Wittgenstein; cf. W.W. Bartley III, "Knowledge Is a Product Not Fully Known to Its Producer; in *The Political Economy of Freedom: Festschrift for F.A.v. Hayek's 85th Birthday,* ed. K. Leube and A. Zlabinger (Munich: Philosphia, 1984). For Wittgenstein's political conservatism, connected to his later philosophizing, cf. S. Schwarzschild, 'Wittgenstein as Alienated Jew," *Telos* 40 (Summer 1979): 163.

111. "Utopia and Violence," p. 361.

112. Ibid., p. 363. See his "Autobiography" in *The Philosophy of Karl Popper,* ed. P. Schilpp (La Salle, Ill.: Open Court, 1974), 1:26 f., for his experiences with communists in Vienna in the early 1920s that led him to this train of thought and, for example, pp. 90, 95, 101, for his relations with v. Hayek. It is not surprising then that the last section "The Place of Values in a World of Facts" (§40, pp. 153-155) must surely be regarded as strikingly thin even by his own standards.

113. "Utopia and Violence," pp. 357-359.

114. W.W. Bartley III argues against his teacher Popper that rationality can be shown itself to be rational in "The Philosophy of K. Popper—Part III. Rationality, Criticsm, and Logic," *Philosophia* (Bar-Ilan University), 11, nos. 1-2 (February 1983), esp. pp. 157-186.

115. "The 'Corroboration' of Theories" in *Philosophy of K. Popper,* p. 238.

116. Cf. Popper's chapter on Hegel in *The Open Society and Its Enemies* (Princeton, N.J.: Princeton University Press, 1950) and H.B. Acton, "Moral Futurism and the Ethics of Marxism," in *The Philosophy of Karl Popper,* 2:876 ff.

117. Cf. M. Buber, *Paths in Utopia* (Boston: Beacon Press, 1958).

118. Cf. H. Cohen, *Ethik des reinen des Willens,* p. ix; cf. also my student H. van der Linden's *Kantian Ethics and Socialism* (Indianapolis, IN: Hacket, forthcoming).

119. This is unfortunately not the place to trace the epistemological and philosophic side if this argument against Popperism. We can say that certain distortions of authentic utopianism in the eighteenth and nineteenth centuries "devalued" and totalitarianized it; cf. J.F. Jones, "Adventures in a Strange Paradise," *Orbis Litterarum* 35 (1980): 200 ff.

120. *The Story of a Novel: The Genesis of "Doctor Faustus"* (New York: Knopf, 1961), p. 215.

121. Cf. n. 58 above.

122. According to Jacob Taubes, "Scholem suppresses with almost steely asceticism his propensity for direct theological and philosophical pronouncements—however strongly it is provoked at every turn of his thinking" ("Der liebe Gott steckt im Detail—G. Scholem und die messianische Verheissung," *Die Welt* [December 10, 1977]).

123. "Zum Verständnis der messianischen Idee im Judentum," Eranos-Jahrbuch 28 (1959-1960): 193-239, = *The Messianic Idea in Judaism* (New York: Schocken, 1971), pp. 1-36, esp. pp. 3, 36.

124. Ibid., p. 36, and *Shabbatai Tzevi* (Hebrew), 1:11.

125. Cf. S. Schwarzschild, "G. Scholem's Recent Writings," *Judaism* 10, no. 1 (Winter 1961): 72-73, and now David Biale, *G. Scholem: Kabbalah and Counter-History* (Cambridge: Harvard University Press, 1979).

126. E.g., *The Messianic Idea*, p. 26, and Biale, op. cit. pp. 80 f., 151 f., 186, 203, etc.

127. *The Messianic Idea*, p. 36, and "Redemption Through Sin." pp. 84 f.

128. In a very late essay, Scholem tries to maintain a problematic dialectic between Israeli politics and Jewish values; cf. "Jewish Theology Today" (Hebrew), *Petachim*, September 1974, pp. 13-16, on messianism.

Chapter 13

1. Arnold M. Goldberg, *Untersuchungen ueber die Vorstellung von der Schekhinah in der fruehen rabbinischen Literatur . . .*, Berlin: de Gruyter, 1969 (a study that gathers and analyzes philologically a great number of texts but unfortunately engages in no conceptual analysis), pp. 1f., shows that the scholarly literature concludes either that the *shekhinah* is an hypostatization or merely another name of God (G.F. Moore: "buffer words"). Goldberg agrees with the second interpretation (cf. ib., e.g., pp. 440, 522). So do I, basically, though I emphasize more than he does the divine-human relationship that *shekhinah* designates.

2. J. Abelson, *The Immanence of God in Rabbinical Literature* (London 1912), N.Y.: Hermon Press, 1969, chapt. xx et al. (I use Abelson a good deal, too, for his

collection of material, although this book suffers of its randomness, Victorian sense of superiority [comp. Goldberg, op. cit., p. 4, n. 29], and the fact, among others, that the femaleness of the *shekhinah* is not taken into account. [Cf. my text, p. 237 below]) Cf. also Goldberg, op. cit., pp. 465-470, A. Marmorstein, "The Holy Spirit in Rabbinic Legend," in *Studies in Jewish Theology,* Oxford University Press, 1950, pp. 127, n. 2, 130f., I. Gruenwald, *Apocalyptic and Merkabah Mysticism,* Brill: Leiden, 1980, pp. 169-173, and Gershom Scholem, *Major Trends in Jewish Mysticism,* N.Y.: Schocken, 1946, pp. 66, 111f., 223. Rivka Horwitz, in her excellent article on *shekhinah* in the *Encyclopedia Judaica,* vol. 14, cols. 1349-54 (which in turn I make grateful use of) also makes the present equation.

3. Cf. Abelson, loc. cit., p. 83 and Appendix II; Maimonides, *Guide for the Perplexed,* Pines translation, p. 50; Scholem, op. cit., p. 111. For *k'vod haShem* in R. Isaac Hutner, in Emmanuel Lévinas, and even in Leibnitz cf. my "Introduction to the Thought of R.I. Hutner," in *Modern Judaism,* Fall 1965, pp. 248-51. Cf. also Abraham J. Heschel, *Between God and Man—An Interpretation of Judaism—From the Writings of A.J. Heschel,* ed. F. Rothschild, N.Y.: Harper & Brothers, 1959, I/6, pp. 55f., "The Glory." D. Schlueter's article about "glory" (*Herrlichkeit*) in the Bible (*Historisches Woerterbuch der Philosophie,* Basel/Stuttgart, vol. 3, col. 1079) shows that the thesis that I advocate here is totally in line with the critical evidence in the Bible; and comp. F. Niewoehner's treatment of this subject in "post-Biblical Judaism," ib., cols. 1080-1083.

4. Cf. Abelson, op. cit., pp. 128f.; Scholem, op. cit., pp. 113, 375, n. 103: "The identity of *kavod, shekhinah, ru'ach hakodesh* is stressed very often" among the German pietists (cf. ib., p. 376, n. 106).

5. Abelson, op. cit., p. 381 and chapt. XII; Scholem, op. cit., p. 216; Robert Hayward, *Divine Name and Presence—The Memra,* 1981; L. Treitel, "Die alexandrinische Lehre von den Mittelwesen . . . ," in *Judaica—Festschrift zu Hermann Cohens 70. Geburtstage,* Berlin: Cassirer, 1912, pp. 179ff.

6. Marmorstein, op. cit., pp. 135ff., and Abelson, op. cit., p. 83. One example of "glory" = *shekhinah* = "daughter voice" = repentance (= morality) can be found in *Lamentation Rabba,* proem xxv. The off beat edition of t. *Berakhot* by E. M. Pinner, Berlin, 1842, p. 24 has an unusual introductory essay about *bat-kol.*

7. Op. cit.

8. Cf. Goldberg, op. cit., p. 442.

9. Cf. n. 7; Horwitz, loc. cit., speaks then of God's immanence, manifestation, and in short as a euphemism for "God."

10. Joseph Dan et al., *The Early Kabbalah,* N.Y. etc.: Paulist Press, 1986, pp. 29f., and Goldberg, op. cit., p. 443: the *shekhinah* never occurs in the Mishnah, nor does it ever occur as a separate entity in earlier rabbinic literature (cf. also ib., p. 462).

11. Scholem op. cit., pp. 229-235, 270f.

12. Ib., p. 111, and J. Dan, "The Emergence of Mystical Prayer," in *Studies in Jewish Mysticism,* eds. J. Dan and F. Talmadge, Cambridge, MA: Association for Jewish Studies, 1982, p. 118, n. 64. (*Allgemeine Juedische Wochenzeitung,* May 13, 1988 [43/19], p. 10, amusingly has to publish an editorial correction: Prof. Navē-Levinson had written, in the present sort of context, about God's "*weibliche Gegenwart*" ["feminine presence"], but a typographcial mistake put an L where a W should be, thus spoke of "*leibliche Gegenwart*" ["corporeal presence"]. "We apologize for this error." [!])

13. Scholem, op. cit., p. 228 (*Zohar* I, 21b-22a).

14. Ib., p. 400, n. 31, et al. Comp. also P. Schaefer, "Adam in der juedischen Ueberlieferung," pp. 87ff., in *Vom alten zum neuen Adam . . . ,* ed. Walter Strolz etc., Freiburg: Herder, 1986.

15. Horwitz, loc. cit., col. 1353; Scholem, op. cit., pp. 233f. (on *d'vekut*) and his essay "Devekut, or Communion with God," in *The Messianic Idea in Judaism . . . ,* N.Y.: Schocken, 1971, pp. 203-227.

16. Op. cit., pp. 227, 230.

17. *Ket.* 111b: "*vekhee 'ephshar lidvukay bishkhinah.*"

18. Cf. A.B. Yehoshua's *A Late Divorce,* Garden City, N.Y.: Doubleday, 1984, in which the mentally disturbed wife Naomi proclaims that the world is ruled by "Elohima," "the glorious she-ness of it all;" also the review by Anne Roiphe in *The N.Y. Times Book Review,* Nov. 9, 1986, p. 12 of Kim Chernin, *The Flame Bearers,* N.Y.: Random House, 1986.

19. Scholem *Major Trends . . . ,* op. cit., p. 235, and his "Schekhina: das passiv-weibliche Moment in der Gottheit," in *Von der mystischen Gestalt der Gottheit,* 1962, pp. 135-195; cf. also *The Holy Letter—A Study in Medieval Jewish Sexual Morality,* tr. Seymour J. Cohen, N.Y.: Ktav, 1976.

20. *B.B.* 25a; Abelson, op. cit., p. 109.

21. *B.B.* 25a, *Sanh.* 39a.

22. Goldberg, op. cit., pp. 361-365.

23. Karl Wolfskehl, *1933—A Poem Sequence,* N.Y.: Schocken, 1947, p. 120.

24. "The Lure of Immanence—The Crisis in Contemporary Religious Thought," this volume, p. 63.

25. Cf. ib., pp. 63f., and H.A. Wolfson, *The Philosophy of the Church Fathers,* vol. I, Harvard University Press, 1964, pp. 223-232, " 'Eternal Generation,' 'by Will' and 'by Nature.' " and chapt. XVI/III, "Orthodox Use of the Analogies of Physical Union."

26. "Lure of Immanence," loc. cit., pp. 63f.

27. *Sifre Numbers* 94, *Midrash Proverbs* 22: 28; comp. Horwitz, loc. cit., cols. 1350, 1352. Comp. also G. S. Rosenthal, "'As-If' Theology and Liberal Judaism," in *Conservative Judaism* 39 (1), 1986, pp. 34-45. (*N.b.* the important role of the *shekhinah* as an "as-if" function in ethics—cf. n. 76 below.)

28. Comp. S. Schwarzschild, "The Religious Stake in Modern Philosophy of Infinity," in *Bar-Ilan Annual . . . Studies in Judaica and Humanities,* XXII-XXIII, Ramat-Gan: Bar-Ilan University Press, 1987, pp. 63-83.

29. Cf. Abelson, op. cit., p. 79, chapt. XIII, et. al.; also Alan F. Segal, *Two Powers in Heaven . . . ,* Leiden: Brill, 1977 (where binatarian, early Christianity and other distortions are addressed), pp. 16, 23, 262, 264, and Treitel, loc. cit., who, however, runs into his own immanentist problems.

30. II/10.

31. *Mishneh Torah,* "Laws on the Foundations of the Torah," 7:1. Cf. Scholem, op. cit., pp. 111f.

32. *The Book of Beliefs and Opinions,* tr. S. Rosenblatt, Yale University Press, 1948, p. 121.

33. *Kuzari* I/109, II/14-18. (Cf. my forthcoming "Proselytism and Ethicism in R. Yehudah HaLevy," Herzog-August Bibliothek, Wolfenbuettel)

34. Cf. Scholem, *Major Trends . . . ,* op. cit., pp. 116, 232, and esp. J. Dan, "The Emergence . . . ," loc. cit., pp. 85-120, esp. p. 119, n. 82.

35. Cf. D. Blumenthal, "A Philosophical-Mystical Interpretation of *Shi'ur Qomah,*" in *Studies in Jewish Mysticism,* op. cit., pp. 153-172, esp. p. 153. Comp. also A. Altmann, "Moses Narboni's 'Epistle on *Shi'ur Qoma,*'" in *Studies in Religion, Philosophy and Mysticism,* Cornell University Press, 1969 (= *Von der mittelalterlichen zur modernen Aufklaerung . . . ,* Tuebingen: J. C. B. Mohr, 1987, chapt. 4): "Among the documents of anthropomorphism in religion the *Shi'ur Qoma* may certainly claim pride of place" (p. 180)—"the most obnoxious document of Jewish mysticism" (p. 195). Note also (ib., pp. 189ff.) that what is here treated as *shi'ur qomah* = "the visible glory" of the German pietists = R. Saadia's "created glory" = *shekhinah.*

36. Blumenthal, ib., p. 154, Cf. Altmann, loc. cit., p. 202, about the *shi'ur qomah* = God as the criterion or yardstick of everything, and J. Dan, "Imago Dei," in *Modern Jewish Religious Thought,* eds. A.A. Cohen and P. Mendes-Flohr, N.Y.: MacMillan, 1987, pp. 474f.

37. Blumenthal, ib., pp. 15, 163.

38. Ib., pp. 158ff., 163, and Altmann, loc. cit., p. 187.

39. Ib., p. 156, and Goldberg, op. cit., pp. 346f.

40. *Guide* . . . , op. cit., I/28 and *Mishneh Torah,* "Laws on Repentance," 8:2; comp. Abelson, op. cit., p. 146.

41. *Some Aspects of Rabbinic Theology,* N.Y.: Behrman, 1936, p. 292.

42. Cf., e.g., Henry Green, *The Economic and Social Origins of Gnosticism,* Atlanta, GA: Scholars Press, 1985, on the fall of *sophia* (something at least close to the *shekhinah*) as heretical Jewish gnosticism.

43. For the role of the *shekhinah* in Sabbateanism and even Frankism as "the way to Edom," i.e., intentional Jewish self-dissolution among the gentiles, cf. Scholem's article "Jacob Frank," *Encyclopaedia Judaica,* vol. 7, and *Major Trends* . . . , op. cit., p. 323, for example. Cf. also Arthur Green, "Hasidism," in *Contemporary Jewish Religious Thought,* op. cit., pp. 474f.

44. Cf. Moshe Idel, "Infities of Torah," in *Midrash and Literature,* eds. G.H. Hartman and S. Burdick, Yale University Press, 1986, p. 144 and n. 9.

45. Op. cit., p. 38; also "The *Shi'ur Qomah,*" p. 180: taking kabbalistic symbolism literally flirts seriously with idolatry. (I might add, in a personal vein, that the current wave of scholarly criticism of Gershom Scholem is threatening to become a deluge: cf. M. Idel, *Kabbalah—New Perspectives,* Yale University Press, 1988—E. Schweid, *Judaism and Mysticism according to G. Scholem* . . . , Chico, CA: Scholars Press, 1985, etc. Although I agree with some of that criticism, I wounder why almost no one, except Baruch Kurzweil, dared raise a voice along such lines while Scholem was alive: cf. Schwarzschild, "G. Scholem's Recent Writings," *Judaism* 10/1, Winter 1961.)

46. "An Introduction . . . ," loc. cit., section IV, "The Nature of Jewish Thought," esp. pp. 257-260.

47. Ib., p. 258

48. Ib., p. 260. Rodal makes essentially this point, too, in his discussion of Blumenthal, "A Philosophical-Mystical Interpretation . . . ," loc. cit.

49. *Negative Dialektik* . . . , Frankfurt: Suhrkamp, 1966, pp. 389ff. (my translation).

50. Tr. Susanne Langer, N.Y.: Dover, 1946.

51. Ib., p. 39.

52. Ib., p. 56.

53. Ib., p. 62.

54. Ib., p. 84.

55. Ib., p. 91.

56. Ib., p. 75.

57. Ib., p. 99. (Notice throughout that this analysis of Cassirer's is also permeated by his earlier distinction of *Substance and Function.*)

58. Abelson, op. cit., basically understand this: cf. pp. 79, 87f., etc., and the very titles of his chapts. V, VI, VIIf.

59. In *Jewish Writings,* ed. F. Rosenzweig, vol. 3, Berlin: Schwetschke & Sohn, 1924 (written in 1915, it is essentially = *Religion of Reason out of the Sources of Judaism,* chapt. 7), p. 195. Comp. the English version, "The Holy Spirit," in *Reason and Hope—Selections from the Jewish Writings of H. Cohen,* tr. Eva Jospe, N.Y.: W.W. Norton & Co., 1971, pp. 133-153. (One might add that this essay, while explicitly and pervasively an exercise in Cohen's strict "scientific idealism," without any intimation of what Rosenzweig invented as "the late Cohen's break with the philosophic system," is filled with Cohen's emotional piety and what he called "inwardness.") Cf. also *Religion of Reason ...,* Frankfurt: Kauffmann, 1929, p. 63, paragr. 18—a sophisticatedly complex paragr; and cf. Andrea Poma, *La Filosofia Critica di Hermann Cohen,* Milan: Mursia, 1988, pp. 196ff.

60. Ib., p. 191 and onward.

61. Ib., pp. 180, 184ff.

62. Cf. L. Ginzburg, *Legends of the Jews,* Philadelphia: Jewish Publication Society, 1946, vol. III, pp. 158f., vol. VI, pp. 37f., n. 206, 65, n. 344.

63. Comp. Abelson, op. cit., pp. 85f.

64. Quoted by Marmorstein, op. cit., pp. 126f., with the references.

65. Ib., pp. 124f., 131, for *Aggadah Gen.,* ed. S. Buber, p. 47 and *Lev. R.* 1:14. Comp. Schechter, op. cit., p. 223 and pp. 241ff., 255.

66. Ginzburg, op. cit., vol. I, p. 63.

67. *Ber.* 6a, *Sabb.* 12b, *Sotah* 17a, *B.B.* 10a, etc.

68. Cf. Horwitz, loc. cit.

69. Cf. Abelson, op. cit., pp. 90, 100, 102, 105, 112.

70. Ib., pp. 140, 378/d.

71. Ib., p. 115, n.

72. Ib., p. 128 and chapt. XI.

73. Ib., pp. 86, 135, and chapt. X.

74. Ib., pp. 139f.

75. *Tankhuma*, ed. Buber, "*nasso*" 6.

76. *B. Hagigah* 16a. In all these rabbinic statements the term "as-if" is often employed. (Cf. n. 27 above)

77. *Sifra* 104a, Onkelos to *Deut.* 31:18 (used by Schechter, op. cit., p. 223).

78. Schechter, op. cit., pp. 229f., with many references.

79. *Sotah* 9:15/14a, *A.Z.* 20b, and Abelson, op. cit., pp. 271f. (Abelson does not fully understand this passage, due to his ingrained Victorianism.) The great classic Jewish ethics in the mystical mode, M. H. Luzzatto's *The Path of the Upright*, is structured by *Sotah* 9:15, as, indeed, are many other standard texts of Jewish ethics.

80. The term "under the wings of the *shekhinah*" seems to be based on *Ruth* 2:2.

81. *Yoma* 56b, *Meg.* 29a, Abelson, op. cit., pp. 120, 127f.

82. *Guide* . . . , op. cit., I/52.

83. Ib., I/53, II/25, and *The Eight Chapters of Maimonides on Ethics*, ed. J. Gorfinkle, N.Y.: AMS Press, 1966, p. 54: "God *is* his attributes (of action), and his attributes are he."

84. Cf. "The Lure of Immanence . . . ," loc cit., p. 63.

85. *Guide* . . . , I/21, Pines tr., p. 48.

86. Ib., I/21, pp. 49f., I/28, p. 60; comp. also Strack-Billerbeck, *Kommentar zum N.T.* . . . , 1924, vol. II, pp. 302-314, and Hayward, op. cit.

87. Ib., I/21, p. 51.

88. Even in the *Shi'ur Qomah* the *shekhinah* came to be reinterpreted as "the active intellect:" cf. Blumenthal, "A Philosophical-Mystical Interpretation . . . ," loc. cit., pp. 159f.

89. *Shulkhan 'Arukh*, "Laws of Idolatry," 141; comp. my "The Legal Foundations of Jewish Aesthetics," this volume, p. 111.

90. H. Cohen, loc. cit., p. 187.

91. *Tikkunay Zohar* VI; comp. *Zohar* I/21a, quoted in Heschel, op. cit., chapt. 12, n. 1; cf. also *Zohar Genesis* I/27b: "The Mishnah is the handmaiden of the *Shekhinah* . . . Moses' sepulcher is the Mishnah." I take it this means: the *shekhinah* is the Law (= Moses, the Mishnah).

92. Scholem, *Major Trends* . . . , op. cit., pp. 234f.

93. Cf., e.g., *3 Enoch* . . ., ed. H. Odeberg, N.Y.: Ktav, 1973, chapts. 5ff. (Note the role of the *shekhinah* and multitudinous similar heavenly agents throughout this text.)

94. Heschel, op. cit., p. 80.

95. Ib., I/6, chapt. "The Glory," p. 56.

96. Ib., p. 85.

97. Cf. *The Early Kabbalah,* op. cit., p. 19, which gives a good one-paragraph introduction to this passage in ibn Ezra. Cf. also Amos Funkenstein, *Theology and the Scientific Imagination from the Middle Ages to the 17th Century,* Princeton University Press, 1986, p. 218, about "Ibn Ezra's Neoplatonic, almost pantheistic interpretation."

98. With thanks for his help to my Arabist colleague Prof. Peter Heath I want here to insert a striking Moslem equivalent of approximately the same period—the beginning of the 11th century, which in most ways completely parallels what I have been pointing to in Judaism and thus, again, illustrates the commonality of what I am inclined to call "Semitic religion."

In a hithero untranslated and very little-studied text attributed to Avicenna, written in Persian, *Mi'raj-nāma* (*Book of the Prophet's Ascension*), filled with a great deal of imaginative description of the heavenly spheres, the *rūh al-qudus* ("spirit of holiness" = *ru'ach hakodesh*) plays a decisive role—is literally called a *wāsita*-"intermediary" and defined as that which exists, but "not as a substance," between God and the first, active intellect (i.e., knowledge). (Its work is carried further downward toward the imagination on the ladder of emanations by the angel Gabriel.) This *rūh al-qudus* in Avicenna (?) is furthermore identified with "the First Command" of the Koran (*rūh wa amr*-"spirit and command")—whatever the command, a command!

99. *Midreshay haZohar, "lekket Sh'mu'el,"* Jerusalem, 1970, p. 800, on *Song of Songs* 7:12.

100. Leo Baeck, "Sefer Ha-Bahir," in *Aus Drei Jahrtausenden. Wissenschaftliche Untersuchungen und Abhandlungen zur Geschichte des juedischen Glaubens,* Berlin 1939 (!), pp. 284f.

101. Tishby and Lachover, *The Wisdom of the Zohar* (Hebr.), I, pp. 219-231, again on the *Song of Songs.*

102. Comp. also F. Rosenzweig, "Atheist Theology," in *Kleinere Schriften,* Berlin: Schocken, 1935, pp. 281, 286f., on Israel as a task, by virtue of the Torah, not a reality. Thomas Sheehan's recent and rather heretical *The First Coming: How the Kingdom of God Became Christianity,* N.Y.: Random House, 1986, eliminates "Christ" from his (Roman Catholic) Christianity by arguing that "God, as God, has *identified himself without a remainder with his people . . .*" (Sheehan's italics) (review by J.M. Cameron, in *N.Y. Review,* Dec. 4, 1986, p. 24). Thus Christian incarnationism is maintained, though "Christ" is eliminated; now *Christendom* is the incarnation—precisely the danger (in the Jewish analogue) against which I am warning.

103. "Judaism and Revolution," in *Du sacré au saint—cinque nouvelles lectures talmudiques,* Paris, 1977, pp. 18f.

104. The anonymous "master" of whom Lévinas here speaks is the mysterious and, I must say, suspect person by the name of Shushani, whom also Elie Wiesel repeatedly depicts: cf. his *Legends of Our Time*, N.Y.: Holt, Rinehart & Winston, 1968, "The Wandering Jew," pp. 87-109, and *One Generation After*, N.Y.: Random House, 1970, "The Death of My Teacher," pp. 120-127.

105. The allusions to "law" and "responsibilities" are, of course, what I am here calling normativity. Lévinas' very French tenses in this passage are a bit unnerving.

106. Abelson, op. cit., p. 268.

107. Ib., p. 378. Comp. Stuart Charme's "Sartre's Jewish Daughter . . . ," in *Midstream*, Oct. 1986, p. 26: "(B)eing Jewish represented [to Sartre] the epitome of the human condition." (Cf. also Schwarzschild, "Sartre as Jew," this volume.)

108. Cf. nn. 45, 76 above.

109. *Ber.* 54a; Schwarzschild, "On Jewish Eschatology," in this volume, p. 100. For this benediction cf. Also E. Borowitz, *The Blessing over a Change of Wine*, Port Washington, N.Y.: Sh'ma, 1987.

110. This established phrase seems to be a colloquial and positive formulation of what the rabbis put negatively, e.g., tr. *Ketubot* 111a (a famous passage for other reasons) —"not to delay the end," etc. Generally for this subject cf. the section "Messianism" in my "On Jewish Meta-Ethics" (unpublished).

111. *Meg.* 15a.

112. *Hullin* 4a. Comp. the great Elie Benamozegh, *Israel et l'humanité*, Paris: E. Leroux, 1914, p. 348: the Messianic Sabbath represents the time when "the mob of men and races becomes humanity."

113. Schwarzschild, "Karl Marx's Jewish Theory of Usury," in *Gesher* (Yeshiva University), 1978, pp. 7-40.

114. Cf., e.g., *Ned.* 25a, *Kidd.* 40b, *Sifre*, "sh' lakh," 33, Maimonides, end of *Commentary to tr. Makkot*, Abarbanel, *Rosh 'amana*, 24, Zalman S. Shapiro, *Tractate on the Thirteen Principles* (Hebr.), Denver, CO, 1959, p. 15.

115. *The Argument to the Other—Reason beyond Reason in the Thought of K. Barth and E. Levinas*, Chico, CA: Scholars Press (American Academy of Religion Series, no. 42), 1983, pp. 87ff. (comp. my review in *International Studies of Philosophy* XIX/3, 1987, pp. 114f.).

116. Ginzburg, op. cit., vol. IV, p. 234. Comp. also *Lamentations R.*, proem XXIV, loc, cit.: ". . . I (God) will not attach myself to (Israel) again until the time of the end arrives" (Soncino ed., p. 41); also Goldberg, op. cit., pp. 318-335, 522-530.

117. Abelson, op. cit., p. 102, n. 2. Hospitality in particular is a Messianic virtue: Ginzburg, op. cit., vol. I, pp. 241f., vol. V, p. 234. Comp. also Goldberg, op. cit., pp. 292ff.

118. Cf. *Lamentations R.,* proem XXV. Indeed, here it is clearly implied that the *shekhinah* is repentance. Comp. on this Abelson, op. cit., pp. 105ff., and R. Aryeh Dessler's *Mikhtav me-Eliyahu,* vol. 2, p. 47, (a totally spiritualized chassidic reading of Messianism).

119. *Meg.* 29a, *Song of Songs Rababa* 6, et al. Comp. Abelson, op. cit., pp. 120, 127f., 136, etc., and pp. 241 above, as well as Ginzburg, op. cit., vol. V, p. 154, n. 199. The fullest statement of the doctrine of the gradual withdrawal from the world and its gradual return, all depending on human and Jewish morality, is probably the one found in *Pesikta deR. Kahana,* ed. B. Mandelbaum, N.Y.: Jewish Theological Seminary, 1962, vol. I, pp. 1-3 and vol. II, Engl. introduction, pp. 3-6.

120. Horwitz, loc. cit., col. 350.

121. *Kuzari* V/23 and II/20, 23, III/23; cf. also *Lamentations R.,* proem XXV, XXXIV, I/6:3; cf. also B. Sack, "The Exile of the *Shekhinah* in *Or Yakar* of R. Moses Cordovero" (Hebr.), in *Jerusalem Studies in Jewish Thought* 4 (1982), pp. 157-178, IXf.

122. Last and separate chapt., part I.

123. Cf. A. Jellinek, *Beth haMidrash,* Jerusalem, 1967, vol. VII, pp. 104-108, chapts. 27-30; Blumenthal, *Understanding Jewish Mysticism . . .,* New York: Ktav, 1978, vol. I, p. 97; and J. Dan, *Three Types of Ancient Jewish Mysticism,* University of Cincinnati, 1984, pp. 24-28 (though I think that Dan misinterprets this notion here by treating it non-Messianically).

124. *Zohar* I, 1b.

125. Horwitz, loc. cit., col. 1354.

126. G. Scholem, *Sabbetai Sevi—The Mystical Messiah,* Princeton University Press, 1973, p. 43.

127. Cf. F. Rosenzweig, *The Star of Redemption,* tr. W. Hallo, N.Y.: Holt, Rinehart and Winston, 1970, pp. 409f. about the universality of the *shekhinah.*

128. Abelson, op. cit., p. 119, chapt. XXI and Appendix I, "The Holy Spirit in its Relations to non-Jews." (Abelson is, I think, much too brief and unanalytical on this particular subject.)

129. Cf. Soncino ed., pp. 16ff, 20f., 22f., et al.

130. *Seder Eliyahu Rabba,* ed. Friedman, p. 48 (quoted by Marmorstein, op. cit., pp. 128f. Marmorstein in this connection interestingly refers to Hermann Cohen, who, indeed, uses this passage in op. cit., p. 187).

131. *Aggada Gen.,* ed. Buber, p. 47 (quoted by Marmorstein, op. cit., pp. 124f.); comp. Also *Lev. R.* 1:14 (quoted ib., p. 131).

132. Cf. Schwarzschild, "An Introduction . . . ," loc. cit., p. 251.

133. Op. cit., p. 57.

134. "The Lure of Immanence . . . ," loc. cit., pp. 75f. and "On Jewish Eschatology," loc. cit., p. 219.

Bibliography of the Writings of Steven S. Schwarzschild

I

Editor, *Judaism—A Quarterly Journal*, N. Y. (1960-1969).

Franz Rosenzweig (1886-1929)—Guide to Reversioners, London 1960.

Hermann Cohen, *Werke*, vol. 7, *Ethik des Reinen Willens*, intro., Hildesheim/N. Y.: Olms, 1981.

II

1948-1950 German newspaper articles

Der Weg, Berlin, Jewish Community:

III/43, Oct. 22, 1948, p. 5, "Simchat Torah."

45, Nov. 5, 1948, p. 6, "Zur Stunde des Gedenkens."

51, Dec. 17, 1948, p. 9, "Judah L. Magnes."

52, Dec. 24, 1948, p. 7, "Zum Chanukkah-Fest."

IV/7, Febr. 18, 1949, pp. 5f., "Israel oder Jesus."

21, May 27, 1949, pp. 1f., "Gott der Vershleppten."

22/23, June 2, 1949, p. 3, "Brief an Bischof Dibelius."

27, July 8, 1949, pp. 1f., "Tatsachen und Zukunft." p. 9, "Abschluss einer Kontroverse."

31, Aug. 5, 1949, pp. 1f., "Deutschland und die Juden."

47, Nov. 25, p. 9, "Freundschaft oder Missionsarbeit," (reprint: *Rundbrief zur Forederung der Freundschaft . . .*, II/7, Apr. 1950, Freiburg, pp. 15-17.

V/3, Jan. 20, 1950, p. 1f, "Religioese Fragan zur Parteipolitik."

Allgemeine Wochenzeitung der Juden in Deutschland, Dusseldorf:

IV/14, July 15, 1949, p. 7, "An der Schwelle des Juedischen Lebens."

42, Jan. 27, 1950, p. 11, "Juedische Geschichtsforschung."

44, Feb. 10, 1950, p. 1, "Wir sind nur Juden."

46, Feb. 24, 1950, p. 1, "Aufruf zur Wahrhaftigkeit."

V/3, Apr. 28, p. 5, "Besuch in Schum."

III

"Help" (F. Rosenzweig) tr., *Hebrew Union College Monthly,* XXXIV/1. Chanukka 1946, p. 10.

"A Rabbi's Book" (F. Rosenzweig) tr. and ed., ib., XXXIV/2 (Purim 1947), pp. 7-9 (reprinted: N. N. Glatzer, *F. Rosenzweig—His Life and Thought*)

1952

"Judaism a la Mode," (review: W. Herberg, *Judaism & Modern Man*), *Menorah Journal,* pp. 102-111.

"Franz Rosenzweig and Existentialism," *Central Conference of American Rabbis Yearbook* LXII (1952), pp. 410-429.

1953

"The *Commentary-Monat* Axis," *Menorah Journal* XLI/1 (Spring 1953) pp. 87-105.

1954

"State and Religion," *Jewish Spectator,* April 1954, p. 18f.

1955

"Two Modern Jewish Philosophies of History: Nachman Krochmal and Hermann Cohen," unpublished dissert., H. U. C.-J. I. R., Cincinnati, Oh.

1956

"The Personal Messiah—Toward the Restoration of a Discarded Doctrine," *Judaism,* V, no. 2 (1956), pp. 123-135. (Reprinted: L. Jacobs, *Jewish Thought Today,* N. Y. 1970, A. A. Cohen, *Arguments and Doctrines,* N. Y. 1970, pp. 519-537, *Faith and Reason,* ed. R. Gordis, 1972).

"The Democratic Socialism of Hermann Cohen," *Hebrew Union College Annual* XXVII (1956) pp. 417-438.

"F. Rosenzweig on Judaism and Christianity," *Conservative Judaism*, Winter 1956, pp. 41-48.

"The Rabbinate Against Itself," *Reconstructionist*, June 15, 1956, pp. 8-12.

1957

"On Jewish Learning: F. Rosenzweig," *Conservative Judaism*, (review) Spring 1957, pp. 56-64.

"The Realities of the Human Spirit," (review of M. Maisels), *Circle—In Jewish Bookland*, September 1957.

1959

"Von Juden in Muenchen," (review), *Historia Judaica* XXI/1 (April 1959), pp. 59-62.

"Survey of Current Theological Literature," quarterly department, *Judaism*, Winter 1959, pp. 26-45.

"Dual Membership in Rabbinic Organizations," *CCAR Journal* April 1959, pp. 23-26.

1960

"Perspectives in American Jewish Life," (review), *Conservative Judaism*, Fall 1960, pp. 53-55.

"The Marquis de Mores: The Story of a Failure," *Jewish Social Studies*, XXII, no. 1 (1960), pp. 3-26.

1961

"Jewish Philosophy and Theology," (review), *Jewish Specatator*, November 1961, pp. 22-25.

"Speech and Silence Before God," *Judaism*, X, no. 3 (1961), pp. 195-204.

"Franz Rosenzweig," *Jewish Spectator*, February 1961, pp. 6-10.

"Theologians and the Bomb," *The Moral Dilemma of Nuclear Weapons*, N. Y. 1961, pp. 22-25, 57f. (*Worldview*, May 1959, pp. 7-10.)

"Tradition modernized" (review), *Saturday Review*, March 4, 1961, p. 41.

1962

"Marilyn Monroe's Death", *Jewish Specator*, November 1962, p. 21 (reprinted: *Southern African Jewish Times*, September 1963, p. 78; *InterMountains-Jewish News*, November 3, 1962, p. 2.)

"Do Noachites Have to Believe in Revelation? (A Passage in Dispute between Maimonides, Spinoza, Mendelssohn, and H. Cohen) A Contribution to a Jewish View of Natural Law," *Jewish Quarterly Review,* LII, no. 4 (April 1962), pp. 297-308; LIII, no. 1 (July 1962), pp. 30-65. ("Deben los Noeidas creer en la Revelation? Un Passje en disputa entre Maimonides, Mendelssohn, Spinoza y H. Cohen. Contribution a una vision judida de la Ley Natural." *Davar-Revista Literaria,* Buenos Aires, December 1964).

"A New Reason for Refraining from Counting Jews," (Hebrew) (letter) *HaDoar,* Tishri 9, 1962, p. 722.

"To Re-Cast Rationalism," ("Directions for Contemporary Jewish Philosophy") *Judaism,* XI, no. 3, (1962), pp. 205-209 (reprinted in A. A. Cohen, *Arguments and Doctrines,* N. Y. 1970, pp. 189-196) ("La Remodelacion del Rationalismo," *Davar-Revista Literaria,* Buenos Aires, September 1964; "To Re-Cast Rationalism," *Jewish Thought in the Diaspora,* Hebrew University, Jerusalem, 1968.)

"Metaphysics and Historicity," (review), *CCAR Journal,* January 1962, p. 62f.

The American Character, Center for the Study of Democratic Institutions, Santa Barbara, Cal. 1962 (pp. 4, 36f.).

"A Sequel to the Story of Herbert Baum," *Judiaca Post (Journal of Philatelic Judaica),* III/3-4 (March-April 1962), pp. 215-217.

"Comment" (on Bruno Bettelheim), *Midstream,* September 1962, pp. 84f.

1963

"The Monk Who was a Jew," (letter), *Commonweal,* January 17, 1963, pp. 464f.

"The Function and Limits of Reason in Contemporary Jewish Theology," *Central Conference of American Rabbis Yearbook,* LXXIII (1963), pp. 199-214.

1964

"New Theology No. 1," (review), *Conservative Judaism,* Summer 1964, pp. 67-69.

"Judaism, Scriptures and Ecumenism," *Judaism,* XIII, no. 3 (Summer 1964), pp. 259-273; *ditto, Scripture and Tradition,* Duquesne U.

"The Messianic Doctrine in Contemporary Jewish History," *Great Jewish Ideas,* Washington, D.C., 1964, ch. 15 (reprint: 1985).

"On Power In Judaism—What is the Junction of Power and Morality," *Worldview,* February 1964, pp. 6-10.

"Negro Nationalism and Black Jews," (review), *Midstream,* December 1964, pp. 106-108.

1965

"Jewish Perspectives on Foreign Policy," *Rediscovering Judaism,* ed. A. J. Wolf, Quadrangle, Chicago, 1965. (Reprinted: *Contemporary Religion & Social Responsibility,* eds. N. Brockman and N. Diediscazi, 1970).

"Torah for Today," *Contemporary Jewish Beliefs,* ed. I. Eisentein, Reconstructionist Foundation, 1965.

"The Necessity of the Lone Man," *Fellowship,* May 1965.

"German-Jewish Lessons for American Jewry," in *Acculturation,* (Report, Federation of Jews from Central Europe), ed. H. Strauss, 1965.

"New Theology 2," (review), *Conservative Judaism,* Fall 1965.

"What Makes Judaism Distinctive?" (Symposium), *Jewish Heritage,* Summer 1965.

"Letter about D. Bonhoeffer," *Commonweal,* November 26, 1965, pp. 251-254.

1966

"From Speculative to Critical Idealism," (review), *Journal of Religion,* January 1966.

"A Little Bit of a Revolution?" ch. in *The Secular City Debate,* ed. D. Callahan, MacMillan, 1966. (Reprinted: *Disputation & Dialogue,* ed. F. Talmage, N. Y.: Ktav, 1975, pp. 145-152.)

"H. Cohen, 'Truth'," (ed. and tr.) *Judaism* XV/4, (Fall 1966), pp. 466-473.

"The Religious Search for Peace," ch. in *National Inter-Religious Conference for Peace,* ed. J. Homer, Beacon, 1966 (and *Judaism,* XV/4 Fall 1966, pp. 1-6.)

"The Anguish of the Jews," (review), *Continuum,* Fall 1966.

"Negro-Jewish Relations," *Midstream,* Fall 1966, pp. 71f.

'Negro and Jew," in *Negro and Jew—An Encounter in America,* ed. S. Katz, N. Y. 1967, pp. 107-110 (reprint of "Negro-Jewish Relations," 1966).

"Torah for our Time," in *Varieties of Jewish Belief,* ed. I. Eisenstein, N. Y.: Reconstructionist Press, 1966, pp. 243-257.

1967

"Jewish Pacifism," *Protest: Pacifism & Politics,* (ed. J. Finn) Random House, N. Y., 1967, pp. 124-138.

"Jewish Values in the Post-Holocaust Future," (symposium moderator), *Judaism,* Summer 1967.

"On Temptation—F. Rosenzweig," (ed. & trans.) *Judaism,* Winter 1967.

"The Lure of Immanence—the Crisis in Contemporary Religious Thought," *Tradition,* Spring-Summmer, 1967, pp. 70-99 (in Hebrew: *Midor Dor* I, 1979, pp. 113-77).

1968

"On the Theology of Jewish Survival," *Central Conference of American Rabbis Journal,* Fall, 1968, pp. 2-21, (reprint: *Judaism and Ethics,* ed. D. J. Silver, N. Y. 1970, pp. 289-314; ACIID, April 1973, pp. 32f.)

"The New Left Meets the Real Thing," *Dissent,* Jan.-Feb. 1968.

"The Day of Atonement—H. Cohen," (introd.), *Judaism,* Summer 1968.

1969

"A Note on the Nature of Ideal Society—A Rabbinic Study," *Curt Silberman Festschrift,* eds. H.A. Strauss, H.K. Reissner, New York, 1969, pp. 86-105.

Congress Bi-Weekly, February 24, 1969 (36/3), "The 6th Annual American-Israel Dialogue," pp. 40-41, 83-84.

"Authenticity and Selflessness: Keys to Creative Jewish Survival," *The Jewish Advocate* (Boston), May 22, 1969, sect. 2, p. 3.

"A Broader View of *Tradition,*" (review), *The Jewish Horizon,* Sep. Oct. 1969, pp. 14-16.

1970

"The Jewish Pathology of the Supreme Court," Sh'ma, I/1, May 22, 1970, p. 5f.

Roots of Jewish Nonviolence, introd., Jewish Peace Fellowship (N. Y., 1970), (2nd ed., 1981).

"The Imperative of Religious Law," *Washington University Law Quarterly,* 1970, Winter 1970, no. 1, pp. 103-109.

"F. Rosenzweig's Anecdotes about H. Cohen," *Gegenwart im Ruckblick . . . ,* ed. H. A. Strauss and K. Grossman, Heidelberg 1970, pp. 209-218.

1971

"Marrano Professors of Jewish Studies," *Association for Jewish Studies Newsletter,* Vol. 2, No. 2 (April, 1971).

"Judaica Collections in Olin Library," *Washington University Librarian,* III/6, March-April 1971, p. 1f.

"More Services, Less Servitude," *Sh'ma,* Vol. 1, No. 9 (March 5, 1971), p. 1.

"The Quaker Report—Eminently Reasonable," *Christianity and Crisis,* Vol. 31, No. 20 (November 29, 1971), pp. 259-261.

"The Star of Redemption," (review) *The Thomist,* Vol. 35, No. 4 (October 1971), pp. 728-737.

"Samuel Atlas," "Covetousness," "Duty," "Justice," "Noachite Law," "Franz Rosenzweig," "Henry Slonimsky," "Suffering," "Truth," in *Encyclopedia Judaica,* Jerusalem, 1971, articles.

1972

"The Radical Imperatives of Judaism," *Judaism,* Vol. 21, No. 1 (Winter 1972), pp. 9-15.

"Judaism and Resistance to Immoral Authority," *Jewish Advocate* (Boston), February 17, 1972, sect. 2, p. 3.

"Lawrence Kohlberg's Theory of Moral Growth," *SIECUS Newsletter,* Vol. 7, No. 4, April, 1972, p. 4.

"Herman Cohen Today," *Sh'ma,* Vol. 2, No. 31 (April 21, 1972), pp. 84-87.

"Jews for McGovern?" *Sh'ma,* II/37, Sept. 15, 1972, pp. 130-132.

"Speech and Silence Before God," (revised) in *Understanding Jewish Prayer,* edited by J. Petuchowski, New York, 1972, pp. 84-99, 167-170. (Excerpted in *Forms of Jewish Worship,* III, London 1985, pp. 774f.)

1973

"The Jewish Key '73 Debate," *Congress Bi-Weekly,* March 9, 1973, pp. 29f.

"The Day of Atonement War," *Sh'ma* 4/61, Nov. 16, 1973, pp. 6f.

"More on Baeck," *CCAR Journal,* Autumn, 1973, p. 85f.

"Chanukkah," *American Report* IV:6, Dec. 24, 1973, pp. 1, 23.

1974

"Analyzing Jewish Counter-Culture," (review) *Review of Books and Religion* III/4, Mid-January 1974, p. 6.

"The Legacy of the German Refugee Intellectuals," (review) *American Jewish Historical Quarterly,* LXIII/3 (March 1974), pp. 296-298.

"The Middle East: Engagement or Disengagement?" *Christianity and Crisis* XXXIV/13, July 22, 1974, pp. 164-167.

"Beth She'arim," (review), *American Anthropologist* 76/2, June 1974.

"Basic Principles Regarding the Problems of the Near East," (pamphlet), Fellowship Publications (Nyack, N. Y.).

"Justice," in *Jewish Values* (Israel Pocket Library), ed. G. Wigoder, Jerusalem, Keter 1974, pp. 194-198.

"Contra Eckardt," *Review of Books and Religion* IV/2, Mid-October 1974, p. 10.

"Two Lectures of Rabbi Isaac Hutner," introduced and translated, *Tradition* XIV/4, Fall 1974, pp. 90-109.

1975

"Disengagement or Engagement in the Near East?" *New Outlook,* 18/8, Dec. 1975, pp. 44-50.

"Old Moves on the Chessboard," (review) *Review of Books and Religion,* V/2, Mid-Oct., 1975, pp. 1, 16.

"The Legal Foundations of Jewish Aesthetics," *Journal of Aesthetic Education,* IX/1, Jan. 1975, pp. 29-42. (Reprint: *A Second Look,* N. Y., Sh'ma, 1978).

"The Legal Foundation of Jewish Aesthetics," in *Melanges Andre Neher,* ed. R. Sidat, Paris: Librarie d'Amerique et de l'Oreint, 1975, pp. 65-72.

"The Jewish Enlightenment Symbiosis," *Jewish Spectator* XL/3, Fall 1975, pp. 26-29.

"The Tenability of H. Cohen's Construction of the Self," *JHP* XIII/3 (July 1975), pp. 361-384.

1976

"On Jewish Pacifism," *Fellowship,* Jan.-Feb. 1976, p. 13.

"The Thirteenth Tribe," (review) *St. Louis Jewish Light,* Sept. 1, 1976, p. 23.

"The Question of Jewish Ethics Today," *Sh'ma* 7/124, Dec. 24, 1976 pp. 29-36 (reprint: *Listening to American Jews Today,* ed. C. T. Oppenheim, N. Y.: *Sh'ma,* 1986, pp. 38-44; N. Y.: Adama Books, 1988, pp. 40-46.

"A Philosophy of Mitzvot," (review) *J.B.L.* 95/3 (1976), p. 519f.

"A Jewish Eschatological Liturgy," *C.C.A.R. Journal,* XXIII/4, (95), Autumn, 1976 pp. 22-26.

1977

"Wake Up . . . ," (review) *St. Louis Jewish Light* (January 5, 1977) p. 19.

"The Question of Jewish Ethics Today: II," *Sh'ma* 7/134, May 13, 1977, pp. 118-124.

"Moral Radicalism and 'Middlingness' in the Ethics of Maimonides," *Studies in Medieval Culture XI,* Western Michigan University Press, 1977, pp. 65-94.

"Beth She'arim," Vols. II, III (review), *American Anthropologist* 79/2 (June 1977), pp. 490f.

1978

"Revelation-Faith-Reason . . . ," (review) *Association of Jewish Studies Newsletter,* no. 22, March 1978, pp. 15, 20.

"Karl Marx's Jewish Theory of Usury," *Gesher* (Yeshiva University) 1978, pp. 7-40.

"Martin Buber—Jewish Education as Spiritual Resistance," *St. Louis Jewish Light,* August 2, 1978, p. 16.

1979

"Wittgenstein as Alienated Jew," *Telos,* no. 40, Summer 1979, pp. 160-165.

"Toward Jewish-Arab Cooperation," *Subject to Change,* (Washington University) VI/1, Oct. 24, 1979, pp. 8-14. (Reprinted: Middle East Project, N. Y.)

" 'Germanism and Judaism'-Hermann Cohen's Normative Paradigm of the German-Jewish Symbiosis," in *Jews and Germans from 1860 to 1933: The Problematic Symbiosis,* ed. David Bronsen; Heidelberg: Carl Winter, 1979, pp. 129-172.

1980

"Violence and Defense in the Jewish Experience," (review), *Journal of Religion* 601, Jan. 1980, pp. 102-106.

"Remembering Erich Fromm," *Jewish Spectator,* Fall 1980, pp. 29-33. (Expanded from "A Remembrance of Erich Fromm," *Subject to Change* [Wash. U.], May 1, 1980, pp. 4, 10.

"Morris B. Margolies, 'Samuel David Luzzatto . . .'," (review) *American Historical Review* 85/4, Oct. 1980, pp. 390f.

1981

"Shalom," *Confrontation* (L.I. University), Winter 1981, no. 21, pp. 166-176. (Reprinted *Holy Land,* Jerusalem: Holy Land Franciscans, VII/4, Winter 1987, pp. 171-180)

"Raphael Levi de Hanovre et la 'Fruhaufklarung' Juive," *Le 18e siecle* 13, 1981, pp. 27-36.

"An Agenda for Jewish Philosophy in the 1980s," in *Studies in Jewish Philosophy: I. Jewish Philosophy in the 1980s,* ed. N. Samuelson, Melrose Park, PA: Academy for Jewish Philosophy, pp. 55-71.

1982

"F. Rosenzweig's Philosophy of Existence . . . ," (review), *International Studies in Philosophy* XIV/1, 1981, pp. 80f.

"Jenseits von Sein und Zeit . . . ," (review), ib., pp. 102-4.

"Authority and Revelation," in *Studies in Jewish Philosophy, vol. II: Reason and Revelation as Authority in Judaism,* Melrose Park, PA: Academy for Jewish Philosophy (1982), pp. 45-63.

"Marx and Wittgenstein . . . ," (review), *Contemporary Sociology* 11/6, March 1982, pp. 733f.

1983

"J-P. Sartre as Jew," *Modern Judaism,* III/1, February 1983, pp. 39-73.

"W. Flach, Thesen zum Begriff der Wissenschaftstheorie," (review), *International Studies in Philosophy* XV/3, 1983, pp. 91f.

1984

"Two Lives in the Jewish 'Fruhaufklarung': Raphael Levy Hannover and Moses Abraham Wolf," *Leo Baeck Institute Year Book,* XXIX, pp. 229-276.

"M. Mendelssohn, *Gesammelte Schriften* . . . ," (review), *Journal of the History of Philosophy* 22:1, January 1984, pp. 124-126.

"The Unnatural Jew," *Environmental Ethics,* VI/4, Winter 1984, pp. 347-362.

1985

"Kantianism on the Death Penalty (and Related Social Problems)," *Archives for Philosophy of Law and Social Philosophy* LXXXI/3 (1985): 343-372.

"An Introduction to the Thought of R. Isaac Hutner," *Modern Judaism* (Fall 1985): 235-277.

"Buber and his Biographer,"*Judaism* XXXIV/4 (Fall 1985): 433-443.

"A Renaissance Man . . . (M. Ficino)," *St. Louis Post Dispatch* (September 6, 1985): 43.

"Paul Celan, 'in egypt'," *Sh'ma* 15/291, April 5, 1985, pp. 85-87.

"What is 'Jewish Art'?" (review), *ARTnews,* January 1985, pp. 35-38.

1986

"Rosenzweig at 100—contemporary," *Sh'ma* 13/316 (September 5, 1986): 121f.

"Jewish Aesthetics," *Reconstructionist* LI/7 (June 1986): 24-27.

"I. Hutner," (volume 6, p. 544), "F. Rosenzweig," (volume 12, pp. 471-473), "H. Cohen," (volume 3, pp. 559-561), (articles in) *Encyclopedia of Religion,* ed. M. Eliade etc., New York: MacMillan, 1986.

"The Title of H. Cohen's 'Religion of Reason Out of the Sources of Judaism'," in *The Life of Covenant . . . Essays in Honor of H. E. Schaalman,* ed. J. Edelheit, Chicago: Spertus College Press, 1986, pp. 207-220.

"A Critique of M. Buber's Political Philosophy—An Affectionate Reappraisal," *Leo Baeck Institute Year Book* XXXI, 1986, pp. 355-388.

"On Jewish Eschatology," in *The Human Condition in the Jewish and Christian Traditions,* ed. F. Greenspahn, New York: Ktav, 1986, pp. 171-211.

"The Halakhic Mind . . . ," (review) *Sh'ma* 13/316 (September 5, 1986): 127f.

"Kant's Theory of Form . . . ," (review) *Idealistic Studies* XVI/2 (May 1986): 182f.

1987

Articles, "Aesthetics," (pp. 1-6), "Conscience," (pp. 87-90), "Modern Jewish Philosophy," (pp. 629-634), in *Contemporary Jewish Religious Thought . . . ,* eds. A. A. Cohen and P. Mendes-Flohr, N. Y.: Scribner's, 1987.

"American History Marked by Racism," *New Politics* I/3 (n.s.), Summer 1987, pp. 56-58.

"H. Cohen, The Challenge . . . ," (review) *Idealistic Studies* XVII/1, January 1987, pp. 83f.

"Shekhinah und juedische Eschatologie," (German), in *Universale Vaterschaft Gottes . . . ,* eds. A. Falaturi, J. Petuchowski, W. Strolz, Freiburg, etc.: Herder, 1987, pp. 88-114.

"Ethik des reinen Willens . . . ," *A Community of Readers: Books That Made a Difference . . . ,* Special Collection—Olin Library, St. Louis, 1987, 2 pp.

"The Theologico-Political Basis of Liberal Christian-Jewish Relations in Modernity," *German Jewry and Liberalism . . .,* Koenigswinter (Germany): Fr.-Naumann-Stiftung, 1986 (actually 1987), pp. 70-95.

"The Religious Stake in Modern Philosophy of Infinity," *Bar-Ilan . . . Annual* XXII-XXIII, 1987, pp. 63-83.

"An Agenda for Jewish Philosophy in the 1980s," (1981), pp. 101-125—"Authority and Reason: *Contra* Gadamer," (1982), pp. 161-190, reprinted in *Studies in Jewish Philosophy . . . ,* ed. N. Samuelson, University Press of America, 1987.

"Steven S. Smith, *The Argument to the Other . . . ,*" (review), *International Studies in Philosophy* XIX/3, 1987, pp. 114f.

1988

"Der Friede ist der hoechste Wert im Judentum," in *Friedensdiskurs aus verschiedener Weltansicht . . . ,* ed. Rudolf Weiler, Berlin: Duncker & Humblot, 1988, pp. 88-102.

"Franz Rosenzweig and Martin Heidegger: The German and the Jewish Turn to Ethnicism," in *Der Philosoph Franz Rosenzweig . . . International Kongress–Kassel 1986,* ed. W. Schmied-Kowarzik, Freiburg/Munich: Karl Alber, 1988, vol. II, pp. 887ff.

1989

"Judentum," in *Evangelisches Kirchenlexikon–Internationale theologische Enzyklopaedie,* 4th ed., vol. 3, cols. 857-868, Goettingen: Vandenhoeck & Ruprecht, 1989.

Index